MARITIME BOUNDARY DELIMITATION: THE CASE LAW

The law of maritime delimitation has been mostly developed through the case law of the International Court of Justice and other tribunals. In the past decade, a number of cases have raised questions about the consistency and predictability of the jurisprudence concerning this subfield of international law. This book investigates these questions through a systematic review of the case law on the delimitation of the continental shelf and the exclusive economic zone. Comprehensive coverage allows for conclusions to be drawn about the case law's approach to the applicable law and its application to the individual case. *Maritime Boundary Delimitation* will appeal to scholars of international dispute settlement as well as practitioners and academics interested in the law concerning the delimitation of maritime boundaries.

ALEX G. OUDE ELFERINK is a Professor of Law at the K. G. Jebsen Centre for the Law of the Sea, University of Tromsø and Utrecht University and Director at the Netherlands Institute for the Law of the Sea, School of Law, Utrecht University.

TORE HENRIKSEN is a Professor of Law at the K. G. Jebsen Centre for the Law of the Sea, University of Tromsø.

SIGNE VEIERUD BUSCH is a post-doctoral research fellow at the K. G. Jebsen Centre for the Law of the Sea, University of Tromsø.

MARITIME BOUNDARY DELIMITATION: THE CASE LAW

Is It Consistent and Predictable?

Edited by

ALEX G. OUDE ELFERINK

University of Tromsø the Arctic University of Norway, Norway and Utrecht University, the Netherlands

TORE HENRIKSEN

University of Tromsø the Arctic University of Norway, Norway

SIGNE VEIERUD BUSCH

University of Tromsø the Arctic University of Norway, Norway

CAMBRIDGE
UNIVERSITY PRESS

CAMBRIDGE
UNIVERSITY PRESS

University Printing House, Cambridge CB2 8BS, United Kingdom

One Liberty Plaza, 20th Floor, New York, NY 10006, USA

477 Williamstown Road, Port Melbourne, VIC 3207, Australia

314-321, 3rd Floor, Plot 3, Splendor Forum, Jasola District Centre, New Delhi - 110025, India

79 Anson Road, #06-04/06, Singapore 079906

Cambridge University Press is part of the University of Cambridge.

It furthers the University's mission by disseminating knowledge in the pursuit of education, learning and research at the highest international levels of excellence.

www.cambridge.org
Information on this title: www.cambridge.org/9781108440943
DOI: 10.1017/9781108344302

First published 2018
First paperback edition 2019

A catalogue record for this publication is available from the British Library

Library of Congress Cataloging in Publication data
Names: Oude Elferink, Alex G., 1962– editor. | Henriksen, Tore, 1964– editor. | Busch, Signe Veierud, editor.
Title: Maritime boundary delimitation: the case law : is it consistent and predictable? / edited by Alex G. Oude, Elferink Universiteit Utrecht, The Netherlands; Tore Henriksen, Universitetet i Tromsø, Norway; Signe Veierud Busch, Universitetet i Tromsø, Norway.
Description: Cambridge,United Kingdom; NewYork, NY, USA : Cambridge University Press, 2018. | Includes bibliographical references and index.
Identifiers: LCCN 2017041998 | ISBN 9781108424790 (hardback)
Subjects: LCSH: Maritime boundaries – Cases.
Classification: LCC KZA1450.M3718 2018 | DDC 341.4/48 – dc23
LC record available at https://lccn.loc.gov/2017041998

ISBN 978-1-108-42479-0 Hardback
ISBN 978-1-108-44094-3 Paperback

CONTENTS

FIGURES

TABLES

CONTRIBUTORS

NUNO MARQUES ANTUNES is a law of the sea specialist who holds degrees in Naval Military Sciences (Portuguese Naval Academy) and Law (Lisbon University) and an MA and PhD from Durham University (UK). He is a member of the list of arbitrators of the LOSC and authored the monograph *Towards the Conceptualisation of Maritime Delimitation: Legal and Technical Aspects of a Political Process* (2003). Currently a Partner at Miranda & Associados (Portugal), Nuno's day-to-day practice focuses on petroleum matters, advising oil companies and state institutions. Nuno worked as petroleum advisor to the Prime Minister of Timor-Leste and advised on the negotiations of the Timor Sea maritime boundaries. He was legal coordinator of the Portuguese project for extension of the continental shelf, appointed expert to the Portuguese Strategic Commission on the Oceans and a member of Portuguese delegations to ocean affairs meetings. He has taught public international law, constitutional law, and petroleum law.

VASCO BECKER-WEINBERG, Dr. iur. (Hamburg), LLM (Lisbon), lectures at the Faculty of Law of the NOVA University of Lisbon on law of the sea and ocean governance subjects as well as at several Portuguese and foreign universities. He is the co-coordinator of the LLM program at NOVA on 'The Law of the Sea and the Sea-Economy' and a researcher at the Centro de Investigação e Desenvolvimento sobre Direito e Sociedade. Professor Becker-Weinberg has researched at prominent academic institutions and written and published extensively in the law of the sea. He was previously legal advisor to the Portuguese Secretary of the Sea and a full-time scholar at the International Max Planck Research School for Maritime Affairs at the University of Hamburg. Professor Becker-Weinberg has taken part in several delegations to international fora and often advises on several law of the sea matters. He has also been involved in the drafting of policies and legislation on many ocean governance subjects.

NAOMI BURKE O'SULLIVAN is an Associate Legal Officer at the International Tribunal for the Law of the Sea. Prior to joining the Tribunal, she was the Arthur Watts Research Fellow in Law of the Sea at the British Institute of International and Comparative Law. Dr. Burke O'Sullivan has previously worked in private practice at a boutique law firm specializing in public international law. She has also worked at the Legal Division of the Irish Ministry of Foreign Affairs, as a clerk at the International Court of Justice and as a research assistant at the International Law Commission. Dr. Burke holds an LLB from Trinity College Dublin, a master's degree from IEP Paris (Sciences Po) specializing in conflict and security studies, an LLM from New York University School of Law and a PhD from the University of Cambridge.

SIGNE VEIERUD BUSCH is a post-doctoral research fellow at the K. G. Jebsen Centre for the Law of the Sea of the University of Tromsø, Norway. Signe teaches public international law and general law of the sea at the Faculty of Law, University of Tromsø. She defended her PhD in 2014, resulting in the publication *Establishing Continental Shelf Limits beyond 200 Nautical Miles by the Coastal State: A Right of Involvement for Other States* (2016).

LUCIE DELABIE is professor of public law and Dean of the Faculty of Law and Political Science at the University of Picardie Jules Verne, France. Specialized in public international law, she is the author of *American Approaches to International Law* (2010). Her research interests include international legal theory, global governance studies, international settlement of disputes, and formal and informal interstate co-operation. She has published on various issues such as the role of G20 in economic co-operation, the interplay between investments and environment and the role of the International Court of Justice in the settlement of maritime delimitation disputes. She is also involved in a research project on the French policy strategies for action on climate change in the Pacific Ocean.

MALCOLM EVANS is Professor of Public International Law at the University of Bristol, UK. His areas of legal specialism include both the international law of the sea, with a particular focus on the delimitation of maritime boundaries, and international human rights protection, where his particular interests concern torture prevention and the protection of religious liberty. Since 2009 he has been a member of the United Nations Subcommittee for the Prevention of Torture (the SPT) and, since 2011, has been serving as its chair. From 2002 to 2013, he was a member of the OSCE ODIHR Advisory Council on the Freedom of Religion or Belief. He is also a member of the UK Foreign Secretary's Human Rights Advisory Group. He is Co-General Editor of the *International and Comparative Law Quarterly* and Editor of *International Law* (4th ed., 2014).

TORE HENRIKSEN is Director at the K. G. Jebsen Centre for the Law of the Sea, the Arctic University of Norway. He has written, *inter alia*, about issues relating to the legal status of the maritime zones off Svalbard.

ØYSTEIN JENSEN is Senior Research Fellow at the Fridtjof Nansen Institute and the K. G. Jebsen Centre for the Law of the Sea, University of Tromsø. He obtained his PhD in international law from the University of Oslo in 2013 with a dissertation on the Commission on the Limits of the Continental Shelf. Jensen has lectured international law at the University of Oslo, and his publications include books and several research articles, particularly on the continental shelf and navigation.

NATALIE KLEIN is Professor at Macquarie Law School, Macquarie University, Sydney, Australia. She served as Dean of Macquarie Law School between 2011 and 2017 as well as Acting Head of the Department for Policing, Intelligence, and Counter-Terrorism at Macquarie in 2013–2014. Professor Klein teaches and researches in different areas of international law, with a focus on law of the sea and international dispute settlement. She provides advice, undertakes consultancies, and interacts with the media on law of the sea issues. Prior to joining Macquarie, Professor Klein worked in the international litigation and arbitration practice of Debevoise & Plimpton LLP, served as counsel to the Government of Eritrea (1998–2002) and was a consultant in the Office of Legal Affairs at the United Nations. Her master's and doctorate in law were earned at Yale Law School, and she is a fellow of the Australian Academy of Law.

COALTER G. LATHROP is principal and owner of Sovereign Geographic, an international boundary consultancy providing legal and cartographic services to clients throughout the world. Lathrop has represented sovereign states in land and maritime boundary disputes and provided negotiation support and advice on related issues to governments and private interests in Africa, Asia, the Middle East, and North and South America. Over the last two decades, he has acted as counsel and advisor in multiple cases before the International Court of Justice and the

International Tribunal for the Law of the Sea. Lathrop holds a Master of Marine Affairs from the University of Washington and a JD and LLM in International and Comparative Law from Duke University. He has published and presented extensively on the law of the sea, the Arctic, island sovereignty and maritime boundaries, and he serves as the editor of *International Maritime Boundaries*, a project of the American Society of International Law.

DONALD MCRAE is Professor Emeritus in the Faculty of Law at the University of Ottawa. He has been counsel in several international fisheries and boundary arbitrations and in cases before the International Court of Justice. He has appeared as counsel before World Trade Organization (WTO) panels and the WTO Appellate Body. He has been a member of several WTO panels as well as member and chair of investment dispute tribunals under ICSID and UNCITRAL rules. Professor McRae is the former Editor-in-Chief of the *Canadian Yearbook of International Law* and serves on the Editorial Board of the *American Journal of International Law*. He is an associate member of the Institute of International Law, a member of the Royal Society of Canada and a Companion of the Order of Canada. He was a member of the International Law Commission from 2007 to 2016.

ALEX G. OUDE ELFERINK is Director at the Netherlands Institute for the law of the sea (NILOS) and an associate of the Utrecht Centre for Oceans, Water and Sustainability Law, School of Law, Utrecht University, the Netherlands. He is also an adjunct professor at the K. G. Jebsen Centre for the law of the sea, University of Tromsø, Norway. His recent publications include *The Delimitation of the Continental Shelf between Denmark, Germany and the Netherlands; Arguing Law, Practicing Politics?* (Cambridge University Press, 2013) and he is the co-editor of *The Oxford Handbook of the Law of the Sea* (2015).

YOSHIFUMI TANAKA is Professor of International Law with Specific Focus on the Law of the Sea at the Faculty of Law, University of Copenhagen, Denmark. He holds a DES and a PhD from the Graduate Institute of International Studies, Geneva (currently the Graduate Institute of International and Development Studies, Geneva) and an LLM from Hitotsubashi University, Tokyo. He is the single author of four books: *Predictability and Flexibility in the Law of Maritime Delimitation* (2006), *A Dual Approach to Ocean Governance: The Cases of Zonal and Integrated Management in International Law of the Sea* (2008), *The International Law of the Sea* (Cambridge University Press, 2012; 2nd ed., 2015) and *The Peaceful Settlement of International Disputes* (Cambridge University Press, forthcoming). He has published widely in the fields of the law of the sea, international environmental law, and peaceful settlement of international disputes.

DAVOR VIDAS is Research Professor in International Law and Director of the Law of the Sea Programme at the Fridtjof Nansen Institute, Norway. He is the Chair of the ILA Committee on International Law and Sea Level Rise and a member of the Anthropocene Working Group of the International Commission on Stratigraphy. Professor Vidas is the Co-Editor-in-Chief of the journal monograph series *Brill Research Perspectives on the Law of the Sea* and of a popular-science book series *Anthropocene*. His authored or edited books include *The World Ocean in Globalisation* (2011), *Law, Technology and Science for Oceans in Globalisation* (2010), *Order for the Oceans at the Turn of the Century* (1999), *Croatian–Slovenian Delimitation* (2009), *Protecting the Adriatic Sea* (2007), *Protecting the Polar Marine Environment* (Cambridge University Press, 2000; 2nd ed., 2006) and *Governing the Antarctic* (Cambridge University Press, 1996). Until 31 July 2015, he served as Counsel for Croatia in the Croatia-Slovenia arbitration.

PREFACE

When the K. G. Jebsen Centre for the Law of the Sea at the University of Tromsø (UiT, the Arctic University of Norway) started operating in 2013, maritime boundaries and limits were one of the main research projects of the Centre. Specifically, it was intended that the research on maritime boundaries and limits would include an assessment of the case law on the delimitation of the continental shelf and the exclusive economic zone. At the time of writing of this preface, the initiation of this case law dates back half a century. In 1967, Denmark, Germany and the Netherlands submitted their disputes concerning the delimitation of the continental shelf in the North Sea to the International Court of Justice. The 1969 Judgment of the Court formed the starting point of a rich and varied jurisprudence dealing with the delimitation of first the continental shelf and subsequently also the exclusive economic zone. As the analysis of the chapters to this volume and the case law itself testify, the concepts that the Court developed in its 1969 Judgment still resonate in the case law today.

This book is a joint effort in more than one respect. As editors, we profited much from working in a team of three. This allowed us to pool our insights on how to proceed with the organization of the project, in providing feedback to our contributors and in drafting the introductory and concluding chapters. Second, we are appreciative of the engagement of the other participants in the project. All of them attended the workshop in the framework of the project, which was convened in Tromsø at the end of May 2016. At the workshop the initial drafts of Chapters 2–13 were discussed. We used this discussion to provide our contributors with detailed feedback in connection with the preparation of a revised version of their drafts. The availability of the draft chapters also allowed us to present and discuss outlines of Chapters 1 and 14 of this volume at the workshop. The input we received greatly assisted us in finding the right focus for these chapters.

For the organization of the workshop in Tromsø we were able to rely on Christin Skjervold of the Jebsen Centre. As always, she did a wonderful job in ensuring that everything was planned perfectly and that we could focus on substantive matters. We would also like to acknowledge the assistance of Sofia Sjögren during the workshop, who at the time was an LLM student at UiT, the Arctic University of Norway. The notes she kept assisted us in reconstructing the discussions and drawing up our feedback to the contributors. We thank Glen Jeffries, one of our current LLM students, for his research assistance in preparing Chapter 14 and his involvement in the stylistic editing of the volume. Anyone familiar with the latter task will appreciate the effort that is required to bring an edited volume of this size into good shape. Finally, our appreciation goes to Finola O'Sullivan and Rebecca Roberts and the other staff at Cambridge University Press for getting this book ready for submission to its intended audience.

Internet materials cited in the chapters that follow were current as of May 2017.

Alex G. Oude Elferink
Signe Veierud Busch
Tore Henriksen
Utrecht and Tromsø, 20 May 2017

ABBREVIATIONS

CLCS	Commission on the Limits of the Continental Shelf
EEZ	Exclusive Economic Zone
ICJ	International Court of Justice
ILC	International Law Commission
ITLOS	International Tribunal for the Law of the Sea
km	kilometre
LOSC	1982 United Nations Convention on the Law of the Sea
nm	nautical mile
UNCLOS I	First United Nations Conferences on the Law of the Sea
UNCLOS II	Second United Nations Conferences on the Law of the Sea
UNCLOS III	Third United Nations Conferences on the Law of the Sea
UNTS	United Nations Treaty Series
Virginia Commentaries	*United Nations Convention on the Law of the Sea 1982: A Commentary* (6 vols., 1985–2002)

TABLE OF CASES

Aegean Sea Continental Shelf (Greece v. Turkey) [1978] ICJ Rep 3
Dispute concerning the MOX Plant, International Movements of Radioactive Materials, and the Protection of the Marine Environment of the Irish Sea, The MOX Plant Case (Ireland v. UK) (Order No. 3, Suspension of Proceedings on Jurisdiction and Merits, and Request for Further Provisional Measures) [2003] 126 ILR 310
Arbitration between Barbados and the Republic of Trinidad and Tobago [2006] XXVII RIAA 147
Case concerning the Delimitation of Continental Shelf between the United Kingdom of Great Britain and Northern Ireland, and the French Republic [1977, 1978] XVIII RIAA 3
Case concerning Land Reclamation by Singapore in and around the Straits of Johor (Malaysia v. Singapore) (Request for Provisional Measures) [2003] 126 ILR 487
Case concerning the Continental Shelf (Tunisia/Libyan Arab Jamahiriya) [1982] ICJ Rep 18
Case concerning the Delimitation of the Maritime Boundary between Guinea-Bissau and Senegal (Guinea-Bissau v. Senegal) [1995] ICJ Rep 423
Case concerning the Delimitation of Maritime Areas between Canada and France [1992] XXI RIAA 265
Case concerning the Continental Shelf (Libyan Arab Jamahiriya/Malta) [1985] ICJ Rep 13
Delimitation of the Maritime Boundary in the Bay of Bengal (Bangladesh/Myanmar) [2012] ITLOS Rep 4
Delimitation of the Maritime Boundary between Guinea and Guinea-Bissau [1985] XIX RIAA 149
Delimitation of the Maritime Boundary in the Gulf of Maine Area (Canada/United States) [1984] ICJ Rep 246
Dispute concerning Delimitation of the Maritime Boundary between Ghana and Côte d'Ivoire in the Atlantic Ocean (Ghana/Côte d'Ivoire) [2015] ITLOS Rep 494
In the Matter of an Arbitration pursuant to an Agreement dated 3 October 1996 between the Government of the State of Eritrea and the Government of the Republic of Yemen (Eritrea/Yemen) [1998] XXII RIAA 211

Fisheries Jurisdiction Case (United Kingdom of Great Britain and Northern Ireland *v.* Iceland) (Request for the Indication of Interim Measures of Protection) [1972] ICJ Rep 4

Grisbadarna Case (Norway v. Sweden) (Award) [1909] 11 RIA 155

In the Matter of an Arbitration between Guyana and Suriname (Guyana v. Suriname) [2007] XXX RIAA 1

In the Matter of the Bay of Bengal Maritime Boundary (Bangladesh v. India) PCA Case 2010–16

Interhandl Case (Switzerland v. US) [1957] ICJ Rep. 105

Land and Maritime Boundary between Cameroon and Nigeria (Cameroon v. Nigeria; Equatorial Guinea intervening) [2002] ICJ Rep 303

Land, Island and Maritime Frontier Dispute (El Salvador/Honduras) [1990] ICJ Rep 130

Maritime Delimitation and Territorial Questions between Qatar and Bahrain (Qatar/Bahrain) [2001] ICJ Rep 91

Maritime Delimitation in the Area between Greenland and Jan Mayen (Denmark v. Norway) [1993] ICJ Rep 38

Maritime Delimitation in the Black Sea (Romania v. Ukraine) [2009] ICJ Rep 61

Maritime Delimitation in the Caribbean Sea and the Pacific Ocean (Costa Rica v. Nicaragua)

Maritime Delimitation in the Indian Ocean (Somalia v. Kenya)

Maritime Dispute (Peru v. Chile) [2014] ICJ Rep 3

M/V Louise (Saint Vincent and the Grenadines v. Spain), Provisional Measures, Order, 23 December 2010, ITLOS Rep 58

Newfoundland and Labrador/Nova Scotia (Award of the Tribunal in the Second Phase) [2002] 128 ILR 504

North Sea Continental Shelf Cases (Federal Republic of Germany/Denmark; Federal Republic of Germany/Netherlands) [1969] ICJ Rep 3

Question of the Delimitation of the Continental Shelf between Nicaragua and Colombia beyond 200 nautical miles from the Nicaraguan Coast (Nicaragua v. Colombia) [2012] ICJ Rep 436

Questions relating to the Obligation to Prosecute or Extradite (Belgium v. Senegal) Provisional Measures Order of 28 May 2009 [2009] ICJ Rep 139

South China Sea Arbitration (Philippines v. China) [2016] PCA Case No 2013–19, ICGJ 495

Southern Bluefin Tuna Cases (Australia v. Japan; New Zealand v. Japan) (Provisional Measures) [1999] 38 ILM 1624

Territorial and Maritime Dispute (Nicaragua v. Colombia) [2012] ICJ Rep 624

Territorial and Maritime Dispute between Nicaragua and Honduras in the Caribbean Sea (Nicaragua v. Honduras) [2007] ICJ Rep 659

The 'Enrica Lexie' Incident (Italy v. India) Provisional Measures Order of 24 August 2015 ITLOS Rep 24

The M/V 'Saiga' *(No. 2) (St. Vincent v. Guinea)* (Order on Provisional Measures) [1998] (11 March 1998) ITLOS Rep 10

INTERNATIONAL INSTRUMENTS

1948 American Treaty on Pacific Settlement, signed 30 April 1948, entered into force 6 May 1949, 30 UNTS 449

1958 Convention on the Territorial Sea and the Contiguous Zone, signed 29 April 1958, entered into force 10 September 1964, 516 UNTS 206

1958 Convention on the Continental Shelf, signed 29 April 1958, entered into force 10 June 1964, 499 UNTS 311

1958 Optional Protocol of Signature concerning the Compulsory Settlement of Disputes arising from the Law of the Sea Conventions, signed 29 April 1958, entered into force 30 September 1962, 450 UNTS 169

1982 United Nations Convention on the Law of the Sea, signed 10 December 1982, entered into force 16 November 1994, 1833 UNTS 397

1993 Convention for the Conservation of Southern Bluefin Tuna, signed 10 May 1993, entered into force 20 May 1994, 1819 UNTS 360

1

The Judiciary and the Law of Maritime Delimitation

Setting the Stage

ALEX G. OUDE ELFERINK, TORE HENRIKSEN, AND SIGNE VEIERUD BUSCH

1.1 Introduction

The development of the regimes of the continental shelf and the exclusive economic zone in the second half of the twentieth century has extended coastal state jurisdiction to almost half of the oceans. One study from 2011 indicates that the oceans cover 335 million square kilometres and that 130 million square miles are exclusive economic zone and continental shelf within 200 nautical miles from the baselines of coastal states. In addition, the continental shelf beyond 200 nautical miles from the baselines covers some 28 million square kilometres of ocean space.[1] This extension of coastal state jurisdiction also dramatically increased the area of overlapping maritime zones of coastal states. Previously, coastal states in principle only had to delimit the territorial sea, which for most states measured only three nautical miles until the 1970s. With the advent of the continental shelf, this situation changed dramatically.[2] For instance, in the

[1] See T. Schoolmeester and E. Baker (eds.), *Continental Shelf; The Last Maritime Zone; Status in Sept. 2010* (UNEP/GRID-Arendal 2011) 16. It may be noted that the latter figure only concerns the continental shelf beyond 200 nautical miles in respect of which coastal states have submitted (preliminary) information in accordance with Art. 76 of the United Nations Convention on the Law of the Sea (LOSC). A number of states with significant continental shelf areas beyond 200 nautical miles, including Canada, Denmark, and the US, had not submitted such information in 2011, indicating that the actual area of continental shelf beyond 200 nautical miles is more than 28 million square kilometres.

[2] As has been remarked by Gilbert Guillaume, the former President of the International Court of Justice (ICJ), '[d]elimitation of [maritime zones] was long considered a secondary question, involving the fixing of the boundaries between narrow territorial seas. Extension of state jurisdiction to the high seas and technological developments have made this into one

North Sea, the entire seabed became part of the continental shelf of the coastal states, among others requiring boundaries between the UK and its neighbours on the European continent. To give one other example, while Norway and the former Soviet Union only shared a territorial sea boundary in the Varanger Fjord, their continental shelf covered the entire Barents Sea and a part of the central Arctic Ocean to the north of Svalbard. While the territorial sea boundary measures 22.7 nautical miles, the continental shelf boundary that was agreed upon in 2010 between Norway and the Russian Federation has a length of more than 920 nautical miles.[3]

Rules on the delimitation of the continental shelf were first included in the 1958 Convention on the Continental Shelf, and the United Nations Convention on the Law of the Sea (LOSC), which was adopted in 1982, contains a delimitation provision for both the continental shelf and the exclusive economic zone.[4] However, the rules contained in these conventions are of a general nature and provide limited guidance to states when they differ about the interpretation and application of the law and the appropriate method(s) to delimit their maritime boundaries. The clarification of the rules on maritime delimitation has been mostly achieved through the case law of the International Court of Justice (ICJ), arbitral tribunals and, more recently, the International Tribunal for the Law of the

of the main territorial issues of the last 30 years' (G. Guillaume, *Speech by His Excellency Judge Gilbert Guillaume, President of the International Court of Justice, to the Sixth Committee of the General Assembly of the United Nations; 31 October 2001*, available at www.icj-cij.org/court/index.php?pr=81&pt=3&p1=1&p2=3&p3=1).

3 Treaty between the Kingdom of Norway and the Russian Federation concerning Maritime Delimitation and Cooperation in the Barents Sea and the Arctic Ocean of 15 September 2010 (English translation available at www.un.org/Depts/los/LEGISLATIONANDTREATIES/PDFFILES/TREATIES/NOR-RUS2010.PDF). Most of the continental shelf delimited by this treaty already was part of the continental shelf under the definition contained in Art. 1 of the 1958 Convention on the Continental Shelf (Convention on the Continental Shelf, signed 29 April 1958, entered into force 10 June 1964, 499 UNTS 311). The figures on the length of these boundaries are mentioned in *Om samtykke til ratifikasjon av overenskomst av 11. juli 2007 mellom Norge og Russland om den maritime avgrensning i Varangerfjordområdet* (St.prp. nr. 3 (2007–2008), 2 and *Samtykke til ratifikasjon av overenskomst av 15. september 2010 mellom Norge og Russland om maritim avgrensning og samarbeid I Barentshavet og Polhavet* (Prop. 43 S (2010–2011) 6–7.

4 The delimitation of the territorial sea is addressed in Art. 12 of the 1958 Convention on the Territorial Sea and Contiguous Zone (Convention on the Territorial Sea and the Contiguous Zone, signed 29 April 1958, entered into force 10 September 1964, 516 UNTS 206) and Art. 15 of the LOSC. See further below for the explanation as to why this volume largely focusses on the delimitation of the continental shelf and the exclusive economic zone.

Sea (ITLOS). As a result, the law of maritime delimitation has also been referred to as judge-made law.[5]

The delimitation of the maritime boundaries is one of the areas of the law of the sea that has been most heavily litigated. At the time of writing, twenty-nine cases on the delimitation of maritime boundaries have either been decided by the judiciary or are pending before a court or tribunal.[6] The majority of this case law is concerned with the delimitation of the continental shelf and exclusive economic zone. Only three of these cases are exclusively concerned with the delimitation of the territorial sea;[7] thirteen with the delimitation of the continental shelf or the continental shelf and the exclusive economic zone;[8] and thirteen with the delimitation of the territorial sea, continental shelf, and exclusive economic zone.[9] In addition, it may be noted that in comparison to the delimitation of the territorial sea, the delimitation of the continental shelf and the exclusive economic zone has led to much more controversy and debate. This may be illustrated by the fact that monographs on the law of maritime delimitation in general focus on the continental shelf and the exclusive economic zone and pay limited attention to the delimitation of the territorial sea.[10] The fate of the delimitation provisions contained in the 1958 Conventions on the Territorial Sea and the Contiguous Zone and the Continental Shelf, respectively, also attests to the larger measure of controversy surrounding the delimitation of the continental shelf and the exclusive economic zone. Article 12 of the former Convention was included almost verbatim as

[5] For instance, President Guillaume of the ICJ in a speech to the Six Committee of the General Assembly of the United Nations submitted that the law in this field had been completely reunified by the Court's judgment in *Maritime Delimitation in the Area between Greenland and Jan Mayen (Denmark v. Norway)* ([1993] ICJ Rep. 38) and that this law 'has reached a new level of unity and certainty' through the development of the case law (Guillaume, n. 2); see also below, Sections 1.2 and 1.5 of this chapter for further references to this speech.

[6] For an overview of these cases, see Table 1.1.

[7] See ibid., entries A.1, A.5 and A.14.

[8] See ibid., entries A.2, A.3, A.4, A.6, A.7, A.8, A.11, B.1, B.2, B.5, B.6, B.7, and B.12. A number of these cases do not concern the delimitation of the exclusive economic zone but concern a 200-nautical-mile fishery zone instead.

[9] See ibid., entries A.9, A.12, A.13, B.3, B.4, B.8, B.9, B.10, B.11, B.13, B.14, and B.15.

[10] See e.g. N. M. Antunes, *Towards the Conceptualisation of Maritime Delimitation* (Martinus Nijhoff Leiden 2003); E. D. Brown, *Sea-bed Energy and Minerals: The International Legal Regime* (Martinus Nijhoff Leiden 1992); T. Cottier, *Equitable Principles of Maritime Boundary Delimitation: The Quest for Distributive Justice in International Law* (Cambridge University Press Cambridge 2015); S. Fietta and R. Cleverly, *A Practitioner's Guide to Maritime Boundary Delimitation* (Oxford University Press Oxford 2015); Y. Tanaka, *Predictability and Flexibility in the Law of Maritime Delimitation* (Hart Oxford 2006); P. Weil, *The Law of Maritime Delimitation: Reflections* (Grotius Cambridge 1989).

Article 15 in the LOSC. The almost identical provision contained in Article 6 of the Convention on the Continental Shelf was found to be unacceptable for a significant number of states at the Third United Nations Conference on the Law of the Sea (UNCLOS III). Articles 74 and 83 of the LOSC on, respectively, the delimitation of the exclusive economic zone and the continental shelf do not have any resemblance to Article 6. One explanation for this difference is that incidental geographical features in general will have limited impact on the equidistance line in the restricted area of the territorial sea. This impact may be much larger where the delimitation of the continental shelf and the exclusive economic zone is concerned. As a matter of fact, the ICJ pointed this out in its judgment in *North Sea Continental Shelf*.[11] While the judgment provided states with strong arguments to reject the rule contained in Article 6 of the Convention on the Continental Shelf,[12] the same does not hold true for the rule contained in Article 12 of the Convention on the Territorial Sea and the Contiguous Zone.

For the above reasons, the current volume focuses on the case law on the delimitation of the continental shelf and the exclusive economic zone and does not pay the same amount of attention to the delimitation of the territorial sea. At the same time, it is recognized that an analysis of the case law on the delimitation of the territorial sea may enhance our understanding of the delimitation of the continental shelf and the exclusive economic zone. For that reason, Chapter 2 of this volume is concerned with the delimitation of the territorial sea. This chapter in particular seeks to determine in which respects the regime of the territorial sea and its delimitation differ from that of the zones beyond the territorial sea.

The remainder of the current chapter provides some additional background information to the chapters that follow. Section 1.2 of the current chapter further introduces the research focus of the project that resulted in this volume. Section 1.3 then briefly comments on the development of the law on the entitlement to and delimitation of the continental shelf and the exclusive economic zone. As is explained in that section, the relevant rules contained in multilateral conventions and customary international law provide the framework against which developments in the case law have to be assessed. Section 1.4 of this chapter discusses the availability of third-party dispute settlement mechanisms to resolve disputes on the delimitation of the continental shelf and the exclusive economic zone.

[11] *North Sea Continental Shelf Cases (Federal Republic of Germany/Denmark; Federal Republic of Germany/The Netherlands)* (Judgment) [1969] ICJ Rep. 18, [8].

[12] See further below at n. 23.

As this discussion illustrates, the option of third-party dispute settlement was considered to be relevant to maritime delimitation from the outset of the debate on substantive delimitation provisions. Section 1.4 also briefly discusses some general trends as regard the delimitation of the continental shelf and the exclusive economic zone through bilateral agreements and third-party dispute settlement procedures. Section 1.5 considers two issues that are not included in the subsequent chapters but still were considered to merit attention. These concern the question how the composition of judicial bodies may shape the law and whether criticism from beyond the bench may have had an impact on the development of the case law. The individual chapters of the volume are introduced in Section 1.6, while a final section presents concluding remarks.

1.2 The Research Focus of the Book

This volume is concerned with the case law of the ICJ, the ITLOS, and arbitral tribunals on the delimitation of the continental shelf and the exclusive economic zone. The title and specific research focus of the current volume and the research project at its basis have been inspired by the ICJ's judgment in *Libya/Malta*, where the Court observed that the justice which the courts had been applying in maritime delimitation cases is

> justice according to the rule of law; which is to say that its application should display consistency and a degree of predictability; even though it looks with particularity to the peculiar circumstances of an instant case, it also looks beyond it to principles of more general application.[13]

It has been submitted that the law as developed by the judiciary has gradually become much more predictable – a development which started in the middle of the 1980s. This view has been regularly expounded in the academic literature.[14] It has also been forcefully argued by influential judges.

[13] *Continental Shelf (Libyan Arab Jamahiriya/Malta)*, (Judgment) [1985] ICJ Rep. 39, [45].

[14] See e.g. R. R. Churchill, 'The Bangladesh/Myanmar Case: Continuity and Novelty in the Law of Maritime Boundary Delimitation,' (2012) 1 *Cambridge Journal of International and Comparative Law* 137, 138, and 151; V. Degan, 'Consolidation of Legal Principles on Maritime Delimitation: Implications for the Dispute between Slovenia and Croatia in the North Adriatic,' (2007) 6 *Chinese Journal of International Law* 601, 609, 616–617, and 619; J. Shi, 'Maritime Delimitation in the Jurisprudence of the International Court of Justice,' 9 (2010) *Chinese Journal of International Law* 271, 290–291; Y. Tanaka, 'Reflections on Maritime Delimitation in the Cameroon/Nigeria Case,' (2004) 53 *International and Comparative Law Quarterly* 369, 405; Y. Tanaka, 'Reflections on Maritime Delimitation in the Romania/Ukraine Case before the ICJ,' (2009) 56 *Netherlands International Law Review* 397, 426; Weil, n. 10, 288.

Of particular note is the speech of Gilbert Guillaume as President of the ICJ to the Sixth Committee of the General Assembly of the United Nations.[15] Referring to the judgments in *Tunisia/Libya* and *Gulf of Maine*, Guillaume observes that

> [a]t this stage, case law and treaty law had become so unpredictable that there was extensive debate within the doctrine on whether there still existed a law of delimitations or whether, in the name of equity, we were not ending up with arbitrary solutions. Sensitive to these criticisms, in subsequent years the Court proceeded to develop its case law in the direction of greater certainty.[16]

Guillaume observes that the Court began this development in *Libya/Malta* and *Jan Mayen*, in which cases the equidistance line was taken as a provisional starting point between opposite coasts. The process was completed in *Qatar/Bahrain*, when the Court found that equidistance also provided the starting point for delimitations involving adjacent coasts.[17] Guillaume concludes that, as a result, 'the Court's case law, has reached a new level of unity and certainty, whilst conserving the necessary flexibility.'[18] More recently, Judge Wolfrum, in a declaration to the judgment of the ITLOS in *Bangladesh/Myanmar*, observed,

> Further objectives to be taken into consideration by international courts and tribunals are to provide for transparency and predictability of the whole process. The ensuing international case law constitutes an *acquis judiciaire*, a source of international law to be read into articles 74 and 83 of the [LOSC].[19]

Notwithstanding these claims, it is open to question whether the case law has been completely successful in this regard. In *Libya/Malta*, a number of judges engaged the Court's claim concerning the consistency and predictability of its decision in the case at hand. Judge Schwebel in his dissenting opinion, while acknowledging that there remained 'considerable room for differences of opinion in the application of equitable principles to problems of maritime delimitation,' submitted that

[15] Guillaume, n. 2. [16] Ibid. [17] Ibid. [18] Ibid.

[19] *Delimitation of the Maritime Boundary in the Bay of Bengal (Bangladesh/Myanmar)*, Judgment of 14 March 2012, [2012] ITLOS Rep. 4, Declaration of Judge Wolfrum, 2. In the subsequent arbitration between Bangladesh and India, under the presidency of Wolfrum, the reference to the significance of the *acquis judiciaire* was included in the Award (*In the Matter of the Bay of Bengal Maritime Boundary (Bangladesh v. India)* [2014] PCA Case 2010-16, [339]. The authors would like to thank Nigel Bankes for drawing their attention to this point.

> the Court's cryptic references to the length of coasts, the distance between coasts, the sparsity of basepoints, and the general geographical context, suffice to justify the selection of the line of delimitation which it has chosen in this case. Nor do these arrested allusions conduce towards building the sense of consistency and predictability at which the Court and the law so rightly aim.[20]

Some of the recent academic literature also continues to voice doubt about the predictability and consistency of the case law.[21]

In the light of these different views concerning the consistency and predictability of the case law, the current volume is intended to further investigate that issue. To that end, the authors of individual chapters will assess to what extent the case law has been consistent in defining the relevant concepts and applying them to the specific case or not.

Contributors were initially requested to focus on the case law of the first two decades of the present century and to consider the previous case law to the extent this would provide the necessary context for understanding the more recent case law. During the first two decades of the present century, the case law has adopted the so-called three-stage approach to the delimitation of the continental shelf and the exclusive economic zone, which consists of first determining a provisional line, then assessing the need to adjust this line in the light of the relevant circumstances and finally carrying out the so-called proportionality test.[22] There were two reasons for this proposing focus. First, this recent case law has received less scholarly attention than the older case law. Second, the existence of a common

[20] *Libya/Malta*, n. 13, Dissenting Opinion of Judge Schwebel, [1985] ICJ Rep., 172, 187. Similar criticisms were voiced by judges Ruda, Bedjaoui, and Jiménez de Aréchaga (ibid., Separate Opinion of Judges Ruda, Bedjaoui and Jiménez de Aréchaga, 76, 90 [37]), Mosler (ibid., Dissenting Opinion of Judge Mosler, 114, 114–115), and Judge ad hoc Valticos (ibid., Separate Opinion of Judge Valticos, 104, 108 [13]).

[21] See e.g. M. D. Evans, 'Maritime Boundary Delimitation: Whatever Next?,' in J. Barrett and R. Barnes (eds.), *Law of the Sea; UNCLOS as a Living Treaty* (British Institute of International and Comparative Law 2016), 41, 78; Fietta and Cleverly, n. 10, 579; A. G. Oude Elferink, 'International Law and Negotiated and Adjudicated Maritime Boundaries: A Complex Relationship,' (2015) 58 *German Yearbook of International Law*; I. Scobbie, 'Tom Franck's Fairness,' (2002) 13 *European Journal of International Law* 909, 924.

[22] The three-stage approach was already used in *Libya/Malta* and *Jan Mayen* (both situations involving the delimitation between opposite coasts) but not in *Canada/France* (which could be said to involve both adjacent and opposite coasts). The Court in *Qatar/Bahrain* for the first time took the position that equidistance also provided the provisional starting point in cases involving adjacent coasts. The authors of this chapter consider the latter case to be the starting point of the consistent application of the three-stage approach (*Maritime Delimitation and Territorial Questions between Qatar and Bahrain (Qatar v. Bahrain)* [2001] ICJ Rep., 91–92 [170] and 111 [230–232].

general approach to the delimitation of the continental shelf and the exclusive economic zone offers the opportunity to assess whether this general approach has been applied in a consistent and predictable manner across cases. However, further consideration of this matter led to the conclusion that it would be counterproductive only to consider the more recent case law in detail. Many concepts of maritime delimitation law have their origins in the earlier case law and cannot be properly understood without an in-depth discussion of that earlier case law.

The editors requested that individual authors, in writing their respective chapters, take into consideration three issues:

1. an analysis of the case law's definition(s) and the characteristics of the main concepts under consideration in the chapter – in this connection, contributors were also requested to consider whether it is possible to distinguish between the approach of the ICJ, the ITLOS and arbitral tribunals;
2. how the main concepts under consideration in the chapter have been applied to the individual case; and
3. an assessment as to how the approach of the case law to the concepts under consideration in the chapter relate to the ICJ's statement in *Libya/Malta* on consistency and predictability.

The choice for an edited volume was deliberate. Current academic practices make it next to impossible to prepare a book of this nature in the form of a monograph. Aside from this practical consideration, the editors hold that an edited volume has the advantage of providing room for different opinions. In particular, in the case of a controversial topic like the law on the delimitation of the continental shelf and the exclusive economic zone, there is a considerable advantage to considering such different views and presenting them to the reader to form her or his own opinion.

1.3 Development of the Law on the Entitlement to and Delimitation of the Continental Shelf and the Exclusive Economic Zone

The relevant rules contained in multilateral conventions and customary international law provide the point of departure for the judiciary in determining the content of that law in more detail while applying it to the individual case. Changes in these relevant rules may be one important factor in explaining the differences in approach to the delimitation process between individual cases. In looking at the development of the case law on the delimitation of the continental shelf and the exclusive economic zone it is necessary to take into account the development of the applicable law as contained in multilateral conventions and customary international law. First, as in any field of law, the specificity of the applicable law will have an impact on the judge or arbitrator in interpreting and applying that law to the specific case. Second, developments in the applicable law, which may make it less or more specific, may provide the judge or arbitrator with greater or lesser leeway in this respect. In the case of the delimitation of the continental shelf and the exclusive economic zone, two aspects of the applicable law are relevant in this connection. First, this obviously concerns the rules that are applicable to the delimitation of the continental shelf and the exclusive economic zone. Second, as will become apparent from what follows, the rules concerning the basis of entitlement of the continental shelf and the exclusive zone are also relevant in this respect.

From its inception, the case law on the delimitation of the continental shelf and the exclusive economic zone has considered the basis of entitlement to these zones pertinent to determining the content of the rules applicable to their delimitation. The 1969 judgment of the ICJ in *North Sea Continental Shelf* is the starting point of the case law on the delimitation of the continental shelf and the exclusive economic zone. At the time, the negotiations that eventually were to result in the LOSC were in an initial phase and the rules on the entitlement to these zones and their delimitation as they would be included in the LOSC did not have an impact on the Court's judgment.[23] The Court was faced with the question whether

[23] As a matter of fact, the impact ran the other way. The Court's finding that the entitlement to the continental shelf is based on natural prolongation of the land territory (*North Sea Continental Shelf*, n. 11, 30 [40] and 54 [101]) was one of the arguments of the so-called broad margin states to support their view that the entitlement to the continental shelf should not be limited by the 200-nautical-mile limit, but extended to the outer edge of the continental margin (see e.g. A. G. Oude Elferink, 'Article 76 of the LOSC on the Definition of the Continental Shelf: Questions Concerning Its Interpretation from a Legal Perspective,' (2006) 21 *International Journal of Marine and Coastal Law* 269, 272–273). The Court's formulation of the rule on the delimitation of the continental shelf to the effect that 'delimitation is to be effected by agreement in accordance with equitable principles, and taking account of all the relevant circumstances' (*North Sea Continental Shelf* (Judgment), n. 11, 54 [101]) provided a group of states at UNCLOS III with an argument to reject the rule on delimitation with its reference to equidistance and special circumstances contained in Art. 6 of the Convention on the Continental Shelf. At the same time, archival material related to *North Sea Continental Shelf* suggests that the Court's approach to the applicable law may have been influenced by a wish to impact on the further development of the law of the sea under consideration at the United Nations (see A. G. Oude Elferink, *The Delimitation of the Continental Shelf between Denmark, Germany and the Netherlands; Arguing Law, Practicing Politics?* (Cambridge University Press Cambridge 2013) 244–245 and 325).

or not the Convention on the Continental Shelf provided the applicable law between the parties. Denmark and the Netherlands maintained that either the Convention itself had become binding on Germany or that the Convention reflected customary international law. According to Denmark and the Netherlands, the Convention's rule on continental shelf entitlement, based on adjacency to the coast, implied that this entitlement was based on proximity to the coast.[24] This distance-based basis of entitlement required that the rule of delimitation also had to be based in distance.[25] Denmark and the Netherlands submitted that Article 6 of the Convention of the Continental Shelf, which refers to delimitation by the equidistance or median line[26] and provides for the possibility of another boundary where this is justified by special circumstances, did indeed accord primacy to the distance-based rule of equidistance. In their view, special circumstances only allowed for limited departures from the equidistance line.[27] The Court did not accept this reasoning. The Convention had not become binding on Germany and its rule of delimitation did not reflect customary law.[28] The Court rejected that the notion of adjacency in the Convention equalled a distance-based entitlement to the continental shelf.[29] Instead, the Court found that entitlement to the continental shelf was based on natural prolongation from the land territory of the coastal state.[30] This finding implied that the equidistance method of delimitation was not directly linked to the basis of continental shelf entitlement. The Court did conclude that there was a linkage between entitlement to and delimitation of the continental shelf, observing that 'delimitation is to be effected [...] in such a way as to leave as much as possible to each party all those parts of the continental shelf that constitute a natural prolongation of its land territory into and under the sea, without encroachment on the natural prolongation of the land territory of the other.'[31]

Having rejected that equidistance constituted an obligatory rule under customary international law, the Court formulated what it considered to constitute the applicable law: 'delimitation is to be effected by agreement in accordance with equitable principles, and taking account of all the relevant circumstances.'[32] Although the Court's judgment provided the

24 *North Sea Continental Shelf* (Judgment), n. 11, 30 [39]. 25 Ibid.

26 Technically speaking, the equidistance line and the median line are the same. Both lines are at equal distance from the baselines from which the breadth of the territorial of the states concerned is measured.

27 *North Sea Continental Shelf* (Judgment) [1969] ICJ Rep., 21 [13].

28 Ibid., 25–28 [25–32]. 29 Ibid., 31–32 [41–42].

30 Ibid., 32 [43]. 31 Ibid., 53 [101(C)(1)]. 32 Ibid.

parties with some indications on how to apply this rule in their further negotiations on the delimitation of their continental shelf, the Court's customary rule cannot be said the have contributed significantly to the certainty and predictability of the law. The Court's refusal to consider the status of the combined rule of equidistance and special circumstance also implied continued uncertainty about the relationship between these two elements of Article 6. The Court's rejection of Article 6 as customary law implied that states and courts and tribunals in the future would be faced with two rules of law of different content, possibly resulting in different outcomes depending on the applicable law in the individual case.

Thc adoption of the LOSC implied a further and final development in the multilateral rules on the entitlement to and the delimitation of the continental shelf. Under the Convention, entitlement to the exclusive economic zone is based on distance from the coast, while entitlements to the continental shelf is based either on distance from the coast or natural prolongation.[33] Like the exclusive economic zone, the continental shelf in any case extends to 200 nautical miles from the baselines, but it extends beyond that distance where the outer edge of the continental margin extends beyond that limit.[34] Although Article 76 in its rules on the precise determination of the outer limits of the continental shelf beyond 200 nautical miles contains two references to distance from the coast, the entitlement to the continental shelf beyond 200 nautical miles otherwise is not linked to that criterion.

The implications of distance-based entitlement to the continental shelf within 200 nautical miles was first considered in *Libya/Malta*. The Court found that this basis of entitlement had to be reflected in 'the choice of the criterion and the method which it is to employ in the first place to arrive at a provisional [delimitation line].'[35] On that basis, the Court adopted an equidistance line as the provisional line of delimitation.[36] A first detailed assessment of the relationship between the basis of continental shelf entitlement beyond 200 nautical miles and the delimitation of that part of the shelf was carried out by the ITLOS in its 2012 judgment in *Bangladesh/Myanmar*.[37]

The LOSC's rule on the delimitation of the exclusive economic zone and the continental shelf contained in its substantively identical Articles 74 and 83 is a compromise that was intended to bridge the insuperable divide between the states at UNCLOS III supporting the rule contained

[33] LOSC, Arts. 57 and 76. [34] LOSC, Art. 76(1). [35] *Libya/Malta*, n. 13, 46–47 [61].
[36] Ibid., 46–47 [60–62]. [37] *Bangladesh/Myanmar*, n. 19, [397–423].

in the Convention on the Continental Shelf and those supporting the rule formulated by the ICJ in *North Sea Continental Shelf*.[38] As a consequence, the judiciary was left with the task of seeking to find an approach to the delimitation of the exclusive economic zone and the continental shelf that ideally should reflect the compromise solution contained in Articles 74 and 83, while at the same time delimiting those boundaries on the basis of a reasoned decision.

How the development of the applicable law relating to entitlement to and delimitation of the exclusive economic zone and the continental shelf has been addressed in the case law will in particular be considered in more detail in Chapters 3, 6, and 13 of this volume.

1.4 Third-Party Dispute Settlement and the Law of Maritime Delimitation[39]

Disputes between states can only be submitted to third-party dispute settlement with the consent of the parties. That consent may either have been given previously under an instrument of general application, or by an agreement between the parties to submit a specific dispute to third-party dispute settlement. Disputes concerning the delimitation of the continental shelf and the exclusive economic zone have been submitted to courts and tribunals through both of these options. The present section briefly outlines the availability of dispute settlement provisions in multilateral instruments on the law of the sea and beyond, and the options that states have used to submit their delimitation disputes to third-party settlement. The section also compares the trends in settlement of delimitation disputes through negotiations and third-party settlement.

The Convention on the Continental Shelf does not contain a provision on third-party settlement. The International Law Commission (ILC), which prepared draft articles on the law of the sea in the 1950s, had provided for this option. As a matter of fact, this proposal originated in a debate on the delimitation provision for the continental shelf. During the 1951 session of the ILC, Scelle had proposed that:

[38] See further e.g. S. N. Nandan and S. Rosenne (eds.), *United Nations Convention on the Law of the Sea 1982: A Commentary*, vol. 2 (Martinus Nijhoff Dordrecht 1993), 796–816 and 948–985.

[39] A part of this section is based on A. G. Oude Elferink, 'International Law and Negotiated and Adjudicated Maritime Boundaries: A Complex Relationship,' (2015) 58 *German Yearbook of International Law* 231, 234–238.

> the Commission should state that, if two governments could not reach agreement as to the partition of the continental shelf, neither State was entitled to exploit it. They must either maintain the status quo or they would be under an obligation to refer the question to the International Court of Justice.[40]

This led the ILC to adopt a draft article providing for arbitration where states could not agree on the delimitation of their continental shelf.[41] Subsequently, the scope of this provision was extended to the continental shelf regime as a whole.[42] The 1956 ILC draft articles that formed the basis of discussion at the 1958 United Nations Conference on the Law of the Sea (UNCLOS I) provided for referral to the ICJ.[43] However, the Conference rejected the possibility of compulsory dispute settlement in relation to the regime of the continental shelf.

The Conference's rejection of a dispute settlement clause did not imply that the delimitation of the continental shelf was altogether beyond the reach of compulsory dispute settlement for prospective parties to the Convention on the Continental Shelf. The 1958 Conference itself adopted the Optional Protocol of signature concerning the compulsory settlement of disputes. Other instruments, such as the ICJ Statute with its optional clause jurisdiction, the Pact of Bogotá[44] and bilateral treaties on dispute settlement, also provided a basis for unilateral recourse to third-party settlement.

The possibility of judicial settlement of maritime boundaries where negotiations would fail to achieve an agreement was again considered at UNCLOS III. It was considered that the content of the substantive delimitation provision was closely related to the regime of compulsory dispute settlement and that they should be treated as one package.[45] The outcome of the negotiations as contained in Articles 74 and 83 of the LOSC explicitly recognizes that negotiations may not lead to an agreement. Common Paragraph 2 provides that '[i]f no agreement can be reached within a reasonable period of time, the states concerned shall resort to the procedures provided for in Part XV.' At the same time, this reference does not imply

40 Yearbook of the International Law Commission, 1951, vol. I, 288, [5]; see also ibid., 292, [65].

41 See ibid., 293–294, [100–101].

42 See ibid., 1953, vol. II, 213 and 216–217.

43 See ibid., 1956, vol. II, 300.

44 American Treaty on Pacific Settlement, signed 30 April 1948, entered into force 6 May 1949, 30 UNTS 449.

45 See further A. G. Oude Elferink, *The Law of Maritime Boundary Delimitation: A Case Study of the Russian Federation* (Martinus Nijhoff Dordrecht 1994) 27–28.

that third-party settlement will always be available to states parties to the Convention to settle their disputes concerning the delimitation of the continental shelf and the exclusive economic zone. First, Section 1 of Part XV imposes a number of procedural hurdles. As Article 279 indicates, Part XV is applicable to disputes concerning the interpretation or application of the LOSC. Maritime delimitation disputes may also involve disputes concerning the sovereignty over land territory or land boundaries.[46] However, such mixed disputes may be submitted to third-party settlement under other instruments, with the LOSC still providing part of the applicable law.[47] Further procedural requirements are contained in Articles 281, 282, and 283 of the LOSC. As a result of Articles 281 and 282 a dispute concerning the delimitation of maritime boundaries may be excluded from the compulsory procedures contained in Section 2 of Part XV. Article 282 implies that the procedures of Part XV do not apply where the parties to a dispute have agreed to settle it through a procedure entailing a binding decision under another agreement. Article 282 does not limit the possibility to settle delimitation disputes through third-party settlement, but does limit the recourse to Section 2 of Part XV.[48] The implications of Article 282 have been considered by the ICJ in its decision on preliminary objections in *Somalia v. Kenya*.[49] This concerned the effect of an optional clause

[46] Admittedly, different views exist over the question to what extent a court or tribunal could deal with all aspects of a mixed dispute that is submitted under the LOSC (for an overview see e.g. I. Buga, 'Territorial Sovereignty Issues in Maritime Disputes: A Jurisdictional Dilemma for Law of the Sea Tribunals,' (2012) 59 *International Journal of Marine and Coastal Law* 27). It would seem that a court or tribunal in any case would be excluded from dealing with matters concerning the sovereignty over territory to the extent this would imply a ruling on a claim that does not arise directly under the LOSC (see also ITLOS *Dispute concerning the MOX Plant, International Movements of Radioactive Materials, and the Protection of the Marine Environment of the Irish Sea (Ireland v. United Kingdom)*, Order No. 3 of 24 June 2003, [19]; *In the Matter of the Arctic Sunrise Arbitration (Netherlands v. Russia)*, Award on the Merits, 14 August 2015, [192].

[47] An example in this respect is *Territorial and Maritime Dispute between Nicaragua and Honduras in the Caribbean Sea (Nicaragua v. Honduras)* [2007] ICJ Rep. 659. Nicaragua submitted this case unilaterally to the ICJ under the Pact of Bogotá. The case involved a sovereignty dispute over islands and the delimitation of the maritime boundary. The LOSC provided the applicable law for the latter matter.

[48] See also *Maritime Delimitation in the Indian Ocean (Somalia v. Kenya)*, Judgment of 2 February 2017, [130].

[49] For a discussion of the judgment, see also N. Bankes, 'The Relationship between Declarations under the Optional Clause of the Statute of the International Court of Justice and Part XV of the Law of the Sea Convention' (K. G. Jebsen Centre for the Law of the Sea blog, available at http://site.uit.no/jclos/files/2017/02/The-relationship-between-declarations-under-the-optional-clause-of-the-Statute-of-the-International-Court-of-Justice-and-Part-XV-of-the-Law-of-the-Sea-Convention.pdf). The only other instance in which Art. 282 was considered is *Barbados v. Trinidad and Tobago*, where the tribunal

declaration under Article 36 of the Court's Statute containing a reservation. The parties were in agreement that optional clause declarations without a reservation constituted an agreement in the sense of Article 282.[50] The Court concurred, observing that the reference to 'otherwise' in Article 282 was 'broad enough to encompass an agreement to the jurisdiction of this Court that is expressed in optional clause declarations.'[51] However, the Kenyan optional clause declaration excluded disputes 'in regard to which the parties to the dispute have agreed or shall agree to have recourse to some other method or methods of settlement.'[52] Kenya submitted that Section 2 of Part XV of the LOSC constituted such an agreement.[53] The Court did not accept this point of view, observing among others that the drafters of Article 282 intended to include optional clause declarations in its scope of application. In that light, the Court considered it unlikely that the drafters would have wanted to exclude the more than half of the declarations that at the time included a reservation.[54] The Court also observed that Kenya's position would achieve exactly the opposite of what Article 282 was intended to do. Instead of giving priority to Article 282 procedures, Kenya's position would give priority to Section 2 of Part XV of the LOSC.[55] Finally, the Court found that declining jurisdiction might mean that there would not be a dispute settlement procedure available. In this connection, the Court referred to Article 286 of the LOSC, which provides that procedures under Section 2 are available *subject to* Section 3 on limitations and exceptions to the applicability of Section 2.[56] The Court's interpretation of Article 282 thus ensures the availability of compulsory dispute settlement in accordance with that article for disputes concerning the interpretation or application of the LOSC even in case a state has made a declaration under Article 298 of the LOSC, which may also pertain to the delimitation of maritime boundaries.

Article 281 provides that recourse to compulsory dispute settlement is excluded when parties have agreed on another means to settle their dispute and that agreement, in case of failure of that means, does not exclude recourse to other procedures. Article 281 has been considered in one case concerning the delimitation of maritime boundaries. In *Barbados v. Trinidad and Tobago*, the arbitral tribunal observed that 'it would appear that Article 281 is intended primarily to cover the situation where the

limits itself to noting that it is not applicable (*Arbitration between Barbados and Trinidad and Tobago* [2006] 27 RIAA 147 (Award), [200(iii)]).

50 *Somalia v. Kenya*, n. 48, [110–111].

51 Ibid., [126]. The Court found that this conclusion was supported by the drafting history of Art. 282 (ibid., [127].

52 Ibid., [31]. 53 Ibid., [110]. 54 Ibid., [129]. 55 Ibid., [130]. 56 Ibid., [132].

Parties have come to an ad hoc agreement as to the means to be adopted to settle the particular dispute which has arisen.'[57] The Tribunal then pointed out that in the present case the parties had agreed to settle their dispute through negotiations, but that this was not done through a formal agreement. The tribunal concluded '[s]ince their *de facto* agreement did not exclude any further procedures, and since their chosen peaceful settlement procedure – negotiations – failed to result in a settlement of their dispute' Article 281 did not exclude recourse to third-party settlement under Section 2 of Part XV of the LOSC.[58] The award does not contain any reference to the award on jurisdiction in *Southern Bluefin*. That award provides a much more detailed discussion of Article 281, and its findings seemingly contradict those of the award in *Barbados v. Trinidad and Tobago* on two points. First, the award in *Southern Bluefin* does not indicate that Article 281 is primarily intended to cover ad hoc agreements. The award was concerned with implications of a dispute settlement provision contained in the Convention for the Conservation of Southern Bluefin Tuna,[59] which sets up a regime for the management of southern Bluefin tuna, for Article 281 of the LOSC. Second, the award found that the exclusion of recourse to further procedures need not be explicitly mentioned in the agreement concerned.[60] This point is not considered by the award in *Barbados v. Trinidad and Tobago*. The implications of Article 281 more recently have been considered by the tribunal in *Philippines v. China*. In its award on jurisdiction the tribunal departed from *Southern Bluefin Tuna*, finding that Article 281 implied that the exclusion of further procedures should be explicitly mentioned in the agreement concerned.[61] Depending on the approach that will be followed in future cases, the impact of Article 281 on the availability of third-party settlement of maritime boundaries may vary considerably.

Article 283 of the LOSC requires parties to exchange views when a dispute arises. In view of the fact that delimitation disputes generally will have been subject to negotiations, Article 283 does not seem to place an additional hurdle before a state can submit a delimitation dispute to third-party settlement. This submission is based on the findings of the tribunal in *Barbados v. Trinidad and Tobago*, which held that:

[57] Ibid., [200(ii)]. [58] Ibid.

[59] Convention for the Conservation of Southern Bluefin Tuna, signed 10 May 1993, entered into force 20 May 1994, 1819 UNTS 360.

[60] *Southern Bluefin Tuna Cases* (Award).

[61] *Philippines v. China* (Award of 12 July 2016), [223–225].

> Article 283(1) cannot reasonably be interpreted to require that, when several years of negotiations have already failed to resolve a dispute, the Parties should embark upon further and separate exchanges of views regarding its settlement by negotiation. The requirement of Article 283(1) for settlement by negotiation is, in relation to Articles 74 and 83, subsumed within the negotiations which those Articles require to have already taken place.[62]

The absence of a requirement to have separate recourse to Article 283, implies that states will not be 'put on notice' by a negotiating partner that they consider that negotiations in their view have been exhausted. states thus cannot use such 'advance notice' to make a declaration under Article 298 of the LOSC to prevent recourse to third-party settlement, where they have not yet done so.

Article 298 of the Convention allows states parties to exclude disputes concerning the interpretation or application of Articles 74 and 83 (and Article 15 on the delimitation of the territorial sea) from the Convention's provisions on compulsory dispute settlement.[63] Only 25 of the 167 states parties to the LOSC currently have used this option.[64] However, the reach of these declarations is much broader than the twenty-five states concerned, as it also affects their neighbours. Interestingly, more than half (thirteen) of the declarations presently in force have been made subsequent to the state concerned becoming a party to the Convention.[65]

[62] *Barbados v. Trinidad and Tobago*, n. 49, [202]. The Tribunal also held that there was no obligation to exchange views on other peaceful means of settlement (ibid.). The Tribunal reached a similar conclusion in respect of Art. 283(2) (see ibid., [205]; see also ibid., [206]). For a recent and detailed discussion on the implications of Art. 283 of the LOSC see *The Matter of the Chagos Marine Protected Area Arbitration between the Republic of Mauritius and the United Kingdom of Great Britain and Northern Ireland*, Award of 18 March 2015, [351–386].

[63] LOSC, Art. 298(1)(a)(i). Art. 298 envisages that delimitation disputes that are covered by a declaration excluding third-party settlement may be submitted to conciliation in accordance with Annex *v.* to the LOSC. This procedure only recently has been used for the first time by East Timor in relation to a delimitation dispute with Australia (see *Timor-Leste's Conciliation with Australia on Maritime Boundaries*; available at http://timor-leste.gov.tl/wp-content/uploads/2016/04/15398-FACT-SHEET-CONCILIATION.pdf). On the role of other modes of third-party dispute settlement in relation to delimitation disputes see also Oude Elferink, n. 39.

[64] This figure is based on the information contained on the relevant page of the website of the Treaty Section of the Office of Legal Affairs of the United Nations (available at http://treaties.un.org/Pages/Treaties.aspx?id=21&subid=0&lang=en&clang=_en). In addition, a limited number of states have indicated that they only accept a specific means of compulsory dispute settlement for these types of disputes (ibid.).

[65] Ibid. In addition, Ghana had made a declaration to this effect on 15 December 2009 but subsequently withdrew that declaration on 22 September 2014 (ibid., n. 18).

Possibly, some of these subsequent declarations may have been triggered by the way in which courts and tribunals have been dealing with the interpretation and application of Articles 74 and 83 of the LOSC.

The possibility of unilateral recourse to third-party dispute settlement under the LOSC seems to have contributed significantly to the use of compulsory dispute settlement mechanisms. Since the entry into force of the LOSC in 1994, five maritime delimitation cases have been brought unilaterally under Part XV of the LOSC. During this same period, nine cases were submitted jointly or unilaterally under other instruments. Recourse to the option of *unilateral* submission of delimitation disputes under the LOSC reflects a broader trend. While until 1988 there had only been one, unsuccessful, attempt by Greece to settle its continental shelf boundaries with Turkey by unilateral recourse to the ICJ, since 1988, fourteen maritime delimitation cases were started unilaterally.[66] By way of comparison, for the same periods the figures for joint submissions are respectively ten and four.[67] Whether this trend will continue will depend, among other factors, on whether or not states will close the possibilities of recourse to this avenue for their neighbours by for instance making a declaration under Article 298(1)(a)(i) of the LOSC or withdrawing or varying their optional clause declaration under Article 36(2) of the Statute of the ICJ.

Third-party settlement may both involve recourse to a standing body – in this case the ICJ and the ITLOS – and ad hoc arbitration. Figure 1.1 provides an overview of recourse to these two modes of dispute settlement over time. As Figure 1.1 indicates, cases have been referred to standing bodies somewhat more often than to ad hoc arbitration. However, in this connection it should not be lost from view that two cases that initially were submitted to ad hoc arbitration (*Bangladesh/Myanmar* and *Ghana/Côte d'Ivoire*) were subsequently transferred to the ITLOS. If these two cases are included in the category of ad hoc arbitration instead of the category of standing courts, the figures for the two categories are closer, being respectively thirteen and sixteen. Figure 1.1 does not suggest that the preference for one or the other mode of dispute settlement has shifted significantly over time. The current project did not make a detailed assessment as to why states opt for arbitration or a standing court.[68] In the case of

[66] The possibility that a state may unilaterally submit a dispute to a court or tribunal may also induce states to seek to agree on joint submission (for an example see Oude Elferink, n. 23, 175).

[67] See Table 1.1 at the end of this chapter.

[68] For a discussion of the merits and drawbacks of standing courts and ad hoc tribunals, see J. G. Merrills, *International Dispute Settlement*, 5th ed. (Cambridge University Press

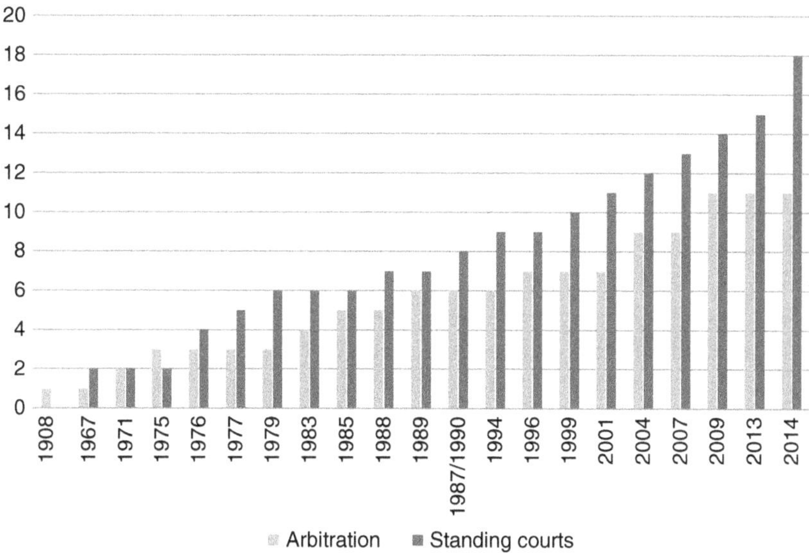

Figure 1.1 Use of *ad hoc* arbitration and standing courts

unilateral applications, the availability of a specific forum, like the ICJ under the Pact of Bogotá or Annex VII arbitration as the default mechanism under Part XV of the LOSC, provides a logical explanation. The additional costs involved in arbitration seem a likely explanation why two cases that were started unilaterally as Annex VII arbitrations were subsequently transferred to the ITLOS. The chapters in this volume will consider the decisions of the ICJ, the ITLOS, and arbitral tribunals, which should allow determining whether standing courts differ significantly from ad hoc tribunals as regards their handling of the applicable law and its application to the individual case. A difference in that regard might be a factor that explains why states opt for a specific dispute settlement body.

To get a proper perspective on the significance of the case law for settling maritime boundaries, a brief comparison to negotiated settlements can be made. Notwithstanding the recurrent use of compulsory dispute settlement mechanisms, negotiations remain the primary mode for dealing with the delimitation of maritime boundaries between neighbouring states. A review of the period 2003–2014 by the authors in the preparation

Cambridge 2011), 111–115, 161–166; C. H. Brower, 'Arbitration,' in *Max Planck Encyclopedia of Public International Law*, online ed. (last updated February 2007) [91].

of this chapter identified fifty-five agreements related to the delimitation of maritime zones.[69] By way of comparison, in the same period eleven cases were submitted to compulsory dispute settlement procedures.[70] A comparison with earlier figures suggests a somewhat increased role for third-party settlement. A study from 1990 lists 154 maritime boundaries that had been settled between 1925 and 1990.[71] Ten boundaries, or some 6.5 per cent of this total, had been settled by adjudication. For the period 2003–2014 the share of adjudicated boundaries in the total is 16.7 per cent.[72]

A major, perhaps even the most important, difference between negotiated and adjudicated settlements may be that cases with a complex legal setting will more often end up in court. One measure to determine this complexity is the method of delimitation that has been used to determine the boundary. Already in *North Sea Continental Shelf*, in which the ICJ found that equidistance did not constitute an obligatory method for the parties, the Court emphasized the advantages of the equidistance method in geographically – and hence legally – straightforward situations.[73] This same distinction has been observed by Legault and Hankey in a statistical analysis of negotiated boundaries.[74] Eighty-nine per cent of the boundaries between opposite coasts included in their sample are based on the equidistance method. On the other hand, only 40 per cent of the cases in their sample involving adjacent coasts employ the equidistance method. In the latter case this figure was split evenly between strict equidistance and modified equidistance.[75] Interestingly, the figures for adjudicated

[69] Based on a review of *Law of the Sea Bulletins* nos. 53–89 and C. Lathrop (ed.), *International Maritime Boundaries*, online ed., including the 2015 update (Martinus Nijhoff). Because some delimitation agreements are not in the public domain immediately after their conclusion, it should not be excluded that the actual figure is higher than fifty-five. The fifty-five agreements concerned also include two agreements on a joint zone and a number of agreements determining tripoints or transforming a continental shelf boundary into a single maritime boundary.

[70] See Table 1.1 at the end of this chapter.

[71] R. W. Smith (ed.), *Maritime Boundaries of the World*, Limits in the Seas 108, 1st revision (US Department of State Washington, DC 1990) 3 and 5.

[72] Based on the number of cases that were submitted to a court or tribunal in this period (see Table 1.1 at the end of this chapter).

[73] *North Sea Continental Shelf*, n. 11, 37, [57].

[74] A recent review in this respect is contained in T. Cottier, n. 10, 242–250. However, Cottier focusses on the period between 1942 and 1992 (ibid., 242), which is basically the period covered by Legault and Hankey. Unsurprisingly, Cottier conclude that his findings are 'roughly appropriate' when compared to the study of Legault and Hankey (ibid., 249).

[75] H. Legault and B. Hankey, 'Method, Oppositeness and Adjacency, and Proportionality in Maritime Boundary Delimitation,' in J. I. Charney and L. M. Alexander (eds.), *International Maritime Boundaries*, vol. 1 (Martinus Nijhoff Dordrecht 1991), 203, 215–216.

boundaries indicate a larger reliance on the equidistance method than is the case for negotiated boundaries involving adjacent coasts. Eleven out of twenty adjudicated boundaries, or 55 per cent, delimiting the continental shelf and/or the exclusive economic zone use the equidistance method.[76] This might suggest that the legal complexity of a delimitation is not the only factor explaining why states resort to adjudication. However, before turning to other explanations, the figure of 55 per cent requires some qualification. Only three out of these eleven cases – 15 per cent of the total number of adjudicated cases – concern strict equidistance for (almost) the entire boundary.[77] In addition, modified equidistance lines at times may have little relationship to the strict equidistance line. In this case, use of the term modified equidistance line might be taken to suggest the absence of a complex legal and geographical situation, while the opposite may be true.

1.5 The Composition of the Bench and the Impact of External Criticism: *Tunisia/Libya* and *Libya/Malta*

People will have different views on the law. Judges are no exception. The 1969 judgment in *North Sea Continental Shelf* was adopted by an eleven to six vote. Not unsurprisingly, the opinions of a number of the dissenting judges indicate that they did not agree with the majority on the role of equidistance in the delimitation process. This existence of different views on the bench raises the question whether developments in the case law on maritime delimitation may (in part) be explained by changes in the composition of third-party dispute settlement bodies. Although this is a topic that because of its breadth and complexity is beyond the scope of the present volume, this section intends to provide the reader with some ideas as to how the composition of the bench and external criticism may impact on the consistency and predictability of the case law. Instead of looking at the case law as a whole, this section opts for the rather more manageable task of comparing the judgments on the merits in *Tunisia/Libya* and *Libya/Malta* with a focus on the latter case. As was noted above, in 2001 then ICJ President Gilbert Guillaume submitted that the unpredictability of *Tunisia/Libya* had led to doubts whether there still existed a law of maritime delimitation. He identified *Libya/Malta* as a first step towards predictability. Guillaume also submitted that this development was due

[76] This concerns entries A.8, A.12, A.13, B.2, B.3, B. 6, B.7, B.8, B.9, B.10, and B. 11 in Table 1.1 at the end of this chapter. In making this count, only boundaries that were established *de novo* by a court or tribunal have been taken into account.

[77] This concerns entries B.3, B.7, and B.8 in Table 1.1 at the end of this chapter.

to criticism from beyond the bench.[78] This section will seek to establish whether there are traces in the judgment and the opinions in *Libya/Malta* to substantiate these positions.[79]

In both *Tunisia/Libya* and *Libya/Malta* the judgment on the merits was supported by a clear majority of respectively ten to four and fourteen to three. The composition of the Court in both cases differed to some extent. Eleven of the judges participating in *Tunisia/Libya* also participated in *Libya/Malta* and the majority in both cases was largely included the same judges. Eight judges were part of the majority in both cases.[80] The majority in *Libya/Malta* also included six judges who were not on the bench in *Tunisia/Libya*.

Judges Schwebel and Mosler, who were part of the majority in *Tunisia/Libya*, dissented in *Libya/Malta*. While Schwebel and Mosler both commend the judgment in *Libya/Malta* for taking the median line as a starting point, they criticize the judgment because it does not lead to greater predictability.[81] The individual opinions of judges voting with the majority in *Libya/Malta* indicate differing appreciations of the judgment. Judge El-Khani's declaration indicates that he does not agree with the approach of the judgment. His argument that the outcome should have given greater weight to proportionality, which would have been in agreement with equity, suggests that he did not support the use of the median line as a starting point.[82] Sette-Camara, while supporting the use of equidistance as a provisional starting point, rejects one of the Court's main argument for taking this approach, namely that entitlement to the shelf is based on distance, requiring a delimitation method that is also based in distance.[83] The linkage between entitlement and delimitation is one way of achieving greater predictability in the applicable law. As the

[78] For both points, see above Section 1.2. In addition to *Tunisia/Libya*, Guillaume also referred to *Gulf of Maine* in his speech. As this case was not decided by the full Court, but a five-member Chamber, *Gulf of Maine* is considered less appropriate for the current comparative exercise (*Case concerning the Continental Shelf (Tunisia/Libyan Arab Jamahiriya)* [1982] ICJ Rep. 18; *Delimitation of the Maritime Boundary in the Gulf of Maine Area (Canada/United States)* [1984] ICJ Rep. 246).

[79] It is acknowledged that the judgment and opinions do not provide a full view on the factors impacting on the internal decision-making process of the Court. However, they are the only readily available sources.

[80] This concerns Elias, Lachs, Morozov, Nagendra Singh, Ago, Sette-Camara, El-Khani, and Jiménez de Aréchaga.

[81] *Libya/Malta*, n. 13, Dissenting Opinion of Judge Schwebel, 186–187; ibid., Dissenting Opinion of Judge Mosler, 114.

[82] Ibid., Declaration of Judge El-Khani, 59.

[83] Ibid., Separate Opinion of Vice-President Sette-Camara, 71.

Court indicated itself, it 'seems logical to the Court that the choice of the criterion and the method which it is to employ in the first place to arrive at a provisional result should be made in a manner Consistent with the concepts underlying the attribution of legal title.'[84] Otherwise, Sette-Camara stresses the importance of reaching an equitable solution.[85]

At its outset, the joint separate opinion of judges Ruda, Bedjaoui, and judge ad hoc Jiménez de Aréchaga in *Libya/Malta* seems to support the judgment's approach, noting that they agree with the Court's exposition of the applicable law and the Court's reasoning in selecting the delimitation line and adjusting the provisional median line.[86] However, their subsequent argument that the provisional delimitation line should have been shifted further north because this would have divided the area of overlapping claims in equal parts and would have better reflected the difference in length of the relevant coasts,[87] indicates that their solution is completely divorced from the two-stage approach of the Court. The solution of Ruda, Bedjaoui and Jiménez de Aréchaga as a matter of fact makes the determination of a provisional line superfluous as their final line results from two factors that operate independently of this line. The opinion of judge ad hoc Valticos does indicate support for the approach of the judgment because of the role it accords to equidistance and the fact this approach is preferable to other approaches.[88] In view of Valticos's opinion as a whole, it seems likely that he is referring to other approaches that are less structured.

The joint opinion of Ruda, Bedjaoui and Jiménez de Aréchaga in *Libya/Malta* is the only opinion that contains a reference to academic criticism of the previous judgments of the Court. However, this does not concern criticisms of the unpredictability of the Court, but rather refers to literature that considers that too little weight has been given to the factor of proportionality.[89]

This brief review of the judgment and individual opinions in *Libya/Malta* allows making a number of tentative conclusions. First, the judgment in *Libya/Malta* does refer to the need for consistency and a

[84] Ibid., 46, [61].
[85] Ibid., Separate Opinion of Vice-President Sette-Camara, 75.
[86] Ibid., Joint Separate Opinion Judges Ruda and Bedjaoui and Judge ad hoc Jiménez de Aréchaga 76, [1].
[87] Ibid., 89–91, [35–38].
[88] Ibid., Separate Opinion of Judge ad hoc Valticos 106–108 [7–13] and 111 [22].
[89] Ibid., Joint Separate Opinion Judges Ruda and Bedjaoui and Judge ad hoc Jiménez de Aréchaga 85, [23].

degree of predictability in judicial decisions. This reference suggests that the majority considered that this was an issue of concern. A number of opinion's share this concern, but other opinions rather indicate that they support an equity-based approach that does not accord specific weight to the equidistance method. The opinion of Ruda, Bedjaoui and Jiménez de Aréchaga confirms that criticism from beyond the bench may impact on the internal decision making of the Court.

The fact that the majority in *Tunisia/Libya* and *Libya/Malta* to a considerable extent consisted of the same judges might indicate that the thinking of the majority about the approach to delimitation did change between 1982 and 1985. The fact that the majority in *Libya/Malta* included six judges that were not on the bench in 1982 may also have contributed to the difference in approach.

Finally, one highly significant difference between the two cases are the facts. As the judgment in *Libya/Malta* also acknowledges, in cases involving opposite coasts, the Court had already recognized the equitable nature of equidistance in *North Sea Continental Shelf*.[90] In the end, this latter circumstance may have played a larger role in adopting a provisional equidistance line than the perceived need for consistency and a degree of predictability. Still, if the Court would have been true to its approach in *Tunisia/Libya* it could also have weighed up the relevant circumstances to immediately arrive at the final delimitation line, an approach that was effectively advocated in the joint separate opinion of judges Ruda, Bedjaoui and Jiménez de Aréchaga in *Libya/Malta*, but was not adopted by the majority.

1.6 Introduction of the Chapters of the Project

The rest of this volume consists of twelve substantive chapters and a final chapter that will draw together the conclusions of these individual chapters. This section briefly introduces these chapters. Chapter 2 of this volume is concerned with the delimitation of the territorial sea and in particular seeks to determine in which respects the regime of the territorial sea and its delimitation differ from that of the zones beyond the territorial sea. This chapter is included because it is considered that an analysis of the case law on the delimitation of the territorial sea may enhance our understanding of the case law on the delimitation of the continental shelf and the exclusive economic zone.

90 *North Sea Continental Shelf*, n. 11, [62].

The actual discussion of the case law on the delimitation of these latter zones starts off with Chapter 3, which addresses the relationship between the entitlement to the continental shelf and the exclusive economic zones and their delimitation, which was briefly introduced in Section 1.3 above. As the case law indicates, the basis of entitlement is one of the critical factors impacting on the development of delimitation law. Chapter 4 deals with the law applicable to these zones as formulated in general terms in the Convention on the Continental Shelf, the LOSC, and customary international law. The existence of these three sources of law also raises the question to which extent they differ or are similar in content.

Chapter 5 looks at the case law in relation to provisional arrangements as defined in Articles 74(3) and 83(3) of the LOSC and provisional measures that may be prescribed by courts and tribunals pending their decision on the merits. The relevant case law indicates that there are significant linkages between these two topics, which Chapter 5 explores. Chapter 6 considers the role of equity, equitable principles, and the equitable solution in the law of maritime delimitation. The ICJ accorded equity and equitable principles a central role in the delimitation process in *North Sea Continental Shelf* and Articles 74 and 83 require that the delimitation of the exclusive economic zone and the continental shelf results in an equitable solution. The recurrent discussion of in particular the nature of equity and equitable principles in the case law indicates that the judiciary has grappled to come to terms with these concepts. Chapter 7 looks at the closely related concepts of relevant coasts and relevant area. As Chapter 7 points out, the development of these concepts by the case law has not been linear.

Most decisions on the delimitation of the continental shelf and the exclusive economic zone first determine a provisional delimitation line and then consider whether there are circumstances calling for the adjustment of that line. In most instances, this provisional line has been an equidistance line. Chapter 8 considers the pronouncements of the case law on the principles and criteria applicable to identifying the provisional delimitation line and assesses how does the actual identification of the provisional delimitation line in the case law relates to those principles and criteria. Chapter 9 looks at the concept of relevant circumstances, which are largely identical to the concept of special circumstances contained in Article 6 of the Convention on the Continental Shelf. In this connection, Chapter 9 investigates to what extent relevant circumstances are also playing a role in the other stages than the second stage, at which the case law explicitly takes into account relevant circumstances. Chapter 10 considers the role of third states in the delimitation of bilateral boundaries in third-party dispute settlement. Third states may impact on the delimitation process mainly in two ways. Their presence may limit the area in which a court or tribunal considers it possible to effect a delimitation. Second, the coast of a third state may be part of the relevant circumstances that need to be taken into consideration in arriving at a final boundary. Chapter 11 focusses on the third-stage proportionality test, which consists of assessing whether the ratio between the relevant coasts of the parties and the ratio of the between the parts of the relevant area attributed to each party does not show a disproportion. Such disproportion would indicate that the delimitation line that is the result of the second stage of the delimitation process does not result in an equitable solution. To put the use of this test in proper perspective, Chapter 11 also considers how the length of the relevant coasts may be used as a relevant circumstance at the second stage of the delimitation process.

Chapters 12 and 13 are concerned with the delimitation of the continental shelf beyond 200 nautical miles. The editors concluded that two characteristics of this part of the continental shelf justified separate treatment of this topic. First, the establishment of the outer limits of the continental shelf beyond 200 nautical miles not only involves the coastal state, but that state is required to submit information on those outer limits to the Commission on the Limits of the Continental Shelf (CLCS) in accordance with Article 76 of the LOSC. The existence of this procedure raises questions concerning its relationship to the delimitation of the continental shelf by dispute settlement bodies. This topic is the subject of Chapter 12. Chapter 13 considers how the case law has addressed the fact that the basis of entitlement to the continental shelf beyond 200 nautical miles, natural prolongation, is different from the distance-based entitlement within 200 nautical miles. Another reason for dealing with the continental shelf beyond 200 nautical miles in two separate chapters is that this concerns a relatively new topic, which may be the subject of further development through the case law as is intimated in these chapters.

Chapter 14 of this volume contains its conclusions and will seek to provide an answer to the central research question of the project: how predictable and consistent has the case law concerning the delimitation of the continental shelf and the exclusive economic zone been? Before drawing together the conclusions of the individual chapters, Chapter 14 will consider the parameters to be used in answering the central research question. As the Statute of the ICJ and the ITLOS indicate a 'judgment shall state the reasons on which it is based.'[91] A similar provision in contained in Annex VII of the LOSC setting out the basic rules applicable to arbitration under the Convention.[92] The Rules of Court of the ICJ and the Rules of the Tribunal of the ITLOS further provide that a judgment shall contain 'a statement of the facts' and 'the reasons in point of law.'[93] Chapter 14 will set out what criteria have been developed to assess whether decisions of international courts and tribunals are rendered in accordance with these requirements.

1.7 Concluding Remarks

The development of the regime of the continental shelf and the exclusive economic zone has led to an expansion of coastal state jurisdiction to almost half of the world oceans. The frequent overlap of these zones between neighbouring states – only some mid-ocean islands do not share maritime boundaries with other land territory – resulted in rules on the delimitation of these zones. The general nature of the rules contained in the Convention on the Continental Shelf and the LOSC has contributed to states making ample use of third-party dispute settlement to establish maritime boundaries with their neighbours. This is a trend that is likely to continue. As was pointed out in Section 1.4, the number of boundary disputes that has been submitted to third-party settlement procedures has actually risen as compared to the number of maritime boundaries that have been settled through direct negotiations. Another notable trend is the rise of unilateral applications to third-party dispute settlement mechanisms. This option already existed under a number of instruments, but a new avenue in this respect was created under Section 2 of Part XV of the LOSC. Whether this trend will continue depends, among other factors, on whether states will make use of options to limit the possibilities for making unilateral applications such as a declaration excluding maritime boundary delimitation from compulsory dispute settlement under the LOSC in accordance with its Article 298.

The main focus of this volume concerns the question how predictable and consistent the case law on the delimitation of maritime boundaries has been through time. Section 1.5 in this connection briefly considers how the composition of the bench may impact on this issues and to what extent

[91] Statute of the ICJ, Art. 56; LOSC, Annex VI, Art. 30.

[92] LOSC, Annex VII, Art. 10.

[93] Rules of Court, Art. 95(1); Rules of the Tribunal, Arts. 125(h) and (j).

criticism from beyond the bench may impact on how judges approach the law. For the reasons set out in Section 1.5, these issues are not pursued in the subsequent chapters of this volume. Section 1.5 briefly compares the judgments on the merits in *Tunisia/Libya* and *Libya/Malta* and discusses the individual opinions appended to the latter judgment. If anything, this assessment shows how difficult it is to second-guess what transpires in the internal deliberations of the judiciary. Individual opinions do indicate that voting with majority does not necessarily mean agreement with the reasoning of the judgment even where it concerns critical issues. A number of individual opinions in *Libya/Malta* moreover indicate that the Court was internally divided as to whether the judgment was successful in making a contribution to the predictability and consistency of the case law on maritime delimitation.

As is set out in Section 1.3, the law on the entitlement to maritime zones and their delimitation has developed through time. This will be one important consideration that has to be factored in while assessing the question whether the case law has been successful in contributing to the predictability and consistence of the law in relation to the delimitation of the continental shelf and the exclusive economic zone. Moreover, as set out in Section 1.6, this volume looks at a number of discrete issues. The development of the case law on these different issues need not necessarily be the same. The significance of the project this project will hopefully consist of making a contribution to the assessment of how the case law has developed the law in an important field and what this may hold in store for the future.

Table 1.1 *Maritime Delimitations Submitted to Compulsory Procedures Entailing Binding Decisions*

A. Joint submission	B. Unilateral submission
1. *Grisbadarna* (Norway/Sweden) BS: SA (1908) O: DM (1909) MZD: TS Decided by: A	1. *Aegean Sea Continental Shelf* (*Greece v. Turkey*) BS: General Act for Pacific Settlement of International Disputes (1928) YA: 1976 O: AJ (1978) MZD: CS Decided by: ICJ

Table 1.1 *(cont.)*

A. Joint submission	B. Unilateral submission
2. *North Sea Continental Shelf* (Germany/Netherlands) BS: SA (1967) O: DM (1969) MZD: CS Decided by: ICJ	2. *Maritime Delimitation in the Area between Greenland and Jan Mayen* (*Denmark v. Norway*) BS: OC YA: 1988 O: DM (1993) MZD: CS/FZ Decided by: ICJ
3. *North Sea Continental Shelf case* (Germany/Denmark) BS: SA (1967) O: DM (1969) MZD: CS Decided by: ICJ	3. *Land and Maritime Boundary between Cameroon and Nigeria* (*Cameroon v. Nigeria*: Equatorial Guinea intervening) BS: OC YA: 1994 O: DM (2002) MZD: TS/CS/EEZ Decided by: ICJ
4. *Case concerning the delimitation of continental shelf between the United Kingdom of Great Britain and Northern Ireland, and the French Republic* BS: SA (1975) O: DM (1977) MZD: CS Decided by: A	4. *Territorial and Maritime Dispute between Nicaragua and Honduras in the Caribbean Sea* (*Nicaragua v. Honduras*) BS: Pact of Bogotá and OC YA: 1999 O: DM (2007) MZD: TS/CS/EEZ Decided by: ICJ
5. *Case concerning a dispute between Argentina and Chile concerning the Beagle Channel* BS: SA (1971) O: DM (1977) MZD: TS Decided by: A	5. *Territorial and Maritime Dispute* (*Nicaragua v. Colombia*) BS: Pact of Bogotá YA: 2001 O: DM (2012) MZD: CS/EEZ Decided by: ICJ

(cont.)

Table 1.1 *(cont.)*

A. Joint submission	B. Unilateral submission
6. *Case concerning the continental shelf* (Tunisia/Libya) BS: SA (1977) O: DM (1982) MZD: CS Decided by: ICJ	6. *Maritime Delimitation in the Black Sea* (*Romania v. Ukraine*) BS: Additional Agreement to the Treaty on the Relations of Good Neighbourliness and Co-operation (1997) YA: 2004 O: DM (2009) MZD: CS/EEZ Decided by: ICJ
7. *Case concerning delimitation of the maritime boundary in the Gulf of Maine area* (Canada/USA) BS: SA (1979) O: DM (1984) MZD: CS/FZ Decided by: ICJ	7. *In the Matter of an Arbitration between Barbados and the Republic of Trinidad and Tobago* (*Barbados v. Trinidad and Tobago*) BS: LOSC YA: 2004 O: DM (2006) MZD: CS/EEZ Decided by: A
8. *Case concerning the continental shelf* (Libya/Malta) BS: SA (1976) O: DM (1985) MZD: CS Decided by: ICJ	8. *In the Matter of an Arbitration between Guyana and Suriname* (*Guyana v. Suriname*) BS: LOSC YA: 2004 O: DM (2007) MZD: TS/CS/EEZ Decided by: A
9. *Case concerning the delimitation of the maritime boundary between Guinea and Guinea-Bissau* BS: SA (1983) O: DM (1985) MZD: TS/CS/EEZ Decided by: A	9. *Maritime Dispute* (*Peru v. Chile*) BS: Pact of Bogotá YA: 2007 O: DM (2014) MZD: TS/CS/EEZ Decided by: ICJ

Table 1.1 *(cont.)*

A. Joint submission	B. Unilateral submission
10. *Case concerning the delimitation of maritime boundary between Guinea-Bissau and Senegal* BS: SA (1985) O: DM (1989) MZD: TS/CS Decided by: A	10. *Dispute concerning delimitation of the maritime boundary between Bangladesh and Myanmar in the Bay of Bengal*[a] BS: LOSC YA: 2009 O: DM (2012) MZD: TS/CS/EEZ Decided by: ITLOS
11. *Case concerning the delimitation of maritime areas between Canada and France* BS: SA (1989) O: DM (1992) MZD: CS/EEZ Decided by: A	11. *In the matter of the Bay of Bengal maritime boundary arbitration (Bangladesh v. India)* BS: LOSC YA: 2009 O: DM (2014) MZD: TS/CS/EEZ Decided by: A
12. *Case concerning maritime delimitation and territorial questions between Qatar and Bahrain* BS: SA (1987/1990)[b] O: DM (2001) MZD: TS/CS Decided by: ICJ	12. *Question of the Delimitation of the Continental Shelf between Nicaragua and Colombia beyond 200 nautical miles from the Nicaraguan Coast (Nicaragua v. Colombia)* BS: Pact of Bogotá YA: 2013 O: Pending MZD: CS Decided by: ICJ
13. *In the matter of an Arbitration pursuant to an Agreement to Arbitrate dated 3 October 1996 between the Government of the State of Eritrea and the Government of the Republic of Yemen* BS: SA (1996) O: DM (1999) MZD: TS/Cs/EEZ Decided by: A	13. *Maritime Delimitation in the Caribbean Sea and the Pacific Ocean (Costa Rica v. Nicaragua)* BS: Pact of Bogotá YA: 2014 O: Pending MZD: TS/CS/EEZ Decided by: ICJ

(cont.)

Table 1.1 *(cont.)*

A. Joint submission	B. Unilateral submission
14. *Territorial and Maritime Arbitration between Croatia and Slovenia* BS: SA (2009) O: Pending MZD: TS Decided by: A	14. *Maritime Delimitation in the Indian Ocean (Somalia v. Kenya)* BS: OC YA: 2014 O: Pending MZD: TS/CS/EEZ Decided by: ICJ
	15. *Dispute concerning Delimitation of the Maritime Boundary between Ghana and Côte d'Ivoire in the Atlantic Ocean (Ghana/Côte d'Ivoire)*[c] BS: LOSC YA: 2014 O: Pending MZD: TS/CS/EEZ Decided by: ICJ

Note: The table only lists cases between states and not between entities that form part of federal states. The table does not lists incidental procedures unless these resulted in a discontinuation of the proceedings. A: arbitration; AJ: finding that there was no basis of jurisdiction; BS: basis of submission; CS: continental shelf; DM: decision on the merits; EEZ: exclusive economic zone; FZ: fishery zone; MZD: maritime zone subject of the proceedings; O: outcome; OC: declarations under Article 36(2) of the Statute of the ICJ; SA: agreement between the parties to submit the specific dispute; TS: territorial sea; YA: year of application.

[a]The case was initiated unilaterally by Bangladesh. The parties subsequently agreed to joint submission to the ITLOS. [b]The case was referred to the ICJ by an Application of Qatar. However, the case is listed as a joint submission because, as was held by the International Court of Justice in a judgment of 1 July 1994, by the terms of two international agreements of respectively 1987 and 1990 'the Parties had undertaken to submit to the Court the whole of the dispute between them' (Judgment of 1 July 1994 ([1994] ICJ Rep. 112 [41(2)]). [c]The case was initiated unilaterally by Ghana. The parties subsequently agreed to joint submission to a Special Chamber of the ITLOS.

2

The Delimitation of the Territorial Sea, the Continental Shelf, and the EEZ

A Comparative Perspective

DAVOR VIDAS

Given the silence of Articles 74 and 83 of the United Nations Convention on the Law of the Sea (LOSC) as to any method for delimiting the continental shelf and exclusive economic zones (EEZ), the international judiciary has gradually developed an elaborate delimitation methodology for those maritime areas.[1] A trend towards consolidation of delimitation methodology distinguishes decisions of international courts and tribunals over the past two to three decades from some earlier cases which often lacked a clear or consistent methodological approach to the delimitation of the continental shelf (and, later, the EEZ).

In contrast to Articles 74 and 83, LOSC Article 15 states the method for delimitation of the territorial sea. Minor stylistic alterations in the text of that article notwithstanding, this still is the same method as in Article 12 of the 1958 Geneva Convention on the Territorial Sea and the Contiguous Zone, and reflects a rule of customary international law.[2] There should therefore exist no legal basis in the applicable sources of international law (codified since the 1950s) for any marked variations or adjustments by the international judiciary of the methodology for delimiting the territorial sea, nor for a trend mirroring the methodology development regarding delimitation of the continental shelf and the EEZ, as witnessed for those two maritime areas in recent decades.

[1] See especially *Maritime Delimitation in the Black Sea (Romania v. Ukraine)* [2009] ICJ Rep. 61, Section 7, 'Delimitation Methodology' [115]–[122].

[2] On the customary nature of Art. 15, see *Maritime Delimitation and Territorial Questions between Qatar and Bahrain (Qatar/Bahrain)* [2001] ICJ Rep. 91 [175]. The Court also commented that the wording of Art. 15 is 'virtually identical' with Art. 12(1) of the 1958 Geneva Convention on the Territorial Sea; ibid., [176].

Our starting hypothesis is that the content of the well established rule itself for territorial sea delimitation is the factor that provides the legal basis and determines the scope for judicial interpretation; and that this leaves no particular need – nor accords much legal room to the judiciary – for analogy with, or adjustments to, how other maritime areas beyond the territorial seas are delimited. This chapter therefore examines the approach of international courts and tribunals to the delimitation of the territorial sea in the light of the delimitation method stated in the rule contained in Article 15, as against the absence of such in Articles 74 and 83. The focus here is not primarily on what has led the judiciary in the development of delimitation methodology for the continental shelf and EEZ, but on whether aspects of that development might have been reflected in the judicial approach to the application of the method for delimitation of the territorial sea as well.

2.1 Basic Considerations on the Territorial Sea, the Continental Shelf, and the EEZ

Any comparative analysis of decisions of international courts and tribunals regarding the delimitation of maritime zones must take into consideration the context provided by the similarities and differences between such zones including their legal nature and spatial extent.

The legal status of the territorial sea, on the one hand, and that of the EEZ and the continental shelf, on the other, is profoundly different. In accordance with the rules and principles of the law of the sea, the coastal state has sovereignty in the territorial sea. Although subject to innocent passage, the nature of the territorial sea as a constituent part of a coastal state's national territory remains unchanged; and, as embodied in the nomenclature, in this belt of the sea a 'territorial' regime applies. The sovereignty of a coastal state in the territorial sea extends to the seabed and subsoil under the water column, as well as to the air space over the territorial sea.[3] An agreement between states, or a judicial decision, on the delimitation of their territorial seas is a matter of determining the state border:[4] separating areas under sovereignty of the respective states, which in turn include all maritime and other space extending to the outer limit of the territorial seas.

[3] Art. 2(2) LOSC. The sovereignty of a coastal state does not extend beyond the outer limit of the territorial sea.

[4] See, e.g., *Black Sea*, n. 1, [64] and [71].

In contrast, the EEZ and the continental shelf are described as 'functional' regimes,[5] thereby indicating that certain sovereign rights and jurisdiction of coastal states in those maritime zones are determined by the specific purpose of those rights extending beyond the state's territory rather than in the performance of coastal states' *territorial* sovereignty there.[6] Once a coastal state declares an EEZ beyond the outer limit of its territorial sea, the rights it has there will overlap with some of the rights it has in the continental shelf: this concerns sovereign rights for the purpose of exploring and exploiting the natural resources of the seabed and subsoil.[7] The rights of the coastal state in the continental shelf do not apply in the superjacent waters, nor do they affect their legal status (which may be the high seas, or the EEZ, or also the contiguous zone). Nonetheless, given the very nature of sovereign rights over submarine areas and their use in practice, aspects of exclusive rights derived from both the continental shelf and EEZ regimes will, *mutatis mutandis*, apply in the water column, insofar as they relate to artificial islands, installations and structures on the continental shelf/EEZ, and the safety zones around these.[8] In the air space over the EEZ (as well as the continental shelf) other states retain freedom of overflight.

Every coastal state has the right to extend its sovereignty beyond its land territory (and internal waters, if applicable) to an adjacent belt of sea,

[5] See, e.g., ibid., [71], describing the zones beyond the territorial seas as 'zones not of sovereignty but of functional competence'; or *Qatar/Bahrain*, n. 2, [174], describing rights of the coastal state in those areas as 'functional' in contrast to territorial rights of a state in its territorial sea. Regarding the EEZ, Art. 55 LOSC uses the term 'specific legal regime,' in the title and in the text of the provision.

[6] While there is no doubt under present international law and judicial practice about the above conclusion, the conceptual construct presented by the International Court of Justice (ICJ) in *North Sea Continental Shelf* regarding the *ipso jure* title of the coastal state to the continental shelf as the natural prolongation or continuation of its 'land territory' or 'land sovereignty' under the sea – and as 'actually part of the territory' – seems to have been made with reliance on the territorial extension rather than functional nature of the rights concerned. See *North Sea Continental Shelf Cases (Federal Republic of Germany/Denmark; Federal Republic of Germany/Netherlands)* (1969) ICJ Rep. 3 [43]. For an analysis of the North Sea Continental Shelf cases, see especially A. G. Oude Elferink, *The Delimitation of the Continental Shelf between Denmark, Germany and the Netherlands: Arguing Law, Practicing Politics* (Cambridge University Press Cambridge 2013).

[7] See a general clause in Art. 56(3) LOSC. Regarding sedentary species, see Arts. 68 and 77(4) LOSC.

[8] See Arts. 60 and 80 LOSC. Art. 60(8) is explicit on the status of such artificial islands, installations, and structures: they do not possess the status of islands and have no territorial sea of their own, and their presence does not affect the delimitation of the territorial sea, the EEZ, or the continental shelf.

described as the 'territorial sea' – although the extent of some of those belts, due to coastal geography and placement in relation to other neighbouring coastal state(s), may in some places be rather limited. Therefore, the very concept of a *coastal* state presupposes that it, per definition, has an adjacent belt of the territorial sea.[9] On the other hand, not every coastal state may have, or may lawfully proclaim, an EEZ, as that right depends on whether there are any high seas beyond and directly adjacent to its territorial sea. The geographical placement of some coastal states prevents them from any extension of maritime zones beyond their territorial sea. For the same reason, since the continental shelf is the area of seabed and subsoil extending beyond the (submarine) outer limit of the territorial sea – and although most coastal states, *ipso facto*, do have a continental shelf – not every coastal state has (or can have) a continental shelf.

The breadth of each of those maritime zones, as allowable under international law, differs. In this connection, Articles 3, 57, and 76(1) are today regarded as reflecting customary law.[10] It is, however, open to debate whether and to what extent the provisions of Article 76, beyond its paragraph 1, constitute customary law.[11]

At this stage, one basic commonality in the setting of the limits and, eventually, also delimiting the territorial sea, the EEZ, and the continental shelf becomes evident. It relates to the shared criterion for determining the breadth of all the three different regimes: *from* the baselines from which the breadth of the territorial sea is measured. This is their 'horizontal' line of commonality: a joint reference-point to the territorial sea baseline, which in turn depends on and is conditioned by the geography of the coastal front.[12]

[9] See Art. 2(1) LOSC. In support of this view, Vladimir Ibler argues that this provision embodies *jus cogens*; V. Ibler, '*Jus cogens* and the Law of the Sea,' in M. G. Cohen (ed.), *Promoting Justice, Human Rights and Conflict Resolution through International Law: Liber Amicorum Lucius Caflisch* (Brill Leiden 2007) 747–765.

[10] Regarding the customary nature of the EEZ, see *Case concerning the Continental Shelf (Libyan Arab Jamahiriya/Malta)* [1985] ICJ Rep. 13 [34]. Regarding the customary nature of Art. 76(1) LOSC, see *Territorial and Maritime Dispute (Nicaragua v. Colombia)* [2012] ICJ Rep. 624 [118].

[11] The comparative approach in this chapter is confined to the delimitation of the continental shelf not extending beyond 200 nm, in addition to the territorial sea and the EEZ, and the use of the term 'continental shelf' here is accordingly restricted. On the delimitation of the so-called outer continental shelf, see Chapters 12 and 13.

[12] The importance of the baseline, insofar as it provides the relevant basepoints in the construction of either median or equidistance line, arises in the delimitation between states

While all three regimes are today codified in the LOSC, their development until and during the Third United Nations Conference on the Law of the Sea (UNCLOS III) was markedly different. The territorial sea entered customary law long ago; however, its breadth was not agreed upon until UNCLOS III. The continental shelf regime had an instant emergence in customary law in the post-1945 period and in the course of the 1950s; however, the criteria for defining its outer limits have been changed profoundly since the 1958 Geneva Conference on the Law of the Sea. And, finally, the EEZ did not figure at all in the Geneva law; it entered customary law, as is reflected in LOSC provisions, during UNCLOS III – regarding both the substance of the regime and its spatial extent.[13] As eventually codified in the LOSC, the criteria of *distance* apply for determining the spatial extent of each of those regimes.

2.2 LOSC Delimitation Provisions in Articles 15 and 74/83: A Similarity and Differences

The LOSC delimitation provision for the territorial sea (Article 15) differs greatly from provisions for the delimitation of the EEZ (Article 74) and the continental shelf (Article 83). The latter two may, due to their mutual correspondence, be conveniently referred to as Article(s) 74/83. Moreover, the text of Article 15 – except for two stylistic alterations in the second sentence – remains the same as in Article 12 of the 1958 Geneva Convention on the Territorial Sea and the Contiguous Zone. In contrast, Article 83, on the delimitation of the continental shelf, is hardly comparable with the delimitation provision contained in the 1958 Geneva Convention on the Continental Shelf. And finally, for Article 74 there is no previous provision for comparison, as this was the first treaty law provision on EEZ delimitation.

The rule on the delimitation of the territorial sea is stated in Article 15 of the Convention:

with both opposite or adjacent coasts. See further C. Lathrop, 'Baselines,' in D. R. Rothwell, A. G. Oude Elferink, K. N. Scott, and T. Stephens (eds.), *The Oxford Handbook of the Law of the Sea* (Oxford University Press Oxford 2015), 71.

13 Solutions adopted for the EEZ were, together with the territorial sea and the regime of straits used for international navigation, in the UNCLOS III 'package deal' approach linked in the same 'package,' in which the continental shelf regime was not included. However, the delimitation provisions for the EEZ and the continental shelf (Arts. 74 and 83 LOSC) were jointly agreed and resulted in the same language for both.

> Where the coasts of two States are opposite or adjacent to each other, neither of the two States is entitled, failing agreement between them to the contrary, to extend its territorial sea beyond the median line every point of which is equidistant from the nearest points on the baselines from which the breadth of the territorial seas of each of the two States is measured. The above provision does not apply, however, where it is necessary by reason of historic title or other special circumstances to delimit the territorial seas of the two States in a way which is at variance therewith.

Prior to the adoption of the LOSC, the only provision relating to the delimitation of maritime areas of sovereign rights of coastal states beyond the territorial sea was Article 6 of the 1958 Geneva Convention on the Continental Shelf. It stated that, in the absence of agreement, and unless another boundary line is justified by *special circumstances*, the boundary of the continental shelf of states with opposite coasts is the *median* line, every point of which is equidistant from the nearest points of the baselines from which the breadth of the territorial sea is measured; and accordingly, for the states with adjacent coasts, that the boundary shall be determined by application of the principle of *equidistance*. The absence of any reference to 'historic title' and the inclusion of the word 'justified' for applying special circumstances were two main differences from the delimitation rule of the territorial sea in Article 12 of the 1958 Convention on the Territorial Sea and the Contiguous Zone.[14]

Conversely, however, there is now only one textual similarity of Articles 74/83 and Article 15 under LOSC. Article 74/83, paragraph 1, reads:

> The delimitation of the [exclusive economic zone] [continental shelf] between States with opposite or adjacent coasts shall be effected by agreement on the basis of international law, as referred to in Article 38 of the Statute of the International Court of Justice, in order to achieve an equitable solution.

A reference to an agreement between states is the only aspect that Article 15 shares with Articles 74/83.[15] This single textual similarity, however,

[14] Regarding Art. 6 as 'placed... in the perspective of customary law,' see *Maritime Delimitation in the Area between Greenland and Jan Mayen (Denmark v. Norway)* [1993] ICJ Rep. 91[46], [51], and [56]. While the similarity in wording of Art. 6 and the rule for the territorial sea delimitation (as today reflected in Art. 15) is, given the negotiating history of those provisions, certainly not coincidental, an important caveat for any interpretation of the legal meaning or effect stemming from the otherwise textually similar or same terms used in those provisions persists: the profoundly different legal nature, substance, and spatial extent of the respective regimes, as described in Section 2.1 above. For further discussion of Art. 6, see Chapter 4.

[15] Even that single similarity between Art. 15 and Arts. 74/83 is not complete: paragraph 2 in Arts. 74/83 states that '[i]f no agreement can be reached within a reasonable period of time,

merely states the pre-eminence of agreement as the source of law for maritime delimitation between the states. In an agreement on (maritime) delimitation, each state retains, *inter alia*, its autonomy over its own rights; it may, for instance, renounce or cede to another state some of the rights it would otherwise have in accordance with international law. Political, economic and other considerations which states may have in their mutual relations may in some circumstances lead to agreements embodying a maritime delimitation line that reflects the outcome of a compromise on their competing claims,[16] to a greater or lesser extent disregarding the legal entitlements otherwise required to support claims under international law.[17] Equally so, states are not bound to follow a particular method of delimitation if they so agree, as long as the outcome does not impact on the rights of third states or violate *jus cogens*.

2.3 The Role of the Judiciary: Distinguishing the Methodology and Law-making?

An international court or tribunal is in a fundamentally different position, in several respects. First, a court or a tribunal does not have the above-described autonomy which states retain, unless – and only to that extent – the parties authorize it, by explicitly agreeing, to decide their maritime boundary dispute *ex aequo et bono*.[18] For this, as yet, there are no precedents to cite. Instead, courts and tribunals are to decide (maritime) disputes on the basis of international law – which means that their decisions must reflect the legal *entitlements* on which claims of the states to a disputed maritime area are based, rather than weighting a decision solely between the claims that parties choose to put forth. Claims may be (and

the states concerned shall resort to the procedures provided for in Part XV' [Settlement of Disputes], and there is no such explicit provision in Art. 15. However, states are in any case under obligation to settle their disputes, including indeed territorial disputes, by peaceful means (Art. 279), to exchange views regarding the settlement of their dispute (Art. 283) and are, moreover, subject to compulsory procedures entailing binding decisions, including means for dispute settlement (Art. 287) – though with limitations and exceptions in accordance with Arts. 297 and 298.

[16] For one such example, see *Jan Mayen*, n. 14, [84].

[17] Although sometimes used as synonyms, 'entitlements' and 'claims' are not always necessarily the same and should be distinguished; whereas overlapping entitlements, such as to a 12 nm territorial sea, create rights pending delimitation, overlapping claims can also be political and without a legal basis (e.g., to a breadth of the territorial sea exceeding 12 nm). See *Black's Law Dictionary*, 6th ed. (West Publishing St. Paul 1990) 246 and 532, for a distinction between an *entitlement* (a 'right to . . . which may not be abridged without due process') and a *claim* (a 'demand' or an 'assertion' . . . 'as one's right').

[18] Regarding the ICJ, see Art. 38(2) of the Statute of the Court.

often are) in the political sphere, whereas entitlements to support these lie within the realm of law. Indeed, there are in law no 'excessive' maritime entitlements – only overlapping entitlements pending delimitation – but there are many excessive maritime claims.[19] Here is one limitation to the extent of autonomy of international courts and tribunals in deciding (maritime delimitation) disputes, equally applicable to all maritime zones.[20] Only those claims that have support in a maritime entitlement can be valid under international law and can receive legal sanction by means of a decision of an international court.

Another more general limitation of jurisprudence, which is in international law also related to the fact that the courts and tribunals are not bearers of sovereignty, concerns their role in the resolution of disputes between states. In principle, the function of an (international) court or tribunal is to decide in disputes by applying (international) law – not by creating the law. The importance of this principle of jurisprudence is further strengthened in matters of international law involving territory, sovereignty, and sovereign rights, as in maritime delimitation cases. Neither codification nor progressive development of international law is a role of an international court or tribunal – and certainly not in terms of Article 13(1)(a) of the UN Charter and Article 16 of the Statute of the International Law Commission.[21] This should not be confused with the role of the international judiciary in contributing to the development of international law, by means of clarification and consistent interpretation of legal principles and rules, and by elaboration of dispute settlement methodology.

Nonetheless, the role of the judiciary in maritime delimitation disputes, and the distinction between the development of methodology, on the one hand, and the legal rule, on the other, does not appear entirely clear-cut regarding the continental shelf and EEZ delimitation. The wording of LOSC Articles 74/83, and their difference from Article 15, may help to

[19] See J. A. Roach and R. W. Smith, *Excessive Maritime Claims*, 3rd ed. (Martinus Nijhoff Leiden 2012).

[20] Delimitations by agreement may therefore differ significantly from the outcome at which an international court or tribunal might arrive if asked to delimit the same boundary; see S. Fietta and R. Cleverly, *A Practitioner's Guide to Maritime Boundary Delimitation* (Oxford University Press Oxford 2016), 115–116. On the distinction by the Court between different legal nature of maritime entitlements, see e.g. *Nicaragua v. Colombia*, n. 10, Section V.5, on 'Entitlements Generated by Maritime Features,' [177]–[182]. See also Section 2.5.1 of this chapter below.

[21] The Statute of the ILC conceives the 'progressive development' of international law as a conscious effort towards the creation of new rules of international law (which is still a long way to go before a rule of international law can receive legally binding force, through the will of sovereign states).

explain one aspect of the role of international judiciary here. Whereas the courts and tribunals are not tasked with the progressive development of international law, the general and vague language of Articles 74/83 has brought the role of the international judiciary 'close to' that – in the sense of *contributing* to the development of international law.[22] That, however, is very different from the role a court or a tribunal can play in applying the well-established and unambiguous rule on the method for the territorial sea delimitation as reflected in LOSC Article 15.

Absent an agreement (or when its existence remains disputed), the international court or a tribunal – especially if tasked with determining a single, all-purpose maritime boundary[23] involving areas within and beyond the territorial sea – faces the key difference between Article 15, on the one hand, and Articles 74/83 on the other. While Article 15 does provide the basic method for the delimitation of the territorial sea (but identifies no particular objective, other than achieving the ultimate purpose – 'to delimit the territorial seas'), Articles 74/83 are silent on any method to be employed in delimiting the EEZ/continental shelf, but do state the objective to be achieved: an 'equitable solution.'[24]

There is, nonetheless, one other shared requirement, albeit not explicitly stated in Article 15 or in Articles 74/83, that a court or a tribunal must be guided by in adjudicating the delimitation of the territorial sea, the continental shelf, or the EEZ. That is the basic principle in accordance with which maritime rights are derived from the coastal State's sovereignty over the land: 'the land dominates the sea.'[25] This axiom was restated by the Court, with reference to its previous judgments, in *Qatar/Bahrain*;[26]

[22] For an early argument in that direction, see B. Vukas, 'Possible Role of the International Tribunal for the Law of the Sea in Interpretation and Progressive Development of the Law of the Sea,' in D. Vidas and W. Østreng (eds.), *Order for the Oceans at the Turn of the Century* (Kluwer Law International The Hague 1999), 102–103. For a more recent view, see 'Declaration of Judge Wolfrum,' n. 95.

[23] In *Qatar/Bahrain*, n. 2, the Court observed that 'the concept of a single maritime boundary does not stem from multilateral treaty law but from State practice, and that it finds its explanation in the wish of States to establish one uninterrupted boundary line delimiting the various – partially coincident – zones of maritime jurisdiction appertaining to them' [173]. Judicial practice was indeed rather conducive here.

[24] Compare this outcome, as now contained in Arts. 74/83, with the view stated by the Court in 1969, regarding the continental shelf delimitation, according to which 'it is necessary to seek not one method of delimitation but one goal' – and in which context 'an equitable solution' was then mentioned; see *North Sea Continental Shelf*, n. 6, [92].

[25] This fundamental principle was, in maritime delimitation jurisprudence, first explicitly stated by the ICJ in ibid., [96].

[26] *Qatar/Bahrain*, n. 2, [185]: '[I]t is thus the terrestrial territorial situation that must be taken as starting point for the delimitation of the maritime rights of a coastal State.'

moreover, in *Cameroon v. Nigeria* the ICJ further explained its reliance on the given geographical features.[27]

The function of an international court or a tribunal tasked with maritime delimitation is not to engage in corrective or redistributive justice. As noted by the UN Secretary-General:

> UNCLOS was not negotiated to correct geographical circumstances. To compensate partially for the latter, the Convention provides adequate remedies for situations where States are at a disadvantage.[28]

Or, as more directly stated by Vaughan Lowe in relation to the function of international judiciary: 'states with short coastlines are not to be compensated by giving them a greater share of the seas adjacent to their coasts.'[29] And conversely, states with long or favourably positioned coastlines are not to be deprived of their rights by a reduction of the effect of their maritime entitlement, except in accordance with international law in case of overlap with the maritime entitlement of another state.

Other than the above general considerations – including the paramount importance of the principle that the 'land dominates the sea' – there is not much guidance for the judiciary offered by Articles 74/83, not least when compared to Article 15 for delimiting the territorial sea. A key difference regarding the role of international judiciary here emerges as a consequence of the content of Article 15, on the one hand, and Articles 73/84, on the other: the method stated in the former contrasts with the lack of any in the latter.

2.4 Delimitation Methodology: As Developed by Judiciary and as Provided for by a Rule

Developing a methodology for maritime delimitation is fundamentally different from amending a rule already provided for by international law. 'Methodology' is here understood in its technical meaning: a set of methods composing a 'due process' that enables a court or a tribunal

[27] *Land and Maritime Boundary between Cameroon and Nigeria (Cameroon* v. *Nigeria: Equatorial Guinea intervening)* [2002], ICJ Rep. 303 [295]: 'the geographical configuration of the maritime areas that the Court is called upon to delimit is a given. It is not an element open to modification by the Court but a fact on the basis of which the Court must effect the delimitation.'

[28] *Oceans and the Law of the Sea: Report of the Secretary-General*, UN Doc. A/59/62, 4 March 2004 [41].

[29] V. Lowe, *International Law: A Very Short Introduction* (Oxford University Press Oxford 2015) 122.

to arrive at what the rule requires.[30] Regarding the delimitation of the EEZ/continental shelf, that requirement consists of the objective stated in Articles 74/83: to achieve an equitable solution. Regarding the delimitation of the territorial sea, the rule in Article 15 does provide the method – and, aside from its interpretation and application, there is not much room for judicial 'development,' nor indeed any legal basis for its amendment by means of judicial practice.

2.4.1 Delimitation Methodology for the Continental Shelf/EEZ as Developed by Judiciary

Upon the conclusion of the LOSC, the ICJ stated in 1985 in *Libya/Malta* that:

> [T]he Convention sets a goal to be achieved, but is silent as to the method to be followed to achieve it. It restricts itself to setting a standard, and it is left to the States themselves or to the courts, to endow this standard with specific content.[31]

The intervening two and a half decades led to a comprehensive restatement of delimitation methodology by the Court in its 2009 judgment in *Black Sea*.[32] Other chapters in this volume explore various aspects of that development and its outcomes so far. Two remarks on the importance of the delimitation rule for the territorial sea also for the judicial development of delimitation methodology for the EEZ/continental shelf are, however, pertinent here. First, although Article 15 and Articles 74/83 contain quite different wording, the ICJ stated in *Qatar/Bahrain*:

> the equidistance/special circumstances rule, which is applicable in particular to the delimitation of the territorial sea, and the equitable principles/relevant circumstances rule, *as it has been developed since 1958* in case-law and State practice with regard to the delimitation of the continental shelf and the exclusive economic zone, are closely interrelated.[33]

30 See e.g. a definition of the method as a 'mode of operating, or the means of attaining an object,' in *Black's Law Dictionary*, n. 17, 991.

31 *Libya/Malta*, n. 10, [28].

32 *Black Sea*, n. 1, Section 7, 'Delimitation Methodology' [115]–[122].

33 *Qatar/Bahrain*, n. 2, [231]. Note the reference to the development 'since 1958,' emphasis added. This judgment, and the one following from the ICJ in the year after (*Cameroon v. Nigeria*, n. 27), are also notable for their terminology of '*equitable principles*/relevant circumstances' in EEZ/continental shelf delimitation. In a quiet judicial 'battle of words,' the '*equidistance*/relevant circumstances' won the day (so far).

And second, the Court explained in its 2002 judgment (and reiterated in 2007) that, when a line applying to several zones of coincident jurisdictions is to be determined, the '*equitable principles*/relevant circumstances' method may usefully be applied, as

> [T]his method, which is very similar to the equidistance/special circumstances method applicable in delimitation of the territorial sea, involves first drawing an equidistance line, then considering whether there are factors calling for the adjustment or shifting of that line in order to achieve an 'equitable result.'[34]

In *Black Sea*, the Court (with reference to its practice in 'recent decades') defined its delimitation methodology as a three-stage approach.[35] First, a provisional 'delimitation' [*sic*] line is to be drawn, 'using methods that are geometrically objective and also appropriate for the geography of the area'; and 'equidistance and median lines'[36] are to be constructed from the 'most *appropriate* points'[37] on the coasts of the two states concerned. At the second stage, consideration of whether there are factors calling for an adjustment or shifting of the provisional equidistance line is to be undertaken, in order to achieve an equitable result. Finally, at the third stage a proportionality test is to be conducted: a further verification of any inequitable result of 'the line (a provisional equidistance line [*sic*])' – as already adjusted if required by the 'relevant circumstances' – against marked disproportion

34 *Cameroon v. Nigeria*, n. 27, [288], referred to also in *Territorial and Maritime Dispute between Nicaragua and Honduras in the Caribbean Sea (Nicaragua* v. *Honduras)* [2007] ICJ Rep. 359 [271]. On the use of the phrase 'equitable result,' which is notable in both 2001 (*Qatar/Bahrain*, n. 2) and 2002 (*Cameroon* v. *Nigeria*, n. 27) judgments by the ICJ, and also different from the wording of Arts. 74/83 ('equitable solution'), see further in Section 2.5.2 below – however, as related to the territorial sea delimitation.

35 *Black Sea*, n. 1, [115]–[122]. This judgment, of 3 February 2009, was the last to be issued during the ICJ presidency of Dame Rosalyn Higgins, whose membership in the Court expired two days later.

36 The Court took great care to explain the 'delimitation line' as an 'equidistance' line between adjacent coasts (yet its use being dependent also on 'compelling reasons' that make equidistance 'unfeasible' in particular cases) and the term 'median' line which 'will' be used insofar as opposite coasts are concerned. It then felt a need to clarify that 'no legal consequences flow from the use of the terms "median line" and "equidistance line" since the method of delimitation is the same for both'; ibid., [116]. Compare the terms used in Art. 6 of the 1958 Geneva Convention on the Continental Shelf.

37 *Black Sea*, n. 1, [117], emphasis added. Some of the terms and formulations used, especially regarding the first stage, leave much to be desired and open for blurring the distinction from the second stage. See the discussion in Chapter 9; also M. D. Evans, 'Maritime Boundary Delimitation: Whatever Next?,' in J. Barrett and R. Barnes (eds.), *Law of the Sea. UNCLOS as a Living Treaty* (British Institute of International and Comparative Law London 2016), 41–79.

between the ratio of the respective coastal lengths and the ratio between the relevant maritime area of each state.

If the extensive development led by the international courts and tribunals in navigating the uncharted waters of Articles 74/83 is distilled into some simple conclusions, two observations can be made. First, while Articles 74/83 identify no method, the delimitation rule found in Article 6 of the 1958 Geneva Convention on the Continental Shelf (on earlier occasions seen by international jurisprudence 'in the perspective of customary law') does state a method: namely, equidistance/special circumstances. It is as if this general content, thoroughly filtered by various sorts of equitable caveats, has gradually spilled over and filled the emptiness of Articles 74/83, resulting in a blend embodied in the methodology recaptured by the ICJ in *Black Sea* methodological passages.[38]

Second, the (basically equidistance/median) line resulting from the territorial sea delimitation in accordance with Article 15, delimiting areas under the sovereignty of states provides, at its terminal point(s), the starting point(s) for the delimitation of more functionally oriented regimes of the EEZ and the continental shelf.[39] Because of this fact, the territorial sea delimitation regularly impacts on the delimitation of further maritime areas adjacent to it – whereas the methodology developed by the judiciary can enable the achievement of the stated objective of an 'equitable solution' in the delimitation beyond the territorial sea. We revert to this black-and-white picture with some colours of the judicial practice added to it in Section 2.5.

2.4.2 Delimitation Method for the Territorial Sea as Provided for under International Law

In accordance with the method based on Article 15, the delimitation of the territorial sea begins with the drawing of a provisional equidistance (or median) line. The basic principle underlying the rule reflected in LOSC Article 15 is, as stated by the tribunal in the *Guyana v. Suriname*, that it 'places the primacy on the median line as the delimitation line between the

[38] This would not be contrary to Art. 311(1) LOSC, in accordance with which the LOSC prevails over the Geneva Conventions (but does not terminate them) – nor does it terminate customary law. See also Chapter 4.

[39] For a specific decision on transition between the terminal point of the territorial sea delimitation (found by the Court to be agreed between the parties but not lying on the equidistance line) and the starting point for a strict equidistance delimitation line beyond the territorial sea, see *Cameroon v. Nigeria*, n. 27, [307].

territorial seas of opposite or adjacent States.'[40] Moreover, stemming from the rule contained in Article 15, in the delimitation of the territorial sea there is a presumption in favour of equidistance.[41] According to Crawford (Brownlie's Principles), while its formal character may be debated, this presumption is 'certainly the norm.'[42] In consequence, any deviation from the presumption of equidistance must be proven. This also means that the burden of proof will be on the party that invokes an exemption from equidistance.

Only in exceptional cases will the equidistance not form the basis of the boundary between overlapping territorial seas.[43] Those exceptions, in accordance with Article 15, could arise when a 'historic title' or other 'special circumstances' make it necessary 'to delimit the territorial seas of the two States in a way which is at variance [with equidistance]' – or where there has been an agreement with such an effect. There is a high threshold for establishing the existence of an agreement on maritime delimitation; as the ICJ stated in *Nicaragua v. Honduras*: 'the establishment of a permanent maritime boundary is a matter of grave importance and agreement is not easily to be presumed.'[44]

Regarding a 'historic title,' neither Article 15 nor other provisions of the LOSC offer a definition. Although the existence of such a title is conceivable, the threshold for proving it is high, due to the lack of a defined criterion and previous jurisprudence. The ICJ defined 'historic waters' in 1951 in the Fisheries Case (*United Kingdom v. Norway*).[45] In state practice, the concept of 'historic waters' or 'historic bays' has been deployed almost exclusively in circumstances where there was a single riparian state bordering the waters in question. One exception, where the concept was

[40] *In the Matter of an Arbitration between Guyana and Suriname* [2007] XXX RIAA 1 [296].

[41] See e.g. V. Prescott and C. Schofield, *The Maritime Political Boundaries of the World*, 2nd ed. (Martinus Nijhoff Leiden 2005) 219; and J. Crawford (ed.), *Brownlie's Principles of Public International Law*, 8th ed. (Oxford University Press Oxford 2012), 283 – explaining also that this presumption is 'justified by the comparatively small distances involved.'

[42] Crawford, n. 41, 285.

[43] M. D. Evans, 'Maritime Boundary Delimitation,' in Rothwell, n. 12, 256; M. D. Evans, 'The Law of the Sea,' in M. D. Evans (ed.), *International Law*, 4th ed. (Oxford University Press Oxford 2014) 676–677.

[44] *Nicaragua v. Honduras*, n. 34, [253]. See also ITLOS reasoning in *Delimitation of the Maritime Boundary between Bangladesh and Myanmar in the Bay of Bengal* [2012] ITLOS Rep. 4[89]–[99] and [112]–[118].

[45] The Court stated: '[B]y "historical *waters*" are usually meant waters which are treated as internal waters but which would not have that character were it not for the existence of an historic title'; *Fisheries Case (United Kingdom v. Norway)*, Judgment, ICJ Rep. 1951 [130], emphasis added.

applied to a situation involving two or more riparian states is the Gulf of Fonseca, decided in 1992 by a Chamber of the ICJ.[46]

The other ground stated in Article 15 – the existence of other 'special circumstances' – is a concept that has in most cases been applied restrictively, and basically reduced to particular geographic features and outstanding configurations which may require that a provisional equidistance line be adjusted to a greater or lesser extent.[47]

2.5 Tendency to Assimilate Legal Principles: A Two-Way Street?

Commenting on the developments until the early 2000s, Anderson noted a 'tendency to assimilate to a certain extent the legal principles relating to maritime delimitation, whether the boundary runs through the territorial sea, the EEZ or the continental shelf,' observing that this trend could be seen most clearly in *Jan Mayen* and *Qatar/Bahrain* (with only the latter involving the territorial sea delimitation).[48] Decisions by the judiciary in later cases seem to have confirmed this early observation. In 2011, Guillaume commented that the ICJ has:

> *unified* the law of maritime delimitation – whether the continental shelf, territorial sea or the exclusive economic zone – in holding that in all these cases it was necessary to first draw the line of equidistance, then adjust it to take account of relevant factors related mainly to the coastline. Finally, it generalized this solution in 2001 in *Bahrain/Qatar*, and resumed it in the 2009 case of *Romania/Ukraine*.[49]

A trend towards certain assimilation was not altogether unexpected, insofar as understood as an assimilation of the legal principles for the delimitation of the territorial sea also in delimiting the zones of functional jurisdiction beyond, but directly adjoining to, the territorial sea. From the substance (or lack of such) in Articles 74/83, on the one hand, and the

[46] *Land, Island and Maritime Frontier Dispute (El Salvador v. Honduras: Nicaragua intervening)* [1992], ICJ Rep. 1992 [394]. In that case, the legal status of that bay is accorded the internal waters under the *joint sovereignty* of the three riparian states – a unique situation to date.

[47] See e.g. *The Bay of Bengal Maritime Boundary Arbitration (Bangladesh v. India)* PCA Case 2010-16 [248], [271]–[272]. See, however, Sections 2.5.3 and 2.5.4 below.

[48] D. Anderson, 'Developments in Maritime Boundary Law and Practice,' in D. A. Colson and R. W. Smith (eds.), *International Maritime Boundaries*, vol. 5 (Martinus Nijhoff Leiden 2005), 3212.

[49] G. Guillaume, 'The Use of Precedent by International Judges and Arbitrators,' (2011) 2 *Journal of International Dispute Settlement* 11–12, emphasis added for 'unified.'

inseparable aspects of the EEZ/continental shelf delimitation from that of the territorial sea, on the other, it was not difficult to foresee such an effect. A statement of the representative of Venezuela (Andrés Aguilar) at the eleventh session of UNCLOS III confirms that this interpretation was present (even if not necessarily endorsed by all) while the LOSC was still in draft form. As stated by Aguilar on that occasion:

> It could be argued that, for lack of any other substantive provision, the criterion established in that regulation [i.e., Article 15 of the then-draft Convention] would apply by analogy not only to the delimitation of the territorial sea but also to the delimitation of the exclusive economic zone and the continental shelf.[50]

Indeed, at UNCLOS III the group of 'pro-equity' states had advocated for the priority of 'equitable principles' for the EEZ/continental shelf delimitation provision, also to balance the adoption of the median/equidistance line criterion in the territorial sea delimitation rule.[51]

But the assimilation of legal principles as relevant for the territorial sea delimitation, which have apparently played a role in informing the judicial development of methodology for delimiting the EEZ/continental shelf, does not imply a sort of *renvoi* effect in which the method for territorial sea delimitation, as provided for in Article 15 of the Convention, would in turn also become 'adjusted' in a process of judicial 'unification.' A comparison of several key aspects undertaken in the rest of this section examines whether, and to what extent, the latter might have happened in the judicial practice upon the entry into force of the Convention.

2.5.1 Distinguishing the Tasks

In *Qatar/Bahrain*, the Court has clearly distinguished its tasks regarding the delimitation of the territorial sea from that of the EEZ/continental shelf. In the words of the Court: '*once it has delimited* the territorial seas,' it *will* determine the rules and principles *to be applied* to the delimitation of

[50] Doc A/CONF.62/SR. 158, of 30 March 1982 [9]. Venezuela had at that point concluded that it could not accept the solution provided by the joint consideration of Arts. 15, 74 and 83 of the draft convention; ibid., [8]. To date, Venezuela is not a party to LOSC.

[51] See B. Vukas, 'The LOS Convention and Sea Boundary Delimitation,' in B. Vukas (ed.), *Essays on the New Law of the Sea* (University of Zagreb Zagreb 1985) 147, 149. The group of states at UNCLOS III advocating a delimitation provision based on 'equitable principles' included, *inter alia*, Bangladesh, Côte d'Ivoire, France, Kenya, Libya, Nicaragua, Nigeria, Romania, Somalia, Turkey, and Venezuela. See an overview in Fietta and Cleverly *Guide* (n. 20), 24–27.

the EEZ/continental shelf – and it will 'further decide whether the method to be chosen for this delimitation differs from or is similar to the approach' it used to delimit the territorial seas.[52] In making this distinction regarding different parts of its task, the Court was led by the difference in the nature of rights in the territorial sea, being territorial and entailing sovereignty, as opposed to the functional rights in the two distinct maritime areas beyond the territorial sea, along with 'taking into account that its ultimate task is to draw a single maritime boundary that serves other purposes as well.'[53]

Although the Court in *Black Sea* was not tasked with delimiting the territorial sea, it nonetheless deemed it pertinent to emphasize that:

> a maritime boundary delimiting the continental shelf and exclusive economic zones is *not to be assimilated* to a State boundary separating territories of States. The former defines the limits of maritime zones where under international law coastal States have certain sovereign rights for defined purposes. The latter defines the territorial limits of State sovereignty.[54]

However, the approach which the Court employed in *Nicaragua v. Honduras* merits special mention. The Court took this opportunity to declare an important distinction: that the 'methods governing territorial sea delimitations have needed to be, and are, more clearly articulated in international law than those used for the other, more functional maritime areas.'[55] It then proceeded to make a rather noteworthy distinction. As a separate task, the Court delimited the territorial seas around the four outer islands of Honduras and one island of Nicaragua, according full effect to the islands and using the unadjusted equidistance line for this part of the delimitation.[56] Within its other delimitation task, however, for which the delimitation line was to be constructed from the mainland, the Court 'grouped' together the delimitation of the territorial sea with that of the continental shelf and the EEZ – thereby subsuming this part of the territorial sea delimitation under the overall, 'single' delimitation line. In doing so, the Court referred to its previous decisions – actually, to those relating mostly to the delimitation of the continental shelf[57] – eventually

[52] *Qatar/Bahrain* [176], n. 2, emphasis added. [53] Ibid., [174].

[54] *Black Sea*, n. 1, [217], emphasis added. [55] *Nicaragua v. Honduras*, n. 34, [269].

[56] For those islands, neither of the parties claimed any maritime areas beyond the territorial sea.

[57] See *Nicaragua v. Honduras*, n. 34, discussing territorial sea delimitation issues with supporting references to e.g. the *North Sea Continental Shelf* [269], *Gulf of Maine* [279], *Tunisia/Libya* [280]. A similar pattern was employed by the arbitral tribunal in *Guyana v. Suriname*, n. 40, in examining the special circumstances requiring adjustment of the

opting for a single delimitation line based on an angle bisector. Moreover, in deciding on the starting point of the delimitation line and also considering its endpoint, the Court failed to indicate any transition point at which the territorial sea delimitation (as determined from the mainland) ends and the continental shelf/EEZ delimitation should commence.[58] Loyal to its own distinction of tasks (and the respective delimitation methods used), the Court identified transition points only between the bisector line and the equidistance line around the outer islands. The delimitation line, as the Court constructed it from the mainland, clearly subsumed the territorial sea delimitation under the single line including the continental shelf and EEZ – as evident already from the way the Court defined its tasks, the supporting references, and the line itself.

The distinction made by the ITLOS in performing its task of territorial sea delimitation is probably best illustrated by two aspects of its *Bangladesh/Myanmar* judgment. First, in drawing the delimitation line of the territorial sea, the ITLOS attributed full effect to St. Martin's Island; in the view of the Tribunal, to decide otherwise would result in giving more weight to the sovereign rights and jurisdiction of Myanmar in its EEZ and continental shelf than to the sovereignty of Bangladesh over its territorial sea.[59] In this way, the 12-mile territorial sea of Bangladesh around St. Martin's Island met, and was delimited with, the EEZ, and continental shelf of Myanmar.[60] Second, the Tribunal made it clear that the question of free and unimpeded navigation for Myanmar in the territorial sea of Bangladesh around St. Martin's Island is *not* an issue to be considered as a part of delimitation, although it is a related matter of particular concern to Myanmar.[61] In addition, there was a third aspect, though related to the arguments of the parties: the Tribunal cautioned against referring to cases (and state practice) related to the delimitation of the continental shelf or

equidistance line: the tribunal used supporting references to cases concerning the continental shelf; see ibid., [302]–[303], also Section 2.5.2 below.

[58] When considering the areas to be delimited, the Court did indicate that the single maritime boundary will 'for some distance' delimit exclusively the territorial seas, *Nicaragua v. Honduras*, n. 34, [262]; it then properly characterized this segment of the maritime boundary as the 'frontier line across the territorial seas' [280] – but it never returned to specify exactly where this 'frontier' ends and the 'more functional maritime areas' begin [see 320]–[321]. The Court did, however, set the 'point of departure of the maritime delimitation' (the starting point) three miles out to sea 'from the point already identified by the Mixed Commission in 1962' [311].

[59] *Bangladesh/Myanmar*, n. 44, [169].

[60] Ibid., [168].

[61] Ibid., [170]; see also [171]–[176], regarding the solution facilitated.

EEZ in the context of the territorial sea delimitation, as that was not seen as directly relevant to the latter.[62]

Arbitral tribunals in recent cases have generally been clear in distinguishing their tasks in different maritime areas. For instance, the tribunal in *Bangladesh v. India* was quite specific in deciding the delimitation of the territorial seas and of the continental shelf/EEZ separately, since 'in delimiting the various maritime spaces different considerations need to be taken into account'; as the tribunal went on to explain:

> in the delimitation of the territorial sea, for instance, it is of considerable significance that the rights of the coastal State are not functional, but territorial, and entail sovereignty,' while 'further to seaward, sovereign rights, rather than sovereignty itself, are at issue, and the relevant considerations differ.[63]

2.5.2 Defining the Objective

Courts and tribunals have consistently reiterated the stated method ('equidistance/special circumstances') and often also the axiom underlying the legal principles ('the land dominates the sea') as key parameters in executing their task: 'to delimit the territorial seas of the two States' (as provided for in Article 15). However, in its first case involving the delimitation of the territorial sea upon the entry into force of the Convention – *Qatar/Bahrain*, decided under the presidency of Gilbert Guillaume – the ICJ, turning to the examination of whether there might be special circumstances requiring an adjustment of the provisional equidistance, stated that such adjustment was made 'in order to obtain an *equitable result* in relation to this part [i.e., the territorial sea] of the single maritime boundary to be fixed.'[64] Moreover, in the abstract of the judgment, it is stated (in the context of territorial sea delimitation): 'method consisting of provisionally drawing an equidistance line and adjusting it to take account of special circumstances *or to obtain an equitable result*.'[65] The Court, however, omitted any explanation for its use of this notion in the part of the judgment concerning the territorial sea, and reverted to such elaborations

[62] Ibid., [150]. Compare this with ICJ's use of supporting references in *Nicaragua v. Honduras*, n. 34, or those of the arbitral tribunal in *Guyana v. Suriname*, n. 40.

[63] *Bangladesh v. India*, n. 47, [191].

[64] *Qatar/Bahrain*, n. 2, [217], emphasis added. The Court here considered it appropriate to make a reference to its judgment in *Jan Mayen*, n. 14 – which, however, did not relate to the territorial sea.

[65] *Qatar/Bahrain*, n. 2, [41], emphasis added.

only when addressing the delimitation *beyond* the territorial sea – where it also reiterated that 'greater importance must be attributed to elements, such as distance from the coast, which are common to both concepts [i.e., the continental shelf and EEZ].'[66]

The choice of this wording ('equitable result'), although frequently used by the judiciary in the context of continental shelf/EEZ delimitation, differs from the term used in Articles 74/83 ('equitable solution'). In *North Sea Continental Shelf*, the ICJ identified the notion of 'equitable solution' as having emerged in the context of drafting history for the territorial sea delimitation provision in 1953. However, the Court identified this notion as not originating from the legal considerations within the ILC but rather from (as it termed it) a 'committee of *hydrographical*' experts, which in 1953 reported to the ILC by recommending the principle of equidistance, but also added that the application of equidistance in some cases 'may not lead to an equitable solution' – and suggested that this outcome should then be 'arrived at by negotiation' (i.e., through an agreement between the states, rather than by reference to 'special circumstances').[67] Moreover, rather than referring to an 'equitable result,' the Court in *North Sea Continental Shelf* referred to a '*reasonable* result' – the one to be achieved through the application of 'equitable principles.'[68] The Court in that connection referred to possible consequences resulting from the application of equidistance in the delimitation of the continental shelf, stating that 'the greater the irregularity and the further from the coastline the area to be delimited, the more *unreasonable* are the results produced.'[69] However, the Court in *North Sea Continental Shelf* was careful to characterize this effect as being 'very slight' or 'comparatively small' in the territorial sea, which – as it also observed – has a different legal nature; for all those reasons the Court stated that it 'does not consider [the territorial sea delimitation] to be analogous to that of the continental shelf.'[70] The 'reasonable result,' to be achieved by the application of 'equitable principles,' here clearly related to the continental shelf delimitation; the Court was concerned with

[66] Ibid., [224]–[234]. Moreover, the Court reverted to 'considerations of equity' when addressing a 'distortion, due to a [tiny] maritime feature located well out to the sea' [248].

[67] *North Sea Continental Shelf*, n. 6, [50–52]. The task of that expert committee was technical rather than legal; see UN Doc. A/CN.4/61/Add.1 (18 May 1953). The term 'special circumstances' was at that time not yet used in the drafting of the territorial sea delimitation provision, however the content and impact of such circumstances in some specific situations (or 'exceptional cases') was present in the ILC deliberations already in 1952; see also n. 89 below.

[68] Ibid., [90], emphasis added.

[69] Ibid., [89], emphasis added.

[70] Ibid., [8], [59] and [80].

abating 'unreasonable results,'[71] rather than facilitating 'equitable results.' This approach is rather different from the formula of 'equitable result/special circumstances' which emerged in the ICJ vocabulary for the territorial sea delimitation in the early 2000s. The notion of delimitation in accordance with 'equitable principles' was, in turn, identified by the Court in 1969 as originating from the 1945 Truman Proclamation and thereby related to the continental shelf delimitation.[72]

Equitableness arises also at the end of the delimitation process of the continental shelf/EEZ, now defined in *Black Sea* as a separate, third stage. In the first case involving the territorial sea delimitation following the entry into force of the Convention, the *Eritrea/Yemen* arbitral tribunal – drawing on the ICJ in *North Sea Continental Shelf* which introduced the notion of proportionality in the continental shelf delimitation context[73] – applied the proportionality test to the *entire* delimitation line, thereby including the territorial sea boundary.[74] Although this eventually meant no practical difference since the tribunal concluded that the line of delimitation resulted in no significant disproportion, it implied the assimilation of criteria.[75]

Beyond those instances, *Nicaragua v. Honduras* is outstanding. In subsuming the territorial sea delimitation under the remaining part of the single delimitation line, the Court could not avoid the assimilation of the objectives either. For instance, in discussing 'the practical advantages of the bisector method,' the Court explained that it 'could adjust the line so as to achieve an equitable result' and referred to Articles 74/83 – omitting any mention of Article 15 altogether.[76]

[71] Ibid., [24] and [89(a)].

[72] Ibid., [47], with reference to Proclamation 2667 of 28 September 1945. In the LOSC preamble (fourth recital), *equitableness* is used in relation to functional (resource use) and not territorial dimension: 'equitable and efficient utilization of [marine] resources.'

[73] *North Sea Continental Shelf*, n. 6, [98]; see also references to the views of Germany, ibid., [7], [15], and [44].

[74] *In the Matter of an Arbitration pursuant to an Agreement dated 3 October 1996 between the Government of the State of Eritrea and the Government of the Republic of Yemen (Eritrea/Yemen)* [1998] XXII RIAA 211 [165]–[168]. See also comments by Anderson, n. 48, 3207; and M. W. Reismann, 'Eritrea–Yemen Arbitration (Award, Phase II: Maritime Delimitation)' (2000) 94 *AJIL* 734.

[75] This approach has been followed in some recent cases involving the delimitation of both the territorial sea and the continental shelf/EEZ; see further on the proportionality test in Chapter 11.

[76] *Nicaragua v. Honduras*, n. 34, [294]. Nicaragua had invoked the 'equitable principles' and 'relevant circumstances' in requesting the Court to delimit the territorial seas, continental shelf and the EEZs alike by determining a single maritime boundary; ibid., [17].

While examining the objective of 'special circumstances' in an adjustment of the equidistance line in the territorial sea delimitation, the arbitral tribunal in *Guyana v. Suriname* based part of its consideration on precedents, such as *Anglo-French Continental Shelf*, according to which 'the notion of special circumstances generally refers to equitable considerations,' as well as other continental shelf-related ICJ judgments, including *Libya/Malta* and *Jan Mayen*.[77]

Other cases decided by the ICJ, ITLOS, and arbitral tribunals over the course of the past fifteen years do not provide – at least as far as the stated objectives are concerned – much that would indicate a *trend* of assimilation of the objective in the delimitation of the areas beyond the territorial sea impacting the delimitation of the latter. It remains to be seen, however, whether application by the judiciary of the method for delimitation of the territorial sea rather than the statements of principle made might point toward different conclusions.

2.5.3 *Application of the Stated Delimitation Method: The Equidistance of Article 15*

In *Nicaragua v. Honduras*, the Court felt the need to declare that equidistance has an 'intrinsic value' and that it 'remains the general rule.'[78] That was, however, the first case in which the ICJ decided to *not* apply equidistance in a territorial sea delimitation: the Court found that the geographical configuration of the area, with the coastline exhibiting highly active morpho-dynamism, 'might render any equidistance line so constructed today arbitrary and unreasonable in the near future'; this amounted to a special circumstance with the meaning of *exception* from applying equidistance.[79] This gives rise to fundamental questions, related both to the two-stage methodology as used in earlier judicial practice in accordance with Article 15, and to consistent judicial interpretation of what could be the constitutive elements of 'special circumstances' (not least given a different approach in *Bangladesh v. India*).[80]

Instead of equidistance, the Court in *Nicaragua v. Honduras* applied the angle-bisector method.[81] Although a simplified variant of equidistance,

[77] *Guyana v. Suriname*, n. 40, [302]–[303].

[78] *Nicaragua v. Honduras*, n. 34, [272] and [281].

[79] Ibid., [277]–[281].

[80] *Bangladesh v. India*, n. 47, [214]–[215]. Further on 'special circumstances' see in Section 2.5.4 below.

[81] On this method see Fietta and Cleverly, n. 20, 99–102.

the bisector method lacks the precision of equidistance and opens the door for considerable subjectivity: instead of basepoints, it relies on the use of 'coastal fronts.' Depending on how the lines of coastal direction are constructed, the angle can vary significantly. Due to its macro-geographic basis, the bisector method can have significant distorting effects already in the territorial sea.[82] It is difficult to disagree with the observation made by Santiago Torres Bernárdez:

> I had always thought that the coasts concerned by a delimitation constituted an objective geographic fact which did not change according to the delimitation method used by the judge. In this Judgment, however, that assumption seems to have been abandoned, since the coasts concerned by the present delimitation expand and contract depending on the method chosen or even the azimuth selected.[83]

With the exception of *Nicaragua v. Honduras*, in all other recent cases equidistance constituted the basis for the territorial sea delimitation. However, a fundamental question may have been opened by several recent cases, due to judicial discretion introduced in the selection of 'appropriate' basepoints (as these are termed in the *Black Sea* methodological 'guide').[84] A trend towards what might be called 'equitable provisional equidistance,' as evident in recent continental shelf/EEZ delimitation cases,[85] may have been reflected in the determination of the provisional equidistance line for delimiting the territorial sea as well. For instance, in selecting the basepoints it considered appropriate for the territorial sea delimitation, the arbitral tribunal in *Bangladesh v. India* referred to the 'criteria elaborated by the [ICJ] in the *Black Sea* case' [in the context of the continental shelf/EEZ delimitation], concluding that the 'Tribunal considers that base points located on low-tide elevations do not fit [these] criteria' [but

[82] The Court, aware of this potential effect, attempted to 'see if it would be possible to start the frontier line across the territorial sea as an equidistance line'; *Nicaragua v. Honduras*, n. 34, [280]

[83] Ibid., Dissenting Opinion of Judge ad hoc Torres Bernárdez [145].

[84] See the description of the first phase of delimitation methodology [for the continental shelf/EEZ] in *Black Sea*, n. 1, [117]. In the LOSC, the term is used in Art. 7 for the method of *straight* baselines joining 'appropriate points,' in the meaning of Art. 7(1), for a coastline deeply indented and cut into or with a fringe of islands along it, and in the meaning of Art. 7(2), where 'appropriate points' may be 'selected' for highly unstable coastlines due to natural conditions such as a river delta. Rules for this 'appropriateness' and 'selection' are, however, provided in Art. 7(3) and, concerning low-tide elevations, in Art. 7(4). Judicial selection of appropriate basepoints seems to rely on terms used, but employed in a different context.

[85] See Evans, n. 43, and Fietta and Cleverly, n. 20, 575–583. See also Chapter 8.

applied to the territorial sea delimitation].[86] This matter should be properly viewed in light of adjustments of the provisional equidistance line, rather than as an integral issue in its determination, and is therefore discussed in the context of the next section.

2.5.4 Adjustments of Equidistance: The Scope of 'Special Circumstances' of Article 15

While Article 15 does not provide a definition of 'special circumstances,' the Court defined them as 'those circumstances which might *modify* the result produced by an unqualified application of the equidistance principle.'[87] This definition, although not formulated exclusively for the territorial sea delimitation, retains relevance due to its general applicability. The difference lies primarily in the higher threshold for adjusting a provisional equidistance line due to 'special' circumstances in the territorial sea, as compared with a continental shelf delimitation context. The set of circumstances that can be considered as being 'special' in a territorial sea context is relatively narrow. The distorting effects of many geographical features are comparatively small within the territorial sea limits; however, such effects may increase considerably with the distances from the coast measured in hundreds of nautical miles. Therefore, some effects, such as those due to the concavity of a coastline, are in the judicial practice excluded from being considered 'special circumstances' in the territorial sea delimitation, while they may be given relevance in the delimitation of zones beyond the territorial sea.[88] On the other hand, there are examples of special circumstances closely linked to the sea–land interaction which are therefore not relevant in the areas beyond the territorial sea. For instance, the ILC in 1952 discussed the situation 'where the line of delimitation had to be drawn through the estuary of a river whose navigable channel did not follow the median line.'[89] Moreover, whereas the

[86] *Bangladesh v. India*, n. 47, [261].

[87] *Jan Mayen*, n. 14, [55], emphasis added.

[88] The reason for this distinction was stated by the ICJ already in the *North Sea Continental Shelf*, n. 6, [8]. See the overview in Fietta and Cleverly, n. 20, 68–71.

[89] UN Doc. A/CN.4/53, (24 July 1952) *ILC Yearbook* vol. I, 180. Moreover, vol. II of the 1952 *ILC Yearbook*, at 38, contains a related report with commentary of the Special Rapporteur Francois (of 4 April 1952). The arbitral tribunal in *Guyana v. Suriname*, n. 40, when concluding in that case that navigation as a special circumstance may justify deviation from the median line [306], referred in support to, *inter alia*, the ILC commentary (in vol. II), and stated that the ILC 'said that the presence of navigable channel could make a boundary based on equidistance *inequitable*' [301] – however, in the ILC report referred to, it is

distorting effects of various minor land features[90] might be given a role in adjustments of equidistance as being both 'special' and 'relevant' circumstances, such effects could not be attributed to segments of the mainland, for instance to a peninsula as a part of the relevant coast.

It is beyond the scope of this analysis to present the full repertoire of special circumstances used under Article 15 in various cases. Rather, the inquiry here examines whether there might be signs of a trend toward methodological assimilation. Some general trends can indeed be discerned, especially if the approach used by the Court in *Qatar/Bahrain* is compared with more recent cases involving delimitation of the territorial sea.

During the past ten years, 'special circumstances' were invoked in the territorial sea delimitation to justify a method used *instead* of provisional equidistance (*Honduras v. Nicaragua*); moreover, 'special circumstances' were considered both *before and* after the provisional equidistance line was drawn (*Bangladesh/Myanmar*, also *Bangladesh v. India*). There seems to be a gradual shift concerning where in the process 'special circumstances' (and thereby adjustments of a provisional equidistance) are actually employed – a trend resembling that emerging in the recent use of 'relevant circumstances.'[91] The method involving a selection of 'appropriate' basepoints in drawing a provisional equidistance line results in (or, in fact, allows for) the judicial discounting of various features that otherwise constitute legal basepoints. This in turn leads to an advance adjustment effect of provisional equidistance, tacitly accompanying the 'selection' of basepoints which judges or arbitrators might consider 'appropriate.'

This might also help to explain an increasingly restrictive approach by the judiciary to what might constitute a 'special circumstance' that would, in accordance with Article 15, justify *adjustment* of a provisional equidistance line. A silent new, but broad and heterogeneous category of pseudo-special circumstances (including various legal basepoints which have *not* been used, due to being interpreted by judges or arbitrators as 'inappropriate'), might thus be entering via the back door and reflecting on the adjustment stage. Article 15 provides no basis for this development. Whether some further quasi-special circumstances might be intruding into the

rather stated that median line is in such a situation not a 'satisfactory solution' ('*solution satisfaisante*': see vol. II, 38), with no mention whatsoever of (in)equity.

[90] On this matter, see P. von Mühlendahl, 'Tiny Land Features in Recent Maritime Delimitation Case Law' (2016) 31 *IJMCL* 1.

[91] Regarding 'relevant circumstances,' see Chapter 9.

delimitation of the territorial sea is a question that leads us to the next section.

2.5.5 Adjusting a State Border in Territorial Sea Delimitation due to Circumstances beyond Article 15?

Two sets of questions could arise in a judicial determination concerning possible adjustments of the territorial sea boundary which may exceed the confines of Article 15. One relates to whether a court or tribunal, in determining a single all-purpose maritime boundary, should consider the delimitation of the territorial sea in isolation, or whether, already in delimiting the territorial sea, it should consider also how the outcome may affect the options for achieving an equitable solution for the delimitation of the continental shelf/EEZ. In this respect, it is essential to make a clear distinction between 'taking into account that the ultimate task is to draw a single maritime boundary that serves other purposes as well,'[92] as the Court did in *Qatar/Bahrain* on the one hand, and subsuming at the outset the territorial sea delimitation under the broader task of determining a single maritime boundary, on the other – as the Court did in *Nicaragua v. Honduras*, with the consequences described above.

The other aspect of this matter concerns the distinction to be made between application of the rule in Article 15 for delimiting a maritime area under state's sovereignty, on the one hand, and solutions that may be determined or facilitated by the courts and tribunals for any related or additional issues with which the parties may task them, or which may arise in the context of a dispute. A clear example of the latter is the solution in *Bangladesh/Myanmar* regarding free and unimpeded navigation for Myanmar in the territorial sea of Bangladesh around St. Martin's Island and the way in which the ITLOS facilitated this. Another example concerning the importance of deciding within the confines of Article 15 is how delimitation of the territorial sea was envisaged under the Arbitration Agreement between Croatia and Slovenia.[93]

[92] See n. 53 above and the related text.

[93] Arbitration Agreement between Croatia and Slovenia (signed on 4 November 2009; entered into force 29 November 2010). On 22 July 2015, one year after the oral pleadings in this case were completed, media (first in Serbia, then in Croatia and Slovenia) revealed that the arbitrator appointed by Slovenia had been in regular contact with the agent of Slovenia, including the exchange of confidential information about the proceedings of the tribunal and the related documentation, as well as planning possible ways to influence other members of the tribunal, the documentary record and the outcome of the case. The public revelation resulted in the immediate resignation of that arbitrator, with further resignations in the course of the next ten days of two additional arbitrators appointed by the

The task of an ad hoc arbitral tribunal under that Agreement was stated in its Article 3(1):

> [T]he Arbitral Tribunal shall determine
>
> (a) the course of the maritime and land boundary [between Croatia and Slovenia];
> (b) Slovenia's junction to the High Sea;
> (c) the regime for the use of the relevant maritime areas.

The law which the tribunal was to apply was stated in Article 4:

> (a) the rules and principles of international law for the determinations referred to in Article 3(1)(a);
> (b) international law, equity and the principle of good neighbourly relations in order to achieve a fair and just result by taking into account all relevant circumstances for the determinations referred to in Article 3(1)(b) and (c).

The interplay of the tribunal's task under Article 3(1)(a) and the applicable law in Article 4(a), on the one hand, and the tasks under Article 3(1)(b) *and* (c) and the applicable law in Article 4(b), on the other hand, was striking and fundamental for how the tribunal was to determine the dispute. The tribunal was to delimit the territorial sea boundary as a distinct part of its task of determining 'the course of the maritime and land boundary' between the two countries. This it had to do in accordance with Article 4(a), by applying 'the rules and principles of international law,' i.e., Article 15 of the LOSC. With this boundary of territorial sovereignty determined, the tribunal would have been in a position to turn its attention to the remaining issues, for which the applicable law (as well as the objective) was jointly stated in Article 4(b) of the Agreement. Those issues were 'Slovenia's junction to the high seas' and 'the regime for the *use* of the relevant maritime areas': both were to be determined by another, wider set of rules of applicable law. Therefore, 'equity' and 'the principle of good neighbourly relations,' which in addition to international law were to play a role here, along with taking into account 'relevant circumstances' so as

parties (one of them was at the time the President of the ICJ). On 31 July 2015, Croatia informed the tribunal that it ceased to apply the Arbitration Agreement, including its participation in the proceedings, as a consequence of a material breach by Slovenia leading to termination of the treaty (Arts. 60 and 65 of the Vienna Convention on the Law of Treaties), and requested the tribunal to discontinue the proceedings. Thereupon, Croatia published the related documentation on its official website; see www.mvep.hr/en/other/termination-of-the-arbitration-process/. Prompted by those events, the tribunal issued a partial award on 30 June 2016 (available at https://pcacases.com/web/sendAttach/1787) and indicated how it intended to proceed.

to achieve the stated objective of a 'fair and just result,' all stood in contrast with the applicable law under Article 4(a) of the Agreement, concerning the 'course of the maritime and land boundary' including the territorial sea delimitation. The determination of the territorial sea boundary by the tribunal was indeed not subject to any proviso about achieving 'a fair and just result,' nor was the tribunal, in determining this boundary, required (nor indeed permitted) to take into account various circumstances which might have been considered 'relevant' in making the determinations concerning the 'junction' and the 'regime.' Accordingly, the tribunal's task in determining the territorial sea boundary was under this Agreement clearly distinguished – also in terms of applicable law – from its additional and subsequent tasks in relation to the 'junction' and the 'regime.' Had the tribunal subsumed the determination of these (functional) issues under the determination of the territorial sea boundary, or assimilated them, it would have contradicted international law as stated in Article 15 of the LOSC as well as gone *ultra petita* regarding its task under Article 3(1)(a) of that Agreement.

2.6 Concluding Remarks

Territorial sea delimitations have been adjudicated since long before the emergence of the continental shelf and the EEZ in international law.[94] With the extension of sovereign rights and jurisdiction to areas beyond the territorial sea, cases involving the delimitation of the continental shelf (and also EEZs) have increasingly featured in international courts and tribunals. The outcome of UNCLOS III as contained in Articles 74/83 brought a rule which stated the objective but provided no method for achieving it, except that it was to be on the basis of international law. To enable the resolution of disputes submitted to them, the judiciary had to develop a delimitation methodology. In the view of Judge Wolfrum, they have exercised in this respect a 'law-making function,' which is legitimized by Articles 74/83 – unlike, however, for the delimitation of the territorial sea.[95]

[94] A notable arbitral award on territorial sea delimitation is the 1909 *Grisbadarna Case (Norway v. Sweden) (Award)* [1909] 11 RIA 155.

[95] See 'Declaration of Judge Wolfrum,' appended to ITLOS Judgment on *Bangladesh/Myanmar*, n. 44, at 2, also arguing that 'the ensuing international case law constitutes an *acquis judiciaire*, a source of international law to be read into Articles 74 and 83 of the Convention.' Compare this with the wording in *Bangladesh v. India*, n. 47, Award (decided by an Annex VII arbitral tribunal presided by Judge Wolfrum), to which, however, several caveats were added [339], notably the reference to Art. 38(1)(d) of the Statute of the ICJ,

Likewise, international law doctrine has increasingly focused on delimitation of the continental shelf and EEZs. Whether the judicially developed '*acquis judiciaire*' for delimiting the continental shelf and EEZs has also affected the approach employed by the courts and tribunals in the delimitation of the territorial sea has so far not attracted much attention in the literature. The analysis undertaken here indicates that such attention may be warranted, both regarding delimitation of the territorial sea as a distinct part of judicially determined single all-purpose maritime boundaries (as predominant in recent jurisprudence),[96] and regarding delimitation of the territorial sea when it is the only maritime area subject to a third-party decision. The latter cases, though not frequent in recent judicial practice, may arise in some geographical settings – as the Croatia/Slovenia maritime dispute and several other pending delimitations may witness.[97]

Upholding the rule of law in the delimitation of the territorial sea, as embodied in Article 15 of the Convention, will remain vital for stability and orderly relations between states. The application of international law is the guarantee of any long-term solution here, and the international judiciary is the main independent agent responsible for enabling this. UNCLOS III was concluded in 1982 and Article 15 is not open to tacit amendments in a court room.

After this chapter was sent to press, the Arbitral tribunal in *Croatia/Slovenia* arbitration issued, on 29 June 2017, its final award which, regarding the territorial sea delimitation, fully confirms – and further aggravates – the reasons for concern expressed here about some recent trends in case law on the territorial sea delimitation.[98]

as well as 'should be' instead of 'to be' for that *acquis* as being 'read into' the articles of the LOSC. Moreover, the insertion of 'still developing' to qualify that *acquis* indicates a sort of 'living charter' character rather than offering a 'final and binding' provision. On some related aspects of arbitral awards, see e.g. S. Talmon, 'The South China Sea Arbitration and the Finality of "Final" Awards,' (2017) 1 *Journal of International Dispute Settlement*.

96 For a recent study, see M. Lando, 'Judicial Uncertainties Concerning Territorial Sea Delimitation under Article 15 of the United Nations Convention on the Law of the Sea' (2017) 66 *ICLQ*.

97 For the broader context of the Croatian–Slovenian delimitation dispute, see D. Vidas, 'The UN Convention on the Law of the Sea, the European Union and the Rule of Law: What Is Going on in the Adriatic Sea?' (2009) 24 *IJMCL* 1.

98 For an analysis, see A. G. Oude Elferink, 'Slovenia/Croatia arbitration – Is the territorial sea delimitation inconsistent with the case law on maritime delimitation?', *JCLOS Blog* of 16 August 2017, at http://site.uit.no/jclos/2017/08/16/sloveniacroatia-arbitration-is-the-territorial-sea-delimitation-inconsistent-with-the-case-law-on-maritime-delimitation/.

3

Entitlement to Maritime Zones and Their Delimitation

In the Doldrums of Uncertainty and Unpredictability

NUNO MARQUES ANTUNES AND VASCO BECKER-WEINBERG

3.1 Introduction

In a collective work on *consistency and predictability* in the case law on maritime delimitation, a chapter on 'Entitlement to Maritime Zones and Their Delimitation' should perhaps focus on validating the legal argumentation surrounding the relationship between *maritime entitlement* and *delimitation of maritime areas*. Particular emphasis should be placed on whether and, if so how and to what extent, judicial discourse explains the relationship between the relevant maritime entitlements and the adjudged delimitation line. Examining the delimitation line alone, without bridging such a chasm, would likely be a spurious exercise.

For those familiar with maritime delimitation case law, there is no surprise in the discussion about uncertainty and unpredictability. A striking feature of delimitation cases is indeed that they resemble at times more an *ex aequo et bono* exercise than a legally reasoned pronouncement. The link between facts, principles and rules, on the one hand, and the ruling, on the other hand, is sometimes left in a haze of unclarity. Since any analysis of consistency and predictability must draw on the canons of legal argumentation and judicial discourse, this is no minor issue. Much of the uncertainty and unpredictability might be related thereto. The line between *obiter dicta* and *ratio decidendi* has been blurred in more than a few instances. Something similar has happened with the emphasis put on each case's 'uniqueness.' Criticism aimed at the 'splitting of the difference between claims' arguably points at subpar legal argumentation, leading to question whether certain such decisions are not in effect *realjurisprudenz*.[1]

[1] Marques Antunes, *Towards the Conceptualization of Maritime Delimitation* (Martinus Nijhoff Leiden 2003) 177–184. The term *realjurisprudenz* may be understood as the

However, there is no room here to delve into this theoretical subject in any depth. All that can realistically be attempted is an enquiry on how the two concepts – *entitlement* and *delimitation* – have intertwined in the reasoning and discourse of courts and tribunals, and the key implications at the level of consistency and predictability.

Evaluating consistency and predictability in the jurisprudential treatment of *maritime entitlement* and *delimitation of maritime areas* requires the adoption of a conceptual understanding of these terms. Section 3.2 provides a gist of such conceptualization, deals with the relationship between the relevant *entitlement* and *delimitation*, and analyses how that *relationship between entitlement and delimitation* appears reflected in the three-stage approach followed by courts.

The final two sections then focus on certain specific issues identified in the case law as a reflection of the relationship between *entitlement* and *delimitation*. Section 3.3 examines issues that concern equidistance as a provisional line; and Section 3.4 looks into issues surrounding the adjustments to that line.

A final preliminary note concerns the scope of this chapter. Chapters 12 and 13 cover specifically the delimitation of the continental shelf beyond 200 nm (outer continental shelf). For reasons of consistency, the decision was made to analyse the entitlement to outer continental shelf together with the other maritime entitlements, i.e., the territorial sea, contiguous zone, and exclusive economic zone. While said chapters discuss in detail the entitlement to the outer continental shelf, we found it important to provide an overarching review.

3.2 'Entitlement' and 'Delimitation'

3.2.1 'The Land Dominates the Sea'

The allocation of maritime zones to states, under international law, is central to the concepts of *entitlement* and of *delimitation*. From the *inter fauces terrae* doctrine to the post-Grotius canon-shot rule, the notion of *dominium maris* evolved over centuries of practice. Just as the pendulum swung from *mare clausum* to *mare liberum* it eventually swung back to a type of refashioned *mare clausum*. The dynamics of international affairs

reflection of *realpolitik* on international judicial decision making. Setting the argument on a somewhat different perspective, but still noting the issue, see T. Cottier, *Equitable Principles of Maritime Boundary Delimitation* (Cambridge University Press Cambridge 2015) 430–435.

so dictated. A new legal balance between interests of coastal states and those of other states, where *internationalized interests* had to be contemplated, was struck in the LOSC. Driven initially by security concerns, and more recently by economic interests, this *appropriation* of maritime areas by states is today consolidated in the LOSC zoning regime.

Customary law emerging from centuries of state practice was codified in treaty law, first in the 1958 Geneva Conventions on the Law of the Sea. At a second moment, custom was codified in the LOSC side-by-side with rules derived from progressive development of international law of the sea. While certain developments flowed from case law, with respect to *entitlement* the central role was played by state practice. Currently, the LOSC maritime zoning regime is acknowledged as customary international law.

The international principle *the land dominates the sea*, as an expression of *entitlement*, was identified in case law since at least one century ago. As stated in *Grisbadarna*, the 'maritime territory is a necessary dependency of the land territory.'[2] Maritime areas are subject to the *dominium* of a coastal state by virtue of its land territory.

Over the second half of the twentieth century, this principle was elaborated upon and reaverred by case law in further detail. The Court also referred to it in *Fisheries*: 'it is the land which confers upon the coastal State a right to the waters off its coasts.'[3]

The principle was restated in *North Sea Continental Shelf*, as to the continental shelf, when the Court inter alia declared that the most fundamental rule was that the rights of a coastal state derive from the 'natural prolongation of its land territory into and under the sea' and that such rights 'exist *ipso facto* and *ab initio*, by virtue of its sovereignty over the land.' It subsequently added that 'the land is the legal source of the power which a State may exercise over territorial extensions to seaward,' and that in respect of both the continental shelf and the contiguous zone 'the principle is applied that the land dominates the sea.'[4]

In *Aegean Sea Continental Shelf*, the Court further elaborated that rights over maritime areas 'are legally both an emanation from and an automatic adjunct of the territorial sovereignty of the coastal State,' and that the land territory regime 'comprises, *ipso jure*, the rights of exploration and exploitation over the continental shelf.'[5]

[2] *Grisbadarna Case (Norway v. Sweden) (Award)* [1909] 11 RIA 155 [159].

[3] *Fisheries Case (United Kingdom v. Norway)* (Judgment) [1951] ICJ Rep. 116 [133].

[4] *North Sea Continental Shelf Cases (Federal Republic of Germany/Netherlands; Federal Republic of Germany/Denmark)* (Judgment) [1969] ICJ Rep. 3 [23, 52].

[5] *Aegean Sea Continental Shelf Case (Greece v. Turkey) (Jurisdiction)* [1978] ICJ Rep. 3 [37].

Emphasizing 'adjacency' within *the land dominates the sea*, in *Tunisia/ Libya* the Court went on to affirm that 'the coast of the territory of [a] State is the decisive factor for title to submarine areas adjacent to it.'[6]

The Chamber's view, in *Gulf of Maine*, was however somewhat odd. It referred to *the land dominates the sea* as one of the 'equitable criteria that may be taken into consideration for an international maritime delimitation,' and viewed one of segments of the boundary as 'a typical illustration of what is meant by [such] adage.'[7] For reasons discussed below, this view is not without criticism.

In *Libya/Malta*, the Court declared that the:

> [l]andmass has never been regarded as a basis of entitlement,' that continental shelf rights derive 'not from the landmass, but from sovereignty over the landmass,' and that 'it is by means of the maritime front of this landmass [...] that this territorial sovereignty brings its continental shelf rights into effect.[8]

The Court observed in *Jan Mayen* 'that the attribution of maritime areas to the territory of a State [...] is a legal process based solely on the possession by the territory concerned of a coastline.'[9]

A complementary note in *Qatar/Bahrain* stressed the idea that the territory is the '*starting point* for the determination of the maritime rights of a coastal State,' which in respect of insular features means that 'islands, regardless of their size, [...] generate the same maritime rights, as other land territory.'[10]

Further elaboration came in *Black Sea*. The Court considered that '[t]he title of a State to [maritime zones] is based on the principle that the land dominates the sea through the projection of the coasts or *the coastal fronts*,' and that it does so 'in such a way that coastal projections in the seaward direction generate maritime claims.'[11] The reference to projection of *coastal fronts* is not entirely clear as to its implications, and is questionable.

6 *Case concerning the Continental Shelf (Tunisia/Libyan Arab Jamahiriya)* (Judgment) [1982] ICJ Rep. 18 [61].

7 *Delimitation of the Maritime Boundary in the Gulf of Maine Area (Canada/USA)* (Judgment) [1984] ICJ Rep. 246 [312–313, 338].

8 *Case concerning the Continental Shelf (Libyan Arab Jamahiriya/Malta)* (Judgment) [1985] ICJ Rep. 13 [41].

9 *Maritime Delimitation in the Area between Greenland and Jan Mayen (Denmark v. Norway)* (Judgment) [1993] ICJ Rep. 38 [74].

10 *Maritime Delimitation and Territorial Questions between Qatar and Bahrain (Qatar/ Bahrain)* (Judgment) [2001] ICJ Rep. 40 [97], emphasis added.

11 *Maritime Delimitation in the Black Sea (Romania v. Ukraine)* (Judgment) [2009] ICJ Rep. 61 [89, 96–97], our emphasis.

It points to 'perpendicular projection,' whereas coasts generate maritime entitlements omni-directionally.

This approach was reaffirmed in both *Bangladesh/Myanmar*[12] and *Bangladesh v. India.*[13] In the latter, the arbitral tribunal went on to state that 'there was no basis for distinguishing between projections within 200 nm and those beyond that point.'[14]

The implications of the principle that *the land dominates the sea* emerged also on a more procedural level. In *Nicaragua v. Honduras*, the Court referred to the principle *the land dominates the sea* when deciding on the sovereignty over certain insular features as a preliminary step to the delimitation.[15]

When examining the case law, the advent of the LOSC cannot go unnoticed in respect of the changes at the level of *maritime entitlement*. The impact of UNCLOS III became patent after *Libya/Malta*, as further elaborated on below.

Within the LOSC framework, the notion of 'proximity' links the land territory with the maritime zones. *The land dominates the sea* through 'closeness,' which is encapsulated in the definition of outer limits of maritime zones based on *distance* from the coast. More properly, the breadth of maritime zones is measured from the *normal baseline*, other lines and points legitimately defined as part of the *baseline*.[16] Distance as basis of entitlement reflects elements of 'certainty' and stability,[17] and consequently predictability.

Distinct is the entitlement to the outer continental shelf, which is based on 'natural prolongation.' It embodies elements of geology that express

[12] *Delimitation of the Maritime Boundary between Bangladesh and Myanmar in the Bay of Bengal (Bangladesh/Myanmar)* (Judgment) [2012] ITLOS Rep. 1 [61–62].

[13] *In the Matter of the Bay of Bengal Maritime Boundary Arbitration (Bangladesh v. India) (Award)* PCA Case 2010-16 [2014] [79].

[14] Ibid., [85].

[15] *Territorial and Maritime Dispute between Nicaragua and Honduras in the Caribbean Sea (Nicaragua v. Honduras)* (Judgment) [2007] ICJ Rep. 659 [697, 699, 702]. The Court could only make such decision on sovereignty because the disputing states had agreed to its jurisdiction. In *Philippines/China*, the tribunal had no jurisdiction to decide on sovereignty over insular features or on maritime delimitation, but still discussed the matter of *entitlement*; *The Republic of the Philippines v. The People's Republic of China (Philippines v. China) (Award)*, available at https://pca-cpa.org/wp-content/uploads/sites/175/2016/07/PH-CN-20160712-Award.pdf [58–67, 119 *et seq*].

[16] LOSC Arts. 5, 6, 7, 9 through 13, 16, 47, and 48. Baselines are to be depicted on charts of adequate scale or alternatively in a list of geographical coordinates of points, specifying the geodetic datum.

[17] D. M. Johnston, *The Theory and History of Ocean Boundary-Making* (McGill-Queen's University Press Kingston-Montreal 1988) 239.

'closeness' on a different basis. The outer continental shelf entitlement is based on 'geological proximity,' to be established through the appurtenance test under Article 76 of the LOSC.[18]

'Natural prolongation' is thus to be construed by reference to the continental margin, whose outermost limits are to be delineated as per said Article 76. In *Bangladesh/Myanmar*, the Tribunal's view on the subject seems to ultimately support this approach.[19] While doubts have been cast on this interpretation,[20] one would side with the Tribunal in considering that the outer continental shelf entitlement corresponds to the area beyond 200 nm that results from the equation of 'natural prolongation' with 'continental margin.'

That 'natural prolongation' is the basis of the outer continental shelf entitlement must not be read as meaning that it is a delimitation criterion, however. 'Natural prolongation' is relevant for ascertaining whether an overlap of outer continental shelf entitlements exists.[21] Once the overlap is confirmed, 'natural prolongation' has arguably no further impact. On the one hand, it is not apt to justify a provisional line other than one based on equidistance. In *Bangladesh/Myanmar*, the Tribunal concluded that 'the delimitation method to be employed [...] for the continental shelf beyond 200 nm should not differ from that within 200 nm,' and resorted to a provisional equidistance line.[22] It is notable that none of the parties sought to justify the use of another line by reference to 'natural prolongation.'

On the other hand, whatever the nature of the underwater geomorphological feature or 'geological' characteristic of the seabed/subsoil, it is doubtful that such an element can be used for adjusting the provisional line. The difficulty might be that, because 'natural prolongation' is the basis of entitlement, conceptually one should in principle not set it aside altogether. But in practice there seems to be no room to act differently. Consider a hypothetical scenario where certain seabed/subsoil areas have a 'geochemical signature' that 'relates' more to the territory of one of the

[18] Marques Antunes, n. 1, 200. Article 76 is often described as focusing on geomorphology. In reality, it also incorporates elements of geology, geophysics, and geochemistry (i.e., 'geological' elements in a wider sense).

[19] *Bangladesh/Myanmar*, n. 12, [127–128].

[20] See Judge Gao's views in his Separate Opinion in ibid., [90]. See also Chapter 13, where it is argued that the question of entitlement is distinct from the specific methods of delineation of the outer edge of the continental shelf. While not disagreeing with this, the question is that *natural prolongation* must necessarily be the area *enclosed inside the outer edge of the margin*.

[21] On the overlapping of entitlements as a requirement for delimitation, see Section 3.2.2.

[22] *Bangladesh/Myanmar*, n. 12, [132].

states concerned. Is this a delimitation factor to be weighed up with others? How would that be done? Similar doubts can be cast on geomorphological features. Either they amount to a 'break' in the entitlement and no overlap exists, or such a 'break' does not exist and it is virtually impossible to weigh-up said features as adjustment to the provisional line.

The reality is that no court has hitherto resorted to 'natural prolongation' as basis for drawing a provisional line or as factor to adjust such line. Recent case law in fact offers grounds to argue the opposite. In *Bangladesh/Myanmar*, no distinction was made between the regime applicable to delimitation within and beyond 200 nm.[23] Similarly, treaty law makes no such distinction. Further, unlike equidistance,[24] 'natural prolongation' elements seem to have no inherent legal content.[25]

All of the above considered, *distance* and *geological proximity* are expressions of the same legal parameter: 'closeness' between land and sea. Where distance is the basis of entitlement, all stretches of a state's coastline are conceivably apt for generating entitlements, omni-directionally from each relevant basepoint. In outer continental shelf entitlements, geological appurtenance (as per Article 76 of the LOSC) must be demonstrated.

No distinction of principle should be made as to insular features (islands, 'rocks' and low-tide elevations),[26] even if the entitlements of islands have given rise to difficulties.[27] Treaty law provides no guidance and the case law has hitherto struggled in providing entirely predictable decisions on the effect of islands in delimitation (if indeed this is possible). The circumstances in which low-tide elevations generate entitlements are clearer in treaty law and the case law, whereas the issue of 'rocks' has until recently remained virtually unaddressed.

In summary, the *vinculum juris* between land and sea has been expressed in the maxim *the land dominates the sea*. All maritime entitlements stem from and depend upon sovereignty over land territory.

[23] As noted in Section 4.3, in *Bangladesh/Myanmar*, ibid., the Tribunal dismissed the argument of 'the most natural prolongation.'

[24] See Section 3.3 below.

[25] When the International Law Commission (ILC) consulted with the Committee of Experts leading to the use equidistance in the 1958 Geneva Conventions, no reference existed to 'entitlement based on distance.' On the contrary, at the time, the basis of continental shelf entitlement was 'natural prolongation.' This evidences the normativity of equidistance in delimitation, irrespective of the 'basis of entitlement.' That the Committee never suggested any line based on 'natural prolongation,' where the 'basis of entitlement' was 'natural prolongation,' should have been considered in the case law, notably in *North Sea Continental Shelf*.

[26] LOSC Arts. 13.1, 121.1, and 121.3.

[27] On the so-called effect of islands in maritime delimitation, see Section 3.4.2.

The LOSC enshrines that principle in two ways: (i) by establishing the outer limits of maritime zones by reference to *distance* (basis of entitlement) from the baselines; or (ii) by reference to the legal notion of *natural prolongation* (basis of entitlement, as translated in geomorphologic, geologic, geophysical, and geochemical assessments[28]) and *distance* from the baselines,[29] which is an expression of *geological proximity*.

3.2.2 *Conceptual Relationship between 'Entitlement' and 'Delimitation'*

The need for conceptualization in maritime delimitation is an issue over which courts, as well as commentators, have been at loggerheads. For example, Evans has argued that, 'despite the amount of theoretical study that both surrounds and obfuscates the subject,' *delimitation* is 'a practical exercise'; and he goes on to state that 'judgments given by Courts cannot be treated as if they were designed as precise expositions of the applicable legal provisions,' as 'it is often easier to agree on the result than on the reasoning that lies behind it.'[30] On the other hand, it has been postulated that conceptualization is 'the operation through which, whilst understanding the *ratio decidendi* of legal decisions, general and abstract principles and rules may be identified,' and that 'over-emphasizing the uniqueness of each case, while under-conceptualizing the maritime delimitation problem, has contributed to the emergence of some misunderstandings.'[31] While the former expresses how courts seem to have actually worked, the latter focuses on how courts should have worked.[32]

[28] The *Scientific and Technical Guidelines of the Commission on the Limits of the Continental Shelf* (CLCS/11, as amended and corrected) posit the ways in which each type of 'geo-evidence' can be provided in support of a claim for extension of the outer continental shelf.

[29] As per Art. 76 of the LOSC, the outer limit of the continental shelf beyond 200 nm can be draw along the 'cut-off line' whose points lie at 350 nm from the baseline. Distance is relevant where the other 'cut-off line' applies, i.e., a line whose points lie at 100 nm from the 2,500 metre isobath.

[30] M. D. Evans, *Relevant Circumstances and Maritime Delimitation* (Clarendon Press Oxford 1989) 63.

[31] Marques Antunes, n. 1,119.

[32] The principle that maritime delimitation is to be effected by agreement has been widely acknowledged and is embedded in the LOSC (Arts. 15, 74(1), and 83(1)), flowing already from the 1958 Geneva Conventions. Here, focus is kept only on situations in which delimitation is effected by a court. On the distinction between maritime delimitation effected by adjudication by comparison to negotiation, see Marques Antunes, n. 1, 177 *et seq*; P. Weil, *The Law of Maritime Delimitation – Reflections* (English translation of *Perspectives du Droit de la Délimitation Maritime*, Grotius Cambridge 1989) 103–114.

That *delimitation* presupposes an *overlapping of entitlements* is undoubted; for only then does *delimitation* become necessary.[33] In *Bangladesh/Myanmar*, the Tribunal confirmed that this view applied to the outer continental shelf, and reviewed the existence of overlapping of entitlements beyond 200 nm before turning to the delimitation.[34] Most notably, the Tribunal stated that it:

> would have been hesitant to proceed with the delimitation of the area beyond 200 nm *had it concluded that there was significant uncertainty as to the existence of a continental margin in the area in question.*[35]

The case law has struggled, however, with certain conceptual elements. A core aspect of *the land dominates the sea* maxim was not immediately grasped unerringly: *basis of entitlement*. Enshrined in said principle, this aspect constitutes the criterion on which the extension of a state's *dominium* offshore is predicated. It embodies essentially the notion of *how* the attribution of maritime areas is 'shaped' by sovereignty over the land territory. Much of the *uncertainty* and *unpredictability* has arguably stemmed from a paucity of a conceptual analysis as to whether and how the *basis of entitlement* bears on delimitation.

For better and worse, delimitation law has developed essentially from *North Sea Continental Shelf*. Many statements by the Court in these cases are cited in case law and legal commentary even today. *Conceptualization* was present in the Court's concerns. Following a review of the (then) recent legal institution of the continental shelf, the Court eventually stated that it would:

> *not be in harmony with the history of the institution of the continental shelf to over-systematize a pragmatic construct* the developments of which have occurred within a relatively short space of time.[36]

Respectfully, the Court took a 'wrong turn' here. The Court's institutional role in the progressive development of international law should have prevailed over the practicalities of the cases. The Court literally opened the door to unnecessary uncertainty and unpredictability in subsequent case law. With such a gambit, it is indeed difficult to see how the case law on maritime delimitation could have developed more consistently.

33 See Marques Antunes, n. 1, 128–145.

34 See *Bangladesh/Myanmar*, n. 12, [117–131].

35 Ibid., [129], emphasis added.

36 *North Sea Continental Shelf*, n. 4, [54], emphasis added.

One striking feature of this judgment, conceptually speaking, is the understanding that 'the process of delimitation is essentially one of drawing a boundary-line between areas which *already appertain* to one or other of the States affected,' and not a matter of 'apportioning an as yet undelimited area.'[37] This illustrates the lack of proper conceptualization in this judgment. For the Court, the delimitation process seemed to be a matter of *finding* a boundary line that separated the seabed areas *already appertaining* to each of the states. This amounts to turning the delimitation process upside down. It *inter alia* fails to grasp the notion that it is through delimitation that the seabed area constituting the overlapping of entitlements is allocated to each state, no areas within the overlapping of entitlements being *naturally appurtenant* to either state.

The Court's approach in *North Sea Continental Shelf* fell short of a clear conceptual reasoning in another respect. While noting the 'geographical configuration of the coastlines' as a relevant aspect of *the land dominates the sea*, emphasis was put on natural prolongation by referring to the extensions seawards of the landmass: 'the stretches of submerged land.'[38] This misperception of 'submerged land territory' (natural prolongation) as delimitation criterion,[39] instead of as basis of entitlement,[40] is the onset of *uncertainty* and *unpredictability* in delimitation law.[41]

In *Tunisia/Libya*, the Court's reasoning followed a similar track. It considered that '*no attempt should be made* [...] *to overconceptualize the application of the principles and rules*' on the continental shelf, and that each dispute '*should be considered and judged on its own merits*, having regard to its peculiar circumstances.'[42] Taken to the limit, such a view emphasizes each case's circumstances (*unicum*) and the determination of an 'equitable line,' without due consideration of the very concept that legally anchors the areas to be delimited: *entitlement*. This is undoubtedly

[37] Ibid., [23], emphasis added. [38] Ibid., [52].

[39] It should be emphasized that the North Sea is a continuous, uninterrupted geological shelf, which could in no way be divided on the basis of underwater features as 'natural boundaries.'

[40] The Court's approach, as expressed throughout the judgment, is clearly not a model of clarity in distinguishing *entitlement* and basis thereof, on one hand, and *delimitation* and delimitation criteria, on the other hand.

[41] Conceptually, the fact that the judgment ultimately hinged on 'coastal configuration' renders this perspective even less understandable. The Court's approach in this germinal case, on a novel international law matter, should have taken particular account of the implications for the subsequent development of international law. How the parties presented their cases should not have been the only concern for the Court.

[42] *Tunisia/Libya*, n. 6, [92], emphasis added.

a matter of result, not reasoning. Because of *North Sea Continental Shelf*, in *Tunisia/Libya* both parties sought to canvass their arguments around the concept of natural prolongation (and 'equity'), diverging however on how to materialize it. Unsurprisingly, there was ultimately no escape from reverting to the coastline as basis for the delimitation, with the Court agreeing that the coastline 'constitute[d] the starting line from which [...] to ascertain how far the submarine areas appertaining to each [state] extend[ed] in a seaward direction.'[43] The Court seemed already on the way to, without expressly saying so, distinguish between *basis of entitlement* and *delimitation criterion*.

Case law took a turn for the better in *Libya/Malta*, which theorized on the relationship between *entitlement* and *delimitation*, as well as the critical notion of *basis of entitlement*. It then declared that:

> the questions of *entitlement* and of definition of continental shelf, on the one hand, and of *delimitation* of continental shelf on the other, are not only distinct but are also complementary [and that the] *legal basis* of that which is to be delimited, and of *entitlement* to it, cannot be other than pertinent to that *delimitation*.[44]

While this pronouncement stems perhaps from the different views taken by Libya and Malta as to the *basis of entitlement*, in conceptualizing terms it was a positive volte-face. Its contribution to 'certainty' in case law cannot be overstated, as it thwarted future exercises in 'distributive justice.' One could go so far as suggesting that there is a law of maritime delimitation pre-*Libya/Malta*, and another post-*Libya/Malta*.

However intertwined and complementary *entitlement* and *delimitation* may be, the two must nevertheless be clearly distinguished.[45] *Entitlement* concerns maritime zones and their limits and is 'unilateral' in nature; whereas *delimitation* relates to maritime boundaries and their delimitation and involves a 'bilateral' ('multilateral') process. The latter aims at 'discovering' – through application of international law, if effected by a court – a line separating the maritime zones of two (or more) states, if and where the maritime entitlements of such states overlap.

An overlap of *entitlements* is an indispensable premise of *delimitation*. Valid, concurring, colliding *entitlements* must be reconciled, through

43 Ibid., [61], emphasis added.

44 *Libya/Malta*, n. 8, [30], emphasis added.

45 'Title' ('sovereign title,' e.g. historic title) and 'maritime entitlement' must be differentiated. Unlike a 'sovereign title,' 'maritime entitlement' is not exclusive of other maritime entitlements. No overlapping of 'sovereign titles' may exist. On title, entitlement and delimitation, see Marques Antunes, n. 1, 132–137.

delimitation, with a view to geographically defining the areas over which each state is entitled to exercise its authority.[46] Practically speaking, *delimitation* results in a geographical 'amputation' of *entitlements*.[47] If effected by a court, however, such an operation must never amount to a practical, non-normative split of a 'disputed area.' It should represent the materially reasoned outcome of the application of international law to the concrete circumstances.[48]

One final conceptual issue that can be found in both conventional law (i.e., Articles 6(1) and 6(2) of the 1958 Convention on the Continental Shelf) and the case law concerns the distinction between *adjacency* and *oppositeness*. Reference is made to 'equidistance line' and 'median line,' respectively, as if a material difference exists. This distinction should not be kept, particularly in light of Articles 74 and 83 of the LOSC. In *Black Sea*, the Court seems to have maintained it.[49] From the standpoint of legal reasoning, however, this does not seem the best approach. The relative position of the coasts is irrelevant when it comes to entitlement. *Adjacency* and *oppositeness* are matters best dealt with when assessing the need for adjustments to the provisional line.

3.2.3 'Maritime Zoning' and the 'Three-Stage Process'

The principle of maritime zoning encapsulates the normative contents of *the land dominates the sea*. While case law treats *the land dominates the sea* as an 'adage' (used to loosely refer to the rights of states over the maritime areas on which their coasts abut),[50] the principle of maritime zoning is in effect a conceptual construction derived from the LOSC.[51]

The LOSC incorporates essentially two types of norms: one, norms geographically defining the 'zones' into which the ocean is divided; and two, norms establishing the rights granted to, and obligations imposed

[46] On concurrence of rights, as an overlapping of two potential positions of exclusiveness, see ibid., 137–138, 201.

[47] Ibid., 139–141. Reference to 'amputation' of entitlements is particularly apt in delimitation to express the idea of geographic curtailment of an otherwise fully valid legal entitlement. This notion was advanced by Germany in *North Sea Continental Shelf*, as reflected in the judgment (French version); *North Sea Continental Shelf*, n. 4, [18, 22]. See Weil, n. 33, 5.

[48] Courts may not render decisions that constitute the application of *realpolitik* to the case. The *ratio decidendi* must be laid down in bridging the gap between the circumstances and the line awarded. See Marques Antunes, n. 1, 181 *et seq*.

[49] *Black Sea*, n. 11, [101–102].

[50] *Gulf of Maine*, n. 7, [338].

[51] Marques Antunes, n. 1, 195 *et seq*. (see also ibid., 193–195).

on, states (but also international entities). The first set of norms constitutes the legal basis for the maritime entitlement of states. The second sets forth the scope and limits of the legal authority exercised by states in such zones. It is not just a matter of which maritime zones may be claimed, but rather conceptually understanding: (1) how coastal states' uses of maritime zones relate with uses by other states; (2) the degree of authority asserted by coastal states in such areas; and (3) the geographical zones to which such uses and authority refer.[52] While not a terminology commonly utilized in the case law, maritime zoning has emerged as a crucial concept in ocean affairs and governance.

One must ask, straightaway, why attention should be drawn to such a principle – rarely if at all mentioned in case law – when conceptualizing maritime delimitation law. The answer is that the principle of maritime zoning (however it may be named) constitutes the conceptual bedrock that underlies the 'three-stage process' stated by and described in case law.[53] All three stages of the delimitation process are related to and derive from maritime zoning.

That equidistance should be the 'provisional line,' to be used as the starting point for delimitation, has long been argued. The preparatory work of the ILC in the 1950s evidenced that no substantive delimitation criteria existed by then.[54] It was after consultation with a Committee of Experts that the ILC went on to draft the articles from which the delimitation provisions in the 1958 Geneva Conventions flowed, all of which prescribe some use of equidistance.[55] The reason is perhaps simpler than it appears when looking into decades of judicial discussion. Equidistance is inherent in delimitation.

First and foremost, equidistance amounts to the allocation of areas over which states hold equally valid entitlements on the basis of 'closer proximity.' Conceptually speaking, this is not only a normative standard that offers certainty, but in abstract terms also reflects a standard of equitableness.[56]

[52] M. S. McDougal and T. Burke, *The Public Order of the Oceans* (Yale University Press New Haven Press 1987) 29, 56–57.

[53] The 'three-stage process' seems to be the most certain, predictable *acquis* of maritime delimitation law. While usually identified as a matter of continental shelf and exclusive economic zone delimitation, in material terms the process does not seem to be significantly different in territorial sea delimitation.

[54] Marques Antunes, n. 1, 19–22.

[55] Art. 12(1) of the Convention on the Territorial Sea and the Contiguous Zone; Arts. 6(1) and 6(2) of the Convention on the Continental Shelf.

[56] It is regrettable that, to deal with the circumstances of the case, the Court failed to acknowledge this in *North Sea Continental Shelf*; see Section 3.3.1 below.

Second, while typically a bilateral matter, delimitation can involve more than two states, as for example in defining tripoints. Equidistance offers an objective parameter for 'protection' of the rights of third states.

Third, equidistance is a reflection of the 'basis of entitlement' in the vast majority of situations (where entitlement is based on distance). This is why, in *Libya/Malta*, the Court stated that the entitlement cannot be 'other than pertinent' to the delimitation of the relevant maritime zone.[57] Although in respect of outer continental shelf entitlements the situation is less obvious,[58] equidistance is still relevant since such entitlement still embodies elements of distance and equidistance offers a measure of equitableness (the result sought by delimitation).

From a conceptual standpoint, one would argue that there are certain corresponding relationships that structure this principle. *Maritime zoning* is for *maritime delimitation* what *entitlement* is for *overlapping of entitlements*, as well as what *basis of entitlement* (proximity) is for *equidistance* (closer proximity). For the first stage, the relevance of the principle of maritime zoning is decisive.

The second stage – i.e., assessing the need to adjust the provisional line in light of the relevant circumstances – is also predicated on the principle of maritime zoning, albeit to a different extent. Put simply, only those circumstances that are relevant in view of the relevant entitlement may be considered. Translated in different terms, as stated in *Libya/Malta*, this means that the principle of maritime zoning is the basis of and the limit for the identification of relevant circumstances. There is a 'filtering process' applied to the circumstances *in casu* through the principle of maritime zoning.

Relevant circumstances must relate either to *geographical elements* concerning the maritime zones (e.g., coastline, 'controlling basepoints,' location and type of insular features, coastal length, coastal direction, overlapping claims, macro-geography, natural prolongation, 'geological proximity,' presence of third states), or to the *legal authority* to be exercised by coastal states in such zones (e.g. defence and security *stricto sensu*, living and non-living natural resources, navigation, traditional rights and livelihood of communities, environmental concerns).

Viewed from this perspective, it is perhaps easier to conceptualize why and how defence and security issues are relevant in territorial sea delimitation, but bear no weight for continental shelf and exclusive economic

[57] *Libya/Malta*, n. 8, [30, 34].

[58] On 'natural prolongation' as basis of entitlement, see Section 3.2.1.

zone delimitation.[59] This perspective can also be used to explain the greater reliance on equidistance in territorial sea delimitation when compared with exclusive economic zone or continental shelf delimitation. Such approach has in fact been reflected, from the outset, in the 1958 Geneva Conventions.[60] Further, it explains equally the greater relevance of living and non-living resources in continental shelf and exclusive economic zone delimitations.

Perhaps as importantly, the role of the 'principle of equity' in adjusting a 'provisional equidistance line' (however canvassed over the years in judicial discourse) can be viewed also on the basis of this conceptualization.[61] Its greater relevance in continental shelf and exclusive economic zone delimitation, when compared to territorial sea delimitation, derives precisely from the different scope and nature of the legal authority of coastal states in the maritime zones in question.

As for the 'proportionality test' constituting the third stage, Weil's reservations as to its use are warranted on a number of grounds.[62] The reality is, however, that courts continue to resort to it as the final delimitation stage (as discussed in Chapter 11). Taking into consideration how the 'proportionality test' is implemented, by reference to key *geographical elements* (i.e., coastline length and the 'relevant area'[63]), it is unsurprising that the conclusion should be that it also stems from the principle of maritime zoning. Equally unsurprising is that this flows consistently from the previous stages.

The realization that said 'proportionality test' is relevant for continental shelf and exclusive economic zone delimitation in a way that is not mirrored in territorial sea delimitation, a distinction to which attention has already been drawn, is significant. In the latter, the very limited room

[59] The reference to 'self-protection' in the Truman Proclamation should be read *latissimo sensu* as referring to general regulatory powers concerning the activities to be conducted, not of military or defense nature proper.

[60] The distinct use of equidistance in Arts. 6(1) and 6(2) of the Convention on the Continental Shelf is arguably already a reflection of a different weighing-up of geographical elements in continental shelf delimitation.

[61] For an approach to the role of equity and equitable principles, see Chapter 6.

[62] In his Dissenting Opinion in *Canada/France*, Weil summarized the most compelling arguments against the use of the 'proportionality test'; see *Case concerning the Delimitation of Maritime Areas between Canada and France* (1992) XXI RIAA 265 [309-312]. Marques Antunes, n. 1, 301–307. In Chapter 11 of this volume, similar reservations appear to be expressed.

[63] For an appraisal on how courts have defined the 'relevant area' in adjudication, see Chapter 7.

to redress inequities resulting from the geographical scope and location of the maritime areas, as well as from the authority involved (i.e., sovereignty in areas closer to shore), contrasts clearly with the former. Manifest disproportion is a test that is virtually unworkable in territorial sea delimitation. Recourse to it in continental shelf and exclusive economic zone delimitation is justified on two grounds that appear in rather distinct terms in territorial sea delimitation. One is the size of the areas involved. The other is the different type of considerations that may be weighed up.

What is clear, nevertheless, is that the 'proportionality test' should be conceptualized under the lenses of the principle of maritime zoning, which is a matter of *entitlement*. The way in which it is implemented is derived from and based on factual circumstances and other considerations that have their roots in said principle.

A final precision point must be made. The role of equity in delimitation law, however viewed as a source of uncertainty and unpredictability, is unavoidable and seeks 'to ensure that the balance of rights and interests attained for the overlapping of entitlements is 'not grossly unreasonable.' The factors by reference to which such a balance is achieved [...] must be selected through the legal regime of the maritime zones to be delimited.' The optimization of the principles of maritime zoning and of equity amounts then to a 'discovery' of the 'case-norm' whereby delimitation is decided. It embodies an inversely proportional relationship whereby if the equidistance line is unreasonable equity becomes predominant.[64]

3.3 Equidistance in the Case Law

3.3.1 Early Misunderstandings

The use of equidistance in maritime delimitation is one of the most discussed aspects in case law. While no explicit statement to that effect has been made, case law eventually came to acknowledge that, in practice, the equidistance line should be the provisional starting point of every delimitation process (first stage). This only came about after some years of hesitation, elaboration, and (why not recognize it) a reversal of position by courts. Even if, in this respect, case law continues to include statements that are unhelpful in promoting consistency and predictability, the prevailing role of equidistance is a fact today.[65]

[64] Marques Antunes, n. 1, 237–238, 244. See also Chapter 6.

[65] For an argument on how priority has been given to the use of equidistance, see F. Olorundami, 'The ICJ and Its Lip Service to the Non-Priority Status of the Equidistance Method

The difficulties go back to *North Sea Continental Shelf*. When the Court considered the arguments advanced by the Netherlands and Denmark as to the use of equidistance, such use had already developed in state practice in the aftermath of the 1958 Geneva Conventions. The finding that such use of equidistance was not customary law, and that customary law consisted of the application of equitable principles,[66] was both legally questionable and detrimental to consistency and predictability.[67] The contrasting of equidistance and equitable principles, as if the two were opposing concepts, embodied an unnecessary 'attack' on equidistance from which maritime delimitation law is yet to fully recover.

A sort of reprieve of equidistance was timidly attempted in *Anglo-French Continental Shelf*, with the tribunal seeking to bring conventional and customary law together.[68] It fell short of what was required in terms of consistency and predictability. By not dismissing the reasoning in *North Sea Continental Shelf* as to equitable principles being part of customary law the tribunal effectively gave it sustenance. The equation of the rule in Article 6 of the 1958 Convention on the Continental Shelf with equitable principles,[69] while a step in the right direction, was conceptually insufficient.

3.3.2 Reversal of Position: The Provisional Equidistance Line

By the early 1980s, the view was expressed that, by suggesting that the principles and rules of international law were only equitable principles and

of Delimitation' (2015) 4(1) *Cambridge Journal of International and Comparative Law* 53. This author also argues elsewhere that maritime delimitation is yet to become objective and predictable, even with the three-stage approach (F. Olorundami, 'Objectivity versus Subjectivity in the Context of the ICJ's Three-Stage Methodology of Maritime Boundary Delimitation' (2017) 32(1) *The International Journal of Marine and Coastal Law* 36.

66 *North Sea Continental Shelf*, n. 4, [36]–[62]. The misrepresentation of equidistance as merely a delimitation method, not a normative standard, was at the heart of the conceptualization difficulties. The reference to equitable principles as customary law can be challenged on various grounds (see Marques Antunes, n. 1, 413). This judgment is unclear also as to the use of natural prolongation as a normative basis for delimitation.

67 Criticizing the Court's approach in *North Sea Continental Shelf*, notably the findings on customary law, see Marques Antunes, n. 1, 46–64. For an in-depth review of the whole delimitation process surrounding *North Sea Continental Shelf*, seemingly taking a different view, A. Oude Elferink, *The Delimitation of the Continental Shelf between Denmark, Germany and the Netherlands* (Cambridge University Press Cambridge 2013).

68 For a review of this case, as a follow-up of *North Sea Continental Shelf*, see Marques Antunes, n. 1, 64–79.

69 *Delimitation of the Continental Shelf between the United Kingdom of Great Britain and Northern Ireland, and the French Republic (UK v. France)* (Award) [1978] XVIII RIAA 3 [45]–[48].

relevant circumstances, the Court merely advanced the 'principle of non-principle.'[70] One had to wait until *Libya/Malta* for a reversal of position (even if not expressly admitted). This occurred when conceptualization became a relevant concern. In a context that already included the LOSC, the premise became that there had to be a sound approach to the relationship between the relevant maritime entitlement and the delimitation process. As the Court concluded:

> It follows that, for juridical and practical reasons, the distance criterion must now apply to the continental shelf [. . .]. This is not to suggest that the idea of natural prolongation is now superseded by that of distance. What it does mean is that where the continental margin does not extend as far as 200 miles from the shore, natural prolongation, which *in spite of its physical origins has throughout its history become more and more a complex and juridical concept*, is in part defined by distance from the shore, irrespective of the physical nature of the intervening sea-bed and subsoil. The concepts of natural prolongation and distance are therefore not opposed but complementary; and both remain essential elements in the juridical concept of the continental shelf.[71]

The Court seems to have attempted (but not entirely succeeded) to harness *judicial subjectivity*, by bringing the notion of *entitlement* into the heart of *delimitation*. Some damage control was attained. Of particular significance was the conclusion that courts are not in the same position as states when choosing which considerations to weigh-up in delimitation.

> For a court, although there is assuredly no closed list of considerations, it is evident that only those that are *pertinent to the institution of the continental shelf* as it has developed within the law, and to the application of equitable principles to *its delimitation*, will qualify for inclusion. Otherwise, *the legal concept of continental shelf could itself be fundamentally changed* by the introduction of considerations strange to its nature.[72]

The Court added that since the law provides for a 200 nm continental shelf entitlement as a minimum, irrespective of the geological characteristics of the seabed and subsoil,

> there is no reason to ascribe any role to geological or geophysical factors within that distance either in *verifying the legal title* of the States concerned or in *proceeding to a delimitation* as between their claims.[73]

[70] Judge Oda, Dissenting Opinion, *Tunisia/Libya*, n. 6, [157].

[71] *Libya/Malta*, n. 8, [33]–[34], emphasis added. On distance and geological proximity, see Section 3.2.1.

[72] Ibid., [40], emphasis added.

[73] Ibid., [35], emphasis added.

The critical point, one would contend, is that when a conceptually solid view of the relationship between *entitlement* and *delimitation* was taken case law made a turn towards more consistency and predictability.[74] While certain 'twists-and-turns' have occurred in case law since *Libya/Malta*, the core normative basis has remained unaltered. It is from here that the three-stage approach was developed, of which the first stage is the computation of a provisional equidistance line.[75] In *Jan Mayen*, the Court restated this view. In a continental shelf and exclusive economic zone delimitation in which the states had not agreed on a single boundary, it found equidistance to be the common starting point (under conventional and customary law) to be adjusted according to the relevant circumstances.[76]

3.3.3 *Exceptions to the Provisional Equidistance Line?*

Whether the provisional equidistance line is mandatory remains a debated issue. Consistency and predictability would certainly be promoted if it were. The case law has unfortunately fallen short of being definitive, as the normative content of equidistance apparently continues to elude the courts. The statement that equidistance has no priority over other methods was unfortunately repeated in *Nicaragua v. Honduras*, with references to the empty formula of 'equitable principles' resurfacing.[77] One should not hesitate in refuting such a view. It is a clear disregard of the need for a consistent and predictable development of international law, and misses entirely the normativity (including equitableness) enshrined in equidistance.

The recourse to a bisector in *Nicaragua v. Honduras* could be easily anticipated, as a bisector is nothing more than a variation of equidistance.[78] Failing to grasp this aspect is a disservice to delimitation

[74] The Court unfortunately continued to state that equidistance was not mandatory even as a provisional step; ibid., [37].

[75] Ibid., [46].

[76] *Jan Mayen*, n. 9, [59]–[64]. The Court recognized that Arts. 74 and 83 of the LOSC reflected customary law.

[77] *Nicaragua v. Honduras*, n. 15, [741]–[742]. See also e.g. *Arbitration between Barbados and the Republic of Trinidad and Tobago (Barbados v. Trinidad and Tobago) (Award)* [2006] XXVII UNRIAA 147 [230]; *Black Sea*, n. 11, [101]; *Territorial and Maritime Dispute (Nicaragua v. Colombia)* (Judgment) [2012] ICJ Rep. 624 [695].

[78] Marques Antunes, n. 1, 165, who argues that a bisector is an 'equidistance line' computed from 'flattened coastlines' (at 161–165).

law. As more recently acknowledged in *Bangladesh/Myanmar*, a bisector is 'an approximation of the equidistance method.'[79]

In *Nicaragua v. Honduras*, all that was necessary was to account for the uncertainties of the relevant basepoints. Paradoxically as it might sound, while stating that the equidistance method had no priority over other methods, the Court effectively applied equidistance as a normative standard. Simplistically put, after 'flattening' the coastlines of the two states, the Court allocated maritime areas on the basis of 'closer proximity' (taking these 'flattened' coasts as a reference).

One would thus argue that the use of bisectors should not be detached from the issue of entitlement. In *Nicaragua v. Honduras*, it was the non-existence of adequate basepoints that allowed for a departure from strict equidistance in determining a line located at 'equal distance' from the 'flattened coasts.'

Another point regarding *entitlement* and *equidistance* concerns the blurring of the computation of the provisional equidistance line through the discarding of basepoints.[80] This happened in *Libya/Malta*, *Black Sea* and *Bangladesh/Myanmar*, in which basepoints on islands – respectively, Filfla Island, Serpents' Island and St. Martin's Island –, relevant for computing the provisional equidistance line, were discarded during the first stage.[81] Serious reservations must be expressed against this procedure. Assessing whether such islands were worthy of adjustments to achieve an equitable delimitation was a matter for the second stage. Unless such islands were 'rocks,' having no continental shelf and exclusive economic zone entitlement, the first stage should result in a strict equidistance line. Uncertainty as to the location of basepoints (in *Nicaragua v. Honduras*) is quite different from discarding basepoints capable of generating an entitlement. Otherwise one is 'refashioning geography.'[82]

An important final point in discussing equidistance is whether the delimitation of the outer continental shelf warrants an exception from the

[79] *Dispute concerning Delimitation of the Maritime Boundary between Bangladesh and Myanmar in the Bay of Bengal (Bangladesh/Myanmar)* (Judgment) [2012] ITLOS Rep. [74–75]. Here, the Tribunal presents a strong case against the use of bisectors due to the uncertainties and subjectivity involved.

[80] See Chapter 8.

[81] *Libya/Malta*, n. 8, [48]; *Black Sea*, n. 11, [109]–[110]; *Bangladesh/Myanmar*, n. 12, [81]–[82]. The reasoning followed by the Tribunal in the latter resembles clearly argumentation discourse that fits best the second stage of delimitation.

[82] For the argument that this assessment of *representativeness of controlling basepoints* is a matter of adjustment of the provisional equidistance line, see Marques Antunes, n. 1, 292–293. Also see the discussion in Chapters 8 and 9 in this volume.

use of equidistance as provisional line, on the grounds that *natural prolongation* – not *distance* – is the basis of entitlement. No doubt there is limited case law to which to resort.

When called upon to address this matter in *Bangladesh/Myanmar*, the Tribunal considered that equidistance should still be used as provisional line in the first of the three stages. It went on to conclude, through a reference to *the land dominates the sea*, that the 'equidistance/relevant circumstances method':

> is rooted in the recognition that sovereignty over the land territory is the basis for the sovereign rights and jurisdiction of the coastal State with respect to both the exclusive economic zone and the continental shelf.[83]

In *Bangladesh v. India*, the arbitral tribunal also used a provisional equidistance line, in line with the position of the two states, which accepted equidistance as starting point for the delimitation. Since the arbitral tribunal and the parties concurred on the existence of a single continental shelf, the view that '[h]aving adopted the equidistance/relevant circumstances method for the delimitation of the continental shelf within 200 nm,' the 'use the same method to delimit the continental shelf beyond 200 nm' should apply raised no difficulties.[84]

From the Tribunal's reasoning in *Bangladesh/Myanmar* it appears that equidistance was applied because it allowed the resolution of the delimitation problems. What remains unaddressed is how, if the equidistance line were not apt to resolve such problems, it would have approached the determination of the provisional line.

It is also unclear whether natural prolongation, as basis of entitlement beyond 200 nm, has any role to play in establishing such a provisional line. No obvious answer seems possible. While in theory the *basis of entitlement* allows the argument that the provisional line should be based on natural prolongation, from a practical perspective this is effectively unworkable.[85] Further, no such example exists in case law. It may well be that the relevance of natural prolongation is a matter to be dealt with only in the second stage (assuming that is possible), by means of adjustments to the provisional equidistance line. But even that can be doubted. For now, the question remains unanswered, with all implications this has at the level of consistency and predictability.

[83] *Bangladesh/Myanmar*, n. 12, [132]. [84] *Bangladesh v. India*, n. 13, [142].

[85] See comments on natural prolongation in Section 3.2.1.

3.4 Adjustment to the Provisional Equidistance Line in the Case Law

Having looked into the concepts of *entitlement* and *delimitation*, and subsequently the recourse to equidistance in the first stage, the purpose of this section is to examine how case law has dealt with other aspects related to the concept of *entitlement* within the second stage. The following subsections are far from exhausting all issues and only drawn attention to the most relevant aspects of adjustment relating to *entitlement*.

3.4.1 Precedence between Different Entitlements

The notion of precedence between entitlements is a conceptual corollary of the different degree of state authority over maritime areas, in the context of amputation of entitlements.[86] No distinction or hierarchy between different entitlements exists in treaty law. However, this distinction is present in the practice of courts.

The most visible illustration is the precedence attributed to territorial sea entitlements over other entitlements, notably in cases involving islands. This occurred for example in *Anglo-French Continental Shelf*,[87] *Guinea/Guinea-Bissau*,[88] *Canada/France*,[89] and *Eritrea/Yemen*.[90]

That the precedence between different entitlements was weighed up by courts within the delimitation process has become clearer in the more recent case law. In *Bangladesh/Myanmar*, the Tribunal recognized the Bangladeshi right to a 12-mile territorial sea around St. Martin's Island where such territorial sea no longer overlapped with Myanmar's territorial sea'; for otherwise, it 'would result in giving more weight to the sovereign rights and jurisdiction of Myanmar in its exclusive economic zone and

[86] On precedence between entitlements, see Marques Antunes, n. 1, 141–145.

[87] *Anglo-French Continental Shelf*, n. 70, [89]–[95].

[88] *Case concerning the Delimitation of Maritime Boundary between Guinea and Guinea-Bissau (Guinea/Guinea-Bissau) (Award)* [1985] IXX UNRIAA 149 [190].

[89] *Canada/France*, n. 63, [289]–[291]. The allocation of additional maritime areas up to 24 nm in the western sector of Saint-Pierre et Miquelon, distinctly from the eastern sector where only 12 nm were considered, seems to indicate that, where geographical scope so allows, precedence between other entitlements might be considered. Various recent cases illustrate how such scope might not exist; e.g. *Territorial and Maritime Dispute (Nicaragua v. Colombia)*, *Black Sea*, and *Bangladesh/Myanmar*.

[90] *In the Matter of an Arbitration pursuant to an Agreement dated 3 October 1996 between the Government of the State of Eritrea and the Government of the Republic of Yemen (Eritrea/Yemen)* [1999] XXII RIAA 335 [354]–[355], [363]–[371].

continental shelf than to the sovereignty of Bangladesh over its territorial sea.'[91] Referring to its judgment in *Nicaragua v. Honduras*, the Court stated similarly in *Territorial and Maritime Dispute (Nicaragua v. Colombia)* that:

> [it] has never restricted the right of a State to establish a territorial sea of 12 nautical miles around an island on the basis of an overlap with the continental shelf and exclusive economic zone entitlements of another State.[92]

The conclusion is that the case law ultimately confirmed that the precedence between different entitlements is a consideration to be weighed up in delimitation, certainly where territorial sea entitlements overlap with other entitlements. At least in one instance, the same appears to have happened in relation to the precedence to be given to areas up to 24 nm (i.e., including the contiguous zone).[93] As between other entitlements, no clear guidance exists, and the emergence of 'grey areas'[94] seems to evidence that no 'hard-and-fast rules' apply and that such consideration must be viewed in light of all relevant circumstances.[95]

3.4.2 Insular Features

This review focuses only on how courts weighed up the entitlements generated by insular features in the context of delimitation, for purposes of the second stage. Although no distinction is made in treaty law between continental and insular territory, adjustments to the provisional equidistance line due to one of the entitlements being generated by an island have often been considered. Vast legal commentary on the so-called full, half or no effect (or other effect) approach has sprung up as a result.[96]

Two types of questions seem to exist. One concerns how different insular features[97] generate entitlements, which relates to the existence and geographical reach of entitlements (and is thus outside the scope of the present discussion). The other refers to the 'discounting' of the effect of

[91] *Bangladesh/Myanmar*, n. 12, [55]–[56].

[92] *Territorial and Maritime Dispute (Nicaragua v. Colombia)*, n. 78, [690]–[691].

[93] See n. 91. [94] See Section 3.4.3.

[95] See Chapter 13, which reviews the 'grey area' issue in *Bangladesh/Myanmar* and *Bangladesh v. India*.

[96] For a succinct overview of case law and legal commentary, see Marques Antunes, n. 1, 293–298.

[97] On the distinction between insular features – islands, rocks, and low-tide elevations – as to the *entitlement* over maritime zones, see *Philippines v. China*, n. 15, [204]–[254]). On the question of controlling basepoints, see Section 3.3.3.

insular features (by granting full, partial, no, or other effect), a matter to which we now turn.

Judicial discretion exercised as to the *effect of (the entitlement generated by) islands* has resulted in uncertainty because the reasoning has not always provided a basis for review of the judicial argumentation. When comparing different cases, it is hard to draw conclusions on the grounds why a different effect was attributed to various insular features. Of course, the standard situation is the full effect of basepoints. However, in *Anglo-French Continental Shelf*,[98] *Gulf of Maine*,[99] *Tunisia/Libya*,[100] and *Qatar/Bahrain*,[101] islands were given half-effect or no effect. Other cases evidence an 'undetermined effect,' as in *Canada/France*,[102] *Eritrea/Yemen*,[103] or *Territorial and Maritime Dispute (Nicaragua v. Colombia)*.[104]

One must recognize that the uncertainty and unpredictability concerning the aforesaid judicial discretion, as perhaps in relation to other issues, is inherent in maritime delimitation. When considering all relevant circumstances together, it is difficult to precisely determine what specific adjustment derives from which circumstance. Even where an adjustment stems from only one circumstance, its relationship with the wider geographical scope varies in terms of room to redress inequities. The same circumstance, in a different context, would likely lead to a different outcome. For example, adjustments resulting from insular features do not always relate to the nature of the territory, but rather concern a delimitation aspect (e.g. disparity in coastline length). As emphasized in *Bangladesh/Myanmar*:

> the effect to be given to an island in the delimitation of the maritime boundary [. . .] depends on the geographic realities and the circumstances of the specific case [and that there] is no general rule in this respect.[105]

The bottom line is that the judicial argumentation on the determination of the boundary line involving islands has not been centred on entitlements. Other factors have been involved. While this is arguably unavoidable, it creates difficulties in striving for legal certainty and predictability.

98 *Anglo-French Continental Shelf*, n. 70, [117].

99 *Gulf of Maine*, n. 7, [336]–[337].

100 *Tunisia/Libya, n.* 6, [63]–[64], [88]–[89].

101 *Qatar/Bahrain*, n. 10, [114]–[115].

102 *Canada/France*, n. 63, [289]–[291].

103 *Eritrea/Yemen*, n. 91, [370]–[371].

104 *Territorial and Maritime Dispute (Nicaragua v. Colombia)*, n. 78, [709]–[710]. An interesting aspect of this case is the use of a 'weighted line'; see Marques Antunes, n. 1, 167–168, 398–399.

105 *Bangladesh/Myanmar, n.* 12, [317].

Accordingly, a particular duty of elaborating in detail on the grounds upon which the findings on entitlements of islands are predicated seems to be imposed on courts. This ought to be done not only by deriving justified analogies with other cases, but also by looking into such analogies in respect of state practice.

3.4.3 Outer Continental Shelf Entitlement

The outer continental shelf entitlement[106] encompasses the areas beyond 200 nm up to the limit of the continental margin delineated as per Article 76 of the LOSC. This entitlement is also encapsulated by *the land dominates the sea* under the guise of 'geological proximity.' As noted above,[107] 'natural prolongation' as basis of entitlement does not necessarily imply the use of a provisional line different from equidistance. Nor does it seem to provide elements that can in practice be used for adjusting the provisional line. This section considers whether, in the second stage, 'natural prolongation' has had any actual bearing in terms of equitable adjustment of the provisional equidistance line (or otherwise dispelling such proposition).

From a theoretical standpoint, it seems difficult to argue that 'natural prolongation' is entirely irrelevant for purposes of adjustment of the provisional equidistance line. As a matter of principle, as legal basis of outer continental shelf entitlements, 'natural prolongation' should not 'be other than pertinent to' the delimitation of outer continental shelf areas.[108] It should be at least one of the circumstances to be weighed up in assessing the equitableness of the provisional equidistance line.

The critical difficulty in this respect is that there is only *one* legal continental shelf, which extends within and beyond 200 nm.[109] The entitlement thereto stems from the same LOSC provision (i.e., Article 76, which expresses 'closeness' to the land territory on two different bases, specifically *distance* and *geological proximity*). Attempting to treat one part of the continental shelf separately from the other might not be warranted under international law.

[106] For a review of the procedural and substantive issues respecting delimitation of outer continental shelf areas, see Chapters 12 and 13, respectively.

[107] See Section 3.2.1.

[108] Application *mutatis mutandis* of the reasoning in *Libya/Malta* as to the continental shelf within 200 nm (see *Libya/Malta*, n. 8, [30]).

[109] The existence of a single continental shelf was explicitly acknowledged by the arbitral tribunal and the parties in *Bangladesh v. India*, n. 13, [142].

Only a handful of cases have thus far addressed the issue of the relationship between entitlement and delimitation beyond 200 nm. The more significant involve the delimitation of maritime boundaries in the Bay of Bengal – *Bangladesh/Myanmar* and *Bangladesh v. India*[110] – where the entitlements of all three states involved overlapped. While there is no question of reviewing in detail all aspects of these decisions, a few points are significant in terms of understanding how the case law has approached the issues of *entitlement* and *delimitation.*

With *Bangladesh/Myanmar* and *Bangladesh v. India* it became clear that an overlapping of outer continental shelf entitlements must exist for delimitation to be required,[111] and the 'equidistance/relevant circumstances method' could be used within and beyond 200 nm.[112] The ensuing corollary was that the circumstances to be assessed in the second stage should not differ in cases of delimitation within and beyond 200 nm, a review of the 'geographical situation as a whole' being required.[113]

The question to be asked in this light is how to conceptualize 'natural prolongation' (the basis of entitlement beyond 200 nm) in terms of, first, the choice of provisional line and, second, the selection of circumstances to be considered in reviewing the equitableness of such provisional line. Most notably, in *Bangladesh/Myanmar*, the dismissal of the argument of 'the most natural prolongation' seems to be a further sign of the evanescing relevance of 'natural prolongation.'[114] By contrast, the geographical circumstance 'coastline concavity' (and the related cut-off effect extending beyond 200 nm)[115] was attributed critical weight in both cases (similarly to previous delimitation cases within 200 nm, since *North Sea Continental Shelf*).

The first proposition that can tentatively be advanced is that the 'equidistance/special circumstances' formula, once disparaged, is finally becoming the reference for delimitations within and beyond 200 nm. Relevant circumstances of a geographical nature seem to have the same role in both instances, the practical impact of 'natural prolongation' on adjustments of the provisional line being apparently non-existent (even for areas

110 For a discussion of the case law before and after *Bangladesh/Myanmar*, see Chapter 12.

111 See discussion in Section 3.2.2.

112 *Bangladesh/Myanmar*, n. 12, [132]; *Bangladesh v. India*, n. 13 [99]–[100], [142].

113 *Bangladesh v. India*, n. 13, [121].

114 *Bangladesh/Myanmar*, n. 12, [133].

115 Ibid, [132]. In *Bangladesh v. India*, the arbitral tribunal viewed the cut-off effect not only from the Bangladeshi perspective but also from the Indian perspective, as limit to the adjustment to be made (*Bangladesh v. India*, n. 13, [143]–[144]).

beyond 200 nm, in which it is the basis of entitlement). The flipside is that the conceptualization in *Libya/Malta*, as to the *pertinence* of the basis of entitlement, could be 'in crisis.'[116]

A second aspect concerns the 'grey areas' that have emerged from the adjustments made to the provisional equidistance line in *Bangladesh/Myanmar* and *Bangladesh/India*.[117] At the level of *entitlement*, first, this allows the argument that there is no precedence between entitlements to continental shelf within and beyond 200 nm. Priority was given in certain areas to the outer continental shelf entitlement of Bangladesh over the continental shelf entitlement within 200 nm of Myanmar and India (without prejudice to their exclusive economic zone entitlements, respecting the water column).[118] The adjustment required in each case due to the cut-off effect of the coastline concavity was deemed to prevail in view of the geographical circumstances. Second, this 'single shelf approach' to delimitation, endorsed by the case law, finds support in the non-existence of distinction in Article 83 of the LOSC, and seems to reinforce the idea that 'natural prolongation' has little if any impact on delimitation.

3.5 Conclusions

Looking back at the case law, in respect of the relationship between maritime entitlements and the delimitation of the relevant maritime zones, it all appears much as a *trial-and-error approach* to maritime delimitation law. The question of the 'basis of entitlement,' and its implications for the boundary line, was at times inconsistently analysed in conceptual terms. The case law has always reflected more the concerns with the outcome. For the sake of certainty and predictability, some restraint on such an approach would be welcome.

On the question of *entitlement* and *delimitation*, one would venture to say that there is an *acquis* of international law: *the land dominates the sea*. While not always expressed in the same fashion, it embodies the *vinculum juris* between land and sea: all entitlements stem from and depend on sovereignty over land territory. Even then, some doubts remain, as

[116] This matter is discussed in further detail in Chapter 13.

[117] *Bangladesh/Myanmar*, n. 12, [134]–[137]; *Bangladesh v. India*, n. 13, [155]–[157]. Maps 10 and 11, in the *Bangladesh v. India* award, illustrate the 'grey areas' in both cases, which overlap to some extent.

[118] The decisions leave it for the states to agree on the appropriate measures in order for each of them to exercise their rights under the LOSC to their fullest extent, including through possible cooperative arrangements.

for example in respect of how entitlements are generated. References to 'coastal projection seawards' (perpendicular projections) do not seem to be entirely aligned with the omni-directional generation of entitlements under the LOSC. In any event, *the land dominates the sea* expresses 'closeness' between land territory and maritime areas, whether through *distance* or *geological proximity* as basis of entitlement.

The conceptual bridge between *entitlement* and *delimitation* has been a far more difficult issue to tackle. No doubt, some aspects seem settled. Only where an *overlapping of entitlements* exists, is *delimitation* required; and delimitation inexorably results in the 'geographical amputation' of the entitlements. Theoretically, the concept of entitlement seems to bear on all three stages of the delimitation process, but far less in the third stage than in the first two stages.

The initial lack of conceptualization created difficulties that remain unresolved hitherto. Much of the uncertainty and unpredictability in the case law stems arguably from said difficulties. Despite recent attempts, a consistent conceptualization has remained elusive. More importantly, the idea of *basis of entitlement* as a central to the *delimitation rule* appears to have suffered a setback in recent cases involving outer continental shelf entitlements (i.e., *Bangladesh/Myanmar* and *Bangladesh v. India*). 'Natural prolongation' (*basis of entitlement*) has apparently been given no relevance, either in establishing the provisional line or for purposes of adjustment thereto. Developments in the case law have been such that one must wonder whether 'natural prolongation' has any practical role in *discovering the boundary line.*

The normativity enshrined in equidistance is an aspect with which courts continue to struggle, as evidenced by the 'step-never-taken' of recognizing it as the inescapable starting point for delimitation. Matters have become conceptually more challenging with the use of a provisional equidistance line in *Bangladesh/Myanmar* and *Bangladesh v. India*, two delimitations involving outer continental shelf entitlements.

The case law points to the 'equidistance/special circumstances' formula (which dates back to the ILC's work) as effectively the only normative parameter for delimitation, the result of which must be an 'equitable solution.' Enshrining the interplay between the principles of maritime zoning and of equity, as discussed in Section 3.2.3, this is another *acquis* in international law. Its relevance must not be underestimated, as it sets the bounds for judicial discretion in the weighing-up of relevant circumstances. A lesser use of judicial discretion (which relies upon the notion of *unicum*) would perhaps have contributed (and would still contribute) to furthering a more consistent and predictable development of delimitation law.

The *ratio decidendi* must henceforth revolve around the judicial argumentation for justifying a boundary-line pursuant to the 'equidistance/special circumstances' parameter, as a balancing-up of the entitlement-related circumstances (in terms of geographical elements or state authority) through equity. It means, first, that equidistance should be the provisional line and, second, that there is no free judicial choice of circumstances to weigh-up. Courts continue to exercise an almost unrestricted freedom in adjusting the provisional line, however. The 'bridging of the gap' towards a *reasoned line* (i.e., justification of the adjustments to the provisional line), which has been the Achilles heel of delimitation law, is an issue on which further light must be shed. It is pivotal to the relation between *entitlement* and *delimitation*.[119]

The case law has in practice (even if not expressly) 'promoted' equidistance to mandatory starting point of delimitation. Exceptions seldom arise. Even where the case law stated it would not apply equidistance as starting point, it resorted to a solution (bisector of coastal façades) that allocated areas on the basis of 'closer proximity,' i.e., the legal rationale underlying equidistance.

In the determination of the provisional equidistance line, courts have at times decided to 'rule out' certain basepoints during the first stage of the delimitation process. This approach should be rejected. One should start from a 'strict equidistance line,' for that is the way of assessing how equitably 'closer proximity' allocates areas within the overlapping of entitlements. Otherwise, one would be refashioning geography. Discarding controlling basepoints that have an inequitable impact upon the line that allocates areas on the basis of 'closer proximity' should be a matter for review in the second stage of the delimitation process.

Courts have clearly stated that the adjustment of the provisional equidistance line is to focus on an examination of the 'geographical situation as a whole.' Relevant circumstances are to be considered jointly in terms of adjustment to be made (i.e., balancing-up *in toto* the adjustment required). This might render it difficult to examine the exact effect resulting from each given circumstance, with the consequent implications on the exercise of judicial discretion. Unless it were possible to 'objectify' the

[119] Marques Antunes, n. 1, 404–405, 417–418.

impact of each such circumstance,[120] in all fairness a different approach seems difficult.

A few other points can be made in respect of the notion entitlement and its treatment in delimitation. The first concerns the notion of *precedence between entitlements*. The case law shows that a territorial sea entitlement is to take precedence over any other entitlement. No 'hard-and-fast rules' seem to exist as to other entitlements. While an entitlement up to 24 nm (i.e., including the contiguous zone) might be given precedence over other entitlements if the geographical scope so allows, the recent emergence of 'grey areas' in outer continental shelf delimitations shows that this is a matter of assessment in light of the whole of the relevant circumstances.

One of the most difficult aspects concerning entitlement relates to the 'effect of insular features.' The way in which courts have handled the cases before them has not contributed to certainty and predictability. From discounting of basepoints in the first stage, to unexplained adjustments to the boundary line in the second stage, much can be improved as a matter of legal argumentation and judicial discourse.

One must accept that the international legal regime on delimitation of maritime boundaries does not render it easy for courts to promote certainty and predictability. While this is true, it is no less true that the case law has not had a model approach. Delimitation may not be a matter of a practical agreement within the court as to what seems an equitable solution. This would pay a disservice to international law. Too many 'practical twists-and-turns' have occurred in judicial discourse. Too little effort has been put on conceptualizing maritime entitlements and maritime delimitation, as well as on bridging the gap between the circumstances of each 'unique case' and the adjudged boundary line. A different approach, with judicial discourse and argumentation at the heart of decision making, would lead to legally sounder outcomes. For the time being, one subsists in the doldrums of uncertainty and unpredictability.

[120] For an attempt to 'objectify' such adjustment in a case study, by reference to the *decision matrix*, see ibid, 392–402.

4

The Applicable Law

The Geneva Convention on the Continental Shelf, the LOSC, and Customary International Law

DONALD MCRAE*

In this chapter I will trace the development of the law relating to maritime boundary delimitation from its origins in Article 6 of the 1958 Convention on the Continental Shelf[1] through its treatment in customary international law and its formulation in the Article 74/83 of the 1982 United Nations Convention on the Law of the Sea (LOSC).[2] I will then consider how international courts and tribunals currently interpret and apply the applicable law and raise some questions about both its content and application.

4.1 Article 6: Equidistance and Special Circumstances

In *North Sea Continental Shelf*[3] the International Court of Justice (ICJ) described the origin of Article 6 of the 1958 Convention on the Continental Shelf as, 'almost impromptu and certainly contingent.'[4] The principle of equidistance had been proposed by the Committee of Experts established by the International Law Commission (ILC) to recommend an appropriate principle for the delimitation of the territorial sea between adjacent or opposite states. In recommending equidistance for the delimitation of

* I am grateful for the research assistance of Erika Schneidereit.

[1] Convention on the Continental Shelf, adopted 29 April 1958, entered into force 10 June 1964, 499 UNTS 311.

[2] Convention on the Law of the Sea, adopted 10 December 1982, entered into force 16 November 1994, 1833 UNTS 397.

[3] *North Sea Continental Shelf Cases (Federal Republic of Germany/Denmark; Federal Republic of Germany/Netherlands)* (Judgment) [1969] ICJ Rep. 3.

[4] Ibid., [53].

the territorial sea, the Committee of Experts added that such a principle would serve as well for the delimitation of the continental shelf.[5]

In the Commission, there was some concern about a simple equidistance or median line rule given the differences in coastal configuration. Initially it was suggested that where the median line could not be simply applied, then the matter would be referred to arbitration.[6] However, after further discussion the provision was elaborated into what it is today. The rule of delimitation became a rather convoluted formulation that in the absence of agreement, unless another boundary was justified by special circumstances, the line was to be a median line (in the case of opposite states) or an equidistance line (in the case of adjacent states).

The Commission clarified the notion of 'special circumstances' as follows: 'provision must be made for departures necessitated by any exceptional configuration of the coast, as well as the presence of islands or of navigable channels.'[7] The Commission also indicated that the rules for the delimitation of the continental shelf ought to be the same as the rules for delimitation of territorial waters.[8] Accordingly, the proposals of the Commission for the delimitation of both the territorial sea and the continental shelf were essentially identical, although the provision on territorial sea delimitation that emerged in Article 12 of the 1958 Convention on the Territorial Sea and Contiguous Zone[9] was modified, without losing the qualification that 'special circumstances' would justify resort to a delimitation that was not based on equidistance.

The rather opaque formulation of the delimitation provision – absence of agreement, no other line justified by special circumstances, then equidistance – left unclear how the rule was to be applied. Certainly, one could start by looking for agreement, but after that was equidistance the primary rule and 'special circumstances' the exception, or in the absence of agreement did one first test for 'special circumstances' and resort to equidistance as a last resort? In a sense, this methodological question was never resolved and remains at the heart of controversies over the applicable law in delimitation. Arguably, however, the law currently applied by courts and tribunals has in principle provided a resolution of this question.

[5] ILC, *Report of the International Law Commission Covering the Work of Its Fifth Session* UN Doc. A/CN.4/SER.A/1953 (1953), vol. 2, 216, [81–82].

[6] Ibid., [81]. [7] Ibid., [82]. [8] Ibid.

[9] Convention on the Territorial Sea and the Contiguous Zone, adopted 29 April 1958, entered into force 10 September 1964, 516 UNTS 206.

4.2 The Emergence of a Customary Rule

No light was thrown on this methodological question in the first judicial examination of Article 6 in *North Sea Continental Shelf*, but a new direction was started – the birth of the notion that there was a customary rule of international law relating to delimitation. In part, the direction the Court would take was dictated by the question put to it. The fundamental dispute between the parties was over the law to be applied to their delimitation. Thus, the question put to the Court was, 'what principles and rules of international law are applicable to the delimitation as between the Parties.'[10]

The Netherlands and Denmark argued that Article 6 of the 1958 Convention on the Continental Shelf was applicable notwithstanding the fact that Germany had not ratified the Convention. Germany took the view that it was not bound by the 1958 Convention and that instead the delimitation had to proceed on the basis of each party being entitled to a 'just and equitable share' of the area in contention. According to Germany, equidistance would only be applicable if it resulted in a 'just and equitable apportionment of the continental shelf among the States concerned.'[11]

The rejection by the Court of the arguments of both parties – Article 6 was not binding on Germany either as a treaty obligation or by virtue of customary international law, and there was no legal basis for apportionment in place of delimitation – left the Court with the task of finding a delimitation rule itself. It did this by returning to the Truman Proclamation,[12] which had provided that if questions arose over the delimitation of the continental shelf between the US and its neighbours, they would be settled in accordance with 'equitable principles.'[13]

The reasoning process by which the Court concluded that there was a rule of law requiring the application of 'equitable principles' is at best elliptical. In its discussion of the argument that equidistance was a logical necessity in delimitation, the Court stated that the concept of 'delimitation in accordance with equitable principles' referred to in the Truman Proclamation, had 'underlain all the subsequent history of the subject.'[14] Later, it described delimitation in accordance with equitable principles as one of the 'basic legal notions' that from the beginning 'reflected the *opinio juris*

[10] *North Sea Continental Shelf*, n. 3, [10]. [11] Ibid., [9].

[12] US Presidential Proclamation No. 2667, Policy of the United States with Respect to the Natural Resources of the Subsoil and Sea Bed of the Continental Shelf, adopted 28 September 1945.

[13] *North Sea Continental Shelf*, n. 3, [47]. [14] Ibid.

in the matter of delimitation.'[15] The Court went on to say in an oft-quoted phrase, 'it is not a question of applying equity simply as a matter of abstract justice, but of applying a rule of law which itself requires the application of equitable principles.'[16]

The essence of this notion, the Court pointed out, was that the parties had to try to negotiate an agreement, that the parties had to act in a way that 'equitable principles' were applied, and that the continental shelf was the natural prolongation of the land territory of a state and could not be permitted to encroach on the natural prolongation of another state.[17] In light of this, the Court identified a number of factors that would have to be considered in any delimitation based on 'equitable principles,' acknowledging nonetheless that there was 'no legal limit to the considerations which States may take account of for the purpose of making sure that they apply equitable procedures, and more often than not it is the balancing-up of all such considerations that will produce this result rather than reliance on one to the exclusion of all others.'[18]

Neither the process by which the Court concluded that there was a customary rule of international law relating to delimitation, nor how the Court described that rule and how it was to be applied, was terribly convincing. And, although it has attracted a substantial amount of scholarly enquiry and criticism, and courts and tribunals have purported to apply it, the application of 'equitable principles' has never been a straightforward implementation of what was articulated in *North Sea Continental Shelf*. Rather, when 'equitable principles' have been invoked, it has often been in conjunction with other approaches and principles of delimitation. Indeed, in the first decision on maritime delimitation after *North Sea Continental Shelf*, a court of arbitration purported to integrate the customary international law rule of 'equitable principles' with the Article 6 combined 'equidistance/special circumstances' rule.[19] Thus, the precise content of *North Sea Continental Shelf's* concept of the customary international law rule has never been clearly articulated or clarified.

Anglo-French Continental Shelf had to deal both with circumstances where Article 6 applied and with circumstances to which customary international law applied.[20] In the course of its judgment the court of

[15] Ibid., [85]. [16] Ibid. [17] Ibid. [18] Ibid., [93].

[19] *Case Concerning the Delimitation of Continental Shelf between the United Kingdom of Great Britain and Northern Ireland, and the French Republic* [1977, 1978] 18 UNRIAA 3.

[20] Both states were party to the 1958 Convention on the Continental Shelf, but the effect of a French reservation and the UK's objection to it was that part of the boundary had to be delimited on the basis of customary international law and not on the basis of Art. 6.

arbitration made clear that the equidistance/special circumstances rule of Article 6 did not embody two rules, one relating to equidistance and the other to special circumstances. Rather, it was a combined equidistance-special circumstances rule. The stipulation unless 'another boundary is justified by special circumstances' is an 'integral part' of the rule providing for the application of equidistance.[21] It also took the view that whether the Article 6 rule for delimitation or the customary international law rule for delimitation was invoked made little practical difference to the result.[22] And, further, whether under customary international law or Article 6, the method of delimitation, whether equidistance or otherwise, was dependent on the geographical circumstances of each case.[23]

4.3 The Decline of Equidistance and the Emergence of the LOSC Rules

These basic propositions were not seriously challenged in the subsequent jurisprudence. What emerged in the decisions of courts and tribunals was a readiness to embrace alternative methods of delimitation and when equidistance was applied, it was frequently adjusted. Indeed, on that basis equidistance could not have been the governing law – it was seen as a method and only one method amongst several possible methods of delimitation.

Subsequent cases defined the applicable law in different ways, although all essentially leading in the same direction. The Court in *Tunisia/Libya* adopted the approach to the applicable law that the parties had agreed on, which was derived from *North Sea Continental Shelf*: 'delimitation is to be effected in accordance with equitable principles, and taking account of all relevant circumstances.'[24] The Court also took into account, as directed by the Special Agreement between the parties, 'the new accepted trends in the Third [United Nations] Conference on the Law of the Sea.'[25]

[21] *Anglo-French Continental Shelf*, n. 19, [68].

[22] Ibid., [70, 82]. The court of arbitration also noted that the shared objective of the customary rules and the equidistance-special circumstances rule rendered customary law a 'relevant and even essential means' for interpreting Art. 6, though the court maintained that Art. 6 itself did not express a rule of customary international law.

[23] Ibid., [84, 125–126].

[24] *Case Concerning the Continental Shelf (Tunisia/Libyan Arab Jamahiriya)* (Judgment) [1982] ICJ Rep. 18, [133].

[25] Ibid., [4]. For example, the Court emphasized that the most recent Art. 83 text produced by the Conference did not impose any specific criteria prescribing how states should pursue

In *Gulf of Maine*, the Chamber of the Court defined the applicable law in terms of a 'fundamental norm,' which in relevant part provided:

> Delimitation is to be effected by the application of equitable criteria and by the use of practical methods capable of ensuring, with regard to the geographic configuration of the area and other relevant circumstances, an equitable result.[26]

The focus thus moved from the applicable law to the methods that could be employed to achieve an equitable result. In this regard, the Chamber made clear that no priority was to be given to equidistance. Indeed, equidistance adjusted to take account of relevant circumstances was utilized in only one of the three boundary segments. The arbitral tribunal in *Guinea/Guinea-Bissau*, while endorsing the approach of the Gulf of Maine Chamber in terms of achieving an equitable result, reformulated it in the terms of the LOSC of achieving an 'equitable solution.'[27]

When it came to drawing the boundary, in none of these cases did the Court or tribunal adopt equidistance as the method for the delimitation as a whole. In *Tunisia/Libya*, the Court drew a line that is roughly an equidistance line adjusted to diminish the impact of the Kerkennah Islands on the boundary. In *Gulf of Maine*, the Chamber of the Court used an adjusted equidistance line where the coasts of the two states were in an opposite relationship. In *Guinea/Guinea-Bissau*, the tribunal did not employ equidistance at all. In short, in all of these cases a variety of factors were taken into account and different methods used. The equidistance principle was given no particular status in delimitation.

Throughout this period the negotiations for a comprehensive convention on the law of the sea were continuing. With respect to maritime boundaries there were now not only territorial sea and continental shelf boundaries to consider, there were also boundaries to be delimited in the emerging exclusive economic zone. The lines of negotiation were predictable. There were states, generally those who preferred the application of equidistance, who wished to retain the Article 6 rule, and there

an equitable solution. Thus, the equidistance approach was only to be adopted in circumstances where it would lead to an equitable solution – otherwise, another method should be applied [50, 109].

26 *Delimitation of the Maritime Boundary in the Gulf of Maine Area (Canada/USA)* (Judgment) [1984] ICJ Rep. 246, [112, 114]. As is clear from this pronouncement, the Chamber determined that customary international law did not specify what rules or practical methods should be used for delimitation.

27 *Delimitation of the Maritime Boundary between Guinea and Guinea-Bissau* [1985] 19 RIAA 149, [88].

were states that preferred the customary international law rule of equitable principles. Earlier drafts contained a reference to both equitable principles and an equidistance or median line,[28] but the final version eliminated them. The rule for delimitation for both the exclusive economic zone (EEZ) (Article 74) and the continental shelf (Article 83) became:

> The delimitation of the [exclusive economic zone/continental shelf] between States with opposite or adjacent coasts shall be effected by agreement on the basis of international law, as referred to in Article 38 of the Statute of the International Court of Justice, in order to achieve an equitable solution.

Gone from the final text were references to equidistance, to special circumstances and to equitable principles.[29]

In *Tunisia/Libya* the Court noted that under the new text, 'the principles and rules applicable to the delimitation of continental shelf areas are those which are appropriate to bring about an equitable result.'[30] The Chamber in *Gulf of Maine* simply noted that this text 'serves to open the door to continuation of the development effected in this field by international case law.'[31]

In this regard, the decision in *Libya/Malta*[32] was an intellectual turning point in thinking about the applicable law, presaging the future use of a 'provisional equidistance line.' The Court took account of the rule for delimitation embodied in Articles 74 and 83 of the LOSC and integrated those provisions into its determination of the applicable law. It noted that the parties agreed that equitable principles were incorporated into and made part of the Article 74/83 regime. It also noted that provision for the delimitation of the EEZ existed alongside that of the delimitation of the continental shelf and the relevance of the fact that entitlement to an EEZ was based on distance.[33]

However, the Court rejected the view, argued by Malta, that the fact that title was based on distance gave a special primacy to equidistance. It said:

[28] Third United Nations Conference on the Law of the Sea, *Informal Composite Negotiating Text*, UN Doc. A/CONF.62/WP.10/Rev.2 (1982), Art. 74.

[29] For further discussion on the drafting history of the LOSC, see the *Virginia Commentaries* and A. O. Adede, 'Toward the Formulation of the Rule of Delimitation of Sea Boundaries between States with Adjacent or Opposite Coasts' (1979) 19 *Virginia Journal of International Law* 207, 210–224 (for a discussion on the competing approaches for delimitation in Arts. 74 and 83).

[30] *Tunisia/Libya*, n. 24, [50].

[31] *Gulf of Maine*, n. 26, [95].

[32] *Continental Shelf (Libyan Arab Jamahiriya/Malta)* (Judgment) [1985] ICJ Rep. 13.

[33] Ibid., [29, 33].

> The Court is unable to accept that, even as a preliminary and provisional step towards the drawing of a delimitation line, the equidistance method is one which *must* be used, or that the Court is 'required, as a first step, to examine the effects of a delimitation by application of the equidistance method.'[34]

In saying this, the Court was reiterating what it had said in its 1982 Judgment, where it had emphasized that equidistance could be applied if it led to an equitable solution.[35] Nonetheless, the Court went ahead and drew a provisional equidistance line, noting the particular applicability of equidistance in the case of opposite coasts. Whether that equidistance line led to an equitable solution could only be determined by the application of equitable principles to the relevant circumstances.[36] Indeed, if one looks at what the Court did in *Libya/Malta*, rather than what it said, the case is really the origin for the first stage in the subsequently developed 'three-stage process.'

4.4 The Emergence of the Provisional Equidistance Line

This apparent contradiction – the Court asserting that it did not have to start with a provisional equidistance line, but starting with one anyway – is in some ways indicative of the inherent ambiguity in the approach to the applicable law that has developed since. In *Jan Mayen*,[37] the Court concluded that although it had been asked to draw a boundary for both the fishery zone and the continental shelf, the parties were bound by Article 6 of the 1958 Convention in respect of the shelf, and by customary international law in respect of the fishing zone.[38] But in any event both bodies of law had the same objective – achieving an 'equitable result.' After pointing out, as had been done in previous cases, that utilizing equidistance was not a necessary or obligatory step, the Court went on to say:

> it is in accord with precedents to begin with the median line as a provisional line and then to ask whether 'special circumstances' require any adjustment or shifting of that line.[39]

[34] Ibid., [43] (emphasis in the original).
[35] *Tunisia/Libya*, n. 24, [109].
[36] *Libya/Malta*, n. 32, [63].
[37] *Maritime Delimitation in the Area between Greenland and Jan Mayen (Denmark v. Norway)* (Judgment) [1993] ICJ Rep. 38.
[38] Ibid., [45]. This was in fact the first occasion on which the Court had applied Art. 6 of the 1958 Convention for continental shelf delimitation.
[39] Ibid., [51].

The Court cited *Gulf of Maine* and *Libya/Malta* as examples of the provisional median or equidistance line approach. But while *Libya/Malta* is certainly an example of that approach, *Gulf of Maine* was not. There the Chamber did not employ a provisional equidistance line. The Chamber adopted equidistance as the appropriate method; it did not see anything provisional about it – equidistance was dictated by the geographical circumstances of the opposite coasts of Nova Scotia and Massachusetts. It was not the application of a method valid for all delimitations. Indeed, the Chamber used different methods for the other parts of the line.

The two-step approach was further consolidated by the Court in *Qatar/Bahrain*, where it said:

> [t]he most logical and widely practised approach is first to draw provisionally an equidistance line and then to consider whether that line must be adjusted in the light of the existence of special circumstances.[40]

Not all of the judges were enamoured with this reliance on provisional equidistance as a methodological approach although in some cases they did not object to its application in the circumstances of the present case.[41] In *Cameroon v. Nigeria* the Court reaffirmed this position, indicating that it 'had on various occasions made it clear what the applicable criteria, principles and rules of delimitation were' and described them as the 'so-called' equitable principles/relevant circumstances method which the Court said, 'involves first drawing an equidistance line, then considering whether there are factors calling for the adjustment or shifting of that line in order to achieve an "equitable result."'[42]

Yet, qualifications continued to exist. In *Nicaragua v. Honduras*, while acknowledging the 'intrinsic value' of equidistance, the Court went on to say:

> however, the equidistance method does not automatically have priority over other methods of delimitation and, in particular circumstances, there may be factors which make the application of the equidistance method inappropriate.[43]

[40] *Maritime Delimitation and Territorial Questions between Qatar and Bahrain (Qatar/Bahrain)* (Judgment) [2001] ICJ Rep. 40, [176].
[41] See ibid., Oda J, Separate Opinion [36]; ibid., Torres Bernárdez J, Dissenting Opinion [485].
[42] *Land and Maritime Boundary between Cameroon and Nigeria (Cameroon v. Nigeria: Equatorial Guinea intervening)* (Judgment) [2002] ICJ Rep. 303, [288].
[43] *Territorial and Maritime Dispute between Nicaragua and Honduras in the Caribbean Sea (Nicaragua v. Honduras)* (Judgment) [2007] ICJ Rep. 659, [272].

In fact, because of the difficulty of identifying base points on the coast, the Court refrained from drawing a provisional equidistance line and instead drew lines representing the coastal fronts of the two states and the 'provisional' boundary was a bisector of the intersection of these coastal fronts. However, in deviating from drawing a provisional equidistance line, the Court added the qualification that equidistance remained the 'general rule.'[44]

The possibility that arbitral tribunals dealing with delimitation would chart their own approach to the applicable law was not realized. In *Barbados v. Trinidad and Tobago*,[45] the tribunal reviewed the factors that had been taken into account in the application of Articles 74 and 83 of the LOSC and then adopted the 'two-step approach' of starting with a provisional equidistance line and then reviewing it in light of relevant circumstances. In *Guyana/Suriname*[46] the Annex VII tribunal endorsed the two-step approach confirming the existing case law, thereby further entrenching the role of equidistance. Courts and tribunals dealing with issues of continental shelf delimitation, the tribunal said, 'have come to embrace a clear role for equidistance.'[47]

4.5 The Three-Stage Approach

The nature of that 'clear role' became clarified, as well as obscured, in the subsequent decision of the ICJ in *Black Sea*.[48] There the Court noted that the applicable law was Articles 74 and 83 of the LOSC, but said no more about what that entailed. In doing so, the Court was continuing what had occurred in other cases since *Gulf of Maine*. The discussion of the applicable law was perfunctory and attention was devoted instead to the way in which delimitation was to be effected. The Court in *Black Sea* spoke in terms of delimitation methodology – how the Court was to go about the delimitation. And it used slightly different terms from the previous cases. Taking account of the approach in *Nicaragua v. Honduras*, where the Court had found itself unable to draw a provisional equidistance line, the Court

44 Ibid., [281].

45 *Arbitration between Barbados and the Republic of Trinidad and Tobago (Barbados v. Trinidad and Tobago)* (2006) 27 RIAA 147.

46 *In the Matter of an Arbitration between Guyana and Suriname (Guyana v. Suriname)* (2007) 30 RIAA 1.

47 Ibid., [335].

48 *Maritime Delimitation in the Black Sea (Romania v. Ukraine)* (Judgment) [2009] ICJ Rep. 61.

in *Black Sea* noted that the first step of the process of delimitation was to establish a 'provisional delimitation line using methods that are geometrically objective and also appropriate for the geography of the area in which the delimitation is to take place.'[49] In the case of adjacent states, the Court said, an equidistance line would be used as the provisional delimitation line 'unless there are compelling reasons that make this unfeasible in the particular case.'[50]

At the second stage, the Court said, it will consider any factors that call for an adjustment of the provisional equidistance line in order to achieve an equitable result. Somewhat obscurely the Court also added that in this second stage, the 'so-called equitable principles/relevant circumstances method may usefully be applied.'[51] What is not clear in the Court's formulation is whether the formula 'equitable principles/relevant circumstances' is simply a different way of stating the second stage requirement of considering whether there are factors warranting the adjustment of the provisional equidistance line in order to achieve an equitable result, or whether it is intended as the mechanism by which the second stage is effected, or whether possibly it is something that is entirely different. The Court does not elaborate.

The Court went on to identify a third stage in the delimitation process. This was an assessment of the provisional equidistance line, adjusted or unadjusted as the case may be, to see whether it 'might lead to an inequitable result by reason of any marked disproportion between the ratio of the respective coastal lengths and the ratio between the relevant maritime area of each State by reference to the delimitation line.'[52] This was a 'disproportionality' test.

The result of *Black Sea* is that a two-stage delimitation process had now become a three-stage process. The need for a reasonable degree of proportionality 'between the extent of the continental shelf appertaining to the states concerned and the lengths of their respective coastlines' was identified as an aspect of the application of equitable principles in *North Sea Continental Shelf*[53] and it has been referred to in a number of subsequent cases. In some instances, it has been dealt with in terms of a comparison of coastal lengths (*Anglo-French Continental Shelf*) and in others a

[49] Ibid., [116].

[50] Ibid. The Court went on to point out that in the cases of opposite states a median line would be used, without adding the qualification relating to compelling reasons making such a line unfeasible.

[51] Ibid., [120].

[52] Ibid., [122].

[53] *North Sea Continental Shelf*, n. 3, [98].

comparison between the ratio of the lengths of coasts and the ratio of the areas attributed to each state (*Gulf of Maine*). What the Court did in *Black Sea* was to elevate the notion of proportionality from one of the factors to be taken into account in considering whether a provisional equidistance line should be adjusted to granting it a separate status as the third stage in a three-stage process. In doing so, it has appeared to give enhanced importance to the question of proportionality.[54]

Black Sea is not just important for its insertion of a third stage into the delimitation process; it also applied the three stages in a way that cast some doubt on whether the 'provisional delimitation line' approach actually provides the degree of certainty and predictability that is behind its rationale.

An equidistance line is a line drawn so that it is an equal distance from the nearest points on the coasts of the two parties. As the Court said in *Black Sea*:

> At this initial stage of the construction of the provisional equidistance line the Court is not yet concerned with any relevant circumstances that may obtain and the line is plotted on strictly geometrical criteria on the basis of objective data.[55]

But that is not what the Court did. Instead, it embarked on a process of selecting base points that were 'appropriate.' Appropriate points, the Court said were:

> points on the Parties' relevant coast or coasts which mark a significant change in the direction of the coast, in such a way that the geometrical figure formed by the line connecting all these points reflects the general direction of the coastlines.'[56]

This is quite different from just selecting the nearest points. It was a process of considering the weight to be given to different geographical features in the drawing of the line – a process that one might have thought was linked to the second stage of the three-stage process. The question whether Serpent's Island should be ignored is classically a second stage issue when looking at 'relevant circumstances.' Although the Sulina Dyke issue was not just a technical matter, the fact that the Sulina Dyke extended

[54] For further discussion of these issues, see Chapter 9 (on relevant circumstances) and Chapter 11 (on proportionality) in this volume.

[55] *Black Sea*, n. 48, [118].

[56] Ibid., [127].

the coast seaward was also a matter that belonged in a consideration of the relevant circumstances in the second stage.[57]

The approach taken in *Black Sea*, with respect to the identification of base points, was essentially followed by the Court in *Territorial and Maritime Dispute (Nicaragua v. Colombia)*.[58] The Court ignored in the drawing of the provisional line a feature that was clearly above the high water mark but was regarded by the Court as a 'miniscule feature,'[59] a matter that was a relevant circumstance to be considered in the second stage. In *Peru v. Chile*,[60] the Court drew a provisional equidistance line in the first stage, but appeared to ignore the fact in the second stage, when considering relevant circumstances, that the starting point for the boundary was not itself an equidistance point. Nor did it consider whether this resulted in a disproportion under the third-stage test.

In *Bangladesh/Myanmar*[61] the International Tribunal on the Law of the Sea (ITLOS) reviewed the approaches taken by the Court and arbitral tribunals to delimitation under Articles 74/83 of the LOSC, including the three-stage approach. It summed them up as the 'equidistance-relevant circumstances' method, which it said had been 'favoured by international courts and tribunals in the majority of the delimitation cases that have come before them.'[62] The 'three-stage' approach was to be applied in application of the equidistance-relevant circumstances method.[63]

Following the approach of the Court in *Black Sea* in making its own judgment about the suitability of base points for the drawing of that line, the Tribunal rejected St. Martin's Island as a base point because it would 'result in a line that blocks the seaward projection of Myanmar's coast.'[64] Thus, the Tribunal took into account in the first stage what was clearly a second stage 'relevant circumstance.'

In *Bangladesh v. India*,[65] an Annex VII tribunal again adopted the three-stage approach. In undertaking the first step in the process, the tribunal adopted most of the base points presented by the parties, but rejected two

[57] For a discussion of these points, see ibid. [129–141] and [149].

[58] *Territorial and Maritime Dispute (Nicaragua v. Colombia)* (Judgment) [2012] ICJ Rep. 624.

[59] Ibid., [202].

[60] *Maritime Dispute (Peru v. Chile)* (Judgment) [2014] ICJ Rep. 3.

[61] *Delimitation of the Maritime Boundary in the Bay of Bengal (Bangladesh/Myanmar)* (Judgment) [2012] ITLOS Rep. 4.

[62] Ibid., [238]. [63] Ibid., [240]. [64] Ibid., [265].

[65] *In the Matter of the Bay of Bengal Maritime Boundary Arbitration (Bangladesh v. India)* (Award) [2014] PCA Case 2010-16.

base points that were on low-tide elevations. Thus, the tribunal did not intervene as much in the determination of the provisional equidistance line as other tribunals have done.[66]

4.6 What Is the Applicable Law Today?

In the light of the way courts and tribunals have articulated their approach to delimitation in respect of both the EEZ and the continental shelf, the starting point for the applicable law is Article 74/83 of the LOSC. While this is obviously true in respect of parties to the LOSC, tribunals have also indicated that these provisions reflect customary international law. But what does Article 74/83 mandate?

To require states to settle their boundaries by agreement on the basis of international law does not say very much. International law prior to the adoption of the LOSC contained a treaty rule in Article 6, for those states that are party to the 1958 Convention on the Continental Shelf and a customary rule on 'equitable principles,' as articulated in *North Sea Continental Shelf* and elaborated by the court of arbitration in *Anglo-French Continental Shelf*, for those that were not. And the reference in Article 74/83 in the LOSC to 'international law as referred to in Article 38 of the Statute of the International Court of Justice' could certainly be treated as a reference to both conventional and customary international law. What is clear is that regardless of how a court or tribunal undertakes delimitation, the ultimate goal is to achieve an 'equitable solution.'

The jurisprudence has responded to this in ways that are not entirely clear or consistent. Three formulations can be identified. First, by developing a three-stage process for delimitation; second by endorsing the 'equidistance-relevant circumstances' approach; and third by saying that resort to equitable principles may also be appropriate. In short, rather than giving a precise definition of what constitutes the applicable law, or precise content to Article 74/83, courts and tribunals have fallen back on allusions and indications focusing chiefly on how to go about delimitation. In doing so, they have blurred any dividing line between delimitation law and delimitation method.

This merging of law and method is not new. In *Gulf of Maine* the Chamber's approach was almost entirely focused on method. In an oft-quoted phrase the Chamber said that:

[66] For a more detailed analysis of these cases, see Chapter 8 in this volume.

> [i]t is therefore unrewarding, especially in a new and still unconsolidated field like that involving the quite recent extension of the claims of States to areas which were until yesterday zones of the high seas, to look to general international law to provide a ready-made set of rules that can be used for solving any delimitation problems that arise.[67]

Under the 'fundamental norm' identified by the Chamber, delimitation was to be effected by the application of equitable criteria and the use of practical methods.'[68] What is different under the contemporary approach to the applicable law is that the 'method' being applied by courts and tribunals today has built into it a particular view of the law.

At present what is lacking is a clear enunciation of the relationship between the three-stage approach and the 'equidistance-relevant circumstances' approach. Some courts have stated that the equidistance-relevant circumstances approach is simply in effect an alternative formulation for the three-stage approach, presumably because the first stage involves a provisional equidistance line, and the second or third stages involve adjusting that line in the light of relevant circumstances. Another approach is to see equidistance-relevant circumstances as inherent in the second stage where the provisional line is tested against 'relevant circumstances.' And in some instances 'equidistance-relevant circumstances' has been referred to as 'equitable principles-relevant circumstances.'[69]

Yet, none of the explanations for treating the issue as one of 'equidistance-relevant circumstances' is completely satisfactory, at least since the *Nicaragua v. Honduras* decision. Up until that point, the first step involved the determination of a provisional equidistance line, but the Court in *Nicaragua v. Honduras* concluded that it was not possible to draw an equidistance line in the circumstances of that case. Due to the particular nature of the coastline in that area, base points from which an equidistance line could be constructed could not be drawn.[70] As a result, the formulation for the first stage was changed in *Black Sea* to the drawing of a provisional 'delimitation' line. And, if the provisional line is not an 'equidistance' line, then the three-stage process cannot be an 'equidistance-relevant circumstances' approach.

In practice, however, courts and tribunals have almost always used an equidistance line in the first phase and *Nicaragua v. Honduras* may be

[67] *Gulf of Maine*, n. 26, [111]. [68] Ibid., [112].

[69] See e.g. *Cameroon v. Nigeria*, n. 43, [288]; *Nicaragua v. Honduras*, n. 43, [271]; *Qatar/Bahrain*, n. 40, [231].

[70] *Nicaragua v. Honduras*, n. 43, [277–281].

simply a unique outlier. Yet, it forced the Court in *Black Sea* to provide a new rationale for the first stage – the provisional delimitation line had to be based on 'methods that are geometrically objective and also appropriate for the geography of the area in which the delimitation is to take place.'[71] While that description may apply to an adjusted equidistance line where the point of the adjustment is precisely to ensure that the line is 'appropriate' for the geography of the area, it is not a description of a strict equidistance line, which by definition has to be 'geometrically objective.' That is, such a line must be drawn so that it is equidistant from the nearest points on the coasts of the two states. The formulation by the Court which refers to the base points being appropriate for the geography of the area may have been a factor in the merging of the first and second phases referred to earlier.

From this it may be suggested that the applicable law today consists of a requirement to utilize a particular methodology and to engage in a particular process of assessment within that methodology in order to delimit a boundary. The methodology involves the three-stage process, in which a line must be drawn, that line must be tested against certain factors, and then the result after that is to be checked to see if it is disproportionate in respect of the areas resulting to each party from the delimitation. The checking phase – the second stage – involves weighing and balancing factors that are alleged to justify a deviation from the provisional equidistance line. This phase essentially requires what had to be done under the 'special circumstances' part of the Article 6 rule, or through the application of 'equitable principles' under the customary international law approach identified by the Court in *North Sea Continental Shelf*.

But, the new approach differs in important ways from the approaches of the past. The equitable principles approach relied on a subjective assessment of what was equitable and did not provide any starting notion of equality of areas as a backdrop for considering whether the requirement of equity had been met. The contemporary three-stage process, by contrast, provides an objective basis against which the relevant factors or circumstances can be measured. Starting with a provisional equidistance line, which has the attribute of equality in terms of distance from the coast, the three-stage approach provides a basis against which relevant circumstances and disproportion can be assessed. Under the equitable principles approach, equity was an abstract concept without a practical manifestation against which various factors or considerations could be evaluated.

[71] *Black Sea*, n. 48, [116].

The Article 6 rule provides the closest resemblance to the contemporary approach, although formulated in reverse terms – unless another line is justified because of special circumstances, equidistance will be applied – the rule required an assessment of a combination of equidistance and relevant (special) circumstances. What the new approach has done is solve the dilemma over Article 6. Was equidistance the rule and special circumstances the exception? The situation under the new approach is clear. The provisional line becomes the final line unless relevant circumstances can be shown to justify a different line.

The result is that the jurisprudence now has achieved what the Third United Nations Conference on the Law of the Sea (UNCLOS III) had been unable to do. It has given equidistance a prominence that states were not prepared to give during UNCLOS III. The Article 74/83 formula was not the result of agreement on a new rule – it was compromise wording in the face of no agreement. The wording allowed each side to take the view that its position had been preserved. What the ICJ has now done, and other international tribunals have endorsed, is to put equidistance as the starting point for delimitation into a favoured position, because unless the relevant circumstances push towards an alternative line then equidistance becomes the boundary. And whether or not that is likely to happen will depend on how willing courts and tribunals are to see the factors in question as justifying a deviation from a provisional equidistance line.

Furthermore, in adopting this approach the Court has made a complete *volte-face* from what it said in *Libya/Malta*. From the position that it could not accept that:

> even as a preliminary and provisional step towards the drawing of a delimitation line, the equidistance method is one which must be used, or that the Court is 'required, as a first step, to examine the effects of a delimitation by application of the equidistance method,'[72]

the Court has come to do precisely that.

4.7 How Adequate Is the New Law?

The rationale for the three-stage approach can variously be described as providing certainty, objectivity, and transparency.[73] An equidistance line

[72] *Libya/Malta*, n. 32, [43] quoting *Tunisia/Libya*, n. 23, [110].

[73] *Bangladesh/Myanmar*, n. 61, [228]; *Bangladesh v. India*, n. 65, [339]. In his Declaration in *Bangladesh/Myanmar*, Judge Wolfrum spoke of transparency and predictability and the need to rely on the decisions of courts and tribunals as an *acquis judiciare* (137).

provides an initial division of the area between the two states, or the area off the coasts of the states in the case of adjacent states, in a *prima facie* equal way – the line is always the same distance from the nearest points on the coasts of each state. This is more obvious in the case of opposite coasts, but in the case of adjacent states an equidistance line corresponds to the actual coastal features of each state. Thus there is a *prima facie* indicator of equity or equality against which the claims that there are relevant circumstances can be measured.

The three-stage approach provides something that did not previously exist in delimitation law, a starting point in the face of competing claims. When two parties put different lines before a tribunal, where does the tribunal start in measuring the equities of the two lines? This was a particular problem when the applicable law was customary international law. In the case of Article 6 there was potentially more guidance, but that depended on what view was taken of the hierarchy between equidistance and special circumstances. The new law has bypassed the starting point issue.

Why choose equidistance as the provisional line? Why not choose an angle bisector in the case of adjacent states, as some states have argued? The principal justification lies in the fact that an equidistance line can be easily drawn – it is to some extent a mechanical process once the nearest points on the coast of each state have been identified. A further justification is that an equidistance line provides a prima facie allocation of equal areas. But this equality can then be questioned to see whether it is the consequence of drawing a line from minor features or whether there are other relevant circumstances that have a significant impact on the location or direction of the line, or there is disproportion that impedes achieving an equitable solution.

In the case of adjacent states an angle bisector can achieve a result similar to that of equidistance. After all, an angle bisector is a simplified equidistance line. But, it requires the determination of lines of coastal direction, which involves choices of starting and end points for the coastal direction lines as well as the orientation of these lines. Depending on the configuration of the coast, this can involve more subjectivity than identifying points on the coast of each state that are at equal distances from points on the coast of the other state. Moreover, if the states have drawn baselines for the determination of their outer limits, these baselines can be used for constructing an equidistance line. However, if base points have to be identified, this is not just a technical matter. There may be questions of legal interpretation, for example does a feature constitute a low-tide elevation? But these questions of interpretation are limited. By contrast, selecting lines of coastal direction requires not legal interpretation but subjective judgments about coastal direction and geographical relationships. In short, an equidistance line has both practical and normative benefits.

Given that the applicable law deriving from Article 74/83 seems increasingly being interpreted to include a direction to apply the three-stage process, the question is whether the way in which the three-stage process is actually used by courts and tribunals can realize the potential benefits from starting with a provisional equidistance line. If not, the three-stage process will be a somewhat futile addition to the law of maritime boundary delimitation.[74]

As pointed out earlier, by making determinations of what constitute appropriate base points and in doing so seeking to construct equidistance lines that reflect the general direction of the coast,[75] the Court in *Black Sea* seems to have moved away from the primary objective of a provisional equidistance line. A provisional equidistance line divides the area on the basis of a form of equality – distance from coasts – which can then be reassessed in the light of features or factors that raise doubts about the equity of the solution thereby achieved and call for some adjustment to the line.

If the provisional equidistance line is already an adjusted equidistance line it is not clear against what standard the so-called relevant circumstances are to be assessed. The first and the second stages of delimitation have become merged which brings us back to the situation that courts were in before the two-stage and now three-stage approach was embarked upon. What is the starting point for considering the potentially competing factors or relevant circumstances other than the subjective views of the court or tribunal? The two-stage process was designed to provide an objective basis for assessing those factors, but if a provisional line has been drawn on the basis of the court's subjective conclusions about some of what are in fact relevant circumstances, then that claim to objectivity has less credibility.

When a court or tribunal makes the decision that an island, which on the basis of an equidistance line drawn strictly would be a base point, should not be included in the drawing of a provisional equidistance line, then it is no longer making decisions about base points – it is making

[74] For further discussion on this issue, see Chapter 8 of this volume.

[75] *Black Sea*, n. 48, [127–150].

decisions about the ultimate equitable solution. And that is something that the second stage, not the first stage, is meant to do.

Thus, in discarding Serpent's Island as a base point as the Court did in *Black Sea*, and disregarding St. Martin's Island as ITLOS did in *Myanmar/Bangladesh*, these tribunals undermined the value of the three-stage process. No longer were the relevant circumstances being measured against a line that reflected the actual geography, but rather they were measuring against refashioned geography, assuming that those two features did not exist. And by peremptorily dismissing those features at the first stage those bodies excluded the possibility of a more nuanced treatment in the second stage, which could involve consideration of the potential for applying a half or otherwise reduced effect. Indeed, avoiding the need to provide the fuller explanation that would be required at the second stage may be a motivation for courts to deal with a relevant circumstance at the first stage.[76]

The second stage should be the critical phase for determining what adjustments should be made to an equidistance line.[77] In the absence of any such adjustments, equidistance becomes the final boundary. In this regard, the decision in *Black Sea* is again instructive. The Court rejected all the claims to adjust the line in light of relevant circumstances. Three of those claims related to geographic considerations – the relative length of coasts, the existence of islands, and the cut-off effect – all of which have been raised in other cases as a justification for modifying equidistance. In respect of the relative lengths of coasts of the two states, the Court concluded that there were no particular marked disparities, although it noted that in determining the relevant coasts it had already excluded the coasts of the Karkinits'ka Gulf from consideration.[78] In respect of offshore islands, principally Serpent's Island, the Court saw no need for adjustment.[79] And in relation to the cut-off effect the Court simply asserted that the provisional equidistance line produced its effects in a 'reasonable and balanced way.'[80]

The second stage as applied in *Black Sea* seems no different from what courts and tribunals have always done in maritime delimitation – considered factors that might indicate where the location of the boundary

[76] See more generally Chapter 9 of this volume.
[77] See Chapter 9 in this volume for a more detailed discussion on relevant circumstances.
[78] *Black Sea*, n. 48, [168].
[79] Ibid., [187] [80] Ibid., [201].

should lie. And it is not evident from this case that any better approach has been developed. The relevance of the circumstances is assessed by the court or tribunal in the light of how such circumstances have been treated by tribunals in the past and on the basis of the tribunal's own subjective assessment of their importance. There do not seem to be any new, objective factors developed to provide assistance in this task.

The conclusion of ITLOS in *Bangladesh/Myanmar* that there was no cut-off because its adjusted line produced 'reasonable and balanced' effects[81] appears to be based more on intuition than analysis. In fact, neither ITLOS nor the Annex VII tribunal in *Bangladesh v. India* provided any clear indication of when cut-off occurs or what is the extent of the adjustment to an equidistance line is required when cut-off is found. The Annex VII tribunal did make the potentially helpful statement that cut-off occurs when the effect of the delimitation line is to block the coastal projection of a state out to its full extension as permitted by international law.[82] That statement has some resonance with the decision of the court of arbitration in *Canada/France*,[83] where the islands of St. Pierre and Miquelon were permitted a narrow projection seaward to the 200 nm limit that did not encroach on the south-facing coast of Newfoundland.

But what does blocking the coastal projection of a state mean in fact? Is there cut-off only when a state cannot get a full projection out to 200 nm or does a partial blocking constitute cut-off as well? And what is the full extent permitted under international law? Does this not beg the question that has to be answered? A state's entitlement under international law is dependent in part on where its maritime boundaries with opposite or adjacent states lie. In short, the jurisprudence on the consideration of relevant circumstances has not clarified the scope of relevant circumstances or the way in which adjustments should be made in the light of a finding of that a circumstance is relevant.

Nonetheless, three observations can be made. First, the category of factors that will be regarded as relevant circumstances is not large – there has been a consistent rejection of geological and geomorphological facts that goes back in time to *Tunisia/Libya*, before the development of the three-stage approach. Similarly, there is limited scope for arguing that fisheries, navigation, and security factors will be regarded as relevant circumstances, although there are some examples to be found in the jurisprudence.

[81] *Bangladesh/Myanmar*, n. 61, [335]. [82] *Bangladesh v. India*, n. 65, [417].

[83] *Case Concerning the Delimitation of Maritime Areas between Canada and France* (1992) 21 RIAA 265.

Second, the confusion between the first and second stages, so that factors that would otherwise be regarded as relevant circumstances have already been taken into account in the drawing of the provisional delimitation line, has made the determination of what constitute relevant circumstances more difficult to understand. In this regard, the rejection of Serpent's Island and St. Martin's Island in the drawing of the provisional equidistance lines, but then considering them again as relevant circumstances is particularly confusing. Presumably what is being considered in the second stage is whether their absence in the delimitation is a relevant circumstance, but this is not made clear in the Court's and the ITLOS's consideration of these issues.

Third, the jurisprudence has not made clear on the basis of what criteria certain circumstances are to be regarded as 'relevant' circumstances. To say that what is being sought is an equitable solution, does not really provide that basis. In a sense, courts and tribunals are no further ahead in trying to determine what should be taken into account in deciding what constitutes an equitable solution. In this regard, Wolfgang Friedmann's criticism of reliance on equity in *North Sea Continental Shelf* because there is no frame of reference for determining what is equitable still resonates today.[84]

The third step in the three-stage process is the test for disproportionality. This test has generally been applied by determining the ratio of the lengths of the relevant coasts of the two parties with the ratios of the relevant areas.[85] A sufficient discrepancy would indicate that there was a disproportionate result. Proportion and disproportion have been dealt with in a variety of ways in earlier cases. There was the notion of proportionality in *North Sea Continental Shelf*, disproportion in *Anglo-French Continental Shelf* and specific proportionality calculations in *Gulf of Maine*. The idea of area ratios compared with ratios of coastal lengths had been rejected in some other cases, and thus it was somewhat surprising to find the Court reverting to that approach in *Black Sea*.

An approach to proportionality that relies on coastal lengths and area relationships is essentially predetermined by conclusions on what constitutes relevant coasts and what constitutes the relevant area.[86] Further, the question also arises of the relationship between proportionality as a

[84] W. Friedmann, 'The North Sea Continental Shelf Cases – A Critique' (1970) 64 *American Journal of International Law* 229, 234–235.

[85] For a discussion of this test, see further Chapter 11 of this volume.

[86] For a discussion of this matter, see further Chapter 7 of this volume.

relevant circumstance and disproportion as a discrete test. The jurisprudence is not clear on this. In fact, if relevant circumstances have been fully assessed, there might be no need for a further disproportionality test.

4.8 Conclusions

Viewed from one perspective, there has been a considerable development in the applicable law relating to maritime boundary delimitation. Courts and tribunals have articulated a process to give effect to the basic rule of Article 74/83 of the LOSC. From a requirement that boundaries be delimited in accordance with international law, the ICJ has crafted a three-stage process involving the drawing of a provisional delimitation line, assessing the equity of the line in the light of relevant circumstances and then providing a final test to determine whether the result is not disproportionate. On the face of it this constitutes major progress in the development of the law applicable to maritime delimitation.

Yet, on closer analysis this development must be viewed with some caution. First, the provisional delimitation line is almost invariably an equidistance line, which in the absence of relevant circumstances or disproportion becomes the final boundary. In the result, maritime boundaries will now become equidistance or adjusted equidistance lines. In effect, equidistance has been elevated into an almost mandatory provision – a result that seems at odds with the objectives behind Article 74/83. Article 74/83 was not intended to privilege equidistance; rather, it was to put the Article 6 rule at the same level as equitable principles. That is not what is being achieved under the three-stage process. It might be said that what courts and tribunals have done is to reverse the result achieved in the LOSC – instead of being a principle or method which has no more weight than any other, equidistance is the primary and often the exclusive method.

One might ask whether this was inevitable. Was there any other way for courts and tribunals to reconcile the requirements of Article 6 with the notion of equitable principles under customary international law in order to come up with a satisfactory application of Article 74/83? To answer this, one has to look at the different aspects of what the courts and tribunals have done. The introduction of a provisional delimitation line to use as a basis for testing the equity of any proposed delimitation is valuable. However, the failure to come to terms with what is required in order to properly assess 'relevant circumstances' has turned the provisional line into a de facto final boundary. Only if a way can be found to provide for a proper assessment of relevant circumstances can the existing law free itself from the charge that it has become a cover for the reification of equidistance.

Second, the trend by courts and tribunals to make subjective judgments in the selection of base points, including disregarding particular features, diminishes the objective value of a provisional line drawn on the basis of geographic criteria against which the effect of relevant circumstances can be measured. If the three-stage process had a rationale, it was surely that it provided a context for considering relevant circumstances. In the absence of that objective basis for assessment, all the three-stage process does is provide a cover for the application of equidistance.

Third, the three-stage process does not provide any guidance on the key question in maritime delimitation – what weight is to be given to particular factors that arguably affect the equity of the final result? That has always been a central problem in maritime delimitation and courts and tribunals are no further ahead in answering that question than they were before the three-stage approach was developed.

Fourth, there is no consistency, and hence no clarity, in the description of the applicable law. Is the term 'equidistance-relevant circumstances' method a synonym for the 'three-stage approach,' or is it a description of methodology utilized in implementing the three-stage approach? And is there a difference between the 'equidistance-relevant circumstances approach' and the 'equitable principles-relevant circumstances approach'? These nuances in language and expression also undermine the transparency that courts and tribunals are seeking to achieve with the three-stage approach.

Fifth, the test of disproportionality, relying on calculations of coastal length and compared with areas allocated as a result of the delimitation, has its limitations. There is as yet not enough consistency in the way in which coastal lengths are calculated (the treatment of the Bay of Fundy in *Gulf of Maine* compared with the exclusion of the Karkinits'ka Gulf in *Black Sea*). Nor are there any agreed criteria for deciding on the relevant area. And there can be wide divergences in the ratios that are found not to be disproportionate. The process remains impressionistic.

What then might be done? Three suggestions can be made. First, the language of a 'provisional delimitation line' should be adopted, instead of provisional equidistance line. That leaves open in any case whether it is appropriate to draw an equidistance line, or for example an angle bisector, and the decision can be made in each case on the form of provisional line to choose in light of the particular geographic circumstances. In the case of adjacent states, an angle bisector might be a way to avoid choices over whether particular base points are appropriate and not just limited to cases where base points cannot be found. An angle bisector might also be seen as a way to adjust a provisional equidistance line in order to achieve an equitable solution.

Second, where equidistance is used as the provisional line, it should be drawn as a strict equidistance line. The determination of whether particular features (relevant circumstances) distort the line and require an adjustment should be left to the second stage.

Third, courts and tribunals should be more explicit in accepting or rejecting particular relevant circumstances and explaining more clearly why any adjustment to the line has to be made and how the extent of any adjustment can be justified.

Of course, there are no simple answers, particularly when the goal is the elusive notion of an 'equitable solution.' It is to the credit of courts and tribunals that they have tried to provide, through the development of the three-stage approach, results that are objectively justified. But, their efforts can hardly be regarded as an unalloyed success.

5

Provisional Measures and Provisional Arrangements

NATALIE KLEIN*

5.1 Introduction

The high stakes involved in maritime boundary disputes may prevent easy or prompt delimitation of the maritime areas in question. Maritime entitlements are inherently connected to a state's sovereignty and that state's exercise of rights and duties in respect of diverse ocean activities. As such, the national interest involved in dividing up those entitlements may trigger the most assertive claims possible. These potentially excessive claims to exclusivity may well clash with the claims of other states to either exclusive or inclusive use of the same ocean space. The disputes that result may prove complex, or even intractable.

Given the considerable national interests of the claimant states, and the possibility that immediate resolution of the competing claims is not evident, temporary solutions may be necessary. Such provisional arrangements reflect agreement between the states concerned as to how to regulate on a joint or agreed basis key maritime activities, such as fishing or other resource exploitation. The policy of allowing for provisional arrangements prior to an agreement on a continental shelf or exclusive economic zone (EEZ) boundary rests in the promotion of stability in the relations between states. To this effect, Charney wrote:

> Such arrangements enable States to make use of the disputed areas and to conduct normal relations there. In the absence of such arrangements, States may feel compelled at some cost, to forcefully challenge each other's actions in the area to maintain their legal rights.[1]

* Parts of this chapter are drawn from my earlier work: N. Klein, 'Provisional Measures and Provisional Arrangements in Maritime Boundary Disputes' (2006) 21 *International Journal of Marine and Coastal Law* 423.

[1] J. I. Charney, 'Progress in International Maritime Delimitation Law' (1994) 88 *American Journal of International Law* 227, 227.

These provisional arrangements will most typically be negotiated as between the states themselves, rather than imposed in the context of any binding dispute resolution process by a third party.

Provisional measures are another means of protecting state's interest in disputed ocean space pending the resolution of a maritime boundary dispute. Rather than agreed between the competing states, these measures will be sought unilaterally when the (usually) neighbouring states are commencing arbitration or adjudication. The justification for provisional measures derives from the:

> elementary juridical principle that the judgment of a court should be effective and that to ensure this it may, while a case is before the Court, be essential to restrain either party, or both, from disrupting the situation, or attempting to present its adversary with a *fait accompli*.[2]

There should be obvious scope for predictability considering that there will be common sources of tension in the context of a maritime boundary dispute. Tension may arise, for example as a result of perceived illegal fishing activities or alleged unlawful exploration activities for seabed resources. However, there is little consistency or predictability emerging from the case law on provisional arrangements and provisional measures as yet. Some recent decisions, when set against earlier incidents or factual settings in cases, provide an interesting insight into what may (or may not) be expected in this space in the years to come. The chapter first considers provisional arrangements as addressed in the United Nations Convention on the Law of the Sea (LOSC)[3] and its case law, highlighting the judicial interpretation of the relevant LOSC provisions in *Guyana v. Suriname*. I also consider how provisional arrangements have impacted on final maritime boundaries that have been delimited by courts and tribunals. There is a tension inasmuch as the LOSC notes that provisional arrangements are to be 'without prejudice to the final delimitation,' yet courts and tribunals have looked to these arrangements as indications of tacit agreements between the states.

The second part of the chapter focuses on provisional measures, examining the criteria for ordering such measures in maritime boundary cases. The final part of the chapter draws out the inter-relationship between

[2] J. G. Merrills, *International Dispute Settlement*, 5th ed. (Cambridge University Press Cambridge 2011) 124.

[3] United Nations Convention on the Law of the Sea, signed 10 December 1982; entered into force 16 November 1994, 1833 UNTS 397.

provisional arrangements and provisional measures in terms of possible overlap of standards and how the two might be expected to work in harmony. I endeavour to set out what elements of consistency have, or may, emerge and to what extent these elements may be predictable in the future.

5.2 Provisional Arrangements

The obligation and the relevant legal standard for provisional arrangements are set out in the LOSC. For the delimitation of the EEZ between states with opposite or adjacent coasts and overlapping entitlements, Article 74(3) of the LOSC provides:

> Pending agreement as provided for in paragraph 1, the States concerned, in a spirit of understanding and cooperation, shall make every effort to enter into provisional arrangements of a practical nature and, during this transitional period, not to jeopardize or hamper the reaching of the final agreement. Such arrangements shall be without prejudice to the final delimitation.

An identical provision is included in Article 83(3) of LOSC in relation to the delimitation of the continental shelf.[4]

The different formulations proposed during the drafting of this paragraph concerned either a preventive rule, or an incentive approach to provisional arrangements.[5] The former refers to preventing any sort of damage by restraining activities in the area of overlapping entitlements, whereas the latter approach sought to provide practical arrangements to allow for provisional utilization pending final delimitation.[6] The preventive approach was not intended to be too extreme, however, as a proposal for a moratorium on economic activities in the disputed area was rejected during the negotiations.[7] Paragraph 3 of Articles 74 and 83 'represent[s] a compromise that combines two basically different views on interim measures: they involve attempts either to promote certain measures or to restrict others.'[8]

Articles 74(3) and 83(3) reflected existing state practice demonstrating joint provisional arrangements between states pending the final

[4] LOSC, Art. 83(3).

[5] R. Lagoni, 'Interim Measures Pending Maritime Delimitation Agreements' (1984) 78 *American Journal of International Law* 345, 351.

[6] Ibid. [7] Ibid., 352. [8] Ibid., 353–354.

determination of their maritime boundary.[9] Since the adoption of the LOSC, states have considered these requirements in reaching agreements on provisional arrangements.[10] However, common paragraph 3 is not a provision of the LOSC that has prompted significant judicial interpretation. This part examines the first, and so far only, judicial interpretation of Articles 74(3) and 83(3) in *Guyana v. Suriname*. Given there is a paucity of case law on the requirement to enter into provisional arrangements, this decision must be tested for the likelihood of creating a benchmark for consistency and predictability going forward. Where there is more consistency and predictability emerging in relation to provisional arrangements is the judicial consideration afforded to this practice in delimiting maritime boundaries. These dimensions are all examined in this part.

5.2.1 Judicial Interpretation in Guyana v. Suriname

In the boundary dispute between Guyana and Suriname, the arbitral tribunal not only delimited a single maritime boundary between the two states, but also considered their respective duties in relation to Articles 74(3) and 83(3). This issue arose because Guyana had issued oil concessions within the disputed area and pursuant to one of those concessions, CGX Resources Inc. had arranged for seismic testing of the area.[11] Following failed diplomatic efforts for CGX to cease its activities, two patrol boats from the Surinamese navy approached a CGX oil rig and drill ship, ordering it to leave within twelve hours or 'the consequences would be theirs.'[12] The CGX crew detached the oil rig from the sea floor and opted

[9] E.g. Davenport has noted ten provisional arrangements agreed between ASEAN member states, even though not all of these arrangements were in effect at the time of writing. T. Davenport, 'ASEAN Approaches to Maritime Boundary Disputes: Wider Implications for ASEAN' (2013) 107 *Proceedings of the Annual Meeting of the American Society of International Law* 281, 282. See further V. Becker-Weinberg, *Joint Development of Hydrocarbon Deposits in the Law of the Sea* (Springer Hamburg 2014) 95–103; Z. Wang, 'Disputes over Fishery Resources and Maritime Boundary Delimitation of the Diaoyu Islands: An Analysis' (2009) 1 *China Oceans Law Review* 310.

[10] This practice has been examined in British Institute of International and Comparative Law, *Report on the Obligations of States under Articles 74(3) and 83(3) of UNCLOS in respect of Undelimited Maritime Areas* (2016) ('BIICL').

[11] *Arbitral Tribunal Constituted pursuant to Art. 287, and in accordance with Annex VII of the United Nations Convention on the Law of the Sea, In the Matter of an Arbitration between Guyana and Suriname (Guyana v. Suriname)*, award of 17 September 2007, 30 RIAA 1, [151]. Drilling for core samples was also commenced as part of this operation. See ibid., [433].

[12] Ibid. See also [150]–[151].

to leave the concession area.[13] This incident prompted allegations before the tribunal that Suriname had violated the prohibition on the threat or use of force as contained in Article 2(4) of the UN Charter and the obligation to settle disputes by peaceful means,[14] and both Suriname and Guyana claimed the other had violated its obligations concerning provisional arrangements as set out in Articles 74(3) and 83(3).

The tribunal considered that provisional arrangements:

> have been recognized as important tools in achieving the objectives of the Convention, and it is for this reason that the Convention imposes an obligation on parties to a dispute to 'make every effort' to reach such arrangements.[15]

Yet reference to provisional arrangements 'of a practical nature' has been criticized as 'so vague that it can be of little practical assistance in establishing interim measures.'[16] The LOSC requirement leaves states with considerable discretion in reaching agreement on what temporary measures should be taken.[17] Most typically, it could be expected that the provisional arrangement would be a temporary boundary line or joint arrangements governing all or distinct aspects of the disputed area.[18]

The *Guyana v. Suriname* tribunal took the view that the LOSC provision was intended 'to promote interim regimes and practical measures that could pave the way for provisional utilization of disputed areas pending delimitation.'[19] On the facts of the case, the tribunal found that Guyana was in violation of this obligation for its failure to engage Suriname in discussions concerning its drilling program at an earlier stage and providing no opportunity for Suriname to participate in any way.[20] Guyana's

13 Ibid., [151]. 14 Ibid., [425]–[431]. 15 Ibid., [464].

16 D. J. Attard, *The Exclusive Economic Zone in International Law* (Oxford University Press Oxford 1987) 228. See also Lagoni, n. 5, 359 ('The content of such arrangements is to be determined by the parties concerned and depends upon the circumstances of each individual case').

17 'The substantive content of this cooperative requirement is uncertain.' D. M. Ong, 'Joint Development of Common Offshore Oil and Gas Deposits: "Mere" State Practice or Customary International Law?' (1999) 93 *American Journal of International Law* 771, 784.

18 See BIICL, n. 10, [51]. 19 *Guyana v. Suriname*, n. 11, [460].

20 Ibid., [477]. The Tribunal noted:

> Steps that Guyana could have taken consistent with efforts to enter into provisional arrangements include (1) giving Suriname official and detailed notice of the planned activities, (2) seeking cooperation of Suriname in undertaking the activities, (3) offering to share the results of the exploration and giving Suriname an opportunity to observe the activities, and (4) offering to share all the financial benefits received from the exploratory activities. (ibid.)

lack of co-operation with Suriname placed it in violation of the LOSC requirements.[21] Suriname had also violated this obligation in resorting to self-help measures against CGX, rather than actively attempting to negotiate with Guyana.[22]

The LOSC text makes clear that states are under no obligation to devise provisional arrangements, but must only endeavour to reach agreement on these arrangements.[23] The importance of this requirement should not be completely dismissed, however. The obligation to negotiate in good faith 'is not merely a nonbinding recommendation or encouragement, but a mandatory rule whose breach would represent a violation of international law.'[24] Lagoni describes the obligation as follows:

> As its purpose is to protect the mutual rights of the States concerned, the obligation to negotiate can generally be assumed to arise whenever one of those States considers it necessary and proper to enter into negotiations on provisional arrangements ... The obligation ceases when the final delimitation agreement is reached.[25]

The tribunal in *Guyana v. Suriname* held that there was a duty to negotiate in good faith in pursuit of provisional arrangements of a practical nature.[26]

In relation to what might constitute an obligation to negotiate in good faith, the International Court of Justice (ICJ) assessed this duty in *North Sea Continental Shelf*. The Court considered that this duty entailed more than merely going through a formal process, but that the negotiations had to be meaningful.[27] To be meaningful, it was not enough for either of the parties 'to insist [...] upon its own position without contemplating any modification of it.'[28] Failure to reach agreement does not nullify the other obligation contained in Articles 74(3) and 83(3), namely not to jeopardize or hamper the reaching of the final agreement.[29]

The *Guyana v. Suriname* tribunal further considered that the LOSC provision entailed a negative obligation not to jeopardize or hamper the

[21] See J. Gao, 'Comments on *Guyana v. Suriname*' (2009) 8 *Chinese Journal of International Law* 191, 203.

[22] *Guyana v. Suriname*, n. 11, [476].

[23] 'This would seem to be an obligation of conduct, not of result.' BIICL, n. 9, [47].

[24] Lagoni, n. 4, 354. See also Ong, n. 17, 784 (noting that the duty to negotiate in good faith is 'widely recognized as a general principle well-founded in international law').

[25] Lagoni, n. 4, 358–359.

[26] *Guyana v. Suriname*, n. 11, [461].

[27] *North Sea Continental Shelf Cases (Federal Republic of Germany/Denmark; Federal Republic of Germany/Netherlands)* [1969] ICJ Rep. 3, [85].

[28] Ibid. See also BIICL, n. 9, [35]–[37].

[29] BIICL, n. 9, [41].

reaching of the final agreement, although the time period for this obligation was unclear.[30] The tribunal's interpretation of this obligation admitted the possibility of some activity in the disputed area, so long as those activities would not prejudice the reaching of a final agreement.[31] The 'acts that do cause physical change would have to be undertaken pursuant to an agreement between the parties to be permissible, as they may hamper or jeopardize the reaching of a final agreement on delimitation.'[32] While the tribunal emphasized activities that could 'lead to a permanent physical change' as a violation of this obligation,[33] it was still acknowledged that Articles 74(3) and 83(3) were 'not intended to preclude all activities in a disputed maritime area.'[34] To this end, the tribunal stated:

> [U]nilateral acts that cause a physical damage to the marine environment will generally be comprised in a class of activities that can be undertaken only jointly or by agreement between the parties. This is due to the fact that these activities may jeopardize or hamper the reaching of a final delimitation agreement as a result of the perceived change to the status quo that they would engender. Indeed, such activities could be perceived to, or may genuinely, prejudice the position of the other party in the delimitation dispute, thereby both hampering or jeopardizing the reaching of a final agreement.[35]

Moreover, '[i]t should not be permissible for a party to a dispute to undertake any unilateral activity that might affect *the other party's rights* in a permanent manner.'[36] The tribunal thus appears to recognize that the duty not to jeopardize or hamper might be breached because of a permanent physical change and also because of a permanent change to the rights of the other party. What precisely might fall into these categories may ultimately depend on the particular factual circumstances existing between the parties concerned and even potentially their subjective views as to how their rights are implicated.[37]

In addition, as discussed immediately below, the likelihood of developing a consistent and predictable approach to the enforcement of Articles 74(3) and 83(3) is further reduced when considering the possible

[30] See discussion in Y. Tanaka, 'Unilateral Exploration and Exploitation of Natural Resources in Disputed Areas: A Note on the Ghana/Côte d'Ivoire Order of 25 April 2015 before the Special Chamber of ITLOS' (2015) 46 *Ocean Development and International Law* 315, 316.

[31] *Guyana v. Suriname*, n. 11, [460] and [465]. [32] *Guyana v. Suriname*, n. 11, [467].

[33] Ibid. [34] Ibid. [35] Ibid., [480]. [36] Ibid., [470] (emphasis added).

[37] Y. van Logchem, 'The Scope for Unilateralism in Disputed Maritime Areas,' in C. Schofield, S. Lee, and M.-S. Kwon (eds.), *The Limits of Maritime Jurisdiction* (Martinus Nijhoff Leiden 2014) 186. See also BIICL, n. 9, [83]–[84].

hurdles to accessing compulsory dispute settlement procedures under the LOSC. Therefore, while the *Guyana v. Suriname* tribunal gave some broad parameters as to what might jeopardize or hamper the reaching of a final agreement, with its emphasis on permanency, there remains a wide scope to assess the activities concerned depending of the particular factual matrix. As a result, consistency and predictability are hard to attain under Articles 74(3) and 83(3).

5.2.2 *Enforcing the* Guyana v. Suriname *Requirements in Future Litigation*

Guyana v. Suriname highlights the possibility of a greater range of inter-state claims in the context of maritime boundary litigation; any state's purported use of the disputed ocean area may be held up as a violation of the LOSC articles on provisional arrangements. These activities may need to be considered in addition to the arguments as to the actual delimitation of the maritime boundary. Yet there are possible barriers to any burgeoning case law on provisional arrangements under the LOSC dispute settlement procedures.

Article 286 of the LOSC provides:

> Subject to section 3, any dispute concerning the interpretation or application of this Convention shall, where no settlement has been reached by recourse to section 1, be submitted at the request of any party to the dispute to the court or tribunal having jurisdiction under this section.

Under Section 1 of Part XV, states are to seek to settle their disputes peacefully,[38] and may be required to utilize pre-existing dispute settlement agreements instead of those set out in the LOSC.[39] Section 3 includes limitations to the availability of compulsory procedures entailing binding decisions and allows for states to exclude delimitation disputes 'concerning the interpretation or application of Articles 15, 74, and 83 relating to sea boundary delimitations' if a state so declares when becoming a party to the LOSC or at any time thereafter.[40] Disputes relating to provisional

[38] See LOSC, Art. 279. This provision reinforces the obligation in Arts. 74(2) and 83(2) to the effect: 'If no agreement can be reached within a reasonable period of time, the states concerned shall resort to the procedures provided for in Part XV.' This latter obligation is discussed further in Part IV, below.

[39] See LOSC, Art. 281 and Art. 282. The relevance of Art. 282 in a maritime boundary delimitation was before the ICJ in *Maritime Delimitation in the Indian Ocean (Somalia v. Kenya)*.

[40] LOSC, Art. 298(1)(a).

arrangements pursuant to Articles 74(3) and 83(3) would be captured by this exclusion because these arrangements directly relate to actions to be undertaken so as not to prejudice the final delimitation.

A state may otherwise have to argue that the activities of the other state violated the exclusive rights afforded to coastal states under Articles 56 and 77 in relation to the EEZ and the continental shelf, respectively. Such a position has been foreshadowed by Côte d'Ivoire's arguments in challenging the potential infringement of its rights by Ghana's activities in the provisional measures stage of *Ghana/Côte d'Ivoire*.[41] In this context, state A would argue that its exclusive right to explore and exploit natural resources has been violated by state B on the assumption that the maritime area in question belonged to state A and not state B. In a contested maritime area, either of the states in dispute could potentially argue that the other has failed to show due regard for the possible rights of the other state in proceeding with activities in the undelimited area.[42] Disputes relating to those provisions would not necessarily fall outside of jurisdiction under the LOSC even where the maritime boundary delimitation itself may not be addressed because of a declaration under Article 298.

In a factual scenario where one state's activities have been challenged by the other, as occurred in *Guyana v. Suriname*, questions concerning the legality of law enforcement activities, or potentially military activities, may also be optionally excluded from compulsory dispute settlement under Article 298 of the LOSC.[43] If Suriname's characterization of its activities as law enforcement had been accepted, it would not necessarily have fallen within the optional exception for law enforcement activities, however, as that exception is only relevant for enforcement activities relating to fishing or marine scientific research. A dispute as to whether commercial research for mineral exploitation falls within the definition of marine scientific research could well be pursued.

There are, though, factual scenarios where one state is considered to be fishing unlawfully in a contested maritime area. Such a claim was raised against China by the Philippines in *South China Sea*. Law enforcement

[41] See discussion below, n. 79–108.

[42] A due regard requirement is imposed on coastal states under Art. 56(2) and on other states in Art. 58(3).

[43] There is a further exception in Art. 298 relating to matters over which the UN Security Council is exercising its functions. This exception may be relevant if there is a situation comparable to the *Aegean Sea Continental Shelf* case wherein Greece also brought its objections to Turkey's seabed activities to the UN Security Council, as well as instituting proceedings before the ICJ.

against this activity would likely fall outside a court or tribunal's jurisdiction where a declaration is in force under Article 298(1)(b) of the LOSC. Presumably, where there are overlapping maritime entitlements that cannot be delimited because of an Article 298(1)(a) exception, it could not be ascertained who was the coastal state entitled to enforce its laws. Once again, only the due regard obligation might be relevant in this setting. In *South China Sea*, the tribunal was able to assess the legality of China's fishing and law enforcement actions because it determined that the Philippines was the relevant coastal state in the absence of any overlapping maritime entitlements.[44]

If the activities of one state in seeking to prevent what it considers illegal exploitation activities in a disputed maritime area prompts a military response, as the tribunal found to be the case in *Guyana v. Suriname*, the military activities exception may then be applicable to prevent the exercise of jurisdiction. In *South China Sea*, the tribunal did not rule on Chinese conduct that prevented the Philippines from undertaking the resupply and rotation of Philippine troops on Second Thomas Shoal on the basis that it was a 'quintessentially military situation.'[45] The tribunal therefore lacked jurisdiction to determine the legality of China's conduct in light of China's declaration under Article 298.[46] This exception was not applicable in *Guyana v. Suriname*. An activity that is found to be an unlawful threat of force would appropriately fall within this exception.

There are therefore a number of hurdles that must be overcome if we are to see a growth in case law in relation to provisional arrangement obligations under the LOSC. Even if jurisdiction is limited because of possible exceptions under Article 298, states may wish to pursue claims that other rights under the LOSC are violated even if Articles 74(3) and 83(3) are not immediately at issue. If states were to pursue claims under, for examples, Articles 56 and 58 rather than Articles 74(3) and 83(3), it would be useful for a court or tribunal to interpret the due regard standards by reference to the obligations not to jeopardize or hamper the resolution of the final maritime boundary in order to promote consistency in standards around state conduct pending the resolution of the maritime boundaries.

Guyana v. Suriname has provided useful guidance as to considerations in deciding whether Articles 74(3) and 83(3) have been violated. Yet even where a case is instituted, commentators have queried whether the permanent change to the seabed standard is appropriate in determining if these provisions have been violated. For instance, in an analysis of the

[44] *South China Sea*, [697]. [45] Ibid., [1161]. [46] Ibid., [1162].

Guyana v. Suriname decision, Fietta has noted the technological developments in seismic surveys since the *Aegean Sea Continental Shelf* order and commented:

> Unilateral seismic exploration could, therefore, in some circumstances, significantly alter the status quo as regards the comparative levels of knowledge of two neighboring States about the value of all (or part) of a disputed maritime area. Such a disequilibrium in knowledge between two States could, in many cases, make a final delimitation agreement more difficult to obtain.[47]

As will be discussed below, *Ghana/Côte d'Ivoire* has acknowledged the sensitivities relating to commercial information and may indicate another dimension to consider in assessing alleged violations of Articles 74(3) and 83(3).

5.2.3 *Effect of Provisional Arrangements in Maritime Boundary Cases*

Articles 74(3) and 83(3) expressly provide that provisional arrangements are 'without prejudice to the final delimitation.' This position was necessary to avoid a scenario whereby states reaching provisional arrangements prior to the final delimitation could prompt a tribunal or court to decide that this arrangement is indicative of an 'equitable solution' for the purposes of the permanent boundary.[48] Oxman observed in this regard:

> Fears that a modus vivendi may, for political or juridical reasons, evolve into a permanent boundary or boundary regime may limit the ability of the parties to find means to control the scope and intensity of their dispute.[49]

While state conduct is scrutinized in maritime boundary cases, a distinction may be appropriate between unilateral conduct (including where that conduct accounts – or appears to account – for the other state's rights) and jointly agreed provisional arrangements. Whereas the latter would seem to fall within Articles 74(3) and 83(3), the former may be examined where one party argues that the working assumption of the parties reflected their recognition of an equitable solution. The ICJ has established

[47] S. Fietta, 'International Court of Justice Judgment on Sovereignty over Disputed Islands, and Delimitation of the Territorial Sea, Exclusive Economic Zone, and Continental Shelf Guyana/Suriname,' (2008) 102 *American Journal of International Law* 119, 127.

[48] Consistent with the requirements of Arts. 74(1) and 83(1) of the LOSC.

[49] B. H. Oxman, 'International Maritime Boundaries: Political, Strategic, and Historical Considerations,' (1994–1995) 26 *University of Miami Inter-American Law Review* 243, 290.

maritime boundaries based on tacit agreement in its earlier decisions.[50] In subsequent cases, the Court has set a relatively high threshold for states to establish that a boundary based on state conduct has been established.[51] Under the LOSC, the *Guyana v. Suriname* tribunal's review of case law on this issue led it to note a 'marked reluctance of international courts and tribunals to accord significance to the oil practice of the parties in the determination of the delimitation line.'[52] The tribunal also acknowledged Suriname's argument that restraint on the part of one of the parties in relation to conduct in the disputed area should not be used to prejudice the position of that party.[53]

In setting a high threshold for the purposes of unilateral conduct demonstrating a tacit agreement, there is an alignment with the concept that provisional arrangements should be without prejudice. That is, states should be able to take action to regulate and use their maritime areas without it prejudicing the agreement on any final maritime boundary. What unilateral conduct is permissible in this context must be informed by the obligation in Articles 74(3) and 83(3) not to jeopardize or hamper the reaching of the final maritime boundary delimitation agreement.

5.3 Provisional Measures

Provisional measures have rarely been sought pending the resolution of a maritime boundary dispute before a court or tribunal. More commonly, the states in dispute have established a moratorium on activities or devised their own interim arrangements pending the outcome of their case.[54] This sort of arrangement has usually been possible where the states are also in agreement to submit their maritime boundary dispute to a court or tribunal. However, where one state institutes proceedings against another state, the unilateral nature of the submission may prompt a greater need for court-ordered provisional measures as the relationship between the

[50] See e.g. *Continental Shelf (Tunisia/Libyan Arab Jamahiriya)* [1982] ICJ Rep. 18.

[51] See e.g. *Territorial and Maritime Dispute between Nicaragua and Honduras in the Caribbean Sea (Nicaragua v. Honduras)* (Judgment) [2007] ICJ Rep. 659, [237]–[258]; *Land and Maritime Boundary between Cameroon and Nigeria (Cameroon v. Nigeria; Equatorial Guinea Intervening)* [2002] ICJ Rep. 303; *Maritime Dispute (Peru v. Chile)* (Judgment), 2014 ICJ Rep. 3, [91].

[52] *Guyana v. Suriname*, n. 11, [390].

[53] *Guyana v. Suriname*, n. 11, [236].

[54] See N. Klein, 'Provisional Measures and Provisional Arrangements in Maritime Boundary Disputes,' (2006) 21 *International Journal of Marine and Coastal Law* 423, 435–438.

states in question may not be sufficiently conducive to permit agreement on temporary arrangements pending the decision.

5.3.1 *Requirements for Provisional Measures*

Although the language of the ICJ and ITLOS Statutes is different in the grant of authority for the use of provisional measures pending the resolution of a dispute, the criteria considered by each institution have been similarly applied in their cases. Tanaka has identified five elements:

> (i) Prima facie jurisdiction; (ii) the plausible character of the alleged rights in the principal request; (iii) a link between the alleged rights and the measures requested; (iv) urgency; and (v) risk of irreparable prejudice.[55]

The prescription of provisional measures under the LOSC specifically references the protection of the marine environment as a consideration for provisional measures.[56] In this regard, the situation is slightly distinct to that before the ICJ when it is acting on a basis of jurisdiction other than the LOSC. The ICJ could well consider risk of environmental harm as a reason to indicate provisional measures, but its mandate in this regard is not as specific as for the courts or tribunals operating under the LOSC.

How these elements have been borne out in the experience of the ICJ and the ITLOS in cases involving provisional measures requests pending the outcome of maritime boundary disputes in particular is considered in the following sections.

5.3.1.1 Before the ICJ

Article 41(1) of the ICJ Statute provides for the indication of provisional measures as follows: 'The Court shall have the power to indicate, if it considers that circumstances so require, any provisional measures which ought to be taken to preserve the respective rights of either party.'

The ICJ has evolved the relevant standard over the course of its decisions. Among the criteria to be established for the indication of provisional measures, there must be *prima facie* jurisdiction. In assessing whether treaty provisions invoked appear on their face to afford grounds on which jurisdiction might be based for the indication of interim measures, the ICJ has stated that the relevant inquiry is whether 'the dispute appears, *prima facie*, to afford a possible basis on which the jurisdiction of the Court might

[55] Tanaka, n. 35, 317. [56] LOSC, Art. 290(1).

be founded.'[57] In explaining this standard in *Interhandl*, Judge Lauterpacht stated:

> The Court may properly act under the terms of article 41 provided that there is in existence an instrument... which prima facie confers jurisdiction upon the Court and which incorporates no reservations obviously excluding its jurisdiction.[58]

One of the rare instances of the ICJ addressing the question of whether provisional measures should be indicated prior to the delimitation of a maritime boundary arose in the context of a dispute between Greece and Turkey as to the delimitation of their respective continental shelves in the Aegean Sea. The issue came before the Court following Turkey's decision to grant its state petroleum company a license covering continental shelf areas that were also claimed by Greece.[59] Upon the grant of this license, a Turkish vessel then proceeded to conduct seismic tests in the contested area.[60] These tests involved the vessel causing small explosions to occur so as to send sound waves that could then indicate the geophysical structure of the earth beneath it.[61] In instituting proceedings, Greece sought interim measures from the ICJ claiming that the exploration activities undertaken by Turkey caused irreparable prejudice and aggravated the dispute.

Greece requested an order from the Court that Turkey 'refrain from all exploration activity or any scientific research' in the disputed areas, as well as 'refrain from taking further military measures or actions which may endanger their peaceful relations.'[62] In seeking this request, Greece sought to emphasize that the coastal state has exclusive rights over continental shelf areas and so any resource-related activity would violate these rights, as the knowledge gained by an entity other than the coastal state risked irreparably prejudicing Greece's rights.[63] Greece clearly sought to preserve the marketability of its title to the areas in question:

> Turkey's seismic exploration threatens in particular to destroy the exclusivity of the rights claimed by Greece to acquire information concerning

[57] See e.g. *Fisheries Jurisdiction Case (UK v. Iceland)* (Request for the Indication of Interim Measures of Protection) [1972] ICJ Rep. 4; *Fisheries Jurisdiction Case (FDR v. Iceland)* (Request for the Indication of Interim Measures of Protection) [1972] ICJ Rep. 30 (hereinafter *Icelandic Fisheries*), [15] and [17].

[58] *Interhandl Case (Switzerland v. US)* [1957] ICJ Rep. 105, 118–119.

[59] *Aegean Sea Continental Shelf Case (Greece v. Turkey)* (Request for the Indication of Interim Measures of Protection) [1976] ICJ Rep. 3, [16].

[60] See ibid., [30]. [61] See ibid. [62] Ibid., [2]. [63] Ibid., [15] and [17].

> the availability, extent and location of the natural resources of the areas; that the acquisition and dissemination of such information without the consent of Greece prejudices its negotiating position in relation to potential purchasers of exploitation licenses, thereby permanently impairing its sovereign rights with respect to the formulation of its national energy policy.'[64]

Turkey, although not appearing in the case, communicated to the Court that the interim measures should not be indicated because *inter alia* Turkey's exploration activities did not cause harm to the rights of Greece and even if there was some prejudice, then it could be remedied through the appropriate reparations.[65]

The ICJ considered that a finding of Greece suffering irreparable prejudice to its potential rights over the continental shelf was a prerequisite for an order of interim measures.[66] The Court recognized that the activity being carried out by the Turkish vessel did not involve any risk of physical damage to the seabed or subsoil or to the natural resources, nor did it involve the establishment of any installations or other permanent structures on the seabed.[67] The ICJ concluded that there was no risk of irreparable prejudice to Greece, and that the exclusivity of the right claimed by Greece could be capable of reparations, should the Court ultimately determine that the contested areas appertained to Greece.[68] In reaching this conclusion, the ICJ appeared more focused on the preservation of rights, rather than seeking to avoid any aggravation of the dispute.[69] Moreover, the ICJ considered that Greece was at most subject to economic harm through Turkey's activities, and this sort of harm could be properly remedied through reparations, if necessary.[70]

64 Ibid., [26]. 65 Ibid., [18]. 66 Ibid., [25].

67 Ibid., [30]. The Court further stated:

> [T]he continued seismic exploration activities undertaken by Turkey are all of the transitory character just described, and do not involve the establishment of installations on or above the sea-bed of the continental shelf; and . . . no suggestion has been made that Turkey has embarked upon any operations involving the actual appropriation or other use of the natural resources of the areas of the continental shelf which are in dispute. (ibid.)

68 Ibid., [32]. But see ibid., [38] (Dissenting Opinion of Judge ad hoc Stassinopoulos) (arguing that irreparable prejudice was caused by the gathering of resource-related information and its possible dissemination).

69 See ibid., [28] (Separate Opinion of Judge Elias). See also ibid., [30] (Separate Opinion of Judge Elias) (emphasizing that the Court allows for a state to violate a coastal state's rights in the knowledge that compensation will be payable, if necessary).

70 Ibid., [33].

The only other occasion that the Court has considered provisional measures in the context of a disputed maritime zone claim was in *Icelandic Fisheries*, which were submitted by Germany and the UK against Iceland. These cases related to Iceland's extension of its exclusive maritime rights into an area that was previously considered high seas and thereby affected the rights of all other users of the area. The UK and Germany sought to challenge the lawfulness of Iceland's extension of its exclusive fisheries jurisdiction to a fifty-mile limit, and requested interim measures from the Court to prevent Iceland from enforcing these claimed rights against British and German fishing vessels in the disputed area. The applicant states also asked the Court to indicate that they were entitled to a specified annual fish catch total from a defined area.[71]

As in *Aegean Sea Continental Shelf*, the Court stated that the object of Article 41 was:

> to preserve the respective rights of the Parties pending the decision of the Court, and presupposes that irreparable prejudice should not be caused to rights which are the subject of the dispute in judicial proceedings and that the Court's judgment should not be anticipated by reason of any initiative regarding the measures which are in issue.[72]

In this regard, the Court considered that Iceland's extension of an area of exclusive fisheries jurisdiction would prejudice the rights of the applicant states and 'affect the possibility of their full restoration in the event of a judgment in [their] favour.'[73] Although acknowledging the potential prejudice to be incurred by the applicants, the Court also took into account the 'exceptional dependence' of Iceland on its coastal fisheries.[74] In seeking to balance the respective rights of the parties pending the resolution of the dispute, the Court decided that it would set a total annual fish catch lower than that requested by the applicants, but based on statistics of the previous five years that accounted for the increasing restriction on the amount of fish harvested.[75]

The Court's approach in these two cases demonstrates that the nature of the resource-related activity is determinative of whether a coastal state's rights in a contested maritime zone are likely to be prejudiced and thereby warrant the indication of provisional measures. In *Aegean Sea Continental Shelf*, mere research activities of a transitory nature could not be viewed as

[71] *Fisheries Jurisdiction Case*, n. 57, [1]. [72] Ibid., [21].
[73] Ibid., [22]. [74] Ibid., [23]. [75] Ibid., [25] and [26].

impacting on Greece's potential rights to the contested continental shelf area, even though such research could have been quite detrimental to the economic value of Greece's rights should that area have been attributed to it in the judgment on the merits.[76] Equally, in *Icelandic Fisheries*, fishing could be continued in the disputed area, presumably because the Court considered that Iceland may also have been entitled to compensation for any economic loss from excess fishing by British and German vessels. The decision may have been distinguishable from *Aegean Sea Continental Shelf*, however, as arguably the catching of fish is more permanent in nature than seismic testing. The Court nonetheless seemed to recognize that excess fish catch amounts may have been prejudicial to Iceland in its decision indicating that a smaller total should be harvested than requested by the applicants. In sum, the Court considered that there was some risk of irreparable prejudice with permanent resource-related activities and that such a risk could be tempered through the indication of provisional measures, but otherwise appropriate reparations would adequately compensate a state for any other infringement of its rights pending the final delimitation of the maritime boundary.

5.3.1.2 Under the LOSC

Article 290(1) of the LOSC permits a court or tribunal with *prima facie* jurisdiction to prescribe provisional measures that are 'appropriate under the circumstances to preserve the respective rights of the parties to the dispute or to prevent serious harm to the marine environment, pending the final decision.' Measures may also be sought from the ITLOS pending the constitution of an arbitral tribunal under the procedure in paragraph 5 of Article 290,[77] where the 'urgency of the situation' so requires.[78] If a state seeks provisional measures before the resolution of a maritime boundary dispute, Article 290 requires certain conditions to be fulfilled prior to the prescription of provisional measures. At time of writing, only one

[76] This case was not ultimately decided on the merits, as the Court decided that it lacked jurisdiction.

[77] Prior to the constitution of an arbitral tribunal, provisional measures can be sought under Art. 290(5) from 'any court or tribunal agreed upon by the parties or, failing such agreement within two weeks from the date of the request for provisional measures, the International Tribunal for the Law of the Sea or, with respect to activities in the Area, the Seabed Disputes Chamber.' LOSC, Art. 290(5).

[78] *Southern Bluefin Tuna Cases (Australia v. Japan; New Zealand v. Japan)* (Provisional Measures) (Order of 27 August 1999) 117 ILR 148 (Separate Opinion of Judge Treves) (commenting on the differing application of 'urgency' in paras. 1 and 5 of Art. 290).

maritime boundary dispute to be resolved under the LOSC dispute settlement procedures has involved a request for provisional measures.

In the 2015 dispute between Ghana and Côte d'Ivoire, Côte d'Ivoire sought provisional measures from the Special Chamber of the ITLOS that was constituted to hear the case.[79] Côte d'Ivoire requested an order from the Special Chamber requiring Ghana to suspend all ongoing oil exploration and exploitation activities in the disputed area, as well as refrain from any new permits for such activity in the disputed area.[80] Further, Côte d'Ivoire sought an order that Ghana refrain from using any information relating to any exploration activities in any way that would be to Côte d'Ivoire's detriment.[81] Côte d'Ivoire also requested that all steps be taken to preserve the continental shelf, its superjacent waters and its subsoil, and that no unilateral actions be taken that would risk prejudicing the rights of Côte d'Ivoire or aggravate the dispute.

The first basic prerequisite is that the relevant court or tribunal has *prima facie* jurisdiction.[82] Similar to the ICJ, tribunals constituted under the LOSC have considered that there was *prima facie* jurisdiction where 'there is nothing which manifestly and in terms excludes the tribunal's jurisdiction.'[83] Jurisprudence under the LOSC has so far indicated that bars to a finding that no jurisdiction exists on a *prima facie* basis include:

[79] Ghana had initially instituted proceedings against Côte d'Ivoire, shortly after removing its declaration under Art. 298 excluding maritime boundary delimitation disputes from compulsory procedures entailing a binding decision. The dispute would normally have been referred to arbitration but the parties agreed that the case would instead be referred to a Special Chamber of the ITLOS. The configuration of this case thus became one of special agreement rather than applicant-respondent as initially instituted.

[80] *Dispute concerning Delimitation of the Maritime Boundary between Ghana and Côte d'Ivoire in the Atlantic Ocean*, [2015] Request for the Prescription of Provisional Measures, Order 25 April 2015, [25].

[81] Ibid., [25].

[82] In respect of Art. 290(1), the court or tribunal makes this determination on its own account whereas under para. 5, the court or tribunal asked to prescribe provisional measures makes this decision for the ad hoc arbitral tribunal that is yet to be constituted.

[83] See e.g. *Arbitral Tribunal Constituted Pursuant to Article 287, and Article 1 of Annex VII, of the United Nations Convention on the Law of the Sea for the Dispute Concerning the MOX Plant, International Movements of Radioactive Materials, and the Protection of the Marine Environment of the Irish Sea, The MOX Plant Case (Ireland v. UK)* (Order No. 3, Suspension of Proceedings on Jurisdiction and Merits, and Request for Further Provisional Measures), 24 June 2003, [14] available at www.pca-cpa.org/ENGLISH/RPC/. See also S. Rosenne, 'The Case-Law of ITLOS (1997-2001): An Overview,' in M. H. Nordquist and J. Norton Moore (eds.), *Current Marine Environmental Issues and the International Tribunal for the Law of the Sea* (2001) 127, 133 (noting that a finding of *prima facie* jurisdiction is a very low threshold and allows the prescription of provisional measures provided 'the absence of jurisdiction is not manifest').

where the requirement in Article 283 to proceed expeditiously to an exchange of views has not been met;[84] the existence of alternative dispute settlement procedures that are to be utilized in lieu of those in the LOSC;[85] and, whether the exclusions and limitations in Section 3 of Part XV apply.[86] In *Ghana/Côte d'Ivoire*, the Special Agreement between the parties clearly provided for *prima facie* jurisdiction.

If there is *prima facie* jurisdiction, the standard that must be met is whether the circumstances warrant the prescription of measures pending the final decision of the court or tribunal in order to preserve the rights of the parties or whether there is a need to prevent serious harm to the marine environment. Both of these elements were at play in *Ghana/Côte d'Ivoire.*

In requesting provisional measures, Côte d'Ivoire set out in its pleadings the relevant disputed area at issue, which reflected overlapping claims between the parties: Ghana was claiming the use of an equidistance line; Côte d'Ivoire claimed that Ghana had not identified the equidistance line accurately and in any event it sought an alternative boundary to achieve an equitable solution.[87] For the purposes of the provisional measures proceedings, the Special Chamber did not need to 'determine definitively whether the rights which they each wish to see protected exist.'[88] Rather, the rights claimed to exist must at least be plausible.[89] This standard of plausibility had not previously been applied in the context of provisional measures under the LOSC, but followed more recent jurisprudence of the ICJ.[90] The Special Chamber considered that Côte d'Ivoire had met this

[84] See e.g. *Southern Bluefin Tuna*, n. 78, [60] and [61]; *MOX Plant Case (Ireland v. UK) (Provisional Measures)*, n. 83 (Order of 3 December 2001) (2002) 41 ILM 405, [68]; *Case Concerning Land Reclamation by Singapore in and around the Straits of Johor (Malaysia v. Singapore)* (Request for Provisional Measures) (Order of 8 October 2003) available at www.itlos.org/start2_en.html, [48].

[85] *Prima facie* jurisdiction may be lacking if either Arts. 281 or 282 clearly bar recourse to the compulsory procedures in Section 2 of Part XV, or if the dispute does not involve the interpretation or application of LOSC. See *Southern Bluefin Tuna*, n. 78, [51] and [55]; *Land Reclamation*, n. 84, [57]; *MOX Plant*, n. 83, [51].

[86] See e.g. *The M/V* 'Saiga' *(No. 2) (St. Vincent v. Guinea)* (Order on Provisional Measures) (11 March 1998) 117 ILR 111, [30].

[87] *Ghana/Côte d'Ivoire*, n. 80, Côte d'Ivoire Pleadings, [6].

[88] Ibid., Order, [57]. [89] Ibid., [58].

[90] Tanaka, n. 35, 318. This requirement was first articulated in *Questions relating to the Obligation to Prosecute or Extradite (Belgium v. Senegal)* Provisional Measures Order of 28 May 2009 [2009] ICJ Rep. 139, 151 and applied subsequently. The ITLOS utilized this standard subsequently in *The 'Enrica Lexie' Incident (Italy v. India)* Provisional Measures Order of 24 August 2015, [84]–[85].

threshold.[91] However, what may be considered 'plausible' is not particularly clear, and there is a risk that this assessment injects an element of uncertainty into provisional measures decisions under the LOSC.[92]

Ghana challenged that there was any urgency in relation to Côte d'Ivoire's requests – commenting that Côte d'Ivoire had not even argued that urgency was a requirement to be met.[93] The Special Chamber confirmed the standard for prescribing provisional measures as requiring 'a real and imminent risk that irreparable prejudice may be caused to the rights of the parties in dispute,'[94] and that urgency is thus required.[95]

Côte d'Ivoire's request for provisional measures also rested on its concerns that serious harm to the marine environment was at stake. Even though the Special Chamber found that Côte d'Ivoire had not discharged its burden of proof to demonstrate that Ghana's activities in the disputed area created an imminent risk of serious harm to the marine environment,[96] the Special Chamber was still minded to address environmental protection pending the resolution of the maritime boundary dispute. The Special Chamber took into account key environmental principles, including the obligation not to cause transboundary harm[97] and the need to act with 'prudence and caution.'[98] Also noted were the core obligations to protect and preserve the marine environment as enshrined in Article 192 of the LOSC and the duty to cooperate in the prevention of pollution of the marine environment.[99]

These environmental principles and concerns were factored into the Special Chamber's consideration of the drilling activities that were being undertaken in Ghana's concession areas. Côte d'Ivoire had observed that the unilateral activities deprived it of the right to determine 'when, how and under what conditions the exploitation of these resources will take place, and even *whether* it should take place.'[100] Moreover, Côte d'Ivoire submitted that drilling was an irreversible activity, preventing any possibility of the subsoil being returned to its prior state.[101] This position was consistent with the approaches taken in *Aegean Sea Continental Shelf* as

[91] *Ghana/Côte D'Ivoire*, n. 80, Order, [62].

[92] Tanaka notes: 'The vagueness of the test may entail the risk of undermining the predictability of orders from ITLOS with regard to provisional measures.' Tanaka, n. 35, 319.

[93] *Ghana/Côte D'Ivoire*, n. 80, Ghana Pleadings, [89].

[94] *Ghana/Côte d'Ivoire*, n. 80, Order, [41], citing the standard used in *M/V Louisa* (Saint Vincent and the Grenadines *v.* Spain), Provisional Measures, Order, 23 December 2010, [72].

[95] *Ghana/Côte d'Ivoire*, n. 80, Order, [42].

[96] Ibid., [67].

[97] Ibid., [71].

[98] Ibid., [72].

[99] Ibid., [69] and [73].

[100] Ibid., [77] (citing Côte d'Ivoire's arguments).

[101] Ibid., [78].

well as in *Guyana v. Suriname.* Ghana resisted any suggestion that it should halt the activities of its concession holders because of the severe financial implications that would flow from such a suspension or cessation of activity.[102] Ghana further considered that Côte d'Ivoire's concerns were ultimately related to financial loss.[103]

The Special Chamber, however, took into account possible modifications to the physical characteristics of the continental shelf that would be significant and permanent and not fully compensable through financial reparations.[104] It therefore unanimously prescribed that 'Ghana shall take all necessary steps to ensure that no new drilling either by Ghana or under its control takes place in the disputed area.'[105] The order is more limited than Côte d'Ivoire had sought.[106] The Special Chamber recognized that *ongoing* activities in respect of which drilling had already taken place would entail considerable financial loss and potentially harm the environment as well.[107] It would therefore fall to the parties to determine what drilling may be construed as new and what is part of an ongoing operation. According to Ghana, the 'activities of exploration and exploitation that it has undertaken or authorized in the disputed areas "are not new."'[108]

To allow any drilling to continue, which would reflect a permanent change to the seabed, appears at odds with the standards discussed in *Aegean Sea Continental Shelf* and *Guyana v. Suriname.* Tanaka has criticized the decision on the basis that the Special Chamber was too deferential to the interests of Ghana, even though those interests were predominantly financial and did not reflect an imminent risk of financial loss.[109] In this respect, the Special Chamber's decision may show a greater tolerance for mining activities in disputed areas than would have been accepted under the previous cases. The threshold for what constitutes a forbidden activity because of the risk of hampering or prejudicing final resolution of the maritime boundary dispute has therefore shifted in *Ghana/Côte d'Ivoire* and opens the door for furthering manoeuvring by ambitious states in future decisions. It may have been acceptable in the factual context of this case, particularly as the parties had both been regulating seabed activity prior to the litigation.[110] There is, therefore, an opening to limit the relevance of the decision in future disputes.

[102] Ibid., [82]–[85]. [103] Ibid., [87]. [104] Ibid., [89]. [105] Ibid., [108].

[106] A tribunal acting under Art. 290 may vary the measures prescribed to what was requested from the applicant state.

[107] *Ghana/Côte d'Ivoire*, n. 80, Order, [99].

[108] Ibid., Separate Opinion of Judge Mensah, [6].

[109] Tanaka, n. 35, 325. [110] *Ghana/Côte d'Ivoire*, n. 80, Order, [51] and [52].

A constraint is placed on Ghanaian activity, however, to the extent that Ghana is required to carry out 'strict and continuous monitoring of all activities' in the disputed area to prevent serious harm to the marine environment.[111] Both parties are to take all necessary steps to prevent serious harm to the marine environment.[112] Arguably, such a provisional measure would not change, or add to, the environmental obligations that already bind Ghana. Yet it does at least underline the commitment of the LOSC dispute settlement process to environmental protection, even in the context of maritime boundary delimitation disputes. Further, the requirements imposed on the parties to report back on the steps taken to conform to the provisional measures order[113] does place a procedural onus and third-party oversight of its actions in relation to Ghana's adherence to environmental norms.[114]

On the request that Ghana take steps to prevent information from being used to the detriment of Côte d'Ivoire, Ghana had challenged that such a right to information existed under the LOSC.[115] The Special Chamber concluded otherwise:

> the Special Chamber considers that the rights of the coastal State over its continental shelf include all rights necessary for and connected with the exploration and exploitation of the natural resources of the continental shelf and that the exclusive right to access to information about the resources of the continental shelf is plausibly among those rights.[116]

The Special Chamber further considered that the risk of prejudice to these rights was imminent pending the decision on the merits. As a result, it prescribed a provisional measure to prevent information that was not already in the public domain being used in any way to the detriment of Côte d'Ivoire. In this regard, Ghana provided an undertaking in the proceedings, which was judicially noted, that it would record information currently being gathered and make it available to Côte d'Ivoire if ordered to do so in the case.[117]

Once prescribed, provisional measures may be modified or revoked if the circumstances justifying their prescription have been changed or cease

[111] Ibid., [108], Operative [1(b)].

[112] Ibid., [108], Operative [1(c)].

[113] Ibid., [108], Operative [2].

[114] This oversight allows for the possibility that a state that fails to report, or even fails to undertake the necessary steps, as required by a provisional measures order, could be found to have violated international law at the merits stage of the dispute.

[115] Ibid., Ghana Pleadings, [107].

[116] Ibid., Order, [94].

[117] Ibid., [92]–[93].

to exist.[118] At the jurisdictional stage of *Southern Bluefin Tuna*, the arbitral tribunal revoked the ITLOS Order but still noted that the revocation did 'not mean that the Parties may disregard the effects of the Order or their own decisions made in conformity with it.'[119] As such, the possibility exists that if a court or tribunal prescribes provisional arrangements, the parties may then use this order as a basis for negotiating their own temporary arrangement and this agreement could be grounds for revoking the order.

At time of writing, the *Ghana/Côte d'Ivoire* dispute remained to be resolved on the merits. The relevance of a provisional arrangement between the parties will likely be a factor taken into consideration by the Special Chamber. At the provisional measures stage, Ghana disputed that Côte d'Ivoire had established there was any new, imminent or urgent concerns about Ghana's exploration and exploitation activities because the parties had long operated on the basis of granting and regulating seabed activity on the basis of the equidistance line.[120] Ghana highlighted at this stage of the case that Côte d'Ivoire's maritime claim was relatively recent and was contrary to the forty years of state practice as between the parties.[121] In disputing that Côte d'Ivoire had a valid maritime claim because of its earlier position, Ghana further argued there could be no imminent risk of harm since none of Côte d'Ivoire's rights were truly at stake. Ultimately, the Special Chamber at the provisional measures stage only had to determine if the claim was plausible, and this low threshold could be established for the purposes of prescribing provisional measures. The impact of the provisional arrangement on the final maritime boundary remains to be seen.

5.4 Connecting Provisional Arrangements and Provisional Measures

In many respects, the requirements of Articles 74(3) and 83(3) are distinct substantive obligations binding coastal states in the process of delimiting their maritime boundaries as compared to states that are engaged in litigation and have immediate requirements imposed to prevent prejudice pending the outcome of a maritime boundary dispute. There are

[118] LOSC, Art. 290(2).

[119] *Southern Bluefin Tuna Cases (Australia v. Japan; New Zealand v. Japan) (Award on Jurisdiction and Admissibility)* (2000) 39 ILM 1359, [67].

[120] *Ghana/Côte d'Ivoire*, n. 80, Order, [51] and [52].

[121] Ibid., Ghana Pleadings, [30].

nonetheless some connections that may be drawn. First, it can be seen that the standards for prescribing provisional measures inform or influence the determination as to whether a state has jeopardized or hampered the resolution of the maritime boundary delimitation. Second, there is a link where states turn to compulsory dispute settlement procedures to ensure that they do not violate the requirements of Articles 74(3) and 83(3). These connections are considered further in this part.

5.4.1 *Standards for Provisional Measures and Provisional Arrangements*

The case law on Articles 74(3) and 83(3) indicates that their interpretation may be influenced by the standards utilized in provisional measures orders. This situation has been seen with the position taken in *Guyana v. Suriname* aligning with the views of the ICJ from *Aegean Sea Continental Shelf* interim measures decision. In this regard, the *Guyana v. Suriname* tribunal commented:

> A distinction is therefore to be made between activities of the kind that lead to a permanent physical change, such as exploitation of oil and gas reserves, and those that do not, such as seismic exploration.[122]

However, the tribunal also recognized that the interim measures judgments were 'far more circumscribed than [those] surrounding activities in disputed waters generally.'[123] As an order for provisional measures requires a demonstration of 'irreparable prejudice,' a lower threshold was to apply in the context of Articles 74(3) and 83(3), which refers to a standard of hampering or jeopardizing the reaching of a final agreement.[124]

The implication that may be drawn from the tribunal's holding is that activities that have been regarded as warranting a prescription of provisional measures because of the irreparable prejudice they would cause pending an arbitration or adjudication of a maritime boundary would necessarily also constitute a violation of the obligation not to hamper or jeopardize the reaching of a final agreement. The outstanding question that therefore remains are what activities might still be considered as hampering or jeopardizing a final agreement even if they do not amount to causing irreparable prejudice to the other party. The answer appears to be found in the tribunal's comments that seek to balance the rights of the parties to pursue economic development in a disputed area against the obligation

[122] *Guyana v. Suriname*, n. 11, [467]. [123] Ibid., [469]. [124] Ibid.

to make every effort not to hamper or jeopardize the reaching of a final agreement.[125]

What exactly will be acceptable economic development may depend on whether the other party can be compensated because of that activity. There may also be consideration as to whether the activity is of such a nature that it would not be possible to provide reparations (in terms of putting any injured party back in the position it would have been in if the wrong-doing had not occurred). In *Ghana/Côte d'Ivoire*, the ITLOS considered the right to information could be irreparably damaged. Ghana, however, had provided an undertaking that it would share whatever information was necessary at the conclusion of the case.[126] As such, arguably this situation may not jeopardize or hamper the reaching of a final agreement, unless perhaps the state concerned considered itself so prejudiced by the actions of the state gathering information that no further negotiations were possible.

The need for provisional measures is also predicated on the preservation of the rights of the parties pending the resolution of the dispute. This aspect of preserving rights resonates with the obligation not to jeopardize or hamper the potential rights of the parties.[127] It could therefore be anticipated that what is needed to protect the rights of the party in the context of provisional measures is also indicative of what is necessary so as not to jeopardize or hamper the reaching of a final agreement between the parties.

5.4.2 Compulsory Dispute Settlement to Satisfy Articles 74(3) and 83(3)

The use of the LOSC dispute settlement procedures is clearly anticipated in relation to disputes that may emerge in relation to overlapping EEZs and continental shelves. Articles 74(2) and 83(2) provide in this regard: 'If no agreement can be reached within a reasonable period of time, the States concerned shall resort to the procedures provided for in Part XV.'

Where a state has infringed the rights of another claimant state and prejudiced reaching a final agreement, there are limited responses that may be pursued. In the case of Suriname's response to the CGX activities, the tribunal found that Suriname was in violation of the prohibition of the threat of use of force.[128] Instead, the alternative path the tribunal proposed

[125] Ibid., [470]. [126] *Ghana/Côte d'Ivoire*, n. 80, Order, [92].
[127] BIICL, n. 9, [124]. [128] *Guyana v. Suriname*, n. 11, [445].

focused on the availability of compulsory litigation and the possible use of provisional measures:

> A State faced with a such a dispute should resort to the compulsory procedures provided for in Section 2 of Part XV of the Convention, which provide among other things that, where the urgency of the situation so requires, a State may request that ITLOS prescribe provisional measures.[129]

In this regard, the tribunal has directly linked the requirements for provisional arrangements with the use of provisional measures to protect against a state that fails to meet those requirements. The tribunal highlighted that Suriname had the option of invoking compulsory dispute settlement under the LOSC, but in resorting to a threat of force in a disputed area, this action violated the obligations under Articles 74(3) and 83(3). While the tribunal did not go so far as to insist that a state 'shall' resort to the compulsory procedures in the LOSC, the alternative course of action followed by the state cannot violate the international prohibition on the threat or use of force. Lawful counter-measures may be an acceptable alternative in this situation.

In some regards, the provisional measures decision of *Ghana/Côte d'Ivoire* forms an appropriate sequel to *Guyana v. Suriname* inasmuch as Côte d'Ivoire's request for provisional measures in the face of exploitation of natural resources from the disputed areas follows the path the tribunal had laid out for Suriname rather than take forceful self-help measures. The decision did, however, deviate from the clear line that had been established in *Aegean Sea Continental Shelf* and *Guyana v. Suriname* in relation to allowing the continuation of some activities that would permanently change the physical seabed. The Special Chamber was also willing to take steps to prevent actions that did not physically change the seabed but negatively impacted on rights in the seabed resources in confirming the need to protect information that may be obtained from the seabed activity.

Although the *Ghana/Côte d'Ivoire* holding suggests that there is an element of unpredictability to be expected in relation to provisional measures orders in maritime boundary disputes, it is necessary to recall that states more commonly reach their own agreement for temporary arrangements pending the outcome of the case. The latter practice may be expected to be more common because companies engaging in exploitation and exploration activities would normally want certainty of title to warrant the investment in the projects at the outset. Unpredictability therefore

[129] Ibid., [446].

comes more so from the very request for provisional measures. Even when account is taken of the fact that it has become far more common for maritime boundary disputes to be referred unilaterally to arbitration or adjudication,[130] states in this litigious posture still rarely request provisional measures. If such a path is actually taken, some predictability exists in relation to the standards for the prescription of provisional measures pending the resolution of the maritime boundary dispute.

5.5 Concluding Remarks

Although the case law addressing the obligation for provisional arrangements under the LOSC and the use of provisional measures in the judicial resolution of maritime boundary disputes is sparse (particularly relative to the number of cases resolving maritime boundary disputes), it must be recalled that this case law sits within a field of active state practice. This state practice shows considerable interest in states working towards joint development agreements, including when negotiations towards the final maritime boundary are ongoing.[131] Ong has commented, '[j]oint development and transboundary unitization are designed to preserve the unity of [a common petroleum deposit], while respecting the inherent, sovereign rights of the interested States.'[132] The tribunal in *Guyana v. Suriname* noted that international courts and tribunals had also sought to encourage states to reach joint arrangements, especially where the unity of deposits was in question.[133] Given the mutual interests involved, states do have an incentive to develop provisional solutions when the higher stakes of a permanent maritime boundary cannot be resolved.

The only judicial interpretation of Articles 74(3) and 83(3), *Guyana v. Suriname*, has highlighted two obligations to be drawn from these provisions: (1) a duty to negotiate in good faith to reach a provisional arrangement and (2) an obligation not to jeopardize or hamper the reaching of the final agreement. Activities that permanently or physically alter the seabed may well violate these LOSC provisions. If that occurs, it is expected that states will refer the matter to the LOSC dispute settlement procedures. However, as discussed, there are potential jurisdictional barriers to enforcing the obligations relating to provisional arrangements as articulated in *Guyana v. Suriname*.

[130] On this point, see further Chapter 1 of this volume. [131] See Klein, n. 54, 433–435.
[132] Ong, n. 17, 771. [133] *Guyana v. Suriname*, n. 11, [463].

If states do proceed to litigation, there is an opportunity to seek provisional measures for the protection of rights prior to the final resolution of the dispute. Judicial resolution of maritime boundary disputes to date indicates that provisional measures will not commonly be needed or sought by the parties in dispute. If a state considers its rights need protection pending the arbitration or adjudication of a maritime boundary, case law at the ICJ has indicated that irreparable prejudice requiring an urgent response was needed for the indication of provisional measures. Permanent changes to the seabed rather than transitory exploration activities were the relevant benchmarks assessed in *Aegean Sea Continental Shelf*. *Ghana/Côte d'Ivoire* has instead suggested some drilling may continue where financial prejudice may result to the opposing state. Also relevant is prejudice to the financial interests from exploitation rights through information gathering about resources in the disputed area. This recognition may well be seen as an appropriate advance from *Aegean Sea Continental Shelf* reflecting current commercial realities.

Ultimately, provisional arrangements and provisional measures should be considered as tools in the overall process of maritime boundary delimitation. As such, they provide states with overlapping entitlements with additional legal avenues to promote peaceful resolution of their disputes as well as the orderly use of maritime resources. In this regard, it may be preferable to contemplate how provisional arrangements and provisional measures might support this overall process and perhaps consider the elements of unpredictability that have thus far emerged as providing welcome flexibility. The parameters created through the obligations concerning provisional arrangements under Articles 74(3) and 83(3) can provide the states concerned with options on how to regulate their relationship in the midst of a disagreement over their maritime boundary. Allowing for unpredictability – alternatively conceived of as flexibility – may ultimately facilitate achieving the final goal of an equitable solution under international law.

6

The Role of Equity, Equitable Principles, and the Equitable Solution in Maritime Delimitation

LUCIE DELABIE

6.1 Introduction

> C'est toujours avec quelque appréhension, et peut-être avec quelque témérité, que le juriste aborde le thème de l'équité, tant la notion en paraît insaisissable, ses rapports avec le droit source de controverse, tant il est malaisé d'en dégager, même sans un domaine limité, l'exacte fonction.[1]

This statement is particularly relevant while examining the place of equity in the maritime delimitation jurisprudence. Used in different fields of international law,[2] equity has for a long time been applied extensively in maritime boundary delimitation, as recalled by the arbitral tribunal in *Barbados v. Trinidad and Tobago*: 'since the very outset, courts and tribunals have taken into consideration elements of equity in reaching a determination of a boundary line over maritime areas. This is also the approach stipulated by UNCLOS Articles 74 and 83.'[3] Some observers even notice an increasing reference to equity in recent ICJ cases and arbitrations in this area.[4]

The important role played by equity in maritime delimitation is first of all due to the inclusion of this concept in the legal rules that the judge or arbitrator is required to apply when a dispute occurs between two states. Explicit reference to these rules is made in Articles 74(1) and 83(1) of the

1 D. Bardonnet, 'Equité et frontières terrestres,' in *Mélanges offerts à Paul Reuter. Le droit international: unité et diversité* (Pedone Paris 1981) 35.

2 F. Francioni, 'Equity in International Law,' in *Max Planck Encyclopedia of Public International Law* (2013).

3 *Arbitration between Barbados and the Republic of Trinidad and Tobago (Barbados v. Trinidad and Tobago)* [2006] 27 RIAA 147, [229].

4 M. Miyoshi, 'Considerations on Equity in Maritime Boundary Cases before the International Court of Justice,' in N. Ando, E. McWhinney, R. Wolfrum, and B. Baker Röben (eds.), *Liber Amicorum Judge Shigeru Oda* (Brill/Nijhoff Leiden 2002) 1087–1101.

United Nations Convention on the Law of the Sea (LOSC),[5] which reflect customary international law.[6] It is also linked with the creative role played by the judges and arbitrators while they interpret these legal rules.[7] This was highlighted in *Jan Mayen* through the formula 'customary law of the continental shelf as developed in the [case law],'[8] and judges Cot and Wolfrum more recently recalled the normative role played by the courts and tribunals in the maritime delimitation process.[9] In line with the transactional function played by the judiciary – namely finding a compromise to definitively resolve a dispute – the concept of equity constitutes a tool of modulation for the judge, who gets a huge margin of appreciation in the maritime delimitation process.

The Hammurabi Code already referred to the relationship between law and equity: 'J'ai placé le droit et l'équité dans la bouche du peuple.' In the same way, the *Institut de droit international* affirmed in a 1937 resolution that 'equity is normally inherent to a sound application of law.'[10] The inherent links between law and equity are more generally revealed by the definition of equity in the *Black's Law Dictionary*:

1. Fairness, impartiality, evenhanded dealing
2. The body of principles constituting what is fair and right; natural law
3. The recourse to principles of justice to correct or supplement the law as applied to particular circumstances[11]

As implied by this definition, equitable considerations appear as a way of accommodating a strict application of a legal norm that could lead to an

[5] The Arts. read: 'The delimitation of the [exclusive economic zone/continental shelf] between States with opposite or adjacent coasts shall be effected by agreement on the basis of international law, as referred to in Article 38 of the Statute of the International Court of Justice, in order to achieve an equitable solution.'

[6] In *Jan Mayen*, the International Court of Justice (ICJ) affirmed the customary nature of the requirement to reach an equitable solution as the aim of any delimitation process, *Maritime Delimitation in the Area between Greenland and Jan Mayen (Denmark v. Norway)* (Judgment) [1992] ICJ Rep. 38, [48]. This statement was recalled by the ICJ in *Maritime Dispute (Peru v. Chile)* (Judgment) [2014] ICJ Rep. 3, [177].

[7] *Barbados v. Trinidad and Tobago*, n. 3, [223].

[8] *Jan Mayen*, n. 6, [51].

[9] See *Delimitation of the Maritime Boundary in the Bay of Bengal (Bangladesh/Myanmar)* (Judgment) [2012] ITLOS Rep. 4. G. Giraudeau, 'La remarquable entrée en scène du TIDM dans le contentieux de la délimitation maritime: l'arrêt du 14 mars 2012 relatif au différend entre le Bangladesh et le Myanmar dans le Golfe du Bengale' (2012) 17 *Annuaire du droit de la mer* 105.

[10] Institut de droit international, Résolution sur 'la compétence du juge international en équité,' 1937 (translation by the author).

[11] *Black's Law Dictionary*, 9th ed. (West Minnesota 2009), 619.

unjust result. It relates more generally to the relations between law and justice.[12]

Nevertheless, equity's exact function within the law remains difficult to identify and has been the source of controversies because of the subjectivity it can introduce in the interpretation and application of the law. Already used in the first delimitation cases – such as *North Sea Continental Shelf* in 1969,[13] the role of equity has progressively evolved in the case law, in particular in the name of consistency and predictability of justice, as affirmed by the ICJ in *Libya/Malta* in 1985.[14]

The purpose of this chapter is to identify the nature and function of equity in the case law on maritime delimitation, and to evaluate to what extent the judge and the arbitrator contribute to ensuring predictability and consistency in maritime boundary delimitation in having recourse to it. The chapter will focus on awards, individual opinions, practice, and doctrine since the 2000s, but will take into account the previous case law as this is necessary to understand the changes that have occurred over the years in interpreting and applying equity in the law of maritime delimitation. In such a context, it is important to take into consideration the risk of fragmentation of the law in the maritime delimitation process, implied by the multiplication of courts and tribunals.[15] Finally, it is important to be aware of the influence of the legal traditions to which scholars and lawyers belong when they make reference to the term equity. While equity is conceived in the common law system as being within the law, the civil law standpoint on equity is more ambivalent about the frontier between legality and extra-legality. This can have an impact on the analysis of the judicial practice and probably will influence the approach developed by a French scholar in the present chapter.

[12] See more generally T. M. Franck, *Fairness in International Law and Institutions* (Clarendon Press Oxford 1995). T. Cottier, *Equitable Principles of Maritime Boundary Delimitation: The Quest for Distributive Justice in International Law* (Cambridge University Press Cambridge 2015).

[13] *North Sea Continental Shelf* (Federal Republic of Germany/Denmark; Federal Republic of Germany/Netherlands) (Judgment) [1969] ICJ Rep. 3, [88 *et seq.*].

[14] 'Justice according to the rule of law; which is to say that its application should display consistency and a degree of predictability; even though it looks with particularity to the peculiar circumstances of an instant case, it also looks beyond it to principles of more general application,' *Continental Shelf (Libyan Arab Jamahiriya/Malta)* (Judgment) [1985] ICJ Rep. 13, [45].

[15] G. Giraudeau, n. 9. G Eiriksson, 'The Bay of Bengal Case before the International Tribunal for the Law of the Sea,' in L. del Castillo, *Law of the Sea, from Grotius to the International Tribunal for the Law of the Sea, Liber Amicorum Judge Hugo Caminos* (Brill/Nijhoff Leiden 2015) 514.

Contrary to the terms of the Convention on the Continental Shelf,[16] the negotiators of the LOSC[17] decided to at least include an indirect reference to equity through the explicit use, in these provisions, of the adjective 'equitable.' We can observe that the noun 'equity' itself is not used. The same remark is valid if we look at in particular the recent case law, where the judge or the arbitrator prefer using the adjective equitable – we mostly find expressions like 'equitable criteria,' 'equitable principles,' 'equitable solution,' 'equitable result' – rather than the noun equity. As an example, in *Black Sea*, whereas Romania refers to 'equity,'[18] the ICJ only uses the adjective 'equitable.'[19] Whereas this might seem a subsidiary issue, this point is important in relation to the objectivity and predictability required in using equitable considerations for resolving a maritime delimitation dispute. It reveals the necessity to distinguish between equity as a principle of justice and equity as a legal norm. It also shows that the judges or arbitrators are confronted with a difficult task in maritime delimitation since they have to find, according to the circumstances of each case and while using equitable considerations, a good balance between the prevalence of a predictable solution and the necessity of some flexibility in applying the legal rule.

After some hesitation between using equity outside the law and equity within the law, it seems that courts and tribunals embarked on a process of rationalization in using equity, more particularly so since the turn of the century. Before examining that process in Section 6.3, Section 6.2 of this chapter gives a brief overview of the links between equitable considerations and maritime boundary delimitation from an historical perspective. Finally, in spite of the rationalization developed in the case law, we cannot ignore the indeterminate character of maritime boundary delimitation.[20] Due to the huge margin of discretion at the disposal of the judges and arbitrators in this field, there remains a risk of subjectivity due to the recourse to autonomous equity. As discussed in Section 6.4, as a consequence, the

[16] Convention on the Continental Shelf, signed 29 April 1958, entered into force 10 June 1964, 499 UNTS 311, Art. 6.

[17] For the context of negotiations, see G. Eiriksson, n. 15, 523–524.

[18] Romania asked for application of 'the principle of equity and the method of proportionality, as applied in state practice and the decisions of international courts regarding the delimitation of continental shelf and exclusive economic zones.' *Maritime Delimitation in the Black Sea (Romania v. Ukraine)* (Judgment) [2009] ICJ Rep. 61, [33].

[19] The Court only uses equity when referring to the arguments of Romania. The Court refers to 'equitable solution,' to 'achieve a delimitation that is equitable' (ibid., [111]).

[20] This remark has been made by the ICJ itself in the judgment in ibid., [211].

recent case law still displays a lack of consistency and predictability, as has been pointed out by some observers on the *Maritime Dispute (Peru v. Chile)* judgment dating from 2014.[21] Section 6.5 draws conclusions on the role of equity in maritime delimitation.

6.2 Historical Relationships between Equity and Law in the Maritime Delimitation Process

We have progressively assisted to the switchover from the central role of equidistance as compared to a subsidiary role of equity, affirmed in the 1958 Convention on the Continental Shelf, to the focus on the equitable solution of the delimitation process resulting from the LOSC. This trend originates from the search for a balance between predictability of the result of delimitation and the necessity of flexibility depending on factual circumstances. Nevertheless, in doing so, the judges and arbitrators introduced autonomous equity, moving away from the traditional corrective function of equity.[22] While looking for obtaining a just result, rather than excluding an inequitable result, they introduced a risk of judgment *ex aequo et bono* – equity outside of the law – which is only possible with the agreement of the parties. The road to autonomous equity in the maritime delimitation jurisprudence (Section 6.2.1) led to a significant risk of subjectivity as illustrated by the case law of the 1980s (Section 6.2.2).

[21] *Peru v. Chile*, n. 6, Separate Opinion of Judge ad hoc Orrego Vicuña:

> This judge is certainly in favour of solutions that might result in the accommodation of the essential interests of the parties to a case, and thus be met with greater acceptance, on the understanding that such exercise is strictly bound by the governing law, which in this case is embodied in treaties and other legal instruments. In the context of this Judgment, however, this limitation placed on the role of equity appears blurred, as if it were called to influence the outcome on its own standing. Consistency with the meaning of the United Nations Convention on the Law of the Sea could thus be compromised. Ibid., [37].

According to Orrego Vicuña, 'this judgment however appears to consider the role of equity as capable of determining the outcome of the dispute on its own standing without strict observance of the governing law as established in treaties and other legal instruments.' F. Orrego Vicuña, 'International Law Issues in the Judgment of the International Court of Justice in the Peru-Chile Maritime Dispute Case,' in L. del Castillo (ed.), *Law of the Sea, from Grotius to the International Tribunal for the Law of the Sea, Liber Amicorum Judge Hugo Caminos* (Brill/Nijhoff Leiden 2015) 581, 581–582.

[22] Linked with the common law conception of equity, as equity within the law.

6.2.1 The Introduction of Equitable Considerations in Maritime Delimitation by the Jurisprudence: The Road to Autonomous Equity

Contrary to what one might think, the use of equity in maritime delimitation law did not appear at the time of the LOSC, some of whose provisions directly refer to that concept. Equitable considerations were already introduced in the delimitation process by the ICJ in the 1969 judgment in *North Sea Continental Shelf*. At that time, the ICJ had been asked to specify the positive law applicable to delimitation of the continental shelf. According to the Netherlands and Denmark, even in a case where there is no agreement between the parties, the legal rule 'equidistance – special circumstances' expressed in Article 6 of the Convention on the Continental Shelf had acquired the status of international custom. This argument was rejected by Germany, which considered that this rule was not applicable to its case. Excluding the customary nature of the equidistance method,[23] the Court decided that 'delimitation must be the object of agreement between the States concerned, and that such agreement must be arrived at in accordance with equitable principles.'[24] In this case, the inapplicability of the Convention on the Continental Shelf – whose provisions exclude any explicit reference to equity – gave to the Court the opportunity to depart from a strict application of the equidistance method that could be unjust. Since then, and until the 1990s, reference to equitable principles has been frequently made by the ICJ, for example in *Tunisia/Libya*,[25] *Gulf of Maine*,[26] and *Jan Mayen*.[27] Arbitrators adopted the same reasoning, as shown in *Anglo-French Continental Shelf* (1977), *Guinea/Guinea-Bissau* (1985), *Canada/France* (1992).

While affirming the importance of equitable principles in the delimitation process, the judges and arbitrators did not point out their exact substance. The ICJ attempted to clarify the concept of equitable principles – in particular in *Tunisia/Libya*, *Gulf of Maine*, and *Jan Mayen* – but did not outline their precise content.[28] Indeed, in *Tunisia/Libya*, the Court affirmed:

[23] *North Sea Continental Shelf*, n. 13, [85]. [24] Ibid.

[25] *Continental Shelf (Tunisia/Libyan Arab Jamahiriya)* (Judgment) [1982] ICJ Rep. 18, [28].

[26] *Delimitation of the Maritime Boundary in the Gulf of Maine Area (Canada/USA)* (Judgment) [1984] ICJ Rep. 246, [39, 44, 70, 71, *et seq.*].

[27] *Jan Mayen*, n. 6, [54 *et seq.*, 66].

[28] See more generally on that question Miyoshi, n. 4, 1088–1089.

> The result of the application of equitable principles must be equitable. This terminology, which is generally used, is not entirely satisfactory because it employs the term equitable to characterize both the result to be achieved and the means to be applied to reach this result. It is, however, the result that is predominant; the principles are subordinate to the goal. The equitableness of a principle must be assessed in the light of its usefulness for arriving at an equitable result. It is not every such principle, which is in itself equitable; it may acquire this quality by reference to the equitableness of the solution. The principles to be indicated by the Court have to be selected according to their appropriateness for reaching an equitable result. From this consideration it follows that the term 'equitable principles' cannot be interpreted in the abstract; it refers back to the principles and rules, which may be appropriate in order to achieve an equitable result.[29]

The Court in this passage explains the inherent links between equitable principles and the equitable result. A principle can be qualified as equitable only if conducing to an equitable result. The main objective is in any case to get an equitable result.

A few years later, in *Libya/Malta*, the ICJ observed:

> That equitable principles are expressed in terms of general application, is immediately apparent from a glance at some well-known examples: the principle that there is to be no question of refashioning geography, or compensating for the inequalities of nature; the related principle of non-encroachment by one party on the natural prolongation of the other, which is no more than the negative expression of the positive rule that the coastal State enjoys sovereign rights over the continental shelf off its coasts to the full extent authorized by international law in the relevant circumstances; the principle of respect due to all such relevant circumstances; the principle that although all States are equal before the law and are entitled to equal treatment, 'equity does not necessarily imply equality' (ICJ Reports 1969, p. 49, para. 9l), [. . .]. The nature of equity is nowhere more evident than in these well-established principles.[30]

This explanation relates to the question directly raised by Elihu Lauterpacht, counsel for Malta, about the silence of the Court in defining the origins of the concept of equitable principles.[31] These principles have also

[29] *Tunisia/Libya*, n. 25, [70]. The Court referred to *North Sea Continental Shelf*: 'This was the view of the Court when it said, in its Judgment of 1969: "it is a truism to say that the determination must be equitable, rather is the problem above all one of defining the means whereby the delimitation can be carried out in such a way as to be recognized as equitable" (*ICJ Reports 1969*, p. 50, para. 92).' The Court confirmed this point in *Libya/ Malta*, n. 14, [45].

[30] *Libya/Malta*, n. 14, [46–47]. See Miyoshi, n. 4, 1089.

[31] Public sitting, 27 November 1984, CR 84/23, 36. Cited by Miyoshi, n. 4, 1090.

been used in *Canada/France* where the tribunal recalled that the parties agreed on the fundamental norm to apply which 'requires the delimitation to be effected in accordance with equitable principles, or equitable criteria taking account of all the relevant circumstances, in order to achieve an equitable result.'[32]

In spite of this additional information, confusion remained, in particular about the links established by the ICJ in *Libya/Malta* case between equitable principles and relevant circumstances. Indeed, as explicitly mentioned in paragraph 46 of the judgment, the Court apparently considers 'the respect due to the all relevant circumstances' as one of the most important equitable principles. Does this imply that relevant circumstances should be considered as equitable principles by themselves? Or, on the contrary, are 'relevant circumstances' different in nature from the equitable principles identified by the judge? Anyway, the vagueness surrounding the notion of the relevant circumstances challenges the objectiveness pursued in the process of delimitation. However, in *Gulf of Maine*, the ICJ seems to have learned from the ambivalent sense of 'equitable principle' and, while referring to relevant circumstances, rather than *principles* used the term *criteria*, which are not in themselves principles and rules of international law.[33] According to the Chamber of the Court, 'delimitation is to be effected by the application of equitable criteria and by the use of practical methods capable of ensuring, with regard to the geographic configuration of the area and other relevant circumstances, an equitable result.'[34]

In spite of these attempts to clarify the role of equity in the maritime delimitation process, strong criticisms have been levelled at the subjectivity and the lack of predictability resulting from this blurred use of the concepts which leads to apply equity outside of the law, in other words 'autonomous equity.'[35]

[32] *Case concerning the Delimitation of Maritime Areas between Canada and France* [1992] 21 RIAA 265, [38].

[33] *Gulf of Maine*, n. 26, [89]: 'any agreement or other equivalent solution should involve the application of equitable criteria, namely criteria derived from equity which – whether they be designated "principles" or "criteria," the latter term being preferred by the Chamber for reasons of clarity.' See R. Kolb, *Case Law on Equitable Maritime Delimitation: Digest and Commentaries*[Jurisprudence sur les délimitations maritimes selon l'équite: répertoire et commentaires] (Nijhoff Leiden 2003) 291.

[34] *Gulf of Maine*, n. 26, [112].

[35] Kolb, n. 33. J.-M. Sorel, 'Le juge international face à l'équité dans le règlement de différends territoriaux,' in P. Weckel (ed.), *Le juge international et l'aménagement de l'espace: la spécificité du contentieux territorial* (Pedone Paris 1998) 161. J. Cazala, 'Retour sur les méthodes

6.2.2 *Implicit Reference to Autonomous Equity and the Risk of Judicial Subjectivity*

One of the main criticisms resulting from the use of equitable principles in maritime delimitation is the risk of granting a judgment *ex aequo et bono*.[36] This legitimate concern had already been highlighted by Judge Koretsky in 1969, in his dissenting opinion in *North Sea Continental Shelf*. Referring to the definition of equity in *Black's Law Dictionary* –'[Equity's] obligations is ethical rather than jural' – Koretsky affirmed that the use of equity in that sense 'may open the door to making subjective and therefore at times arbitrary evaluations, instead of following the guidance of established general principles and rules of international law.'[37]

Despite this first warning, the judges in The Hague gave priority to autonomous equity rather than to equity *infra legem*, in particular in *Tunisia/Libya*.[38] This case provided the point of departure for such a conception of equity. As has been observed by Orrego Vicuña: 'it seems that the ICJ moved on from a period where equitable principles are that ordered by the law (*North Sea Continental Shelf* case) behind a direct application of equity as law (*Tunisia v. Libya* case).'[39] The same criticism has been made by Judge Gros, in *Gulf of Maine*, in which case the Chamber of the Court also used a vague conception of equity. According to Gros, this approach departs from the firmly controlled equity of the *North Sea Continental Shelf* judgment of 1969 and the award in *Anglo-French Continental Shelf* of 1977 and leads to the disappearance of any legal rule governing maritime delimitation, since each judge decides at his discretion what is equitable or not.[40] Prosper Weil goes even further, considering this case law as being 'l'extrême limite de la déjuridisation.'[41]

Until the 1990s, the reasoning of the judges and arbitrators remained influenced by this conception of equity, used independently from any

de délimitation juridictionnelle d'espaces maritimes mises en œuvre dans quelques affaires récentes' (2008) 54 *Annuaire français de droit international* 412.

36 Miyoshi, n. 4, 1099.

37 Judge Koretsky, *North Sea Continental Shelf*, n. 13, Dissenting Opinion, 166.

38 Sorel, n. 35, 161 and 169.

39 F. Orrego Vicuña, 'Le pied du chancelier continue de s'allonger: les principes généraux et l'équité en droit international: à la recherche de limites à la flexibilité du droit,' in M. Kohen, R. Kolb, and D. Liva Tehindrazanarivelo (eds.), *Perspectives of International Law in the 21st Century: Liber Amicorum Professor Christian Dominicé in Honour of his 80th Birthday* (Martinus Nijhoff Leiden 2012) 81.

40 See *Gulf of Maine*, n. 26, Dissenting Opinion of Judge Gros, [29, 37].

41 P. Weil, *Perspectives du droit de la délimitation maritime* (Pedone Paris 1988) 190.

predetermined rule.[42] In spite of some criticisms about the risk of rendering arbitrary decisions, the majority of judges agreed with this use of equitable considerations in maritime delimitation process.[43] Consequently, equity could be said to have superseded the law and become the 'main actor of the trial.'[44] For example, as highlighted by Judges Oda and Schwebel in *Jan Mayen*,[45] whereas the Court applied the three-stage approach to arrive at an equitable solution, its insufficiently elaborated analysis implied a lack of objectivity. To accept such a lack of objectivity would be 'contrary to the elementary principle of legal security.'[46] Nevertheless, we do not observe any significant change in the case law until the 2000s. From then on, the courts and tribunals initiated a process of rationalization of the use of equity in the delimitation process.

6.3 Rationalization of the Use of Equity in the Maritime Delimitation Process

The reinforcement of the predictability of law has been obtained through a strict rationalization in the use of equity within the maritime delimitation process. In order to achieve this, the courts and tribunals have highlighted that the entire process of delimitation must be guided by the aim of

[42] R. Kolb, n. 33, xxii.

[43] E. Jiménez de Aréchaga, 'The Conception of Equity in Maritime Delimitation,' in P. L. Zanardi et al. (eds.), *Le droit international à l'heure de sa codification. Etudes en l'honneur de Roberto Ago* (Milan 1987) t. II, 229 *et seq*.

[44] F. Orrego Vicuña, n. 39, 78. Also P. Weil, 'Towards Relative Normativity in International Law,' (1983) 77 *American Journal of International Law* 413; P. Weil, 'Le droit international en quête de son identité: cours général de droit international public,' (1992) 237 in *Collected Courses of the Hague Academy of International Law* (Brill Leiden 1992) 245.

[45] According to Judge Schwebel:

> the Court by this holding of distributive justice has departed from the accepted law of the matter, as fashioned pre-eminently by it. It is not suggested that this departure from principle and precedent is legally fatal. If what is lawful in maritime delimitation by the Court is what is equitable, and if what is equitable is as variable as the weather of The Hague, then this innovation may be seen as, and it may be as defensible and desirable as another.' *Jan Mayen*, n. 6, Separate Opinion of Judge Schwebel, 118.

Also Sorel, n. 35, 161. Separate Opinion of Vice President Oda, ICJ Rep. 89, [118]. Oda stresses the lack of objectivity in the examination of the relevant circumstances and the potential realization of a delimitation *ex aequo et bono* [89, 98]. On judge Oda's positions, see O. Schachter, 'Linking Equity and Law in Maritime Delimitation,' in N. Ando, E. McWhinney, R. Wolfrum, and B. Baker Röben (eds.), *Liber Amicorum Judge Shigeru Oda* (Brill/Nijhoff Leiden 2002) 1163.

[46] P. Daillier, M. Forteau, and A. Pellet, *Droit international public* (LGDJ Paris 2009) 356.

obtaining an 'equitable solution' according to positive law (Section 6.3.1) and make, at least prima facie, a strict use of equitable considerations in its method of delimitation (Section 6.3.2).

6.3.1 *Equity* infra legem, *a General Aim in Order to Achieve an Equitable Solution as Required by Positive Law*

Since the 2000s, the practice of the courts and tribunals shows that equity does not provide a method of delimitation, even if there can be recourse to equitable considerations in the delimitation process. According to the judges and arbitrators, the 'equitable solution' is an aim to achieve. This was already said by the ICJ in 1969, and it has since then been clearly reaffirmed as a guideline that can be derived from the reasoning of the judge, as best illustrated by the statement of the Court in *Cameroon v. Nigeria*:

> The Court is bound to stress that in this connection that delimiting with a concern to achieving an equitable result, as required by current international law, is not the same as delimiting in equity. The Court's jurisprudence shows that, in disputes relating to maritime delimitation, equity is not a method of delimitation but solely an aim that should be borne in mind in effecting the delimitation.'[47]

The first objective is to get an equitable solution for a stable resolution of the dispute between the states. This objective is associated with the principle of reasonableness recognized in international law, which is encompassed in the notion of the 'equitable solution,' called for in Articles 74 and 83 of the LOSC.[48] The standard of 'reasonable regard' is not entirely new in maritime delimitation. It was discussed in the 1950s by the International Law Commission (ILC) during its codification of the regime of the high seas.[49] This standard is used more generally while interpreting and

[47] *Land and Maritime Boundary between Cameroon and Nigeria (Cameroon v. Nigeria; Equatorial Guinea intervening)* (Judgment) [2002] ICJ Rep. 303, [294].

[48] D. Anderson, 'The Principle of Reasonableness in the Law of the Sea,' in H. P. Hestermeyer, D. Köning, N. Matz-Lück, V. Röben, A. Seibert-Fohr, P.-T. Stoll, and S. Vöneky (eds.), *Coexistence, Cooperation and Solidarity, Liber Amicorum Rüdiger Wolfrum* (Martinus Nijhoff Leiden 2012) 667. Also D. Anderson, 'Recent Judicial Decisions Concerning Maritime Delimitation,' in L. del Castillo (ed.), *Law of the Sea, from Grotius to the International Tribunal for the Law of the Sea* (Brill/Nijhoff Leiden 2015) 500. The idea of reasonable result was already mentioned in *North Sea Continental Shelf*, n. 13, [90].

[49] The reasonable regard test implies to take into account the rights of the other users while applying the rule of freedom of the high seas (in case of conflicts between claims of navigation, claims of fishing and other claims). See Anderson, n. 48, 658–659. More generally

applying LOSC provisions. This has been recently illustrated by the ICJ in relation to the maritime delimitation process. In *Territorial and Maritime Dispute (Nicaragua v. Colombia)*, the Court stated that 'an equitable solution requires that each State enjoy reasonable entitlements in the areas into which its coasts project.'[50]

This last point refers to the ground used by the judge and the arbitrator to justify the use of equity in maritime delimitation. As recalled by the tribunal in *Barbados v. Trinidad and Tobago* in 2006, 'some early attempts by international courts and tribunals to define the role of equity resulted in distancing the outcome from the role of law and thus led to a state of confusion in the matter.'[51] Indeed, faced with these criticisms, the judiciary progressively specified that in applying equity it applies a normative principle that is well established in positive international law. Equity is therefore understood as a quality of law which guides its interpretation.[52] To this end, the ICJ has gradually relied on its previous decisions, and more particularly on *North Sea Continental Shelf*, where it observed that it did not intend to use equity outside the law:

> it is not a question of applying equity simply as a matter of abstract justice, but of applying a rule of law which itself requires the application of equitable principles, in accordance with the ideas which have always underlain the development of the legal regime of the continental shelf in this field.[53]

For example, in *Libya/Malta*, relying respectively on *North Sea Continental Shelf* and *Tunisia/Libya*, the Court observed that:

> the justice of which equity is an emanation, is not abstract justice but justice according to the rule of law; which is to say that its application should display consistency and a degree of predictability; even though it looks with particularity to the peculiar circumstances of an instant case, it also looks beyond it to principles of more general application [. . .] as the Court has also said, 'the legal concept of equity is a general principle directly applicable as law.' (ICJ Reports 1982, p. 60, para. 71)[54]

It seems quite surprising that the Court relies on *Tunisia/Libya* whereas it had been criticized at that time for applying equity without real regard for

on reasonableness and international law, see O. Corten, *L'utilisation du 'raisonnable' par le juge international: discours juridique, raison et contradictions* (Bruylant Bruxelles 1997).

[50] *Territorial and Maritime Dispute (Nicaragua v. Colombia)* (Judgment) [2012] ICJ Rep. 624, [216].

[51] *Barbados v. Trinidad and Tobago* case, n. 3, [230].

[52] Orrego Vicuña, n. 39, 79.

[53] *North Sea Continental Shelf*, n. 13, [85].

[54] *Libya/Malta*, n. 14, [45].

the law.[55] But, in this case, the Court adds: 'Yet the "Application of equitable principles is to be distinguished from a decision *ex aequo et bono.*"'[56]

Therefore, a differentiation is clearly made between autonomous equity and equity *infra legem*, which is implied by the reference to an 'equitable solution.' According to that case law (*Libya/Malta, Tunisia/Libya*), the latter approach should prevail. With this clarification in mind, the ICJ certainly wanted to answer the criticism about the subjectivity of previous decisions. The reference to equitable principles, considered as a normative concept, allows the judge to justify that his decision is based on positive law. Even if such principles are flexible,[57] they are legal norms giving different relevant circumstances their respective weight.[58]

This explanation is associated with the introduction of the concept of 'equitable solution' in the LOSC, as a part of the legal rule relating to the delimitation process.[59] Therefore, the reference to equity is legally expressed; it is part of a normative rule. In 2014, in his separate opinion in *Maritime Dispute (Peru v. Chile)*, Orrego Vicuña recalled the evolution of the jurisprudence on the place of equity within the law through the LOSC provisions:

> in its first attempts to use equity in the context of maritime delimitation, the Court did not clearly rely on this source in keeping within the bounds of the law, which was largely left undetermined. Following the evolution of its jurisprudence, the Court then turned to a more precisely bound form of equity. This is the very understanding of Article 74, paragraph 1, of the 1982 United Nations Convention on the Law of the Sea in considering equitable results of maritime delimitation, not in isolation from, but in conjunction with agreements between the parties, all of it effected on the basis of international law.[60]

These provisions have led the judiciary to use equity *infra legem*, as an adjustment factor of the legal rule to allow for the individualization of situations that a strict application of law would render unjust.[61] As rightly highlighted in *Barbados v. Trinidad and Tobago*,

> The Tribunal must exercise its judgment in order to decide upon a line that is, in its view, both equitable and as practically satisfactory as possible while at the same time in keeping with the requirement of achieving a stable

[55] See e.g. the Dissenting Opinion of Judge Oda, *Tunisia/Libya*, n. 25, [157]. Also Dissenting Opinion of Judge Gros, ibid., [143].

[56] Ibid. [57] Kolb, n. 33, 332.

[58] M Bedjaoui, 'L'énigme des principes equitables dans le droit des délimitations maritimes,' (1990) *REDI* 382.

[59] See LOSC, Arts. 74(1) and 83(1). [60] *Peru v. Chile*, n. 6, [36]. [61] Sorel, n. 35, 133.

> legal outcome. Certainty, equity, and stability are thus integral parts of the process of delimitation.[62]

To conclude, equity has not totally disappeared from judicial reasoning, but it has been reduced to the use of equitable considerations within the law. For that reason, we can affirm that equity has been rationalized in order to further the reliability and predictability of decisions in this matter.

6.3.2 *The Strict Use of Equitable Considerations in the Three-Stage Method of Delimitation*

The section does not aim to make a detailed analysis of the process of delimitation, which is part of other chapters of the present volume.[63] It is nevertheless important to recall the three stages of maritime delimitation and the role given to equity in each of them, since the introduction of those three stages has been a way for the judiciary to progressively ensure more objectivity.

The privileged method of delimitation was clearly recalled by the ICJ in *Black Sea* in 2009, and has, since then, been systematically repeated by courts and tribunals in almost all cases.[64] At that time, the ICJ did not pretend to create the three-stage process, but applied it on the basis of its previous jurisprudence.[65] As well-summarized in *Territorial and Maritime Dispute (Nicaragua v. Colombia)* in 2012,[66] in the first stage, the Court establishes a provisional delimitation line between territories, consisting of the construction of an equidistance line; then, it adjusts this provisional line depending on the existence of relevant circumstances and, in the final stage, the Court conducts 'a disproportionality test in which it assesses whether the effect of the line, as adjusted or shifted, is that the Parties' respective shares of the relevant area are markedly disproportionate to their respective relevant coasts.'[67]

62 *Barbados v. Trinidad and Tobago* case, n. 3, [244].

63 See Chapters 2, 3, and 8.

64 Recalled in *Peru v. Chile* case, n. 6, [179–180]. See also e.g. *In the Matter of the Bay of Bengal Maritime Boundary (Bangladesh v. India)*, PCA Case 2010-16, [341]. On that point, Eiriksson, n. 15, 519–520. See Anderson, n. 48, 591.

65 See *Black Sea*, n. 18, [115–122]. In *Territorial and Maritime Dispute (Nicaragua v. Colombia)*, n. 50, the Court observed that it 'has made clear on a number of occasions that the methodology which it will normally employ when called upon to effect a delimitation between overlapping continental shelf and exclusive economic zone entitlements involves proceeding in three stages,' [190].

66 Ibid., [191–193].

67 Ibid.

The strict use of equitable considerations in this method appears as a way of constraining equity to legal considerations. Therefore, as mentioned by the arbitral tribunal in *Barbados v. Trinidad and Tobago*, 'the process of achieving an equitable result is thus constrained by legal principle'[68] and, on the other hand, 'certainty is [. . .] combined with the need for an equitable result.'[69]

First, we witness to the apparent exclusion of equity at the first stage of delimitation. As the arbitral tribunal in *Guyana v. Suriname* observed, 'in the course of the last two decades international courts and tribunals dealing with disputes concerning the delimitation of the continental shelf and the exclusive economic zone have come to embrace a clear role for equidistance.'[70] The priority given by courts and tribunals to the establishment of a provisional equidistance line is due to its 'scientific' character, as clearly set out by the ICJ in *Nicaragua v. Honduras*:

> The jurisprudence of the Court sets out the reasons why the equidistance method is widely used in the practice of maritime delimitation: it has a certain intrinsic value because of its scientific character and the relative ease with which it can be applied.[71]

In giving priority to the line of equidistance during the first stage of the delimitation, based on equality in the process of delimitation, equitable considerations seem to be relegated prima facie to a secondary role.[72]

But equitable considerations are introduced in the second step of the delimitation process, while examining the existence of relevant circumstances to ensure an equitable result. At this point, the equidistance-relevant circumstances principle appears to be the best combination between certainty and an equitable result, as an expression of equity *infra legem*.[73] As affirmed by Judges ad hoc Mensah and Oxman in *Bangladesh/Myanmar*:

68 Ibid., [243].

69 *Barbados v. Trinidad and Tobago*, n. 3, [242], referring to *Qatar/Bahrain* and *Cameroon v. Nigeria*.

70 *In the Matter of an Arbitration between Guyana and Suriname (Guyana v. Suriname)* [2007] 30 RIAA 1, [335].

71 In this case, Nicaragua asked for the delimitation of the territorial sea, the continental shelf, and the exclusive economic zone. *Territorial and Maritime Dispute between Nicaragua and Honduras in the Caribbean Sea (Nicaragua v. Honduras)* (Judgment), [2007] ICJ Rep. 649, [272].

72 For a more detailed assessment of this apparent relegation and its limits, see Chapters 8 and 9 of this volume.

73 As explicitly expressed by the tribunal in *Barbados v. Trinidad and Tobago*, n. 3, [242].

> The law applicable to delimitation of the exclusive economic zone and the continental shelf, as articulated and applied by international courts and tribunals, entails neither a unyielding insistence on mathematical certainty nor an unbounded quest for an equitable solution. The equidistance/relevant circumstances method of delimitation seeks to balance the need for objectivity and predictability with the need for sufficient flexibility to answer circumstances relevant to a particular delimitation.[74]

Within this second step of delimitation, equity seems to be reintroduced at two levels in the examination of an individual case – the search for an equitable result and the examination of potential relevant circumstances – even if these two aspects are mostly interlinked. In any case, it is strictly intended as equity *infra legem*, to go beyond a strict reading of the law,[75] but no to go beyond the law. This objective has been progressively explained by the ICJ in its jurisprudence, and was clearly formulated in *Black Sea* in 2009:

> once the provisional equidistance line has been drawn, [the Court] shall 'then [consider] whether there are factors calling for the adjustment or shifting of that line in order to achieve an "equitable result"' [. . .]. Such factors have usually been referred to in the jurisprudence of the Court, since the *North Sea Continental Shelf (Federal Republic of Germany/Denmark; Federal Republic of Germany/Netherlands)* cases, as the relevant circumstances (*Judgment, ICJ Reports 1969*, p. 53, para. 53). Their function is to verify that the provisional equidistance line, drawn by the geometrical method from the determined base points on the coasts of the Parties is not, in light of the particular circumstances of the case, perceived as inequitable.[76]

While making a reference to *North Sea Continental Shelf*, the use of such a method was not that clear for a long time. The 2000s judgments have attempted to specify this matter. First of all in *Cameroon v. Nigeria*, where the ICJ affirmed that:

> The Court has on various occasions made it clear what the applicable criteria, principles and rules of delimitation are when a line covering several zones of coincident jurisdiction has to be determined. They are expressed in the so-called equitable principles/relevant circumstances method. This method, which is very similar to the equidistance/special circumstances

[74] *Bangladesh/Myanmar*, n. 9, Joint Declaration Mensah & Oxman [4–8].
[75] O. Schachter, n. 45, 1163. [76] *Black Sea*, n. 18, [155].

> method applicable in delimitation of the territorial sea, involves first drawing an equidistance line, then considering whether there are factors of that line in order to achieve an 'equitable result.'[77]

Since then, it has been confirmed in *Nicaragua v. Honduras*[78] and *Black Sea*[79] that the method of delimitation is guided by the need of obtaining an equitable result.

Arbitral tribunals have taken the same point of view, as shown by *Guyana v. Suriname* dating from 2007. It is interesting to observe that, contrary to the ICJ, the tribunal mentions the objective of obtaining an equitable solution and not of equitable result.[80] If we look at the ICJ jurisprudence, it seems that the expressions 'equitable result' and 'equitable solution' are not used exactly in the same way. Indeed, in the Court's decisions, the expression 'equitable result' only appears as part of the method of delimitation (at the second stage) while the entire process of delimitation (including the three steps) is used to get an 'equitable solution' – as said the main goal of maritime delimitation as expressed in the LOSC (Articles 74 and 83). In spite of the lack of differentiation by the tribunal, the final objective remains the same: to obtain an 'equitable solution.' By the way, we notice that in its reasoning the tribunal, in using the expression 'equitable solution,' explicitly makes a reference to Articles 74 and 83 of the LOSC.[81]

77 *Cameroon v. Nigeria*, n. 47, [288].

78 *Nicaragua v. Honduras*, n. 71, [271]: 'As to the plotting of a single maritime boundary the Court has on various occasions made it clear that, when a line covering several zones of coincident jurisdictions is to be determined, the so-called equitable principles/relevant circumstances method may usefully be applied, as in these maritime zones this method is also suited to achieving an equitable result.'

79 As the Court observed: '[it] should adjust the line in order to achieve the "equitable solution" as required by Articles 74, paragraph 1, and 83, paragraph 1, of UNCLOS' (*Black Sea*, n. 18, [155]). Recalling *Nicaragua v. Honduras*, the Court stated that '[it] has also made clear that when the line to be drawn covers several zones of coincident jurisdictions, the "so-called equitable principles/relevant circumstances method may usefully be applied, as in these maritime zones this method is also suited to achieving and equitable result"' (ibid., [120]).

80 'The case law of the International Court of Justice and arbitral jurisprudence as well as state practice are at one in holding that the delimitation process should, in appropriate cases, begin by positing a provisional equidistance line which may be adjusted in the light of relevant circumstances in order to achieve an equitable solution' (*Guyana v. Suriname*, n. 70, [342]).

81 The first part of the reasoning is: 'Articles 74 and 83 of the Convention require that the Tribunal achieve an "equitable" solution. The case law of the International Court of Justice and arbitral jurisprudence . . . ' (ibid.).

These terminological remarks confirm that equity remains present at least two levels of the whole process of delimitation: as a general aim to achieve and as being part of the technical tool at the disposal of the judges and arbitrators for obtaining a delimitation line. In this second operational aspect, equity is not only used in the determination of an equitable result, but also in the identification of potential relevant circumstances. As regards the latter, the question remains to determine what these relevant circumstances, which are designated in case law as 'factors calling for the adjustment or shifting' of the provisional line.[82]

Here again, even if this question is covered in another chapter,[83] it is important to recall the criteria used by the judiciary in order to evaluate to what extent equitable considerations are taken into account to decide a case. As indicated below, in the case law dating from the 1980s, these factors/relevant circumstances where linked by the Court with 'equitable principles.'[84] According to Bedjaoui, it is nevertheless important to distinguish these two concepts.[85] In any case, the factors usually taken into account in the case law are mostly those linked with the geographical context, such as a substantial difference in the length of the respective coasts. Except for the geographical context, the judiciary traditionally has refused to take into consideration either the economic (fisheries, oil, and gas concessions etc.) or the political context of a case.[86] This reluctance can easily be explained by the subjectivity inherent in those contexts and, more generally, by the subjectivity inherent in the second stage of delimitation, as outlined by Judges Nelson, Chandrasekhara Rao and Cot in their declaration appended to the judgment in *Bangladesh/Myanmar*. As they observe, equity can only come into play at the second step of delimitation because it contains an inevitable part of subjectivity.[87] On the contrary, there apparently is a tendency of the judges and arbitrators to rely on a very mathematical reasoning while examining the relevant circumstances. *Territorial and Maritime Dispute (Nicaragua v. Colombia)*[88] is a good example: relying

[82] See abstracts mentioned in *Black Sea* and *Cameroon v. Nigeria*, below.

[83] See Chapter 8.

[84] See Section 6.2 of this chapter. *Tunisia/Libya*, n. 25, [85]. Miyoshi, n. 4, 1099.

[85] 'Equitable principles are legal norms giving to different pertinent circumstances their respective weight.' Bedjaoui, n. 58, 382.

[86] J. Cazala, 'Retour sur les méthodes de délimitation juridictionnelle d'espaces maritimes mises en œuvre dans quelques affaires récentes' (2008) 54 *Annuaire français de droit international* 411.

[87] Giraudeau, n. 9, 106.

[88] See *Territorial and Maritime Dispute (Nicaragua v. Colombia)*, n. 50, [215–216]. Also L. Delabie, 'Le fragile équilibre entre prévisibilité juridique et opportunité judiciaire en

on a ratio between the relevant Colombian coast and that of Nicaragua of 1:8.2, the Court concludes that 'this is undoubtedly a substantial disparity [...] that requires an adjustment or shifting of the provisional line.'[89]

Finally, to achieve an appropriate balance between equality and equity in this second stage of the delimitation, it is important to keep in mind that the judicial reasoning should be guided by transparency. Such a principle is not restricted to maritime delimitation law.[90] However, it is of particular importance in this field since the judges and arbitrators have stressed the need for objectivity in their reasoning. This has been clearly expressed by the tribunal in *Bangladesh v. India*, stating that 'a high degree of transparency can be achieved'[91] in the adjustment process. The question however is knowing how to arrive at such transparency. Judge Rao in this case argued that the tribunal failed to meet the test of transparency and, therefore did not achieve an equitable result.[92] The rather obscure explanations of the Tribunal – in particular its choosing of Sandy Point as defining the extent of India's relevant coast and the creation of a grey area as part of achieving an equitable result[93] – suggest that the quest for transparency is not necessarily the best way to get an equitable result. It is submitted that these two concepts do not necessarily go hand in hand. Not only has the concept of transparency itself to be legally defined more clearly, but the requirement of a high degree of transparency could lead to a strict application of predefined delimitation criteria which would be counterproductive to reaching an equitable and a predictable result.

Finally, in the last stage of the delimitation process, the judiciary makes, at least apparently, a restrictive use of equity through the disproportionality test.[94] As the Court explained in *Black Sea*:

> at a third stage, the Court will verify that the line [...] does not, as it stands, lead to an inequitable result by reason of any marked disproportion between the ratio of the respective coastal lengths and the ratio between the relevant maritime area of each State by reference to the delimitation line.'[95]

matière de délimitation maritime: l'arrêt de la Cour internationale de Justice du 19 novembre 2012 dans l'*affaire du différend territorial et maritime (Nicaragua c. Colombie),*' (2012) *Annuaire français de droit international* 223.

89 *Territorial and Maritime Dispute (Nicaragua v. Colombia)*, n. 50, [211].

90 On transparency in international law, see A. Bianchi and A. Peters (eds.), *Transparency in International Law* (Cambridge University Press Cambridge 2013) 620.

91 *Bangladesh v. India*, n. 64, [344].

92 Ibid., Rao Declaration, [5–6].

93 Ibid., *award* [301].

94 For a discussion of the disproportionality test, see Chapter 11 of this volume.

95 *Black Sea*, n. 18, [122].

Subsequently, the Court in *Territorial and Maritime Dispute (Nicaragua v. Colombia)* pointed out that the objective is to ensure that 'there is not a disproportion so gross as to '"taint" the result and render it inequitable [. . .].'[96] The case law indicates that proportionality has never been considered as being in itself a method of delimitation,[97] but rather an aspect of equity, a means of checking whether a provisional delimitation established by the use of equitable principles/criteria is satisfactory.[98] As clearly affirmed by the ICJ in *Black Sea*, it is a '*final check* for an equitable outcome';[99] a tool of verification. In *Barbados v. Trinidad and Tobago*, the tribunal concluded in the same way, demonstrating consistency with the existing case. According to the Tribunal, it used the test of proportionality 'to ensure that the result is not tainted by some form of *gross disproportion*.'[100]

To conclude, in the whole process of delimitation – whether in the global objective pursued or in the material tools used, equity is apparently mainly conceived by the judge or the arbitrator as being *infra legem*. But such a rationalization of equity, even if firmly stated in the case law, should not obscure the reappearance of subjectivity due to the judicial power of the judge or the arbitrator, which allows him to implicitly reintroduce autonomous equity in his reasoning.

6.4 The Judge's and Arbitrator's Judicial Power and the Irreducible Subjectivity in the Process of Maritime Delimitation

The process of rationalization by the courts and tribunals since the 2000s does not completely hide the significant role played by equity in judicial reasoning. Equity is reintroduced through the search for a good balance of interests that the judge or the arbitrator seems to have in mind while resolving a case. Linked with the judge's or arbitrator's judicial power in deciding the individual case, this observation is particularly striking in the maritime delimitation field. As observed by Sorel, the role of equity

[96] Confirmed in *Peru v. Chile*: 'The next and third step is to determine whether the provisional equidistance line drawn from Point A produces a result which is significantly disproportionate in terms of the lengths of the relevant coasts and the division of the relevant area. The purpose is to assess the equitable nature of the result,' n. 6, [192].

[97] *Black Sea*, n. 18, [110].

[98] See *Tunisia/Libya*, n. 25, [130–131]; *Gulf of Maine*, n. 26, [185].

[99] *Black Sea*, n. 18, [122] (emphasis provided).

[100] *Barbados v. Trinidad and Tobago*, n. 3 [232] (emphasis provided). This conception should be nuanced when considering the use of the proportionality test in practice (see Section 6.4 of the present chapter).

in international law – autonomous equity or equity infra legem – depends on the position adopted by the judge or the arbitrator.[101] Associated with the judicial power of the judge in the maritime delimitation area – even considered by some observers as implying a normative function[102] – the use of equity challenges the objectiveness of the judge's reasoning.

This phenomenon is perceived at each stage of the method of delimitation. Firstly, in the possibility for the judge to choose between equidistance – including itself a certain margin of appreciation in the selection of basepoints – and another method of delimitation as the provisional delimitation line; secondly, in examining the relevant circumstances in an individual case; and then in the implementation of the disproportionality test. In any case, a gap may be observed between the judicial discourse consisting of limiting the role of equity, and the reality of the material result obtained in individual cases.

6.4.1 *Equidistance versus Other Methods of Delimitation in Looking for an Equitable Result: A Subjective Choice?*

According to the jurisprudence, the equidistance principle is considered as the favoured means used by the judge for the first step of the delimitation process because of its scientific character.[103] This has been confirmed recently by the ICJ[104] and arbitral tribunals.[105] But this does not guarantee a complete objectivity in the judicial reasoning. As observed by Judge Cot in *Bangladesh/Myanmar*, a change of methodology can highlight the subjectivity of the judge.[106] If more appropriate, another method should be used, as illustrated in recent decisions and awards, such as the *Nicaragua v. Honduras* and the *Bay of Bengal* cases. Indeed, the judiciary can choose not to use the equidistance-relevant circumstances method. As already affirmed by the ICJ in 1969, the functional primacy given to the equidistance method does not mean a legal primacy:

[101] Sorel, n. 35, 159–163.

[102] Giraudeau, n. 9, 106. See *Bangladesh/Myanmar*, n. 9, Declaration of Judge Wolfrum, [2].

[103] See further n. 71.

[104] *Nicaragua v. Honduras*, n. 71, [272]; *Black Sea*, n. 18, [116]. On this point, see J. Cazala, n. 35, 414.

[105] *Barbados v. Trinidad and Tobago*, n. 3, [306]. *Guyana v. Suriname*, n. 70, [335]. G. Giraudeau, n. 9, 105.

[106] *Bangladesh/Myanmar*, n. 9, Separate Opinion of Judge Cot, 189. For Judge Cot, there is a 'perversion of methodology,' ibid., 184. See also G. Giraudeau, n. 9, 107.

> It would probably be true to say that no other method of delimitation has the same combination of practical convenience and certainty of application. Yet these factors do not suffice of themselves to convert what is a method into a rule of law, making the acceptance of the results of using that method obligatory in all cases in which the parties do not agree otherwise, or in which 'special circumstances' cannot be shown to exist. Juridically, if there is such a rule, it must draw its legal force from other factors than the existence of these advantages, important though they may be. It should also be noticed that the counterpart of this conclusion is no less valid, and that the practical advantages of the equidistance method would continue to exist whether its employment were obligatory or not.[107]

More recently, in *Barbados v. Trinidad and Tobago*, the Tribunal confirmed that 'no method of delimitation can be considered of and by itself compulsory.'[108] In *Guyana v. Suriname*, the tribunal is more nuanced. While answering to Suriname's argument that there is no legal presumption in favour of the equidistance method,[109] it recalls that 'it has become normal to begin by considering the equidistance line and possible adjustments and to adopt some other method of delimitation only if the circumstances justify it.'[110]

However, the judiciary still remains free to replace the equidistance method by another tool of delimitation. According to some observers this position is even beneficial. As Judge Abraham explained in *Territorial and Maritime Dispute (Nicaragua v. Colombia)*:

> there are cases which are presented in such specific terms that it is, on the whole, preferable to acknowledge that the Court needs to depart from its usual technique, and to explain why, rather than to sacrifice clarity and intelligibility to the semblance of an illusory continuity.[111]

107 *North Sea Continental Shelf*, n. 13, [23].

108 *Barbados v. Trinidad and Tobago*, n. 3, [304–306].

109 *Guyana v. Suriname*, n. 70, [222].

110 Ibid., [335 and 339], making reference to the Award of the Tribunal in *In the Matter of an Arbitration Pursuant to an Agreement to Arbitrate Dated 3 October 1996 between the Government of the State of Eritrea and the Government of the Republic of Yemen (Eritrea/Yemen)* [1998] 12 RIAA 211, [2.28].

111 *Territorial and Maritime Dispute (Nicaragua v. Colombia)*, n. 50, separate Opinion of Judge Abraham, [35]. Judge Abraham also observed that

> I understand that the Court wishes to give all its observers, and first and foremost States, the impression that it does not use arbitrary methods to achieve an equitable solution, but that it implements proven and consistent techniques. And it is perfectly true that there is nothing arbitrary about the Court's approach, which is characterized merely by a scrupulous search for the best solution. (ibid.)

However, such a choice is surprising since the jurisprudence over the years has made a significant effort to give primacy to the equidistance principle, in the name of predictability of the maritime delimitation process. In this context, at least the question remains to know how the judiciary justifies not resorting to equidistance in specific cases. We must say that the grounds used are wrapped in mystery. In *Guyana v. Suriname*, whereas the tribunal started with a provisional equidistance line and considered that there were no geographical peculiarities requiring it to adopt a different methodology, it observed that such geographical peculiarities might 'be taken into account as relevant circumstances, for the purpose, if necessary, of adjusting or shifting the provisional delimitation line.'[112] Less than one month later, in *Nicaragua v. Honduras*, the ICJ was confronted with the same question. In this case, the Court observes that 'the equidistance method does not automatically have priority over other methods of delimitation and, in particular circumstances, there may be factors which make the application of the equidistance method inappropriate.'[113] In conclusion, the Court observes that the geographical context does not permit to use the equidistance method: the unstable nature of the relevant coasts would lead to inherently unstable base points.[114] Therefore, it applies the bisector method, insisting precisely on its objectivity:

> The use of a bisector [...] has proved to be a viable substitute method in certain circumstances where equidistance is not possible or appropriate. The justification for the application of the bisector method in maritime delimitation lies in the configuration of and relationship between the relevant coastal fronts and the maritime areas to be delimited. [...] Like equidistance, the bisector method is a geometrical approach that can be used to give legal effect to the 'criterion long held to be as equitable as it is simple, namely that in principle, while having regard to the special circumstances of the case, one should aim at an equal division of areas where the maritime projections of the coasts of the States ... converge and overlap.' (Delimitation of the Maritime Boundary in the Gulf of Maine Area, Judgment, ICJ Reports 1984, p. 327, para. 195)[115]

But such a justification, based on the geographical result, is not entirely convincing. According to Judge Ranjeva, the recourse to 'particular circumstances' to depart from the application of the provisional median line rule and to justify the use of a different rule, that of the bisector, is problematic:

[112] *Guyana v. Suriname*, n. 70, [372]. [113] *Nicaragua v. Honduras*, n. 71, [272].
[114] Ibid., [280–281, 287]. [115] Ibid.

> The major problem is that the majority of the Members of the Court base themselves upon those circumstances, as distinct from the circumstances known as 'special or relevant,' are no longer assigned the merely corrective function prescribed by the law and all jurisprudence to date, but instead a rule-making function. [. . .] Contrary to the Court's jurisprudence, which excludes from the field of directly applicable rules any principle other than that of preliminary and provisional equidistance, the present Judgment challenges the creative exercise progressively undertaken by the Court. It opens up the way for new uncertainties which may lead to a direct normativity of equitable principles at the expense of the rule of positive law.[116]

The use of the bisector method appears a way of reintroducing autonomous equity in the first stage of the delimitation process. More generally, the Court's decision not to use the equidistance method raises the question of a reversal of the jurisprudence[117] and of its consequences on the predictability of justice advocated by the judges and arbitrators since the 1980s. Last but not least, the way the judges and arbitrators respectively used equidistance, the bisector method, and relevant circumstances in recent case law could lead to a risk of confusion between the different stages of the method of delimitation. Indeed, what is considered by the jurisprudence as the prevalent method is the 'equidistance-relevant circumstances' method – as said, the first two stages of the delimitation process – rather than the 'equidistance method' by itself. In mixing equidistance (including the selective use of basepoints in determining the provisional line), the bisector method, and relevant circumstances, the judiciary reintroduces equity at the outset of the delimitation, conducing to a renewal of equity as an autonomous source of law which departs from the effort of rationalization of the solutions elaborated in the jurisprudence since the early 2000s. As observed by Judge Torres Bernárdez, 'there is a return to the idea of *sui generis* solutions for each delimitation, in other words a relapse into pragmatism and subjectivity.'[118] In that case, the bisector line is inequitable, creating much more serious problems of law and equity than the equidistance line.[119] This difference would reinforce the lack of predictability and of certainty in the process of delimitation. Such a threat is also perceptible in the examination of the relevant circumstances made by courts and tribunals.

[116] Ibid., Separate opinion of Judge Ranjeva, [16–17]. [117] Ibid., [9].
[118] Ibid., Dissenting opinion of Judge ad hoc Torres Bernárdez, [122].
[119] Ibid., [128–130].

6.4.2 *A Limited Role of Equitable Considerations While Examining Relevant Circumstances: A Risk for Legal Certainty?*

Courts and tribunals mostly take into account relevant circumstances of a geographical nature as a factor of adjustment of the provisional line. Yet, they are confronted with the arguments of parties who rely on economic and political considerations – mainly based on fishery activities[120] and on the exploitation of natural resources – in order to justify an adjustment of the provisional delimitation line.

It must be said, as observed by the tribunal in *Barbados v. Trinidad and Tobago*, that there is no 'magic formula' in the process of delimitation.[121] In that context, while referring to equitable principles to assess the role of specific circumstances, the judiciary gets, once again, a significant margin of appreciation depending upon the specific factual circumstances of the case. This opportunity is accentuated by there is not exhaustive list of relevant circumstances used by the judiciary to explain its reasoning.

Nevertheless, in practice, we observe that the judges and arbitrators are very reluctant to qualify economic considerations as relevant circumstances. As observed by the ICJ in *Cameroon v. Nigeria*: 'it follows from the jurisprudence that, [. . .] oil concessions and oil wells are not in themselves to be considered as relevant circumstances justifying the adjustment or shifting of the provisional delimitation line.'[122] This finding has been confirmed in *Barbados v. Trinidad and Tobago* in relation to the relevance of fishing resources. The sole example in which the judges accept to take into account these circumstances is in cases where the parties have expressly or implicitly agreed[123] to adjust the delimitation line, as recalled – but not recognized – in *Barbados v. Trinidad and Tobago*.[124] On the other hand, the ICJ specifies that evidence of a tacit agreement must be compelling.[125]

The reluctance of the judiciary to take into account economic circumstances is understandable in order to escape the criticism of subjective reasoning within the process of delimitation through the use of subjective considerations to resolve the case. As recalled by the Annex VII

[120] See e.g. *Gulf of Maine*, n. 26, [237]; *Jan Mayen*, n. 6, [76]; argument of Barbados in *Barbados v. Trinidad and Tobago*, n. 3, [125].

[121] *Barbados v. Trinidad and Tobago*, n. 3, [373].

[122] *Cameroon v. Nigeria*, n. 47, [304].

[123] J. Cazala, n. 35, 423 and following.

[124] *Barbados v. Trinidad and Tobago*, n. 3, [270].

[125] *Nicaragua v. Honduras*, n. 71, [253]. J. Cazala, n. 35, 426.

Tribunal in *Bangladesh v. India*, while examining the relevant circumstances invoked by the parties,[126] 'the purpose of adjusting an equidistance line is not to refashion geography, or to compensate for the inequalities of nature; there can be no question of distributive justice.'[127] This attitude contrasts with the margin of appreciation operated in the first step of delimitation.[128] Moreover, it is only an apparent self-restraint that is affirmed here. As the tribunal in *Bangladesh v. India* noted, a diversity of adjustments may be necessary to obtain an equitable solution.[129] The adjustments, made up of 'considérations d'opportunité,'[130] through implementation of equity considerations, stem from judicial alchemy.[131] In fact, the judges seem to conjure up what will be the equitable result.

Finally, in refusing to take into consideration economic circumstances, is there no risk for the judiciary to grant an inequitable solution, contrary to the objective of the law of maritime delimitation? Indeed, if we adopt a realist point of view, it is difficult to exclude, while resolving a dispute, its economic and political context. Of course, the sole role of the court/tribunal is to apply the positive law. But, since the positive law in the field of maritime delimitation allows taking into account the factors that would lead to an equitable solution for getting a long-term resolution of the dispute, why should this opportunity not be fully used? Refusal to include these economic factors could be counterproductive.[132]

6.4.3 *The Ambivalent Role of Equity Consideration in the Test of Proportionality*

Even if proportionality has always been a central element in the delimitation process, there is no consensus about the role played by that principle.[133] Proportionality has been used in different ways: as a tool in the process of delimitation or as a test of its result.[134] For some observers proportionality is regarded as a test of equity; for others as a way of adjusting the provisional boundary; whereas still others qualify it as an equitable

[126] Coastal instability, concavity, or economic circumstances (*Bangladesh v. India*, n. 64, [395]).
[127] Ibid., [397].
[128] See the discussion on the use of the equidistance and bisector methods above at Section 6.4.1.
[129] See *Bangladesh v. India*, n. 64, [327]. G. Giraudeau, n. 9, 109.
[130] G. Giraudeau, n. 9, 106.
[131] Ibid., 109.
[132] This point has been addressed in different cases (see e.g. *Tunisia/Libya*, n. 25, [106–107]; *Libya/Malta*, n. 14, [48, 50].
[133] See further Chapter 11 of this volume.
[134] Miyoshi, n. 4, 1099.

principle.[135] These different views imply that the role of proportionality varies, as does the place of equity in its context.

Does the strict application of proportionality by the judge mean a limited role of equity in this last stage of the delimitation process? The answer is in the negative. Even if proportionality is guided by quantitative parameters, the judge or the arbitrator has recognized the subjectivity involved in the method. On this point, whereas in the first stage of delimitation, the judge carefully adopts a mathematical methodology, it seems to be excluded in this last stage. Such a phenomenon is accentuated by a different application of the test depending on the situation. As the ICJ has observed examining disproportion:

> is not a question capable of being answered by reference to any mathematical formula but is a matter, which can be answered only in the light of all the circumstances of the particular case.[136]

Certainly, the court or the tribunal takes care of defining the relevant area and the relevant coast[137] in order to evaluate a potential disproportion. Again, the 'calculation of the relevant area does not purport to be precise and is approximate since the first objective of delimitation is to achieve a delimitation that is equitable.'[138] In *Barbados v. Trinidad and Tobago*, the Tribunal affirms that the test of proportionality is not mathematically determined.[139] The refusal to follow a strict mathematical calculation, which could lead to an 'inequitable result,'[140] is not entirely new in the case law. It was already implicit in the ICJ's decisions such as *North Sea Continental Shelf*, *Libya/Malta* and *Jan Mayen*.[141] It is nevertheless interesting to highlight that these decisions have been largely interpreted as exemplifying a recourse to autonomous equity in the judicial reasoning, which could lead to a subjective decision.[142] Moreover, it seems that, contrary to the necessity of using mathematical tools in the previous stages, at this third stage, using such a tool seems inappropriate. This argument leaves the observer quite sceptical. Whereas the Tribunal affirmed that the identification of the relevant coasts is a means for objectiveness,[143] the way

[135] R. Kolb, 33, 332.

[136] *Territorial and Maritime Dispute (Nicaragua v. Colombia)*, n. 50, [242].

[137] For a discussion of the roles of relevant coasts, see *Black Sea*, n. 18, [78]. See further Chapter 7 of this volume.

[138] Ibid., [111]. See also *Territorial and Maritime Dispute (Nicaragua v. Colombia)*, n. 50, [158]. More recently, *Peru v. Chile*, n. 6, [192].

[139] Ibid., [328]. [140] Ibid. [141] See Section 6.2 of the present chapter.

[142] See Section 6.2.2 of the present chapter.

[143] *Barbados v. Trinidad and Tobago*, n. 3, [231].

in which judges and arbitrators apply this last step contrasts with the aim of an objective process of delimitation. It apparently reintroduces some degree of uncertainty in the use of equitable considerations. At least, it recalls the huge difficulty to find in the maritime delimitation process a proper balance between legal certainty and an equitable solution and the subsequent impossibility to ignore the part of subjectivity inherent to the judiciary reasoning in the whole maritime delimitation process.

6.5 Conclusions

In 1995, Paul Reuter said about equity: 'Few words are as pleasing to the mind and heart, deeply affecting as little waiting inscribed in the depths of human nature, but instead few remain as mysterious.'[144] As we look at the role of equity in maritime delimitation law, the mystery is still not solved. Although mainly linked with the equity *infra legem* in the recent case law, the use of equitable considerations can sometimes be a way for the judge or the arbitrator to go beyond the law in his legal reasoning, leading to a reminiscence of autonomous equity.

More generally, despite the judiciary's reluctance to use a concept that could introduce subjectivity into the legal reasoning, equitable considerations, on the condition that they are not completely outside the law, can be a way of obtaining legal certainty by resolving a dispute in a sustainable manner. Indeed, it allows the judge or the arbitrator to take into consideration the peculiar context of a case beyond the strict application of a legal rule to the extent it leads to an unjust result. Of course, the balance between flexibility and predictability of the law is hard to find. But at the same time, it is impossible for the judiciary to ignore the intrinsic relationship between law and justice; and it is, to some extent, a guarantee for the effectiveness of the legal norm. For all these reasons, equity conceived as a general standard to take into account while applying a legal rule will always be part of the case law not only in the maritime delimitation field, but also beyond it.

[144] P. Reuter, *Le développement de l'ordre juridique international, écrits de droit international* (Economica Paris 1995) 28.

7

Relevant Coasts and Relevant Area

The Difficulty of Developing General Concepts in a Case-Specific Context

ALEX G. OUDE ELFERINK*

7.1 Introduction

Geography no doubt is at the heart of the law of maritime delimitation. As the case law has time and again noted, 'the land dominates the sea.'[1] States have entitlements to maritime zones because they have a coastline and the extent of these maritime zones in general is measured from the baselines along that coast. Similar considerations apply to the delimitation of maritime boundaries between states. However in this case, it is not only a requirement to establish the seaward extent of the maritime domain of one coastal state. Maritime delimitation requires the determination of the relationship between the coasts of the states concerned and the maritime area in which delimitation has to be affected. In this connection, the case law has developed and applied the concepts of relevant coasts and relevant area.[2] However, the case law has not been consistent in this respect. For instance, a number of cases – including cases that have been decided in

* I would like to thank Catherine Blanchard for her assistance in identifying and analyzing the relevant academic literature and her comments on an earlier version of the chapter. I would like to thank my coeditors and the participants to the workshop in the framework of this book project for their comments on an earlier version of the chapter. Any errors or omissions remain the sole responsibility of the author.

[1] In the context of maritime delimitation law, this principle was first formulated in *North Sea Continental Shelf (North Sea Continental Shelf Cases (Federal Republic of Germany/Denmark; Federal Republic of Germany/The Netherlands)* [1969] ICJ Rep. 3, Judgment of 20 February 1969, [96]).

[2] See L. Lucchini and M. Vœlckel, *Droit de la mer* tome II, *Délimitation* (Pedone Paris 1996) 219, where the authors point out that other terms have been used next to the term relevant area. They submit that this reflects the uncertainty surrounding the concept of the relevant area (ibid.). Apart from the relevant area, the case law may also define the broader

the first decade and a half of this century – has refrained from defining the relevant area or has only defined it in general terms, while other cases have defined it in precise terms with reference to limits defined by geographical coordinates or with reference to specific points.

The concepts of relevant coasts and relevant area serve three purposes. First, the relevant coasts and the relevant area serve to identify the coasts that have to be considered in the delimitation process and the area in which the delimitation between the parties has to be affected. Second, a disparity between the lengths of the relevant coasts of the parties may constitute a relevant circumstance justifying an adjustment of the provisional delimitation line. Third, the relevant coast and the relevant area are used to assess whether the boundary line resulting after an evaluation of the relevant circumstances of a case leads to an equitable solution. The present chapter will focus on the first of these issues.[3] The other two issues are considered in, respectively, Chapters 9 and 11 of this volume.

Section 7.2 of this chapter focusses on the definition of the concepts of relevant coasts and relevant area. The first sub-section traces the origins of these concepts and aims to provide a further understanding of their purpose. Section 7.2.2 briefly considers the normative nature of the concepts of relevant coasts and relevant area. Section 7.2.3 discusses the different criteria that have been advanced by the case law to identify the relevant coasts and relevant area. As the analysis in Section 7.2.3 indicates, the general criteria that have been formulated by the International Court of Justice (ICJ) in *Tunisia/Libya* have been most often relied upon by the judiciary. Section 7.2.3 looks at the question how the general direction and length of the relevant coast have been determined in the case law. Section 7.3 further assesses how the general criteria to determine the relevant coasts and the relevant area have been applied in the circumstances of the specific case. Section 7.3 concludes that the application of these general criteria raises a number of questions. In that light, Section 7.4 considers whether there are other general criteria that are more easily applicable across the board. Section 7.4.1 discusses possible alternatives, while

geographical framework in which the delimitation takes place (see e.g. M. D. Evans, *Relevant Circumstances and Maritime Delimitation* (Oxford University Press Oxford 1989) 125–131; Lucchini and Vœlckel, n. 2, 238–239). This broader geographical framework may also impact on the delimitation exercise (see e.g. the discussion in Evans, n. 2, 126–131).

[3] The case law at times has defined the relevant area having reference to (1) an area in which a third state has an interest or (2) a boundary between one of the parties and a third state. This specific issue is considered in more detail in Chapter 10 of this volume.

Section 7.4.2 considers their merits and shortcomings. Section 7.5 contains concluding remarks.

7.2 Defining the Relevant Coasts and the Relevant Area

7.2.1 Genesis of the Concepts

The concepts of relevant coast and relevant area, like other key concepts in the law of maritime delimitation, have their origin in the case law. However, the drafting history of the delimitation provisions of the Geneva Conventions could be said to contain the seeds for the subsequent development of the concept of relevant coast. During the debate in the International Law Commission (ILC), it was suggested that a departure from the equidistance line might be justified on account of 'any exceptional configuration of the coast, as well as the presence of islands.'[4] At the 1958 United Nations Conference on the Law of the Sea (UNCLOS I), there was some further consideration of the role of islands in the delimitation process. Very small islands located beyond the territorial sea of the mainland on a continuous continental shelf need not be taken into account in determining the equidistance line. As a general criterion, it was proposed that 'islands should be treated on their merits.'[5] A couple of points are to be noted about these references. Determining what constitutes an exceptional configuration of the coast would seem to require an assessment of the coast concerned in its broader context. This could imply either looking at the coast of the state concerned or looking at that coast and its relationship with the coasts of one or more other states. Although the references to islands are similarly general in nature, it would seem that one of the criteria to assess their role in the delimitation process is their size. More specifically, in view of the fact that maritime entitlements are generated by the coast, this criterion would seem to require looking at coastal lengths. The fact that the treatment of very small islands was placed in the context of the presence of mainland coasts suggests that the assessment of the weight to be attributed to islands is a comparative exercise, requiring to look both at the island and other coasts involved in the delimitation process. The context in which these remarks were made – determining the impact of exceptional coastal configurations or islands

[4] *Yearbook of the International Law Commission* 1953, vol. I, 216, [82].

[5] Statement by the UK, *United Nations Conference on the Law of the Sea; Official Records* (A/CONF.13/37), vol. VI, 93, [3]; the latter point was supported by the US (ibid., 95, [23]).

on the equidistance line – suggests the underlying assumption of these remarks. As the discussions in the ILC and at UNCLOS I indicate departures from the equidistance line in specific instances may be required to guarantee that the outcome of a delimitation is equitable.[6]

The judgment in *North Sea Continental Shelf*,[7] the first case dealing with the delimitation of the continental shelf, did not explicitly refer to or define the concepts of relevant coasts and relevant area, but key elements in the ICJ's reasoning presuppose the need to rely on them. Having concluded that equitable principles and the rule of equity were basic legal notions in the matter of continental shelf delimitation,[8] the Court turned to considering the implications of the rule of equity.[9] After an explanation as to why the equidistance method 'leads unquestionably to inequity' in certain circumstances,[10] the Court turned to the implications of equity for looking at the coasts of the parties involved in a delimitation. As the Court observed:

> equity does not require [...] rendering the situation of a State with an extensive coastline similar to that of a State with a restricted coastline. Equality is to be reckoned within the same plane, and it is not such natural inequalities as these that equity could remedy.[11]

However, the situation in the North Sea was different. The coastlines of Denmark, Germany and the Netherlands were 'comparable in length and [...] have been given broadly equal treatment by nature' and that light it would be 'unacceptable [...] that a State should enjoy continental shelf rights considerably different from those of its neighbours.'[12] As is apparent, making this assessment both requires a determination of the coasts of the parties and the area of continental shelf that would belong to them as a consequence of its delimitation. This requirement is also implicit in the proportionality test the Court introduced as a final element of the delimitation process.[13]

7.2.2 Normative Nature of the Concepts

The case law has not given a clear and unequivocal answer as regards the normative nature of the concepts of relevant coasts and relevant area.

[6] For a discussion of this point, see e.g. A. G. Oude Elferink, *The Law of Maritime Boundary Delimitation: A Case Study of the Russian Federation* (Martinus Nijhoff Dordrecht 1994) 16–20.

[7] *North Sea Continental Shelf*, n. 1. [8] Ibid., [85]. [9] Ibid., [88] and following.

[10] Ibid., [89]. [11] Ibid., [91]. [12] Ibid. [13] Ibid., [98].

For instance, the ICJ in a number of recent decisions has referred to the 'legal concept of the "relevant area."'[14] On the other hand, the International Tribunal for the Law of the Sea (ITLOS) and the arbitral tribunal in the Bay of Bengal cases did not address the legal status of the concepts of relevant coast and relevant area, while the tribunal in *Barbados v. Trinidad and Tobago* in its 2006 Award observed that the 'identification of the relevant coasts abutting upon the areas to be delimited is one [. . .] objective criterion, relating to the very source of entitlement to maritime areas.'[15]

The case law, as further discussed below, does not indicate that there is rule of law prescribing the definition of the relevant area and the relevant coasts in a specific manner. For instance, the Court in *Maritime Dispute (Peru v. Chile)* observed that while in some previous cases it had made a precise calculation of the relevant coasts and the relevant area, it did not do so in other cases, in which the specific circumstances of the case made such precise calculations problematic.[16] The Court also took the latter approach in *Maritime Dispute (Peru v. Chile)*.[17] This approach to the concepts of relevant coasts and relevant area indicates that it is critical to look at their operationalization in the individual case and whether such operationalization has been approached consistently, rather than focusing on their normative nature.

7.2.3 General Criteria to Identify the Relevant Coasts and Relevant Area

The case law has not provided a clear definition of the concepts of relevant coasts and relevant area. Rather, starting from the basic precept of 'the land dominates the sea,' the case law has defined criteria that allow the identification of the relevant coasts and the relevant area in the particular case.[18] The case law displays a twofold division as regards these general criteria: (1) reliance on the criteria as first defined in *Tunisia/Libya* and (2) a number of approaches different from those defined in *Tunisia/Libya*.

[14] *Maritime Delimitation in the Black Sea (Romania v. Ukraine)* (Judgment), [2009] ICJ Rep. 61, 99, [110]; *Territorial and Maritime Dispute (Nicaragua v. Colombia)* (Judgment) [2012], ICJ Rep. 624, 682, [157].

[15] *Arbitration between Barbados and Trinidad and Tobago* [2006] Award, 27 RIAA 147, [231].

[16] *Maritime Dispute, Peru v. Chile* [2014] ICJ Rep. 3, [193].

[17] Ibid., [194].

[18] See e.g. *In the Matter of the Bay of Bengal Maritime Boundary (Bangladesh v. India)* PCA Case 2010–2016, [279].

7.2.3.1 The *Tunisia/Libya* Criteria

Clearly stated general criteria to define the relevant coasts and the relevant area were first expressed by the ICJ in *Tunisia/Libya*:

> 74. The coast of each of the Parties, therefore, constitutes the starting line from which one has to set out in order to ascertain how far the submarine areas appertaining to each of them extend in a seaward direction, as well as in relation to neighbouring states situated either in an adjacent or opposite position.
>
> 75. Nevertheless, for the purpose of shelf delimitation between the Parties, it is not the whole of the coast of each Party which can be taken into account; the submarine extension of any part of the coast of one Party which, because of its geographic situation, cannot overlap with the extension of the coast of the other, is to be excluded from further consideration by the Court. It is clear from the map that there comes a point on the coast of each of the two Parties beyond which the coast in question no longer has a relationship with the coast of the other Party relevant for submarine delimitation. The sea-bed areas off the coast beyond that point cannot therefore constitute an area of overlap of the extensions of the territories of the two Parties, and are therefore not relevant to the delimitation.[19]

These criteria indicate an inextricable link between the relevant coasts and the relevant area, in which both concepts reciprocally define each other. The relevant coasts of the parties are identified by determining which parts of their coasts contribute to overlapping areas of continental shelf, while the area of overlapping continental shelf is determined by the coastal relationship(s) between the coasts of the parties.[20]

According to *Tunisia/Libya* the determination of the relevant area is achieved by looking at the *seaward* extension of the relevant coasts.[21]

[19] *Case Concerning the Continental Shelf (Tunisia/Libyan Arab Jamahiriya)* [1982] ICJ Rep. 18, [74] and [75].

[20] As Evans observes: 'whilst the relevant coasts do generate the area of potential overlap and frame the relevant framework area, these bounds themselves are a reflection of their ability to do so. It is by reference back to the possibility of overlap that the relevance of the coasts is assessed' (Evans, n. 3, 127); see also D. R. Rothwell and T. Stephens, *The International Law of the Sea* (Hart Oxford 2009) 429. However, subsequently, Evans has observed that 'the idea of the 'relevant area' within which the delimitation is to be conducted has become secondary to, and largely a function of, the identification of the 'relevant coasts.' M. D. Evans, 'Maritime Boundary Delimitation,' in D. R. Rothwell, A. G. Oude Elferink, K. N. Scott, and T. Stephens (eds.), *The Oxford Handbook of the Law of the Sea* (Oxford University Press Oxford 2015) 255, 267.

[21] Different terms have also been used to characterize the relationship of the coast to the maritime entitlements it generates. For instance, a number of cases employ the formulation of

The judgment does not provide a further definition of the term 'seaward.' The ordinary meaning of 'seaward' connotes that something is pointing towards or facing the sea,[22] while 'facing' implies being placed with the face towards something.[23] The term 'facing' is also used in combination with cardinal points (e.g., in a northwards-facing direction). Taken together, it would seem that the term seaward extension in its ordinary meaning implies that it includes maritime areas that are bounded by lateral limits perpendicular to the relevant coast. As will be discussed below, this conclusion on the ordinary meaning of the term seaward (extension) does not accord with the Court's actual determination of the relevant area in *Tunisia/Libya* or that determination in other cases.

The general criteria to determine the relevant coasts and relevant area stated in *Tunisia/Libya* have been explicitly adopted in a number of subsequent cases: *Black Sea*,[24] *Territorial and Maritime Dispute (Nicaragua v. Colombia)*,[25] and *Bangladesh v. India*.[26] *Bangladesh/Myanmar*, without explicitly quoting *Tunisia/Libya* on this point, also adopts these general criteria.[27]

7.2.3.2 Other Approaches to Defining the Relevant Coasts and the Relevant Area

In a number of cases – *Nicaragua v. Honduras*, *Jan Mayen*, and *Guyana v. Suriname* – the general criteria to define the relevant coasts of the parties have been defined differently than in *Tunisia/Libya*. In these cases, the relevant coasts of the parties have been identified by reference to the delimitation method that is selected, i.e., respectively a bisector of the general

coasts 'abutting' on a maritime area (see e.g. *Case Concerning the Delimitation of Continental Shelf between the United Kingdom of Great Britain and Northern Ireland, and the French Republic* [1978] 18 RIAA 3, [28], [70], [79], and [192]; *Maritime Delimitation and Territorial Questions between Qatar and Bahrain (Qatar/Bahrain)* [2001] ICJ Rep. 91, [247]). An analysis of those cases indicates that there is no material difference between the term 'abutting' and 'seaward' (see e.g. ibid. and the text below at n. 51 and 100).

22 *Oxford Dictionary of English*, 3rd ed., online version (2015). See also S. Fietta and R. Cleverly, *A Practitioner's Guide to Maritime Boundary Delimitation* (Oxford University Press Oxford 2016) 49 and Figure A2.7 at 48.

23 See e.g. the definition of the verb 'to face' in the online edition of *Merriam-Webster*.

24 *Black Sea*, n. 15, [99].

25 *Territorial and Maritime Dispute (Nicaragua v. Colombia)*, n. 15, [150].

26 *Bangladesh v. India*, n. 27, [279] (reference is to the judgment in *Black Sea*, which in turn refers to *Tunisia/Libya*).

27 *Delimitation of the Maritime Boundary in the Bay of Bengal (Bangladesh/Myanmar)* [2012] ITLOS Rep. 4, [489]; see also [185].

directions of the coasts of the parties[28] and the equidistance method.[29] It may be noted that neither *Nicaragua v. Honduras* nor *Guyana v. Suriname* provide criteria to determine the relevant area. In the former case the ICJ did not define a relevant area,[30] while in the latter case the tribunal did not explicitly define the relevant area, but did provide a ratio for the division of the relevant area by the boundary it determined.[31] In *Nicaragua v. Honduras*, the choice for different criteria may be explained by the fact that the criteria formulated in *Tunisia/Libya* would not result in the definition of relevant coasts and a relevant area that would allow a meaningful evaluation. Honduras's relevant coast as determined by the ICJ measured along a straight line projects seaward in a north-easterly direction and the same coast of Nicaragua projects in a seaward direction slightly south of east.[32] By no stretch of the imagination is it possible to maintain that these coasts generate overlapping entitlement in a seaward facing direction. To the contrary, in *Guyana v. Suriname* the adoption of the general criteria of *Tunisia/Libya* would have allowed the identification of relevant coasts and a relevant area. In *Jan Mayen*, the ICJ defined the relevant area in part by

[28] *Territorial and Maritime Dispute between Nicaragua and Honduras in the Caribbean Sea (Nicaragua v. Honduras)* [2007] ICJ Rep. 659, [287]–[289].

[29] *In the Matter of an Arbitration between Guyana and Suriname (Guyana v. Suriname)* [2007] 30 RIAA 1, [352]; *Maritime Delimitation in the Area between Greenland and Jan Mayen (Denmark v. Norway)* [1993] ICJ Rep. 38, [20] and [67]. The methodology involved in these three cases is further discussed below in Section 7.4.2.

[30] Another example of a case in which the relevant area was not defined is *Guinea/Guinea-Bissau (Delimitation of the Maritime Boundary between Guinea and Guinea-Bissau* [1985] 19 RIAA 149). The reason for this approach is provided by [120] of the Award, which discusses the proportionality test. As the tribunal points out, its determination of the relevant coasts result in relevant coasts that are similar in length. As a consequence, the tribunal considers it unnecessary to effect proportionally test, observing that 'au regard de la proportionnalité, aucune des deux parties ne saurait prétendre à un avantage supplémentaire.' It may be observed that that the fact that states have similar relevant coasts does not necessarily imply that the relevant area is divided in a similar manner by the selected delimitation line.

[31] *Nicaragua v. Honduras*, n. 28, [392]. The Award indicates that the boundary established by the tribunal attributes 51 per cent of the relevant area to Guyana and 49 per cent to Suriname. Almost the same figures (51.8 per cent and 48.2 per cent) are attained if the maritime areas within 200 nm of the baselines of Suriname and Guyana bounded by equidistance lines of Guyana with its neighbours and the notional boundary between Suriname and France is assumed to be the relevant area. That presumed definition of the relevant area accords with the coastal frontages that the tribunal uses to determine the ratio between the coasts of the parties (see ibid., [132] and [392]). A division of 51 per cent to 49 per cent is attained if the areas within 200 nm from the baselines of both states are considered, excluding the relevant area beyond Suriname's notional boundary with France. However, the coastal frontage of Guyana used by the tribunal extends west of these relevant areas.

[32] For the definition of the coastal front lines of Honduras and Nicaragua, see *Nicaragua v. Honduras*, n. 28, [296] and [298] and Sketch-map 3.

reference to the area of overlapping entitlements. However, it also included areas that are only part of the maritime entitlements of one of the parties that are located between the relevant coasts of the parties.[33]

In the majority of cases, courts and tribunals have either been less clear on the general criteria to identify the relevant coasts or have directly focused on the definition of the relevant coasts and area for the specific case at hand, without explicating relevant criteria in any detail. For instance, in *Barbados v. Trinidad and Tobago*, the arbitral Tribunal in looking at the coastal frontages relevant for the delimitation limited itself to observing that 'what matters is whether they abut as a whole upon the disputed area by a *radial* or *directional* presence relevant to the delimitation.'[34] An example of the second approach is provided by *Libya/Malta*.[35] Without first identifying criteria for determining the relevant coasts of the parties, the Court considers and defines these coasts in the context of identifying relevant circumstances that may require an adjustment of the provisional equidistance line.[36] For Malta, no explanation for the identification of the relevant coast is offered.[37] In the case of Libya, the Court observes that 'the terminus of the frontier with Tunisia, must clearly be the starting point,'[38] without providing any explanation as to why that is the case. To the east, Libya's relevant coast is bounded by Ras Zarruq.[39] This point had also been identified by Libya and the Court observes that Ras Zarruq is close to the meridian of 15° 10′ E. Italy had stated to have claims to the area east of this meridian and the Court found that it could not delimit a boundary between Malta and Libya in this area also claimed by Italy.[40] It may be noted that this latter finding would seem to disqualify the Court's selection of the western limit of Libya's relevant coast. That western limit is some 215 kilometres to the west of the point at which the meridian of 13° 50′ E intersects the coast of Libya. This meridian

[33] For a criticism of this approach, see N. M. Antunes, *Towards the Conceptualisation of Maritime Delimitation* (Martinus Nijhoff Leiden 2003) 305. In support of the approach of the Court, it could be argued that not taking into account a maritime area directly in front of the relevant coasts of the parties would sever the link between the relevant coasts and the relevant area, which would seem to be contrary to the principle that the land dominates the sea through the projection of the coasts.

[34] *Barbados v. Trinidad and Tobago*, n. 15, [331] (emphasis provided).

[35] This choice may be explained by the fact that the Court found that 'the geographical context [of the case] is such that the identification of the relevant coasts and the relevant areas is so much at large that virtually any variant could be chosen, leading to widely different results' (*Case concerning the Continental Shelf (Libyan Arab Jamahiriya/Malta)* [1985] ICJ Rep. 13, [74]).

[36] Ibid., [66] and [68].

[37] Ibid., [68].

[38] Ibid.

[39] Ibid. *Ras* is the Arabic word for 'cape.'

[40] Ibid.

had also been used by Italy to identify the extent of its claims. The Court's identification of Libya's relevant coast also begs the question how the relevant area off that coast is identified. While the eastern terminus of Libya's relevant coast as selected suggests the facing projection of that coast to be determinative, that explanation clearly is not available for its western terminus. The Court itself observes that in looking at the disparity of the coastal lengths as a relevant circumstance it does not need to look at the relevant area.[41] In effecting the proportionality test, the Court indicates that the relevant area is bounded by the meridians of 13° 50′ E and 15° 10′ E that identify the limits of Italy's claim. In its reasoning the Court in this connection refers to the relevant coasts of the parties. As was mentioned above, Libya's relevant coast is located in large part beyond this relevant area, making the link between the two concepts tenuous at best.

The language that is used to define the relevant coasts and the relevant area in other cases does suggest that the coasts, which face the area in which the delimitation has to be effected, provide the relevant coasts for that delimitation. For instance, the tribunal in *Eritrea/Yemen* defined the extent of the relevant coasts of the parties by drawing a perpendicular to the general direction of the coast from the terminus of the land frontier of one of the parties to the opposite coast of the other party. The coast of the other party beyond the intersection with that perpendicular (respectively the coast of Eritrea in the north and that of Yemen in the south) did not constitute part of the relevant coasts.[42] In *Anglo-French Continental Shelf* the Court of Arbitration, in defining the coastal relationship between the relevant coasts of France and the UK in the Atlantic region, refers to the fact that

> the further extension south-westwards of the United Kingdom's coast has a tendency to make it obtrude upon the continental shelf situated to seawards of the more westerly facing coast of the French Republic in that region.[43]

The ICJ in *Cameroon v. Nigeria* considered that

> [t]he part of the Cameroon coastline beyond Debundsha Point faces [Equatorial Guinea's island of] Bioko. It cannot therefore be treated as facing Nigeria so as to be relevant to the maritime delimitation between Cameroon and Nigeria.[44]

41 Ibid., [67].

42 *Eritrea v. Yemen, Award on Territorial Sovereignty and Scope of the Dispute (Eritrea v. Yemen)* [1998] 22 RIAA 211, [167].

43 *Anglo-French Continental Shelf*, n. 21, [235].

44 *Land and Maritime Boundary between Cameroon and Nigeria (Cameroon v. Nigeria; Equatorial Guinea Intervening)* [2002] ICJ Rep. 303, [291].

Finally, courts and tribunals in some cases refrain from (explicitly) defining the relevant coasts and the relevant area. In *Maritime Dispute (Peru v. Chile)* the Court explained the absence of the definition of the relevant coasts and the relevant area by the unusual situation of that case.[45] In *Cameroon v. Nigeria*, the Court determined the relevant coast of Cameroon, but refrained from defining the relevant coast of Nigeria. The Court was considering this matter in light of a Cameroonian argument that its longer relevant coasts constituted a relevant circumstance. Having itself determined what constituted Cameroon's relevant coast, the Court concluded that it was no longer needed to determine the relevant coast of Nigeria: 'whichever coastline of Nigeria is regarded as relevant, the relevant coastline of Cameroon [. . .], is not longer than that of Nigeria.'[46] This conclusion of the Court might seem to indicate that the Court in this case considered that implementing the general criteria as stated in *Tunisia/Libya* would not have allowed a definitive conclusion on this point. It may also be noted that application of the criteria of *Tunisia/Libya* to the coasts of Cameroon and Nigeria would seem to result in the conclusion that all of the south-facing coast of Nigeria generates seaward projections overlapping with the seaward projection of the west-facing coast of Cameroon north of Debundsha Point. At the same time, it would seem difficult to maintain that the western part of the south-facing coast of Nigeria is relevant for the delimitation with Cameroon. The absence of a defined relevant coast of Nigeria excluded the definition of the relevant area and the Court indeed did not do so.[47]

7.2.4 *Determination of the General Direction and Length of the Relevant Coast*

In view of the uses of the concepts of relevant coasts and relevant area, two further determinations are required in respect of the relevant coasts. One is how to determine the general direction(s) of those coasts from which to assess their seaward projection. The other is how to determine the length of the relevant coasts.

Determining the general direction of the relevant coast should be a straightforward exercise. Once the relevant coast has been determined,

[45] *Maritime Dispute (Peru v. Chile)*, n. 16, [193].

[46] *Cameroon v. Nigeria*, n. 44, [301]. The Court in its judgment does not identify the various coastlines it considered potentially relevant in this respect.

[47] A further example of a case that only deals with the relevant coasts and relevant area fleetingly is *Qatar/Bahrain*, n. 21, [170], [187], [224], and [247]).

its general direction may be determined by drawing a straight line along that coast. Such a straight line represents the average of the direction of all individual segments of that relevant coast. The case law does not contain any indication that it looks at the direction of relevant coasts by assessing the seaward direction of individual coastal features.

In measuring the length of the relevant coast, the case law has taken two approaches. Where the coasts of the parties are relatively straight they may be measured along their natural configuration.[48] How these coasts are exactly measured is not clear from the case law. For instance, the ICJ in *Territorial and Maritime Dispute (Nicaragua v. Colombia)* indicates that the relevant coasts are measured along 'the general direction of the coast.'[49] This reference to general direction might suggest the use of straight lines.[50] However, from the coastal length figures the Court provides for the relevant coasts, it is clear that they are not measured along straight lines.[51] Sketch-map 6 included in the judgment identifying the relevant coasts of the parties suggests that in particular in the case of the Colombian coast, the line representing the relevant coast follows the actual coast closely.

At the same time, the case law also provides examples where relatively straight coasts are measured along a straight line. One example is provided by *Libya/Malta*. Libya's relevant coast as determined by the Court is measured 'following its general direction,'[52] although this coast is without marked indentations. The figure that the Court provides for the length of this coast,[53] indicates that it is represented by one straight line. The Court does not provide an explanation for this approach. An explanation might be that Malta's coast is measured along its straight baselines.[54] Another explanation might be that the Court looked at coastal lengths to check whether there was a disparity justifying an adjustment of the provisional equidistance line. As the Court observed 'the degree of such adjustment does not depend upon a mathematical operation.'[55] In that light it would also not be necessary to make a very precise determination of the relevant

[48] See e.g. the discussion on relevant coasts in *Black Sea*, where the ICJ in general measures the length of the relevant coast along its natural configuration, but in the case of the Yahorlyts'ka Gulf and the Dmiepr Firth represents the relevant coast of Ukraine by a straight line along the mouth of these features (n. 16, [100] and Sketch-map 4); *Territorial and Maritime Dispute (Nicaragua v. Colombia)*, n. 15, [145] and [151]–[152].

[49] *Territorial and Maritime Dispute (Nicaragua v. Colombia)*, n. 14, [145] and [151].

[50] See also below, n. 57.

[51] For Nicaragua, the Court provides a figure of 531 kilometres (*Territorial and Maritime Dispute (Nicaragua v. Colombia)*, n. 14, [145]) while its mainland measured along a straight line measures around 450 kilometres.

[52] *Libya/Malta*, n. 35, [68]. [53] Ibid. [54] Ibid. [55] Ibid.

coasts.[56] Another example of measuring coastal length by straight lines along relatively smooth coasts is provided by *Guyana v. Suriname*.[57] The tribunal does not offer an explanation for this choice.

Straight lines have also been used to determine coastal length along highly indented and irregular coastlines. For instance, in *Jan Mayen*, the Court determines the length of the relevant coasts of both Greenland and Jan Mayen by one straight line segment.[58] While the coast of Greenland is highly irregular with many deep fjords, the coast of Jan Mayen facing Greenland is relatively straight. The Court also measures the length of the relevant coasts along the baselines of the parties. In the case of Greenland this concerns straight baselines, while the baseline of Jan Mayen is the low-water line.[59] The numbers for both these measurements are similar and result in almost identical ratios between the relevant coasts of respectively 1:9.1 and 1:9.2.[60] The judgment does not explain why it adopts these two approaches for measuring the relevant coasts.

A justification for using straight lines to determine the lengths of the relevant coast is provided by *Bangladesh/Myanmar*. The ITLOS observes that for Bangladesh it measures the coast by two straight lines '[t]o avoid difficulties caused by the complexity and sinuosity of that coast.'[61] Two straight lines are also employed in the case of Myanmar. This is done 'to avoid difficulties caused by the sinuosity of the coast and to ensure consistency in measuring the respective coasts of the Parties.'[62]

In other instances, the judiciary has refrained from determining the length of the relevant coasts of the parties.[63] In *Barbados v. Trinidad and Tobago* the tribunal engages in a detailed discussion of the relevance of the length of the coasts of the parties in the delimitation process.[64] However, the tribunal does not commit itself to providing a specific figures for these

[56] However, it may be noted that the Court excluded Malta's straight baselines to and from the islet of Filfla in determining the length of Malta's relevant coast (ibid.). Use of these baselines would have extended Malta's relevant coast by about two kilometres. This would hardly seem to be a relevant difference in the light of determining a disparity between the relevant coasts.

[57] *Guyana v. Suriname*, n. 29, [132]. For the relationship between these coastal frontages and the relevant coasts, see below at n. 109. The tribunal characterizes these coasts as 'unremarkable' (ibid., [375]).

[58] *Jan Mayen*, n. 29, [61].

[59] Ibid. and Sketch-map 2.

[60] Ibid.

[61] *Bangladesh/Myanmar*, n. 27, [201].

[62] Ibid., [204]. See also *North Sea Continental Shelf*, n. 1, [98].

[63] For another example, see above n. 48 for a discussion of the relevant coasts of Cameroon and Nigeria.

[64] *Barbados v. Trinidad and Tobago*, n. 15, [321]–[334].

coast to which the tribunal refers as 'coastal frontages abutting upon the area of overlapping claims.'[65] The tribunal also refrained from determining the size of the relevant area.[66]

7.3 Application of the General Criteria Formulated in *Tunisia/Libya* to the Specific Case

As discussed in Section 7.2.3, a number of judicial decisions have explicitly relied on the general criteria to identify the relevant coasts and the relevant area as formulated by the ICJ in *Tunisia/Libya*: *Black Sea*, *Bangladesh/Myanmar*, *Territorial and Maritime Dispute (Nicaragua v. Colombia)*, and *Bangladesh v. India*. The present section considers how these general criteria have been applied to the facts in *Tunisia/Libya* and these other cases. In *Tunisia/Libya* itself, the Court found that these criteria implied that the relevant coast of Tunisia extended as far north as Ras Kaboudia and that of Libya as far east as Ras Tajoura. The judgment does not offer any further explanation for the selection of these specific points.[67] In the case of Ras Kaboudia, this selection seems uncontroversial. The coasts to the south and north of this point clearly face in different directions. In the case of Ras Tajoura, the choice is less obvious, except perhaps for the fact that it is an easily identified point. The general direction of the coast west and east of this point is not different and the overlapping entitlements of the two states extend east beyond the meridian passing through Ras Tajoura.

The relevant area in *Tunisia/Libya* is defined for the purposes of the proportionality test, and the Court observes that for this purpose 'the essential aspect [. . .] is simply that one must compare like with like, the exact method of drawing the outer boundaries is not critical, provided the same approach is adopted to each of the two coasts.'[68] The limits of the relevant area are then defined by a parallel and a meridian running through respectively Ras Kaboudia and Ras Tajoura. As the Court observes, this choice has the 'advantage of cartographical convenience.'[69] Convenience apart, it can be questioned whether the Court really adopts the same approach for both coasts. In the case of Tunisia, the parallel passing through Ras

[65] Ibid., [350].

[66] The tribunal refers to the concept of relevant area in paragraph [377] of the Award.

[67] *Tunisia/Libya*, n. 19, [75]. For a criticism of this aspect of the judgment, see also Y. Tanaka, 'Reflections on the Concept of Proportionality in the Law of Maritime Delimitation,' (2001) 16 *Journal of Marine and Coastal Law* 433, 439.

[68] *Tunisia/Libya*, n. 19, [130]. [69] Ibid.

Kaboudia includes a large area in the relevant area that is located north of the seaward facing projection of Tunisia's mainland coast. The angle between that projection and the parallel is 42°.[70] On the Libyan side the choice of a meridian instead diminishes the relevant area as compared to the seaward projection of Libya's relevant coast. The lateral limit of Libya's seaward facing projection is about 9° north of east.[71] In defence of the Court, it might be submitted that the term 'seaward' should not be equated with a projection from the coast at a straight angle (i.e., and angle of 90°) and that a projection bounded by an angle of 132° to the general direction of the relevant coast still is a seaward projection of that coast. However, if that argument is accepted, the selection of Ras Kaboudia and Ras Tajoura as identifying the western and eastern extremities of the relevant coasts becomes untenable as the coasts beyond these points under that broader definition of seaward projection also are contributing to the relevant coasts. More importantly, the approach of the Court conflicts with its premise that 'the same approach [has to be] adopted to each of the two coasts.'[72]

In *Black Sea* the Court first indicated that all coasts generating overlapping entitlements could potentially contribute to the definition of the relevant coasts.[73] In determining the relevant coasts of Ukraine, the Court excluded the Karkinits'ka Gulf because its 'submarine extension cannot overlap with the extensions of Romania's coast.'[74] This approach is debatable. Even if the exacting standard of projection at a straight angle to the coast were to be applied, a part of the promontory at the northern entrance of the Gulf generates projections that overlap with the seaward projections of Romania. The same applies to a part of the coast at the back of the Gulf. A comparison with other parts of the relevant coasts and the relevant area as determined by the Court further underscores this point. First, the Court considers that the east- and west-facing coast of Ukraine in the general

[70] The Court determined the general direction of Tunisia's mainland coast in connection with the delimitation of the second part of the continental shelf boundary (ibid., [128] and Map Number 3 at 76). The Court in this connection also determined that the Kerkennah Islands should be given half weight in effecting this delimitation. If a general direction line giving half weight to the Kerkennah Islands would be taken into account the angle between that general direction and the parallel would be 52°.

[71] This figure has been obtained by representing the Libyan relevant coast by one straight line segment passing through the terminus of the land boundary with Tunisia and Ras Tajoura, which corresponds to the method use by the Court to determine the general direction of the relevant coast of Tunisia up to Ras Kaboudia.

[72] *Tunisia/Libya*, n. 19, [130]. [73] *Black Sea*, n. 14, [78].

[74] Ibid., [100] and Sketch-map 5.

area of Odessa are part of Ukraine's relevant coast.[75] Like the coasts of the Karkinits'ka Gulf, these coasts face each other and their seaward extensions do not overlap with the extensions of Romania's coast in a seaward direction. Second, the south-eastern corner of the relevant area is defined as a meridian starting at Cape Sarych.[76] That meridian makes and angle of about 130° with the general direction of the relevant coast of Ukraine on the Crimea between Cape Khersones and Cape Sarych. If that same angle were to be applied to determine whether the coasts of the Gulf of Karkinits'ka and the coast of Romania produce overlapping projections, a large part of the coast of the Gulf would be part of Ukraine's relevant coast.

In *Territorial and Maritime Dispute (Nicaragua v. Colombia)* the Court concluded that the entire coast of Nicaragua, except for a short stretch of coast south of Punta de Perlas constituted Nicaragua's relevant coast.[77] Although the Court concluded that Nicaragua's coast was east-facing,[78] the relevant area to the north is not bounded by a parallel of latitude. Instead, the northern limit is bounded by the maritime boundary between Nicaragua and Honduras, which in large part is constituted by an azimuth. That azimuth makes an angle of around 20° with a parallel of latitude. The area up to the boundary with Honduras certainly can be considered to be relevant to the delimitation between Colombia and Nicaragua. The maritime entitlements of both states overlap in this area and a maritime boundary could potentially have extended into this area.[79]

The Court's definition of Colombia's relevant coast in *Territorial and Maritime Dispute (Nicaragua v. Colombia)* also points to the difficulties that may arise from looking at the seaward projection of the relevant coasts to determine the relevant area. The Court rejected Nicaragua's argument that only the west-facing coasts of the Colombian islands of San Andres and Providencia should be taken into account. As the Court pointed out the area of overlapping entitlements extended well to the east of the islands.[80] Consequently, the Court considered that the entire coast of San Andres and Providencia should be taken into account.[81] Although

[75] Ibid., Sketch-map 4. [76] Ibid., [106] and [114] and Sketch-map 5.

[77] *Territorial and Maritime Dispute (Nicaragua v. Colombia)*, n. 14, [145] and Sketch-map 5.

[78] Ibid., where the Court observes the east-facing coasts of islands fringing the Nicaraguan mainland are parallel to that mainland coast.

[79] See also ibid., Sketch-map 8, for the provisional equidistance line determined by the Court.

[80] Ibid., [151].

[81] Ibid. The Court reached the same conclusion for smaller Colombian islands ([152]). These smaller islands will not be further considered in the present context as they do not materially affect the conclusions that area presented.

the Court seemingly presents its argument in terms of facing coasts,[82] its definition of the relevant area can only be explained on the basis of a radial projection from the coasts of the islands.[83] Dividing the coast of San Andres and Providencia in a number of segments facing in different directions would not result in an omni-directional overlapping entitlement with the east-facing coast of Nicaragua.

The most notable aspects of the two Bay of Bengal cases as regards the relevant coasts and relevant area is perhaps that the arbitral tribunal in *Bangladesh v. India* provided some operationalization of the term 'seaward extension.' The parties differed about the southern end point of India's relevant mainland coast. In this connection, the tribunal observed:

> there is a margin of appreciation in determining the projections generated by a segment of coastline and a point at which a line drawn at an acute angle to the general direction of the coast can no longer be fairly said to represent the seaward projection of that coast.[84]

The tribunal did not further consider when this would be the case, as it deferred to the view of the parties. Neither India nor Bangladesh had argued that the relevant coast extended beyond Sandy Point, which projects seaward at a straight angle into the relevant area.[85] However, a further indication of the tribunal's view on this matter can be gleaned from its discussion on the Andaman Islands. The tribunal considered that the northern part of the Andaman Islands (the northern part of Smith Island and adjacent islands) formed part of the relevant coast of India, but that the southern part did not.[86] The seaward extension of the northern part of the Andaman Islands projects into the relevant area at an angle of around 90° to the general direction of that coast. For the southern (excluded) part of the Andaman Islands these angles would range between approximately 70° and 80°.[87] This difference in treatment of the northern and southern

[82] Ibid., [151].

[83] See also P. Reichler, 'A Case of Equitable Maritime Delimitation: Nicaragua and Colombia in the Western Caribbean Sea,' (2013) 2(3) *Revista Tribuna Internacional*, 129, 135.

[84] *Bangladesh v. India*, n. 18, [302]. Although this pronouncement might suggest that the tribunal only expressed itself on acute angles (i.e., an angle of less than 90°), this finding implicitly also applies to obtuse angles (i.e., an angle of more than 90°). A line that intersects a line representing the general direction of the coast at a point A on one side of point A will form an acute angle with that general direction line and at the other side an obtuse angle.

[85] Ibid., and Map 4. [86] Ibid., [304]; see also ibid., Map 4.

[87] These figures have been established on the basis of a general direction of approximately 10° east of true north of the coast of Smith Island between the latitudes 12° 35′ N and 11° 49′ N. The angles have been determined by measuring the angle of a line starting at points on the coast at these latitudes and the southern limit of the relevant area as defined by the tribunal.

part of the Andaman Islands suggests that the tribunal largely adhered to the ordinary meaning of the term 'seaward projection' as set out above in Section 7.2.2.1.

7.4 Alternatives to the General Criteria Formulated in *Tunisia/Libya*?

7.4.1 Possible Alternatives

The determination of the relevant coasts and the relevant area in accordance with the general criteria formulated in *Tunisia/Libya* raises a number of concerns. As the preceding analysis indicates, these criteria may not allow the identification of relevant coasts and a relevant area due to the specific geography of the specific case unless the ordinary meaning of the term 'seaward projection' is stretched beyond recognition. That problem is illustrated in a telling way by the discussion of *Nicaragua v. Honduras*. However, if the coasts of the parties face each other, solely looking at the seaward projections of these coasts may not result in including all of the area of overlapping entitlements that are relevant to the delimitation in the relevant area. This issue is illustrated by *Territorial and Maritime Dispute (Nicaragua v. Colombia)*, in which case the relevant area was determined on the basis of the east-facing projection of the mainland coast of Nicaragua and a radial projection from the islands of San Andres and Providencia. The present section further considers possible alternatives to the general criteria of *Tunisia/Libya* as they have been proposed by the case law and academic literature, and which are also discussed in Section 7.2.2.2. Section 7.4.2 provides an assessment of these alternatives.

In *Anglo-French Continental Shelf* one of the issues concerned the delimitation of the continental shelf between the French mainland coast and the English mainland coast in the region of the Channel Islands. A median line between the two mainland coast is located to the north of the Channel Islands. As the court of arbitration observed, because of their location the Channel Island and their territorial sea block the natural prolongation of France to the median line with the UK.[88] The court of arbitration rejected the geographically based theory of France that the natural prolongation of the French coast 'turns in some manner around the

[88] *Anglo-French Continental Shelf*, n. 22, [165] and [192]. It is clear from the reasoning of the court of arbitration that it held that in assessing the natural prolongations of territory it is required to look at their projection to seaward (see also above text n. 44).

Channel Islands.'[89] Instead of relying on this geographical argument, the court of arbitration held that

> in these cases the effect to be given to the principle of natural prolongation of the coastal State's land territory is always dependent not only on the particular geographical and other circumstances but also on any relevant considerations of law and equity.[90]

The fundamental consideration for the court in this connection was the 'equality of the two States in their geographical relation to the continental shelf of the Channel.'[91] The ICJ in *Territorial and Maritime Dispute (Nicaragua v. Colombia)* was faced with a similar issue as the court of arbitration. In this case, the Colombian islands of San Andres and Providencia and a number of smaller islands and their territorial seas could be said to block the seaward projection of the east-facing coast of the Nicaragua. The Court did not explicitly address this question, but determined the relevant area by first establishing the area of overlapping entitlements.[92] As the Court observes, Nicaragua's coasts project a potential maritime entitlement up to 200 nautical miles from the Nicaraguan baselines. The fact that Colombia's islands are located inside that potential entitlement does not block that projection.[93] The relevant area as defined by the Court also includes all of the maritime area directly to the east of the islands.[94]

In *Guyana v. Suriname* the arbitral tribunal adopted as relevant coasts of the parties those coasts on which basepoints that generated the full course of the equidistance line between the parties were located. In justifying this choice, the tribunal explained that since the provisional starting point of the delimitation was an equidistance line, 'it seems logical and appropriate to treat as relevant the coasts of the Parties which generate' that line.[95] Interestingly, the tribunal does not use these relevant coasts in connection with the proportionality test it effectuates. Instead it uses the 'coastal frontages' of the parties between the mouth of the Corentyne River, whose western bank is the boundary between Guyana and Suriname, and the terminus of their land boundary with respectively Venezuela and French

89 Ibid., [165] and [192]. 90 Ibid., [194]. 91 Ibid., [195].

92 *Territorial and Maritime Dispute (Nicaragua v. Colombia)*, n. 14, [159].

93 Ibid. It may be questioned whether the terms 'projection' and 'project' are the most appropriate to convey the idea that entitlement exists in the entire maritime area up to the outer limit of the maritime zone concerned.

94 See ibid., Sketch-map 7. 95 *Guyana v. Suriname*, n. 29, [352].

Guiana.[96] The award does not explain why it takes this approach. The relevant paragraph even refers to the 'relevant coastal lengths.'[97]

The approach of using the coast between the basepoints as the relevant coast was also adopted by the ICJ in *Jan Mayen.*[98] The Court in this connection limits itself to observing that this approach is 'not arbitrary' and 'appropriate.'[99] This approach has also found support in the literature. Lucchini justifies this approach with reference to the role of equidistance within the delimitation process.[100] It has also been suggested that only the coasts that contribute to the existence of overlapping entitlements should be taken into account.[101]

As was mentioned above in Section 7.2.3, the ICJ's determination of the relevant area in *Territorial and Maritime Dispute (Nicaragua v. Colombia)* implies that the coasts of the Colombian islands were considered to project radially and not in the direction in which their coasts face. In rejecting Nicaragua's contention that only the west-facing coasts of the islands formed part of Colombia's relevant coast, the Court only provided the justification that the overlapping entitlements of the parties extended 'well to the east of the Colombian Islands.'[102] Another example of using radial projections – or not looking only at seaward projection – is provided by *Jan Mayen*. This case is concerned with the delimitation of the continental shelf and fisheries zones between the opposite coast of Greenland and Jan Mayen. In view of the geography of the area, the coast of Greenland projects seaward for the entire course of a potential maritime boundary. On the other hand, the coast of Jan Mayen which faces Greenland, to which the Court refers as the 'coastal front' of Jan Mayen, only measures around fifty-five kilometres.[103] If the seaward projection of this coastal front would have been taken into consideration in determining the relevant area, the relevant area would not have included a large part

[96] Ibid., [132] and [392]; [392] refers to the coastal frontages and the percentages for these frontages that are provided in this paragraph match with the lengths of the coastal frontages as provided in [132].

[97] Ibid., [392]. [98] *Jan Mayen*, n. 29, [20] and [67]. [99] Ibid.

[100] L. Lucchini, 'La délimitation des frontièes maritimes dans la jurisprudence international: vue d'ensemble,' in R. Lagoni and D. Vignes (eds.), *Maritime Delimitation* (Leiden Martinus Nijhoff 2006) 1, 12; see also D. Anderson, 'Baselines in the Modern Law of the Sea,' in M. Lodge and M. Nordquist (eds.), *Peaceful Order in the World's Oceans* (Leiden Brill 2014) 51, 65–66; Antunes, n. 33, 305; Tanaka, n. 67, 461. Antunes does indicate that this approach may not be appropriate in all circumstances (305).

[101] See e.g. Lucchini 2006, n. 100, 12; Tanaka, n. 67, 462.

[102] *Territorial and Maritime Dispute (Nicaragua v. Colombia)*, n. 14, [151].

[103] *Jan Mayen*, n. 29, [61].

of the area of overlapping entitlements and the area in which a potential boundary would be located.[104] From the Court's reasoning in discussing the relevant area it is clear that it considered that it was required to include the entire area of overlapping entitlements that is subject to delimitation in the relevant area.[105] That definition implies that the radial projection of the coast of Jan Mayen was taken into consideration to determine the relevant area. The idea that the relevant area should be determined by looking at the radial projections of the coasts of the parties has also been argued in the literature.[106] Weil provides a theoretical basis to this approach, observing that the entitlements of coasts project omni-directional and that there is no reason why this should be otherwise where these entitlements overlap with the entitlements of another coast.[107]

A final alternative to determine the relevant coasts is provided by *Nicaragua v. Honduras*. The ICJ in this case found that the circumstances of the case did not allow it to determine a provisional equidistance line[108] and instead decided to delimit the boundary by a bisector line between the relevant coasts of the parties.[109] The key element in this respect was the geographical configuration of the coast.[110] In determining the relevant coasts the Court considered how different options for the relevant coasts represented by straight lines would impact on the bearing of a bisector line. In this connection two considerations had to be balanced. First, such lines would have to provide a proper representation of the coast of the parties and e.g., not cut off a significant part of the coast concerned.[111] Second, the coastal segment to be selected should be of sufficient length 'from which to reflect a coastal front more than 100 nautical miles out to sea.'[112]

7.4.2 *Assessment of the Alternatives to the General Criteria of* Tunisia/Libya

The preceding sub-section provides a number of alternatives to the general criteria of *Tunisia/Libya* for determining the relevant coasts and the relevant area. The proposition to define the relevant coasts by reference to the basepoints that generate the equidistance line at first sight might seem

[104] See ibid., Sketch-map 1. [105] Ibid., [19]–[20], [67], and [71].
[106] See e.g. P. Weil, *The Law of Maritime Delimitation: Reflections* (Grotius Cambridge 1989) 63–69; Y. Tanaka, *Predictability and Flexibility in the Law of Maritime Delimitation* (Hart Oxford 2006), 141.
[107] Weil, n. 106, 63–66. [108] *Nicaragua v. Honduras*, n. 28, [280].
[109] Ibid., [287]. [110] Ibid., [292]. [111] Ibid., and following. [112] Ibid., [296].

to offer a more objective and predictable approach than the selection on the basis of the criterion that the relevant coasts are those that generate overlapping entitlements in a seaward direction. The almost total absence of any attempt to define the term 'seaward' more precisely and the inconsistencies in identifying the relevant coast in the individual case have made this criterion subjective and the outcome of its application unpredictable. In *Jan Mayen* and *Guyana v. Suriname* the definition of the relevant coasts of the parties by selecting the coasts on which the basepoints generating the equidistance line are located works well. The relevant coasts can be determined without difficulty and there does not seem to exist any clear ground to criticize these relevant coasts.[113] These coasts do not give any reason to assume that they do not contribute to the overall goal of delimitation of achieving an equitable solution. However, when this criterion for defining the relevant coasts is applied to other cases, its usefulness as a generally applicable criterion is no longer apparent.[114]

For instance, in *Nicaragua v. Honduras* the Court found that it could not apply the equidistance method because of the disagreement between the parties over the title to islands that were formed at the mouth of the boundary river and the uncertainty of the basepoints for determining the equidistance line due to the configuration and unstable nature of the coast at that mouth.[115] If there would have been no dispute over the islands in the mouth of the river, and the Court would have used basepoints on these islands to generate the equidistance line, that line would have been generated solely by those basepoints and basepoints on a number of small islets and rocks off the mainland coasts of Honduras and Nicaragua. As a consequence, the relevant coasts of the both states would have been defined by two points at the mouth of the boundary river and small stretches of coast on a number of insignificant features, while completely disregarding the mainland coasts of the parties, which constitute the main geographical features of this case.

Territorial and Maritime Dispute (Nicaragua v. Colombia) further illustrates that using the equidistance line's basepoints may lead to debatable

[113] In *Guyana v. Suriname*, there might be some argument about the exact starting point of the relevant coast of both parties at their common land boundary (*Guyana v. Suriname*, n. 29, [352]). However, any differences in this respect are of limited significance in view of the location of the most western and eastern basepoint of the equidistance line.

[114] See also *Barbados v. Trinidad and Tobago*, n. 15, [329]; S. M. Punzhin, 'Printsipy Razgranicheniia Morskikh Prostranstv,' in R. A. Kolodkin and S. M. Punzhin (eds.), *International Law of the Sea*, Essays in Memory of A. L. Kolodkin (Statut Moscow 2014) 61, 68.

[115] *Nicaragua v. Honduras*, n. 28, [280].

results. In this case, the equidistance line is determined by basepoints on small islands fringing the Nicaraguan mainland coast and basepoints on Colombia's San Andres and Providencia and a number of smaller features. Adopting these coasts as the relevant coast would completely ignore the main geographical feature of this delimitation, the mainland coast of Nicaragua.

Apart from these difficulties in using the basepoints generating the equidistance line as an alternative for defining the relevant coasts, it also raises a more fundamental concern. The concept of relevant coasts is intended to contribute to an assessment of how an equitable solution may be achieved in delimiting the continental shelf and the exclusive economic zone. In most cases this requires an evaluation as to whether the equidistance line leads to an equitable solution. Accepting that the relevant coasts should be determined with reference to the basepoints of the equidistance line would make the determination as to whether the equidistance line result in an equitable solution dependent on the very method that needs to be evaluated.[116] A similar concern would seem to apply to an approach that takes into account the coasts that contribute to the existence of overlapping entitlements. Where entitlement is based on distance, this approach implies that it includes all coasts that are within that distance from each other.[117] Where entitlement is not based on distance, as is the case for the continental shelf beyond 200 nm, this approach does not allow determining the relevant coasts.[118]

Determining the relevant area by looking at the radial projections of the relevant coasts resolves one of the problems inherent in determining the relevant area by looking at the seaward projections of the relevant coasts. As a coast viewed along its general direction never faces seaward in all directions, applying that seaward projection to determine the relevant area may result in excluding areas that are part of the overlapping entitlements of the parties in which a part of the delimitation line will be located from the relevant area. At the same time, the concept of radial projections does not resolve the question how to determine the stretch of the coast that is the relevant coast for the purposes of the delimitation. In *Jan Mayen*the ICJ, while impliedly using a radial projection from the relevant coast of the island of Jan Mayen to determine the relevant area,

[116] See also Fietta and Cleverly, n. 22, 597.

[117] Moreover, this approach raises a similar concern as the approach based on the radial projection of the coasts (see further below).

[118] See also Fietta and Cleverly, n. 22, 48–49.

determined the relevant coast of Jan Mayen by selecting the coast between basepoints generating the equidistance line. This coast is also the part of coast of Jan Mayen that faces the relevant coast of Greenland in a seaward direction. In the case of the island of Jan Mayen there might be little debate about the selection of that coast, but as the current discussion shows this may not be so in many other instances. For Weil the starting point for looking at the radial projections of the coasts of the states concerned is the determination of which coasts have a facing relationship.[119] This again raises the question how to determine which parts of the coast display such a facing relationship. In other words, the concept of radial projection is more appropriate in conceptualizing the relevant area, but it does not really assist in identifying the relevant coasts unless it is accepted that all coasts that are contributing to generating overlapping entitlements are included.[120]

The method employed by the ICJ in *Nicaragua v. Honduras* at first sight is specific to the circumstances of that particular case. However, at the same time it could be argued that the reasoning underlying the selection of the relevant coasts is in line with the general precepts of equity and leads to a careful assessment of the individual case.[121] Something similar could be said about the court of arbitration's determination in *Anglo-French Continental Shelf* that the location of the Channel Islands in relation to the mainland coast of France did not imply that this mainland coast did not disqualify a part of France's coast as relevant coast. It may be noted that *Anglo-French Continental Shelf* stands out for not relying on geometric methods to determine the relevant coast. On the one hand, it could be submitted that this contributes to the unpredictability of the case law. On the other hand, the court of arbitration's approach could be said to allow for the flexibility to deal with the particularities of the individual case and avoids relying on general criteria that cannot be applied to all individual cases.

7.5 Concluding Remarks

The concepts of relevant coasts and relevant area no doubt are part and parcel of the conceptual toolbox for maritime boundary delimitation. At

[119] Weil, n. 106, 72. Weil, among others, relies on *Anglo-French Continental Shelf*, n. 21, which refers to the coasts abutting on the area to be delimited.

[120] For a discussion of the latter point, see above n. 128 and following.

[121] See further above.

the same, the case law has not come up with a consistent approach in relation to these concepts. For instance, a number of cases – including cases that have been decided in the first decade and a half of this century – has refrained from defining the relevant area or has only defined it in general terms, while other cases have defined the relevant area with reference to limits defined by geographical coordinates or specific points.

The case law's engagement with the concepts of relevant coasts and relevant area illustrates the difficulties involved in establishing general criteria defined at a certain level of precision that can be applied in a consistent manner to all geographical situations with which the case law has been confronted.[122] The general criteria formulated in *Tunisia/Libya*, which have been accepted by a considerable number of cases,[123] do not allow the identification of meaningful relevant coasts and a meaningful relevant area in all geographical situations. Key to these criteria is the identification of the overlapping maritime entitlements extending from the coasts of the parties in a seaward direction. In this approach the coasts of the parties drive the identification of the parts of those coasts that constitute the relevant coasts for the purpose of the delimitation of their maritime boundary and the relevant area. In this sense, the *Tunisia/Libya* criteria are in full accord with one of the basic precepts of the law of the sea, namely that 'the land dominates the sea.'[124]

At the level of application, the *Tunisia/Libya* criteria have been mired by a number of difficulties. As was already noted above, it may not be possible to apply them in practice. In addition, the case law has, with the exception of *Bangladesh v. India*,[125] failed to come up with a further operationalization of the concept of 'seaward projection.' As was set

[122] In that sense, the present discussion calls to mind the idea that each boundary delimitation represents a unique situation, due to the great variety of geographical circumstances that may be found. This variety in turn would make it difficult if not impossible to define rules of general application (see e.g. L. D. M. Nelson, 'The Roles of Equity in the Delimitation of Maritime Boundaries,' (1990) 86 *American Journal of International Law* 837, 838–839. For a criticism of the notion of *unicum* see e.g. Antunes, n. 33, 259–260; Lucchini and Vœlckel, n. 2, 93; Weil, n. 106, 180–185; see also below, n. 141.

[123] These cases do show a refinement of *Tunisia/Libya* in the sense that they first explicitly identify the area of overlapping entitlements before proceeding to identify the relevant coasts and the relevant area. This arguably makes the process of identifying the relevant coasts and relevant area more transparent an predictable.

[124] As noted above, this principle formed the starting point of the Court's analysis of the concepts of the relevant coasts and the relevant area in *Tunisia/Libya* (*Tunisia/Libya*, n. 19, [73]). This same approach has been followed in other cases following the precedent of *Tunisia/Libya* (see e.g. *Bangladesh v. India*, n. 18, [279]).

[125] See also below next paragraph.

out in Section 7.2.3.1, the ordinary meaning of this term would imply a projection to the general direction of the relevant coast at a straight angle and, as was argued, *Bangladesh v. India* largely seems to subscribe to that view. A review of the case law indicates that courts and tribunals have not always adopted this ordinary meaning in identifying the lateral limits of the relevant area. As was set out in *Tunisia/Libya*, one of the lateral limits of the relevant area makes an angle of 42° with the general direction of the relevant mainland coast of Tunisia. Not dissimilar differences have been pointed out in respect of other cases. Such divergences from the ordinary meaning of the term seaward seem to make the use of this term a misnomer. The discussion of, among others, *Tunisia/Libya* and *Black Sea* moreover shows that the case law has not only been inconsistent when cases are compared, but also in respect of the treatment of different stretches of coast in the same, individual case.

As was pointed out above, *Bangladesh v. India* is the one case in which an attempt was made to quantify the meaning of the term 'seaward' projection. The tribunal in that case takes projection at a straight angle as a starting point of its analysis and observes that too acute an angle of the seaward projection to the general direction of a coast implies that such a coast cannot be part of the relevant coast. The tribunal did not consider this question in relation to the Indian coast south of Sandy Point, because neither party had argued that part of the coast to be part of the relevant coast.[126] Although this no doubt relieved the tribunal of a difficult if not impossible task – the relevant coast south of Sandy Point is straight for a considerable distance, implying that the tribunal might have had to find that an acute angle of x° still leads to a seaward projection, but an angle of x − 1° does not – it can be questioned whether such deferral to the views of the parties leads to predictability and consistency.

The case law also reveals different approaches to measuring the lengths of the relevant coast of the parties. Coastal length may both be measured along the actual coast and by straight lines along the coast. This is only in part explained by coastal geography. One other factor partly explaining these differences is the overall approach to the specific delimitation concerned. Where a court or tribunal wants to make a numerical proportionality test it obviously needs to put a figure on the length of the relevant coasts, while this need not be done in other cases.

In view of the fact the criteria developed in *Tunisia/Libya* appear problematic in their practical application, Section 7.4 considers a number of

[126] *Bangladesh v. India*, n. 18, [302].

alternatives that have been used in the case law or have been advocated in the academic literature. First, in *Jan Mayen*and *Guyana v. Suriname*, the relevant coasts were determined by selecting the coasts of the parties between the basepoints that generate the provisional equidistance line. As is observed, in the context of those two cases that approach suggests itself as a viable alternative. However as Section 7.4.2 concludes, on closer consideration this approach is not generalizable in a meaningful sense and raises methodological concerns. Second, the concept of radial projection, rather than being a full-fledged alternative to the concept of seaward projection, only addresses one of the shortcomings of the latter concept.

In light of the difficulties quantifiable geometric criteria run into, Section 7.4.2 posits that a preferable approach might have been to solely rely on more general precepts underlying maritime delimitation law. That approach would have provided the flexibility to deal with the particularities of the individual case and avoided relying on general criteria that cannot be applied (equally) to all individual cases. In fact, one of the main lessons that may be drawn from the current discussion is the risk inherent in developing general criteria in the context of a specific case (i.e., *Tunisia/Libya*), without apparently having a clear understanding of or considering how these general criteria would play out in the geographical framework of other bilateral delimitations. As a consequence subsequent cases have had to disavow those criteria explicitly or impliedly. As a result the case law on this point can neither be characterized as wholly predictable nor wholly consistent.[127]

[127] As has been argued by Evans: '[w]hile determining the relevant area for the purposes of delimitation is critical, it remains unclear and controversial. Given also the significance attached to the "relevant coasts" for this purpose, and the relationships between them in terms both of geographical alignment and length, this too becomes a central question and this is reflected in their increasing prominence in recent cases. Yet even a cursory survey indicates the high degree of arbitrariness which attaches to these calculations' (Evans, n. 20, 270–271). See also ibid., 267–268 and 272; Antunes, n. 33, 305 and 324–325; Lucchini, n. 100, 11–12; Lucchini and Vœlckel, n. 2, 220, 223, and 227; Tanaka, n. 67, 458; Tanaka, n. 106, 178). On the other hand, Fietta and Cleverly submit that '[w]hile there has been some inconsistency, the process of identifying the relevant coasts and the relevant area broadly involves [...] three stages' (Fietta and Cleverly, n. 22, 45). However, they subsequently observe that the judiciary has 'taken some markedly different approaches to the identification of relevant coasts and relevant areas' (ibid., 594).

8

The Provisional Equidistance Line

Charting a Course between Objectivity and Subjectivity?

COALTER G. LATHROP

8.1 Introduction

The International Court of Justice (ICJ) and other international courts and tribunals have developed what is now described as a three-stage maritime delimitation methodology which has been applied in one form or another in almost every delimitation case in the modern, post-*North Sea Continental Shelf* era in order to achieve an equitable delimitation solution.[1] Ostensibly, the first stage consists of the objective, geometric process of constructing a line that is at an equal distance from the nearest points on the coasts of the parties. This provisionally drawn equidistance line, which is subject to adjustment in the second stage when accounting for relevant circumstances and the third stage in the event that gross disproportionality is discovered between coastal length and maritime area ratios, has come to be known as the 'provisional equidistance line'[2] or, alternatively,

[1] Evans addresses the second-stage consideration of relevant circumstances in Chapter 9, and Tanaka addresses the third-stage consideration of disproportionality in Chapter 11 in this volume. As Tanaka notes, the concept of a reasonable degree of proportionality between coastal lengths and maritime area arose in *North Sea Continental Shelf Cases (Federal Republic of Germany/Denmark; Federal Republic of Germany/Netherlands)* [1969] ICJ Rep. 3. While proportionality has long been described as 'a test of equitableness of a delimitation arrived at by some other means' (*Award of the Arbitral Tribunal in the second stage of the proceedings between Eritrea and Yemen (Maritime Delimitation)* [1999] XXII RIAA 335, 372 [165]), it was not until *Black Sea* that the disproportionality test formally became the third stage of a three-stage delimitation procedure. *Maritime Delimitation in the Black Sea (Romania v. Ukraine)* (Judgment) [2009] ICJ Rep. 61.

[2] See *In the Matter of the Bay of Bengal Maritime Boundary (Bangladesh v. India)* PCA Case 2010-16 (Award) 7 July 2014; *Maritime Dispute (Peru v. Chile)* (Judgment) [2014] ICJ Rep. 3; *Territorial and Maritime Dispute (Nicaragua v. Colombia)* (Judgment) [2012] ICJ Rep. 624; *Delimitation of the Maritime Boundary in the Bay of Bengal (Bangladesh/Myanmar)* (Judgment) ITLOS, Case No 16, 14 March 2012; *Black Sea*, n. 1; *Territorial and Maritime Dispute between Nicaragua and Honduras in the Caribbean Sea (Nicaragua v. Honduras)* (Judgment)

as the 'provisional median line,'[3] the 'provisional equidistance/median line,'[4] or the 'provisional delimitation line.'[5] By whatever name it is known, the provisional line is 'posited as a hypothesis and a practical starting point' subject to examination and adjustment in light of relevant circumstances.[6]

The topic of this chapter is the purportedly objective first-stage construction of the equidistance line. In an area of international law described as result oriented,[7] vague,[8] imprecise,[9] open-textured,[10] and arbitrary,[11] a clear procedural method with an objective starting point could provide much welcomed certainty to litigants, who want predictability from third-party resolution of their maritime boundary disputes, and to negotiators, who have an interest in narrowing the differences between neighboring states in an effort to achieve an agreed solution. This chapter

[2007] ICJ Rep. 659; *In the Matter of an Arbitration between Guyana and Suriname (Guyana v. Suriname)* (Award) 30 RIAA 1; *Arbitration between Barbados and the Republic of Trinidad and Tobago, Relating to the Delimitation of the Exclusive Economic Zone and the Continental Shelf between Them (Barbados v. Trinidad and Tobago)* (Award) [2006] 27 RIAA 147; *Maritime Delimitation and Territorial Questions between Qatar and Bahrain (Qatar/Bahrain)* (Judgment) [2001] ICJ Rep. 91.

3 See *Territorial and Maritime Dispute (Nicaragua v. Colombia)*, n. 2; *Black Sea*, n. 1; *Maritime Delimitation in the Area between Greenland and Jan Mayen (Denmark v. Norway)* (Judgment) [1993] ICJ Rep. 38; *Continental Shelf (Libyan Arab Jamahiriya/Malta)* (Judgment) [1985] ICJ Rep. 13.

4 See *Territorial and Maritime Dispute (Nicaragua v. Colombia)*, n. 2. The Court, in *Black Sea*, assures that '[n]o legal consequences flow from the use of the terms "median line" and "equidistance line" since the method of delimitation is the same for both.' *Black Sea*, n. 1, [116].

5 The use of this phrase has always been in reference to a median or equidistance line provisionally drawn and does not appear to be intended to distinguish a provisional equidistance line from a provisional line drawn on some other basis. See *Territorial and Maritime Dispute (Nicaragua v. Colombia)*, n. 2; *Black Sea*, (n. 1); *Land and Maritime Boundary between Cameroon and Nigeria (Cameroon v. Nigeria; Equatorial Guinea intervening)* (Judgment) [2002] ICJ Rep. 303; *Libya/Malta*, n. 3.

6 *Barbados v. Trinidad and Tobago*, n. 2, [242].

7 J. I. Charney, 'Ocean Boundaries between Nations: A Theory for Progress,' (1984) 78 *American Journal of International Law* 582, 583.

8 E. D. Brown, 'The Tunisia-Libya Continental Shelf Case: A Missed Opportunity,' (July 1983) *Marine Policy* 142, 162.

9 Ibid., 142.

10 M. D. Evans, 'Maritime Boundary Delimitation,' in D. R. Rothwell, A. G. Oude Elferink, K. N. Scott, and T. Stephens (eds.), *The Oxford Handbook of the Law of the Sea* (Oxford University Press Oxford 2015) 255, 257.

11 Specifically in regard to the judgment in *Concerning the Continental Shelf (Tunisia/Libyan Arab Jamahiriya)* [1982] ICJ Rep. 18, see *Tunisia/Libya* (Diss. Op. Oda); *Tunisia/Libya* (Diss. Op. Gros); *Tunisia/Libya* (Diss. Op. Evensen).

considers whether courts and tribunals indeed have been faithful to their much-vaunted methodology; do their descriptions of the first stage match their actions?

Tunisia/Libya, decided in 1982, months before the adoption of the United Nations Convention on the Law of the Sea (LOSC),[12] is one of the few cases in which the Court declined to construct such a provisional equidistance line. The judgment, separate opinions, and dissenting opinions in that case provide the springboard for a discussion of equidistance as a provisional starting point from which an equitable maritime boundary may be delimited.

The following section sets the stage with a review of *Tunisia/Libya* and the different approaches applied in that judgment and advocated for in the separate opinion of Judge ad hoc Jiménez de Aréchaga and the dissenting opinions of Judges Oda and Gros. To some degree these judicial opinions reflected the negotiating positions of the opposing camps contemporaneously debating the exclusive economic zone and continental shelf delimitation provisions (eventually Articles 74(1) and 83(1)) during the Third United Nations Conference on the Law of the Sea (UNCLOS III).[13] Judge Oda's dissent, in particular, sowed the seeds from which the provisional equidistance line jurisprudence would grow over the following three decades and more. The chapter turns, in Section 8.3, to the ideal of equidistance as an objective, scientific methodology for anchoring the delimitation process, relying in part on the case law that purports to apply this method in the first stage of the delimitation process and describing the stated rationale for doing so (i.e., the inherent value of applying an objective method on which to base any subsequent assessment in the search for an equitable delimitation solution). Section 8.4 contrasts the ideal of blindly constructing a provisional line using geometry and objective data as the first, distinct stage of delimitation with the concepts of simultaneity and preemptive modification of baselines, and presents examples of the actual practice of the Court and other international courts and tribunals with respect to the selection of basepoints from which to construct the provisional line, a practice which introduces relevant circumstances and a significant level of subjectivity to the first stage of the delimitation process. Section 8.5 contains some concluding remarks.

[12] Adopted 10 December 1982, entered into force 16 November 1994, 1833 UNTS 397.

[13] For further discussion of these negotiations, see *Virginia Commentaries*, vol. 2, 796–816, 948–985.

8.2 *Tunisia/Libya*: Crystallizing the Debate

As the Court deliberated in the continental shelf delimitation case between Tunisia and Libya, from the end of oral argument in October 1981 to the release of the judgment and appended opinions in February 1982, delegations at UNCLOS III were tying up loose ends left over from nearly a decade of negotiation. By then the draft convention was available to the Court with its draft Articles 74(1) and 83(1), the delimitation provisions applicable to the newly established, *sui generis* exclusive economic zone and the continental shelf, respectively. By the time the Court was deciding *Tunisia/Libya*, the word 'equidistance' had disappeared from both provisions which had assumed their now familiar form in what would soon be adopted as the LOSC.[14]

The mandate of the Court in *Tunisia/Libya*, as set out in the parties' *compromis*, was to 'take its decision according to equitable principles, and the relevant circumstances which characterize the area, as well as the new accepted trends in the Third Conference on the Law of the Sea.'[15] The Court recognized the equidistance-less draft text of Article 83(1) as representing one of those trends.[16] Judge ad hoc Jiménez de Aréchaga, voting with the Court, seized on the absence of any reference to equidistance in his separate opinion. Referring to UNCLOS III he wrote 'the whole process of the Conference is indicative of a new accepted trend, which is to minimize or 'tone down' the role assigned to equidistance.'[17]

Jiménez de Aréchaga's identification of a 'new accepted trend' in relation to the minimized role of equidistance undoubtedly was correct, especially when juxtaposed to Article 6 of the 1958 Convention on the Continental Shelf[18] and in light of the ongoing but nearly completed negotiations at UNCLOS III. Beginning with the rejection of Article 6 as a reflection of customary international law in *North Sea Continental Shelf*, there clearly was a trend toward minimizing the role of equidistance and removing any misconception that delimitation-by-equidistance had risen

[14] 'The delimitation of the [exclusive economic zone/continental shelf] between states with opposite or adjacent coasts shall be effected by agreement on the basis of international law, as referred to in Article 38 of the Statute of the International Court of Justice, in order to achieve an equitable solution.'

[15] *Tunisia/Libya*, n. 11, [4] quoting the Libyan translation of the Tunisia/Libya Special Agreement, Art. 2.

[16] Ibid., [47 *et seq.*].

[17] Ibid. (Sep. Op. Jiménez de Aréchaga), [35].

[18] Adopted 29 April 1958, entered into force 10 June 1964, 499 UNTS 311.

to the level of legal rule or principle. The language of Articles 74(1) and 83(1) embodied that trend.

As a result, neither party argued for an equidistance delimitation, and the Court did not entertain equidistance or construct an equidistance line in that case. Following the decision in *Tunisia/Libya* one might have asked whether the new accepted trend required the wholesale elimination of equidistance from the jurists' tool box? And, if yes, what would replace this method, a method incomparable in respect of its 'combination of practical convenience and certainty of application'?[19] Without recourse to equidistance in *Tunisia/Libya*, the Court's search for a practical delimitation method seemed to be adrift.

Recognizing and reiterating the axiomatic rule that title to maritime areas is derivative of title to territory ('the land dominates the sea') and that geography is the starting point for delimiting those areas,[20] the Court constructed a two-segment line by reference to several coastal features but without any objective methodology for linking the coastal geography to the delimitation line or for choosing the directions or lengths of the line segments. Taking aim, not at the result in *Tunisia/Libya*, but at 'the way in which the Court set about the search for an equitable delimitation,' Judge Gros described the arbitrary approach in which the Court '[chose] to draw lines of direction which no principle dictates and to adopt angles without justifying their selection in terms of any relevant facts.'[21] He continued his critique by noting that the 'lack of a systematic search for the equitable has produced a result the equity of which remains to be proved,'[22] and concluded that 'the judgment has strayed into subjectivism.'[23]

Judge Oda was more specific in his criticism of the Court's practical method and the illusory link between the coastal geography and the resulting delimitation. Oda could 'neither share, nor even understand, the view which the majority of the Court, in describing the practical method to be employed for the delimitation between the Parties, has expressed to the effect that the delimitation line should be composed of two segments.'[24] Writing about the location of the inflection point between the two segments he asked, 'What significance, moreover, from any objective viewpoint, has the point of intersection of this line with the parallel passing through the most westerly point of the Gulf of Gabes?'[25] With regard to the direction of the second segment, he asked, 'Why should

[19] *North Sea Continental Shelf*, n. 1, [23]. [20] *Tunisia/Libya*, n. 11, [73, 114].
[21] Ibid. (Diss. Op. Gros), [17]. [22] Ibid., [11]. [23] Ibid., [24].
[24] Ibid. (Diss. Op. Oda), [177]. [25] Ibid., [178].

this segment of the line be parallel with the coast of Tunisia rather than the coast of Libya?'[26] He concluded that 'the Court fails to adduce any cogent ground for either segment of the line, or for the line as a whole, a line which does not exemplify any principle or rule of international law.'[27] Oda rounded out his assessment with a damning critique of a decision ostensibly based in law: '[t]he Judgment appears, to my eyes, simply as one appropriate to a case *ex aequo et bono* such as might have been decided, if the Parties so agreed, in accordance with Article 38, paragraph 2, of the Statute.'[28]

Did this decision, perceived as unsystematic, subjective, and made solely on the basis of what is fair and just, produce an equitable solution nonetheless? Perhaps it did. The parties accepted the Court's judgment and adopted the line in their 1988 boundary agreement implementing the judgment.[29] Narrowly construed, the Court may have discharged its duty to clarify the practical delimitation method to be applied in the specific situation between these parties in this geography. But did the manner in which the Court arrived at its equitable solution in *Tunisia/Libya* strengthen consistency with past delimitations, predictability for those still to come, fairness for participants, transparency of process, and legitimacy of this area of international law?[30]

Devoid of discernible process, the judgment in *Tunisia/Libya* stands at the nadir of consistency and predictability in the maritime boundary jurisprudence.[31] Without method, the Courts' approach sounded in magic, conjuring Jiménez de Aréchaga's metaphorical description of the Court's delimitation method in which '[all the relevant circumstances] are to be thrown together into the crucible and their interaction will yield the correct equitable solution of each individual case'[32] without any attempt to explain how one might reproduce, much less predict, the result. Exactly what invisible interactions were at work in Jiménez de Aréchaga's crucible? And what alternative approach could contribute to the predictability and

[26] Ibid., [179]. [27] Ibid., [180]. [28] Ibid., [1].

[29] See T. Scovazzi, 'Libya-Tunisia,' in J. I. Charney and L. M. Alexander (eds.), *International Maritime Boundaries*, vol. 2 (Martinus Nijhoff Dordrecht 1993) 1663.

[30] The tribunal formed to delimit the boundary between Bangladesh and India stated that, aside from the 'paramount objective' – achieving an equitable result – 'transparency and the predictability of the delimitation process as a whole are additional objectives to be achieved in the process.' *Bangladesh v. India*, n. 2, [339].

[31] Brown writes of *Tunisia/Libya* that, 'so far as the clarification and development of the law are concerned, the Judgment is a distinct step backwards [. . .].' Brown, n. 8, 143.

[32] *Tunisia/Libya*, n. 11 (Sep. Op. Jiménez de Aréchaga), [35].

consistency of maritime delimitation decisions in the future? Notwithstanding the new accepted trend, Oda urged equidistance as the starting point.[33] Three years later the Court adopted his recommendation.

The Court's opaque, 'crucible' approach in *Tunisia/Libya*, in which the inputs (coastal geography and historical conduct of the parties) and outputs (a two-segment maritime boundary) are visible but the process by which the outputs are created is difficult to discern,[34] combined with the illogic of ignoring distance in the delimitation of the continental shelf, title to which was, by then, determined in large part by distance from shore,[35] could not stand for long. Within three years, and immediately next door, the Court changed course with respect to process, invoking for the first time equidistance as a *procedural* starting point in *Libya/Malta*, a case that has been attributed with moving the law of maritime delimitation 'dramatically... toward a more secure legal foundation.'[36]

In that case the Court explained its approach as a two-stage process. In the first stage, the Court would 'make a provisional delimitation by using a criterion and a method both of which are clearly destined to play an important role in producing the final result.'[37] The Court's criterion, 'distance from the coast,' was 'linked with the law relating to a State's legal title to the continental shelf.'[38] The Court continued: 'it therefore seems logical to the Court that the choice of the criterion and the method which it is to employ in the first place to arrive at a provisional result should be made in a manner consistent with the concepts underlying the attribution of legal title.'[39] With distance from the coast as the criterion, equidistance was the logical method. As the Court explained, '[i]t is clear that, in these circumstances, the tracing of a median line between those coasts, by way of a provisional step in a process to be continued by other operations, is the most judicious manner of proceeding with a view to the eventual achievement of an equitable result.'[40]

[33] Ibid., (Diss. Op. Oda), [181] ('[t]he qualified equidistance method is thus the equitable method *par excellence*, and for this reason along should be tried before all others').

[34] Charney notes that '[w]hat is missing, however, is an articulate statement of how the Court took the law and applied it to all of the facts it found relevant in order to reach that particular boundary line.' Charney, n. 7, 584.

[35] Distance is the sole criterion for attributing legal title to the exclusive economic zone and the main criterion for attributing legal title to the continental shelf in areas within 200 nautical miles from shore. See Chapter 3 in this volume.

[36] *Case concerning the Delimitation of Maritime Areas between Canada and France* (Canada/France) (Diss. Op. Weil) [1992] 31 *International Legal Materials* 1145, 1197 [1].

[37] *Libya/Malta*, n. 3, [60]. [38] Ibid., [61]. [39] Ibid. [40] Ibid., [62].

8.3 Equidistance: The Ideal

Considering the newly codified distance basis of title to water column and seabed areas for all LOSC zones within 200 nautical miles from shore, by 1985 distance from shore had become an obvious choice for starting any delimitation analysis. It is not surprising, on that basis alone, that equidistance was quickly adopted and used as a starting point in subsequent delimitation analyses.

In the context of distance-based title, the equidistance method 'has a certain intrinsic value,'[41] and that value comes from its objectivity: distance measurements are exemplars of objective fact. As long as there is agreement on the starting point, any competent measurer will produce, within a margin of error, the same result as the next measurer. The starting point for measuring distance in maritime boundary delimitation is on the law of the sea baselines, either the normal baselines or straight line baselines. Considering that an equidistance line is a line every point of which is equidistant from the nearest points on the baselines of the two states, constructing an equidistance line should start with the interpretation of the LOSC baseline rules, including the rules related to the normal baseline (Articles 5, 6, 11, and 13) and to straight line baselines (Articles 7, 9, 10, and 47). A court or tribunal may also be required to interpret LOSC rules related to the status and location of a feature, including Article 13 (vertical and horizontal criteria for low-tide elevations) and Article 121 (definition of an island and criteria islands have to meet for generating all LOSC coastal state zones), before constructing a provisional equidistance line. Once the legal baselines have been discerned through the application of these rules to the coastal geography of the parties, the equidistance line may be constructed by any competent cartographer. In theory, these are the steps that make up the first stage of delimitation as it has been described in the case law: identify legal baselines; construct provisional equidistance line therefrom.

An example of the Court strictly adhering to this stepwise process is provided by *Qatar/Bahrain*. For the purpose of the delimitation in that case, the Court turned first to an assessment of the status of Fasht al Azm (based on the geographic facts, was it a stand-alone low-tide elevation or was it part of Sitrah Island?),[42] Qit'at Jaradah (was it an island or a low-tide elevation?),[43] and Fasht ad Dibal (was it a valid source of basepoints under

[41] *Nicaragua v. Honduras*, n. 2, [272].

[42] *Qatar/Bahrain*, n. 2, [188–190]. [43] Ibid., [191–195].

international law considering its status and location?).[44] The Court also assessed Bahrain's coast against the criteria of Article 7 and Part IV of the LOSC and rejected the notion that Bahrain was entitled to draw straight or archipelagic baselines for the purpose of the delimitation.[45] After discerning the legal baselines, the Court constructed two versions of the provisional equidistance line to account for factual ambiguity related to the status of Fasht al Azm.[46] Only after the completion of this objective[47] first stage did the Court turn to a consideration of special circumstances in the territorial sea and relevant circumstances beyond the territorial sea that might 'call [. . .] for an appropriate correction to the delimitation line provisionally arrived at.'[48] Only after applying the law to the geographic facts and plotting an equidistance line on strictly geometrical criteria did the Court entertain considerations of appropriateness: the appropriateness of treating Fasht al Azm as part of Sitrah Island,[49] the appropriateness of giving no effect to Qit'at Jaradah,[50] the appropriateness of simplifying the line,[51] the appropriateness of correcting the line to account for disparate coastal lengths[52] or the disproportionate effect of Fasht al Jarim.[53]

In *Qatar/Bahrain*, the Court executed its own process as described:

> In keeping with its settled jurisprudence on maritime delimitation, the first stage of the Court's approach is to establish the provisional equidistance line. At this initial stage of the construction of the provisional equidistance line the Court is not yet concerned with any relevant circumstances that may obtain and the line is plotted on strictly geometrical criteria on the basis of objective data.[54]

This approach to the first stage brings with it the benefits of convenience and certainty, qualities of equidistance recognized by the Court as early as *North Sea Continental Shelf*. In that judgment, famous for undercutting the customary status and central role of equidistance in delimitation, the Court nonetheless heaped praise on the method, observing that:

[44] Ibid., [199–209]. [45] Ibid., [210–215].

[46] Ibid., [216] ('After careful analysis of the various reports, documents and charts submitted by the Parties, the Court has been unable to establish whether a permanent passage separating Sitrah Island from Fasht al Azm existed before the reclamation works of 1982 were undertaken' [190]).

[47] The Court's application in this case of the law, as codified in the baselines provisions of the LOSC, to the facts, as discerned from scientific and technical sources, in order to ascertain the legality of the use of certain features as basepoint-generating features, was not subject to assessments of appropriateness. The Court waited until the second stage to make this subjective assessment in *Qatar/Bahrain*.

[48] Ibid., [241]. [49] Ibid., [218]. [50] Ibid., [220]. [51] Ibid., [221].

[52] Ibid., [241–243]. [53] Ibid., [245–249]. [54] *Black Sea*, n. 1, [118].

> 22 ... It has never been doubted that the equidistance method of delimitation is a very convenient one, the use of which is indicated in a considerable number of cases. It constitutes a method capable of being employed in almost all circumstances, however singular the results might sometimes be, and has the virtue that if necessary ... any cartographer can *de facto* trace such a boundary on the appropriate maps and charts, and those traced by competent cartographers will for all practical purposes agree.
>
> 23. In short, it would probably be true to say that *no other method of delimitation has the same combination of practical convenience and certainty of application.*[55]

Further praise for equidistance as a starting point has continued throughout the maritime delimitation jurisprudence of the Court and other courts and tribunals. In *Nicaragua v. Honduras*, the Court noted that '[equidistance] has a certain intrinsic value because of its scientific character and the relative ease with which it can be applied.'[56] In *Bangladesh/Myanmar*, the International Tribunal for the Law of the Sea (ITLOS) acknowledged 'the objective precision of equidistance,'[57] and in *Black Sea* the Court referred to equidistance as 'geometrically objective.'[58] Because of these desirable characteristics, equidistance has been applied in delimitations between States and by adjudicators and 'has rendered undeniable service in many concrete situations, ... '[59] But it has not always been applied as scientifically or as objectively as one might expect from a first reading of the judgments and awards.

8.4 Equidistance: The First Stage as Applied

Jiménez de Aréchaga described the delimitation process as a simultaneous one, expressly disavowing 'distinct and successive phases.' As he wrote in his separate opinion in *Tunisia/Libya*:

> [t]he application of equidistance and of equitable principles are not to be viewed as two distinct and successive phases, nor as requiring that equitable principles are only to be resorted to after applying equidistance, in

[55] *North Sea Continental Shelf*, n. 1, [22–23] (emphasis provided); cf. ibid., [57] (distinguishing role of equidistance in opposite versus lateral delimitations).

[56] *Nicaragua v. Honduras*, n. 2, [272]. [57] *Bangladesh/Myanmar*, n. 2, [228].

[58] *Black Sea*, n. 1, [116].

[59] *Delimitation of the Maritime Boundary in the Gulf of Maine Area (Canada/United States)* [1984] ICJ Rep. 4 [107].

> order to correct its result. There is no such succession in time and the process must be a simultaneous one.'[60]

In direct contrast to Jiménez de Aréchaga's simultaneity, and beginning only a few years after the judgment in *Tunisia/Libya*, the Court and other courts and tribunals have repeatedly and consistently described their process as a stepwise process of two (or three) distinct and successive phases. In *Black Sea*, the Court clearly separated the objective first stage in which 'the Court is not yet concerned with any relevant circumstances that may obtain'[61] from 'the next, second stage' when the Court will 'consider whether there are factors calling for the adjustment or shifting of the provisional equidistance line in order to achieve an equitable result.'[62]

This structure has value. As conceived, the first stage of the methodology creates procedural predictability and an objectively determined starting point: the provisional equidistance line. If the Court's process of applying distinct and successive stages to a delimitation were followed with rigor, one would not expect any consideration of 'appropriateness' of base points in the first stage, only a consideration of whether they were legally justified under the applicable baseline rules. The Court's approach in *Qatar/Bahrain* epitomizes a considered application of the LOSC baseline rules to coastal geographic facts followed by the mechanical application of equidistance. Only after the first-stage construction of the provisional equidistance line in that case did the Court embark on the less objective task of considering relevant circumstances that might require an adjustment of the first-stage line. Perhaps surprisingly, considering the repeated assertions of and praise for an objective first stage, the Court's approach in *Qatar/Bahrain* is an outlier. Instead, the case law is rife with examples of first-stage subjective assessments of coastal geography that, according to the Court's own process, should not appear until the second stage.

In more than half of the cases in which a provisional line has been constructed, the inherent value of an objective first stage has been reduced by using subjectively chosen base points to construct that line. This practice is described, without any apparent irony, by the tribunal in *Bangladesh v. India*:

> In the view of the Tribunal, the advantage of the equidistance/relevant circumstances method lies in the fact that it clearly separates the steps to be taken and is thus more transparent. The identification of a

[60] *Tunisia/Libya*, n. 11 (Sep. Op. Jiménez de Aréchaga), [35].
[61] *Black Sea*, n. 1, [118]. [62] *Black Sea*, n. 1, [120].

> provisional equidistance line is based on geometrically objective criteria, while at the same time account is taken of the geography through the selection of appropriate base points.[63]

The objectivity of the equidistance method is severely undercut when base points are 'selected'; all the more so when judges are doing the selecting and when 'appropriateness' is the criterion for that selection.[64]

Selection of base points is an inherently subjective process. The intrinsic value of equidistance is that base points need not be 'selected' in order to construct such a line. Instead, the legal coast lines must be identified through the application of the baseline rules discussed above and then represented mathematically with coordinates. With these inputs – data representing two states' coasts – the output – a line every point of which is equidistant from the nearest points on those coasts – will be substantially the same every time.[65] With equidistance, the interactions in the crucible are a matter of mathematics, not magic, but with judge-selected inputs, the promise of objectivity fades.

In fact, inserting subjective choice into the purportedly objective first stage was embedded in the provisional equidistance line construction process advocated by Judge Oda in his dissent in *Tunisia/Libya*. In that opinion, Oda staunchly supported equidistance as a method to be applied in the search for an equitable solution, but his suggested application of the method was not blind. He asked, rhetorically, 'Should the real configuration of the coast of each state be the sole baseline for measuring equidistance?'[66] In short, he answered 'no.' According to Oda, the 'real configuration' of the coast may need to be modified before equidistance may be applied. He explained:

[63] *Bangladesh v. India*, n. 2, [343].

[64] As Anderson notes, 'appropriateness is a relative concept containing an element of appreciation. In contrast, the identification of the "nearest points" is an objective exercise, as is the construction of an equidistance line between them.' D. H. Anderson, 'Maritime Delimitation in the Black Sea Case (Romania *v.* Ukraine),' (2009) 8 *Law and Practice of International Courts and Tribunals* 305, 316.

[65] The technical aspects of constructing or calculating an equidistance line using spherical trigonometry is beyond the scope of this chapter. I hope the reader will trust that the available measurement and calculating tools will result in largely the same line when applied to the same coastal geography on the same spheroid, irrespective of who pushes the 'calculate' button. To the extent that there is a significant difference between provisional equidistance line A and provisional equidistance line B, it will be because the inputs (baselines and base points) are fundamentally different. Fundamental differences in these inputs arise from subjective decisions made by judges.

[66] *Tunisia/Libya*, n. 11 (Diss. Op. Oda), [168].

> 168 ... While the sole use of the equidistance method can be expected to lead to an equitable result, this is on the understanding that the baseline to be employed for the purpose of the geometrical construction will vary from case to case, from the strict version used in measuring the limit of the territorial sea to certain modified baselines employed because of special circumstances in the geography of the region.
>
> 169. If I may put the conclusion first, 'irregularities in coastlines' and the 'existence of islands' have always, even if only implicitly, been regarded as circumstances to be taken into account. Certainly, not just any existing geographical condition may be regarded as an anomaly, and it will not be easy to define what irregularities should be rectified in determining the baseline for application of the equidistance method. However, an irregular overall shape of the coastline, significant configurational irregularities and the existence of narrow promontories or peninsulae, or even of islands, might be agreed upon as constituting irregularities *the effect of which is to be mitigated in settling the baselines.*[67]

In theory, it is the 'strict version [of the baseline] used in measuring the limit of the territorial sea' that one would expect courts and tribunals to use in the construction of the provisional equidistance line. This is not the approach Oda advocated. Instead, Oda expressed the same concerns shared by the majority in *North Sea Continental Shelf* about 'abating the effects of an incidental special feature from which an unjustifiable difference of treatment could result.'[68]

The question presented in this chapter is not whether to abate unjustifiable effects, but at what stage in the delimitation process that abatement should occur. This is a question of timing and sequence. While courts and tribunals are clear in their statements about timing and sequence – that they matter and are to be followed – a close assessment of the actual practice of these same bodies reflects a substantial adherence to Jiménez de Aréchaga's concept of simultaneity and to Oda's approach of modifying baselines before calculating the equidistance line.

8.4.1 Libya/Malta: *The Precursor*

From the start of the equidistance renaissance in *Libya/Malta*, the Court conflated 'the tracing of a median line between [the] coasts [of Libya and Malta], by way of a provisional step'[69] with the distinct and subsequent step of assessing the equitableness of the result. The Court echoed Oda's

[67] Ibid., n. 11 (Diss. Op. Oda), [168–169] (emphasis provided).

[68] *North Sea Continental Shelf*, n. 1, [91].

[69] *Libya/Malta*, n. 3, [62].

concern about using strict law of the sea baselines even for the limited purpose of constructing a provisional line. Before constructing that line, the Court wrote, '[a]n immediate qualification of the median line which the Court considers must be made concerns the basepoints from which it is to be constructed.'[70] The Court then proceeded to eliminate Malta's 'uninhabited islet of Filfla' from the basepoints to be used in the construction of its provisional median line. The Court explained this modification of Malta's baseline:

> The Court does not express any opinion on whether the inclusion of Filfla in the Maltese baselines was legally justified; but in any event the baselines as determined by coastal States are not *per se* identical with the points chosen on a coast to make it possible to calculate the area of continental shelf appertaining to that State. In this case, the equitableness of an equidistance line depends on whether the precaution is taken of eliminating the disproportionate effect of certain 'islets, rocks and minor coastal projections,' to use the language of the Court in its 1969 Judgment, quoted above. The Court thus finds it equitable not to take account of Filfla in the calculation of the provisional median line between Malta and Libya. Having established such a provisional median line, the Court still has to consider whether other considerations, including the factor of proportionality, should lead to an adjustment of that line being made.[71]

It is worth unpacking this paragraph because the issues raised here arise in the subsequent cases.

Was the inclusion of Filfla in the Maltese baselines legally justified? While the Court declined to ask or answer this question, it seems to be a necessary prerequisite for constructing a median line from legally justifiable baselines. Malta included Filfla in a system of straight baselines authorized by its 1971 Territorial Waters and Contiguous Zone Act.[72] As a state party to the 1958 Territorial Convention on the Territorial Sea and the Contiguous Zone[73] (the LOSC was not yet in force), it may not have satisfied the conditions of Article 4 for drawing straight baselines, but Filfla would have qualified as an island under Article 10 of the 1958 Convention, with baselines of its own and, in any event, is situated within the territorial sea measured from Malta's main island.[74] On the facts, yes, the

70 Ibid., [64]. 71 Ibid.

72 Malta, Territorial Waters and Contiguous Zone Act. No. XXXII of 1971.

73 Adopted 29 April 1958, entered into force 10 September 1964, 516 UNTS 206.

74 Even if Filfla had been a low-tide elevation, it would have been legally justifiable to include the feature in Malta's baselines on the basis of Art. 11(1) of the 1958 Convention related to low-tide elevations situated within the territorial sea.

inclusion of Filfla in the Maltese baselines, at least normal baselines, was legally justified under the baseline rules of both the 1958 Convention and the LOSC.

The Court found it unnecessary to opine on Filfla because 'the baselines as determined by coastal States are not *per se* identical with the points chosen on a coast to make it possible to calculate the area of continental shelf appertaining to that State.' This statement raises two points. First, it must certainly be correct that states participating in a judicial process do not have the last word on the veracity of the facts presented, including facts related to baselines and base points. This is left to the fact finder, here the Court. The Court could have applied the baseline rules to the coasts of Libya and Malta to determine their legally justifiable baselines. Instead, and this is the second point, the Court moved directly to the important distinction between the legally justifiable baseline (a product of the law applied to the facts), on the one hand, and 'the points chosen on a coast' for the purpose of delimitation (a product of subjective selection), on the other. By making this distinction during the first stage of the delimitation process, the Court mixed ingredients from the second stage into the first. There is no dispute that legally justified baselines are not *per se* identical to the baselines ultimately to be used to determine the extent of one state's maritime zones vis-à-vis another state's maritime zones,[75] which is to say the baselines relevant in the final delimitation, but to eliminate parts of a legally justifiable baseline *before* constructing the provisional line is to work out of sequence bringing second-stage relevant circumstances into the first stage.

In the next sentence the Court cites the *North Sea Continental Shelf* cases as it explains that an equidistance line may not be equitable unless precautions are taken to eliminate the disproportionate effect of certain coastal and insular features, concluding that '[t]he Court thus finds it equitable not to take account of Filfla in the calculation of the provisional median line between Malta and Libya.' Thereby, the Court inserts subjective considerations of equitableness into the objective first stage resulting in the construction of what would more properly be called the provisional *modified* median line. Under an objective approach, Filfla would have

[75] The Court reiterated this point in *Black Sea*, noting that 'the issue of determining the baseline for the purpose of measuring the breadth of the continental shelf and the exclusive economic zone and the issue of identifying base points for drawing an equidistance/median line for the purpose of delimiting the continental shelf and exclusive economic zone between adjacent/opposite States are two different issues,' n. 1, [137].

been included in the first-stage construction, possibly to be eliminated in the second stage when considerations of equitableness are purportedly to be made. Ultimately (considering the Court's substantial adjustment of its provisional median line to account for other relevant circumstances, including disparity in coastal lengths), the question of including Filfla in the calculation of the provisional line would not have made any difference in the final outcome. Therefore Filfla's first-stage elimination was not only contrary to objectivity, but also unnecessary in the circumstances.[76]

In several of the subsequent delimitation cases before the Court and other courts and tribunals, no provisional line was constructed in the delimitation process.[77] In several others, the provisional line was constructed properly without considerations of equity at that stage.[78] In most of the cases in this second group the basepoints presented by the parties for their own coasts were accepted, without modification, as legally justified basepoints to be used in the first stage. But in a substantial number of other cases the cross contamination between the objective construction of a provisional equidistance line and the subjective considerations of relevant circumstances and equity recurred. Those cases have been heard by the ICJ, ITLOS, and a LOSC Annex VII tribunal, and they include *Black Sea*, *Bangladesh/Myanmar*, *Territorial and Maritime Dispute (Nicaragua v. Colombia)*, *Maritime Dispute (Peru v. Chile)*, and *Bangladesh v. India*. The cases are considered below in chronological order.

8.4.2 Black Sea *and Its Progeny*

The practice of separating the objective first stage from the subjective second stage changed with the Court's decision in *Black Sea* and its treatment of Serpents' Island and Sulina Dyke,[79] which was especially surprising considering the Court's description of its process in that case. That

[76] *Libya/Malta*, n. 3, [68 *et seq.*].

[77] See *Nicaragua v. Honduras*, n. 2; *In the Matter of an Arbitration pursuant to an Agreement to Arbitrate dated 3 October 1996 between the Government of the State of Eritrea and the Government of the Republic of Yemen (Eritrea/Yemen)* (1999) XXII RIAA 335; *Canada/France* (n. 36); *Delimitation of the Maritime Boundary between Guinea and Guinea-Bissau (Guinea/Guinea-Bissau)* [1985] 19 RIAA 149.

[78] See *Guyana v. Suriname*, n. 2; *Barbados v. Trinidad and Tobago*, n. 2; *Cameroon v. Nigeria*, n. 5; *Qatar/Bahrain*, n. 2; and *Jan Mayen*, n. 3.

[79] Evans refers to the decision in *Black Sea* as 'the high water mark of equidistance.' Evans, n. 10, 260. Indeed, once the provisional equidistance line was constructed, the Court did not adjust it in subsequent phases. However, the subjective selection of basepoints, including the non-use of Serpents' Island, seems to undermine the place of equidistance in this case.

description bears repeating here: 'At this initial stage of the construction of the provisional equidistance line the Court is not yet concerned with any relevant circumstances that may obtain and the line is plotted on strictly geometrical criteria on the basis of objective data.'[80] And yet the Court did concern itself at length with 'choosing its own basepoints for [the] purpose [of constructing the provisional equidistance line].'[81] Noting that the Court may 'deviate from the base points selected by the parties for their territorial seas,'[82] the Court went on to describe the process of choosing its own base points:

> In this stage of the delimitation exercise, the Court will identify the appropriate points on the Parties' relevant coast or coasts which mark a significant change in the direction of the coast, in such a way that the geometrical figure formed by the line connecting all these points reflects the general direction of the coastlines. The points thus selected on each coast will have an effect on the provisional equidistance line that takes due account of the geography.[83]

This approach in *Black Sea* represented a significant shift in the Court's practice. In *Qatar/Bahrain*, only eight years earlier, the Court considered the legal status and baseline eligibility of every questionable insular feature in the delimitation area and then applied equidistance without further questioning the coasts of the parties or the overall geography of the area to be delimited. The resulting first-stage line emphasized and responded to the micro-geographic configurations of the natural coastlines of the parties. Natural coastlines tend to be sinuous and irregular, and the location and direction of an equidistance line, therefore, can be unduly influenced by an otherwise insignificant piece of coastal territory. This, of course, is one of the criticisms of equidistance as a delimitation method. Nonetheless, the Court in *Qatar/Bahrain* conducted the exercise of constructing an equidistance line on the basis of the actual coast as a provisional step.

In *Black Sea*, the Court, before applying equidistance, selected points that, in the Court's view, were 'appropriate,' 'mark[ing] a significant change in the direction of the coast,' and, when taken together 'reflect[ed] the general direction of the coastlines.' Applying this strikingly macro-geographic approach to coasts, the Court reduced the parties' 1,000 kilometres of coast to five points. This led to the elimination (among many others) of the coastal features that would have provided the nearest basepoint on the Romanian coast at the seaward end of Sulina Dyke, and the

[80] *Black Sea*, n. 1, [118]. [81] Ibid., [117]. [82] Ibid. [83] Ibid., [127].

nearest basepoint on the Ukrainian coast on Serpents' Island: the two points that would have played the most prominent role in the construction of the provisional equidistance line. While there is nothing inherently wrong with this approach, it does not result in a provisional line drawn 'on the basis of objective data.' It results in a provisional line drawn on the basis of subjective, judge-modified data.

Although the Court started to apply the baseline rules to Sulina Dyke, specifically Article 11 of the LOSC regarding the inclusion of harbor works in the normal baseline, it did not reach a conclusion about whether Sulina Dyke was a legally justifiable part of Romania's baseline. Instead, the Court eliminated the seaward end of Sulina Dyke so that it would not give 'greater importance to an installation than to the physical geography of the landmass.'[84] The treatment of Sulina Dyke involved at least a partial application of the baseline rules to the feature in question. The rationale for the elimination of Serpents' Island was unsupported by any such justification.

In its explanation for eliminating Serpents' Island from the construction of the provisional equidistance line, the Court wrote:

> To count Serpents' Island as a relevant part of the coast would amount to grafting an extraneous element onto Ukraine's coastline; the consequence would be a judicial refashioning of geography, which neither the law nor practice of maritime delimitation authorizes.[85]

In a bizarre twist, the Court used its own famous phrase from *North Sea Continental Shelf*, cautioning against 'totally refashioning geography' when eliminating incidental features,[86] to support the elimination of an incidental feature. No other rationale, such as an analysis of the Article 121 status of Serpents' Island, was forthcoming to justify the elimination of Serpents' Island from the calculation of the provisional equidistance line at this initial stage, when the Court purportedly is 'not yet concerned with any relevant circumstances.' The spillover from the second stage into the first in this case was substantial. It directly contradicted the purported use of distinct, successive stages. And we have seen a similar disregard for the distinction between the first and second stages in every delimitation case since.

[84] Ibid., [139]. [85] Ibid., [149].

[86] 'It is therefore not a question of totally refashioning geography whatever the facts of the situation but, given a geographical situation of quasi-equality as between a number of States, of abating the effects of an incidental special feature from which unjustifiable difference of treatment could result.' *North Sea Continental Shelf*, n. 1, [91].

The practice of subjectively eliminating islands prior to the 'objective' construction of the provisional equidistance line continued in the subsequent cases even as those courts and tribunals paid lip service to the inherent value of equidistance and the distinct and successive phases in the oft-touted delimitation methodology. In *Bangladesh/Myanmar*, citing *Black Sea*, the ITLOS excluded 'as the source of any base point' St. Martin's Island, a substantial, inhabited Bangladeshi island just off the coast near the land boundary terminus.[87] The Tribunal's reasoning was not based in an analysis of St. Martin's Island as a legally justifiable source of basepoints for the purpose of constructing a provisional line. Instead the Tribunal wrote:

> because it is located immediately in front of the mainland on Myanmar's side of the Parties' land boundary terminus in the Naaf River, the selection of a base point on St. Martin's Island would result in a line that blocks the seaward projection from Myanmar's coast . . . result[ing] in an unwarranted distortion of the delimitation line.[88]

Cut-off of seaward projections and considerations of small insular features that unduly distort the direction of a delimitation line are quintessential relevant circumstances appropriately to be assessed in the second stage of delimitation.

In *Territorial and Maritime Dispute (Nicaragua v. Colombia)*, again citing *Black Sea*, the Court took it upon itself to select 'the basepoints which it considers appropriate.'[89] Without any explanation, the Court eliminated base points on Colombia's Low Cay, 'a small uninhabited feature near Santa Catalina,' from the construction of the provisional median line.[90] Colombia's Quitasueño and Serrana received slightly more attention, but base points on those features were not used because they 'would have a marked effect upon the course of the provisional median line which would be out of all proportion to [their] size and importance.'[91] Again, any consideration of a feature's disproportionate effect on the course of a delimitation line is, according to the descriptions of this process in the jurisprudence, appropriately to be considered in the second stage of delimitation.

87 *Bangladesh/Myanmar*, n. 2, [265]. 88 Ibid.

89 *Territorial and Maritime Dispute (Nicaragua v. Colombia)*, n. 2, [200].

90 Ibid., [202]. Like Filfla in *Libya/Malta*, subsequent severe adjustments to the provisional line would have wiped out any influence of Low Cay, making its first-stage elimination both contrary to the objectivity of the first stage and unnecessary as a matter of reaching an equitable solution.

91 Ibid., [202].

The treatment of base points and the construction of a provisional equidistance line in the Court's 2014 judgment in *Maritime Dispute (Peru v. Chile)* is an extreme outlier, unmatched for its subjectivity. Faced with an agreed, non-equidistant boundary for the first eighty nautical miles of its length, the Court still felt compelled to apply its three-stage methodology to delimit the remaining maritime area. In order to get around the problem of starting an equidistance line at a non-equidistant point, the Court developed a new approach to the selection of 'appropriate base points' by eliminating all base points on the Peruvian coast that were *closer* than eighty nautical miles from the agreed segment of the boundary, all the while insisting that 'base points for the construction of the provisional equidistance line have been selected as the most seaward coastal points "situated nearest to the area to be delimited."'[92] Tortured and arbitrary, the Court's first-stage provisional line is not related to equidistance or the actual coasts of the parties in any real way.[93]

Finally, in the most recent maritime boundary decision, the 2014 decision in *Bangladesh v. India*, the tribunal formed pursuant to LOSC Annex VII followed *Bangladesh/Myanmar* in its non-use of basepoints on St. Martin's Island because neither party proposed such use.[94] With respect to other features, the Tribunal undertook to 'choose the base points it consider[ed] appropriate.'[95] In that process, the tribunal reviewed Article 13 of the LOSC and acknowledged that '[l]ow-tide elevations may certainly be used as baselines for measuring the breadth of the territorial sea.'[96] It did not 'follow, however, that low-tide elevations should be considered as appropriate base points for use by a court or tribunal in delimiting a maritime boundary...'[97] The tribunal concluded that it would not use base points located on low-tide elevations for the construction of its provisional line thus eliminating otherwise legally justifiable base points from its first-stage calculation.[98]

8.5 Conclusions

Despite an oft-cited delimitation methodology consisting of distinct and successive stages, an element of Jiménez de Aréchaga's simultaneity has

[92] *Maritime Dispute (Peru v. Chile)*, n. 2, [185], quoting *Black Sea*, [117].

[93] For a further assessment of the Court's deviation from equidistance in this case, see A. G. Oude Elferink, 'International Law and Negotiated and Adjudicated Maritime Boundaries: A Complex Relationship,' (2015) 58 *German Yearbook of International Law* 231.

[94] *Bangladesh v. India*, n. 2, [367]. [95] Ibid., [253]. [96] Ibid., [259].

[97] Ibid., [260]. [98] Ibid., [261], quoting *Black Sea*, [117, 127].

crept back into the method applied by courts and tribunals. He insisted that 'the [delimitation] process must be a simultaneous one,' and where the construction of the provisional equidistance line and considerations of the effect of specific features on that line are concerned, simultaneity is now prevalent in the case law. Indeed, considerations of second-stage relevant circumstances have crept into the first-stage construction of the provisional equidistance line to such an extent that the second stage has been rendered unnecessary in some of the cases.[99] Ironically, considering Jiménez de Aréchaga and Oda's diametrically opposed positions in *Tunisia/Libya*, Jiménez de Aréchaga's simultaneity has, in practice, taken the form of Oda's suggested application of the equidistance method to modified baselines in order to address, preemptively, 'special circumstances in the geography.'[100]

The practice of simultaneity does not match the language of distinct, successive stages. Why have the actions of courts and tribunals, with respect to the first stage, not matched the words describing that stage? Perhaps by cloaking subjective considerations of equity and appropriateness in the language of objectivity, judges are attempting to avoid the critique of arbitrariness and imprecision often leveled at the second stage consideration of relevant circumstances.[101] Perhaps considerations of appropriateness in the first stage may be used to avoid difficult or incidental questions of law or fact, such as whether a feature is above water at low tide, the status of an island under LOSC Article 121, or the validity of a party's baselines under LOSC Part II.[102] Or perhaps it is an indication that judges are reluctant to fetter their own discretion with rigid procedural steps, even if those steps have arisen from the case law.

Does the apparent disregard for these separate steps have an effect on the delimitation result? Would a stricter adherence to the methodology as described change the substantive outcomes of the cases? In many instances, probably it would not. For example, if Serpents' Island had been included in the first stage in *Black Sea*, probably the Court would have eliminated it in the second stage and perhaps on the same grounds that it was eliminated in the first stage: it 'would amount to grafting an extraneous element onto Ukraine's coastline.'[103] If St. Martin's Island had

[99] See Anderson, n. 61, 326 ('This may deprive the second and third stages of much of their salience').

[100] *Tunisia/Libya*, n. 11 (Diss. Op. Oda) [168].

[101] See Evans, n. 10, 261 ('Once again, "equity" rather than "equidistance" may be re-emerging as the dominant approach, though couched in the language of equidistance').

[102] See Anderson, n. 61, 327.

[103] *Black Sea*, n. 1, [149].

been included in the first stage in *Bangladesh/Myanmar*, probably the Tribunal would have eliminated it in the second stage and perhaps on the same grounds that it was eliminated in the first stage: its use 'would result in an unwarranted distortion of the delimitation line.'[104]

Maritime delimitation under the LOSC is result oriented; achieving an equitable solution is the goal. If the result would have been the same, perhaps it is unimportant whether courts and tribunals approach delimitation the way the Court did in *Qatar/Bahrain* – eliminating a distorting feature in the second stage – or the way the Court did in *Black Sea* – eliminating an extraneous feature in the first stage. But *how* a court decides is often as important as *what* a court decides, especially in the international legal system where legitimacy is such a valuable commodity. Consistency, predictability, fairness, transparency, and legitimacy are all served by a clear process that is followed reliably, and these are all characteristics that international maritime boundary delimitation could use more of. The three-stage methodology as described in the decisions provides a clearly articulated process for moving through the deliberations in pursuit of an equitable solution. The first-stage construction of a provisional equidistance line from the legal coasts of the parties provides a solid foundation from which to consider, in particular, the effect of coastal irregularities and other features. When a sound procedural methodology has been developed and a court or tribunal claims to apply it, that application should be faithful to the process as described. Courts and tribunals that ignore or distort their own process undermine the legitimacy of their decisions unnecessarily.

[104] *Bangladesh/Myanmar*, n. 2, [265].

9

Relevant Circumstances

MALCOLM EVANS

9.1 The Nature and Role of Relevant Circumstances within the Delimitation Process

Does the extensive case law concerning the delimitation of maritime boundaries contribute to – or does it distract from – the consistency and the degree of predictability which is reflective of a rules-based approach to the delimitation process?[1] The oscillation between 'predictability and flexibility' in maritime boundary delimitation has become something of a leitmotiv in recent times[2] but it is important to recall that whilst the delimitation process may well require a particular focus on the particularities of each situation – and it has long been acknowledged that each situation is 'an unicum'[3] – it is still (or is still meant to be) a legal process. As such, it must evidence the essential hallmarks of a rules-based approach or it is fundamentally defective.[4] There are two aspects to this. The first concerns the rules of the process itself, the second concerns the manner in which those rules are applied. In the sections which follow, both aspects will be explored in relation to the concept of 'relevant circumstances.'

[1] See *Continental Shelf (Libyan Arab Jamahiriya/Malta)* (Judgment) [1985] ICJ Rep. 13, [45], which emphasizes the importance of such a rules-based approach, describing equity as a mean of achieving 'justice in accordance with the rule of law' as opposed to an exercise in *ex aequo et bono* determination.

[2] See Y. Tanaka, *Predictability and Flexibility in the Law of Maritime Boundary Delimitation* (Hart Oxford 2006) for a study of the subject couched in these terms.

[3] *Delimitation of the Maritime Boundary in the Gulf of Maine Area (Canada/USA)* (Judgment) [1984] ICJ Rep. 246, [81]; *Delimitation of the Maritime Boundary between Guinea and Guinea-Bissau* [1985] 19 RIAA 149, [89].

[4] For an innovative exploration viewing the rules relating to maritime delimitation in quasi-constitutional terms, as providing an imperfect framework for achieving equitable outcomes on a case-by-case basis, see T. Cottier, *Equitable Principles of Maritime Boundary Delimitation: The Quest for Distributive Justice in International Law* (Cambridge University Press Cambridge 2015).

This opening section will consider the concept of relevant circumstances itself; its origins, its role in the delimitation process and our understanding of its nature. This provides essential background for understanding what, in practice, are considered to be relevant circumstances today, which is considered in Section 9.2. Approaching the subject in this fashion paves the way for considering whether the practice of courts and tribunals really does accord relevance to those things which are said to be 'relevant' and whether they do so in the manner which might be expected of a rules-based approach to the delimitation process; and likewise, whether matters which are said not to be relevant are in fact accorded a role, or are treated in a manner at odds with such an approach. This allows the final section to consider whether the case law has strayed beyond being 'predictably flexible' (which is consonant with a rules-based approach) to become disingenuously manipulative (which is not at all consonant with a rules-based approach), and thus permitting some overall conclusion concerning the manner in which the case law has engaged with relevant circumstances, a key component of the delimitation process.

9.1.1 The Emergence of 'Relevant' Circumstances and Their Relationship with 'Special Circumstances'

There is a certain oddity in considering the extent to which the case law has been faithful to the concept of 'relevant circumstances', since that concept is actually a product of the case law itself, with no mention being made of it in either the Geneva Conventions on the Law of the Sea or in the Law of the Sea Convention (LOSC). Article 15 of the 1982 Law of the Sea Convention, concerning the delimitation of the territorial sea, refers to 'special circumstances,' this being directly carried over from Article 12 of the 1958 Geneva Convention on the Territorial Sea and Contiguous Zone. The origins of that Article, in turn, are found in the work of the International Law Commission (ILC), whose 1956 draft articles on the delimitation of the territorial sea had also referred to 'special circumstances' which might cause the equidistance or median line which would otherwise be drawn to be altered.[5] The language of 'special circumstances, found its way into the provisions of continental shelf delimitation as a result of its being

[5] For the latter, see ILC Final Draft Articles and Commentary, Arts. 12(1) and 14 (1), reproduced in Sir A. Watts, *The International Law Commission 1948–1998*, vol. 1 (Oxford University Press Oxford 1999) 43–44.

decided that the provisions proposed for the delimitation of the territorial sea should also be applicable to the continental shelf, it being recognized that '[a]s in the case of the boundaries of the territorial sea, provision must be made for departures necessitated by an exceptional configurations of the coast, as well as the presences of islands or of navigable channels.'[6] It was also understood that 'this case may arise fairly often, so that the rule adopted in fairly elastic.'[7]

This ultimately found reflection in Article 6 of the 1958 Geneva Convention on the Continental Shelf (1958 Convention),[8] which provides that '[i]n the absence of agreement, and unless another boundary is justified by special circumstances, the boundary' would be the equidistance or median line. It seems clear that such circumstances were to be understood in a fairly restrictive sense, although it was also accepted that they might be somewhat more extensive than in the case of the territorial sea. For current purposes, what needs to be stressed is that the clarity or certainty of the rule as a whole was not thought to be undermined by such 'special' circumstances being somewhat inchoate and only identifiable on the facts of each. Indeed, it was considered necessary in order for there to be agreement on a general rule. Thus in terms of the dialectic of this work, such an approach remained 'predictable,' even if the special circumstances might be undefined, unknown or, indeed, unknowable.

What is well known, however, is that in *North Sea Continental Shelf*, the first judicial exploration of the question, the International Court of Justice (ICJ) determined that Article 6 was not reflective of customary international law.[9] A variety of reasons was given for this but, at the end of the day, the ultimate reason seems to have been that its application to the physical and political geography of the North Sea would produce an

[6] See ILC Final Draft Articles and Commentary, Art. 72, reproduced in Watts, ibid., 106.

[7] Ibid.

[8] See generally J. A. C. Gutteridge, 'The 1958 Geneva Convention on the Continental Shelf' (1959) 53 *British Yearbook of International Law* 102. For an overview of the background to these articles, see M. D. Evans, *Relevant Circumstances and Maritime Delimitation* (Oxford University Press Oxford 1989) 8–12; G. J. Tanja, *The Legal Determination of International Maritime Boundaries* (Kluwer Law Deventer 1990) 21–45. The general literature on the Convention in general and Art. 6 in particular is too voluminous to usefully cite.

[9] *North Sea Continental Shelf Cases (Federal Republic of Germany/Denmark; Federal Republic of Germany/The Netherlands)* (Judgment) [1969] ICJ Rep. 3, [56], [69] and [81]–[82]. For an exhaustive analysis of all aspects of the presentation and consideration of the case, see A. G. Oude Elferink, *The Delimitation of the Continental Shelf between Denmark, Germany and the Netherlands* (Cambridge University Press Cambridge 2013).

inequitable result.[10] A number of things need to be said about this which are relevant to the question currently under investigation. The first is that there was little in the work of the ILC or in the *travaux préparatoires* of the 1958 Convention which suggested that the outcome of the delimitation was to be 'equitable.' This is not to suggest that the drafters may not have hoped or anticipated that the outcome would be equitable: it is just that the equitability of the outcome was not seen as being an element of the process as such. That process comprised the application of a method – equidistance – which was to be applied unless special circumstances suggested otherwise. The second is that it must be remembered that in *North Sea Continental Shelf* the Court was not tasked with determining the boundary itself, but with identifying the principles on which that determination should be undertaken by the states concerned.[11] If the Court had been undertaking the task itself it could, perhaps, have decided to 'apply' Article 6 in an 'equitable' fashion – but this was not an option which was open to it. Given the desire of Denmark and the Netherlands to apply Article 6 as such, and in a fairly narrow and literal manner, and given the Court's belief that this ought not to provide the framework for the delimitation between the parties, it was virtually inevitable that the Court would articulate a different approach. And so it said that 'Delimitation is to be effected by agreement in accordance with equitable principles and taking account of all relevant circumstances.'[12]

We may never really know just how different the Court thought an approach based on equitable principles and taking account of relevant circumstances was to the 'equidistance/special circumstances' approach as set out in Article 6. Nor are we likely to ever know what the Court really meant by 'taking account of all relevant circumstances,' not least because it had virtually nothing to say about relevant circumstances as a concept in its judgment.[13] It is important to note that in the subsequent 1977 *Anglo-French Continental Shelf* the Arbitral Tribunal went out of its way to

[10] *North Sea Continental Shelf*, n. 9, [24]. See also S. Fietta and R. Cleverly, *A Practitioner's Guide to Maritime Boundary Delimitation* (Oxford University Press Oxford 2016) 175, for a similar conclusion.

[11] *North Sea Continental Shelf*, n. 9, [2]. For the background to this, see Oude Elferink, n. 10, 185–181.

[12] *North Sea Continental Shelf*, n. 9, [101].

[13] In [101 (D)] the Court listed a number of factors which it said the parties were to take into account in their negotiations and it has become a commonplace for these to be considered to be examples of relevant circumstances. They may well be. But the Court did not say that they were. Cf. Oude Elferink, n. 10, 329, who notes that the Court 'did not define what it understood by relevant circumstances.'

suggest that it really made no difference which rubric was used since they would in practice lead to much the same result,[14] and the ICJ subsequently took a very similar approach in *Jan Mayen*.[15] What was important about *North Sea Continental Shelf* was its introduction of 'equitable principles' as opposed to the equidistance method, not its introduction of 'relevant circumstances' as opposed to 'special circumstances.' Nevertheless, since 'equitable principles' and 'equidistance' thus came to be seen as competing approaches, it was perhaps inevitable that 'relevant' circumstances' came to be seen as being in some way different to 'special circumstances.' And as 'special circumstances' were, from the outset, considered to be fairly limited in scope,[16] it was probably inevitable that 'relevant circumstances' would come to be considered potentially more broad-ranging, reflecting their connection with a more equitably oriented, rather than methods-based, approach.[17]

Against this polarized and polarizing background, it was perhaps also inevitable that all four terms were abandoned in the 1982 Convention as being too contentious. As a result, Article 74(1) (delimitation of the exclusive economic zone (EEZ)) and 83(1) (delimitation of the continental shelf) scrupulously avoided using any of them, and provides that 'the delimitation of the [EEZ/continental shelf] between states with opposite or adjacent coasts shall be effected by agreement on the basis of international law, as referred to in Article 38 of the Statute of the International Court of Justice, in order to achieve an equitable solution.'[18] These articles are now understood to reflect customary international law.[19] It might,

[14] *Delimitation of the Continental Shelf between the United Kingdom of Great Britain and Northern Ireland and the French Republic* (1977) XVIII RIAA 3 [73], [148]; see also ibid., [65]. See also P. Weil, *The Law of Maritime Delimitation – Reflections* (Grotius Cambridge 1989), 144–146.

[15] *Maritime Delimitation in the Area between Greenland and Jan Mayen (Denmark v. Norway)* (Judgment) [1993] ICJ Rep. 38, [46].

[16] At the same time, however, it is worth noting that special circumstances were also quite loosely described, holding out the prospect of a broad interpretation – such as references to 'exceptional' coastal configurations or the 'presence' of islands.

[17] See e.g. E. D. Brown, *Legal Regime of Hydrospace* (Stevens London 1971) 62–70 (written in the immediate aftermath of the *North Sea* cases); R. R. Churchill and A. V. Lowe, *The Law of the Sea*, 3rd ed. (Manchester University Press Manchester 1999) 187–188.

[18] For the background to this, see the *Virginia Commentaries*, vol. 2, 796–816, 948–985.

[19] See *Territorial and Maritime Dispute (Nicaragua v. Colombia)* (Judgment) [2012] ICJ Rep. 624, [139]. The Court cites as authority for this its decision in *Maritime Delimitation and Territorial Questions between Qatar and Bahrain (Qatar v. Bahrain)* (Judgment) [2001] ICJ Rep. 91, [167]. This is not entirely accurate, as all this does is note that the parties considered most of the relevant provisions of the LOSC to be rules of customary International law. The Court does not in that judgment categorically state that it believed them to be so.

therefore, be tempting to argue that since there is no mention of relevant or special circumstances (or indeed, of equitable principles or of equidistance) in that article, these concepts cannot be relevant to delimitations conducted under them. However, those articles do refer to Article 38 of the ICJ Statute and so customary law is of direct relevance to delimitations conducted under them. The customary law status of those articles cannot therefore be used to downplay the role of relevant circumstances either as a matter of customary law or under the provisions of the LOSC. On the contrary, it supports it.[20] It is therefore no surprise that the failure of the 1982 Convention to mention either 'special' or 'relevant' circumstances in its articles concerning the delimitation of the continental shelf and the EEZ has had no discernible effect on the readiness of states to resort to these concepts in all subsequent cases, or on the willingness of courts and tribunals to engage with them. They are firmly established as a part of the customary international law matrix. But this says nothing of what they are.

This is not the place to trace the long and tortuous history of the use of these terms in the subsequent case law.[21] What does need to be noted is that by the time the ICJ came to restate its approach to delimitation in *Black Sea* (2009), it no longer spoke of 'special circumstances' at all. The Court said that a delimitation should commence with the drawing of a provisional equidistance line, which would then be followed by a consideration of whether there were 'factors calling for the adjustment or shifting of the provisional equidistance line in order to achieve an equitable result.'[22] Later, it confirmed that 'Such factors have usually been referred to in the jurisprudence of the Court, since the *North Sea Continental Shelf (Federal Republic of Germany/Denmark; Federal Republic*

[20] This is made very clear by the Tribunal in the *Arbitration between Barbados and the Republic of Trinidad and Tobago (Barbados/Trinidad and Tobago)* (2006) 27 RIAA 147; (2006) 45 ILM 798 [222] and by the ITLOS in *Delimitation of the Maritime Boundary in the Bay of Bengal (Bangladesh/Myanmar)* [2012] ITLOS Rep. 4, [183]. See also [184], making a similar point as regards the inclusion of decisions of courts and tribunals as a subsidiary source of law.

[21] Virtually all works on maritime delimitation consider special and relevant circumstances in some detail, though from varying perspectives. Key overarching works devoting substantial sections to the topic include S. P. Jagota, *Maritime Boundary* (Nijhoff Dordrecht 1985); Weil, n. 15; Evans, n. 9; Tanja, n. 9; N. M. Antunes *Towards the Conceptualisation of Maritime Delimitation* (Martinus Nijhoff Leiden 2003); Tanaka, n. 2; Cottier, n. 4; Fietta and Cleverly, n. 11.

[22] *Maritime Delimitation in the Black Sea (Romania v. Ukraine)* (Judgment) [2009] ICJ Rep. 61, [120], this being derived from *Land and Maritime Boundary between Cameroon and Nigeria (Cameroon v. Nigeria: Equatorial Guinea Intervening)* (Judgment) [2002] ICJ Rep. 303, [288].

of Germany/Netherlands) cases, as the relevant circumstances (*Judgment, ICJ Reports 1969*, p. 53, para. 53).'[23]

This, it should be said, is completely untrue: the paragraph referred to discusses 'special circumstances' and does not mention relevant circumstances at all. The Court blithely forgets that there was a debate over whether there was a distinction between them. Be that as it may, this only serves to emphasize the essential point, which is that the 'equidistance-special circumstances' rule has, de facto, become a 'provisional equidistance-relevant circumstances' rule. In *Black Sea* the Court addressed all such factors under the rubric of 'relevant circumstances.' This has now been followed in subsequent cases by the ITLOS,[24] the ICJ itself,[25] and an Annex VII Arbitral Tribunal.[26] As a consequence, it can now be concluded with some confidence that all such factors as might affect the delimitation process concerning the continental shelf and the EEZ should be considered as 'relevant circumstances,' that in this context the language of special circumstances can be set aside but, importantly, all those things which were previously addressed under the language of special circumstances retain their potency as potential forms of relevant circumstances. Although the courts have not been consistent and, indeed, have recently upturned the language of the 1958 Convention, this has probably been a helpful development since it removes the scope for arguing that 'relevant' circumstances might be different in some ways from 'special' circumstances. Even if once they may have been different (and this is by no means obvious), today they are not.[27]

[23] *Black Sea*, n. 22, [155].

[24] *Bangladesh/Myanmar*, n. 20, [229], where it says, 'This general approach has proven to be suitable for use in most of the subsequent judicial and arbitral delimitations. As developed in those cases, it has come to be known as the *equidistance/relevant circumstances* method' (emphasis added).

[25] *Nicaragua v. Colombia*, n. 19, [192], where it says, 'In the second stage, the Court considers whether there are any relevant circumstances which may call for an adjustment or shifting of the provisional equidistance/median line so as to achieve an equitable result.'

[26] *In the Matter of the Bay of Bengal Maritime Boundary Arbitration (Bangladesh v. India)* (2014) PCA Case 2010-16, Award of the LOSC Annex VII Tribunal, [395], where it says, 'The Tribunal will now turn to the question whether relevant circumstances exist and call for an alternative delimitation method, or for an adjustment of the provisional equidistance line established on the basis of the *equidistance/relevant circumstances* method' (emphasis added).

[27] Reflecting this development, the remainder of this chapter refers only to 'relevant circumstances,' unless the context or quotation requires the use of 'special circumstances.' Cf. Fietta and Cleverly, n. 11, 67 at n. 73, who conclude that it is now appropriate to use these terms interchangeably.

9.1.2 *The Role of Relevant Circumstances within the Delimitation Process*

9.1.2.1 The Twin Roles of Relevant Circumstances

More important than knowing what to call such factors is understanding the role that they are to play within the delimitation process. This too has shifted over time but, in essence, there have been two basic approaches. The first has been to see relevant circumstances as factors which affect the manner in which a primary methodology is to be applied. The second is the idea of using relevant circumstances as a means of determining what that primary methodology is to be.

Article 6 of the 1958 Convention is usually considered to reflect the first approach by providing that the equidistance method is to be applied, unless it is necessary to take account of any 'special circumstances'.[28] As a general approach, it was implicitly rejected by the ICJ in *North Sea Continental Shelf*, which, as has been seen, indicated a list of factors which the parties were to take account of in their negotiations.[29] The Court said little else about the role of such factors – that is, how in methodological terms they would take their place within an ordered legal process.[30] Given that the Court was not seeking to set out or to conduct such a process, however, this is unsurprising.[31]

As a result, it was necessary to determine how, from a methodological point of view, such relevant circumstances might be used as a means of bringing about an equitable result. From a practical perspective, one has to start somewhere. If that starting point is not provided for as a matter of law, then unless there is to be an unfettered discretion, there has to be some

[28] Strictly speaking, this is not what Art. 6 says: it says that, in the absence of agreement, the equidistance line will be the boundary 'unless another boundary line is justified by special circumstances.' This does not necessarily mean that such factors would affect the course of an equidistance line. Its more natural meaning (or its just as natural meaning) is that the presence of such factors would mean that the equidistance line need not be used. Nevertheless, this is not the general approach to its interpretation.

[29] *North Sea Continental Shelf*, n. 9, [101(D)].

[30] The nearest it came to providing some guidance is in [93] where it rather unhelpfully observes that 'more often than not it is the balancing-up of all such considerations that will produce this result rather than reliance on one to the exclusion of all others. The problem of the relative weight to be accorded to different considerations naturally varies with the circumstances of the case.' The Court is telling us, in other words, that 'it all depends.'

[31] What is more surprising is that the Court does not really make it clear whether the factors it identifies as those necessary to be taken into account are 'equitable principles' or 'relevant circumstances' (see [101 (D)]). This alone renders it almost impossible to determine the relationship between the concepts in the Judgment.

means of determining what it is be. Clearly, if the parties to a dispute are in agreement over the methodology to be used, that helps settle the question, but what if they are not?

The second general approach – using relevant circumstances as a means of determining what that primary methodology was to be – arose as a response to this problem. Under this approach, the role of the relevant circumstances was to help identify the applicable method,[32] or to indicate how the delimitation might otherwise be undertaken. This, it must be stressed, was not instead of, but in addition to their role as factors which might affect the practical application of that method. So relevant circumstances came to have two different, but complementary, functions: first, as an indicator of the method (or determinant of the process) and, secondly, as a potential element within that process.

The importance of this development for the concept of relevant circumstances cannot be understated: it was not just their role which changed, but the nature of what was considered to be a potential relevant circumstance changed too. If, in the light of these circumstances, equidistance was considered to be an appropriate method, then it would be used: if these circumstances pointed towards a different approach being preferable, then that other approach would be used – all this being entirely consonant with the overarching idea of producing an equitable result. It therefore became commonplace for the case law to consider an ever broader range of issues under the general rubric of 'relevant circumstances' which could be indicators of what the appropriate approach to the delimitation might be.[33] At the same time, because relevant circumstances also might have a role to play in the implementation of the chosen method, they could in fact influence the process twice over – or at the very least might have

[32] A clear example of this is *Continental Shelf (Tunisia/Libya)* (Judgment) [1982] ICJ Rep. 18 [110], where it said that 'a finding in favour of a delimitation by an equidistance line could only be based on considerations derived from an evaluation and balancing up of all relevant circumstances.' This is made even clearer in the *dispositif* ([133]), which is structured in terms of (A) applicable law, (B) relevant circumstances, (C) the resulting practical method.

[33] *Libya/Malta*, n. 1, provides some good examples, including the arguments advanced by Malta that the relative economic strengths of the parties might be of relevance (which was rejected by the Court, [50]) and that its being an Island Developing Nation was also a relevant consideration (see Maltese Memorial, para. 226, an argument the Court's judgment does not even engage with). Not to be outdone, Libya suggested that the fact of its having an extensive continental hinterland gave its coasts a greater 'seawards thrust' than did the coasts of Malta, which were not similarly endowed with rearwards bulk – an argument also rejected by the Court [49].

varying impacts at various points of the process. Thus they not only become a series of broad-ranging considerations, as opposed to being relatively concrete and factual matters that needed to be considered when applying a particular methodology, but such broad-ranging factors as might be used at a number of points within the process, since there was no clear differentiation between those factors which might help identify the method and those which might affect its application. In short, as the range of factors which might be considered relevant within the delimitation process expanded, so did the role that they might play within it.[34]

The problem with genies is that once they are out of the bottle they are difficult to put back in again. As a result, even though the high water mark of the equitable principles/relevant circumstances approach appears to have been in the past following the establishment of the three-stage approach in *Black Sea*,[35] it has proven difficult to roll back the concept of relevant circumstances to its being understood as a relatively narrow set of factors modifying the application of the primary methodology at the second stage of that approach. To be sure, previous to that decision courts and tribunals seemed to be diminishing the impact of relevant circumstances.[36] But this has been more of a reconfiguration of the manner in which account has been taken account of broadly understood relevant circumstances, rather than a rolling back of the expansive nature of the concept. This will be illustrated by looking in some detail at the manner in which the Court addressed the question relevant circumstances in *Black Sea*, which on the face of it relegates the role of relevant circumstances to a modest ameliorative function at its second stage and then on the facts declined to accord them any relevance at all. On closer analysis, it appears that this is not in fact the case and that there is less discontinuity of approach between *Black Sea* and those cases which preceded – and which have followed – it than has been thought.

[34] See generally the examples considered in the literature cited in n. 22 above. For an early consideration of this as a trend, see M. D. Evans, 'Maritime Delimitation and Expanding Categories of Relevant Circumstances' [1990] 40 *ICLQ* 1.

[35] More recent decisions have, however, indicated a preference for a return to more results-oriented approaches. See M. D. Evans, 'Maritime Boundary Delimitation: Whatever Next?,' in J. Barrett and R. Barnes (eds.), *Law of the Sea: UNCLOS as a Living Treaty* (BIICL London 2016) 41.

[36] Indeed, in a number of cases during that period, the provisional equidistance line was adopted as the final boundary and the relevance of all potential relevant circumstances rejected. See *Cameroon v. Nigeria*, n. 22, [293]–[306]; *In the Matter of an Arbitration between Guyana and Suriname (Guyana v. Suriname)* [2007] 30 RIAA 1, [392].

9.1.2.2 The Role of Relevant Circumstances under the 'Three-Stage Approach'

On the face of it, the Court in *Black Sea* endorsed the first of the two general approaches to the role of relevant circumstances set out above and rejected the second. The first stage of its three-stage approach involves the application of equidistance and the role of relevant circumstances is limited to indicating whether there is a need for that line to be altered in some way in order to ensure an equitable result at the second stage of the delimitation process.[37] To that end, the Court considered a range of potential relevant circumstances presented by the parties at some length, but concluded that there was in fact no need for it to alter its provisional line.[38] It might therefore seem that 'relevant circumstances' played no role at all in the case, as they did not affect the choice of the method, nor did they call for its adjustment. This, however, would be a misunderstanding, for two reasons.

First, it is important to note that a considerable part of the judgment is devoted to considering the lengths of the 'relevant coasts' and determining the 'relevant area.' Both these concepts have been routinely understood as being 'relevant circumstances' and have been used to help determine not only what the appropriate method of delimitation might be, but also how that method might be applied in practice.[39] That is to say, the 'relevant coasts' and 'relevant area' have been understood as being 'relevant' to both the first and second stages of the 'three-stage approach' in previous cases. Remarkably, in *Black Sea*, the Court said that it considered them irrelevant to the first stage[40] and, whilst in principle applicable to the second,[41] in fact relegated their use to its third stage, that of determining whether the outcome showed a degree of 'disproportionality'

[37] The Court could hardly be clearer about the irrelevance of relevant circumstances to the first stage of the process, saying that 'At this initial stage of the construction of the provisional equidistance line the Court is not yet concerned with any relevant circumstances that may obtain and the line is plotted on strictly geometrical criteria on the basis of objective data' (*Black Sea*, n. 22, [118]).

[38] Ibid., [155]–[218].

[39] Whilst this is well attested as regards coastal lengths, this may be less clear as regards the 'relevant area.' However, since the nature of the general geographical relationship (e.g. whether coasts are opposite or adjacent) impacts upon the choice of method – and this can depend on the relevant area – the capacity of the relevant area to influence the delimitation process is clear.

[40] *Black Sea*, n. 22, [163].

[41] Ibid., [164].

between the ratios of the relevant coasts and the area pertaining to each state.[42] At the same time, however, it also granted them an additional *a priori* role at the very commencement of the exercise – what one might call 'stage zero' – when it noted that 'it is necessary to identify the relevant coasts in order to determine what constitutes in the specific context of a case the overlapping claims to these zones.'[43] By this, it means that identifying those coasts whose projections overlap serves to define the area within which there is a dispute and that the ratio between the lengths of those coasts is a vital factor in the determination of disproportionality. And yet they are said not to be 'relevant circumstances' on the facts of the case.

This is as remarkable as it is nonsensical. If one steps back from the formalism of the three-stage approach, it is quite obvious that the 'relevant coasts' were factors which helped determine the overall appropriateness of the method to be applied and the outcome of the delimitation as a whole. Clearly, given the approach taken by the Court to the first stage of the process in *Black Sea*, they could not have been accorded a direct effect in this case at that point. However, since the Court did return to them at its final, third, stage, when determining whether the outcome produced by the first two stages was 'disproportionate' to the ratios between the relevant coastal lengths and relevant areas, these factors continued to be 'of relevance' to the delimitation as a whole. All that has happened, then, was that factors traditionally considered relevant at the first and second stages of the three-stage approach were banished from them, but have been given a relevance elsewhere. That does not mean that they have ceased to be, or to function as, relevant circumstances.

Indeed, the Court suggests that it is more a question of choosing where to allow the relevance of this disparity to take effect. As has been noted, it accepted that the disparity in coastal lengths *could* be a relevant circumstance with an operative impact at the second stage of the approach.[44] On the facts, however, it concluded that there was 'no such particularly marked disparities between the relevant coasts of Ukraine and Romania that would require it to adjust the provisional equidistance line *at this*

[42] Ibid., [78]: 'the relevant coasts need to be ascertained in order to check, in the third and final stage of the delimitation process, whether any disproportionality exists in the ratios of the coastal length of each State and the maritime areas falling either side of the delimitation line.'

[43] Ibid. See also at n. 64 below.

[44] Ibid., [165].

juncture.'[45] As this suggests, it could always adjust the line on this basis subsequently at the third stage of the process if it wished.

This all suggests that taking a rigid approach to the classification of what is, or is not, a relevant circumstance for the purposes of the second stage of the three-stage approach is likely to be an unhelpful exercise. Indeed, the entire exercise as conducted by the Court here – and elsewhere – is vaguely absurd. The entire point about relevant circumstances is that they are circumstances which are relevant to the delimitation. It makes little sense to dismiss the 'relevance' of a potentially relevant circumstance simply because account is taken of it at another stage of the delimitation process and in a manner which does not involve the shifting of a previously drawn provisional line. If account is taken of something, that is enough to make it a relevant circumstance – irrespective of where in a process that occurs.

This is illustrated by the Court's approach to other 'relevant circumstances' in *Black Sea*. As has been said, the Court dismissed the relevance of all 'relevant circumstances' to the course of its provisional equidistance line. Having considered the disparity in coastal lengths, the Court then considered the relevance of other delimitations concluded within the Black Sea. It concluded that 'no adjustment to the equidistance line as provisionally drawn is called for,'[46] but it had also noted that 'The Court will bear in mind the agreed maritime delimitations between Turkey and Bulgaria, as well as between Turkey and Ukraine, when considering the end-point of the single maritime boundary it is asked to draw in the present case'.[47] It is difficult to understand how this is not according it relevance – albeit at another point in the exercise and not as a 'relevant circumstance' as such.

The third potential 'relevant' circumstance which the Court dismissed concerned the effect of 'Serpents' Island,' the capacity of which to generate extended maritime zones at all was also in question. The presence of small islands in the area to be delimited is a quintessential example of a potential 'relevant circumstance' and the Court acknowledges that 'In this phase the Court may be called upon to decide whether this line should be adjusted because of the presence of small islands in its vicinity.'[48] It concluded however, that the presence of Serpents' Island did not call for an adjustment to the provisional equidistance line[49] and so was not, presumably, a relevant circumstance. Yet this is entirely disingenuous

[45] Ibid., [168] (emphasis added). [46] Ibid., [178].
[47] Ibid., [177]. [48] Ibid., [185]. [49] Ibid., [187].

since, as the Court notes, it had already decided that the island could not be used as a basepoint for the generation of the provisional equidistance line and so its effect on that line had already been subject to consideration.[50] Likewise, the Court noted that Ukraine had not sought to extend the relevant area on the basis of the island's potential generative capacity.[51] In other words, it was not that the island was 'not relevant,' but that its relevance, or lack of relevance, had already been accounted for in other stages of the delimitation process. Indeed, the Court itself noted that 'in the context of the present case, Serpents' Island should have no effect on the delimitation in this case, other than that stemming from the role of the 12-nautical-mile arc of its territorial sea.'[52] This sounds very much like a finding that the island was a relevant circumstance, the relevance of which had been taken into account in other ways.

The Court then considered a number of other issues concerning the conduct of the parties, which, whilst potentially relevant to the question of prior agreement, did not 'in the circumstances of the present case' amount to relevant circumstances.[53] Once again, the potential relevance of such factors was, therefore, not entirely discounted.[54] Similar points can be made about the final two potential relevant circumstances considered by the Court. The first concerns potential 'cut-off,' an acknowledged factor[55] – but one which the Court had already addressed when choosing basepoints for the construction of its provisional equidistance line.[56] Finally, the Court considered a range of security issues advanced

[50] Ibid., [149] and [186]. See further Fietta and Cleverly, n. 11, 489. They make the more general point related that the Court adopted an 'inherently subjective approach to the selection of basepoints,' thereby undermining the claim that they were adopting a 'geometrically objective' approach. Approaching the matter in this way also meant that the Court could avoid having to determine whether the island was entitled to generate extended zones of maritime jurisdiction under LOSC Art. 121(3).

[51] Ibid., [187]. [52] Ibid., [188]. [53] Ibid., [198].

[54] Cf. *Maritime Dispute (Peru v. Chile)* (Judgment) [2014] ICJ Rep. 3, where evidence of a prior agreement displaced the application of the 'three-stage approach.' Whether such evidence is properly described as a relevant circumstance is unclear. Fietta and Cleverly, n. 11, 544, note that it is the first example of the ICJ accepting a prior agreement as determining a portion of an extended zone of maritime jurisdiction.

[55] In *North Sea Continental Shelf*, n. 9, [101(C)], no 'cut-off,' or 'non-encroachment' was seen as an aim of the delimitation process. As such, whether a provisional delimitation would have such an effect has become routinely considered to be a relevant circumstance. See e.g. *Bangladesh/Myanmar*, n. 20, [292]–[294]; *Nicaragua v. Colombia*, n. 19, [215]. For a recent discussion, see Cottier, n. 4, 530–536.

[56] See e.g. its decision to use the landward rather than the seaward end of the Sulina Dyke for these purposes. *Black Sea*, n. 22, [138].

by the parties, but again concluded that there was no need to adjust the provisional equidistance line because it already 'fully respects the legitimate security interests of either Party.'[57] This is one of the Court's more forthright statements concerning the potential relevance of security issues,[58] but once again, it is not made clear where or how within the process its effect might be felt; the Court merely notes that whilst 'the legitimate security considerations of the parties may play a role in determining the final delimitation line,'[59] and although considered a relevant circumstance, its relevance had been accounted for in other ways.

Thus what we see when looking at the Court's approach to relevant circumstances in *Black Sea* is that rather than confining them to a rather narrow role at the second stage of the three-stage approach as a means of determining whether the provisional equidistance line is in need to adjustment, they actually infuse the entire process. The stages of the process are not rigid, they are blurred and permeable: the relevance of the potentially relevant geographical or geographically related circumstances *as* relevant circumstances at the second stage of the process turns out to be entirely contingent on decisions taken by the Court when generating its provisional equidistance line at the first stage of the process. Indeed, the discussion of the generation of that line betrays concern for the effect of coastal geography, including the effect of dykes and islands, protrusions, and general coastal configuration – all examples of factors claimed to be, and acknowledged to be, relevant circumstances within its general jurisprudence. If the Court had not decided as it did at the first stage of the case, then it may well be that some of the relevant circumstances considered in the case might have been taken into account at the second stage. This suggests that the three-stage approach, from the outset, was not, nor ever could be, quite so rigid in its approach to the function of relevant circumstances within the delimitation process.

It also suggests that there may be a preference for avoiding the second stage wherever possible in favour of the first, since that first stage – perhaps paradoxically – tends to come in for less scrutiny. It is a commonplace in the literature to focus on the failure of Courts and Tribunals to offer plausible explanations for their decisions concerning how 'relevant

[57] Ibid., [204].

[58] For a consideration of security as a relevant circumstance more generally, see Tanaka, n. 2, 306–314. Cf. Weil, n. 15, 264–266, who considered security to be 'relevant' as a form of legitimate political consideration when boundaries generated on the basis of geography are 'deemed undesirable.'

[59] Ibid.

circumstances' justify shifting the location of a provisional line.[60] It has been less common to focus on the manner in which a provisional boundary is generated, though this is now gaining more attention.[61] Since it is far easier to demonstrate why it is not necessary to alter the course of a boundary determined in accordance with a given method than it is to demonstrate why and how it should be altered, there is an increasing tendency to address 'relevant circumstances' at other points in the process. It should be remembered that the generation of the provisional equidistance line can be as much the product of choice as it is of geography.

If we look again at the three-stage approach, this is in some ways 'wired into' its formulation. In *Black Sea* the Court argued that at its first stage the equidistance line would always be used unless it was 'unfeasible' to do so.[62] This recalls the decision of the ICJ in *Nicaragua v. Honduras* not to use a provisional equidistance line in the case of a territorial sea delimitation because it was 'impossible' to identify basepoints from which it might be generated given both the configuration and the highly unstable nature of the coasts.[63] In essence, the Court in that case was drawing on a 'relevant circumstance' in order to justify the use of a different method at the initial stage of the process. This is exactly what the second of the two basic approaches outlined at the start of this section proposed should happen, and precisely what the 'three-stage approach' purports to reject. As this author has observed elsewhere,[64] the three-stage approach as set out in *Black Sea* has been progressively watered down to admit of increasing flexibility at the first stage of the process. In other words, courts and tribunals are finding it increasingly useful to deflect consideration of 'relevant circumstances' into the decision making concerning the method to be employed and the manner of its application. To that extent, any need to

[60] Among the more recent writings, see e.g. Fietta and Cleverly, n. 11, 584–593, on 'the inconsistent approach of Courts and Tribunals in the adjustment of provisional equidistance lines to accommodate geographical relevant circumstances.' Cf. Cottier, n. 4, 614–635, who, noting the same problems, urges us 'to embrace the need for a creative judgment process and selection from a variety of possible solutions within the concept of equity' (635).

[61] See Fietta and Cleverly, n. 11, 575–583, on 'the creeping subjectivity of base-point selection: A lurch toward a "four stage approach" (or a return to equitable principles)?'

[62] *Black Sea*, n. 22, [116].

[63] *Territorial and Maritime Dispute between Nicaragua and Honduras in the Caribbean Sea (Nicaragua v. Honduras)*, [2007] ICJ Rep. 659, [280].

[64] M. D. Evans, 'Maritime Boundary Delimitation,' in D. R. Rothwell, A. G. Oude Elferink, K. N. Scott, and T. Stephens (eds.), *The Oxford Handbook of the Law of the Sea* (Oxford University Press Oxford 2015) 255; Evans, n. 36.

resort to 'relevant circumstances' in order to justify a departure from the provisional method as applied in practice becomes tantamount to a failure to properly undertake the first stage of the process. As the Court said in *Black Sea*:

> once the provisional equidistance line has been drawn, it shall 'then [consider] whether there are factors calling for the adjustment or shifting of that line in order to achieve an "equitable result"... Their function is to verify that the provisional equidistance line, drawn by the geometrical method from the determined base points on the coasts of the Parties is not, in light of the particular circumstances of the case, perceived as inequitable.'[65]

On this basis, a judgment which requires an adjustment at the 'second stage' because there is a relevant circumstances which needs to be taken into account begins to look like a judgment which is defective. The point of the second, as well as the third, stage has become to demonstrate that the Court has made the right choices at the prior stage.[66]

9.1.2.3 The Approach after *Black Sea*

The approach to the role of 'relevant circumstances' in *Black Sea* has been explored in some detail since this is the case which, above all others, seems to elevate the role of equidistance as a methodology and relegate the role of relevant circumstances to the corrective margins. As has been seen, if it did so, it was more as a matter of rhetoric than reality. We might therefore conclude that there has been little real change regarding the nature, roles and functions of relevant circumstances, even if the Court's rather rigid methodological approach makes this more difficult to discern than hitherto. Subsequent decisions reinforce this conclusion.

Turning more briefly to subsequent cases, the same approach can be seen. For example, and most strikingly, the Arbitral Tribunal in *Bangladesh v. India* seems to have resurrected the idea that the use of the provisional equidistance line within the three-stage approach is itself a matter for debate. It was ultimately decided that a provisional equidistance line was to be used in preference to an angle-bisector line at the first stage of the delimitation process because of its 'transparency,' this being the quality which justified its use unless it is 'impractical' to do so.[67] The Tribunal thought:

[65] *Black Sea*, n. 22, [155].

[66] Unless, of course, the court or tribunal wishes to be seen to be taking account of a particular factor – in which case it can highlight this by addressing it at the 'second stage.'

[67] *Bangladesh v. India*, n. 26, [345].

> 'the argument of Bangladesh that the "coastal configuration renders the identification of equidistance base points impractical or unreliable" is not sustainable. Nor does the Tribunal find the depiction of the coastal façade proposed by Bangladesh to be convincing as it does not reflect the geography of the northern part of the Bay of Bengal. For this reason also, the Tribunal considers it appropriate to apply the equidistance/relevant circumstances method in this case.'[68]

This suggests that the Tribunal considered both the availability of basepoints and the general geographical situation to be 'relevant' (along with the overarching principle of 'transparency') to its decision to use the provisional equidistance line in the first place. This looks very much like determining the applicable method on the basis of 'relevant circumstances' rather than on the basis that its use is provided for as a matter of law. Indeed, the Tribunal seems to confirm that this is so when it subsequently says that it 'will now turn to the question whether relevant circumstances exist and call for an alternative delimitation method, or for an adjustment of the provisional equidistance line established on the basis of the equidistance/relevant circumstances method.'[69] Clearly, the role of relevant circumstances is not confined to the second of a three-stage process as far as the Tribunal is concerned.

Turning to its application of that method (the 'hidden' stage in the process), the Tribunal focussed greatly on the choice of basepoints. Following *Black Sea*, it decided it was free to choose those which it felt most appropriate,[70] believing that it ought to do so 'by reference to the physical geography at the time of the delimitation and to the low-water line of the relevant coasts.'[71] This meant that it was able to take account of a range of factors which it considered to be 'relevant' even before proceeding to produce its provisional equidistance line and then moving on to the second stage of the process.

The Tribunal prefaced its considering of the 'relevant circumstances' with the rather striking and unusual observation that

> 'any delimitation – with or without adjusting an equidistance line – results in limiting the exercise of coastal states' sovereign rights over the continental shelf off its coast to the full extent authorized by international law. *These limits have to be borne in mind when assessing whether relevant*

[68] Ibid., [346]. [69] Ibid., [395].

[70] See e.g. ibid., [353]: Fietta and Cleverly, n. 11, 570, comment that this 'continues the modern trend, started by the ICJ on the *Black Sea* case, of allowing for the subjective selection of the "most appropriate" base points, as opposed to the construction of a pure equidistance line based on objective criteria, at the first stage of the delimitation process.'

[71] Ibid., [223].

> *circumstances exist, whether they call for an adjustment of the equidistance line and, if so, to what extent.*'[72]

The idea that relevant circumstances should be seen as a limitation on sovereign rights is both unusual and, presumably, intended to underline the need for a cautious approach to be taken. This is not, however, entirely reflected in the approach taken in the Award.

The first relevant circumstance considered was the 'instability of the coastline.' The Tribunal rejected the relevance of this on the grounds that it was dealing with the situation as it was today, not as it might become in the future.[73] It did accept that instability could be a relevant circumstance, but only if it precluded the identification of appropriate basepoints, which was not the case here. To that extent, then, it had already taken account of this potential 'relevant circumstance' at that earlier stage of the process. Another potential relevant circumstance advanced concerned the ability of Bangladesh to access the fish stocks on which its population were heavily dependent. The Tribunal rejected this on the grounds that the extent of that dependency had not been demonstrated to be such as to justify its being taken into account.[74] Once again, however, it did accept its potential relevance.

The other potential relevant circumstance advanced concerned the generally concave nature of the coastal configuration. Whilst it did not think this was a relevant circumstance as such, the Tribunal did accept that the 'cut-off' effect which the use of the provisional equidistance line produced in such circumstances was a relevant circumstance and that 'the provisional equidistance line... must be adjusted in order to avoid an unreasonable cut-off effect to the detriment of Bangladesh.'[75] Remarkably, the Tribunal then 'adjusted' the provisional equidistance line by abandoning it altogether, replacing it with an azimuth – a straight line with a specific bearing.[76] Thus the Arbitral Tribunal abandoned its chosen methodology within the second stage of the three-stage approach, on the grounds that an azimuth better reflected the relevant circumstances of the case. Whether this was really a 'stage two' amelioration or whether it is better seen as a 'stage one' determination of the appropriate method is hardly that important. The key point is that, once again – and despite the narrow scope accorded to relevant circumstances by the three-stage

[72] Ibid., [398] (emphasis added). [73] Ibid., [399].

[74] Ibid., [424]. See also Section 2(b)(ii). [75] Ibid., [421]. See also ibid., [475].

[76] Ibid., [478], this being a geodetic line with an initial azimuth of 177° 30′ 00″.

approach – 'relevant circumstances, in practice, had a much broader and more general – one might say pervasive – influence across the process as a whole.'

This was not, however, unheralded. The ITLOS in *Bangladesh/Myanmar* had, in fact, done exactly the same thing some years earlier. Although it had claimed to be applying the three-stage approach, the ITLOS noted that:

> the issue of which method should be followed in drawing the maritime delimitation line should be considered in light of the circumstances of each case . . . the method to be followed should be one that, under the prevailing geographic realities and the particular circumstances of each case, can lead to an equitable result.[77]

It then said that the three-stage approach was to be used, without explaining why. It determined its own basepoints[78] and, having generated the provisional line, proceeded to consider the three issues advanced by Bangladesh as relevant circumstances.[79] It decided that the geology and geomorphology of the seabed area to be delimited was not relevant.[80] It also decided that the island of St. Martin was 'not a relevant circumstance' and that it should have no effect on the delimitation.'[81] On the face of it, this seems to make little sense: if it is not a relevant circumstance, why should the Tribunal stress that no effect be given to it? The answer is that the ITLOS had already decided not to give effect to it when choosing the basepoints for the generation of the provisional equidistance line[82] – so no account was being taken of it for the purposes of the delimitation of the EEZ and the continental shelf at all. This once again underlines the fluid nature of the categorizations. The island was not a relevant circumstance because of the decisions already taken concerning the equidistance

[77] *Bangladesh/Myanmar*, n. 20, [235]. Other authors have, however, tended to see the Award as supporting the application of the three-stage approach. See e.g. R. R. Churchill, 'The Bangladesh/Myanmar Case: Continuity and Novelty in the Law of Maritime Boundary Delimitation,' (2012) 1 *Cambridge Journal of International and Comparative Law* 137, 143; B. M. Magnusson, 'Judgment in the Dispute Concerning the Delimitation of the Maritime Boundary between Bangladesh and Myanmar in the Bay of Bengal,' (2012) 27 *IJMCL* 623, 632.

[78] Ibid., [264].

[79] Myanmar claimed there were no relevant circumstances.

[80] Ibid., [322]. This will be discussed further below.

[81] Ibid., [319].

[82] Ibid., [265]. It should be noted the St. Martin's Island was, however, used as a basepoint and given full effect for determining the territorial sea and so was not without some effect on the overall course of the boundary (ibid., [168]).

line. Had a different decision been made then, it might well have been a relevant circumstance at the later stage.[83]

Then, as subsequently in *Bangladesh v. India*, the ITLOS concluded that 'the concavity of the coast of Bangladesh is a relevant circumstance in the present case, because the provisional equidistance line as drawn produces a cut-off effect on that coast requiring an adjustment of that line.'[84] And it did so by 'an adjustment of the provisional equidistance line by drawing a geodetic line starting at a particular azimuth. In the view of the Tribunal the direction of any plausible adjustment of the provisional equidistance line would not differ substantially from a geodetic line starting at an azimuth of 215°.'[85] Once again, a relevant circumstance, identified at the second stage of the process, justified the remodelling of the whole delimitation exercise by the adoption of a different primary methodology.

Finally, *Territorial and Maritime Dispute (Nicaragua v. Colombia)* again illustrates the extent to which relevant circumstances remain a key determinant within the delimitation process. At first sight, this seems to be the most faithful of the subsequent cases to the *Black Sea* approach, in that it drew a provisional equidistance line – in highly unpropitious circumstances[86] – and then considered a range of relevant circumstances in order to identify which, if any, justified a change in that line.[87] It identified the relative disparities in the coastal lengths of the parties as being of such magnitude as to justify an adjustment,[88] and also identified the 'cut-off' effect which the presence of the Colombian islands located opposite the coast of Nicaragua caused, in as much as it prevented the Nicaraguan coast from generating maritime entitlements beyond them.[89] This, it must be said, is an unusual use of the term, which is more traditionally associated with the swinging of an equidistance line in front of the coast of an adjacent state.[90] Nevertheless, on the basis of these two relevant

[83] Cf. Fietta and Cleverly, n. 11, 507, who argue that the Tribunal ought to have used the island to generate the provisional line and then ameliorated its impact upon it if it thought it right to do so. Doubtless they are correct if one wants to maintain the integrity of the three-stage approach.

[84] *Bangladesh v. India*, n. 26, [297]. [85] Ibid., [334].

[86] Fietta and Cleverly, n. 11, 528, observe that 'the appropriateness of [the three-stage methodology] was, perhaps, not readily apparent.'

[87] *Territorial and Maritime Dispute (Nicaragua v. Colombia)*, n. 19, [205]–[228].

[88] Ibid., [211]. The disparity in this was calculated as being 1:8.2, which the Court considered 'substantial' and similar to those which had justified an adjustment of a provisional line in other cases.

[89] Ibid., [215]–[216].

[90] Fietta and Cleverly, n. 11, 529, describe it as 'a novel application of the so-called cut-off principle.'

circumstances, the Court 'adjusted' the provisional equidistance line in accordance with the second stage of the approach.[91] That 'adjustment,' however, involved such radical shifts in the equidistance line that it is almost impossible to consider it to be an equidistance line at all.[92] Though the approach of the ICJ is fully in accordance with the letter of *Black Sea*, once again its application is so far removed from anything which looks an equidistance line 'adjusted' to account for relevant circumstances as to call into question the real nature of the three-stage approach and, as a result, the place of relevant circumstances within the delimitation process as a whole.

It therefore seems that our understanding of the role of relevant circumstances within the delimitation process needs to be reassessed. Even after the introduction of the three-stage approach, they appear to be as open-textured and as decisive – yet as nebulous – as ever, and continue to operate at all stages of the delimitation process as a means of influencing its outcome, however described or addressed. Despite what is said in the case law, there is a greater degree of consistency over time than is immediately apparent.

9.1.3 The Nature(s) of Relevant Circumstances

This preliminary conclusion needs to be nuanced by a consideration of the nature of the zones to be delimited. It has always been understood that 'special circumstances' for the purposes of the delimitation of the territorial sea might be different from 'special' or 'relevant' circumstances for the purposes of continental shelf delimitation, and this has recently been reaffirmed in *Bangladesh v. India*.[93] There has also been a recognition that the different nature of the continental shelf and the EEZ means that, at least in principle, different factors might be relevant to them, or they might have different weight depending on which zone is at issue. Since the EEZ encompasses the jurisdictional competencies of the continental shelf, all factors potentially relevant to the delimitation of the continental shelf have a potential relevance to the delimitation of the EEZ.[94] But not all factors

[91] See *Territorial and Maritime Dispute (Nicaragua v. Colombia)*, n. 19, [236]–[237].

[92] Even if the boundary line in the area between the Nicaraguan mainland coast and the Colombian Islands can be understood as a substantially modified equidistance line, the northern and southern boundaries clearly cannot, since they follow parallels of latitude. Ibid.

[93] *Bangladesh v. India*, n. 26, [191].

[94] A possible exception to this concerns situations in which the factors relating to the continental shelf beyond 200 nm are considered relevant to the delimitation of the continental

potentially relevant to the delimitation of the EEZ are necessarily relevant to the delimitation of a continental shelf. This is most obviously the case as regards factors concerning fisheries, which are not normally at issue in the delimitation of the continental shelf.[95] Navigational factors are also of potentially less direct relevance to the continental shelf,[96] although they are not altogether without relevance given the need to be able to undertake exploration and exploitation of the shelf areas.

This leads in the direction of a larger question concerning the relationship between the continental shelf and the EEZ more generally. Although there has been surprisingly little detailed consideration of this issue,[97] it is quite clear that whilst it is entirely possible to have an exclusive fishing zone boundary which is different from that of the continental shelf, since they delimit different things, it is impossible to have an EEZ boundary within 200 nm of a coastline which is different from that of the continental shelf, as they delimit, in part, jurisdiction over the same sovereign rights.[98] It is also possible to argue that since rights over the continental shelf exist *ipso facto* and *ab initio*,[99] whereas rights over the EEZ have to

shelf within 200 nm, since, as such factors are outside of the EEZ, they ought not – in theory – be of relevance to its determination.

[95] See e.g. *Jan Mayen*, n. 15, [90], where although access to fisheries was relevant to the placement of an exclusive fishing zone boundary, but not the separate continental shelf boundary, the Court felt it lay within the bounds of its 'equitable discretion' to ensure that they, in practice, coincided.

[96] See e.g. *Nicaragua v. Colombia*, n. 19, [222], noting that control over the EEZ and continental shelf 'does not affect rights of navigation.' Tanaka, n. 2, 315, concluded that navigational factors were of 'minimal' influence.

[97] For an early exploration of this question at a theoretical level, see M. D. Evans, 'Delimitation and the Common Maritime Boundary,' (1993) 64 *British Yearbook of International Law* 283. This question has subsequently been explored as an aspect of the debate of 'grey zones,' an early example of which is A. Oude Elferink, 'Does Undisputed Title to a Maritime Zone Always Exclude Its Delimitation: The Grey Area Issue,' (1998) 13 *International Journal of Marine and Coastal Law* 143. The recent delimitations in the Bay of Bengal have given rise to two such grey areas, which have re-invigorated the debate on this question. See e.g. T. M. Ndiaye, 'The Judge, Maritime Delimitation and the Grey Areas,' (2015) 55 *Indian Journal of International Law* 493.

[98] Thus in *Bangladesh/Myanmar*, n. 20, [474], the ITLOS made it clear that where the delimitation line extended into an area more than 200 nm from the coasts of Bangladesh into an area within 200 nm of the coasts of Myanmar, that boundary served to divide the seabed and subsoil jurisdictions, with Myanmar continued to exercise jurisdiction over other rights associated with the EEZ out to its 200 nm limit This, in effect 'subtracts' the continental shelf from the EEZ of Myanmar at that point, thus ensuring there is no overlap of jurisdictions. The same approach was followed by the Arbitral Tribunal in *Bangladesh v. India*, n. 26, [505]. It is perhaps confusing to describe such an area as being an 'EEZ' at all, as it does not really appear to be one.

[99] *North Sea Continental Shelf*, n. 9, [19] and LOSC, Art. 76(1).

be claimed,[100] then there is a strong doctrinal reason flowing from this to prioritize factors connected to the delimitation of the continental shelf even when delimiting the EEZ.

States with multiple zones of jurisdiction may choose to seek to delimit a single maritime boundary for all zones at issue.[101] The first case to do was *Gulf of Maine*. The Chamber of the Court responded to this challenge by deciding that it should seek to apply 'neutral' criteria – that is, criteria which were equally relevant to both the continental shelf and EEZ.[102] Drawing on the idea, set out in *North Sea Continental Shelf*, that 'the land dominates the sea,' it concluded that such criteria were largely to be drawn from coastal geography, this being a common point of departure for both zones and reflective of this general principle.[103] This approach has gained general approval and has been adopted in many subsequent cases.[104] It has also been supported by another important development.

Under both the 1945 Truman Proclamation[105] and the 1958 Convention the basis on which states were said to enjoy sovereignty over seabed and subsoil resources was that the seabed was a continuation of the land territory into and under the sea. In the words of the Court in *North Sea Continental Shelf*, it was the 'natural prolongation' of the land territory.[106] At the same time, there only was jurisdiction if there was a 'natural prolongation' in a physical sense. Whilst that prolongation obviously began at a coast, there was no reason why it should reflect or follow the coastline. Hence in early cases much of the argument regarding both entitlement and delimitation focussed on the physical nature of the area to be delimited, rather than the coastal geography.[107] The resort to 'neutral criteria' in the *Gulf of Maine* case served to exclude the relevance of physical geography on the grounds that it related only to one of the zones to be delimited by

[100] Although not spelt out in the LOSC, this is implicit in the text and long been understood to be the case. See *Libya/Malta*, n. 1, [33] and Churchill and Lowe, n. 18, 161.

[101] See *Qatar/Bahrain*, n. 19, [173], where it was emphasized that this is driven by the wishes of the states concerned, as the concept of a single maritime boundary is not found in treaty or customary law.

[102] *Gulf of Maine*, n. 3, [194]. [103] Ibid., [195].

[104] See e.g. the comments of the Tribunal in the *Barbados/Trinidad and Tobago*, n. 20, [234] and of the ICJ in *Maritime Dispute, Peru v. Chile*, n. 54, [111].

[105] Presidential Proclamation No. 2667, concerning the Policy of the United States with respect to the Natural Resources of the Subsoil and Sea Bed of the Continental Shelf of 28 September 1945 (UNLS, ST/LEG/SER.B/1, 38).

[106] *North Sea Continental Shelf*, n. 9, [19].

[107] See in particular the discussions concerning submarine troughs and other seabed features or characteristics as potential limits to entitlement in the *Anglo-French Continental Shelf*, n. 14, [104]–[109] and in *Tunisia/Libya*, n. 32, [51]–[68].

the single maritime boundary.[108] In the meanwhile, the basis of title to the continental shelf had itself shifted towards being a 'distance' based zone, at least within the first 200 nm, and as such aligned with the doctrinal basis for jurisdiction over the EEZ. As a result, the Court in *Libya/Malta* was able to draw on the changing basis of title to again reinforce the primacy of coastal geography within the delimitation process and diminish the significance of physical geography,[109] even when the continental shelf alone might be at issue, at least within 200 nm of the coasts.

As a result of the changing doctrinal conventional basis of jurisdiction and the trend towards the delimitation of single, rather than separate, boundaries, there has inevitably been a tendency to merge the approach to relevant circumstances. In a sense, this was most graphically illustrated – perhaps paradoxically – in *Jan Mayen*, in which the Court was asked to delimit a continental shelf and a separate exclusive fishing zone boundary between Norway and Denmark. There was in fact no reason (unusually) why the Court could not have produced different boundaries for these different purposes. Yet it chose not to,[110] and moreover, chose (entirely properly) to grant weight to access to fisheries in relation to the fishing zone.[111] Although this was entirely irrelevant to the delimitation of the continental shelf, it nevertheless placed value on there being a single line and so utilized this for them both. This was, as the Court put it, 'within the measure of discretion conferred on [it] in order to arrive at an equitable result.'[112] As this shows, there has, then, been a retreat from the 'neutral criteria' approach, and the potential relevance of factors is not dismissed merely because they do not have a doctrinal connection with both zones at issue. To that extent, the approach adopted in *Gulf of Maine* has been abandoned. However, given the changing basis of entitlement within 200 nm and the willingness to see a reflexive relationship between the zones where possible, it appears that we have reached a point at which the precise nature of the zone to be delimited, and of the line to be drawn, is less significant than might be expected.

This is important in terms of our approach to the case law as well as to relevant circumstances themselves. Whilst it is important not to assume that issues relevant to the territorial sea will be of similar relevance to the delimitation of the continental shelf and the EEZ, it is perhaps less

[108] *Gulf of Maine*, n. 3, [194]. [109] *Libya/Malta*, n. 1, [33].

[110] *Jan Mayen*, n. 15, [90]. It did, however, consider both strands of law separately throughout its judgment. See ibid., [44].

[111] Ibid., [76]. [112] Ibid., [90].

important to be overly concerned with whether a particular case was, or is, delimiting a continental shelf, an EEZ, or a single maritime boundary. Whilst matters concerning fisheries will clearly not have an automatic relevance to a 'pure' continental shelf delimitation, it seems neither necessary nor desirable to dwell too much on whether a court or tribunal was or was not engaged in the delimitation of single maritime boundary when considering its approach to delimitation. Whilst this may have been an important consideration in the past, it would seem to be an unnecessary scruple today. Whilst the nature of the zones to be delimited obviously remains important, the precise nature of the line to be drawn in order to delimit them does not: the core messages, trends, and approaches within the cases retain their general relevance to our understanding of the subject as a whole. To that extent, it is the case law, and not each case, which is today has become 'an unicum.'[113] At the same time, it does mean that when looking at older cases which were operating under a different set of assumptions – and in particular *Tunisia/Libya* – some caution is needed.

9.2 Towards an Understanding of Relevant Circumstances in Practice

The previous section made the claim that over time different roles have been accorded to relevant circumstances within the delimitation process and that this is at least in part due to evolving understandings of the basis of title as well as shifting understandings of the nature of the delimitation process. Naturally, the claims made by states regarding what amounts to a relevant circumstance reflect this: when, for example, the courts seem interested in broad, expansive claims based on coastal geography, and not interested in claims based on geology or geomorphology, this is what tends to get presented to them. This is entirely predictable, but also tends towards the solidifying of a relatively small number of factors as being 'potentially relevant,' in a manner somewhat akin to 'natural selection.' The practice has – literally – evolved away from certain types of claims. This does not, however, mean that such claims may not retain relevance – it may be just be that their relevance is not identified or acknowledged in those terms. It is a fair supposition that if states continue to raise the relevance of factors which are not, on the face of it, accorded direct

[113] See above, n. 3.

relevance in the case law as a relevant circumstance within the delimitation process, they do so because they believe that they nevertheless may have some impact upon the overall evaluation which is being made.

This section will survey the types of circumstances which have been accepted as having potential relevance to the delimitation process. Once again, it must be stressed that these have changed over time and can only be properly understood by relating them back to the evolving (or oscillating) place of relevant circumstances in the delimitation process as a whole. Thus some particular factors which previously were considered as relevant circumstances have now become to be seen as largely separate elements of the process. The clearest examples of this concern the idea of the 'relevant coasts,' 'relevant area' and 'proportionality.' These no longer tend to be considered to be 'relevant circumstances' as such, but are looked at separately in most recent cases in order to help both 'frame' the dispute and to assessing the equitability (whether described in terms of proportionality or disproportionality) of the result. As such, these all are considered elsewhere in this volume, and rightly so.[114] But this does not mean that they are not also 'relevant circumstances,' broadly understood. Nor does it mean that on the facts of a given case they might not also function as a 'relevant circumstance,' narrowly understood.

This makes it virtually impossible to provide a sensible 'list' of very specific factors which have been considered as relevant circumstances in the case law and attempt to deduce from that much that is meaningful in terms of what might or might not be a relevant circumstance in future cases. There is just far too much complexity, related to changing approaches over time as well as to the specific contexts of each case, to make this a particularly helpful approach. It is, however, possible to consider in more general terms the nature or types of factors which have generally been considered to have been relevant and which have been accorded an effect within the process. In this way, it is possible to identify those issues which are likely to have a bearing on the process, even if precisely how that will occur is not necessarily clear, or indeed, consistent. It can be argued that there are two overarching categories into which most of what are generally considered to be 'relevant circumstances' now fall. Identifying these overarching categories can provide a starting point: if a particular issue can be located within them, then the likelihood of its having a practical relevance is enhanced.

[114] See Chapters 7 and 11 of this volume.

9.2.1 *Factors Relating to Coastal Geography*

By far the most important category of relevant circumstances are those associated with coastal geography. From *North Sea Continental Shelf* onwards, the general coastal configuration has been considered to be the dominant consideration in any delimitation exercise,[115] as a reflection of the idea that the 'land dominates the sea.'[116] Thus the starting point has to be the identification of those portions of the coast which bear upon the delimitation process in some ways. Once this has been determined, a number of generic sub-factors emerge which have the potential to be 'relevant,' in either of the two general senses discussed in the previous section. These will include:

9.2.1.1 The General Geographical Relationship between the Coastlines

It should be remembered that this has been identified as a 'relevant circumstance' from the outset, it being recognized that equidistance lines were more prone to inequitable outcomes in the context of adjacent state delimitations than in the case of opposite coast delimitations because of their propensity to magnify the effect of features as lines projected seawards. The emergence of the three-stage approach has had the effect of lessening the discussion of whether the relationship between the coasts is 'opposite' or 'adjacent,' but the importance of that general relationship remains. It is, for example, reflected in the discussion of the effect of concavities, as in *North Sea Continental Shelf* and in the Bay of Bengal cases (*Bangladesh/Myanmar* and *Bangladesh v. India*). It also finds reflection in the discussions concerning the disparities in coastal length facing onto the areas, which has been a feature of many cases.[117]

9.2.1.2 Natural Prolongation of the Landmass

The issue of natural prolongation as a relevant circumstance must be separated off from the discussion of natural prolongation as a basis of title.

[115] It should be stressed that for the purposes of this discussion, it is assumed that there are overlapping areas of entitlement. Without overlapping entitlements there cannot be a delimitation at all. See e.g. *South China Sea Arbitration (Philippines v. China)* (Jurisdiction) [2015], [156]; ibid., Merits [2016], [155].

[116] *North Sea Continental Shelf*, n. 9, [96].

[117] See e.g. *Gulf of Maine*, n. 3; *Libya/Malta*, n. 1; *Case concerning the Delimitation of Maritime Areas between Canada and France* [1992] 21 RIAA 265; *Territorial and Maritime Dispute (Nicaragua v. Colombia)* (Judgment), n. 19; *Bangladesh v. India*, n. 26.

Nevertheless, the emergence of the 'distance principle' has re-emphasized the role of the coastline as the starting point for the delimitation and has lent force to the idea that the delimitation process should 'allow the coasts of the parties to produce their effects in terms of maritime entitlements in a reasonable and mutually balanced way.'[118] This has at least two distinct – and controversial – aspects.

The first aspect concerns whether coasts may be treated unequally. As far back as *Libya/Malta* a claim was made – and rejected by the Court – that the sheer size of Libya's landmass when compared to that of Malta meant that its coasts had greater 'thrust' and so could project further seawards than (or, at least, vis-à-vis) those of Malta.[119] Though rejected, the idea that the effect of some coasts is greater than the effect of others is well entrenched in the case law when considering the effect of islands. Notoriously, in *Anglo-French Continental Shelf*, the tribunal took the view that the Channel Islands were 'on the wrong side' of a median line, and used this to help justify an enclave approach to their delimitation. In effect, the coasts of the islands were 'in the wrong place' as far as the tribunal was concerned.[120]

Thirty-five years later, the ICJ in *Territorial and Maritime Dispute (Nicaragua v. Colombia)* vigorously rejected the idea that Colombian islands located off the coast of Nicaragua were in any sense located 'on' the continental shelf of Nicaragua[121] but instead noted that, giving effect to the Colombian islands as if there were the 'opposite coast,' meant that 'The effect of the provisional the median line is to cut Nicaragua off from some three-quarters of the areas into which its coast projects.'[122] It should be recalled that the outcomes in both *Libya/Malta* and *Territorial and Maritime Dispute (Nicaragua v. Colombia)* were, essentially, the same: the provisional line was shifted towards the islands in order to give greater effect to the coastal lengths of the mainland. In all these cases, the common factor is that whilst the entitlement of islands to generate zones of maritime jurisdiction was fully respected, their capacity to do so on an equal

[118] *Black Sea*, n. 22, [201]; *Territorial and Maritime Dispute (Nicaragua v. Colombia)* (Judgment), n. 19, [215].

[119] *Libya/Malta*, n. 1, [49].

[120] *Anglo-French Continental Shelf*, n. 14, [199]. This might also be compared with the treatment of the Isles of Scilly contrasted with Ushant, the former being given a half-effect, the latter full effect: Ushant, it seems, was in 'the right place' as far as the Tribunal was concerned. Ibid., [251].

[121] *Territorial and Maritime Dispute (Nicaragua v. Colombia)*, n. 19, [214].

[122] Ibid., [215].

basis with 'mainland' coasts in the context of the delimitation was not: this was, therefore, a relevant circumstance. The 'land' dominates the sea, and islands are 'features within the sea' and so are prone to 'domination' by the landmass. As the Court put it, 'islands should not be treated as though they were a continuous mainland . . . cutting off Nicaraguan access to the sea-bed and waters to their east.'[123] It is difficult to avoid the conclusion that the Court felt that the Colombian islands were just 'getting in the way' of the entitlement generated by the Nicaraguan coastline.

This leads into the second aspect of natural prolongation, and this is the idea of 'cut-off' itself. The origins of this as a factor are impeccable, being found in *North Sea Continental Shelf* themselves.[124] It has recently found reflection not only in *Nicaragua v. Honduras*, as quoted above, but in both the Bay of Bengal cases (*Bangladesh/Myanmar* and *Bangladesh v. India*) too. Indeed, and as has been seen, in those cases it was used to justify not only altering the provisional median line, but of abandoning it altogether for an alternative methodology. The essential idea is that the areas lying seawards of the coast ought to pertain to the coastal state. In the context of adjacent states, this means that anything other than a vertical line to a horizontal plane will produce a 'cut-off' and so be a relevant circumstance. The issue is, however, whether any adjustment to the provisional equidistance line needs to be made in the light of this.[125] In *Bangladesh v. India*, the Tribunal set out its thoughts on this, saying that in order to justify an adjustment: first, such cut-off 'must prevent a coastal state from extending its maritime boundary as far seawards as international law permits' and, if not adjusted, 'it would fail to achieve the equitable solution required.'[126] This is considerable less helpful than it seems – and as the Tribunal itself noted,[127] and as the Court noted in *Territorial and Maritime Dispute (Nicaragua v. Colombia)*,[128] any adjustment in favour of one state should not produce an unreasonable result for the other.

[123] Ibid., [215].

[124] *North Sea Continental Shelf*, n. 9, [8] and [15], where Germany argued against the applicability of equidistance on those grounds that it 'cut off' access to its continental shelf. This is reflected by the idea of 'non encroachment' in the Court's judgment ([101 (C) (1)]. See also Oude Elferink, n. 10, 330–331.

[125] See *Bangladesh v. India*, n. 26, [408], 'As a result of the concavity of the coast, the provisional equidistance line *in fact produces* a cut off . . . For that reason the tribunal considers the cut-off to constitute a relevant circumstance which *may* require the adjustment of the provisional equidistance line' (emphasis added).

[126] Ibid., [417]. [127] Ibid., [419].

[128] *Territorial and Maritime Dispute (Nicaragua v. Colombia)*, n. 19, [216].

Issues of cut-off inevitably lead back to the general geographic relationships between the parties, and it might more naturally be thought of as linked with that relationship rather than with 'natural prolongation.' Nevertheless, it does seem more helpful to see 'cut-off' as linked to natural prolongation because this helps explain the differing effects accorded to the coasts of mainlands and of islands: cutting off islands from their entitlements is not considered to be particularly problematic, whereas cutting mainlands from theirs is. This can best be explained by thinking in terms of the domination of the sea by the landmass, which is more linked to natural prolongation than to coastal geography *per se*. But at the end of the day, it really may not matter too much how these issues are presented and classified. The important and overarching point is that factors connected to the configuration of mainland coasts, how they relate to and how they project into the areas to be delimited are, and always have been, central to the process of delimitation, and are therefore most certainly a key form of 'relevant circumstance'.

9.2.2 *Factors Related to Interests and Activities*

A second key form of relevant circumstances relates to what might generally be described as interests and activities of the parties. Once again, this has a powerful heritage: as outlined at the start of this chapter, the need to reflect such interests has long been recognized.

The case law is littered with examples of parties pleading examples of their practice, or highlighting their interests, over the area to be delimited. Whilst some of these are clearly advanced as 'relevant circumstances' in their own right, others appear to be intended to contribute to what in *Anglo-French Continental Shelf* was described as the 'predominant interest' of a state in relation to the area in question.[129] This might be thought of as an indirect way in which factors can influence the outcome, even if they are not formally recognized as being directly 'relevant' as such. Thus even when the direct relevance of such factors is rejected, they may not be without influence in shaping views concerning what might be an 'equitable solution.' Unsurprisingly, then, a broad range of matters are often raised during the course of a delimitation dispute[130] which might be linked to

[129] *Anglo-French Continental Shelf*, n. 14, [163]. For predominant interests as a possible form of relevant circumstances, see Evans, n. 9, 208–213.

[130] It should be stressed that this relates to situations in which there are overlapping entitlements. It is not concerned with situations in which states argue that their particular

these considerations and an exhaustive listing is neither necessary nor desirable. Rather, and as in the previous section, a number of the more well-acknowledged forms of interests or activities will be outlined.

9.2.2.1 Resource-Related Factors

There is no doubt that issues concerning access to fisheries can be a relevant circumstance as regards the delimitation of the water column and so is of potential relevance to the delimitation of the EEZ and a single maritime boundary. We have already seen how, in *Jan Mayen*, fisheries-related factors were allowed to influence the placing a continental shelf boundary too. Moreover, in *North Sea Continental Shelf* the ICJ noted the potential relevance of resource-related factors to the delimitation of the continental shelf.[131] Nevertheless, the case law does not generally give much weight to economic factors as relevant circumstances in the delimitation of extended zones of maritime jurisdiction. As the Arbitral Tribunal noted in *Barbados v. Trinidad and Tobago*, '[r]esource-related criteria have been treated more cautiously by the decisions of international courts and tribunals, which have not generally applied this factor as a relevant circumstance.'[132] The ICJ endorsed this statement in *Black Sea*,[133] and *Territorial and Maritime Dispute (Nicaragua v. Colombia)*,[134] as did the Arbitral tribunal in *Bangladesh v. India*.[135] It is difficult to resist the conclusion that whilst there is a clear willingness to recognize the potential relevance of this factor, there is a clear reluctance to take it into account unless there is compelling evidence that it is necessary to do so,[136] and in

interests in an area generates an entitlement. The Tribunal in *Philippines v. China*, n. 115, [246]–[247], rejected the argument that China enjoyed historic rights within the area of it 'nine dash line' on the grounds that it is now the LOSC which, as between states parties, provides the source of title to both the continental shelf and EEZ. *A fortiori*, any claim to an entitlement based on factors which would have fallen short of historic title are thus also bound to fail to ground an entitlement. This does not, however, mean that such factors cannot play a role within the delimitation process.

131 *North Sea Continental Shelf*, n. 9, [101(D)(2)].

132 *Barbados v. Trinidad and Tobago*, n. 20, [241]. For a helpful overview, see Fietta and Cleverly, n. 11, 84–89.

133 *Black Sea*, n. 22, [198].

134 *Territorial and Maritime Dispute (Nicaragua v. Colombia)*, n. 19, [223].

135 *Bangladesh v. India*, n. 26, [423].

136 It might be that there is a greater willingness to take account of relatively small-scale artisanal fisheries, as evidenced by *Eritrea/Yemen, Award on Territorial Sovereignty and Scope of the Dispute* [1999] 22 RIAA 335 and the ICJ's judgment in *Maritime Delimitation in the Caribbean Sea and the Pacific Ocean (Costa Rica v. Nicaragua)* (Judgment) [2009] ICJ Rep. 213. This, however, may be open to doubt in the light of comments in *Philippines v.*

all the cases mentioned this was not thought to be the case. Indeed, there may still be traces of the preference for 'neutral criteria' here. In *Maritime Dispute (Peru v. Chile)*, the ICJ, whilst acknowledging that the entire purpose of the maritime agreement entered into between the states was to control access to fish stocks, observed that 'the all-purpose nature of the maritime boundary means that evidence concerning fisheries activity, in itself, cannot be determinative of the extent of that boundary.'[137]

This is paradoxical, to say the least, since the entire point of the continental shelf regime was to facilitate orderly exploration and exploitation of its natural resources and the EEZ is by its very name an exclusive *economic* zone. Whilst there has been much focus on the basis of title, there is surprisingly little focus on the underlying reason for having such title in the first place.[138] This is doubly strange, since in *North Sea Continental Shelf* the ICJ included the 'unity of deposits' (by which it meant natural resource deposits) as a factor which might be taken into account either when undertaking the delimitation itself[139] or where, as a result of a delimitation, a resource deposit straddled the delimitation line[140] and in practice outside of the case law this is an important consideration.[141] The difficulty, however, is that rarely will there be existing patterns of exploitation of seabed or subsoil resources in an area yet to be delimited.[142] To that extent, the

China, n. 115, [803], where the Tribunal said that 'the Tribunal does not consider it possible that the drafters of the Convention intended for traditional or artisanal fishing rights to survive the introduction of the exclusive economic zone. In this respect, the Tribunal disagrees with the conclusions of the tribunal in *Eritrea v. Yemen*.' This would suggest that all patterns of fishing predating the establishment of the EEZ are not only not determinative, but would be irrelevant to the delimitation exercise beyond the territorial sea. It would seem premature to build too greatly on this view.

137 *Maritime Dispute (Peru v. Chile)*, n. 54, [111].

138 See also Cottier, n. 4, 458, who perceptively notes that this is because equity in this context has become associated with spatial issues and thus of space allocation, thus ignoring issues of resource allocation. This, he argues, means that 'the ultimate goals and purposes of delimitation are at variance with its underlying concepts.' *Cf. Libya/Malta*, n. 1, [50].

139 *North Sea Continental Shelf*, n. 9, [97]. 140 Ibid., [99].

141 *Gulf of Maine*, n. 3, [240], cast some doubt on this – even in the context of fisheries – when it was 'unable to discern any inevitable source of insurmountable disputes in the fact that its decision has not endorsed the single management of the Bank's fisheries.' It may be, however, that changing attitudes towards fisheries management would mean that this approach would not be taken today.

142 Though rare, this does not mean never. In the provisional measures phase of *Ghana/Côte d'Ivoire*, Côte d'Ivoire argued that Ghana should cease its drilling operations until the case was concluded in order to preserve the interests at stake. Whilst the Special chamber of the ITLOS which heard the application ordered that new activities should not be commenced, it also permitted existing activities to continue (*Delimitation of the Maritime*

claim is likely to be one of potential economic significance and this is so speculative as to make it very difficult indeed for a court to determine what might or might not be equitable.[143] As in *North Sea Continental Shelf*, this is seen as a matter best left to the parties.

It is, then, existing, rather than potential, resource-related interests which might be of relevance to the delimitation process: but even this has been questioned. In *Cameroon v. Nigeria*, the ICJ took the view that even existing oil wells did not amount to a special circumstance, unless this was reflective of an agreement between the parties.[144] As a result, it would be exceptional for resource issues to be taken into account as a 'relevant circumstance' at the second stage of a delimitation undertaken in accordance with the three-stage approach set out in *Black Sea*. So, for example, in *Nicaragua v. Honduras* the Court did not see arguments relating to natural resources as being 'so exceptional as to warrant it treating them as a relevant consideration.'[145]

But this does not mean that they are not of relevance to the process as a whole. In *Gulf of Maine*, for example, the Chamber noted that the result of its delimitation must not have any 'catastrophic repercussions for the livelihood and well-being of the population of the countries concerned'[146] and it has since become accepted that such an outcome would render the result inequitable, and so not in accordance with both conventional and customary international law. Once again, there are few instances in which such as adjustment has proven necessary: in *Barbados v. Trinidad and Tobago* the Tribunal felt that the 'catastrophic nature' of the consequences suggested had not been demonstrated,[147] and a similar finding was made in *Bangladesh v. India*.[148] In *Barbados v. Trinidad and Tobago*, however, the Tribunal went even further, saying that, even if it had been demonstrated:

Boundary between Ghana and Côte d'Ivoire (Ghana/Côte d'Ivoire) (Provisional Measures) [2015] ITLOS Rep. [99]–[102] and [108(1)(a)]). Whether the presence of the oil wells will affect the outcome of the delimitation is, of course, a different question.

143 See *Libya/Malta*, n. 1, [50].

144 *Cameroon v. Nigeria*, n. 22, [202]. See also *Barbados v. Trinidad and Tobago*, n. 20, [364].

145 *Territorial and Maritime Dispute (Nicaragua v. Colombia)*, n. 19, [223].

146 *Gulf of Maine*, n. 3, [237].

147 *Barbados v. Trinidad and Tobago*, n. 20, [267]. It would seem that the threshold for such a finding is high: in the *Barbados v. Trinidad and Tobago* case the Tribunal, whilst recognizing that 'this deprivation is profoundly significant for them, their families, and their livelihoods, and that its deleterious effects are felt in the economy of Barbados,' also felt that 'injury does not equate with catastrophe' (ibid.).

148 *Bangladesh v. India*, n. 26, [424].

> it does not follow that, as a matter of law, its case for adjustment would be conclusive. Determining an international maritime boundary between two States on the basis of traditional fishing on the high seas by nationals of one of those States is altogether exceptional. Support for such a principle in customary and conventional international law is largely lacking.[149]

As a result, it can be concluded that, whilst it is generally accepted to be a potential relevant circumstance, issues concerning access to resources will rarely be taken account of as a relevant circumstance at the second stage of the three-stage approach. They may, however, feed into broader assessments of equitability.

9.2.2.2 Security

It is often forgotten that one of the original rationales for the continental shelf doctrine set out in the Truman Proclamation was that 'self-protection compels the coastal nation to keep close watch over activities off its shore which are of the nature necessary for the utilization of these resources.'[150] The legitimacy of the security interests which coastal states have in the ways in which waters off their coasts are used is well attested, but does this extend as far as influencing the delimitation of competing entitlements?

In both early and recent cases the potential relevance of security concerns has been accepted. As long ago as *Anglo-French Continental Shelf*, the Court of Arbitration agreed that defence and security interests were of relevance, and, whilst it felt that since both states had similar interests they tended to cancel each other out, it also thought that they 'tend to evidence the predominant interest of the French Republic in the southern areas of the English Channel'.[151] Latent in this is the idea of proximity, and this was brought out more clearly some years later in *Libya/Malta*, where the Court again accepted the relevance of security issues but concluded that the delimitation line would not be 'so near to the coast of either party as to make questions of security a particular consideration'.[152]

This has been a feature of more recent cases too. In *Black Sea*, Romania argued that Ukraine's proposed delimitation line ran 'unreasonably close to the Romanian coast and thus encroaches on the security interests

149 *Barbados/Trinidad and Tobago*, n. 3, [269]. See also *Philippines v. China*, n. 115, [803], and see n. 139 above.

150 Proclamation No. 2267, (1945) 12 *Federal Register* 12303.

151 *Anglo-French Continental Shelf*, n. 14, [188].

152 *Libya/Malta*, n. 1, [73]. See also the *Delimitation of the Maritime Boundary between Guinea and Guinea-Bissau* (*Guinea/Guinea-Bissau*) [1985] 19 RIAA 149, [124].

of Romania,'[153] whereas Ukraine argued that '"the predominant interest Ukraine has for security and other matters as a function of its geographical position along this part of the Black Sea on three sides of the coast."'[154] The Court confined itself to saying that whilst:

> legitimate security considerations of the parties may play a role in determining the final delimitation line... The provisional equidistance line determined by the Court fully respects the legitimate security interests of either Party. Therefore, there is no need to adjust the line on the basis of this consideration.'[155]

Moving forward to *Territorial and Maritime Dispute (Nicaragua v. Colombia)*, a similar point is made: the Court noted that 'legitimate security concerns might be a relevant consideration, if a maritime delimitation was effected particularly near to the coast of a State and the Court will bear this in mind in determining what adjustment to make to the provisional median line or in what way that line should be shifted.'[156] In fact, the Court in that case adopted a rather different approach, with potentially far reaching implications. When it considered its approach to the principal Colombian islands facing Nicaraguan territory, it noted that if it were to 'enclave' each island, this would:

> produce a disorderly pattern of several distinct Colombian enclaves within a maritime space which otherwise pertained to Nicaragua with unfortunate consequences for the orderly management of maritime resources, policing and the public order of the oceans in general, all of which would be better served by a simpler and more coherent division of the relevant area.[157]

The security issue here is not so much the security of the islands, or the absolute security concerns of Colombia; rather, it relates to Colombia's capacity effectively to assert its jurisdiction ('policing') in those waters. This is an interesting development, focussing as it does on broader public order issues, and its identification as a relevant circumstance in this case, in this guise, is novel.[158] Nevertheless, too much ought not to be read into this. The primary reason for the Court not adopting an 'enclave' approach

[153] *Black Sea*, n. 22, [202]. [154] Ibid., [203]. [155] Ibid., [204].
[156] *Territorial and Maritime Dispute (Nicaragua v. Colombia)*, n. 19, [222].
[157] Ibid., [230].
[158] Cf. the related, though even more far reaching, claim of the Philippines that security and public order issues pointed in favour features in the South China Seas being unable to generate broader zones of maritime jurisdiction (*Philippines v. China*, n. 115, [421] and [1187], a claim the Tribunal did not find it necessary to address [1199]).

was that doing so would 'cut-off' Colombia from potential maritime entitlements – that is, a factor associated with natural prolongation (or projection) of the coasts of the islands. Its concerns about the security and public order of the oceans are very much 'supplemental'; being said to be 'in addition'.[159]

Even though the continental shelf and EEZ are not 'security' zones as such, security issues are clearly accepted as being potentially relevant to their delimitation. Although *Black Sea* seems to suggest that this might take place at the second stage of the delimitation process, the weight of evidence suggests that it is more likely to be seen as relevant to assessing the overall equitability of the result, rather than as a discrete factor in its own right.

9.2.2.3 Conduct

A third category of factors concerns the conduct of the parties. This is a large and complex subject which will only be sketched here because of its connection with interest-based relevant circumstances. In essence, those interests which are evidenced by conduct are likely to have greater effect within the delimitation process than those which are not. Of course, the parties may already have determined the outcome of the delimitation by having already agreed upon a delimitation line, and a number of cases have turned on whether such agreements either exist, or how they are to be interpreted.[160] These are not issues concerning relevant circumstances as such. What is of concern here are instances in which it is claimed that the practice of the parties in relation to essential interests provides some indication of what an equitable solution might be. A 'hard' form of this approach would be claims that that practice amounts to a '*modus vivendi*,' that is, a settled practice which, whilst not amounting to a formal agreement as such,[161] is so well reflected in mutual practice that it would be inequitable not to take account of it in determining the boundary. An early example of this approach is found in *Tunisia/Libya*, where the Court felt that the pattern of oil concessions evidenced a 'de facto' boundary.[162] A

[159] *Territorial and Maritime Dispute (Nicaragua v. Colombia)*, n. 19, [230].

[160] See e.g. *Maritime Dispute (Peru v. Chile)*, n. 54, which largely concerned the implications of the parties' treaty practice on the course of their maritime boundary.

[161] Cf. *Barbados v. Trinidad and Tobago*, n. 20, [98] and [270], where the Tribunal rejected the argument of Barbados that an agreement it had entered into with Trinidad and Tobago was 'merely' a modus vivendi rather than a binding arrangement.

[162] *Tunisia/Libya*, n. 32, [117]. The Court expressly said [118] that this was not the same as saying there was a tacit agreement, despite later cases equating *tacit agreement* with a *modus vivendi*.

similar claim was more recently made by Ghana in its claim against Côte d'Ivoire.[163] In such cases there may be no room for drawing a provisional equidistance line at all (if that *modus vivendi* points towards another solution) or – and which may amount to much the same thing – that a provisional equidistance line would then be altered so as to reflect the *modus vivendi* between the parties.[164]

This might be contrasted with a 'soft' approach, in which the conduct of the parties evidences the significance which it places on the interests or concerns it has raised, and so enhances their potential relevance. A good example of this approach is found in *Black Sea*. Ukraine was not trying to show a *modus vivendi* but was said it was seeking to 'assess the claims of the Parties in relation to their actual conduct'[165] in order to demonstrate that its substantive claims were consonant with its practice, whereas the claims of Romania were not.[166] The Court's handling of this was not as clear as it might have been. Whilst it rejected the relevance of resource-related criteria 'in the circumstances of this case',[167] it did not directly address the security and law enforcement practice which Ukraine had raised. Moreover, it never really engaged with the substance of the Ukrainian argument concerning the extent to which the conduct of the parties supported the Ukrainian position more generally, it felt that arguments based on conduct in relation to such factors were not relevant.

A similar situation arose in *Territorial and Maritime Dispute (Nicaragua v. Colombia)*, in which Colombia argued that it had for many years regulated fishing, undertaken scientific exploration and undertaken naval patrols in areas in which Nicaragua had not done so, and that this supported the use of an equidistance line.[168] The Court, however, seems to have taken this as an argument that the provisional median should be shifted to reflect such conduct, rather than seeing the conduct as evidence of *other* relevant circumstances which *themselves* warranted such a shift and, whilst accepting the potential relevance of conduct in exceptional cases, it concluded that it was of no relevance here as such.[169]

Whether conduct is seen as a potential relevant circumstance in its own right, or as providing evidence in support of the relevance of other interest-based circumstances, it seems clear enough that the case law has

[163] See *Ghana/Côte d'Ivoire*, n. 142, [52].

[164] See e.g. *Cameroon v. Nigeria*, n. 22, [304], where the ICJ said, 'Only if they [the location of oil concessions and oil wells] are based on express or tacit agreement between the parties may they be taken into account.'

[165] *Black Sea*, n. 22, [189]. [166] Ibid., [190]–[191]. [167] Ibid., [198].

[168] *Territorial and Maritime Dispute (Nicaragua v. Colombia)*, n. 19, [217].

[169] Ibid., [220].

taken a largely consistent approach over time. Whilst recognizing the potential relevance of all such factors, it has tended to discount them as relevant circumstances on the facts of each case and only very rarely draws on them at the second stage of the three-stage process. Nevertheless, the persistence with which such factors are advanced suggests that they do have an impact on perceptions of what amounts to an equitable outcome, even if that impact is rarely clearly articulated or quantified. Such interests do, then, remain 'relevant' and, despite rarely being given direct effect, they are correctly considered as a distinct species of 'relevant circumstances'. However, it is also true that they are a subservient species, and that issues connected to coastal geography will almost always take priority over conduct within the delimitation process, unless the conduct in question amounts to evidence of an agreement.

9.3 Conclusion

This chapter has *not* attempted to give a comprehensive account of how relevant circumstances operate within the delimitation process. Nor has it attempted to explore exhaustively the use of relevant circumstances within the case law of the courts and tribunals – let alone in state practice. That would require a far greater canvass than can be provided by a single chapter. The aim has been to probe the nature of the delimitation process and to present a picture of how relevant circumstances have been understood over time, taking into account our evolving understanding of that process. Against this background of constant flux, some clear commonalities of approach can be seen across the case law.

Has there been any radical disjuncture over time in the approach taken to, and our understanding of, relevant circumstances? The conclusion is that there has not. Whilst there has been a welcome change in nomenclature, with 'relevant circumstances' now eclipsing the use of 'special circumstances' in the context of continental shelf and EEZ delimitation, this does not reflect a change of substance. The factors which influence the delimitation process have largely been those which reflect coastal geography, even the practical manner in which this has been recognized and given effect to have changed significantly as the underlying methodologies have changed. The relationship of the coasts to the area to be delimited is the key consideration, and other factors – such as the presence of islands, promontories, coastal lengths, etc., all take their place as specific examples of this more general factor.

Alongside this, we can see that there are a whole host of other factors which reflect the interests of the parties in the area to be delimited and which are also of relevance. These will not displace the primary significance of coastal geography as the dominant category of relevant circumstances but they may be of relevance when determining *how* effect is given to them. They might also be taken into account by the court or tribunal in question when it assesses the overall equitability of the solution produced by whatever method or approach is has followed.

Whilst we can be sure that, in the absence of agreement between the parties, recourse to relevant circumstances within the delimitation process represents a principle of customary law, it may be going too far to claim that particular matters or issues *will be* relevant circumstances as a matter of customary international law. Nevertheless, the approach to understanding relevant circumstances within that process presented in this chapter represents a largely settled and stable practice, discernible through the seemingly endless permutations of, and perturbations within, the case law of courts and tribunals over many years. If the chapter has been written at a certain level of generality, this merely reflects the inevitably general level of the conclusions that can be drawn from their practice.

Does this meet the challenge of providing sufficient certainly so as to reflect a rules-based approach to maritime boundary delimitation? In *Libya/Malta* the ICJ observed that the justice which the courts had been applying in maritime delimitation cases was:

> justice according to the rule of law; which is to say that its application should display consistency and a degree of predictability; even though it looks with particularity to the peculiar circumstances of an instant case, it also looks beyond it to principles of more general application.[170]

If that be the test, the conclusion must be that it is met, since those more general principles concerning relevant circumstances can – and, it is hoped, here have been – identified and presented in a sufficiently coherent and consistent fashion.

[170] *Libya/Malta*, n. 1, [45].

10

The Case Law's Handling of Issues Concerning Third States

NAOMI BURKE O'SULLIVAN*

10.1 Introduction

Issues involving third states may arise in maritime boundary delimitation cases in several ways. This includes situations of potential or claimed overlap of maritime zones of a third state with those of the parties to a delimitation case, as well as situations where the presence of a third state has a bearing on the geographic circumstances of a delimitation. This chapter examines how international courts and tribunals have dealt with issues concerning third states while at the same time have attempted to settle maritime delimitation disputes to the fullest extent possible. Despite some initial inconsistencies, the recent case law indicates a reasonably consistent approach towards third-state issues, with a preference emerging for the indication of boundaries without a defined end point. However, the 2012 decision of the ICJ in *Territorial and Maritime Dispute (Nicaragua v. Colombia)* took a somewhat different approach and highlighted the impact a delimitation decision may have on third states.

When considering third-state issues in delimitation cases, it is useful to distinguish between how third states may be affected by decisions to which they are not a party on the one hand, and the way in which third-state interests may affect the delimitation between the parties to a case on the other. For this reason, Section 10.2 first examines the potential effects of a maritime delimitation decision on third states. Section 10.3 then sets out how third-state issues arise in delimitation cases and how, in the practice of delimiting maritime boundaries between two states, international courts and tribunals have taken third-state interests into account. Finally, Section 10.4 offers some conclusions on the case law's handling of issues concerning third states.

* This chapter is written in my personal capacity and does not reflect the views of the International Tribunal for the Law of the Sea.

10.2 Impact of Delimitation Decisions on Third States

Whether maritime delimitation cases are brought to a dispute settlement mechanism under the LOSC or settled by non-LOSC *ad hoc* arbitration or the International Court of Justice (ICJ) by agreement of the parties, the jurisdiction of an international court or tribunal is based on the consent of the parties. The consensual nature of international dispute settlement mechanisms is reflected in the fact that a decision of an international court or tribunal delimiting a maritime boundary has no binding force for states not party to the dispute. This principle is set out in Article 59 of the ICJ Statute and Article 33 of the International Tribunal for the Law of the Sea (ITLOS) Statute.[1] It has also been followed by arbitral tribunals, for example, in *Anglo-French Continental Shelf*, where the tribunal held that its decision:

> will neither be binding upon nor create any rights or obligations for any third State, and in particular for the Republic of Ireland, for which the Decision will be *res inter alios acta*.[2]

In *Bangladesh/Myanmar*, Myanmar had submitted that the ITLOS did not have jurisdiction to delimit the maritime boundary beyond 200 nm 'because any judicial pronouncement on these issues might prejudice the rights of third parties and those relating to the international seabed area.'[3] The ITLOS held that as its decision would, in accordance with its Statute, only be binding on the parties, 'the delimitation of the continental shelf by the Tribunal cannot prejudice the rights of third parties.'[4]

The principal way in which the rights and interests of third states are recognized and protected in delimitation cases is thus the relative binding effect of the decision, that is, the fact that third states are not bound by any decision to which they are not a party. Given this relative effect, it might appear that delimitation tribunals need not be concerned with third-state issues since their decisions will always be *res inter alios acta* for third states, and techniques described in Section 10.3 such as delimitation without a fixed endpoint should be unnecessary.

[1] Art. 59 of the ICJ Statute provides: 'The decision of the Court has no binding force except between the parties and in respect of that particular case.'

[2] *Case concerning the Delimitation of Continental Shelf between the United Kingdom of Great Britain and Northern Ireland, and the French Republic* [1977] XVIII RIAA 3, [28].

[3] *Delimitation of the Maritime Boundary in the Bay of Bengal (Bangladesh/Myanmar)* [2012] ITLOS Rep. 4, Counter-Memorial of Myanmar [1.16].

[4] *Bangladesh/Myanmar*, n. 3, [367].

However, the case law reveals that the character of maritime delimitation is such that a delimitation decision will often have an impact on third states. As the ICJ noted in *Cameroon v. Nigeria*:

> in the case of maritime delimitations where the maritime areas of several States are involved, the protection afforded by Article 59 of the Statute may not always be sufficient. In the present case, Article 59 may not sufficiently protect Equatorial Guinea or Sao Tome and Principe from the effects – even if only indirect – of a judgment affecting their legal rights.[5]

While courts and tribunals have consistently underlined that their decisions are not binding on third states, in the majority of delimitation decisions additional steps have been taken to ensure the rights of third states are not affected. Third states have also sought to intervene in delimitation cases before the ICJ, both as parties and non-parties, on the basis of Article 62 of the ICJ Statute.[6] To date, formal intervention has not been requested before the ITLOS. The majority of intervention requests at the ICJ have been in maritime delimitation cases.

The case law of the ICJ indicates a high threshold must be met in order for permission to intervene to be granted. It is necessary for the intervening state to have a legal interest that may be affected 'in its content and scope, by the court's future decision in the main proceedings.'[7] Permission to intervene under Article 62 has been granted only three times, and only once regarding aspects of maritime delimitation.[8] In its

[5] *Land and Maritime Boundary between Cameroon and Nigeria (Cameroon v. Nigeria; Equatorial Guinea intervening)* [2002] ICJ Rep. 303, [238].

[6] Art. 62 of the ICJ Statute and Art. 31 of the ITLOS Statute permit a state that considers that 'it has an interest of a legal nature which may be affected by the decision' of either body in a dispute to request to intervene in the case. The ICJ and the ITLOS respectively have the competence to decide whether to allow such requests. Art. 31 of the ITLOS Statute provides that if a state is granted permission to intervene 'the decision of the Tribunal in respect of the dispute shall be binding upon the intervening State Party in so far as it relates to matters in respect of which that State Party intervened.' The ICJ Statute does not contain an equivalent provision. This has led to the development of the procedure of intervention as a non-party, where the intervening state is not bound by the judgment in the case.

[7] *Territorial and Maritime Dispute (Nicaragua v. Colombia)* [2011] (Application for Permission to Intervene, Judgment) ICJ Rep. 358, [26].

[8] The ICJ denied the following requests for intervention: Malta in *Case concerning the Continental Shelf (Tunisia/Libyan Arab Jamahiriya)* (Application for Permission to Intervene by Malta, Judgment) [1981] ICJ Rep. 3); Italy in *Libya/Malta Case Concerning the Continental Shelf (Libyan Arab Jamahiriya/Malta)* (Application for Permission to Intervene by Italy, Judgment [1984] ICJ Rep. 3); and Honduras and Costa Rica in *Territorial and Maritime Dispute (Nicaragua v. Colombia)*, (Application for Permission to Intervene), Judgment [2011] ICJ Rep. 240; and ibid., (Application for Permission to Intervene), Judgment [2011] ICJ

application to intervene in *El Salvador/Honduras*, Nicaragua referred to several different ways in which its legal interest would be affected by the Court's decision. Its application to intervene was only accepted in relation to the question of whether the waters of the Gulf of Fonseca were subject to a condominium, on the basis that a decision as to the regime applying in the waters of the Gulf would affect all three riparian states.[9] However, the aspect of the intervention relating to the delimitation was denied on the basis that Nicaragua had not indicated any maritime spaces in which it had a legal interest that would be affected by a possible delimitation.[10] This decision indicates that the interest of a third state would only be affected by a delimitation decision such as to justify intervention if the state identifies maritime spaces in which it has a legal interest that would be potentially affected by the decision. The Court considered that this threshold was met by Equatorial Guinea in relation to its application to intervene in the maritime boundary aspect of *Cameroon v. Nigeria*, but not by Costa Rica in relation to its application to intervene in *Territorial and Maritime Dispute (Nicaragua v. Colombia)*, as will be discussed further below.[11]

From the perspective of a third state, at first glance it may appear that whether permission to intervene is granted or not is not of great importance. Through the procedure of applying for permission to intervene, and outlining its legal interest in a dispute, a third state will generally succeed in drawing a tribunal's attention to its interest in a particular delimitation case. This makes it easier for the tribunal to evaluate the impact of its delimitation on a third state. However, the ICJ noted in *El Salvador/Honduras* that in its application for permission to intervene, a third state should not provide 'an exhaustive account' of its interest in a dispute.[12] In respect of the application of Honduras to intervene in *Territorial and Maritime Dispute (Nicaragua v. Colombia)*, the Court held that proceedings concerning an application for intervention 'are not an

Rep. 348. Outside the context of maritime boundary delimitation, the ICJ has denied permission to intervene in the following cases *Nuclear Tests (Australia v. France)*, (Application for Permission to Intervene by Fiji, Order of 12 July 1973) [1973] ICJ Rep. 320; *Nuclear Tests (New Zealand v. France)* (Application for Permission to Intervene by Fiji, Order of 12 July 1973) [1973] ICJ Rep. 324.

9 *Land, Island and Maritime Frontier Dispute (El Salvador/Honduras)* (Application to Intervene, Judgment) [1990] ICJ Rep. 121, [72].

10 Ibid., 125, [78]–[79].

11 *Cameroon v. Nigeria* (Application to Intervene, Order of 21 October 1999) [1999] ICJ Rep. 1029; *Territorial and Maritime Dispute (Nicaragua v. Colombia)* (Application for Permission to Intervene, Judgment) [2011] ICJ Rep. 348.

12 *El Salvador/Honduras*, n. 9, [89].

occasion for the State seeking to intervene or for the Parties to discuss questions of substance relating to the main proceedings.'[13] This suggests that successful intervention offers greater scope for outlining the potential effects of a decision on the interests of a third state.[14]

Even when the interests of third states are not 'affected' so as to meet the ICJ's threshold for intervention, a delimitation decision may nevertheless have an impact on a third state, particularly as regards a future maritime boundary with one of the parties to the delimitation dispute. This section analyses the ways in which delimitation decisions can impact third states.

10.2.1 Recognition of Entitlements

From the perspective of a third state claiming maritime zones that overlap with one or both parties to a delimitation dispute, the most important effect of a delimitation decision will be its validation of the maritime entitlements of the parties. The delimitation of overlapping claims to maritime zones involves an initial determination that both states parties have an entitlement under the LOSC to sovereignty or sovereign rights in the area in dispute. Thus the arbitral tribunal in *Philippines v. China* noted that 'fixing the extent of parties' entitlements and the area in which they overlap will commonly be one of the first matters to be addressed in the delimitation of a maritime boundary.'[15]

The parties' entitlements to maritime zones arise by operation of law as a result of their sovereignty over land territory. A court or tribunal must ascertain the extent of the parties' entitlements, but does not create or award them.[16] In *Libya/Malta*, the Court described this stage of the delimitation process as one of 'verifying the legal title of the States concerned.'[17] This raises the question of whether the validation of the entitlements of the parties underlying a delimitation decision amounts to the recognition of the existence of an objective situation with *erga omnes* effect, despite the

[13] *Territorial and Maritime Dispute (Nicaragua v. Colombia)*, n. 7, [45].

[14] See B. Bonafe, 'Interests of a Legal Nature Justifying Intervention before the ICJ,' (2012) 25 *Leiden Journal of International Law* 3, 739.

[15] *South China Sea Arbitration (Philippines v. China)* [2016] PCA Case No. 2013-19, ICGJ 495, [156].

[16] See *Bangladesh/Myanmar*, n. 3, Separate Opinion of Judge Ndiaye, [88]; T. Ndiaye, 'The Judge, Maritime Delimitation and the Grey Area,' (2015) 55 *Indian Journal of International Law* 493, 522.

[17] *Case concerning the Continental Shelf (Libyan Arab Jamahiriya/Malta)* (Judgment) [1985] ICJ Rep. 13, [39].

fact that the decision is only binding on the parties to the dispute.[18] Does the recognition of the entitlements of the parties amount to a determination of exclusive title?

In its application to intervene in *Libya/Malta*, Italy argued that by including a certain area within the delimitation, the Court would implicitly decide that given areas did not appertain to Italy.[19] In response, the Court noted that it would 'so far as it may find it necessary to do so, make it clear that it is deciding only between the competing claims of Libya and Malta.'[20] At the merits stage, the Court drew a distinction between 'the areas of shelf which '"appertain" to the parties, as distinct from the areas to which one of the parties has shown a better title than the other, but which might nevertheless prove to "appertain" to a third State.'[21] The Court also noted, in relation to areas of continental shelf within 200 nm of the coast that 'title depends solely on the distance from the coast of the claimant States of any areas of sea-bed claimed by way of continental shelf.'[22]

As entitlement within 200 nm is basely solely on distance, the overlapping entitlements of coastal states to maritime zones are equally valid.[23] If the concept of 'better title' is still considered to have a place in the modern law of maritime delimitation, it is only to the extent that when a court or tribunal delimits a boundary, the effect of the delimitation is that each state can be considered to have 'better title' than the other on its respective side of the delimitation line.

The case law indicates that if there are no overlapping entitlements of other states, the delimitation of maritime areas effected by the delimitation decision is definitive and has *erga omnes* effects. A maritime delimitation decision thus transforms the parties' pre-existing overlapping entitlements to maritime areas into defined areas in which each party is entitled to exercise exclusive sovereignty or sovereign rights. The consideration that a maritime delimitation decision has a definitive or determinative character is reflected in the award of the arbitral tribunal in

[18] See E. Jouannet, 'L'impossible protection des droits du tiers par la Cour internationale de Justice dans les affaires de délimitation maritime,' in *La mer et son droit, Mélanges offerts à L. Luchini et J. P Quéneudec* (Pedone Paris 2003) 315; S. Rosenne, *Intervention in the International Court of Justice* (Martinus Nijhoff Leiden 1993) 155; cf. I. Scobbie, 'Res Judicata, Precedent and the International Court: A Preliminary Sketch,' (1999) 20 *Australian Year Book of International Law* 299.

[19] *Libya/Malta*, n. 8, [16]. [20] Ibid., [43]. [21] *Libya/Malta*, n. 17, [21]. [22] Ibid., [39].

[23] On the equal validity of overlapping distance-based entitlements, see P. Weil, 'Délimitation maritime et délimitation terrestre,' in Y. Dinștein and M. Tabory (eds.), *International Law at a Time of Perplexity: Essays in Honour of Shabtai Rosenne* (Martinus Nijhoff Leiden 1989) 1023.

Guyana v. Suriname, which states: 'as a result of this Award, Guyana now has undisputed title to the area where the incident occurred.'[24] In relation to Honduras's application to intervene in *Territorial and Maritime Dispute (Nicaragua v. Colombia)*, the ICJ held that as a result of its delimitation in *Nicaragua v. Honduras*, Honduras had no rights south of the *Nicaragua v. Honduras* delimitation line, regardless of the existence of a 1986 delimitation treaty with Colombia establishing a boundary in that area. The Court described its delimitation between Honduras and Nicaragua as 'definitive' and stated that '[s]o long as there are no third-State claims, the boundary is to run indisputably on the course defined by the Court.'[25]

However, the recognition of the entitlements of the parties underlying a delimitation decision can only amount to a definitive determination of title where no overlapping entitlements of third states exist. If a delimitation decision includes within its scope areas in which third states have entitlements, it cannot be considered as being determinative. At a later point, it may be decided that neither of the two parties to the dispute have title over the area in question, so that the delimitation decision is without legal effect in that area. Nevertheless, in practice, a maritime boundary determined by a tribunal takes on a 'presumption of finality,' as noted by Tanaka.[26]

This may create difficulties if the parties to the case decide to exercise their sovereign rights in the area subject to third-state claims on the basis of a delimitation decision. A third state, while not bound by the decision, would have to take positive action to prevent the parties to the case from exercising their sovereign rights in the area of overlapping entitlements. Such a scenario illustrates the benefit of intervention by a third state in a delimitation case. As Thirlway notes, intervention allows third states:

> to explain to the Court what should be the limits of its decision, to avoid the inconvenience of having subsequently to convince the parties to the case that the judgment they have obtained extends too far, into the areas appertaining to the third State.[27]

[24] *In the Matter of an Arbitration between Guyana v. Suriname* (2007) 30 RIAA 1 [451].

[25] *Territorial and Maritime Dispute (Nicaragua v. Colombia)*, n. 7 (Application for Permission to Intervene, Judgment), [64].

[26] Y. Tanaka, *Predictability and Flexibility in the Law of Maritime Delimitation* (Hart Oxford 2006), 255. See also Y. Tanaka, 'Reflections on the Territorial and Maritime Dispute between Nicaragua and Colombia before the International Court of Justice,' (2013) 26 *Leiden Journal of International Law* 4, 929.

[27] H. Thirlway, 'The Law and Procedure of the International Court of Justice 1960–1989: Part Thirteen,' (2003) 74 *British Yearbook of International Law* 1, 52.

The problems arising from the presumption of the finality of delimitation decisions are clearly evident in the case law, particularly with respect to references to potential 'prejudice' to the rights of third states. In *Nicaragua v. Honduras*, the Court examined the effect of its delimitation on a 1986 delimitation treaty between Colombia and Honduras. The delimitation line set out in the 1986 Treaty started at the 82nd meridian and ran east. Honduras had drawn the Court's attention to a potential third-state claim of Colombia pursuant to the 1986 Treaty. The Court considered the argument that any 'extension of the delimitation line in this case past the 82nd meridian could be interpreted as indicating that Honduras negotiated a treaty involving maritime areas that did not actually appertain to it and could thereby prejudice Colombia's rights under that treaty.'[28] The Court rejected this argument on the basis that the delimitation line it drew ran north of the 15th parallel and thus 'would not actually prejudice Colombia's rights because Colombia's rights under this Treaty do not extend north of the 15th parallel.'[29] Thus, even though the effect of the delimitation between Nicaragua and Honduras was that Honduras did not have title over an area in which it had concluded a delimitation treaty with Colombia, the Court considered that Colombia's rights were not prejudiced, as the delimitation line did not cross into an area awarded to Colombia under the treaty. However, implicit in the Court's decision is the consideration that Colombia's rights would be prejudiced if the delimitation between Nicaragua and Honduras crossed into an area allocated to Colombia under the 1986 Treaty.

Similarly, in *Cameroon v. Nigeria*, the Court considered that the interest of Equatorial Guinea would be prejudiced if the Cameroon/Nigeria delimitation line were to cross over a Cameroon/Equatorial Guinea median line, representing the undelimited boundary. In its written statement, Equatorial Guinea referred to the fact that Cameroon, relying on the 'apparent support given to its claim of title by an award of the Court,' might act upon the judgment and exercise sovereign rights in an area in which Equatorial Guinea claimed an overlapping entitlement.[30] Equatorial Guinea further considered that what Cameroon sought from the Court was a determination of title, and not simply a judgment of whether it or Nigeria

[28] *Territorial and Maritime Dispute between Nicaragua and Honduras in the Caribbean Sea (Nicaragua v. Honduras)* [2007] ICJ Rep. 659, [316].

[29] Ibid.

[30] *Cameroon v. Nigeria*, n. 5. Written Statement of the Republic of Equatorial Guinea, 4 April 2001, [18].

had a better claim to an area which might nevertheless belong to a third state.[31]

An argument based on the determinative effect of a boundary delimited by an international tribunal was also made by Costa Rica in its application to intervene in *Territorial and Maritime Dispute (Nicaragua v. Colombia)*. Costa Rica submitted that a delimitation by the Court:

> implies much more than the allocation of the column of water and sea-bed to the parties. It entails title to maritime areas, the right to exercise their sovereign rights and jurisdiction under international law in those areas, the right to exclude others from them and the right of enjoyment.[32]

Costa Rica's application to intervene was rejected. Costa Rica was required to demonstrate not only that it had an interest of a legal nature in the maritime area bordering the area in dispute between Nicaragua and Colombia, but that such an interest needed 'a protection that is not provided by the relative effect of decisions of the Court under Article 59 of the Statute.'[33] The ICJ held that Costa Rica's interest of a legal nature would only be affected if the maritime boundary were to be extended beyond a certain latitude southwards, and that the Court would, if necessary, stop its delimitation line before it reached this point.[34] The Court thus indicated that Costa Rica's rights would be protected, not by the relative effect of its decision, but by the fact that the delimitation line would not cross into areas of overlap with Costa Rica's entitlement. This approach was markedly different from that taken towards the application of Equatorial Guinea in *Cameroon v. Nigeria*, although at the merits stage, the protection afforded to Equatorial Guinea and Costa Rica's rights was similar. The Court's reluctance to allow Costa Rica to intervene is somewhat difficult to understand. Forlati considers the decision to give the impression that the Court had already decided that Colombia would no longer have a boundary with Costa Rica in the relevant area as a result of the delimitation.[35] However, in acknowledging that the legal interests of Costa Rica would be affected if the delimitation line were to extend 'beyond a certain latitude southwards,'[36] the Court cannot be considered to have rejected Costa Rica's argument that the delimitation award would be determinative of title.

[31] Ibid., [11]. [32] *Territorial and Maritime Dispute Nicaragua v. Colombia*, n. 7, [80].
[33] Ibid., [87]. [34] Ibid., [89].
[35] S. Forlati, *The International Court of Justice, an Arbitral Tribunal or a Judicial Body* (Springer Switzerland 2014) 195.
[36] *Territorial and Maritime Dispute Nicaragua v. Colombia*, n. 7, [89].

The effect of the recognition of entitlements underlying a delimitation award is also evident in the way in which the arbitral tribunal in *Bangladesh v. India* treated the ITLOS decision in *Bangladesh/Myanmar*. Regarding entitlement to the continental shelf beyond 200 nm, the arbitral tribunal noted that 'the Judgment in *Bangladesh/Myanmar* has *established* the entitlement of Bangladesh to the continental shelf beyond 200 nm.'[37] Thus, even though the Commission on the Limits of the Continental Shelf (CLCS) had not made recommendations on the submission of Bangladesh, the tribunal considered that the effect of the ITLOS decision was to establish the existence of Bangladesh's entitlements to the continental shelf beyond 200 nm. While the existence of entitlement to the continental shelf beyond 200 nm in the Bay of Bengal was already accepted during the negotiation of the LOSC, the language of the arbitral tribunal is interesting, particularly as the tribunal highlights in the next paragraph of its decision that it must consider the decision of the ITLOS as *res inter alios acta*. In this case, the parties agreed that they both had entitlements to the continental shelf beyond 200 nm, but it is worth considering whether the *Bangladesh* v. *India* tribunal would still have used the language of 'establishing' entitlement if the parties had objected to each other's continental shelf claims. The language of the arbitral tribunal suggests that the recognition of entitlements inherent in a delimitation award may be considered to have an objective effect.

It is also noteworthy that the endpoint of the delimitation carried out by the arbitral tribunal was a point on the line decided in *Bangladesh/Myanmar*. The effect of the decision is that India is bound by the division of entitlements carried out by the ITLOS in *Bangladesh/Myanmar*.

The case law thus indicates that while a state's exclusive sovereign rights over its continental shelf are inherent and a state's entitlement to maritime zones pre-exists a delimitation decision, such a decision, by confirming the existence of the parties' entitlements and fixing the precise scope of the parties' sovereign rights, has a greater than neutral effect in practice.

10.2.2 *Delimitation Methodology*

A neighbouring state may also have an interest in the way in which an international court delimits a boundary, including certain findings of fact

[37] *In the Matter of the Bay of Bengal Maritime Boundary (Bangladesh v. India)*, PCA Case 2010-16, [410], emphasis added.

or law underlying the delimitation. An example is to be found in the application of Malta to intervene in *Tunisia/Libya*, on the basis that the Court's 'appreciation of certain geographical and geomorphological features in the area and [. . .] its assessment of their legal relevance and value as factors in the delimitation of areas of the continental shelf' would inevitably affect its own interest.[38] Malta gave as examples the adoption of any special baselines, including bay closing lines[39] and the 'identification of any particular geographical or other factors found to be relevant either as constituting "special circumstances" or as a matter of the application of equitable principles',[40] stating that the decision could 'have a prejudicial effect on Malta's own legal interests in future settlement of its own continental shelf boundaries with Libya and Tunisia.'[41] The ICJ rejected Malta's application to intervene, on the basis that Malta's interest was 'of the same kind as the interests of other states' in the region, and could not be considered a legal interest that would be affected by its decision.[42] The Court held that the indirect impact on Malta arising from its determination of the applicable principles and rules of international law was not sufficient to justify intervention.[43]

However, the Court noted that 'no conclusions or inferences may legitimately be drawn' from its findings or reasoning with 'respect to rights or claims of other States not parties to the case.'[44] In *El Salvador/Honduras*, the Chamber of the Court cited to the decision regarding Malta's application with approval and held that 'an interest of a third State in the general legal rules and principles likely to be applied by the decision' could not justify an intervention.[45]

Nevertheless, the way in which a delimitation is carried out can have a considerable impact on third states.[46] First, the choice of delimitation methodology may have an impact on existing or future delimitations in the region. In *Guinea/Guinea-Bissau*, the arbitral tribunal referred to the integration of the delimitation into existing and future delimitations in the

[38] *Tunisia/Libya*, n. 8, [19]. [39] Ibid., [30]. [40] Ibid., [13]. [41] Ibid., [29].

[42] Ibid., [33]. See H. Thirlway, *The International Court of Justice* (Oxford University Press Oxford 2016) 183.

[43] *Tunisia/Libya*, n. 8 (Judgment, Application to Intervene) [33].

[44] Ibid., [35]. [45] *El Salvador/Honduras*, n. 9, [76].

[46] See A. G. Oude Elferink, 'Third States in Maritime Delimitation Cases: Too Big a Role, Too Small a Role or Both?,' in A. Chircop, T. L. McDorman, and S. J. Rolston (eds.), *The Future of Ocean Regime-building: Essays in Tribute to Douglas M. Johnston* (Martinus Nijhoff Leiden 2009) 611.

region as a factor justifying its choice of methodology.[47] It may be considered that the choice of methodology by a tribunal, when based on regional geography, will have consequences for other states in the region, particularly if a tribunal considers that it must follow the approach used in similar delimitations in the same region.

Second, for neighbouring states, certain findings of fact or law underlying a delimitation decision may be difficult to challenge in future delimitations. For example, a determination that a certain feature is an island rather than a rock could have an impact on third states. It will be difficult for a third state to advocate for a different application of Article 121 to the same maritime feature, whether in negotiations or before a new tribunal. This impact is not unique to delimitation decisions and arises as a result of the structure of the international legal system, where, in practice, precedential weight is given to previous decisions. In this example, the grounds for intervention are reasonably clear.

10.2.3 Effect on Existing Delimitation Agreements

Another way in which the interests of third states can be affected by a delimitation decision is with respect to delimitation agreements in existence between a third state and one or both of the parties to the dispute.

As noted above, the ICJ in *Nicaragua v. Honduras* suggested that the rights of a third state would be prejudiced if the delimitation line indicated by the Court crossed into an area allocated to the third state under a bilateral agreement with one of the parties to the delimitation. If the delimitation line drawn by the Court in *Nicaragua v. Honduras* had crossed over the boundary between Honduras and Colombia established in the 1986 Treaty, the rights of Honduras as against Nicaragua would extend into an area previously agreed by Honduras to appertain to Colombia. In order to comply with both the ICJ decision and the 1986 Treaty with Colombia, Honduras would have to refrain from exercising rights in the area south of the boundary set out in the 1986 Treaty. To the east of the where the *Nicaragua v. Honduras* delimitation line would cross the 1986 Treaty line, the rights of Nicaragua against Honduras would extend to an area previously agreed by Colombia and Honduras to appertain to Colombia. As Colombia would not be bound by the *Nicaragua v. Honduras* delimitation decision and Nicaragua would not be bound by the 1986 Treaty, the

[47] *Delimitation of the Maritime Boundary between Guinea and Guinea-Bissau*, [1985] XIX RIAA 149, [108].

delimitation of entitlements between Nicaragua and Colombia would have to be agreed between them. In effect, the prejudice suffered by Colombia would be that a previously delimited boundary would become undelimited and the boundary would have to be negotiated with a new state. There is also the risk that Nicaragua would consider itself entitled to act in the area allocated to it under the *Nicaragua v. Honduras* decision.

While this 'prejudicial' effect was only hypothetical in *Nicaragua v. Honduras*, *Territorial and Maritime Dispute (Nicaragua v. Colombia)* illustrates how a delimitation decision may have an effect on existing delimitation agreements entered into by the parties. Colombia had concluded a maritime boundary agreement with Jamaica in 1993, which left undelimited a 'Joint Regime Area.' Colombia had also entered into an agreement with Panama on the boundary between the Colombian islands and the Panamanian mainland and had signed an agreement with Costa Rica on the boundary extending from the Colombia/Panama boundary.[48] Colombia argued that these agreements amounted to a recognition by those states of Colombian entitlements in parts of the relevant area, which the ICJ should take into account.[49] The Court rejected this argument, recalling that it 'is a fundamental principle of international law that a treaty between two States cannot, by itself, affect the rights of a third State.'[50] The Court held that its decision 'addresses only Nicaragua's rights as against Colombia and vice versa and is, therefore, without prejudice to any claim of a third State or any claim which either Party may have against a third State.'[51]

Nevertheless, as a result of the delimitation, along part of the former Colombia/Panama boundary and Colombia/Costa Rica boundary, the maritime zones on the other side of the boundary from Panama and Costa Rica are areas where Colombia has no entitlement to exercise sovereign rights. Judge Xue considered that:

> [t]he boundary line in the south would virtually produce the effect of invalidating the existing agreements on maritime delimitation that Colombia has concluded with Panama and Costa Rica respectively and drastically changing the maritime relations in the area.[52]

Judge *ad hoc* Cot considered that the agreements ceased to exist 'since their object disappears with the substitution of Nicaragua for Colombia as

[48] *Territorial and Maritime Dispute (Nicaragua v. Colombia)* (Judgment) [2012] ICJ Rep. 683, [160].

[49] Ibid., [224]–[226]. [50] Ibid., [227] [51] Ibid., [208].

[52] Ibid., Declaration of Judge Xue, [15].

the holder of sovereignty or of sovereign rights in the spaces concerned.'[53] Judge Cot referred to the 'nullity ab initio' of the agreements made by Colombia with its neighbours, in respect of maritime spaces determined by the Court to fall under the sovereignty of Nicaragua. The effect of a delimitation decision on a pre-existing delimitation agreement of the parties merits further consideration. Where a treaty is based on a presumed entitlement to exercise sovereign rights over an area, the absence of such entitlement may be considered to constitute a fundamental change of circumstances. In this context, it should be recalled that Article 62(2)(a) of the Vienna Convention on the Law of Treaties provides that fundamental change of circumstances may not be invoked as a grounds for termination of a treaty that establishes a boundary. Árnadóttir considers that Article 62 does not automatically apply to maritime boundaries as it does to land boundaries, due to the particular characteristics of maritime boundaries.[54] In any event, the rule in Article 62 deals with the situation of unilateral termination of a boundary treaty by one of the parties. Arguably, it would remain open to the parties to agree to terminate the treaty.

As the Court's determination of the relevant area indicating the limits of overlapping entitlements of Colombia and Nicaragua was based on agreements concluded by Colombia that are not binding on Nicaragua, there is the possibility that the scope of Panama and Costa Rica's entitlements may be reduced (in comparison with the situation existing before the delimitation) in any future negotiations or judicial settlements with Nicaragua. Moreover, Colombia may have exercised its sovereign rights in good faith in areas in which it is now considered to have no entitlements. The sovereign rights previously exercised by Costa Rica and Panama can be considered to be prejudiced in that they may no longer exist in a certain area. On the other hand, it is also possible that the scope of said entitlements will be increased.

This legal effect of a delimitation decision arises because of the bilateral nature of delimitation treaties. In concluding such treaties, states are not prevented from including within their scope areas subject to claims by third states. These treaties are *res inter alios acta* for third states. A court delimiting a boundary between states A and B cannot give effect to a delimitation agreement between states B and C when to do so would

[53] Ibid., Declaration of Judge Cot, [10].

[54] S. Árnadóttir, 'Termination of Maritime Boundaries due to a Fundamental Change of Circumstances,' (2016) 32 *Utrecht Journal of International and European Law* 83, 104.

prejudice the rights of state A. If states B and C have included an area of overlapping entitlements of state A within their delimitation agreement, then the decision of the court may well have an impact on the B/C delimitation agreement. This effect can only be avoided if states exclude from the scope of bilateral delimitation agreements areas in which third states have overlapping entitlements. This becomes more difficult when the entitlements of any of the states concerned arises as a result of sovereignty over maritime features, and sovereignty over such features is disputed.

10.3 Third-State Issues in Delimitation Cases

10.3.1 Overlapping Entitlements

The most pertinent way in which the interests of third states can be relevant to a maritime delimitation case is where the maritime entitlements of a third state overlap or potentially overlap with the entitlements claimed by the parties to that case. A tribunal delimiting a boundary in such a situation must take a position on whether the existence of overlapping claims of third states should be taken into account.

The first option for a tribunal is not to take the claims of third states into account at all since the delimitation decision will not be binding on third states, as in *Anglo-French Continental Shelf*.[55] The advantage of this approach is that it prevents a non-party to the dispute from the defining the scope of the tribunal's task, and allows the tribunal to fully delimit any overlapping entitlements of the parties. However, it raises the possibility that the boundary delimited will be subject to alteration in future, depending on what is agreed upon with the third state or determined by judicial settlement. The parties are left in a position where it is unclear as to whether their sovereign rights in an area determined by the delimitation are relative or absolute.

In order to ensure that the boundary delimited is stable and final, a tribunal may decide to take the overlapping entitlements of a third state into account, whether the third state makes a representation to the tribunal or not. However, this approach is also not without difficulty. A tribunal will be faced with a choice of either taking the claims of the third state, where known, at face value or making at least a preliminary determination as to the extent of third state entitlements. The case law of the ICJ indicates that the Court's evaluation of the extent of third-state entitlements is to some

[55] *Anglo-French Continental Shelf*, n. 2, [28].

degree dependent on submissions made by those states, and on the positions of the parties. In *Cameroon v. Nigeria*, the Court accepted Equatorial Guinea's submission that its rights would be prejudiced if the delimitation line crossed a median line between it and Cameroon.[56] In *Libya/Malta*, Italy's claims went beyond a median line and the Court took them into account, noting that 'it has not been suggested by either of the parties that they are obviously unreasonable.'[57] In contrast, in rejecting Costa Rica's application to intervene in *Territorial and Maritime Dispute (Nicaragua v. Colombia)*, the Court stated that it was 'not called upon to examine the exact geographical parameters' of Costa Rica's area of interest.[58] It considered that it was possible to determine that Costa Rica's interests would only be affected by its decision if it extended 'beyond a certain latitude southwards,' without specifying the precise extent of those interests.[59]

How should a court or tribunal go about defining the scope of potential third-state entitlements in the area to be delimited? In the absence of a better option, reliance on a hypothetical equidistance line as defining the scope of third-state entitlements appears to be a prudent and transparent approach. However, insistence on a hypothetical equidistance boundary, when the boundary has already been delimited by agreement is unlikely to bring about the desired effect of stability and permanence of the boundary to be delimited.

The issue of potential overlapping entitlements of a third state was first considered by the ICJ in *Tunisia/Libya*. Malta based its request for intervention on the existence of a legal interest in the Court's determinations regarding certain geographical and geomorphologic features in the area, rather than on the basis that it had overlapping entitlements with the parties.[60] However, the ICJ considered that Malta had emphasized that 'its object and interest in intervening does relate to the general area in which those two States also claim continental shelf rights' and considered that Malta's application 'assumes existing rights of Malta to areas of continental shelf opposable to the claims of the two States Parties to the dispute before the Court.'[61]

Although the Court dismissed Malta's request to intervene, it stated that it understood Malta's preoccupations and that it would be 'be sensible of the limits of the jurisdiction conferred upon it by its Statute and by the parties to the case.'[62] At the merits stage, the ICJ ruled that in the northern

[56] *Cameroon v. Nigeria*, n. 5, [307]. [57] *Libya/Malta*, n. 17, [23].
[58] *Nicaragua v. Colombia*, n. 7, [65]. [59] Ibid., [89].
[60] *Tunisia/Libya*, n. 8, [29]. [61] Ibid., [31]. [62] Ibid., [35].

and north-eastern parts of the Pelagian Block, where conflicting claims of the parties existed, it had 'no jurisdiction to deal with such problems [. . .] and must not prejudge their solution in the future.'[63] The Court held that 'the extension of this line north-eastwards is a matter falling outside the jurisdiction of the Court in the present case, as it will depend on the delimitation to be agreed with third States.'[64]

Three years after *Tunisia/Libya*, the Court, in a different configuration, addressed the issue of the overlapping entitlements of Italy with the parties to *Libya/Malta*. Libya and Malta had asked the ICJ to indicate the principles and rules of international law applicable to the delimitation of 'the area of the continental shelf which appertains to the Republic of Malta and the area of continental shelf which appertains to the Libyan Arab Republic.'[65] Italy applied to intervene in the case, 'to enable it to defend the rights which it claims over some of the areas claimed by the Parties.'[66] According to Italy, the purpose of its intervention was to enable the Court to give the parties guidance to ensure non-encroachment on areas over which Italy had rights.[67] Both Libya and Malta objected to the intervention of Italy on the grounds that Italy's claims regarding its area of legal interest were too vague to establish the existence of an interest of a legal nature and the absence of a jurisdictional link.[68] The Court rejected Italy's application to intervene.[69]

In its decision on the merits, noting that Italy had been denied permission to protect its interests through formal intervention in the case, the ICJ held that its decision 'must be confined to the area in which, as the Court has been informed by Italy, that State has no claims to continental shelf rights.'[70] Although noting that the scope of its judgment had been limited, the Court framed the issue as one of the parties' choice, since they had not consented to Italian intervention.[71] The Court held that Libya and Malta, by objecting to the intervention of Italy, had 'indicated their own preferences' between a more limited judgment and allowing Italy to intervene.[72] The Court also considered it necessary to clarify that its decision was 'only between the competing claims of Libya and Malta.'[73] As the Court explained in the later case of *El Salvador/Honduras*, the reason for the refusal of permission to intervene in that case was 'not that the Court was already sufficiently informed of Italy's interests by those

[63] *Tunisia/Libya*, n. 8, [33]. [64] Ibid., [130].
[65] *Libya/Malta*, n. 8 (Application for Permission to Intervene, Judgment), [16].
[66] Ibid., [17]. [67] Ibid. [68] Ibid., [19]–[24]. [69] Ibid., [43].
[70] *Libya/Malta*, n. 17, [21]. [71] Ibid., [23]. [72] Ibid., [43]. [73] Ibid.

proceedings. Nor was it a finding that Italy had not sufficiently indicated the interests to be protected or presented them in an inappropriate manner.'[74] The application was rejected because of the lack of consent of Libya and Malta, though the Court highlighted that the opposition of the parties to a case 'is, though very important, no more than one element to be taken into account by the Court.'[75] The decision has been criticized on the basis that 'the determination of the extent of the Court's jurisdiction is placed into the hands of a third State and depends on that State's claims.'[76]

A similar approach was adopted by the *ad hoc* arbitral tribunal in *Eritrea/Yemen*, which noted that 'the progress of the boundary line' had been halted 'well short of where the boundary line might be disputed by any third State.'[77] Summarizing its jurisprudence in *Territorial and Maritime Dispute (Nicaragua v. Colombia)*, the ICJ noted 'the Court has always taken care not to draw a boundary line which extends into areas where the rights of third States may be affected.'[78]

The first technique used by delimitation tribunals to take third-state interests into account is thus to avoid delimiting a boundary in an area where the interests of third states may be affected. This approach has the advantage of ensuring the interest of third states are fully protected, provided that the court or tribunal is adequately informed about the extent of such rights. It also ensures that the boundary delimited is final, and the recognition of title to maritime spaces determinative. However, it also circumscribes the jurisdiction of the tribunal, in that it does not fully resolve the dispute submitted to it by the parties.

An alternative technique employed by courts and tribunals is to delimit the maritime boundary without a fixed endpoint, which has been described by Pellet as 'an elegant, simple and globally satisfactory solution.'[79] The court or tribunal indicates the direction that boundary will take, generally along an azimuth. When the extent of the title of the third state is determined, the boundary becomes definitive. This

[74] *El Salvador/Honduras*, n. 9 (Application to Intervene, Judgment), [89].

[75] *Libya/Malta*, n. 8 (Application to Intervene, Judgment), [46].

[76] Tanaka, n. 26 (2006), 244.

[77] *In the Matter of an Arbitration pursuant to an Agreement dated 3 October 1996 between the Government of the State of Eritrea and the Government of the Republic of Yemen (Eritrea/Yemen)* [1998] XXII RIAA 211, [164].

[78] *Territorial and Maritime Dispute (Nicaragua v. Colombia)*, n. 48, [228].

[79] A. Pellet, 'Land and Maritime Tripoints in International Jurisprudence,' in H. Hestermeyer et al. (eds.), *Coexistence, Cooperation and Solidarity: Liber Amicorum Rüdiger Wolfrum* (Martinus Nijhoff Leiden 2011) 245.

approach was used by the ICJ in *Qatar/Bahrain*, *Cameroon v. Nigeria*, *Nicaragua v. Honduras* and *Black Sea*.[80]

In its application to intervene in *Cameroon v. Nigeria*, Equatorial Guinea defined its rights and interests in the area by reference to a median line boundary, considering that its rights would be prejudged if the boundary determined by the Court crossed over this median line representing the undelimited boundary between it and Cameroon.[81] The Court considered that Equatorial Guinea had sufficiently established that it had an interest of a legal nature that could be affected by the decision. In its written statement, Equatorial Guinea submitted detailed information on its area of legal interests, which was taken into account by the Court.

At the merits stage, the Court stated that it 'must ensure that it does not adopt any position which might affect the rights of Equatorial Guinea and Sao Tome and Principe.'[82] To achieve this result the Court indicated the loxodrome along which the boundary should proceed from point X along the equidistance line, noting that 'the equidistance line adopted by the Court cannot be extended very far' as it could not take a 'decision that might affect rights of Equatorial Guinea.'[83] The Court thus considered that an extension of the delimitation line across the median line would prejudice Equatorial Guinea, presumably in part because of its impact on the Nigeria-Equatorial Guinea Agreement of 2000.

In *Nicaragua v. Honduras*, the ICJ summarized its previous jurisprudence noting 'it is usual in a judicial delimitation for the precise endpoint to be left undefined in order to refrain from prejudicing the rights of third States.'[84] In *Black Sea*, the ICJ stated that it would 'stay north of any area where third party interests could become involved' and determined that the boundary should follow an equidistance line south until the point beyond which the interests of third states may be affected.[85]

The use of a delimitation line without a fixed endpoint approach was confirmed by the ITLOS in *Bangladesh/Myanmar*, where the Tribunal held that:

[80] See C. G. Lathrop, 'Tripoint Issues in Maritime Boundary Delimitation,' in D. Colson and R. W. Smith (eds.), *International Maritime Boundaries*, vol. 5 (2005) 3321.

[81] *Cameroon v. Nigeria* (Application to Intervene, Order of 21 October 1999) [1999] ICJ Rep. 1031.

[82] *Cameroon v. Nigeria* (Judgment) [2002] ICJ Rep. 421, [238].

[83] Ibid., [307].

[84] *Nicaragua v. Honduras*, n. 28, [312].

[85] *Maritime Delimitation in the Black Sea (Romania v. Ukraine)* [2009] ICJ Rep. 61, [112]; [207]–[209].

> it is established practice that the direction of the seaward segment of a maritime boundary may be determined without indicating its precise terminus, for example by specifying that it continues until it reaches the area where the rights of third parties may be affected.[86]

This approach is also not free from difficulties. It assumes that any circumstances relevant to the delimitation will continue to operate in an equal way along the course of the boundary. This presents particular problems with respect to the continental shelf beyond 200 nm, where geomorphological circumstances may be relevant.[87] It also prevents a proper evaluation of the proportionality of the maritime spaces allocated by the boundary line in relation to the lengths of the relevant coasts. However, in that it avoids the parties having to begin new negotiations on the boundary once the issue of third-state entitlements have been settled, it can be considered as preferable to the technique of avoiding the area of third-state interests completely.

10.3.2 Geographical Circumstances

The presence of third states will often constitute the relevant geographical context to a delimitation. In *El Salvador/Honduras*, the Court held that

> the taking into account of all the coasts and coastal relationships within the Gulf as a geographical fact for the purpose of effecting an eventual delimitation [...] in no way signifies that by such an operation itself the legal interest of a third riparian State of the Gulf, Nicaragua, may be affected.[88]

Conversely, the presence of third states may affect the interests of the parties to a delimitation. Submissions regarding the presence of third states as relevant to the construction of delimitation line have been raised by the parties in several delimitation cases.

The first way in which the presence of third states may have an impact on the way in which a delimitation is carried out is in the determination of the relevant area. In *Black Sea*, the Court noted that although third states might have entitlements in the area of overlapping entitlements of Romania and Ukraine, this did not preclude the inclusion of those parts in the relevant area 'without prejudice to the position of any third State regarding its entitlements in this area.'[89] In contrast, agreements between

[86] *Bangladesh/Myanmar*, n. 3, [367].
[87] See Chapter 13 of this volume, which discusses this issue in detail.
[88] *El Salvador/Honduras*, n. 9, [77]. [89] *Black Sea*, n. 85, [114].

one of the parties to the delimitation and a third state have been used to define the extent of the parties overlapping entitlements. In *Barbados v. Trinidad and Tobago*, the arbitral tribunal held that the existence of the Barbados/Guyana Joint Cooperation Zone Treaty could only 'influence the delimitation [. . .] in so far as it would reflect the limits of Barbados' maritime claim'[90] on the basis that the maritime areas which Trinidad and Tobago had, 'in the 1990 Trinidad-Venezuela Agreement, given up in favour of Venezuela do not any longer appertain to Trinidad and Tobago and thus the Tribunal could not draw a delimitation line the effect of which would be to attribute to Trinidad and Tobago areas it no longer claims.'[91]

In *Territorial and Maritime Dispute (Nicaragua v. Colombia)*, when setting out the relevant area, the Court excluded an area subject to a joint development agreement between Jamaica and Colombia, noting that more than half of the Joint Regime Area was located more than 200 nautical miles from Nicaragua.[92] The Court also treated the agreements between Colombia and Panama and Colombia and Costa Rica as defining the limits of the relevant area, on the basis that as Colombia had given up its claims in a particular area, there could be no overlap of the parties' entitlements beyond the area. However, the Court did not deal with the 1986 Honduras/Colombia Treaty in the same manner. The Court ignored this agreement for the purpose of defining the relevant area and instead fixed the northern limit of the relevant area as the delimitation line it had effected in *Nicaragua v. Honduras*. In respect of this agreement, the Court noted '[w]hatever concessions one State party has made to the other shall remain bilateral and bilateral only, and will not affect the entitlements of the third State.'[93] Thus, while Colombia was assumed to have no entitlements that could overlap with Nicaragua in the area south and west of its agreed boundary with Panama, it was considered to have overlapping entitlements with Nicaragua in the area north of its agreed boundary with Honduras.

The presence of third states has also been raised as an element having a bearing on the methodology to be adopted. In *Guinea/Guinea-Bissau* the arbitral tribunal considered that the somewhat concave nature of the coastline from Guinea-Bissau to Sierra Leone and the convex character

[90] *Arbitration between Barbados and the Republic of Trinidad and Tobago* [2006] XXVII RIAA 147, [349].

[91] Ibid., [347].

[92] *Territorial and Maritime Dispute (Nicaragua v. Colombia)*, n. 48, [163].

[93] *Territorial and Maritime Dispute (Nicaragua v. Colombia)* (Application for Permission to Intervene, Judgment), [2011] ICJ Rep. 444, [72].

of the West African coastline as whole rendered the equidistance method unsuitable, and called for a method which could be integrated with existing and future delimitations in the region.[94] Although the coast of Guinea is only slightly concave, an unadjusted equidistance line would have left Guinea with a narrow wedge of maritime zones if its boundary with Sierra Leone was also delimited on the basis of an equidistance line. The tribunal's resort to the angle-bisector delimitation method as a result of existing or future delimitations in the area has not been followed in subsequent cases, and has been the subject of scholarly criticism.[95] However, the consideration that other delimitations in the region should be a relevant factor in a delimitation exercise is not without merit, as will be discussed further below.

In *Bangladesh/Myanmar*, Bangladesh argued that the Tribunal should apply the angle-bisector method 'on account of the specific configuration of its coast in the northern part of the Bay of Bengal and of the double concavity characterizing it.'[96] The ITLOS rejected this argument and concluded that the equidistance/relevant circumstances method was appropriate.[97] Taking into account the decision of the ICJ in *Nicaragua v. Honduras*, the case-law since *Guinea/Guinea-Bissau* appears reasonably consistent, and indicates that the presence of third states is not a relevant factor in the choice of delimitation methodology.

In *Ghana/Côte d'Ivoire*, Côte d'Ivoire argued for the application of the angle-bisector methodology on several grounds, including the future delimitation of Togo's overlapping entitlements with Ghana. Côte d'Ivoire submitted that the use of the equidistance method would create a precedent with a 'a follow-on effect on the region' and that the precedent established 'will serve as reference for the delimitation of the boundaries of the States in the sub-region, and this should not be of such a nature as to be to the detriment of the interests of those States.'[98] The decision of the Special Chamber is expected at the end of September 2017 and represents an

[94] *Guinea/Guinea-Bissau*, n. 47, [19].

[95] See A. G. Oude Elferink, *The Law of Maritime Boundary Delimitation: A Case Study of the Russian Federation* (Martinus Nijhoff Leiden 1994) 89; S. Fietta and R. Cleverly, *A Practitioner's Guide to Maritime Boundary Delimitation* (Oxford University Press Oxford 2016) 279; *Bangladesh v. India*, Transcript, 13 December 2013, 623; *Ghana/Côte d'Ivoire*, Transcript, 10 February 2017, 12.

[96] *Bangladesh/Myanmar*, n. 3, [213]. [97] Ibid., [239].

[98] *Dispute Concerning Delimitation of the Maritime Boundary between Ghana and Côte d'Ivoire in the Atlantic Ocean (Ghana/Côte d'Ivoire)* [2015] ITLOS Rep. 494, Statement of Mr. Pitron, 10 February 2017, PV5, 24.

opportunity for further judicial pronouncement on the relevance of third states in the choice of delimitation methodology.

When the appropriate methodology has been identified, a tribunal may choose to take into account the coastline of neighbouring states when constructing the delimitation line. In *Guinea/Guinea-Bissau*, when constructing a perpendicular to the general direction of the coast the arbitral tribunal did not limit itself to the direction of the coastlines of the parties, but took into account the coastline including neighbouring states.[99] In contrast, in *Cameroon v. Nigeria*, the ICJ rejected Cameroon's contention that the coastline from Akasso in Nigeria to Cap Lopez in Gabon should be taken into account when constructing a provisional equidistance line noting that 'the maritime boundary between Cameroon and Nigeria can only be determined by reference to points on the coastlines of these two States and not of third States.'[100] It is logical that an equidistance line should only be determined from basepoints situated on the coastlines of the parties to a delimitation. Considering that an angle-bisector, is at its heart, a different method for drawing an equidistance line, the argument that the coastlines of third states should be taken into account is not compelling. Arguably, it is preferable when constructing an angle bisector to draw the general direction of the coasts only on the basis of the coasts of the parties and then to adjust the bisector if necessary in order to take into account relevant circumstances arising from the regional geography. As Fietta and Cleverly note 'the identification of a simplified coastal front is inherently subjective.'[101] Given the possible impact of such actions on third states, as noted in Section 10.2.2 above, it seems prudent for a tribunal to avoid any subjective determinations involving third states.

A more complex issue is whether the presence of third states and their maritime entitlements is a relevant circumstance which should be taken into account by a tribunal when adjusting a provisional equidistance line. In *Black Sea*, the ICJ considered that '[t]hird party entitlements would only be relevant if the delimitation between Romania and Ukraine were to affect them.'[102] The effect of the presence of third states is particularly evident in respect of concavity of the coast as a relevant circumstance. The jurisprudence indicates that concavity will only be a relevant circumstance when it generates a cut-off effect. In practice, a cut-off effect can arise solely as a result of the concave shape of the coast of one state party to a delimitation, or as a result of the concavity of a state's coast combined

[99] *Guinea/Guinea-Bissau*, n. 47, [110]. [100] *Cameroon v. Nigeria*, n. 5, [291].
[101] Fietta and Cleverly, n. 95. [102] *Black Sea*, n. 85, [114].

with the location of that state between two other states when the coastline of all three generally has a concave configuration. In the latter situation, the presence of a third state may contribute to the cut-off effect arising as a result of the concavity of the coast. It is difficult to discern a consistent position regarding the impact of the entitlements of third states from the jurisprudence.

In *North Sea Continental Shelf*, the ICJ considered the situation of a state with a concave coast between two adjacent states. The Court stated that when two equidistance lines are drawn at different points on a concave coast,

> they will [...] cause the continental shelf area they enclose, to take the form approximately of a triangle with its apex to seaward [...] 'cutting off' the coastal State from the further areas of the continental shelf outside of and beyond this triangle.[103]

The Court thus indicated that the cut-off effect is produced by the combined effect of two equidistance lines, and not just the concavity of the coast itself.

The Court first noted that each of the cases could have been brought separately, and that different conclusions could have been reached in each case. However, referring to the fact that the Netherlands and Denmark had made identical submissions and presented them in common or in close co-operation, the Court then held:

> [t]o this extent therefore, the two cases may be treated as one; and it must be noted that although two separate delimitations are in question, they involve – indeed actually give rise to – a single situation. The fact that the question of either of these delimitations might have arisen and called for settlement separately in point of time, does not alter the character of the problem with which the Court is actually faced, having regard to the manner in which the Parties themselves have brought the matter before it.[104]

Although this passage is somewhat opaque, it can be read to mean that since the Netherlands and Denmark had effectively treated the two delimitations as a single situation, and that no distinction had been made in terms of factors which would be relevant to one delimitation but not the other, the Court could regard the effects of the two equidistance lines as

[103] *North Sea Continental Shelf Cases (Federal Republic of Germany/Denmark; Federal Republic of Germany/Netherlands)* [1969] ICJ Rep. 3, [8].
[104] Ibid., [11].

whole, rather than in each case, treating the existence of the other delimitation line as irrelevant. The Court considered that the parties had pleaded the case on the basis that the drawing of two delimitation lines created a 'single situation.' The Court, in evaluating the cut-off effect could, as a result, consider the combined effect of the two delimitation lines. The Court's emphasis on the way in which the parties brought the case suggests that if only one of the cases had been brought to the Court, for example, Germany/Netherlands, then the Court would only have been able to evaluate the cut-off effect produced by the Netherlands/Germany delimitation line in isolation, without taking into account any existing or possible future delimitation between Denmark and Germany.

In *Guinea/Guinea-Bissau*, the tribunal dealt with concavity as relevant to choice of delimitation method rather than as a circumstance justifying adjustment of provisional equidistance line. However, it is notable that the tribunal specifically referred to the situation of Guinea between Guinea-Bissau and Sierra Leone and referred to the fact that the drawing of two equidistance lines would join the boundary between Guinea and Sierra Leone 'too quickly.'[105] In contrast, in *Cameroon v. Nigeria*, the Court emphasized that concavity was only to be assessed with respect to the relevant parts of the parties' coasts, and not the geographic situation of the region as a whole.[106] The Court considered that the relevant part of Cameroon's coast was not concave and that it was thus not necessary to take the overall concavity of Cameroon's coast into consideration as a relevant circumstance.

In *Bangladesh/Myanmar*, Bangladesh referred to its situation between Myanmar and India, stating that two equidistance lines 'create a "cut-off" effect that deprives Bangladesh of the overwhelming majority of its maritime entitlement'[107] and referred to the 'inequity of limiting Bangladesh to the small wedge of maritime space that equidistance would give it.'[108] The ITLOS considered that the whole of Bangladesh's coast was relevant[109] and stated that the 'coast of Bangladesh, seen as a whole, is manifestly concave.'[110] Citing to *North Sea Continental Shelf* and *Guinea/Guinea-Bissau*, the ITLOS held that 'the concavity of the coast of Bangladesh is a relevant circumstance in the present case, because the provisional equidistance line as drawn produces a cut-off effect on that coast requiring an adjustment of that line.'[111] Although the ITLOS referred to

[105] *Guinea/Guinea-Bissau*, n. 47, [104]. [106] *Cameroon v. Nigeria*, n. 5, [297].
[107] *Bangladesh/Myanmar*, n. 3 (*Memorial of Bangladesh*), [6.30]. [108] Ibid., [6.39].
[109] *Bangladesh/Myanmar*, n. 3, [201]. [110] Ibid., [291]. [111] Ibid., [417].

the 'the concavity of the coast in question,'[112] the citation to the consideration of three state situations in the North Sea and *Guinea/Guinea-Bissau* cases suggests that the cut-off produced as a result of Bangladesh's situation between Myanmar and India in a concave configuration may also have been taken into consideration.

The arbitral tribunal in *Bangladesh v. India* was more explicit. While it stated that it would 'base its decision solely on consideration of the relationship between Bangladesh and India' it also held that it would take into account

> any compensation Bangladesh claims it is entitled to due to any inequity it suffers in its relation to India as a result of its concave coast and its location in the middle of two other States, sitting on the top of the concavity of the Bay of Bengal.[113]

The arbitral tribunal considered that the 'south facing coast of Bangladesh is given insufficient weight by the provisional equidistance line'[114] and that accordingly the provisional equidistance line required adjustment to achieve an equitable result.[115]

A separate but related question is whether existing maritime boundaries of one of the parties to a case with a third state should be taken into account by a tribunal as a relevant circumstance.[116] The parties' delimitation agreements with third states have been treated as irrelevant to the determination of whether a provisional equidistance line achieves an equitable result. In *Barbados v. Trinidad and Tobago*, the tribunal held 'Barbados cannot be required to "compensate" Trinidad and Tobago for the agreements it has made by shifting Barbados' maritime boundary in favour of Trinidad and Tobago [. . .] The treaty is quite evidently *res inter alios acta* in respect of Barbados and every other country.'[117]

As discussed above, a prudent approach for a tribunal wishing to estimate the extent of third-state interests in a delimitation area could be to assume a hypothetical equidistance boundary between the third state and the party to the dispute. This raises the question of whether a delimitation tribunal should, when relevant, consider delimitations with neighbouring states as consisting of hypothetical equidistance lines, even when such boundaries have already been delimited. In this regard a distinction can be

[112] Ibid., [293]. [113] *Bangladesh v. India*, n. 37, [411].
[114] Ibid., [474]. [115] Ibid., [475].
[116] See P. Weil, *The Law of Maritime Delimitation – Reflections* (Grotius Cambridge 1989) 256.
[117] *Barbados v. Trinidad and Tobago*, n. 90, [346].

made between bilateral boundary agreements and judicially determined boundaries. While a bilateral agreement with a third state is a *res inter alios acta* for the other party to a delimitation, as noted in Section 10.2.1 above, in the absence of overlapping claims of third states, a delimitation decision can be regarded as a definitive determination on the title of the parties to maritime zones, with *erga omnes* effects.

In *Bangladesh v. India*, India argued that the concavity of Bangladesh's coast had already been ameliorated by the ITLOS in *Bangladesh/Myanmar* and thus should not be taken into account by the arbitral tribunal as a relevant circumstance.[118] The arbitral tribunal rejected this argument, considering that non-adjustment of the line 'would provide no redress to Bangladesh from the cut-off resulting from the concavity of its coast.'[119]

However, in the context of three states along a concave coast, where the cut-off effect is generated by two equidistance lines, there may be circumstances where a prior delimitation would be relevant to determining the equitable result produced by an equidistance line.[120] The ICJ in *North Sea Continental Shelf* held that one of the factors to be taken into account in the course of negotiations on the maritime boundary was proportionality between coastal lengths and the extent of the areas of continental shelf appertaining to the coastal state, 'account being taken for this purpose of the effects, actual or prospective, of any other continental shelf delimitations between adjacent States in the same region.'[121] The ITLOS in *Bangladesh/Myanmar* took a different approach and noted that 'the fact that a third party may claim the same maritime area does not prevent its inclusion in the relevant maritime area for purposes of the disproportionality test. This in no way affects the rights of third parties.'[122]

The assessment of proportionality at the third stage of the three-stage delimitation approach has never been treated as an exact science, and it is reasonable that the inclusion of a particular area as lying within the entitlements of a state has no effect on a third state's rights. However, in order for the proportionality test to have some meaning it is necessary to estimate the maritime area that will appertain to a state as a result of the delimitation.[123]

[118] *Bangladesh v. India*, n. 37, [391]. [119] Ibid., [470].

[120] Though Fietta and Cleverly consider that '[d]elimitation agreements with third States should be irrelevant in the context of cut-off arguments.' Fietta and Cleverly, n. 95, 72.

[121] *North Sea Continental Shelf*, n. 103, [101].

[122] *Bangladesh/Myanmar*, n. 3, [494]. See *Black Sea*, n. 85, [114].

[123] See Chapter 11 of this volume, which discusses the proportionality test in detail.

10.4 Conclusions

In accordance with the consensual character of international dispute resolution and the principle of the relative effect of decisions, maritime delimitation decisions should have no legal effect on the interests of third states. The reality is more complicated. As Brown notes 'the reality is that this strictly *inter partes* binding effect cannot be maintained in certain cases of treaty interpretation or decisions on the status of territories or maritime delimitation.'[124] The particular character of maritime delimitation decisions means that in practice, they may affect the legal interests of third states, even though in theory they are only binding on the parties to the case. Parties to a delimitation case may rely on a decision to justify their exercise of sovereign rights in an area subject to the claims of a third state. Moreover, where no overlapping entitlements of third states exist, a delimitation decision can be regarded as a definitive determination of the title of the parties to maritime zones, with *erga omnes* effects.

When courts and tribunals refer to 'prejudice' to the interests of third states, what is generally at stake is the finality of the boundary delimited. A third state may suffer prejudice if it is forced to take steps to prevent a party to delimitation from exercising its sovereign rights in an area included in a delimitation decision but subject to overlapping claims. If the dispute with the third state is brought to judicial settlement, the finality of the initial delimitation may be called into question. The prejudice suffered is thus not only to the third state but to the validity of the delimitation decision itself.

International courts and tribunals, while insisting on the relative effect of their decisions, have taken steps to protect the legal interests of third states. In this regard, the dominant trend is to draw a delimitation line without a fixed end point. From the perspective of a third state, the effect of such a line is to determine which state it has overlapping claims it, with the potential side effect of invalidating bilateral agreements. This approach is inherently contradictory with the position that delimitation decisions are not binding on third parties but has been adopted in recognition of the legal effects of delimitation decisions on third states, in order to ensure the stability and finality of boundaries delimited by international judicial bodies. Compared with the approach of avoiding any delimitation of an area subject to third part claims, it presents the advantage of delimiting the

[124] C. Brown, 'Article 59,' in A. Zimmerman et al. (eds.), *The Statute of the International Court of Justice: A Commentary* (Oxford University Press Oxford 2012) 1434.

parties' entitlements to the fullest extent possible. In practice however, it involves a determination, however preliminary, as to the extent of third-state entitlements, a determination which can raise problems of its own.

This chapter has described the inconsistencies in the case law, particularly with regard to the question of overlapping entitlements of third states. For the most part, these inconsistencies can be ascribed to the fact that a delimitation tribunal is attempting to anticipate in advance the scope of third-state entitlements, with the aim of ensuring its delimitation is final and binding. If dealing with a request from a third state to intervene, the court or tribunal may be constrained by the fact that it has not yet reached a merits determination on the course of the delimitation, or by the fact that it has reached such a determination, but cannot allude to it in responding to a request for intervention.

The decision in *Territorial and Maritime Dispute (Colombia v. Nicaragua)* introduced several new elements to the jurisprudence on third-state issues. Notably the Court accepted Colombia's argument that in concluding a bilateral delimitation agreement with Honduras it had not given up claims in the area north of that agreement as against Nicaragua. Moreover, the Court's refusal to allow Costa Rica to intervene was somewhat surprising, given that the Court accepted that Costa Rica had identified an area where its legal interests might be affected by the decision in the case. Despite these findings, an application for intervention would still appear to be a useful exercise for third states, even if unsuccessful, as it allows such states to present their view on whether and how their interests should be taken into account.

With regard to issues other than overlapping entitlements, the impact of delimitation decisions on third states is more difficult to quantify. In part, this is a reflection of the character of international dispute settlement more generally, in that decisions are only binding upon the parties, yet are often treated as binding precedent by both the parties and by courts and tribunals themselves in subsequent cases. The consistent approach of the case law to deny intervention in such cases does not appear unreasonable, given that this approach is also followed in other fields of international law.

11

The Disproportionality Test in the Law of Maritime Delimitation

YOSHIFUMI TANAKA

11.1 Introduction

While the concept of proportionality performs an important role in various branches of international law,[1] its role is of particular importance in the law of maritime delimitation. Given that proportionality has been discussed in almost all cases concerning maritime delimitation, it would be no exaggeration to say that proportionality constitutes one of the key elements in the law of maritime delimitation. Thus it is important to examine the function and limitations of the concept of (dis)proportionality in the law.[2] As we shall discuss in Section 11.3 of this chapter, the International Court of Justice (ICJ), in *Black Sea*, formulated disproportionality as an *ex post facto* test to verify the equitableness of the delimitation line at the third and final stage of maritime delimitation.[3] In the words of the Court:

> [T]he Court will verify that the line (a provisional equidistance line which may or may not have been adjusted by taking into account the relevant circumstances) does not, as it stands, lead to an inequitable result by reason of any marked disproportion between the ratio of the respective coastal lengths and the ratio between the relevant maritime area of each State by reference to the delimitation line.[4]

1 Generally on this subject, see M. Newton and L. May, *Proportionality in International Law* (Oxford University Press Oxford 2014).

2 In the early cases concerning maritime delimitations, the terminology of 'proportionality' or 'disproportionality' has not been used consistently. In principle, this chapter will follow the terminology adopted in each decision.

3 The role of equity will be discussed in Chapter 6 of this volume.

4 *Maritime Delimitation in the Black Sea (Romania v. Ukraine)* [2009] ICJ Rep. 61, 103, [122].

This chapter seeks to examine the role of (dis)proportionality as an *ex post facto* test.[5]

The concept of (dis)proportionality in the law of maritime delimitation has been elaborated through the jurisprudence. In a broad perspective, this process can be divided into two phases. A first phase was devoted to the emergence and development of the concept of (dis)proportionality, while the second phase concerns the establishment of the disproportionality test as the third stage of maritime delimitation. Following this introduction, the next section of this chapter will examine the emergence and development of the concept of (dis)proportionality by analysing the jurisprudence concerning the delimitation of the continental shelf and the single maritime boundary. This chapter will then analyse the application of disproportionality test in the jurisprudence of the ICJ and the two *Bay of Bengal* cases. On the basis of this analysis, possible shortcomings of the (dis)proportionality test will be considered, before offering conclusions.

11.2 Emergence and Development of Proportionality in the Jurisprudence Concerning Maritime Delimitation

11.2.1 (Dis)proportionality in the Jurisprudence Concerning Continental Shelf Delimitation

11.2.1.1 Emergence of the Concept of Proportionality

The origin of the concept of proportionality in the law of maritime delimitation can be traced to the 'façade approach' formulated by the Federal Republic of Germany (Germany) in *North Sea Continental Shelf.*[6] Germany contended that each state concerned should receive a 'just and equitable share' of the available continental shelf, proportionate to the length of its coastline or sea-frontage.[7] Although the ICJ rejected the idea of a 'just and equitable share,' it held that:

[5] Issues concerning the identification of the relevant coasts/maritime areas are discussed in Chapter 7 of this volume. See also Chapter 9 of this volume.

[6] *North Sea Continental Shelf Cases (Federal Republic of Germany/Denmark; Federal Republic of Germany/The Netherlands)* [1969] ICJ Rep. 3. The 'façade approach' was advocated primarily by Oda, Counsel for Germany. See Argument of Professor Oda, ICJ, Pleadings, Oral Arguments Documents, North Sea Continental Shelf Cases, vol. II, 1968, 62–63; see also Reply of Professor Oda, ibid., 195–196. Related to this, it is to be noted that as early as 1946, Sir Francis Vallat suggested an idea of proportionality in the context of a bay. F. Vallat, 'The Continental Shelf' (1946) 23 *British Yearbook of International Law* 333, 336.

[7] *North Sea Continental Shelf*, n. 6, 20, [15].

> [I]n the present case there are three States whose North Sea coastlines are in fact comparable in length and which, therefore, have been given broadly equal treatment by nature except that the configuration of one of the coastlines would, if the equidistance method is used, deny to one of these States treatment equal or comparable to that given the other two. [. . .] What is unacceptable in this instance is that a state should enjoy continental shelf rights considerably different from those of its neighbours merely because in the one case the coastline is roughly convex in form and in the other it is markedly concave, *although those coastlines are comparable in length*.[8]

Thus, the Court did accept the concept of proportionality as a final factor to be taken into account in the course of the negotiations between the parties concerned. In the words of the Court,

> A final factor to be taken account of is the element of a reasonable degree of proportionality which a delimitation effected according to equitable principles ought to bring about between the extent of the continental shelf appertaining to the States concerned and the lengths of their respective coastlines, – these being measured according to their general direction *in order to establish the necessary balance between States with straight, and those with markedly concave or convex coasts or to reduce very irregular coastlines to their truer proportions*.[9]

In cases where concavity or convexity exists in adjacent coasts that are comparable in length, a distorting effect would be produced by the application of the equidistance method. For the Court, such a result was unacceptable.[10] As Higgins rightly observed, it was in this particular geographical situation that proportionality came into play.[11] In this regard, Judge Oda, who advocated the concept of proportionality as Counsel for Germany in *North Sea Continental Shelf*, stated that:

> [W]hat the Court intended to say in 1969 was that in such specific circumstances, in which the States concerned were located as adjacent States

[8] Ibid., 50, [91] (emphasis added).

[9] Ibid., 52, [98] (emphasis added). However, Judge ad hoc Sørensen rejected the concept of proportionality on the ground that it lacked any basis in law. Dissenting Opinion of Judge Sørensen, ibid., 255.

[10] Judgment, ibid., 50, [91].

[11] R. Higgins, *Problems and Process: International Law and How We Use It* (Clarendon Press Oxford 1994) 229. See also R. Ida, 'The Role of Proportionality in Maritime Delimitation Revisited: The Origin and Meaning of the Principle from the Early Decisions of the Court,' in N. Ando et al. (eds.), *Liber Amicorum Judge Shigeru Oda* (Kluwer The Hague 2002) 1037, 1039; R. Kolb, *Case Law on Equitable Maritime Delimitation: Digest and Commentaries* (Nijhoff The Hague 2003) 257–258.

> in similar situations, but where the existence of a marked concave or convex coastline produced a somewhat distorting effect, the proportion of the length of the coast as rectified by its general direction [. . .] was in principle useful in the verification of geographical equity [. . .].[12]

The learned Judge further stated that: 'The 1969 Judgment nowhere implied the possibility of generally applying the concept of proportionality in other cases, particularly in cases of delimitation between opposite States.'[13] In interpreting the *North Sea Continental Shelf* judgment, Bowett also argued that:

> Indeed, it would seem that the proportionality factor might only be applied, or be meaningful, in the case of adjacent States (not 'opposite') where the existence of a markedly concave or convex coastline will produce a cut-off effect if the equidistance principle is applied.[14]

In the *North Sea Continental Shelf* judgment, proportionality was suggested as a factor to be taken into account in the course of the negotiations between the three states concerned. Overall there appears to be some scope to argue that originally the role of proportionality was limited to a particular geographical situation, even though the paragraphs of the judgment concerning proportionality seemed to be formulated in somewhat general terms.

The above observations are confirmed by *Anglo-French Continental Shelf*. With regard to the geographical circumstances which would justify recourse to proportionality, the Court of Arbitration stated that:

> In particular, this Court does not consider that the adoption in the *North Sea Continental Shelf* cases of the criterion of a reasonable degree of proportionality between the areas of continental shelf and the lengths of the coastlines means that this criterion is one for application in all cases. On the contrary, it was *the particular geographical situation of three adjoining*

[12] Dissenting Opinion of Judge Oda in *Continental Shelf (Libyan Arab Jamahiriya/Malta)*, [1985] ICJ Rep. 13, 134–135, [18].

[13] Ibid. Judge Oda's view was echoed by Judges Schwebel and Valticos. Dissenting Opinion of Judge Schwebel, ibid., 184; Separate Opinion of Judge Valticos, ibid., 110, [19].

[14] D. W. Bowett, *The Legal Regime of Islands in International Law* (Oceana Publications New York 1979) 164. Similar views were taken by writers including Higgins, above n. 11, 229. J.-H. Paik, 'The Role of Proportionality in Maritime Delimitation: State of Jurisprudence,' in H. P. Hestermeyer et al. (eds.), *Coexistence, Cooperation and Solidarity, Liber Amicorum Rüdiger Wolfrum*, vol. 1 (Nijhoff Leiden 2012) 199, 201. See also S. Fietta and R. Cleverly, *A Practitioner's Guide to Maritime Boundary Delimitation* (Oxford University Press Oxford 2016) 608.

> *States situated on a concave coast* which gave relevance to that criterion in those cases.[15]

In addition, it further clarified the role of proportionality as follows. First, according to the Court:

> [t]he concept of 'proportionality' merely expresses the criterion or factor by which it may be determined whether such a distortion results in an inequitable delimitation of the continental shelf as between the coastal States concerned. [...] [I]t may also appear, and more usually does, as a factor for determining the reasonable or unreasonable – the equitable or inequitable – effects of particular geographical features or configurations upon the course of an equidistance-line boundary.[16]

Since proportionality is merely a criterion, it does not constitute an independent source of rights over the continental shelf. This is made clear in the following statement:

> Proportionality, therefore, is to be used as a criterion or factor relevant in evaluating the equities of certain geographical situations, not as a general principle providing an independent source of rights to areas of continental shelf.[17]

Second, proportionality is a criterion for evaluating *disproportions* in particular geographical situations. In the words of the Court, 'it is disproportion rather than any general principle of proportionality which is the relevant criterion or factor.'[18] In *Anglo-French Continental Shelf*, proportionality only plays a role in appreciating whether the Scilly Isles are to be considered a 'special circumstance' having distorting effects on the equidistance boundary as between the French Republic and the UK and, if so, the extent of the adjustment appropriate to abate the inequity.[19] Thus, this case did not involve the application of an *ex post facto* test of proportionality.

11.2.1.2 Development of Proportionality in the Jurisprudence

In subsequent cases, courts and tribunals have enlarged the role and geographical scope of the concept of proportionality. A change was perceptible in *Tunisia/Libya*. In this case, the coastline of the parties was neither concave nor comparable to that of the North Sea. However, the

[15] *Case concerning the Delimitation of Continental Shelf between the United Kingdom of Great Britain and Northern Ireland, and the French Republic* [1977] 18 RIAA 3, [99] (emphasis added).

[16] Ibid., 58, [100]. [17] Ibid., 58, [101]. [18] Ibid. [19] Ibid., 116–17, [250].

ICJ held that: '[T]he Court considered that that element [of proportionality] is indeed required by the fundamental principle of ensuring an equitable delimitation between the States concerned.'[20] By referring to the term 'fundamental principle,' the Court appeared to highlight proportionality at the level of a general rule. Furthermore, no reference was made to the particular geographical conditions in the *Tunisia/Libya* judgment.[21] According to Judge Gros, '[t]he present judgment drastically alters the restricted role which properly belongs to the proportionality factor, and the justice of the calculations it employs is not borne out by any of the precautions taken in a delimitation which took account of the proportionality of the areas concerned.'[22]

In the *Tunisia/Libya* judgment, the Court saw the role of proportionality as an *ex post facto* check of the equitableness of a delimitation line. In applying the test of proportionality, the ICJ made a mathematical calculation. On the one hand, it held that the ratio between the relevant coastlines of Libya and Tunisia was approximately 31:69. The ratio between the coastal front of Libya, represented by a straight line drawn from Ras Tajoura to Ras Ajdir, and that of Tunisia, represented by straight lines connecting Ras Kaboudia to the most westerly point of the Gulf of Gabes and from that point to Ras Ajdir, was about 34:66.[23] On the other hand, the areas of the continental shelf below the low-water mark appertaining to Libya and Tunisia stood in a proportion of approximately 40:60. The Court thus found that the result met the requirements of the test of proportionality.[24] In the process of calculation, however, the Court offered scant explanation why the Kerkennah Archipelago was totally disregarded.[25]

The earlier cases related, although not exclusively, to delimitations between adjacent coasts. In *Libya/Malta*, however, proportionality was applied to a delimitation between states with opposite coasts. According to the ICJ, the coast of Libya from Ras Ajdir to Ras Zarruq is 192 miles long, while the coast of Malta from Ras il-Wardija to Delimara Point, excluding the islet of Filfla, measures twenty-four miles.[26] In light of this difference

[20] *Case concerning the Continental Shelf (Tunisia/Libyan Arab Jamahiriya)* [1982] ICJ Rep. 18, 75, [103].

[21] H. Thirlway, *The Law and Procedure of the International Court of Justice: Fifty Years of Jurisprudence*, vol. 1 (Oxford University Press Oxford 2013) 500.

[22] Dissenting Opinion of Judge Gros, *Tunisia/Libya*, 152, [17]. See also the Dissenting Opinion of Judge Evensen, ibid., 314, [23].

[23] Judgment, ibid., 91, [131].

[24] Ibid.

[25] Dissenting Opinion of Judge Evensen, ibid., 313, [23].

[26] *Libya/Malta*, n. 12, 50, [68].

of coastal lengths,[27] the Court adjusted a provisional median line by shifting it 18' to the north.[28] Thus the Court took into account the difference of coastal lengths in the delimitation process as a relevant circumstance. At the final stage, the Court applied proportionality as a test for the equitableness of the result of the delimitation. The area to be delimited was a small one owing to the presence of a third state. As the Court itself accepted, it would be unrealistic to apply the test of proportionality to such a limited area, as future delimitations with third states would change the situation.[29] According to the Court, however, this did not debar it from applying the test of proportionality, and it was possible to make a broad assessment of the equitableness of the result. Having checked the equitableness of the result from the angle of proportionality, the Court concluded that there was no evident disproportion in this case.[30] Yet, the application of proportionality in a delimitation between opposite coasts was criticized by the members of the Court and commentators.[31]

11.2.2 *(Dis)proportionality in the Jurisprudence Concerning Single Maritime Boundaries*

11.2.2.1 Proportionality in the Jurisprudence of the ICJ

In *Gulf of Maine*, the Chamber of the ICJ took proportionality between coastal lengths only into account for the second segment of the delimitation line, where the situation was one of opposite coasts.[32] Thus proportionality was applied as a factor in correcting a median line for both the continental shelf and the fishery zone. However, the Chamber did not

[27] Ibid.

[28] A northward shift of 18′ on the 15° 10′ E meridian resulted in a delimitation line intersecting the reference line at 34° 30′ N. Even though the ICJ did not mention it, this point was the same as the southwestern corner of the Italian claim in the Ionian Sea. It would follow that the line was dictated by a third-party claim. For a criticism on this point, see Dissenting Opinion of Judge Oda, ibid., 137–138, [23–25].

[29] Judgment, ibid., 53, [74].

[30] Ibid., 53–55, [75]. See also Fietta and Cleverly, n. 14, 604–605.

[31] Dissenting Opinion of Judge Oda, *Libya/Malta*, n. 12, 134–135, [18]. Dissenting Opinion of Judge Schwebel, ibid., 184; Separate Opinion of Judge Valticos, ibid., 110, [19]; P. Weil, *Perspective du droit de la delimitation maritime* (Pedone Paris 1988) 258; Y. Tanaka, *Predictability and Flexibility in the Law of Maritime Delimitation* (Hart Oxford 2006) 167–169; Fietta and Cleverly, n. 14, 604–605 and 606–608.

[32] *Delimitation of the Maritime Boundary in the Gulf of Maine Area (Canada/United States)* [1984] ICJ Rep. 246, 322–323, [184]. Ibid., 334–35, [218]. Ibid., 336–337, [222]. In this regard, see J. Cooper, 'Delimitation of the Maritime Boundary in the Gulf of Maine Area,' (1986) 16 *Ocean Development and International Law* 59, 82.

apply proportionality as an *ex post facto* test to check the equitableness of the single maritime boundary.

In *Jan Mayen*, the parties' views with regard to the role of proportionality were sharply divided. Claiming a maritime zone of 200 nautical miles, Denmark requested the Court to take into account the ratio of the relevant coastal lengths, which was 9.2:1 in favour of Greenland. For Denmark, proportionality had to play a double role: as a relevant circumstance in the adoption of an appropriate method, and as a test of equity.[33] In contrast, Norway rejected this view by advocating a median line.[34] The ICJ adjusted the median line in all the three zones in such a way as to locate the delimitation line closer to the coast of Jan Mayen,[35] since 'the differences in length of the respective coasts of the Parties are so significant.'[36] The Court did not apply proportionality as an *ex post facto* test.

In *Qatar/Bahrain*, Qatar argued proportionality as a test of the equitableness of a single maritime boundary.[37] According to Qatar, the ratio of its mainland coasts to that of Bahrain's principal islands was 1.59:1.[38] In applying the proportionality test to the single maritime boundary proposed by Qatar in the northern sector, the ratio between the maritime areas on either side of the boundary was 1.68:1 in favour of Qatar. It thus argued that the proportionality test was sufficient to permit the conclusion that the proposed boundary was equitable.[39] By contrast, Bahrain contended that the above calculation relied on the assumption that the Hawar Islands were under Qatar's sovereignty. It stated that, if these islands were considered as appertaining to Bahrain, the lengths of the relevant coasts would be almost equal.[40]

The ICJ supported Bahrain's view. After having decided that Bahrain had sovereignty over the Hawar Islands, the Court held that 'the disparity in length of the coastal fronts of the Parties cannot be considered such as to necessitate an adjustment of the equidistance line.'[41] The Court's view calls for two comments. First, proportionality was not regarded as a

[33] *Maritime Delimitation in the Area between Greenland and Jan Mayen (Denmark v. Norway)* [1993] ICJ Rep. 38, 65–66, [62]; Argument by Bernhard, CR 93/4, 14 January 1993, 32.

[34] Ibid., Argument by Mr. Haug, CR 93/11, 27 January 1993, 45; Argument by Mr. Weil, CR 93/9, 21 January 1993, 8–31.

[35] *Jan Mayen*, n. 33, ICJ Rep. 79–81, [92].

[36] Ibid., 68, [68].

[37] *Maritime Delimitation and Territorial Questions between Qatar and Bahrain (Qatar/Bahrain)* [2001] ICJ Rep. 91, [168]; Memorial submitted by Qatar, vol. 1, 30 September 1996, 301–302, [12.65]. See also 279–283, [12.30–12.36].

[38] *Qatar/Bahrain*, n. 37, 114, [241].

[39] Memorial submitted by Qatar, n. 37, 304–305, [12.70–12.71].

[40] *Qatar/Bahrain*, n. 37, 114, [242].

[41] Ibid., [243].

relevant circumstance in this case. As the Court indicated, however, this was because there was no disparity between the coastal lengths of the parties which called for an adjustment of an equidistance line. This appears to suggest that, where there is a disproportion between coastal lengths, proportionality may be considered.[42] Second, the Court's reasoning relied on the fact that the lengths of the relevant coasts between the parties were approximately equal. As Judge ad hoc Torres Bernárdez pointed out, however, no precise figures were given in the judgment to support that conclusion.[43]

In *Cameroon v. Nigeria*, Cameroon invoked the disparity between the length of coastlines of the parties in the Gulf of Guinea as a relevant circumstance that could justify shifting the delimitation line towards the north-west.[44] In this connection, Cameroon divided the relevant area into three sectors. In the first sector, connecting Bonny (Nigeria) and Campo (Cameroon), Cameroon maintained that the ratio of the relevant coastline is about 2.3:1 in favour of Cameroon. The second sector is the area bounded by the Bonny-Campo line and by a construction line running from Akasso in Nigeria to Cabo San Juan in Equatorial Guinea. According to Cameroon, in this sector, the ratio of the relevant coastlines is approximately 1.25:1 in favour of Cameroon. The third area is subtended by a line running between Akasso in Nigeria and Cap Lopez in Gabon, with the same ratio of coastal lengths of 1.25:1. Applying the above ratios to constructing lines of each sector, Cameroon proposed an equitable line.[45] By contrast, Nigeria contended that the ratio of coastal lengths was in favour of Nigeria by a factor of between 1:1.3 and 1:3.2 depending on the precise coasts being used. In Nigeria's view, Cameroon's line was questionable since it failed to take due account of the criterion of proportionality.[46] In this regard, the Court noted that substantial differences in the lengths of the parties' coastlines may be a factor to be taken into account in order to adjust the provisional delimitation line. In the present case, however, the Court held that whichever coastline of Nigeria was regarded as relevant,

42 This is in line with the other cases discussed above. As will be seen, this view is also supported by subsequent cases.

43 Dissenting Opinion of Judge ad hoc Torres Bernárdez, ibid., 436, [521].

44 *Land and Maritime Boundary between Cameroon and Nigeria (Cameroon v. Nigeria; Equatorial Guinea intervening)*, [2002] ICJ Rep. 303, 446, [330].

45 For the method of drawing Cameroon's line, see Memorial of Cameroon, vol. 1, 16 March 1995, 553–555, [5.119–5.128]; Reply of Cameroon, vol. 1, 4 April 2000, 421–426, [9.81–9.95]; Argument by Mendelson, Verbatim Record, CR 2002/6, 25 February 2002, 51–55, [16–28]; Argument by Kamto, Verbatim Record, CR 2002/7, 26 February 2002, 28–31, [31–42].

46 Rejoinder of Nigeria, 4 January 2001, [13.13]; [13.41]; *Cameroon v. Nigeria*, n. 44, [278].

the relevant coastline of Cameroon was not longer than that of Nigeria.[47] In this connection, the Court did not define the relevant coasts and area of Nigeria[48] and it eventually denied the relevance of proportionality in this case.[49] Nor did it apply the proportionality as an *ex post facto* test.

Finally, in *Nicaragua v. Honduras*, no mention was made of the proportionality test, although Nicaragua argued this point.[50] Nor did the Court define the relevant coast and area of the parties in dispute for the purpose of the proportionality test.

11.2.2.2 Proportionality in the Arbitral Awards

In *Guinea/Guinea-Bissau*, the Court of Arbitration considered proportionality at the verification stage. Thus, it regarded proportionality as an *ex post facto* test of equitableness. However, the Court compared the coastal lengths of the parties without calculating the maritime areas attributed to each of them. It merely stated that the coastlines of the two states were the same length and that, therefore, neither party could claim any advantage.[51]

In *Canada/France*, the Court of Arbitration used the concept of proportionality to test the equitableness of the delimitation. According to the Court of Arbitration, while the ratio between the Canadian and French coastlines was 15.3:1,[52] the ratio of the actual maritime spaces appertaining to the parties was 16.4 (Canada):1 (France).[53] The Court thus concluded that there was no disproportion. Nevertheless, this application of the proportionality test was sharply criticized by two of the arbitrators, Gotlieb and Weil.[54] As Weil indicated, the parties submitted divergent views concerning the identification and measurement of these coasts and area. While Canada contended that the ratio of coastal lengths was 21.4

[47] For an analysis of the Court's approach to the determination of relevant coasts and relevant areas in this case, see Chapter 7 of this volume.

[48] The ICJ did not define the relevant coast and area of Nigeria. See Chapter 7 of this volume.

[49] *Cameroon v. Nigeria*, n. 44, 446–447, [301].

[50] *Territorial and Maritime Dispute between Nicaragua and Honduras in the Caribbean Sea (Nicaragua v. Honduras)* [2007] ICJ Rep. 659. Reply of Nicaragua, vol. 1, 193, paras. 9.53–9.54; Argument by Mr. Brownlie, Verbatim Record, CR 2007/5, 39–40, [64–66]; Argument by Mr. Brownlie, Verbatim Record, CR 2007/12, 51–52, [63–66].

[51] *Delimitation of the Maritime Boundary between Guinea and Guinea-Bissau* [1985] 19 RIAA 149, [120].

[52] *Case concerning the Delimitation of Maritime Areas between Canada and France* [1992] 21 RIAA 265, [33].

[53] Ibid., 1176, [93].

[54] Dissenting Opinion of Mr. Gotlieb, ibid., 1181–1188, [5–37]; Dissenting Opinion of Mr. Weil, ibid., 1204–1207, [20–26].

(Canada):1 (France), France arrived at a ratio of 6.5:1.[55] Yet, the Court of Arbitration adopted a ratio of 15.3:1 that significantly differed from the figures submitted by the parties. Likewise, the parties submitted divergent figures as to the size of the relevant areas and the Court of Arbitration made its own determination area, which embraced the whole economic zone generated in the south by the southern coast of Newfoundland.[56] As Weil observed, however, '[t]he figures indicated by the Decision at paragraphs 33 and 93 for the lengths of the coastlines, the size of the relevant area and *their respective ratios* are no more and no less convincing than those put forward by the Parties.'[57] Overall, this award illustrated the uncertainties with the proportionality test.[58]

The parties in *Eritrea/Yemen* agreed that the role of proportionality was a test of equitableness and that manifest disproportionality must be avoided.[59] However, there was strong disagreement about how to measure the length of the respective coasts and the significance of that operation once executed.[60] On the one hand, Yemen suggested that a line dividing the areas concerned into almost equal parts correctly reflected the proportion between the lengths of the respective coasts. On the other hand, Eritrea alleged that its own historic median line between the mainland coasts would produce areas favouring Eritrea by a proportion of 3:2. According to Eritrea, this reflected accurately the proportion of the lengths of the coasts.[61] Furthermore, in calculating the areas resulting from the delimitation, Eritrea insisted that account should not be taken of the internal waters within the Dahlaks or the bays along its coast, including the Bay of Assab.[62]

In the Tribunal's view, there was no doubt that the calculation of the Eritrean coastal length should follow the outer circumference of the Dahlak group of islands.[63] However, an issue was how far north the Eritrean coast should go for the purposes of establishing its length. Eritrea wished to include in the proportionality calculation the whole of its mainland coast up to the latitudinal line of 16° N, the line that was also used by

[55] Dissenting Opinion of Mr. Weil, ibid., 1207, [24], n. 19. [56] Judgment, ibid., 1176, [93].

[57] Dissenting Opinion of Mr. Weil, ibid., 1206, [24] (emphasis added). See also Dissenting Opinion of Mr. Gotlieb, ibid., 1192, [52].

[58] Dissenting Opinion of Mr. Weil, ibid., 1206, [24]; H. Ruiz-Fabri, 'Sur la délimitation des espaces maritimes entre le Canada et la France, sentence arbitrale du 10 juin 1992,' (1993) 97 *Revue générale de droit international public* 67, 95.

[59] *Second Stage of the Proceedings between Eritrea and Yemen (Maritime Delimitation)*, 17 December 1999, 22 RIAA, 343, [39].

[60] Ibid., 343, [39]. [61] Ibid., 344, [42]. [62] Ibid., [43]. [63] Ibid., 372, [166].

Yemen to define its northern sector of the area in question. However, the Tribunal had doubts about the appropriateness of employing a line of latitude to divide, for the purposes of the proportionality test, as the coasts of the parties lie at an angle of roughly 45° to this line of latitude. The Tribunal thus considered the relevant proportion of the Eritrean coast as ceasing where the general direction of that coast met a line drawn from what seems to be the northern terminus of the Yemeni land frontier at right angles to the general direction of the Yemeni coast. In the same way, the Tribunal determined the southern end point to be considered for the computation of the length of the Yemeni coast.[64] According to the calculations of the Tribunal, the ratio of coastal lengths of Yemen and Eritrea, was 387,026 metres to 507,110 metres, or 1:1.31. On the other hand, the ratio of water areas, including the territorial seas of Yemen and Eritrea, was 25,535 to 27,944 square kilometres (km), or 1:1.09. On this basis, the Tribunal concluded that the delimitation line it had decided upon engendered no disproportion.[65]

In *Barbados v. Trinidad and Tobago*, proportionality was at issue in the delimitation of the eastern part of the area to be delimited. While delimiting this area, the Arbitral Tribunal found that proportionality is a relevant circumstance to be taken into consideration in reviewing the equity of a tentative delimitation line, but not in any way to require the application of ratios or mathematical determinations in the attribution of maritime areas. The Tribunal thus decided that it would not resort to any form of 'splitting the difference' or other mathematical approaches or use ratio methodologies that would entail attributing to one party what as a matter of law might belong to the other.[66]

At the operational stage of the maritime delimitation, the Tribunal adjusted the equidistance line in light of the existence of the significant coastal frontage of Trinidad and Tobago. As a consequence, the delimitation line was drawn from this point in a straight line in the direction of its terminal point, which is located at the point of intersection of Trinidad and Tobago's southern maritime boundary with its 200 nm exclusive economic zone (EEZ) limit.[67] The Tribunal examined this outcome in the light of proportionality as the ultimate test of the equitableness of the solution. By applying the proportionality test, the Tribunal concluded that

[64] Ibid., 373, [167]. [65] Ibid., 373, [168].

[66] *Arbitration between Barbados and the Republic of Trinidad and Tobago* [2006] 27 RIAA 147, Decision of 11 April 2006, 237, [337]–[338].

[67] Ibid., 243, [373]–[374].

the bending of the equidistance line reflects a reasonable influence of the coastal frontages on the overall area of delimitation, with a view to avoiding reciprocal encroachments which would otherwise result in some form of inequity.[68] However, the Arbitral Tribunal did not specify the relevant coastal lengths of the parties and the relevant areas belonging to each party.[69] Nor did it determine the validity of the arguments of the parties with regard to proportionality. Furthermore, it seems that the Tribunal focused on the question whether the adjusted equidistance line reflects *the coastal frontages* on the overall area of delimitation, not the disproportion between the relevant coastal lengths and relevant areas belonging to each party. This is an original approach of *Barbados v. Trinidad and Tobago*. In consequence, the proportionality test in this case was not applied on the basis of the ratios of the relevant coastal lengths and the maritime areas attributed to each party.

Finally, in *Guyana v. Suriname*, Guyana claimed that its relevant coastline is materially longer than Suriname's rather than shorter, as Suriname claimed.[70] In this regard, Guyana explained that the ratio of the lengths of the parties' relevant coastlines is thus 1.4:1 (215 km to 153 km) in its favour.[71] Guyana thus argued that its calculation of the maritime areas appurtenant to the parties' relevant coasts using the relevant coastal lengths presented by it revealed Guyana to have a larger appurtenant maritime area than Suriname, rather than a smaller one as Suriname claims.[72] However, Suriname contended that the relevant coasts identified by Guyana were excessive in length and that the disparity in relative relevant coastal lengths favoured Suriname in this case. It also disputed the basis on which Guyana calculated appurtenant maritime areas, asserting that the area of overlapping maritime entitlements was to be determined using lines perpendicular to the angles of the states' coastal fronts.[73]

The Arbitral Tribunal did not consider that there were any relevant circumstances in the continental shelf or EEZ which would require an adjustment of the provisional equidistance line.[74] Thus there are no factors which would render the equidistance line determined by the Tribunal inequitable. The Tribunal then checked the relevant coastal lengths for proportionality and concluded that the ratio of the coastal lengths 'comes up with nearly the same ratio of relevant areas (Guyana 51 per cent:

[68] Ibid., 244, [379]. [69] Further, see Chapter 7 of this volume.

[70] *In the Matter of an Arbitration between Guyana and Suriname* [2007] 30 RIAA 1, Award of 17 September 2007, [224].

[71] Ibid., 96, [346]. [72] Ibid., 59, [225]. [73] Ibid., 60, [228]. [74] Ibid., 109, [392].

Suriname 49 per cent) as it does for coastal frontages (Guyana 54 per cent: Suriname 46 per cent).'[75]

11.2.3 Summary

On the basis of the above analysis, three points can be made.

First, even though the concept of proportionality first emerged in the particular geographical situation of *North Sea Continental Shelf*, subsequently the ICJ and arbitral tribunals considered proportionality in every geographical situation.

Second, the application of the proportionality test has not been applied consistently in the jurisprudence concerning maritime delimitation. While, in some cases, the ICJ and arbitral tribunals applied proportionality as an *ex post facto* test, in other cases, the ICJ did not do so.[76]

Third, the proportionality test has not been applied in a consistent manner. In *Tunisia/Libya, Canada/France, Eritrea/Yemen* and *Guyana v. Suriname*, the ICJ and the arbitral tribunals presented the specific figures for the relevant coastal lengths and maritime areas belonging to each party when applying the proportionality test. In other cases, however, no specific figure was presented by the ICJ and arbitral tribunal.

11.3 Disproportionality as an *Ex Post Facto* Test at the Third State of Maritime Delimitation

11.3.1 The Disproportionality Test in Black Sea *and After*

11.3.1.1 *Black Sea*

The *Black Sea* judgment marked an important landmark in the jurisprudence concerning maritime delimitation in the sense that the ICJ clarified what might be called the three-stage approach of maritime delimitation. According to this approach, at the first stage, a provisional delimitation line, which will usually be an equidistance line, is to be established and, at the second stage, the Court will examine whether there are relevant circumstances calling for the adjustment of this provisional line in order to achieve an equitable result. At the final and third stage, the Court, by applying the disproportionality test, will verify whether the delimitation line does not lead to an inequitable result.[77] Under this approach, notably disproportionality was given an independent status distinct from other

[75] Ibid. [76] See also Chapter 7 of this volume. [77] *Black Sea*, n. 4, 101–103, [118–122].

relevant circumstances. In this regard, the ICJ clarified the principal elements of the disproportionality test. Four points can be made.

First, by referring to the *dictum* of *Anglo-French Continental Shelf*,[78] the ICJ used the negative formula of *dis*proportionality. In the Court's view, 'it is disproportion rather than any general principle of proportionality which is the relevant criterion or factor.'[79]

Second, according to the Court, the continental shelf and EEZ allocations are not to be assigned in proportion to length of respective coastlines. Disproportionality comes into play an *ex post facto* test of equitableness of the delimitation line it has constructed.[80]

Third, the disproportionality test is not in itself a method of delimitation. For the Court:

> It is rather a means of checking whether the delimitation line arrived at by other means needs adjustment because of a significant disproportionality in the ratios between the maritime areas which would fall to one party or other by virtue of the delimitation line arrived at by other means, and the lengths of their respective coasts.[81]

Fourth, the checking of the equitableness of the delimitation line by the disproportionality test can only be approximate. In this regard, the ICJ in *Black Sea* admitted a certain degree of flexibility with regard to the calculation of coastal length, stating that:

> [d]iverse techniques have in the past been used for assessing coastal lengths, with no clear requirements of international law having been shown as to whether the real coastline should be followed, or baselines used, or whether or not coasts relating to internal waters should be excluded.'[82]

In addition, the Court further stated that:

> The Court cannot but observe that various tribunals, and the Court itself, have drawn different conclusions over the years as to what disparity in coastal lengths would constitute *a significant disproportionality* which suggested the delimitation line was inequitable and still required adjustment. This remains in each case a matter for the Court's appreciation, which it will exercise by reference to the overall geography of the area.[83]

The above passage did seem to imply that currently there is no objective criterion for checking whether there is a significant disproportionality in

[78] *Anglo-French Continental Shelf*, n. 15, 58, [101]. [79] *Black Sea*, n. 4, 129, [210].
[80] Ibid., [211]. [81] Ibid., 99–100, [110]. [82] Ibid., 129, [212].
[83] Ibid., 129, [213] (emphasis added).

coastal lengths that requires an adjustment of a provisional line drawn at the second stage of the delimitation.

According to the Court, the length of Romania's relevant coast is approximately 248 km,[84] while the length of the Ukraine's relevant coast is approximately 705 km.[85] The ratio for the coastal lengths between Romania and Ukraine is approximately 1:2.8, while the ratio of the relevant area between Romania and Ukraine is approximately 1:2.1.[86] The Court thus held that the equidistance line as constructed required no alteration.[87]

11.3.1.2 *Territorial and Maritime Dispute (Nicaragua v. Colombia)*

The three-stage approach was also applied in *Territorial and Maritime Dispute (Nicaragua v. Colombia)*. In carrying out the disproportionality test at the third stage of the maritime delimitation, the ICJ noted that it was not applying a principle of strict proportionality. In the view of the Court, '[m]aritime delimitation is not designed to produce a correlation between the lengths of the Parties' relevant coasts and their respective shares of the relevant area' and '[t]he Court's task is to check for a significant disproportionality.'[88] The Court clarified its approach to the disproportionality test as follows:

> The Court thus considers that its task, at this third stage, is not to attempt to achieve even an approximate correlation between the ratio of the lengths of the Parties' relevant coasts and the ratio of their respective shares of the relevant area. It is, rather, to ensure that there is not a disproportion so gross as to 'taint' the result and render it inequitable. Whether any disproportion is so great as to have that effect is not a question capable of being answered by reference to any mathematical formula but is a matter which can be answered only in the light of all the circumstances of the particular case.[89]

The ICJ calculated that the length of Nicaragua's relevant coast is approximately 531 km taking the general direction of this coast and that of Colombia's relevant coast is 65 km.[90] According to the Court, the ratio for the coastal lengths is approximately 1:8.2 in Nicaragua's favour and the ratio of the relevant area is approximately 1:3.44 in Nicaragua's favour. In the words of the Court, '[t]he question, therefore, is whether this

[84] Ibid., 93, [88].

[85] Ibid., 98, [103]. The Court drew a line across the entrance of Karkinits'ka Gulf in order to make clear the relevant coasts and areas. However, this line is not taken into account in the calculation of the total length of the Ukrainian relevant coasts. Ibid., 97, [100].

[86] Ibid., 130, [215]. [87] Ibid., [216].

[88] *Territorial and Maritime Dispute (Nicaragua v. Colombia)* [2012] ICJ Rep. 624, 715, [240].

[89] Ibid., 716, [242]. [90] Ibid., 680, [153].

disproportion is so great as to render the result inequitable.'[91] This statement did seem to suggest that in itself the Court admitted the existence of disproportion.[92] Nevertheless, the Court eventually concluded that, taking account of all the circumstances of the present case, the result achieved by the application of the provisional line did not entail such a disproportionality as to create an inequitable result.[93] Given that the ratio of the relevant area is over twice as great as the ration between the relevant coastal lengths, it is debatable whether there is no disproportionality between the ration of the coastal lengths and that of the relevant area.[94] In support of its conclusion, the Court referred to two precedents: *Libya/Malta* and *Jan Mayen*.

First, the Court observed that in *Libya/Malta*, the ratio of relevant coasts was approximately 1:8, a figure that is almost identical to that in *Territorial and Maritime Dispute (Nicaragua v. Colombia)*. The Court, in *Libya/Malta*, considered that this disparity required an adjustment or shifting of the provisional median line. It eventually stated that there was no significant disproportionality, without examining the precise division of shares of the relevant area. Nonetheless, the Court accepted that: '[I]t is clear that the respective shares of Libya and Malta did not come anywhere near a ratio of 1:8.'[95]

Second, in *Jan Mayen*, the ratio of the coastal lengths was approximately 1:9 in Denmark's favour.[96] As the ICJ observed in *Territorial and Maritime Dispute (Nicaragua v. Colombia)*, that disparity led the Court to shift the provisional median line in *Jan Mayen*. The description in the *Jan Mayen* Judgment and the depiction of the boundary on the maps attached thereto show that the precise shares of the relevant area were approximately 1:2.7. The Court, in *Jan Mayen*, did not consider the result to be significantly disproportionate.[97] The ratio of the coastal lengths and that of the relevant area in *Jan Mayen* may seem to be similar to the ratio presented by the ICJ in *Territorial and Maritime Dispute (Nicaragua v. Colombia)*. However, some doubts could be expressed regarding whether there was no disproportionality between the ratio for the coastal lengths and the ratio of the maritime area in *Jan Mayen*. In fact, the majority opinion's view

[91] Ibid., 716, [243] (emphasis provided).

[92] M. D. Evans, 'Maritime Boundary Delimitation: Whatever Next?,' in J. Barrett and R. Barnes (eds.), *Law of the Sea: UNCLOS as a Living Treaty* (British Institute of International and Comparative Law London 2016) 41, 62.

[93] *Territorial and Maritime Dispute (Nicaragua v. Colombia)*, n. 88, 717, [247].

[94] Evans, n. 92, 62.

[95] *Territorial and Maritime Dispute (Nicaragua v. Colombia)*, n. 88, 717, [245].

[96] *Jan Mayen*, n. 33, 65, [61].

[97] *Territorial and Maritime Dispute (Nicaragua v. Colombia)*, n. 88, 717, [246].

on proportionality in Jan Mayen was questioned by Judge ad hoc Fischer, stating that: 'I do not see how this partition [of some 3 to 1] can be equitable considering the ratio of the costal length.'[98] In addition, *Jan Mayen* is not a case where the ICJ applied proportionality as an *ex post facto* test. Overall there appears to be some scope to reconsider the question whether *Libya/Malta* and *Jan Mayen* can adequately support the reasonableness of the disproportionality test in *Territorial and Maritime Dispute (Nicaragua v. Colombia)*.

11.3.1.3 *Maritime Dispute (Peru v. Chile)*

In *Maritime Dispute (Peru v. Chile)*, Peru and Chile adopted fundamentally different positions.[99] Chile claimed that the maritime zones of Chile and Peru had been fully delimited by agreement, while Peru argued that no agreed maritime boundary existed between the two countries.[100] Thus, the ICJ was first of all required to ascertain whether an agreed maritime boundary existed as Chile claimed.[101] After examining the competing claims of the parties, the Court ruled that there existed a maritime boundary between the parties that extended up to Point A situated at a distance of eighty nautical miles up to (Point A) along the parallel from its starting point of the single maritime boundary, namely, the intersection of the parallel of latitude passing through Boundary Marker No. 1 with the low-water line.[102] The Court then determined the course of the maritime boundary from Point A.[103]

According to the Court, the situation in this case was unusual in that the starting point for the delimitation was eighty nautical miles from the closest point on the Chilean coast and about forty-five nautical miles from the closest point on the Peruvian coast.[104] Even so, the Court decided to apply the three-stage approach to the delimitation of the maritime area that begins at the endpoint of the agreed maritime boundary. First, the Court drew a provisional equidistance line which starts at the endpoint of the existing maritime boundary (Point A).[105] At the second stage of maritime delimitation, the Court envisaged whether there are any relevant circumstances calling for an adjustment of the provisional equidistance line to achieve an equitable result. In this regard, the Court

[98] Dissenting opinion of Judge ad hoc Fischer in *Jan Mayen*, n. 33, 309.

[99] While Chile is a party to the LOSC, Peru is not. However, the ICJ proceeded with the maritime delimitation on the basis of Arts. 74(1) and 83(1) of the LOSC since the Court recognised these provisions as part of customary international law. *Maritime Dispute (Peru v. Chile)*, [2014] ICJ Rep. 3, 65, [179].

[100] Ibid., 16, [22–23]. [101] Ibid., [24]. [102] Ibid., 58, [151] and 61, [176]

[103] Ibid., 65, [177]. [104] Ibid., 66, [183]. [105] Ibid., [184].

found no relevant circumstances that require an adjustment of the provisional equidistance line.

At the third stage, the Court determined whether the provisional equidistance line drawn from Point A produced a result which was significantly disproportionate in terms of the lengths of the relevant coasts and the division of the relevant area.[106] As the Court noted, however, the existence of the agreed maritime boundary, which extends for a significant distance (eighty nautical miles), gave rise to novel questions about how to assess proportionality in respect of the area delimited on the basis of equidistance.[107] In fact, the Court had to admit that: 'The existence of that line would make difficult, if not impossible, the calculation of the length of the relevant coasts and of the extent of the relevant area, were the usual mathematical calculation of the proportions to be undertaken.'[108] If so, together with Evans, one can ask the question: '[W]here does this leave the third stage of the test?'[109] In this regard, the Court recalled that in some instances in the past, it had not undertaken that calculation because of the practical difficulties arising from the particular circumstances of the case; and that it engaged in a broad assessment of disproportionality. Given the unusual circumstances of this case, the Court decided that it would follow the same approach and concluded that no significant disproportion was evident, such as would call into question the equitable nature of the provisional equidistance line.[110] However, the Court provides scant explanation as to why there is no significant disproportion in this case.[111] Thus, *Maritime Dispute (Peru v. Chile)* revealed that the application of the disproportionality test encounters considerable difficulty in a situation where agreed maritime boundary that does not rely on the equidistance method already exists.

11.3.2 The Disproportionality Test in the Bay of Bengal Cases

11.3.2.1 *Bangladesh/Myanmar*

The disproportionality test has been applied in the two cases concerning maritime delimitation of the Bay of Bengal. The International Tribunal of the Law of the Sea (ITLOS) in *Bangladesh/Myanmar* ruled that it would

[106] Ibid., 69, [192]. [107] See Declaration of Judge Donoghue, ibid., 110.
[108] *Maritime Dispute (Peru v. Chile)*, n. 100, 69, [193]. [109] Evans, n. 92, 65.
[110] *Maritime Dispute (Peru v. Chile)*, n. 100, 69–70, [193–194].
[111] M. D. Evans, 'Maritime Boundary Delimitation,' in D. R. Rothwell, A. G. Oude Elferink, K. N. Scott, and T. Stephens (eds.), *The Oxford Handbook of the Law of the Sea* (Oxford University Press Oxford 2015) 254, 272. See also Separate Opinion, partly concurring and partly dissenting, of Judge ad hoc Orrego Vicuña, 131, [28] and 133, [34].

follow the three-stage approach as developed in the most recent case law concerning maritime delimitation and that at the third and final stage in the process of maritime delimitation, the Tribunal would check whether the line, as adjusted, resulted in any significant disproportion between the ratio of the respective coastal lengths and the ratio of the relevant maritime areas allocated to each party or not.[112] The application of the disproportionality test was also accepted by the parties, and both Bangladesh and Myanmar invoked the test to support the equitableness of their own delimitation lines.

Bangladesh claimed that the maritime delimitation line between Bangladesh and Myanmar should be a 215° bisector line. To support the equitableness of the 215° line, Bangladesh submitted that the respective coastal façades of Bangladesh and Myanmar are 349 and 369 km and that the maritime areas appertaining to the parties by the 215° bisector line is 69,717 square km for Bangladesh and 86,931 square km for Myanmar. According to Bangladesh, the ratio of the lengths of the parties' coastal façades is 1.06:1 in favour of Myanmar, while the ratio of maritime spaces is 1.25:1 in favour of Myanmar. Bangladesh argued that if these figures are at all disproportionate, it is disproportionately unfavourable to Bangladesh and Myanmar therefore had no argument that the 215° line was inequitable to it.[113]

However, Myanmar submitted that the length of Bangladesh's coast is 364 km and that of its own coast 740 km,[114] while the maritime areas belonging to each state on the basis of equidistance are 80,406 square km (Bangladesh) and 156,133 square km (Myanmar).[115] According to Myanmar, the ratio of coastal lengths is 1 (Bangladesh):2.03 (Myanmar), while the ratio of maritime areas is 1 (Bangladesh):1.94 (Myanmar).[116] Myanmar thus submitted that: '[T]he test of proportionality – or, more precisely, the absence of excessive disproportionality – confirms the equitable character of the solution resulting from the provisional equidistance line.'[117] In summary, Bangladesh and Myanmar presented different figures concerning the ratio of the coastal lengths and that of the maritime areas belonging to each state.[118]

[112] *Delimitation of the Maritime Boundary in the Bay of Bengal (Bangladesh/Myanmar)* [2012] ITLOS Rep. 4, Judgment of 14 March 2012, 67–68, [240].

[113] *Bangladesh/Myanmar*, n. 112, Memorial of Bangladesh, vol. 1, 1 July 2010, 92–93, [6.75–6.76].

[114] *Bangladesh/Myanmar*, n. 112, 57, [190] and 58, [197]. See also Counter-Memorial of the Union of Myanmar, vol. 1, 1 December 2010, 157, [5.151].

[115] Ibid. [116] Ibid. [117] *Bangladesh/Myanmar*, n. 112, 80, [289].

[118] The parties disagreed on the relevant area. See Chapter 7 of this volume.

When applying the disproportionality test, the ITLOS used its own figures. According to the ITLOS, the length of Bangladesh's relevant coast is approximately 413 km and that of Myanmar's coast 587 km, resulting in a ratio between these coastal lengths of approximately 1:1.42 in favour of Myanmar.[119] According to the Tribunal, the adjusted delimitation line allocates approximately 111,631 square km of the relevant area to Bangladesh and approximately 171,832 square km to Myanmar. The ratio of the allocated areas is approximately 1:1.54 in favour of Myanmar. When calculating the size of the relevant area, an issue arose with regard to a claim of a third state in the same maritime area.[120] In this regard, the ITLOS simply stated that: 'The fact that a third party may claim the same maritime area does not prevent its inclusion in the relevant maritime area for purposes of the disproportionality test.'[121] In conclusion, the ITLOS ruled that the above-mentioned ratio did not lead to any significant disproportion between the respective lengths of the coasts of the parties and the maritime areas allocated to the parties.[122]

11.3.2.2 *Bangladesh v. India*

In *Bangladesh v. India*, the parties agreed that the final step in the delimitation process involves a test to ensure that the delimitation line does not yield a disproportionate result.[123] Yet, the parties submitted different figures with regard to the relevant coastal lengths and the size of the relevant area. According to Bangladesh, the length of the relevant coast of Bangladesh and India was 424 km and 708 km respectively, and the ratio of the relevant coasts was 1:1.67 in favour of India, while the Bangladesh's proposed boundary line allocated Bangladesh and India maritime areas of 145,364 square km and 211,490 square km respectively, the ratio of which is 1:1.52 in favour of India.[124] Bangladesh thus asserted that this result passed the disproportionality test. On the other hand, India submitted that the ratio of relevant coasts of the parties was 1:1.015, while the ratio of the

119 *Bangladesh/Myanmar*, n. 112, 65–66, [202–205].

120 As Churchill pointedly observed, the size of the area appertaining to Bangladesh could be affected by the location of a future maritime boundary with India. R. Churchill, 'The *Bangladesh/Myanmar* Case: Continuity and Novelty in the Law of Maritime Boundary Delimitation,' (2012) 1 *Cambridge Journal of International and Comparative Law* 137, 145. See also Chapter 10 of this volume.

121 *Bangladesh/Myanmar*, n. 112, 142, [494].

122 Ibid., 142–143, [499].

123 *In the Matter of the Bay of Bengal Maritime Boundary (Bangladesh v. India)*, PCA Case 2010-16, Award of 7 July 2014, 151, [481]. See also Reply of Bangladesh, vol. 1, 31 January 2013, 125, [4.150]; Counter-Memorial of India, 31 July 2012, vol. 1, 195, [6.108].

124 *Bangladesh v. India*, n. 123, 152, [486].

relevant areas resulting from India's proposed line as 1:0.942.[125] Hence, India asserted that its proposed line satisfied the disproportionality test.

When applying the disproportionality test, the Arbitral Tribunal confirmed the function of the test, stating that the responsibility of the Tribunal was to check, *ex post facto*, the equitableness of the delimitation line it had constructed.[126] In this regard, the Tribunal stressed that: '[P]roportionality is not a mathematical exercise that results in the attribution of maritime areas as a function of the length of the coasts of the Parties or other such ratio calculations.'[127] According to the Tribunal, to produce a correlation between the relevant coastal lengths and the relevant maritime areas could itself produce inequity. In addition, the Tribunal clearly stated that: 'Whether or not significant disproportionality exists remains a matter for the Tribunal's appreciation, which it will exercise by reference to the overall geography of the area.'[128]

According to the Tribunal, the length of the relevant coast of Bangladesh and India was 418.6 km and 803.7 km, respectively. Accordingly, the ratio between the lengths of the relevant coasts of the parties was 1:1.92. The Tribunal's delimitation line allocates approximately 106,613 square km of the relevant area to Bangladesh and approximately 300,220 square km to India. Thus the ratio of the allocated areas is approximately 1:2.81. The Tribunal found that this ratio did not produce any significant disproportion in the allocation of maritime areas to the parties that would require alteration of the adjusted equidistance line to ensure an equitable solution.[129]

11.3.3 Summary

The above considerations can be summarized in two points.

First, the ICJ in *Black Sea* ruled that the disproportionality test is to be applied at the final and third stage to verify whether the delimitation line does not lead to an inequitable result. In subsequent cases, the disproportionality test was applied not only by the ICJ itself but also by the ITLOS and an Annex VII arbitral tribunal.

Second, in *Black Sea*, *Territorial and Maritime Dispute (Nicaragua v. Colombia)*, *Bangladesh/Myanmar* and *Bangladesh v. India*, the ICJ, the ITLOS and an Annex VII arbitral tribunal presented specific figures for the relevant coastal lengths and maritime areas accorded to each party in

[125] Ibid., 153, [489]. [126] Ibid., 153–154, [492]. [127] Ibid., 153, [492].
[128] Ibid., 154, [494]. [129] Ibid., 154, [495–497].

their decisions. In *Maritime Dispute (Peru v. Chile)*, however, the ICJ concluded that there was no significant disproportion, without calculating the relevant coastal lengths and maritime areas. In this regard, serious doubts could be expressed with regard to the objectiveness of the broad assessment of disproportionality in this case.

11.4 Normativity of the Disproportionality Test

On the basis of the above analysis, two issues may be examined: the legal basis of the disproportionality test and limitations associated with that test.

11.4.1 The Legal Basis of the Disproportionality Test

The first issue to be examined is from where the concept of (dis)proportionality derives. Courts and tribunals offer scant explanation in this regard. The striking fact in this regard is that courts and tribunals make no reference to state practice and *opinio juris* with regard to the disproportionality test in maritime delimitation.

As delimitation treaties rarely seldom explain why and to what extent a factor was taken into account when drawing a maritime boundary, it is difficult to find evidence of *opinio juris* in state practice. Furthermore, as discussed elsewhere, the state practice concerning (dis)proportionality remains limited.[130] Even in cases where considerations of proportionality may be presumed to have been present, it is difficult to determine its effect on the negotiated boundary with any degree of precision. Thus it will be difficult to find evidence to argue that the concept of proportionality is supported by 'extensive and virtually uniform' state practice and *opinio juris* which can generate customary rules.[131] One can thus argue that (dis)proportionality in the jurisprudence concerning maritime delimitation is the product of a 'judge-made law,' detached from actual state practice.

It is arguable that the disproportionality test can be regarded as an operationalization of the equitable principles that require to resulting in an equitable result. Even if this is the case, such an operationalization must

[130] Tanaka, n. 31, 179–182.

[131] Ibid., 182. Concerning customary-law making, the ICJ always supports the two-elements theory that combines an objective element of 'extensive and virtually uniform' state practice and the subjective or psychological element known as the *opinio juris*. *North Sea Continental Shelf*, n. 6, 42–44, [73–77]; *Libya/Malta*, n. 12, 29–30, [27].

be undertaken in the framework of law, not *ex aequo et bono*.[132] It seems questionable whether the disproportionality test developed through the jurisprudence is adequately objective and scientific as a norm of international law.[133]

11.4.2 Limitations Associated with the Disproportionality Test

The disproportionality test is open to criticism particularly in five respects.[134] First, when applying the disproportionality test, it is necessary to calculate the relevant coastal lengths and maritime areas belonging to each party. Yet, it is debatable whether any objective methods to scientifically calculate relevant coastal lengths and maritime areas concerned exist in the law of maritime delimitation.[135] In fact, the jurisprudence shows that parties to a dispute often present different figures of the relevant coastal lengths maritime areas to prove the equitableness of their own delimitation line and courts and tribunals have presented their own figures of the coastal lengths that significantly differ from the figures submitted by the parties in dispute. As Weil observed in *Canada/France*, however, there is no guarantee that the calculation made by a court or tribunal is scientifically more convincing than that put forward by the parties.[136]

The second problem relates to the excessive subjectivity with regard to the evaluation of (dis)proportionality between the coastal lengths and maritime areas appertaining to each party. On the basis of the jurisprudence in this field, it is difficult to identify an objective standard for determining disproportion between the ratio of the relevant coastal lengths and

[132] In this regard, it may be relevant to recall Judge Oda's view in *Jan Mayen*, according to which judgments regarding maritime delimitation may be rendered only as decisions according to *ex aequo et bono*. Separate Opinion of Judge Oda in *Jan Mayen*, n. 33, [85]. For critics of the subjectivity of the concept of equity, see Chapter 6 of this volume. See also Tanaka, n. 31, 326–327.

[133] In *Canada/France*, Weil already voiced his misgivings about the uncertainties of the proportionality test in its quantified form, n. 52, Dissenting Opinion of Mr. Weil, 1206, [24]. See also P. Weil, n. 31, 259. More recently, some writers also have pointed to the subjective elements of the disproportionality test. Fietta and Cleverly, n. 14, 609. See also Evans, n. 111, 270–272.

[134] Y. Tanaka, 'Reflections on the Territorial and Maritime Dispute between Nicaragua and Colombia before the International Court of Justice,' (2013) 26 *Leiden Journal of International Law* 909, 922–926.

[135] See further Chapter 7 of this volume.

[136] Dissenting Opinion of Mr. Weil, *Canada/France*, n. 52, 1206, [24].

maritime areas belonging to each party.[137] An eminent instance is *Territorial and Maritime Dispute (Nicaragua v. Colombia)* where the ratio of maritime areas was 1 (Colombia):3.44 (Nicaragua), while the ratio of coastal length was 1 (Colombia):8.2 (Nicaragua). Thus the ratio of coastal length is more than twice as great as that of maritime areas. If this is not disproportionate, what is the meaning of the 'disproportionality' test?[138] Furthermore, in some cases, the ICJ ruled that the disproportionality test was met, without presenting any specific figures of the relevant coastal lengths and maritime areas accorded to each party. The disproportionality test without calculation of the ratio of the coastal length and the maritime area is merely legal impressionism. As the ICJ stated in *Black Sea*, the disproportionality test is a means of checking whether there is a 'significant' disproportionality in the ratios between the maritime areas which would fall to one party or other by virtue of the delimitation line arrived at after the second stage of the delimitation process, and the lengths of their respective coasts. However, the adjective 'significant' is too vague to be very useful. The existence of a significant disproportionality is merely a matter of subjective appreciation by judges.[139]

Third, as Judge Oda pointedly observed, (dis)proportionality cannot determine any concrete delimitation line since the number of lines capable of producing the same proportion is limitless.[140] Accordingly, the role of the disproportionality test is limited to check the equitableness of the maritime boundary established by a court or tribunal only in a *retrospective* manner. As a matter of theory, it cannot objectively constrain discretion of judges in the adjustment of the provisional equidistance line. Hence it seems debatable whether the disproportionality test can contribute to enhancing the transparency and objectiveness of the process of maritime delimitation.

Fourth, the striking fact is that, to date, there is no single case where courts and tribunals admitted the existence of disproportion between the ratio of coastal lengths and the ratio for maritime areas appertaining to the parties. This hardly can be a mere coincidence. In this regard, it is

137 For statistics on the proportionality test, see Fietta and Cleverly, n. 14, 605–606.

138 Evans, n. 92, 62.

139 According to Evans, the concept of proportionality is a means to demonstrate that 'the delimitation line settled upon [...] has an equitable "feel" to it.' M. Evans, 'Maritime Boundary Delimitation: Where Do We Go from Here?,' in D. Freestone, R. Barnes, and D. Ong (eds.), *The Law of the Sea: Progress and Prospects* (Oxford University Press Oxford 2006) 155.

140 Dissenting Opinion of Judge Oda, *Tunisia/Libya*, n. 20, 258, [162]; Thirlway, n. 21, 500–501.

difficult to resist the temptation to submit that, at the second stage of maritime delimitation, the maritime boundary was already drawn in such a way as to pass the disproportionality test. In any case, one cannot deny that the application of the disproportionality test may be only formalistic in the sense that the delimitation line determined by a court or tribunal will always pass the disproportionality test.

Last but not least, there is the risk that the concept of (dis)proportionality may blur the distinction between delimitation and apportionment. The importance of this distinction was repeatedly highlighted by the ICJ in *North Sea Continental Shelf*, stating that: '[I]ts task in the present proceedings relates essentially to the delimitation and not the apportionment of the areas concerned or their division into converging sectors.'[141] In *Tunisia/Libya*, the Court also affirmed that the application of the equitable principle and consideration of relevant circumstances are not an operation of distributive justice.[142] Even though the ICJ stressed that the disproportionality test is not in itself a method of delimitation, it cannot pass unnoticed that the very idea of 'ratios' necessarily entails that of shares.[143] Thus it may have to be admitted that the concept of proportionality contradicts the rejection of the idea of apportionment in maritime delimitation. According weight to the consideration of proportionality in the delimitation process raises a serious concern that the process of maritime delimitation may be transformed to 'apportionment' or 'award of a just and equitable share' of marine spaces which was rejected by the Court itself.

11.5 Conclusions

This chapter has analysed the role and limitations of (dis)proportionality as an *ex post facto* test. The findings of the analysis can be summarized in four points.

First, the concept of (dis)proportionality in the law of maritime delimitation has been developed through the jurisprudence. In the jurisprudence prior to *Black Sea*, it can be observed that the application of the (dis)proportionality test remained inconsistent and uncertain. In fact, even though the ICJ applied the (dis)proportionality test in some cases, it did not apply that test in other cases. In some cases, such as *Gulf of Maine*

141 *North Sea Continental Shelf*, n. 6, 22, [18].

142 *Tunisia/Libya*, n. 20, 60, [71]. See also *Libya/Malta*, n. 12, 39–40, [46]; *Jan Mayen*, n. 33, 66–67, [64].

143 Thirlway, n. 21, 500.

and *Jan Mayen*, the Court considered proportionality between coastal lengths as a factor in adjusting a provisional equidistance line at the second stage of maritime delimitation. In *Black Sea*, however, the disproportionality test was given an independent status as the third and final stage of maritime delimitation. In subsequent cases, the disproportionality test has been always applied by the ICJ, ITLOS, and Annex VII Arbitral Tribunal.

Second, according to the jurisprudence, the disproportionality test is not in itself a method of delimitation. The function of the disproportionality test is to avoid a *significant* disproportionality, not to achieve an approximate correlation between the ratio of the lengths of the parties' relevant coasts and the ratio of their respective shares of the relevant area. The checking of the equitableness of the delimitation line by the disproportionality test can only be approximate.

Third, the application of the disproportionality test is not free from difficulty. In particular, it is debatable whether, for the purpose of that test, objective criterion for calculating relevant coastal lengths and the size of the relevant areas exist in the law of maritime delimitation.[144] It is also difficult to identify objective criteria for determining a significant disproportionality between coastal lengths and the maritime areas attributed to the parties. Furthermore, in some cases, the ICJ did not calculate the relevant coastal lengths and maritime areas accorded to each party when applying the (dis)proportionality test. Even if the disproportionality test can only be approximate, the application of the disproportionality test seems to be highly subjective. The striking fact in this regard is that the disproportionality test at the third stage is always met, even though the ratios of the relevant coastal lengths and maritime areas belonging to each party considerably differ between cases. Here some doubt could be expressed whether the disproportionality test is merely formalistic.

Fourth, given that the number of lines capable of producing the same proportion is limitless, the disproportionality test cannot verify the validity of the location of the maritime boundary established by a court or tribunal. Hence, it is debatable whether the application of the disproportionality test can contribute to securing the validity of the maritime boundary.

All in all, it may have to be admitted that the application of the disproportionality test is far from being objective. It is difficult to disagree with the observation of Higgins that: 'the concept of proportionality in maritime delimitation remains, for me, full of uncertainties and problems.'[145] If courts and tribunals continue to apply the disproportionality test, it is

[144] Further, see Chapter 7 of this volume. [145] Higgins, n. 11, 230.

necessary to enhance the objectiveness of the disproportionality test by specifying the ratio of the relevant coastal lengths and maritime areas belonging to each party in a scientific manner. This would be highly difficult, however.[146] As Evans suggests, an option may be to deny the role of (dis)proportionality in the process of maritime delimitation.[147] Yet, one cannot easily expect that a court or a tribunal would deny the disproportionality test on this point. Hence, there appears to be some scope to consider a more moderate option that the application of the disproportionality test should be limited to the situations where a provisional equidistance line would create the cut-off effect by a markedly concave or convex coastline, even though relevant coasts are comparative in length.[148]

[146] In fact, as Evans observes, the ICJ, in *Maritime Dispute (Peru v. Chile)*, seems to have 'thrown in the towel' by admitting that it is 'difficult if not impossible' to calculate the relevant coastal lengths and the extent of the relevant area. Evans, n. 92, 65.

[147] Evans, n. 139, 156.

[148] Fietta and Cleverly, n. 14, 608.

12

The Delimitation of the Continental Shelf beyond 200 nm

Procedural Issues

SIGNE VEIERUD BUSCH

12.1 Introduction

When a court or tribunal is requested to delimit the continental shelf beyond 200 nautical miles (nm) from the baselines, a number of procedural and substantive circumstances may affect the jurisdiction of the court or tribunal, and its decision on whether it could and should exercise jurisdiction. This chapter sets out to examine how the relationship between delimitation of the continental shelf beyond 200 nm and the procedure to determine the outer limits of the continental shelf beyond 200 nm (OCS limits) in accordance with Article 76 of the United Nations Convention on the Law of the Sea (LOSC), has been conceptualized by the international jurisprudence. This chapter will only focus on the procedural aspects of delimitation of the continental shelf, whilst Chapter 13 focuses on the substantive issues in relation to continental shelf delimitation.

The jurisprudence on delimitation of the continental shelf beyond 200 nm is relatively limited, and only on nine occasions over the past twenty-four years has an international court or tribunal been requested to undertake a delimitation between opposite or adjacent states of the continental shelf beyond 200 nm from the baselines, five of which have been adjudicated over the past five years. In addition, *Newfoundland and Labrador/Nova Scotia* is also considered as relevant, although it did not concern an interstate arbitration, and accordingly not being opposable to any international process for the determination of the outer limit of the Canadian continental shelf.[1] The available jurisprudence stems from the

[1] *Newfoundland and Labrador/Nova Scotia* (Award of the Tribunal in the Second Phase) [2002] 128 ILR 504.

International Court of Justice (ICJ), the International Tribunal for the Law of the Sea (ITLOS) and arbitral tribunals.

In Section 12.2 of this chapter, the procedure for delineating the continental shelf beyond 200 nm through the Commission on the Limits of the Continental Shelf (CLCS) submission procedure under Article 76 is first briefly introduced. The principal procedural issues in delimiting the continental shelf beyond 200 nm is whether or not such delimitation falls within the jurisdiction of the relevant court or tribunal, and secondly, if there is any reason why the court or tribunal should refrain from exercising its jurisdiction, in instances in which the CLCS has not yet issued its recommendations on the location of the outer limit of the continental shelf.

The *Bangladesh/Myanmar* delimitation from 2012 marks a clear shift in how courts and tribunals have addressed the question of delimitation beyond 200 nm.[2] For the past five years, there has been a considerable development in the jurisprudence concerning the delimitation of the continental shelf. The ICJ, the ITLOS, and an Annex VII arbitral tribunal have all moved in the same direction, explicitly and critically addressing the relationship between delimitation between states as opposed to delineation of outer limits, the submission procedure under Article 76(8), and the role of the CLCS in dispute settlement. For that reason, this chapter discusses the case law before and after *Bangladesh/Myanmar* separately in Sections 12.3 and 12.4.

The concluding Section 12.5 addresses the question whether the practice of international courts and tribunals is consistent or inconsistent, contributing to predictability or uncertainty in maritime boundary delimitation.

12.2 Delineation and Delimitation of the Continental Shelf

Delimitation of the continental shelf presupposes that the parties to the delimitation dispute have overlapping entitlements to the continental shelf, continuing beyond 200 nm measured from their baselines in accordance with Article 76(1) of the LOSC.

The LOSC provides that all coastal states are entitled to a continental shelf, defined as the natural prolongation of its land territory, and that such

[2] *Delimitation of the Maritime Boundary in the Bay of Bengal (Bangladesh/Myanmar)* (Judgment) [2012] ITLOS Rep. 16.

entitlement exists without occupation or any express proclamation.[3] In cases where a coastal state's continental margin extends beyond 200 nm from the baselines, it is entitled to establish continental shelf limits beyond such distance, to a distance of 350 nm from the baselines or not exceeding 100 nm from the 2,500 metre isobath.[4] Although the coastal state's sovereign rights for the purpose of exploring and exploiting the natural resources of the continental shelf in such areas are inherent and do not depend on occupation or proclamation, the LOSC obligates the coastal state whose entitlement extends beyond 200 nm to submit information on the limits to the CLCS.[5]

The CLCS is a treaty body established for the purpose of considering the data and other material submitted by coastal states concerning the location of their OCS limits, and to make recommendations on matters related to the establishment of such limits.[6] In addition, the CLCS is mandated to provide scientific and technical advice to coastal states in the process of preparing data for submission to the CLCS.[7] The coastal state may establish final and binding OCS limits on the basis of the CLCS recommendations.[8]

Article 76(10) however specifies that '[t]he provisions of this article are without prejudice to the question of delimitation of the continental shelf between States with opposite and adjacent coasts.' Article 9 of Annex II to the LOSC provides explicitly that '[t]he actions of the Commission shall not prejudice matters relating to the delimitation of boundaries between States.' These provisions contribute to determining the scope of the CLCS' mandate and competence, and are commonly referred to as the saving clauses of Article 76. The rationale of the saving clauses is to ensure that the CLCS in exercising its functions will not prejudice the sovereign and exclusive right of coastal states to establish their continental shelf boundaries. When the CLCS was established, it prepared Rules of Procedure (RoP) for the purpose of ensuring the implementation of Article 76(8) and Annex II to the LOSC.[9] The CLCS found a need to further clarify its role with regard to, amongst other, delimitation disputes. The CLCS therefore provided procedures in its RoP for avoiding prejudicing the delimitation

[3] LOSC, Art. 76(1) and Art. 77(3). [4] LOSC, Art. 76(5).

[5] LOSC, Art. 76(8). [6] LOSC, Art. 76 and Annex II, Art. 3.

[7] LOSC, Annex II, Art. 3(b). [8] LOSC, Art. 76(8).

[9] CLCS, *Rules of Procedure of the Commission on the Limits of the Continental Shelf* (17 April 2008), Doc. CLCS/40/Rev.1, available at https://documents-dds-ny.un.org/doc/UNDOC/GEN/N08/309/23/PDF/N0830923.pdf?OpenElement.

of the continental shelf between opposite or adjacent states. This work resulted in the current Rule 46 in the RoP, stipulating that

> [i]n case of a dispute in the delimitation of the continental shelf between opposite or adjacent States [...] submissions may be made and shall be considered in accordance with Annex I to these Rules.

There is accordingly nothing in the LOSC or the CLCS's RoP precluding coastal states from making submissions to the CLCS concerning areas that are subject to unresolved delimitations with opposite or adjacent states. However, paragraph 1 of Annex I to which Rule 46 refers, provides that the competence in case of disputes which arise in connection with the establishment of OCS limits rests with the states concerned, not the CLCS. In fact, if such delimitation dispute exists, the CLCS may only consider a submission made under Article 76(8) by any of the states concerned in the dispute if all states parties to the dispute have given their prior consent.[10] There are currently fifty-six continental shelf submissions awaiting the CLCS' consideration and recommendation, and forty-two of these submissions are subject to unresolved delimitation. In relation to seventeen of these submissions, the parties to the dispute have withheld their consent in accordance with paragraph 5(a) of Annex I of the RoP, and blocked the CLCS from considering the submission.[11] This leaves the CLCS procedure at a standstill, awaiting the parties' settlement of the dispute either by agreement or adjudication, or revoking their objections. This is the case for several of the disputes discussed in the current chapter.

Whereas Article 76 provides a definition of the continental shelf, the CLCS is not ascribed any function in relation to the delimitation of the continental shelf. The delimitation of the continental shelf is described in Article 83, providing that

> The delimitation of the continental shelf [...] shall be effected by agreement on the basis of international law [...]. If no agreement can be reached within a reasonable period of time, the States concerned shall resort to the procedures provided for in Part XV.[12]

10 RoP, Annex I, Para. 5(a).

11 These numbers are based on an analysis of coastal state submissions and third party *notes verbales* publicly available on the CLCS website at www.un.org/depts/los/clcs_new/commission_submissions.htm. See also S. V. Busch, *Establishing Continental Shelf Limits beyond 200 Nautical Miles by the Coastal State: A Right of Involvement for Other States?* (Brill/Nijhoff Leiden 2016) 122.

12 LOSC, Art. 83(1)–(2).

The states are obligated to try to reach an agreement on the delimitation, but if they do not succeed, they are required to resort to dispute settlement procedures available under Part XV. Part XV provides the applicable procedure for settlement of disputes where not settlement has been reached by the parties to the dispute,[13] and Article 288(1) provides that courts and tribunals operating under the LOSC 'have jurisdiction over any disputes concerning the interpretation or application of this Convention.'

Although Articles 76 and 83 seem to exist independently from each other, they are at the same time intertwined. They both set out to determine the size of a coastal state's continental shelf, and they both require the existence of a continental shelf.[14] They are also very different, in the sense that Article 76 provides a detailed definition of the nature and extent of the continental shelf, based on a number of scientific and legal phrases, such as 'outer edge of the continental margin' and 'natural prolongation,' whilst Article 83 provides no specific method for delimiting the continental shelf between states.[15] In addition, they both presuppose the existence of an entitlement to the continental shelf as basis for either delineation or delimitation.

Article 83 does not differentiate between the continental shelf within and beyond 200 nm, an inner and an outer continental shelf, and is equally applicable in cases of delimitation beyond 200 nm from the baselines. In *Barbados v. Trinidad and Tobago*, the arbitral tribunal raised the question if it 'should [...] make a distinction between areas within 200 nm of the Parties' coasts and areas beyond 200 nm [...].'[16] The tribunal observed that 'there is in law only a single "continental shelf" rather than an inner continental shelf and a separate extended or outer continental shelf.'[17]

Even though the text of Articles 76 and 83 may suggest that the relationship between delineation and delimitation is relatively unproblematic, the jurisprudence on the delimitation of the continental shelf proves that the interrelationship between delineation and delimitation is not as clear in practice.

[13] LOSC, Art. 281.

[14] Ø. Jensen, 'Maritime Boundary Delimitation beyond 200 Nautical Miles: The International Judiciary and the Commission on the Limits of the Continental Shelf,' (2015) 84 *Nordic Journal of International Law* 580, 583.

[15] Ibid.

[16] *Arbitration between Barbados and the Republic of Trinidad and Tobago* [2006] 27 RIAA 147, 172 [2]. See also below Section 12.4.2.1.

[17] Ibid., 209 [213].

12.3 Early Jurisprudence Addressing Continental Shelf Delimitation beyond 200 nm

12.3.1 Introduction

The current section discusses the case law prior to *Bangladesh/Myanmar*. Four cases are relevant within the scope of this section, three of which have been decided by international courts or tribunals, and the fourth being a domestic arbitration. In two of these cases, both parties had ratified the LOSC at the time of the proceedings. Part XV of the LOSC provided the legal basis for the tribunal's jurisdiction in *Barbados/Trinidad and Tobago*.[18] In *Nicaragua v. Honduras*, Nicaragua brought the case under the Pact of Bogotá.[19]

Accordingly, in the four cases concerned, the jurisdiction of the relevant courts and tribunals stems from different legal bases. This may impact the court's or tribunal's jurisdiction and approach in addressing the delimitation and how they relate to the CLCS submission procedure included in Article 76(8). A common starting point in all these cases is that the courts or tribunals incontestably are competent to delimit the continental shelf within 200 nm from the baselines between the opposite or adjacent states concerned. The courts and tribunals express uncertainty on whether their jurisdiction extends to the delimitation of the continental shelf beyond the 200 nm limit or not, and how it should relate to the CLCS and the procedure included in Article 76 of the LOSC.

12.3.2 Canada/France

In *Canada/France*, the court of arbitration was requested to establish a single delimitation line of the maritime areas as between the parties, a line which was to govern all rights and jurisdiction which the parties may exercise under international law.[20]

The court observed that its competence to pronounce on the disagreement between the parties as to the existence of a continental shelf beyond 200 nm must be considered in accordance with the Arbitration

[18] *Barbados/Trinidad and Tobago*, n. 16.

[19] American Treaty on Pacific Settlement (Pact of Bogotá) adopted 30 April 1948, entered into force 6 May 1949, OAS Treaty Series, No. 17 and 61; *Territorial and Maritime Dispute between Nicaragua and Honduras in the Caribbean Sea (Nicaragua v. Honduras)* (Judgment) [2007] ICJ Rep. 659, 738 [1–2].

[20] *Case concerning the Delimitation of Maritime Areas between Canada and France* [1992] 31 ILM 1145, 1163 [36].

Agreement.[21] Referring to the Agreement, the court noted that it did not suggest that there was any difference in the delimitation of the maritime areas within and beyond 200 nm.[22] However, the Arbitration Agreement only provided the court jurisdiction to delimit the maritime areas 'between the parties,' and the court feared that a delimitation beyond 200 nm could potentially affect other states and the international community.[23] The court of arbitration upon this basis observed that it 'is not competent to carry out a delimitation which affects the rights of a Party which is not before it.'[24]

Although the LOSC was not applicable in *Canada/France*, the court of arbitration continued that:

> [i]n this connection the Court notes that in accordance with Article 76, para. 8 and Annex II of the [LOSC], a Commission is to be set up, [. . .], to consider the claims and data submitted by coastal States and issue recommendations to them. In conformity with this provision, only 'the limits of the shelf established by a coastal State on the basis of these recommendations shall be final and binding.'[25]

However, at the time of the judgment, the CLCS had not yet been established, and its potential role was not the most important reason why the court of arbitration refrained from delimiting the shelf beyond 200 nm.

In addition to observing the factual uncertainty in terms of entitlement to the continental shelf, the court of arbitration observed that the special agreement between the parties which enjoins it to 'establish a single delimitation which shall govern all rights of jurisdiction which the parties may exercise under international law in these maritime areas,' posed certain restraints to its competence.[26] The court of arbitration interpreted this phrase to mandate a single boundary line that would apply both to the seabed and the superjacent waters in the area subject to delimitation, and therefore the court was only competent to effect a delimitation reaching as far as the 200 nm limit.[27] Upon this basis, the court decided not to effect a delimitation of the shelf beyond 200 nm.[28]

[21] Ibid., 1172, [77]. [22] Ibid. [23] Ibid. [24] Ibid., 1172, [79].

[25] Ibid. [26] Ibid., 1172, [81–82]. [27] Ibid., 1172, [82].

[28] It is noted that France made a submission to the CLCS concerning the Saint-Pierre and Miquelon in 2014 and that Canada shortly after submitted a *note verbale* requesting the CLCS not to consider the submission in accordance with Rule 46 and Para. 5(a) of Annex I to the RoP, as Canada and France have overlapping claims to the area which were not resolved by the 1992 judgment.

12.3.3 *Newfoundland and Labrador/Nova Scotia*

In *Newfoundland and Labrador/Nova Scotia* an arbitral tribunal was established to resolve the dispute relating to the line dividing the respective offshore areas of the Canadian provinces of Nova Scotia and of Newfoundland and Labrador.[29] The arbitral tribunal observed that the *Accord Acts* defined the offshore areas to be attributed to the parties as extending to the outer edge of the continental margin, incorporating the provisions of Article 76 of the LOSC, and that both parties to the dispute agreed that the line determined by the tribunal should extend so far out.[30] The arbitral tribunal concluded that its 'jurisdiction clearly permits it to do so.'[31]

At the same time the tribunal observed that no international tribunal had yet delimited to the outer edge of the continental shelf between adjacent States, and acknowledged that it in any case did not have either 'the competence or mandate to delimit the outer limit of the continental shelf.'[32] Although lacking the competence to delineate the outer limits of the continental shelf, the arbitral tribunal was satisfied with simply noting that 'a continental shelf wider than 200 [nm] from the territorial sea baselines probably exists through most, if not all, of the seaward area [concerned].'[33]

The arbitral tribunal sought to distance itself from the *Canada/France* award, first observing that

> the Court of Arbitration held it had no jurisdiction to delimit the continental shelf beyond 200 nautical miles, on the ground that to do so would involve the legal position of a third party, the 'international community' as represented by the Commission on the Limits of the Continental Shelf.[34]

The arbitral tribunal then observed that it found itself in a quite different position, asserting that as its mandate did not concern an interstate arbitration, 'there is no question of any decision which might be opposable to any international process for the delimitation of the outer edge of the Continental shelf.'[35] The arbitral tribunal maintained that it was only called upon to specify the offshore areas of the two parties inter se for the purpose of the *Accord Acts*, which it could do by providing that 'the [delimitation] line shall not extend beyond the point of intersection with the outer limit of the continental margin as determined in accordance with international law.'[36]

[29] *Newfoundland and Labrador/Nova Scotia*, n. 1. [30] Ibid., [2.29]. [31] Ibid.
[32] Ibid., [2.30]; see also *Canada/France*, n. 20. [33] Ibid., n. 1, [2.30].
[34] Ibid., [2.31]. [35] Ibid. [36] Ibid.

12.3.4 *Barbados v. Trinidad and Tobago*

In February 2004 Barbados filed its notice of arbitration and Statement of Claim, requesting an Annex VII arbitral tribunal to decide on a

> single unified maritime boundary line, delimiting the exclusive economic zone and continental shelf between it and the Republic of Trinidad and Tobago, as provided under Articles 74 and 83 of UNCLOS.[37]

In its Counter-Memorial, Trinidad and Tobago set out its own positive claim, requesting the arbitral tribunal to delimit the continental shelf between the two states, 'extending to the outer limit of the continental shelf as determined in accordance with international law.'[38] The tribunal raised the question if it had jurisdiction to consider Trinidad and Tobago's claim, and in particularly asked if

> the Tribunal [should] make a distinction between areas within 200 nm of the Parties' coasts and areas beyond 200 nm and, if so, what, if any, are the consequences of making the distinction?[39]

The arbitral tribunal observed that 'there is in law only a single "continental shelf" rather than an inner continental shelf and a separate extended or outer continental shelf,' and considered that the dispute to be dealt with included the delimitation of the continental shelf beyond 200 nm.[40] Although having concluded that the delimitation was within its jurisdiction, the arbitral tribunal ultimately determined a boundary ending at the 200 nm limit of Trinidad and Tobago.

12.3.5 *Nicaragua v. Honduras*

The following year, the ICJ issued its judgment in *Nicaragua v. Honduras*, where both parties requested the Court to determine the course of the single maritime boundary between the areas of territorial sea, continental shelf and exclusive economic zone appertaining respectively to Nicaragua and Honduras in the Caribbean Sea.[41]

When considering the starting point and endpoint of the single maritime boundary, the Court observed that neither party had specified a precise seaward end to the boundary in their submissions to the Court. The Court maintained that 'it will not rule on an issue when in order to do so the rights of a third party that is not before it, have first to

[37] *Barbados v. Trinidad and Tobago*, n. 16, 163 [57]. [38] Ibid., 165 [63(c)].
[39] Ibid., 172, Section B (2). [40] Ibid., 209 [213].
[41] *Nicaragua v. Honduras*, n. 19, 685, [72], [261].

be determined.'[42] Having analysed the potential interests of third states in the region that may be relevant for the boundary between Nicaragua and Honduras, the ICJ found that it may, without specifying a precise endpoint, delimit the maritime boundary without affecting third state rights.[43] In addition, the ICJ explicitly provided that

> in no case may the line be interpreted as extending more than 200 nautical miles from the baselines from which the breadth of the territorial sea is measured; any claim of continental shelf rights beyond 200 miles must be in accordance with Article 76 of UNCLOS and reviewed by the Commission on the Limits of the Continental Shelf established thereunder.[44]

It can be argued that this statement does not seem to be part of the rationale for the Court's decision, and must rather be considered an *obiter dictum* of the Court.

12.3.6 An Obiter Dictum *Relating to Maritime Delimitation beyond 200 nm*

The meaning of the ICJ's *obiter dictum* in *Nicaragua v. Honduras* has been considered by a number of legal scholars, and it has also played a role in subsequent case law on maritime delimitation. In this study, addressing the question of transparency, consistency, and predictability in maritime delimitation case law, it is therefore timely not only to analyse the meaning of the *obiter dictum*, but also to discuss whether it has kept its ground in more recent case law, or if it has lost its relevance.

Kunoy interprets the statement of the ICJ in *Nicaragua v. Honduras* as supporting his assumption that a delimitation of the continental shelf between neighbouring states beyond 200 nm presupposes entitlement to the continental shelf. In his opinion, there is a temporal relationship between delimitation and delineation of the continental shelf, as could also be read from the decision in *Canada/France*.[45] Kunoy argues that entitlement to the continental shelf is only hypothetical until the CLCS has endorsed the outer limits in accordance with Article 76 of the LOSC. As it is not the role of an adjudicative body to advise states on a hypothetical basis, he asserts that a court or tribunal cannot accept proceedings on

[42] Ibid., 756, [312]. [43] Ibid., 759, [318]–[319]. [44] Ibid., 759, [319].

[45] B. Kunoy, 'The Admissibility of a Plea to an International Adjudicative Forum to Delimit the Outer Continental Shelf prior to the Adoption of Final Recommendations by the Commission on the Limits of the Continental Shelf,' (2010) 25 *The International Journal of Marine and Coastal Law* 237, 262.

the delimitation of the OCS in the absence of recommendations by the CLCS.[46]

Kwiatkowska, on the other hand, asserts that the interpretation suggested by Kunoy is not in accordance with the saving clauses of the LOSC, implemented in the RoP of the CLCS, clearly prescribing that the CLCS has no role in the delimitation of boundaries between states. Instead, Kwiatkowska argues that the statement by the ICJ in *Nicaragua v. Honduras* 'should be regarded as a courtesy recognition by the principle organ of the United Nations, ICJ, of the work of the CLCS.'[47] She continues that

> were the ICJ or any other court, or states themselves, to delimit the outer CS beyond 200 miles prior to the completion of the CLCS process, the CLCS review [. . .] will be confined to its being informed about, or its using such boundary lines.[48]

Magnusson shares the view of Kwiatkowska, and observes that '[t]his statement cannot be read as implying that the ICJ decided that the delineation must precede delimitation.'[49] Jensen, observes along the same line that

> there is nothing wrong legally about using Article 83 [. . .] before the Article 76 process has run its course; indeed this possibility is implied by the LOSC itself, since the Convention does not seem to indicate which provisions should be implemented first.[50]

Jensen observes that in practice states tend to delimit their continental shelf beyond 200 nm before they delineate the outer limit, and they also invoke third-party dispute settlement mechanisms to delimit the continental shelf between them prior to delineation the OCS limits.[51] Therefore, he argues, we must ask whether and to what extent Article 76 and the CLCS submission procedure have legal significance for the international judiciary when dealing with issues of continental shelf delimitation beyond 200 nm. Oude Elferink also addresses the extent to which Article 76 is relevant for delimitation in accordance with Article 83, and

[46] Ibid., 248 and 262. Similar wording was used by the court of arbitration in *Canada/France*, n. 20, 1172 [81].

[47] B. Kwiatkowska, 'Submissions to the UN CLCS in Cases of Disputed and Undisputed Maritime Boundary Delimitations or Other Unresolved Land or Maritime Disputes of Developing States,' Farewell Lecture of Prof. B. Kwiatkowska, 9 December 2011, available at http://dspace.library.uu.nl/handle/1874/23543019, 19.

[48] Ibid.

[49] B. M. Magnusson, *The Continental Shelf beyond 200 Nautical Miles – Delineation, Delimitation and Dispute Settlement* (Brill/Nijhoff Leiden 2015) 252.

[50] Ø. Jensen, n. 14, 584. [51] Ibid.

observes that '[d]elimitation of the continental shelf beyond 200 nautical miles requires the existence of a valid claim of more than one state to the same area.'[52] He seems to establish a certain temporal relationship between entitlement to the continental shelf and delimitation, as overlapping entitlement is a necessary prerequisite for delimitation of the continental shelf, thus without going as far as requiring that the CLCS submission procedure must be completed before the outer continental shelf between neighbouring states may be delimited.

It is submitted that nothing in Article 83, which provides the legal basis for continental shelf delimitation, suggests that the delimitation of the continental shelf beyond 200 nm differs from the delimitation within 200 nm, neither in terms of procedure or substance, and the LOSC does not provide any provision concerning the order in which Articles 76 and 83 shall be implemented by states.[53] However, the fact that delimitation of the continental shelf beyond 200 nm presupposes entitlement to the continental shelf raises the question of who has the competence to decide on the existence of such entitlement.[54] Is this a situation where two bodies, the CLCS and a court or tribunal, both have the competence to decide on entitlement or is it rather a situation where one of them has the competence to deal with entitlement, and the other to deal with outer limits? This is a question which has come up in more recent jurisprudence concerning the delimitation of the continental shelf, and is addressed in the following section. The discussions in the following section will also shed light on if and how international courts and tribunals have addressed the ICJ's *obiter dictum* from *Nicaragua v. Honduras.*

12.4 Recent Jurisprudence Addressing Continental Shelf Delimitation beyond 200 nm

12.4.1 Bangladesh/Myanmar

12.4.1.1 Introduction

Bangladesh/Myanmar concerning delimitation in the Bay of Bengal is considered a milestone in the delimitation jurisprudence, not only as the first delimitation dispute decided by the ITLOS, but also because the ITLOS was the first adjudicative body to undertake a thorough discussion of the

[52] A. G. Oude Elferink, 'The Impact of the Law of the Sea Convention on the Delimitation of Maritime Boundaries,' in D. Vidas and W. Østreng (eds.), *Order for the Oceans at the Turn of the Century* (Kluwer Law International The Hague 1999) 462.

[53] Jensen, n. 14, 584.

[54] See also Chapter 6 above.

relationship between courts and tribunals on the one hand, and the CLCS on the other.[55] According to Judge Treves, the ITLOS built on and adopted the methodology developed in previous jurisprudence by the ITLOS and in recent arbitral awards, but in addition

> the Tribunal has also contributed its own grain of wisdom and particular outlook. This contribution consists, in my view, especially in the [...] [Tribunals] decision to delimit the continental shelf beyond 200 miles.[56]

As indicated by Treves, several of the issues discussed in *Bangladesh/ Myanmar* build on the previous jurisprudence, by either choosing different formulations, or developing them further. Whereas early jurisprudence focused on whether delimitation of the continental shelf beyond 200 nm would affect the potential rights of third states and the international community as a decisive factor for the court or tribunal's jurisdiction, the ITLOS phrased these concerns in terms of a more clear-cut distinction between delimitation on the one hand, and delineation on the other, by means of undertaking a contextual analysis of Articles 76, 77, and 83 of the LOSC. After having decided on its jurisdiction *ratione materiae*, the ITLOS raised the question if there was any reason why it should refrain from exercising such jurisdiction.[57]

12.4.1.2 Jurisdiction *Ratione Materiae* of the ITLOS

The *Bangladesh/Myanmar* dispute was submitted to the ITLOS by Bangladesh in 2009, requesting the Tribunal to secure 'the full and satisfactory delimitation of Bangladesh's maritime boundaries with [...] Myanmar in the territorial sea, the exclusive economic zone and the continental shelf in accordance with international law.'[58] Both Bangladesh and Myanmar accepted the Tribunal's jurisdiction to settle the delimitation dispute. Bangladesh argued that such jurisdiction also included the delimitation of the continental shelf beyond 200 nm from the baselines.[59] Myanmar shared the view that, in principle, the Tribunal could be competent to delimit the shelf beyond 200 nm, but asserted that in the present case the Tribunal did not have jurisdiction with regard to the continental

[55] See e.g. R. Churchill, 'The Bangladesh/Myanmar Case: Continuity and Novelty in the Law of Maritime Boundary Delimitation,' (2012) 1 *Cambridge Journal of International and Comparative Law* 137, 152; and *Bangladesh/Myanmar* (Judgment), n. 2, Declaration of Judge Wolfrum, 140.

[56] *Bangladesh/Myanmar*, n. 2, Declaration of Judge Treves [2].

[57] See further Section 12.4.2.

[58] *Bangladesh/Myanmar*, n. 2, 9 [1].

[59] Ibid., 22, [43].

shelf beyond 200 nm as the delimitation line terminates before reaching the 200 nm line.[60]

The ITLOS dealt only briefly with the issue, observing that the LOSC does not make any distinction between an inner and an outer continental shelf. Article 76 embodies the concept of a single continental shelf, and Article 77 provides that the coastal state can exercise its sovereign rights over the entire continental shelf without any distinction being made between a continental shelf within and beyond 200 nm. Likewise, Article 83 concerning the delimitation of the continental shelf does not make any such distinction.[61] This understanding is in accordance with the arbitral tribunal's interpretation in the *Barbados v. Trinidad and Tobago* delimitation.[62] Upon this basis, the ITLOS concluded that it had jurisdiction *ratione materiae* to delimit the continental shelf in its entirety.

12.4.1.3 Delineation and Delimitation Distinguished

After having decided that it had jurisdiction *ratione materiae* to decide the dispute, ITLOS considered whether it would be appropriate to exercise such jurisdiction. ITLOS briefly noted that the exercise of its jurisdiction would not prejudice the rights of third parties, as Article 33 (2) of its Statute provides that its decision has no binding force except between the parties in the dispute.[63] However, the Tribunal found that due to the location of the disputed areas, the delimitation would neither affect the potential rights of the international community in the Area.[64]

Next, the Tribunal discussed whether it should refrain from exercising its jurisdiction to delimit the continental shelf beyond 200 nm until such the CLCS had issued its recommendations.[65] The similar question was raised in *Nicaragua v. Honduras*, where the ICJ pronounced that delimitation of the shelf beyond 200 nm cannot be effectuated until the CLCS submission procedure under Article 76(8) was completed. The ITLOS took note of this *obiter dictum*, and observed that 'the determination of whether an international court or tribunal should exercise its jurisdiction depends on the procedural and substantive circumstances of each case.'[66]

ITLOS argued that 'the absence of established outer limits of a maritime zone does not preclude delimitation in that zone,' and maintained that there is a clear distinction between the delimitation of the continental

[60] Ibid., 102, [343]. [61] Ibid., 108, [361].
[62] Ibid., 108, [363]; see also *Barbados v. Trinidad and Tobago*, n. 16, 209, [213].
[63] *Bangladesh/Myanmar*, n. 2, 109, [366–367].
[64] Ibid., 109, [368]. [65] Ibid., 109, [369]. [66] Ibid., 113, [384].

shelf under Article 83 and the delineation of its outer limits under Article 76.[67] The CLCS is a body set up for the implementation of Article 76, and its mandate is to make recommendations to coastal states on matters related to the establishment of OCS limits, in relation to which the Commission members have a special expertise.[68] In fact, Article 76(10) and Article 9 of Annex II to the LOSC specifically provide that the provisions of Article 76 are without prejudice to questions of delimitation of the continental shelf between states with opposite and adjacent coasts, and that the actions of the CLCS shall not prejudice the delimitation of such limits. The Tribunal upon this basis asserted that

> [j]ust as the functions of the Commission are without prejudice to the question of delimitation of the continental shelf between States with opposite or adjacent coasts, so the exercise by international courts and tribunals of their jurisdiction regarding the delimitation of maritime bondages, including that of the continental shelf, is without prejudice to the exercise by the Commission of its functions on matters related to the delineation of the outer limits of the continental shelf.[69]

Bangladesh further asserted that, in the current dispute, the CLCS was precluded from making recommendations on the OCS limits until the time the ongoing dispute between Myanmar and Bangladesh was resolved, as the parties to the disputes has invoked the application of Rule 46 and paragraph 5(a) of Annex I to the RoP, blocking the work of the CLCS on the disputed submissions.[70] If the Tribunal was to await the recommendations of the CLCS, this would not only leave the situation in a deadlock, but it would also mean that the compulsory proceedings entailing binding decisions would have no practical application in disputes regarding the continental shelf beyond 200 nm.[71] The Tribunal shared Bangladesh's view that a decision not to exercise its jurisdiction over the dispute, would not be conducive to the efficient operation of the Convention, and would be contrary to the object and purpose of the Convention:

> Inaction in the present case, by the Commission and the Tribunal, two organs created by the Convention to ensure the effective implementation of its provisions, would leave the parties in a position where they may be unable to benefit fully from their rights over the continental shelf.[72]

[67] Ibid., 111, [373]. [68] Ibid., 111, [373]–[375].
[69] *Bangladesh/Myanmar*, n. 2, 112, [379]. [70] Ibid., 107, [358], 114, [387].
[71] Ibid. [72] Ibid., 115, [393].

Upon this basis, the Tribunal found that it had an obligation to adjudicate the dispute and delimit the continental shelf beyond 200 nm, without prejudice to the delineation of the OCS in accordance with Article 76(8).[73]

12.4.1.4 Entitlement as a Prerequisite for Delimitation

The decisive factor for the ITLOS' choice to exercise jurisdiction in *Bangladesh/Myanmar*, however, seemed to be the undisputed entitlement of the parties to the continental shelf beyond 200 nm. Early jurisprudence suggests that an international court or tribunal should not delimit the continental shelf beyond 200 nm unless the CLCS has decided on the entitlement of the parties to the continental shelf in accordance with Article 76(8) of the LOSC.

In *Bangladesh/Myanmar*, the ITLOS could not delimit the boundary, without first having assured itself that the parties had overlapping entitlements to the disputed parts of the continental shelf.[74] The ITLOS observed that a clear distinction has to be made between the notion of entitlement to the continental shelf, and the delineation of the continental shelf, and argued that entitlement to the shelf does not depend on any procedural requirement.[75] Quite the opposite, Article 77(3) of the LOSC provides that entitlement exists without a requirement of occupation or proclamation, and accordingly entitlement to the OCS exists regardless of the submission procedure in accordance with Article 76(8). This led the ITLOS to raise the question if there was any reason why it would be inappropriate for the Tribunal to interpret Article 76 for the purpose of determining the parties' entitlement to the continental shelf. The Tribunal observed that 'as this article contains elements of law and science, its proper interpretation and application requires both legal and scientific expertise.'[76] Whilst the CLCS is a scientific and technical body with recommendatory functions to consider scientific and technical issues under Article 76, the ITLOS can interpret and apply all provisions of the Convention, including Article 76.[77]

In the present case, the ITLOS observed that the parties did not disagree on the scientific aspects of the seabed and the subsoil in the Bay of Bengal, but rather they disagreed on the interpretation and the legal significance of the phrase 'natural prolongation' in Article 76(1).[78] As the question of the parties' entitlement are predominantly legal in nature, the Tribunal

[73] Ibid., 115, [393]–[394]. [74] R Churchill, n. 55, 148.
[75] *Bangladesh/Myanmar*, n. 2, 119, [406–408]. [76] Ibid., 120, [411].
[77] Busch, n. 11, 153. [78] *Bangladesh/Myanmar*, n. 2, 121, [412].

found that it could and should determine the entitlement of the parties in this particular case.[79]

In doing so, the Tribunal did not have to assume the functions of the Commission in order to decide on entitlement. The Tribunal observed that its exercise of jurisdiction could not be seen as an encroachment of the functions of the CLCS, as the settlement of disputes regarding delimitation does not preclude examination of a submission, or hinder the CLCS from issuing appropriate recommendations. In addition, there was no potential risk of encroachment upon the Area, due to the special circumstances in the Bay of Bengal, and its distance from the Area, where the international community could potentially have legitimate interests. This is where the ITLOS seemingly departs from the ICJ's *obiter dictum*, finding that there is no requirement that the CLCS has issued recommendations before the Tribunal may proceed with the delimitation beyond 200 nm. As Treves puts it, the Tribunal, although being '[part] of a collective interpretative endeavour, in which, while keeping in mind the need to ensure consistency and coherence, [. . .] contributes its grain of wisdom and its particular outlook.'[80]

However, the Tribunal acknowledged that it

> would have been hesitant to proceed with the delimitation of the area beyond 200 nautical miles had it concluded that there was significant uncertainty as to the existence of a continental margin in the area in question.[81]

This statement suggests that the relationship between the CLCS and the ITLOS may be more complex than at first sight appears from what the ITLOS says about their relationship. Although their roles and functions are separate, they are also clearly intertwined. As the ITLOS found that it could decide on entitlement in the Bay of Bengal without encroaching on or assuming the functions of the CLCS, it was unproblematic in that specific case to undertake the delimitation beyond 200 nm. However, this may not necessarily be the case for other delimitation disputes, if there are significant uncertainties as to the existence of a continental margin in the disputed area. The statement of the ITLOS suggests that in such cases, the court or tribunal may decide not to exercise its jurisdiction to delimit the shelf beyond 200 nm. Interestingly, a similar point was made already during *Canada/France*, where the court of arbitration observed that there

[79] Ibid., 121, [413]. [80] Ibid., Declaration of Judge Treves, 1 [2].
[81] Ibid., n. 2, 129, [443].

was a factual uncertainty in terms of entitlement to the continental shelf, and observed that it did not have the competence to give a pronouncement on the French claim, as the competence to consider continental shelf claims was rather vested in the CLCS under Article 76(8) and Annex II to the LOSC.[82]

12.4.2 *Territorial and Maritime Dispute (Nicaragua v. Colombia)*

12.4.2.1 Jurisdiction and Admissibility

Only months after the ITLOS's decision in *Bangladesh/Myanmar*, the ICJ issued its ruling in *Territorial and Maritime Dispute (Nicaragua v. Colombia)*, where the Court was requested to delimit the exclusive economic zone and continental shelf between Nicaragua and Colombia.[83]

In 2007, the Court had already ruled on its jurisdiction as regards the question of maritime delimitation between the states, and finding that it had jurisdiction under Article XXXI of the Pact of Bogotá to delimit the continental shelf.[84] Although Nicaragua appeared to be making a new claim during the subsequent proceeding, now including the areas beyond 200 nm, the Court found that 'the claim to an extended continental shelf falls within the dispute between the Parties relating to maritime delimitation, and cannot be said to transform the subject matter of the dispute.'[85] Upon this basis the Court decided that Nicaragua's request to the Court to delimit the continental shelf beyond 200 nm was admissible.[86]

12.4.2.2 The Distinction between Delineation and Delimitation

Next, the ICJ turned to the question if it was 'in a position to' determine the continental shelf boundary as requested by Nicaragua.[87] Nicaragua claimed that its entitlement to the continental shelf beyond 200 nm overlapped with Colombia's 200 nm continental shelf, and requested the ICJ to divide by equal parts the overlapping entitlements to a continental shelf of both parties. It is noted that due to the geographic location of the parties in the dispute, a potential delimitation line in the course of what was claimed by Nicaragua, would not only constitute a delimitation line

[82] *Canada/France*, n. 20, 1172, [79–80].
[83] *Territorial and Maritime Dispute (Nicaragua v. Colombia)* (Judgment) [2012] ICJ Rep. 624.
[84] Ibid., (Preliminary objections) [2007] ICJ Rep. 832, 869, [121].
[85] Ibid., 665, [111]. [86] Ibid., 665, [112]. [87] Ibid., 665, [113].

between the parties, but in practice constitute a seaward delineation line of Nicaragua's continental shelf beyond 200 nm. The ICJ noted that in none of the previous cases referred to by Nicaragua had the court or tribunal been requested to determine the outer limits of a continental shelf beyond 200 nm.[88] Upon this basis, the Court looked into the relationship between Article 83 and Article 76 of the LOSC.

In its argumentation before the Court, Nicaragua relied heavily on the ITLOS' ruling in *Bangladesh/Myanmar* that it had jurisdiction to decide the dispute, but the ICJ observed a number of differences between *Bangladesh/Myanmar* and *Territorial and Maritime Dispute (Nicaragua v. Colombia)*. In particular, the ICJ observed that 'ITLOS in its judgement did not [. . .] determine the outer limits of the continental shelf beyond 200 nautical miles.'[89] However, the delimitation methodology proposed by Nicaragua would require the Court to delineate the outer limits of the continental shelf, as a first step in the delimitation of the continental shelf between the states. For the purpose of determining entitlement, the Court observed that Nicaragua had made a preliminary submission to the CLCS, and the Court had been provided with the same preliminary information. However, by its own admission, preliminary information submitted to the CLCS does not meet the requirements of a submission under Article 76(8), and the Court found that the preliminary information was not sufficient for pronouncing itself in relation to the potential overlap between Nicaragua's continental margin and the shelf of the Colombian islands.[90]

In *Bangladesh/Myanmar*, both parties had already made complete submissions to the CLCS in accordance with Article 76(8), and the

> Tribunal's ruling on the delimitation of the continental shelf in accordance with Article 83 of UNCLOS, does not preclude any recommendations by the Commission as to the outer limits of the continental shelf in accordance with Article 76, paragraph 8, of the Convention.[91]

If the ICJ was to decide on the location of the outer continental shelf limits of Nicaragua and Colombia, its fear was that it would do just that; prejudice recommendations by the CLCS. The fact that Colombia was not party to the LOSC, did not relieve Nicaragua of its obligation under Article 76. Upon this basis, the ICJ reiterated the *obiter dictum* from *Nicaragua v. Honduras*, stating that

[88] Ibid., 668, [125]. [89] Ibid., 668, [125].
[90] Ibid., 669, [127–129]. [91] Ibid., 668, [125].

> any claim of continental shelf rights beyond 200 nautical miles must be in accordance with Article 76 of UNCLOS and reviewed by the Commission on the Limits of the Continental Shelf established thereunder.[92]

For this reason, the ICJ found that it was not in a position to delimit the continental shelf boundary between Nicaragua and Colombia beyond 200 nm from Nicaragua's baselines. Such a decision also seems to be in accordance with the pronouncement by ITLOS in *Bangladesh/Myanmar*, that it 'would have been hesitant to proceed with the delimitation of the area beyond 200 nautical miles had it concluded that there was significant uncertainty as to the existence of a continental margin in the area in question.'[93]

Judge ad hoc Mensah argues that the uncertain factual situation alone would have been sufficient grounds for the Court to decide not to delimit the continental shelf of Nicaragua beyond 200 nm, without any need for going into the *obiter dictum* in *Nicaragua v. Honduras*.[94] Judge Donoghue agrees that the Court did not have the required information for reaching a factual conclusion on the location of the outer limits of Nicaragua's continental shelf.[95] Accordingly, it was precluded from undertaking both a delineation and delimitation of the continental shelf beyond 200 nm due to the particular method suggested by Nicaragua and the lack of factual information.

For this reason, several of the judges in *Territorial and Maritime Dispute (Nicaragua v. Colombia)* criticized paragraph 126 of the judgment, reiterating the *obiter dictum* from *Nicaragua v. Honduras*. Judge ad Hoc Mensah observed in his declaration that although agreeing with the Court's conclusion, he did 'not believe that the reason given in paragraph 126 of the Judgment for rejecting Nicaragua's request is correct in the circumstances of this case.'[96] He observes that the application of the *obiter dictum* from *Nicaragua v. Honduras* is neither correct nor relevant in the present case, as Colombia is not a party to UNCLOS. Also, as the parties disagree on the extent to which Article 76 is part of customary law, having in mind that ICJ only decided that paragraph 1 of Article 76 is customary law, he notes that 'it is reasonable to operate under the assumption that other provisions

[92] Ibid., 669, [126]. See also *Nicaragua v. Honduras*, n. 19, 759, [319].
[93] *Bangladesh/Myanmar*, n. 2, 129, [443].
[94] *Territorial and Maritime Dispute (Nicaragua v. Colombia)*, n. 83, Declaration of Judge ad hoc Mensah, 762, [1].
[95] Ibid., Declaration of Judge ad hoc Mensah, 754, [12].
[96] Ibid., 762, [2].

of Article 76 [. . .] are not included in the provisions deemed to be applicable in this case.'[97] Mensah observes that the reference to the statement in *Nicaragua v. Honduras*, taken to its logical conclusion

> suggests that a State which is a party to UNCLOS can only assert its right to a continental shelf beyond 200 nautical miles, as against a State which is not a party to the Convention, if it follows the procedure in paragraphs 8 and 9 of Article 76 [. . .].[98]

Judge Donoghue also expressed her misgivings about the Court's reason for rejecting the delimitation beyond 200 nm and describes that she has been 'puzzled' by the quoted statement from *Nicaragua v. Honduras*.[99] She regrets that the judgment in *Territorial and Maritime Dispute (Nicaragua v. Colombia)* reaffirms the *dictum*, without acknowledging that delimitation is not precluded in every case in which a LOSC state party seeks delimitation before delineating its OCS limit, and points out that *Bangladesh/Myanmar* illustrates that in cases where the existence of the continental shelf is not in dispute and the methodology and geography do not require the Court to make any factual findings regarding the OCS limits, the exercise of delimitation and delineation may proceed in parallel, regardless of whether a state has established its OCS limits in accordance with Article 76(8).[100] Another weakness of the Court's decision in *Territorial and Maritime Dispute (Nicaragua v. Colombia)*, Judge Donoghue notes, is that the Court even extended the reasoning from *Nicaragua v. Honduras* to also include non-parties of the LOSC.[101]

Upon this basis, it is timely to raise the question if the ICJ's statement included in paragraph 126 of the judgment was necessary for the ICJ to reach its conclusion, or if it should be considered another *obiter dictum*, similar to that in *Nicaragua v. Honduras*. If it is concluded that the statement in paragraph 126 in *Territorial and Maritime Dispute (Nicaragua v. Colombia)* is *not* intended as an *obiter dictum*, but rather a necessary premise for the ICJ' decision, it can be argued that the latter decision deviates from *Bangladesh/Myanmar*, where ITLOS found that recommendations by the CLCS were *not* a prerequisite for delimiting the continental shelf beyond 200 nm in situations where the court or tribunal could pronounce itself on entitlement without encroaching on the functions of the CLCS.[102]

[97] Ibid. [98] Ibid., 764, [6]. [99] Ibid., 758, [25]. See also Magnusson, n. 49, 256–257.
[100] Ibid. [101] Ibid., 758, [26]. [102] Magnusson, n. 49, 258.

As Judge Donoghue and Judge ad hoc Mensah quite accurately point out, it does not seem that the reference to the *obiter dictum* from *Nicaragua v. Honduras* in paragraph 126, was necessary for the Court to reach its decision. Rather, in line with the reasoning provided by ITLOS in *Bangladesh/Myanmar*, the considerable factual uncertainly in *Territorial and Maritime Dispute (Nicaragua v. Colombia)* could be sufficient basis for the Court to decide not to delimit the shelf beyond 200 nm. The fact that Nicaragua had only made a preliminary submission to the CLCS at the time of proceedings supports that approach. Another argument pulling in the same direction is the fact that a delimitation of the continental shelf would encroach upon the function of the CLCS, as the method suggested by Nicaragua presupposes the delineation of its OCS limit. These arguments alone suggest that the ICJ was not in a position to delimit the shelf beyond 200 nm in *Territorial and Maritime Dispute (Nicaragua v. Colombia)*. On this basis, this author tends to agree with Donoghue and Mensah that the reference to the *obiter dictum* seems unnecessary for the Court's decision. But does this mean that paragraph 126 of *Territorial and Maritime Dispute (Nicaragua v. Colombia)* constitutes another *dictum* of the Court? The core of the criticism towards paragraph 126 is that it simply repeats the *dictum*, without providing any nuance as to how it should be interpreted, as done by ITLOS in Bangladesh/Myanmar. This is a clear weakness of the judgment issued by the ICJ in *Territorial and Maritime Dispute (Nicaragua v. Colombia)*, and contributes to blur the predictability and transparency in maritime delimitation beyond 200 nm.

The critique of Donoghue and Mensah on the Article 76 obligation as an obligation also towards non-parties to the LOSC, is in the opinion of this author not a great drawback in the judgment. In fact, this may partially provide an explanation as to why the Court chose to include the *dictum* in the first place. The Court rules that the fact that Colombia is not party to the LOSC does not relieve Nicaragua from its obligation to make a submission to the CLCS in accordance with Article 76. It is argued, that such a reminder is called for, and that states non-parties to the LOSC enjoy the same privilege as states parties to invoke the consequences of Rule 46 and Annex I of the RoP in case of ongoing land or maritime disputes with a state party to the LOSC. Upon the 2013 continental shelf submission by Nicaragua, Colombia submitted several *notes verbales* to the CLCS, requesting the CLCS not to consider the submission by Nicaragua until the delimitation dispute has been settled. The CLCS accepted the *note verbale* by Colombia.[103] The fact that Colombia is not party to the LOSC does not relieve Nicaragua from its obligations under Article 76 or Annex II to the LOSC.

12.4.3 *Bangladesh v. India*

12.4.3.1 Jurisdiction *Ratione Materiae* of the Arbitral Tribunal

In October 2009, Bangladesh requested an arbitral tribunal to

> delimit [. . .] the maritime boundary between Bangladesh and India in the Bay of Bengal, in the territorial sea, the EEZ, and the continental shelf, including the portion of the continental shelf pertaining to Bangladesh that lies more than 200 nautical miles from the baselines [. . .].[104]

Both parties agreed that the tribunal had jurisdiction to delimit the continental shelf beyond 200 nm.[105] *Bangladesh v. India* resembles *Bangladesh/Myanmar* in many respects, as they both concern a delimitation in the Bay of Bengal, and the parties in both disputes have made complete submissions to the CLCS in accordance with Article 76(8).[106] For that purpose, the entire line of argument of the tribunal need not be repeated in detail.

12.4.3.2 The Distinction between Delineation and Delimitation

Although the parties agreed on the tribunal's jurisdiction, the tribunal devoted a considerable amount of paragraphs to discussing if there was any reason why it should refrain from exercising such jurisdiction.[107] Noting that the jurisprudence on the topic was fairly limited, the tribunal

[103] *Note verbale* of the Ministry of Foreign Affairs of Colombia to the Secretary-General of the United Nations (24 September 2013) in response to the submission by Nicaragua (Submission to the Commission on the Limits of the Continental Shelf pursuant to Art. 76, para. 8 of the United Nations Convention on the Law of the Sea, 1982, Republic de Nicaragua, Executive summary, 24 June 2013) (Subm.no. 66); and *Note verbale* of the representatives of the Government of Colombia, Costa Rica, and Panama to the Secretary-General of the United Nations (5 February 29014) in response to the submission by Nicaragua (Submission to the Commission on the Limits of the Continental Shelf pursuant to Art. 76, para. 8 of the United Nations Convention on the Law of the Sea, 1982, Republic de Nicaragua, Executive summary, 24 June 2013) (Subm.no. 66); see also Busch, n. 11, 292.

[104] *In the Matter of the Bay of Bengal Maritime Boundary (Bangladesh v. India)* (Award) [2014] 20 [74].

[105] Ibid., 1, [2]. [106] Ibid. [107] Ibid., 20–23, [74–83].

in particular took note of *Barbados v. Trinidad and Tobago*, *Bangladesh/Myanmar* and *Territorial and Maritime Dispute (Nicaragua v. Colombia)*.

The tribunal briefly observed that the parties to the dispute had yet to delineate the outer limits of their continental shelf beyond 200 nm in accordance with Article 76, but recalled *Bangladesh/Myanmar* in which it was observed that this alone did not provide grounds for the tribunal to refrain from exercising its jurisdiction.[108]

In *Bangladesh v. India*, both parties to the dispute had made a submission to the CLCS in accordance with Article 76(8). India did not object to the CLCS's consideration of Bangladesh's submission, but Bangladesh, on the other hand, had not given its consent to the consideration of India's submission by the CLCS.[109] The tribunal therefore found itself in the same position as the ITLOS in *Bangladesh/Myanmar.* A refusal to delimit the continental shelf beyond 200 nm would leave the continental shelf limits unresolved, unless the parties were able to reach an agreement. Taking into account the many rounds of unsuccessful negotiations between the parties, the tribunal did not see such an agreement as likely.[110] Upon this basis, the tribunal found that it could and should exercise its jurisdiction to delimit the overlapping continental shelves beyond 200 nm.[111]

12.4.3.3 Entitlement as a Prerequisite for Delimitation

India and Bangladesh agreed they have entitlements beyond 200 nm in the Bay of Bengal. The tribunal observed that '[t]he Convention assigns to different bodies functions regarding decisions on the entitlement of coastal States to the continental shelf beyond 200 nm.'[112] Although the CLCS is ascribed the main function to consider OCS entitlement, courts and tribunals are not entirely prevented from considering the entitlement of the parties to the continental shelf, if the factual situation comes across as clear and is undisputed. Given the sedimentary thickness in the Bay of Bengal, the tribunal was in no doubt that the parties' entitlement to the continental shelf continued beyond 200 nm, and would satisfy the criteria contained in Article 76(4)–(5). The tribunal accordingly reached the same result as the ITLOS in *Bangladesh/Myanmar*.[113]

The question may be raised if the two Bay of Bengal cases will serve as a precedent for future cases concerning maritime delimitation beyond 200 nm, as they both relate to a very limited and unique geographic area.

[108] Ibid., 21, [76]. [109] Ibid., 22, [81]. [110] Ibid., 22, [82].
[111] Ibid., 23, [83]. [112] *Bangladesh v. India*, n. 104, 21, [78–79].
[113] Ibid., 21, [76–82]; see also *Bangladesh/Myanmar*, n. 2, 109, [369–394].

The ITLOS clearly indicated that its decision is not necessarily only relevant to Bay of Bengal, and it contributes new interpretative perspectives on the relationship between Article 76 and 83, and on the relationship between the CLCS and courts and tribunals. It is submitted that the main contribution of the Bay of Bengal judgments are first and foremost that the determination of whether a court or tribunal should exercise its jurisdiction to delimit the continental shelf depends on the procedural and substantive circumstances of each case, and that the obiter dictum in *Nicaragua v. Honduras* does not apply across the board.[114] Second, if there is significant uncertainty as to the existence of a continental margin, and hence also the overlapping entitlement of the parties in the area subject to dispute, a court or tribunal will most likely to be hesitant to proceed with the delimitation beyond 200 nm, as such consideration would then be hypothetical.

12.4.4 Continental Shelf *(*Nicaragua v. Colombia*) (Preliminary objections)*

After having finalized its submission to the CLCS, Nicaragua instituted proceedings against Colombia in the dispute concerning the delimitation of the continental shelf beyond 200 nm between Nicaragua and Colombia, requesting the Court to determine 'the precise course of the boundary of the continental shelf between Nicaragua and Colombia in accordance with the principles and rules of international law.'[115]

Colombia raised five preliminary objections to the jurisdiction of the Court and the admissibility of Nicaragua's application, of which the fifth and final objection is relevant for this chapter.[116] In that final objection, Colombia asserted that the request to the ICJ to determine a delimitation line between Nicaragua and Colombia beyond 200 nm was inadmissible, since the CLCS had 'not made recommendations to Nicaragua with respect to whether, and if so how far, Nicaragua's claimed

[114] *Bangladesh/Myanmar*, n. 2, 113, [384].

[115] *Continental Shelf (Nicaragua v. Colombia)* (Application instituting proceedings) [2013] ICJ (16 September 2013), [2]. In addition, Nicaragua requested the Court to adjudge and declare 'the Principles and rules of international law that determine the rights and duties of the two States in relation to the area of overlapping continental shelf claims and the use of its resources, pending the delimitation of the maritime boundary between them beyond 200 nautical miles from Nicaragua's coast.' Only the first request is relevant in the context of this chapter. Ibid., [2].

[116] *Continental Shelf (Nicaragua v. Colombia)* (Preliminary objections) [2016] ICJ Rep. 1, 34 [15].

outer continental shelf extends beyond 200 nautical miles.'[117] Colombia argued that a state cannot establish a continental shelf without a valid entitlement. Although the potentiality of such entitlement is confirmed in Article 76(1), Colombia, with reference to the *obiter dictum* in *Nicaragua v. Honduras* and the Court's ruling in *Territorial and Maritime Dispute (Nicaragua v. Colombia)*, argued that

> [t]he recommendations of the CLCS is thus the prerequisite for transforming an inherent but inchoate right into an entitlement whose external limits is 'final and binding' under Article 76(8) and opposable *ergo omnes*.[118]

The Court acknowledged that it had already established in *Territorial and Maritime Dispute (Nicaragua v. Colombia)* that Nicaragua was under an obligation to make a submission to the CLCS pursuant to Article 76(8), and that this was a prerequisite for the delimitation beyond 200 nm by the Court.[119] As Nicaragua seven months after the 2012 Judgment made a complete submission to the CLCS for the southwestern part of the Caribbean Sea, covering the disputed area, the ICJ observed that it must at this stage 'determine whether a *recommendation* made by the CLCS [...] is a prerequisite in order for the Court to be able entertain the Application filed by Nicaragua in 2013.'[120] The Court observed that the role of the CLCS only relates to the delineation of the outer limits of the continental shelf, and not its delimitation. This is confirmed by the saving clauses included in Article 76(10) and Article 9 of Annex II to the LOSC, and is also expressed through Rule 46 and Annex I to the RoP of the CLCS. The Court maintained that the CLCS procedure is distinct from the delimitation of the continental shelf, which is rather governed by Article 83, and effected either by agreement between the states concerned, or by recourse to dispute settlement procedures.[121] Upon this basis, the Court found that delimitation can be undertaken independently of the CLCS's recommendations.

It accordingly seems that the ICJ departed from its *obiter dictum* in *Nicaragua v. Honduras*. Rather, the ICJ followed the interpretation provided by ITLOS and the Annex VII arbitral tribunal in the Bay of Bengal cases, adjusting the scope of the *dictum*. However, the factual basis in the Bay of Bengal cases is very different from that in *Continental Shelf (Nicaragua v. Colombia)*. Although Nicaragua has made a complete

[117] Ibid., 12, [15].
[118] *Continental Shelf (Nicaragua v. Colombia)* (Preliminary Objections of the Republic of Colombia, vol. 1) [2014] ICJ (14 August 2014), 162 [7.11] (footnote omitted).
[119] Ibid., n. 116, 36, [105]. [120] Ibid., 36, [106] (emphasis added). [121] Ibid., 37, [112].

submission to the CLCS in accordance with Article 76(8), factual uncertainty may still be present, and if the ICJ is to undertake delimitation in accordance with the method as provided by Nicaragua during *Territorial and maritime Dispute (Nicaragua v. Colombia)*, the exercise of jurisdiction may constitute an encroachment on the functions of the CLCS.[122] If delimitation requires the Court to undertake an in-depth assessment of the parties' entitlement to the continental shelf, it is likely that the Court in the merits phase of the dispute will desist from delimiting the continental shelf beyond 200 nm from the coast of Nicaragua. In that connection, it remains to be seen how the Court will apply 'significant uncertainty test' formulated by the ITLOS in *Bangladesh/Myanmar*.

Another interesting aspect the Court will have to consider is the position of Colombia as a non-party to the LOSC, and whether its entitlement within 200 nm trumps the potential entitlement of Nicaragua beyond 200 nm. In addition, it may be required to decide on the entitlement of Colombia to the continental shelf beyond 200 nm. As Colombia as a non-party to the LOSC is excluded from making a submission to the CLCS, such consideration would presumably not encroach upon the functions of the CLCS.

12.4.5 Somalia v. Kenya *(Preliminary Objections)*

In *Somalia v. Kenya*,[123] the ICJ had to consider whether the parties through the Memorandum of Understanding (hereinafter the MOU) had agreed on a temporal order where the delineation process it the CLCS were to precede the delimitation between the parties, and if this agreement constituted 'other methods' of settlement of their maritime boundary dispute.[124] Kenya asserted that Somalia's application was inadmissible as paragraph 6 of the MOU prohibited delimitation prior to the CLCS' recommendations.[125] Paragraph 6 reads as follows:

[122] However, it may be noted that the Court following its 2012 Judgment will also have to delimit a continental shelf boundary between Nicaragua and Colombia's islands, which does not require determining the outer limits of Nicaragua's continental shelf.

[123] *Somalia v. Kenya* (Preliminary Objections) [2017] ICJ Rep. 1.

[124] The Memorandum of Understanding (MOU) is an agreement negotiated between Somalia and Kenya, granting each other no-objection in respect of submissions on the continental shelf beyond 200 nm to the CLCS, in accordance with Rule 46 and Para. 5(a) of Annex I to the CLCS RoP. The full text of the MOU is available at www.innercitypress.com/los2somalia.pdf.

[125] *Somalia v. Kenya*, n. 123, 22, [52–53].

> The delimitation of maritime boundaries in the areas under dispute, including the delimitation of the continental shelf beyond 200 nautical miles, *shall* be agreed between the two coastal States on the basis of international law *after* the Commission has concluded its examination of the separate submissions made by each of the two coastal States and made its recommendations to two coastal States [. . .].[126]

Somalia's turning to the Court clearly indicated another view, and Somalia observed that 'the MOU cannot be considered as an 'agreement not to agree' in the sense that '[i]t would provide for negotiation of the maritime boundary dispute, but only so long as *no* agreement was *reached*.'[127] Rather, Somalia argued, the wording of paragraph 6 only means that the limit cannot be finalized because its seaward terminus can only be fixed after the CLCS has issued its recommendations.[128] Therefore, neither the parties nor the Court have to wait for the CLCS' recommendations before proceeding to a delimitation.[129]

The ICJ observed that paragraph 6 of the MOU is:

> at the heart of the first preliminary objection currently under consideration. It is, however, difficult to understand that paragraph without a prior analysis of the text of the MOU as a whole, which provides the context in which any particular paragraph should be interpreted and gives insight into the object and purpose of the MOU.[130]

After having analysed the MOU as a whole,[131] the Court turned to a more explicit analysis of paragraph 6, by means of defining the maritime zones to which the paragraph is applicable. The Court also observed that according to Article 31 (3)(c) of the Vienna Convention, any relevant rules of international law should be taken into account, together with context.[132]

The ICJ noted that there are similarities in language between Article 83 of the LOSC and paragraph 6 of the MOU, and considered it reasonable to read the latter in light of the former. The similarity in text allegedly suggests that the parties intended to acknowledge the usual approach to delimitation under Article 83, namely engaging in negotiations with the purpose of reaching an agreement, and not to prescribe a method of dispute settlement.[133] Having discussed Article 83, the ICJ observes that 'the text of the sixth paragraph of the MOU reflects that of Article 83.'[134]

[126] Ibid., 17, [37] (emphasis added). [127] Ibid., 24, [61] (original emphasis).
[128] Ibid., 25, [61]. [129] Ibid. [130] Ibid., 26, [65]. [131] Ibid., 25–30.
[132] Ibid., 32, [89]. [133] Ibid., 35, [97]. [134] Ibid.

In addition, the ICJ noted that the MOU repeatedly distinguished between delineation and delimitation, and maintained that the delineation is without prejudice to delimitation, implying that delimitation can be undertaken independently of CLCS's recommendations, consistently with the jurisprudence of the Court.[135] Upon this basis, the Court concludes that the text of paragraph 6 could not have been intended to establish a method of dispute settlement, and therefore it does not bind the parties to await the CLCS's recommendations, nor does it obligate the parties to settle their boundary dispute through a particular method of settlement.[136]

The decision that delineation does not precede delimitation and that there is no temporal relationship between the two, is in line with recent jurisprudence. However, one may question if the Court's interpretation of the content of paragraph 6 reflects the 'ordinary meaning' of the parties to the MOU In his dissenting opinion, Judge Bennouna strongly criticizes the methodology of the Court, observing that the Court has inverted the order set out in Article 31 of the Vienna Convention, analysing the context of paragraph 6, before even considering the ordinary meaning to be given to the terms in the treaty.[137] Judge Bennouna asserts that the Court should have begun with the terms whose meaning posed difficulties and then, when necessary, placed those terms in their context. The inverted reasoning allegedly leads the ICJ to find that the purpose of the MOU is to enable the CLCS to consider the submissions by Kenya and Somalia, and this creates the basis for the Court's examination of paragraph 6.[138] Bennouna is also very critical to the Court's comparison of paragraph 6 and Article 83 of the LOSC, observing that

> the Court ultimately gives a different meaning to the terms of the sixth paragraph, one which is at odds with their ordinary meaning. The Court considers that 'the text of the sixth paragraph of the MOU reflects that of Article 83 [...],' [...]. And thus, as if by magic, the obligation, agreed on in this paragraph, to negotiate and conclude a maritime delimitation agreement in the area in dispute once the CLCS has made it[s] recommendations, vanishes.[139]

[135] Ibid., 35, [97]. See also *Continental Shelf (Nicaragua v. Colombia)* n. 116, 36, [114].

[136] *Somalia v. Kenya*, n. 123, 35, [98].

[137] Ibid., Dissenting Opinion Judge Bennouna, 2.

[138] Ibid. See also ibid., 28 [75].

[139] Ibid., Dissenting Opinion Judge Bennouna, 4. See also 34 [97]. Note also joint declaration by Judges Gaja and Crawford, observing that the plain language of Para. 6, and in particular the word 'shall,' suggests that the parties have an obligation to agree on maritime

This author certainly shares the concern of Judge Bennouna concerning to the Court's method of interpretation of paragraph 6 of the MOU. Although not being entirely convinced that paragraph 6 of the MOU constitutes an agreed method of dispute settlement between Kenya and Somalia, this author is neither convinced by the Court's reasoning for the opposite. It is quite clear that paragraph 6 says *something* on when and how the limits shall be decided, and this is hardly reflected in the Court's decision. A more traditional method of interpretation, with a stronger focus on ordinary meaning in accordance with Article 31 of the Vienna Convention would presumably have given a more accurate picture of the parties' intent in concluding the MOU.

12.5 Concluding Remarks

Courts and tribunals have considered the relationship between the procedure of delineating the outer limits of the continental shelf in accordance with Article 76, involving the CLCS, and the delimitation of the continental shelf beyond 200 nm between neighbouring states on a limited number of occasions.

The *France/Canada* award suggests that delimitation cannot be undertaken until the coastal state has established its continental shelf limits in accordance with Article 76. Similarly, the ICJ's *obiter dictum* in *Nicaragua v. Honduras* indicates that the boundary the Court had established should not be interpreted as extending beyond the 200 nm limit. Continental shelf rights beyond 200 nm had to be reviewed by the CLCS.

In *Newfoundland and Labrador/Nova Scotia* and *Barbados v. Trinidad and Tobago*, the tribunals considered that they could address the delimitation beyond 200 nm. However, in the latter case, the tribunal delimited a boundary that ended at the 200 nm limit and the previously agreed upon boundary between Trinidad and Tobago and Venezuela, and in the former, the arbitral tribunal maintained that its decision involving two Canadian provinces would not be opposable to the international process for the determination of OCS limits.

boundaries after the CLCS has issued its recommendations. In para. 6, 'the Parties effectively agreed that the dispute would not be ripe for resolution of any kind until after this date' (ibid., Joint Declaration by Judges Gaja and Crawford, 2 [8]). However, according to Gaja and Crawford, the following conduct of the parties by means of negotiations of the maritime boundaries between the parties, have modified the content of para. 6 (ibid., 2 [10]).

In *Bangladesh/Myanmar* and *Bangladesh v. India*, the ITLOS and an arbitral tribunal observed that the parties had made a full submission to the CLCS in accordance with Article 76(8) and found that they could proceed with the delimitation beyond 200 nm in the absence of CLCS recommendations, without encroaching upon the CLCS functions, as there was no factual uncertainty relating to the existence of a continental margin in the disputed area. However, the tribunals also pointed out that they might have decided otherwise if there would have been significant uncertainty as to the existence of a continental margin in the area in question. Accordingly, the Bay of Bengal cases contributed to circumscribe the *obiter dictum* of the ICJ in *Nicaragua v. Honduras*.

In *Continental Shelf (Nicaragua v. Colombia)*, the ICJ concluded, concurring with *Bangladesh/Myanmar* and *Bangladesh v. India*, that there was no requirement for the CLCS to have reviewed the submission and issued its recommendations in accordance with Article 76(8) before a court or tribunal could undertake a delimitation of the continental shelf. Similarly, the lack of CLCS recommendations was not considered an obstacle to the Court's jurisdiction in *Somalia v. Kenya*, however bearing in mind that this decision was based on a more specific agreement between the parties, and not the LOSC.

Summarizing the jurisprudence, it does not seem to reveal an absolute uniformity on how courts and tribunals deal with the relationship between delimitation of the continental shelf beyond 200 nm and the procedure to determine the outer limits of the continental shelf contained in Article 76 of the LOSC. There may be several explanations for this. The jurisprudence on continental shelf delimitation beyond 200 nm is somewhat sparse, with eight cases over the past twenty-four years. The limited number of cases, with a number of different variables, may suggest that they are not very suitable for comparison. However, as pointed out in the foregoing analysis, there are clear differences that cannot easily be explained away by the factual circumstances of each case.

Notably, the most recent jurisprudence seems to be arriving at a more uniform interpretation of the relationship between Articles 76 and 83; between the functions of the CLCS on the one hand and the functions of courts and tribunals on the other. It now seems well established that there exists no requirement for the coastal state to establish its OCS limits in accordance with Article 76(8) prior to the delimitation of the continental shelf beyond 200 nm. A few common factors seem to affect the courts' and tribunals' willingness to undertake delimitation beyond 200 nm. One of these relates to the factual certainty concerning continental shelf entitlement in the disputed area. Courts and tribunals to date seem to have been reluctant to encroach upon the function of the CLCS involved in its consideration of submissions of coastal states, if there are significant uncertainties as to the extent of entitlement of the parties to the dispute. Another factor that has been taken into account in the Bay of Bengal cases is the absence of a prospect of the parties settling the dispute between them by other means. Where the parties have blocked the CLCS's consideration of each other's continental shelf submissions, they are left in an unfortunate deadlock if a court or tribunal would refuse to delimit the continental shelf beyond 200 nm between them.

13

The Delimitation of the Continental Shelf beyond 200 nm

Substantive Issues

ØYSTEIN JENSEN

13.1 Introduction

Until recently, dispute settlement relating to continental shelf delimitation almost exclusively concerned the delimitation of the continental shelf within 200 nm from the territorial sea baselines. Thus the 2012 judgment of the International Tribunal for the Law of the Sea (ITLOS) in *Bangladesh/Myanmar*[1] broke new legal ground. Despite being the sixteenth case to be heard by the ITLOS, this was only the second case in which the Tribunal gave a judgment on the merits of a dispute,[2] and the first that concerned maritime boundary delimitation. The *Bangladesh/Myanmar* case was also the first instance in which an international court or tribunal delimited a continental shelf boundary beyond 200 nm and considered the issue of 'grey zones.'[3]

[1] *Delimitation of the Maritime Boundary between Bangladesh and Myanmar in the Bay of Bengal (Bangladesh v. Myanmar)* (Judgment) [2012] ITLOS Rep. 4, [342]–[349]. Text of the judgment retrieved from the ITLOS website (www.itlos.org), 10 April 2016. For a commentary, see R. Churchill, 'The Bangladesh/Myanmar Case: Continuity and Novelty in the Law of Maritime Boundary Delimitation,' (2012) 1 *Cambridge Journal of International and Comparative Law* 137; and A. G. Oude Elferink, 'ITLOS's Approach to the Delimitation of the Continental Shelf beyond 200 Nautical Miles in the Bangladesh/Myanmar Case: Theoretical and Practical Difficulties,' in R. Wolfrum, M. Seršić, and T. Šošić (eds.), *Contemporary Developments in International Law – Essays in Honour of Budislav Vukas* (Brill/Nijhoff Leiden 2015) 230.

[2] The other being *The M/V 'Saiga' (No. 2) (St. Vincent v. Guinea)* (Judgment) [1998] 117 ILR 111.

[3] A 'grey zone' is an area on one side of a continental shelf boundary beyond 200 nm from the state on that side of the boundary, but within 200 nm of the state on the other side of the boundary. See further Section 13.3.3.

The second – and to date the last – time a tribunal delimited a continental shelf boundary beyond 200 nm and considered the issue of grey zones is the *Bangladesh v. India*,[4] rendered by an arbitral tribunal established under Annex VII of the United Nations Convention on the Law of the Sea (LOSC)[5] on 7 July 2014. Taken together with the *Bangladesh/Myanmar* case, the decisions not only end many years of uncertainty as to the allocation of maritime entitlements within the Bay of Bengal, but will also be important for future cases dealing with the delimitation of the continental shelf beyond 200 nm. But while the decisions have contributed to greater certainty in some respects, several substantive legal uncertainties remain.

This chapter highlights key substantive legal issues arising from the Bay of Bengal cases and examines what this jurisprudence may mean for future disputes relating to the delimitation of the continental shelf beyond 200 nm. It begins by providing an overview of case law dealing with the delimitation of the continental shelf beyond 200 nm. This is followed by a section that examines the approach taken by the judiciary specifically as it relates to the delimitation of the continental shelf beyond 200 nm. Section 13.4 assesses this approach, particularly as pertaining to the relationship between entitlement and delimitation, the method of delimitation and the concept of grey zones. The chapter concludes with a summation of the main points.

13.2 The Case Law Relating to the Delimitation of Continental

13.2.1 Bangladesh/Myanmar

The 2012 *Bangladesh/Myanmar* case was the first time an international tribunal actually performed the delimitation of continental shelf areas beyond 200 nm.[6] Pursuant to Annex VII of the LOSC, Bangladesh

[4] *In the Matter of the Bay of Bengal Maritime Boundary Arbitration (Bangladesh v. India)* (Award) [2014]. Text of the judgment retrieved from the website of the Permanent court of Arbitration (www.pca-cpa.org/showpage.asp?pag_id=1376). For a comment on the case, see D. Anderson, 'Bay of Bengal Maritime Boundary (Bangladesh *v.* India),' (2015) 105 *American Journal of International Law* 146, and R. Churchill, 'Dispute Settlement in the Law of the Sea: Survey for 2014,' (2015) 13 *International Journal of Marine and Coastal Law* 585, 608–617.

[5] Adopted 10 December 1982, entered into force 16 November 1994, 1833 UNTS 397.

[6] In *Case Concerning Delimitation of Maritime Areas between Canada and France*, the arbitral tribunal took the view that it could not delimit the continental shelf boundary beyond 200 nm, [1992] 31 ILM 1145, 1171–1172. In the judgment of the International Court of Justice (ICJ) relating to the territorial and maritime dispute between Nicaragua and Colombia, the Court also declined to delimit the continental shelf beyond 200 nm (*Territorial and*

commenced arbitral proceedings in October 2009.[7] A few weeks later Myanmar lodged a Declaration under the LOSC to accept the jurisdiction of the ITLOS to hear the dispute. Bangladesh then withdrew the separate arbitral proceedings and submitted a similar Declaration accepting the jurisdiction of the ITLOS on 12 December 2010.[8]

There was agreement between the parties that the territorial sea, the exclusive economic zone (EEZ) and the continental shelf *within* 200 nm should be delimited by the ITLOS. However, the parties disagreed as to whether the ITLOS had jurisdiction to delimit the continental shelf *beyond* 200 nm, and if so, whether it should exercise that jurisdiction.[9] The ITLOS found to have jurisdiction also with respect to the delimitation of the continental shelf beyond 200 nm and on 14 March 2012, it issued its judgment, delimiting the maritime boundary between Bangladesh and Myanmar in the Bay of Bengal with respect to the territorial sea, the EEZ, and the continental shelf – within and beyond 200 nm.

13.2.2 *Bangladesh v. India*

The second case involving an actual delimitation of continental shelf areas beyond 200 nm was the *Bangladesh v. India* award. On 8 October 2009,

Maritime Dispute (Nicaragua v. Colombia) (Judgment) [2012] ICJ Rep. 624). And while the Arbitral Tribunal in the case between Barbados and Trinidad and Tobago of 11 April 2006 concluded that it had jurisdiction to decide upon the delimitation of a maritime boundary in relation to the part of the continental shelf extending beyond 200 nm, in practice it did not do so because the single maritime boundary which the Tribunal determined was such that, as between the Parties, it did not extend beyond 200 nm (*Arbitration between Barbados and the Republic of Trinidad and Tobago* [2006] 27 UNRIAA, 147, 209, [217], [242], [368]). Note also in *Newfoundland and Labrador/Nova Scotia* [2002] 128 ILR 504, decided by a three-member arbitral tribunal established in order to determine the maritime boundary between the two Canadian provinces of Nova Scotia, and Newfoundland and Labrador. According to the Tribunal's Terms of Reference the Arbitral Tribunal was established to treat the provinces as sovereign states and thus to apply principles of international maritime boundary law in order to determine the boundary dividing their respective maritime entitlements as defined under domestic legislation, including the seabed beyond 200 nm. Thus the Tribunal's award basically amounted to a regular inter-state continental shelf delimitation. See further J. Currie, 'Maritime Boundary Delimitation in a Federal Domestic Setting: The Newfoundland and Labrador v. Nova Scotia Arbitration,' (2004) 17 *Leiden Journal of International Law* 155. For more detail on these cases, see Chapter 12 of this volume.

[7] *Bangladesh/Myanmar*, n. 1, [39].

[8] For an extensive discussion of the background of the case, see M. Shah Alam and A. Al Faruque, 'The Problem of Delimitation of Bangladesh's Maritime Boundaries with India and Myanmar: Prospects for a Solution,' (2010) 25 *International Journal of Marine and Coastal Law* 405.

[9] See further Chapter 12 of this volume.

Bangladesh initiated arbitral proceedings against India, pursuant to Article 287 and in accordance with LOSC Annex VII. Bangladesh requested the tribunal to delimit, in accordance with the principles and rules set forth in the LOSC, the maritime boundary between Bangladesh and India in the Bay of Bengal with respect to the territorial sea, the EEZ, and the continental shelf, including the portion of the continental shelf pertaining to Bangladesh and India that lies more than 200 nm from the territorial sea baselines.[10]

The Arbitral Tribunal was established pursuant to Article 3 of Annex VII to the LOSC. In accordance with subparagraph (a) of Article 3 of Annex VII, the tribunal would include five members, three of whom were serving as ITLOS judges in the Bangladesh/Myanmar case. Similar to the *Bangladesh/Myanmar* case, the tribunal decided unanimously that it had jurisdiction to delimit the continental shelf beyond 200 nm. While the parties agreed that both had entitlements to the continental shelf beyond 200 nm, each disagreed with the delimitation lines proposed by the other, and, accordingly, the appropriate method for delimiting the continental shelf beyond 200 nm.

13.3 Approaches to the Delimitation of the Continental Shelf beyond 200 nm

13.3.1 Entitlement and Delimitation

The first question that both the ITLOS and the Arbitral Tribunal addressed with respect to the delimitation of the continental shelf beyond 200 nm was whether the coastal states in question had entitlements to that part of the continental shelf. In the *Bangladesh v. India* arbitration, this point was not much debated: the parties agreed that they both had entitlements to the continental shelf beyond 200 nm, and both had made submissions to the Commission on the Limits of the Continental Shelf (CLCS) to that effect.[11]

However, the question of entitlement posed challenging issues for the ITLOS in *Bangladesh/Myanmar*. The first step in any delimitation, the Tribunal noted, was to determine 'whether there are entitlements and whether they overlap.'[12] Being parties to the LOSC, Bangladesh and Myanmar agreed that the applicable law was the Convention and other rules of international law not incompatible with it.[13] LOSC Article 83 thus

[10] *Bangladesh v. India*, n. 4, [2]. [11] Ibid., [438].
[12] *Bangladesh/Myanmar*, n. 1, [397]. [13] Ibid., [53].

established the law applicable to the delimitation of the continental shelf. In determining entitlement to the continental shelf beyond 200 nm, however, Article 76 of the LOSC had to be taken into consideration. The Tribunal emphasized:

> While entitlement and delimitation are two distinct concepts addressed respectively in articles 76 and 83 of the Convention, they are interrelated. The Parties also recognize the interrelationship between entitlement and delimitation. Bangladesh states that '[t]he Tribunal must answer this question before it can delimit the shelf: does either Party have an entitlement to a continental shelf beyond 200 [nm]?' Likewise, Myanmar observes that 'the determination of the entitlements of both States to a continental shelf beyond 200 [nm] and their respective extent is a prerequisite for any delimitation.'[14]

Considering these positions of the parties, the Tribunal addressed the main point disputed by Bangladesh and Myanmar: whether or not they had any entitlement to the continental shelf beyond 200 nm. The ITLOS divided this analysis into a four-step approach. *First*, the Tribunal dealt with the question of whether it could and should determine the entitlements of the parties to an extended continental shelf. Bangladesh argued that the Tribunal was required to decide on the question of the parties' entitlements to the continental shelf beyond 200 nm.[15] Myanmar, by contrast, argued that the ITLOS did not need to, and in fact could not, deal with the issue of the entitlement of Bangladesh or of Myanmar to an extended continental shelf. In the view of Myanmar, determination of continental shelf entitlements beyond 200 nm and their respective extent was a prerequisite for any delimitation, in which the CLCS plays a crucial role.[16] However, the ITLOS noted that, since the question of the parties' entitlement to a continental shelf beyond 200 nm in the Bay of Bengal raised issues that were predominantly legal in nature, it could and should determine the entitlements of the parties.[17]

Second, the Tribunal considered the positions of the parties regarding entitlements. Interestingly, each party argued that it alone was entitled to the entire area of the continental shelf beyond 200 nm. Bangladesh, by reason of the significant geological discontinuity that divides the Burma plate from the Indian plate, argued that Myanmar was not entitled to an extended continental shelf in any of the seabed areas.[18] However, Myanmar claimed, first, that it indeed had a continental shelf extending beyond 200 nm, referring to the 'Gardiner formula,' embodied in LOSC

[14] Ibid., [398.] [15] Ibid., [403]. [16] Ibid., [405]. [17] Ibid., [413]. [18] Ibid., [419].

Article 76, paragraph 4(a)(i), and under which Myanmar had demonstrated that the outer edge of its continental margin was located well beyond 200 nm. Myanmar also argued that it was Bangladesh that did not have a continental shelf beyond 200 nm, because the *delimitation* of the continental shelf between them would end well before reaching the 200 nm limit measured from the baselines of both states. Thus, according to Myanmar, the issue was not about Bangladesh not having a natural prolongation beyond 200 nm, but rather that the question of the delimitation of the continental shelf beyond 200 nm had no practical relevance and did not need to be considered further by the ITLOS.[19]

Third, when the Tribunal analysed the meaning of natural prolongation, it basically found that Bangladesh's contention was incorrect. The reasoning of the Tribunal on this point merits closer attention. The Tribunal did not enter into an analysis of the said geological discontinuity, simply stating that it found 'it difficult to accept that natural prolongation referred to in Article 76, paragraph 1, constitutes a separate and independent criterion a coastal State must satisfy in order to be entitled to a continental shelf beyond 200 nm.'[20] What was decisive for the Tribunal was to define the precise outer limits of the continental shelf; apparently, according to the Tribunal, entitlement to a continental shelf beyond 200 nm should be determined *exclusively* by reference to the outer edge of the continental margin, to be ascertained in accordance with Article 76, paragraph 4. To interpret otherwise – to include also natural prolongation as a separate and independent criterion that a coastal state must satisfy in order to be entitled to a continental shelf beyond 200 nm – was, in the Tribunal's view, warranted neither by the text of Article 76 nor by its object and purpose.[21]

It may be queried, however, whether this was an error of judgment on the part of the ITLOS. The term 'natural prolongation' – used in conjunction with the term 'submerged prolongation' in Article 76, paragraph 3 – is *the* criterion that determines the breadth of a state's continental shelf where it extends beyond 200 nm. Thus, when the ITLOS held that 'the notion of natural prolongation and that of continental margin under Article 76, paragraphs 1 and 4, are closely interrelated' and that '[t]hey refer to the same area,' the Tribunal actually seems to be confusing the question of entitlement (regulated by Article 76, paragraphs 1 and 3) with the specific methods by which the outer edge of the continental margin is determined (regulated by Article 76, paragraph 4). Given the ITLOS' premise – that all that matters for determining the outer edge of the

[19] Ibid., [423]. [20] Ibid., [435]. [21] Ibid., [437].

continental margin is Article 76, paragraph 4 – it never reached the point where it evaluated the legal significance of the geological discontinuity dividing the Burma plate from the Indian plate at 50 nm from the territorial sea baselines. The result – that Myanmar was entitled to a shelf beyond 200 nm – is probably not incorrect. The ITLOS noted that the floor of the Bay of Bengal is covered by a thick layer of sediment some 14–22 km deep. This certainly fulfils the sedimentary rocks criterion in Article 76, paragraph 4 (a)(i) – but does it also fulfil the criterion 'natural prolongation' in paragraph 1? On the basis of geomorphology, probably yes. But in (less convincingly) wrongly dismissing 'natural prolongation' as a separate criterion for entitlement beyond 200 nm, the Tribunal simply did not enter into that discussion.

Finally, the Tribunal turned to the determination of the parties' entitlements to a continental shelf beyond 200 nm. As noted, Myanmar did not deny that the continental shelf of Bangladesh extends beyond 200 nm but that the delimitation of the continental shelf between the two states stops well before reaching the 200 nm limit and therefore that the question of the delimitation was moot and did not need to be considered further by the ITLOS.[22] Bangladesh, on the other hand, while not denying the continental margin off Myanmar's coast, argued on the basis of its interpretation of LOSC Article 76 that this margin has no natural prolongation beyond 50 nm off that coast. The Tribunal, however, found that both Bangladesh and Myanmar have entitlements to a continental shelf extending beyond 200 nm in the Bay of Bengal. The ITLOS' conclusion seems to be based on the following arguments: First, both parties had taken this position in their submissions to the CLCS, so there was no significant uncertainty as to the existence of a continental margin in the area in question.[23] Second, referring to the negotiations at the Third United Nations Conference on the Law of the Sea, the Tribunal noted that the Bay of Bengal presents a unique situation, being covered by a thick layer of sediments some 14 to 22 km deep, that certainly would fulfil the criteria for thickness of sedimentary rocks pursuant to the formula contained in LOSC Article 76, paragraph 4(a)(i). Third, since the Tribunal had already found that the 'natural prolongation' under paragraph 1 of Article 76 did not constitute a separate and independent criterion that a coastal state must satisfy in order to be entitled to a continental shelf beyond 200 nm, it did not consider Bangladesh's assertion regarding the geological discontinuity dividing the Burma plate from the Indian plate. However, the Tribunal held that

[22] Ibid., [423]. [23] Ibid., [445].

it was satisfied that there was a 'continuous' layer of sedimentary rocks extending from Myanmar's coast to the area beyond 200 nm.[24]

13.3.2 *Delimitation Methodology*

13.3.2.1 Bangladesh/Myanmar

As to the actual delimitation of the continental shelf beyond 200 nm, the ITLOS began by emphasizing that LOSC Article 83 'applies equally to the delimitation of the continental shelf both within and beyond 200 nm.'[25] Thus in the view of the Tribunal 'the delimitation method to be employed in the present case for the continental shelf beyond 200 nautical miles should not differ from that within 200 nm.'[26]

On the fundamental level, Bangladesh and Myanmar were in agreement that the equidistance method must be applied if there are no circumstances requiring a different approach to the delimitation.[27] Bangladesh, however, challenged the validity of the equidistance method advocated by Myanmar, emphasizing that this method could 'under certain circumstances produce results that appear on the face of them to be extraordinary, unnatural, or unreasonable.'[28] Notably, Bangladesh pointed out that concave coasts like those in the northern Bay of Bengal were among the recognized situations where equidistance produces 'irrational results,' referring to *Libya/Malta*.[29] In that case, the International Court of Justice (ICJ) stated that an equidistance line 'may yield a disproportionate result where a coast is markedly irregular or markedly concave or convex,'[30] and also that equidistance is 'not the only method applicable [and does] not even have the benefit of a presumption in its favour.'[31] Thus, Bangladesh held that, given the specific configuration of its coast in the northern part of the Bay of Bengal, and the double concavity characterizing it, the Tribunal:

> should apply the angle-bisector method in delimiting the maritime boundary between Bangladesh and Myanmar in the exclusive economic zone and on the continental shelf. In its view, this method would eliminate the inequity associated with equidistance and lead to an equitable result.[32]

[24] Ibid., [446]. [25] Ibid., [454]. [26] Ibid., [455].
[27] Ibid., [206–240]. [28] Ibid., [210]. [29] Ibid., [211].
[30] *Case Concerning the Continental Shelf (Libyan Arab Jamahiriya/Malta)* (Judgment) [1985] ICJ Rep. 13, [44].
[31] Ibid., [47]. [32] *Bangladesh/Myanmar*, n. 1, [213].

Myanmar responded, however, that Bangladesh was attempting to cast doubts on well-established principles for the delimitation of the EEZ and the continental shelf, deliberately ignoring the developments of many decades in maritime boundary delimitation law.[33] It rejected the arguments advanced by Bangladesh that the equidistance line failed to take account of the relevant circumstances in the case, notably the cut-off effect it produced and the concavity of Bangladesh's coast. Myanmar therefore requested the Tribunal to apply the equidistance method for drawing an all-purpose line with respect to the maritime boundary between the parties.[34]

The Tribunal started from the premise that the method to be followed should be one that, under the prevailing geographic realities and the particular circumstances of each case, could lead to an equitable result.[35] It noted that the bisector approach proposed by Bangladesh would fail to give adequate effect to the southward projection of its coast.[36] However, the Tribunal also emphasized that the jurisprudence had developed 'in favour' of the equidistance/relevant circumstances method advanced by Myanmar and that this was 'the method adopted by international courts and tribunals in the majority of the delimitation cases that have come before them.'[37] The Tribunal thus found that the appropriate method for delimiting the EEZ and the continental shelf between Bangladesh and Myanmar was the equidistance/relevant circumstances method.[38] That methodology included a three-stage approach. First, the Tribunal constructed a provisional equidistance line, based on the geography of the parties' coasts and mathematical calculations. Second, it proceeded to determine whether there were any relevant circumstances requiring adjustment of the provisional equidistance line for the delimitation line to produce an equitable result. And third, the Tribunal checked whether the line, as adjusted, resulted in any significant disproportion between the ratio of the respective coastal lengths and the ratio of the relevant maritime areas allocated to each of the parties.

The equidistance/relevant circumstances method continued to apply for the delimitation of the continental shelf beyond 200 nm. The Tribunal noted that this method permitted resolution also as regards the problem of the cut-off effect created by the equidistance line where the coast of one party is markedly concave. After this, but without describing the provisional equidistance line specifically as it relates to the shelf beyond

[33] Ibid., [218]. [34] Ibid., [222]. [35] Ibid., [235].
[36] Ibid., [237]. [37] Ibid., [238]. [38] Ibid., [239].

200 nm,[39] the Tribunal proceeded to re-examine the question of possible relevant circumstances.[40]

Given its position that Bangladesh's continental shelf did not extend beyond 200 nm, Myanmar did not present any arguments regarding the existence of relevant circumstances relating to the delimitation of the continental shelf beyond 200 nm. However, the Tribunal did consider two relevant circumstances beyond 200 nm advanced by Bangladesh. First, Bangladesh contended that geology and geomorphology of the seabed and subsoil were relevant circumstances for adjusting the provisional equidistance because entitlement beyond 200 nm depends entirely on natural prolongation, whereas within 200 nm it is based on distance from the coast. According to Bangladesh, while its entitlement to the continental shelf beyond 200 nm rested firmly on the geological and geomorphological continuity between its land territory and the entire seabed of the Bay of Bengal, Myanmar enjoyed at most only geomorphological continuity between its own landmass and the outer continental shelf. Thus, in Bangladesh's view, an equitable delimitation consistent with Article 83 should take full account of the fact that Bangladesh had the 'most natural prolongation' into the Bay of Bengal, whereas Myanmar had little or no natural prolongation beyond 200 nm.[41]

The ITLOS, however, rejected Bangladesh's arguments that geological and geomorphological factors were relevant in the delimitation beyond 200 nm:

> The Tribunal is of the view that 'the most natural prolongation' argument made by Bangladesh has no relevance to the present case. The Tribunal has already determined that natural prolongation is not an independent basis for entitlement and should be interpreted in the context of the subsequent provisions of article 76 of the Convention, in particular paragraph 4 thereof. The Tribunal has determined that both Parties have entitlements to a continental shelf beyond 200 nm in accordance with article 76 and has decided that those entitlements overlap. The Tribunal therefore cannot accept the argument of Bangladesh that, were the Tribunal to decide that Myanmar is entitled to a continental shelf beyond 200 nm, Bangladesh would be entitled to a greater portion of the disputed area because it has 'the most natural prolongation.'[42]

The second relevant circumstance indicated by Bangladesh was the continuing effect of Bangladesh's concave coast and the cut-off effect

[39] Perhaps because the basepoints for drawing the equidistance line beyond 200 nm were the same as the basepoints for drawing the equidistance line within 200 nm.

[40] *Libya/Malta*, n. 30, [456].

[41] *Bangladesh/Myanmar*, n. 1, [457].

[42] Ibid., [460].

generated by Myanmar's equidistance line, or by any other version of an equidistance line. According to Bangladesh, '[t]he farther an equidistance or even a modified equidistance line extends from a concave coast, the more it cuts across that coast, continually narrowing the wedge of sea in front of it.'[43]

The ITLOS found that the concavity of Bangladesh's coastline continued to be a relevant circumstance beyond 200 nm.[44] The Tribunal therefore decided that the adjusted equidistance line delimiting the EEZ and the continental shelf within 200 nm[45] should continue in the same direction beyond the 200 nm limit of Bangladesh until it reached the area where the rights of third states (here: India) might be affected.[46] Thus, the delimitation line beyond 200 nm is a geodetic line starting at an azimuth of 215° from 'point 11' and for which no specific terminus is adopted.

Having reached the third stage in the delimitation process, the ITLOS conducted the test of proportionality (actually, this test is more about the absence of disproportionality). The concept of proportionality is about the relationship between the area of maritime space to be allocated to each of the parties by delimitation on the one hand, and the lengths of the relevant coasts of the states whose maritime zones have been delimited. Basically it involves testing the equitableness of a result obtained after other methods of delimitation have been applied, by comparing the ratio of the areas accruing to each party from the provisional delimitation with the ratio of their relevant coasts.[47]

The ITLOS found that the ratio of the relevant coasts of the parties was 1:1.42 in Myanmar's favour.[48] The relevant area was divided between the parties in the ratio of 1:1.54, also in favour of Myanmar.[49] Thus, there was no 'significant disproportion in the allocation of maritime area to the parties relative to the respective lengths of their coasts that would require the shifting of the adjusted equidistance line in order to ensure an equitable solution.'[50]

13.3.2.2 Bangladesh v. India

In terms of methodology for delimitation beyond 200 nm, the Annex VII Arbitral Tribunal in *Bangladesh v. India* very closely mirrors that of the

[43] Ibid., [458]. [44] Ibid., [461].
[45] Ibid., [505]. See also [323]–[336], in which the Tribunal describes the adjustment of the provisional equidistance line.
[46] Ibid., [462]. [47] See further Chapter 11 of this volume.
[48] *Bangladesh/Myanmar*, n. 1, [498]. See also [185]–[205]. [49] Ibid., [499]. [50] Ibid.

ITLOS in *Bangladesh/Myanmar*. Unlike the ITLOS judgment, however, the Arbitral Tribunal devoted a separate section to describing the provisional equidistance line specifically as it related to the continental shelf beyond 200 nm.[51]

The Arbitral Tribunal determined that the same method of delimitation should be applied both within and beyond 200 nm because 'there is a single continental shelf.'[52] According to the tribunal, the method for delimiting the continental shelf should therefore be the same, irrespective of whether the area to be delimited lied within or beyond 200 nm. So, having adopted the equidistance/relevant circumstances method for the delimitation of the continental shelf within 200 nm (thereby rejecting Bangladesh's contention that the angle-bisector method should be utilized), the tribunal used the same method to delimit the continental shelf beyond that distance.[53]

As in *Bangladesh/Myanmar*, however, each party disagreed with the delimitation lines proposed by the other. India contended that the provisional equidistance line did not call for any adjustment, but should be prolonged into the area beyond 200 nm until it met the delimitation line established by the ITLOS in the *Bangladesh/Myanmar* case.[54] Bangladesh, on the other hand, held that the provisional equidistance line would not produce an equitable solution beyond 200 nm, and that there was a need to adjust the boundary westwards.[55] On the basis of the ITLOS judgment in the *Bangladesh/Myanmar* case, Bangladesh no longer relied on the 'most natural prolongation' argument concerning its coast.[56] Bangladesh upheld its argument that the concavity of its coast was a relevant circumstance – and proposed a substantial departure from the provisional equidistance line beyond 200 nm.[57]

The Arbitral Tribunal accepted neither Bangladesh's nor India's claims *in toto*. It found that the implementation of Bangladesh's approach would lead to 'a significant cut-off to the detriment of India's entitlement to the area beyond 200 nm and cannot be accepted for that reason.'[58] Here – without going into much detail – the Tribunal pointed out that

> international jurisprudence on the delimitation of the continental shelf does not recognize a general right of coastal States to the maximum reach of their entitlements, irrespective of the geographical situation and the rights of other coastal States.[59]

[51] *Bangladesh v. India*, n. 4, [464]. [52] Ibid., [465]. [53] Ibid. [54] Ibid., [468]. [55] Ibid., [467]. [56] Ibid., [439]. [57] Ibid., [467]. [58] Ibid., [469]. [59] Ibid.

On the other hand, India's proposal, that no adjustment should be made to the provisional equidistance line, was not accepted, on the grounds that such a solution would not compensate Bangladesh with respect to the cut-off effect resulting from the concavity of its coast. Thus the provisional equidistance line required some adjustment.

As in *Bangladesh/Myanmar*, the Arbitral Tribunal adjusted the equidistance line by drawing an azimuth: a geodetic line with a horizontal angle in degrees from a reference direction. The tribunal determined that this azimuth – 177° 30′ 00″ – should continue until the line met the maritime boundary established by the ITLOS in the Bangladesh/Myanmar case.[60] Such a delimitation line – beginning from point 'Delim-3' – would, in the tribunal's view, lead to an equitable result and also ameliorate the excessively negative impact that implementation of the provisional equidistance line would have on the entitlement of Bangladesh to the continental shelf beyond 200 nm.[61] Here it is worth nothing Judge Rao's concurring and dissenting opinion with respect to the adjustment of the provisional equidistance line. He disagreed that the adjustment of the line should start at 'Delim-3,' because that point lies well *before* a significant 'cut-off' effect occurs resulting from the concavity of Bangladesh's coast.[62]

The Tribunal, borrowing the terminology of the ITLOS, also performed a 'disproportionality test' to see whether there should be any further adjustment of the equidistance line. The Tribunal found that the coast of Bangladesh measured 418.6 km, and the relevant Indian coast measured 803.7 km, i.e., a ratio of 1:1.92. The relevant area was determined by the Tribunal to be approximately 406,833 km^2.[63] After the provisional equidistance line had been adjusted, approximately 106,613 km^2 of the relevant area was allocated to Bangladesh and approximately 300,220 km^2 of the relevant area was allocated to India, i.e., a ratio of approximately 1:2.81. Thus, even though India's coastline is 'only' twice as long as Bangladesh's, India obtained nearly three times as much of the delimitation area. However, the tribunal found that 'this ratio does not produce any significant disproportion in the allocation of maritime areas to the Parties that would require alteration of the adjusted equidistance line to ensure an equitable solution.'[64]

60 Ibid., [478]. 61 Ibid.

62 Ibid., Concurring and Dissenting Opinion of Judge Rao, [9]. Text of the Opinion available at website of the Permanent Court of Arbitration (www.pca-cpa.org/showpage.asp?pag_id=1376).

63 *Bangladesh v. India*, n. 4, [306]–[311]. 64 Ibid., [497].

Viewed together with *Bangladesh/Myanmar*, the delimitation result appears rather peculiar: while the EEZ of Bangladesh is totally surrounded by those of Myanmar and India, and Bangladesh would, due to its disadvantageous coastal geography, be 'shelf-locked' by equidistance lines, Bangladesh was found to be entitled to a continental shelf beyond 200 nm. In some places, however, these continental shelf areas lie beneath the EEZs of Myanmar and India. One consequence of both cases is thus that they create so-called grey zones.

13.3.3 Grey Zones

The Bay of Bengal cases are special not merely because they mark the first time the judiciary delimited continental shelf areas beyond 200 nm. The cases also serve to illustrate another problem dealt with for the first time explicitly under international litigation: the concept of 'grey zones' (labelled 'grey areas' in both *Bangladesh/Myanmar* and *Bangladesh v. India*).[65] The Arbitral Tribunal in *Bangladesh v. India* described a grey zone as follows:

> The Tribunal's delimitation of the Parties' exclusive economic zones and of the continental shelf within and beyond 200 nm gives rise to an area that lies beyond 200 nm from the coast of Bangladesh and within 200 nm from the coast of India, and yet lies to the east of the Tribunal's delimitation line. The resulting 'grey area' is a practical consequence of the delimitation process. Such an area will arise whenever the entitlements of two States to the continental shelf extend beyond 200 nm and relevant circumstances call for a boundary at other than the equidistance line at or beyond the 200 nm limit in order to provide an equitable delimitation.[66]

In other words, a grey zone is an area on one side of a continental shelf boundary beyond 200 nm from the state on that side of the boundary, but within 200 nm of the state on the other side of the boundary.[67] The result of the ITLOS delimitation in *Bangladesh/Myanmar* was the creation of such a zone on Bangladesh's side of the boundary.[68] This means that Myanmar has sovereign rights over the water column in that area,

[65] The concept of grey areas was argued by the Parties in the *Gulf of Maine* case, n. 92. See A. Oude Elferink, 'Does Undisputed Title to a Maritime Zone Always Exclude Its Delimitation: The Grey Area Issue,' (1998) 13 *International Journal of Marine and Coastal Law* 143. The article examines in detail earlier state practice and jurisprudence with respect to grey areas.

[66] *Bangladesh v. India*, n. 4, [498].

[67] Churchill, n. 1, 150.

[68] For illustration, see map included in the Judgment at [138] (*Bangladesh/Myanmar*, n. 1).

while Bangladesh – due to the delimited boundary – has continental shelf jurisdiction.

This would appear to be a curious conflict of norms, since a coastal state's sovereign rights under the LOSC regime for the EEZ include the seabed and subsoil. Would Myanmar's jurisdiction over the superjacent waters then not 'trump' Bangladesh's continental shelf rights in the grey zone? There is no explicit provision in the LOSC on the fundamental question on the relation of the two entitlements. However, according to LOSC Article 56, paragraph 3, the rights of the coastal state with respect to the seabed and subsoil of the EEZ shall be *exercised* in accordance with Part VI of the Convention, which includes Article 83.[69] This indicates that legally, it is indeed possible that the seabed of a grey zone is subject to a coastal state's continental shelf jurisdiction (Bangladesh), while the superjacent waters are subject to the EEZ-jurisdiction of its neighbour (Myanmar).

The Tribunal held that it was for the parties to determine what measures they deemed appropriate for the purpose of resolving the practical difficulties that might arise when one state has jurisdiction over the continental shelf and the neighbouring state has jurisdiction over the superjacent waters.[70] In that regard, the ITLOS remarked that the legal regime of the continental shelf has in fact always coexisted with another legal regime in the same area – the high seas – and that the LOSC also contains regulations that prompt states to exercise their rights and perform their duties with due regard for the rights and duties of other states.[71] The Tribunal hints that Bangladesh and Myanmar should discharge their obligations by concluding specific agreements or by establishing appropriate cooperative arrangements.[72]

In *Bangladesh/Myanmar* the parties differed as to the status and treatment of the grey zone created by the continental shelf boundary beyond 200 nm. Myanmar argued primarily that the problem of a grey zone did not arise, since the equitable delimitation line did not extend beyond 200 nm. However, it also contended that any allocation of areas to Bangladesh extending beyond 200 nm off Bangladesh's coast would trump Myanmar's rights to the EEZ and continental shelf rights within 200 nm. It argued that to 'advance' Bangladesh's claim to an extended continental shelf 'against' its own continental shelf jurisdiction within 200 nm and its right to extend its EEZ up to 200 nm would 'inevitably infringe on [its own] indisputable

[69] Also, Art. 68 provides that Part *v.* on the EEZ does not apply to sedentary species of the continental shelf as defined in LOSC Art. 77.

[70] *Bangladesh/Myanmar*, n. 1, [476]. [71] Ibid., [475]. [72] Ibid., [476].

rights'[73] and also be 'contrary to both the Convention and international practice.'[74] The ITLOS was thus faced with a claim that the grey zone should be avoided and this could be done either by implementing the equidistance line or giving priority to the EEZ over the continental shelf beyond 200 nm.

This argumentation, however, did not figure in *Bangladesh v. India*, where India held that there were no relevant circumstances that would call for an adjustment of the provisional equidistance line. India did not address the grey zone issue. Since the Arbitral Tribunal in Bangladesh/India also adopted a delimitation line beyond 200 nm that deviated from equidistance, the problem of grey zones did emerge in that case as well. The delimitation along the 177° azimuth created a grey zone, in fact one that overlapped in part with the grey zone described in *Bangladesh/Myanmar.*[75]

The Arbitral Tribunal followed the same approach as in *Bangladesh/Myanmar* on the grey zone (albeit with Rao dissenting).[76] The conclusion was the same: the delimitation would not limit India's sovereign rights to the superjacent waters in its EEZ. With respect to the overlap, the Tribunal also noted that the delimitation did not prejudice the rights of India vis-à-vis Myanmar with respect to the water column in the area where the EEZ claims of those two states overlap.[77] The Tribunal also emphasized that it was for the parties to determine the measures they deemed appropriate for solving any practical problems arising from the grey zone phenomenon, hinting at the possibility of concluding further agreements and creating cooperative arrangements.[78]

13.4 An Assessment of the Bay of Bengal Cases

13.4.1 Delimitation Methodology

The decisions of the ITLOS and the Arbitral Tribunal are very similar in terms of approach and the delimitation method chosen. In both cases the resulting continental shelf boundary beyond 200 nm is a linear continuation of the single maritime boundary delimited for the EEZ and the

[73] Ibid., [469]. [74] Ibid., [468].

[75] Thus India and Myanmar later will have to delimit their water column rights in that area.

[76] *Bangladesh v. India*, n. 4, Concurring and Dissenting Opinion of Judge Rao, [10] and [24]–[37].

[77] Ibid., [506]. [78] Ibid., [508].

continental shelf within 200 nm. In *Bangladesh v. India*, the Arbitral Tribunal justified this as follows:

> The Parties and the Tribunal agree that there is a single continental shelf. The tribunal considers that the appropriate method for delimiting the continental shelf remains the same, irrespective of whether the area to be delimited lies within or beyond 200 M.[79]

It is unclear what is actually the justification for the tribunal's conclusion that the equidistance/relevant circumstance method is the appropriate approach also for the delimitation of the continental shelf beyond 200 nm. The explanation offered by the ITLOS in *Bangladesh/Myanmar* is somewhat more comprehensive:

> [The equidistance/relevant circumstances] method is rooted in the recognition that sovereignty over the land territory is the basis for the sovereign rights and jurisdiction of the coastal State with respect to both the exclusive economic zone and the continental shelf [...] The Tribunal notes [...] that this method can, and does in this case, permit resolution also beyond 200 nm of the problem of the cut-off effect that can be created by an equidistance line where the coast of one party is markedly concave.[80]

However, neither of the decisions takes up the point that LOSC Article 83 does not prescribe any specific method for continental shelf delimitation: the only requirement is that the solution shall lead to an equitable result. Thus, Article 83 does not *preclude* the selection of other approaches in different parts of the continental shelf, notably within and beyond 200 nm.

It should also be noted that the mandate for the judiciary in both cases was to draw a single maritime boundary for the water column and the continental shelf out to a distance of 200 nm, and then delimit overlapping continental shelf areas beyond that distance. So while the boundary out to 200 nm delimits both the EEZ and the continental shelf, the boundary beyond 200 nm delimits *only* the continental shelf. In my view, this calls for a further explanation as to why the same methodology of delimitation is deemed appropriate both within and beyond 200 nm, notably if there are not any particular considerations that come into play when only the shelf is being delimited.

The Bay of Bengal cases could have taken further pains to justify the use of a provisional equidistance line as a starting point for the delimitation of the continental shelf beyond 200 nm. Contrary to what is the case in the Bay of Bengal, there are seabed areas where drawing a provisional

[79] Ibid., [465]. [80] *Bangladesh/Myanmar*, n. 1, [455].

equidistance line as a starting point for the delimitation of the continental shelf beyond 200 nm clearly is improper, notably when such a line is located beyond the area of overlapping entitlements. The continental shelf beyond 200 nm between Greenland and Iceland in the Irminger Sea is one example,[81] which then prompts discussion of alternative approaches to the methodology of delimitation, one being to proceed directly to the stage of weighing all relevant circumstances?[82] In the Bay of Bengal, however, the situation is very different to that between Greenland and Iceland in the Irminger Sea. There is no uncertainty with respect to overlap of entitlements and the final outcome with respect to overlap does not in the same way depend upon the implementation of LOSC Article 76 and the role of the CLCS. Thus the justification of the ITLOS and the Arbitral Tribunal for drawing a provisional equidistance line beyond 200 nm could have been strengthened.

We clearly see the distinction between Article 83 and Article 6 of the 1958 Convention on the Continental Shelf. Both articles apply beyond 200 nm; but while Article 83 only prescribes the result that is to be achieved, Article 6 also prescribes a specific method – basically the three-step approach that is the 'standard' in maritime boundary delimitation for 200 nm zones and continental shelf areas. Dispute resolution bodies thus have greater flexibility in the selection of delimitation method under the LOSC than under older treaty law, a flexibility that theoretically may also be utilized to choose a different approach to delimitation regarding the continental shelf beyond and within 200 nm.

In addition, the ITLOS and the Arbitral Tribunal do not always explain their findings and conclusions amply. For example, fuller reasoning should have been employed with respect to why the provisional equidistance line was adjusted as it was. In *Bangladesh v. India*, the explanation for choosing an azimuth of 177° was thin.[83] The Tribunal merely noted that its choice of azimuth 'does not unreasonably limit the entitlement of India'[84] and 'avoids turning points and is thus simpler to implement and administer by the Parties.'[85] We may note the opinion of Dr. Rao, who dissented with respect to how the equidistance line should be adjusted, and was critical of the tribunal's failure to provide further explanation of its decision.[86]

Third, there is the question of 'relevant circumstances.' Bangladesh – also beyond 200 nm – was compensated for having a concave coastline, in

[81] A. Oude Elferink, n. 1, 243–245. [82] Ibid., 247.
[83] *Bangladesh v. India*, n. 4, [334]–[335]. [84] Ibid., [479]. [85] Ibid., [480].
[86] Ibid., Concurring and Dissenting Opinion of Judge Rao, [9], [14]–[23], and [38]–[42].

which case the equidistance method would be disadvantageous and result in the country being shelf-locked. Due to this concavity, the provisional equidistance lines produced cut-off effects on the maritime projection of Bangladesh and hence required adjustments to produce an equitable solution. In this instance, the Bay of Bengal cases contribute first and foremost to consolidating the principle that a concave coastline *may* be a relevant circumstance for adjusting the equidistance line – but that it not necessarily is.[87] And it is worth noting that the extent of the cut-off effect was established taking into account the whole area in which competing claims have been made, i.e., not making a distinction between the continental shelf within and beyond 200 nm.[88]

However, the cases also show that there is indeed a limit to the importance to be attached to concavity as a relevant circumstance. Myanmar and India argued that the judiciary should be cautious about choosing a boundary that cuts off – encroaches – areas that more *naturally* belong to one party than the other. For instance, India held that the tribunal could not 'refashion' nature by treating concavity as a relevant circumstance.[89] The tribunal's decision did not, however, accept the arguments of both parties in full.

An important point in relation to the relevance of concavity is that the ITLOS and the Tribunal did not find reason to adjust the equidistance line, the further out from the coast it extends. Bangladesh argued that the results of the equidistance method become increasingly inequitable as the equidistance line moves further from the coast. Concavity as a relevant circumstance should thus have been given increasing weight, to compensate for the increasingly severe inequity of the resulting line. Nevertheless, the ITLOS and the Tribunal decided that the delimitation line should continue in the same direction, also beyond 200 nm. In *Bangladesh/Myanmar*, this was justified on the basis of 'the geographic circumstances of this case' and, furthermore, that the concavity had a 'continuing effect' beyond 200 nm. The Arbitral Tribunal seemed to endorse this position by simply

[87] That the establishment of an equidistance line may produce a cut-off effect has been recognized since the decision in *North Sea Continental Shelf*, in which the ICJ explained: 'It has been seen in the case of concave or convex coastlines that if the equidistance method is employed, then the greater the irregularity and the further from the coastline the area to be delimited, the more unreasonable are the results produced. So great an exaggeration of the consequences of a natural geographical feature must be remedied or compensated for as far as possible, being of itself creative of inequity' (*North Sea Continental Shelf (Germany/Netherlands; Germany/Denmark)* (Judgment) [1969] ICJ Rep. 3, [49]).

[88] *Bangladesh v. India*, n. 4, [404].

[89] Ibid., 391.

referring to *Bangladesh/Myanmar* with respect to the direction of the maritime boundary.[90]

The Bay of Bengal cases did not place any weight on geological or geomorphological factors when determining the placement of the continental shelf boundary, within 200 nm or beyond. Concerning the shelf within 200 nm, this is hardly surprising, as the ITLOS and the Tribunal were tasked with drawing a single maritime boundary.[91] As the ICJ observed in *Gulf of Maine*, the argument for excluding geological or geomorphological features within 200 nm is not that they are irrelevant *per se*, but basically because they have no relevance for the delimitation of the superjacent waters that are also being delimited.[92] This justification, however, does not apply beyond 200 nm.

It should be emphasized that case law in other respects has not deemed geomorphological or geological features irrelevant for determining an 'equitable solution' with respect to potential delimitations *beyond* 200 nm from the territorial sea baselines. Already in the *North Sea Continental Shelf*, the ICJ took into consideration the geological and geomorphological nature of the area under dispute and held that certain configurational features could be relevant to the delimitation of the continental shelf.[93] In the *Tunisia/Libya*, the ICJ also noted that 'identification of natural prolongation may, where the geographical circumstances are appropriate, have an important role to play in defining an equitable delimitation, in view of its significance as the justification of continental shelf rights in some cases.'[94] However, weight was not given to the parties' arguments that geological conditions on the seabed should have relevance for the delimitation of the seabed, because such circumstances could not be easily proven.[95] Furthermore, what the ICJ actually stated in *Tunisia/Libya* was that geological

90 For the EEZ and the continental shelf within 200 nm, see ibid., [333], and ibid., Award, [471]–[472]. For the continental shelf beyond 200 nm, see ibid., [461]–[462], and ibid., Award, [471]–[472].

91 Ibid., [179]–[180]. Ibid., Award, [60] and [62].

92 *Delimitation of the Maritime Boundary in the Gulf of Maine Area (Canada/USA)* (Judgment) [1984] ICJ Rep. 246, [326–327].

93 The Court argued: '[I]t can be useful to consider the geology of that shelf in order to find out whether the direction taken by certain configurational features should influence delimitation because, in certain localities, they point-up the whole notion of the appurtenance of the continental shelf to the State whose territory it does in fact prolong.' *North Sea Continental Shelf*, n. 87, [51].

94 *Case concerning the Continental Shelf (Tunisia/Libyan Arab Jamahiriya)* [1982] ICJ Rep. 18, [47].

95 Ibid., [57].

features of the seabed would basically without interest for the delimitation of the continental shelf *within* 200 nm – not with respect to delimitation beyond that distance.[96]

Therefore, the previous case law can by no means be interpreted as dealing any kind of deathblow to geology and geomorphology as factors relevant for delimiting the continental shelf. And, in the view of this author, neither can the Bay of Bengal cases.

Two factors weaken the precedential value. First, the dismissal of Bangladesh's 'most natural prolongation' argument' in *Bangladesh/Myanmar* has a double effect: If the ITLOS concluded that 'natural prolongation' was irrelevant for *entitlement* beyond 200 nm, how could 'natural prolongation' possibly be relevant in the delimitation? If the ITLOS had concluded differently (i.e., that 'natural prolongation' is a separate criterion for entitlement under Article 76), then it would perhaps not *automatically* disregard the 'degree' of natural prolongation as a circumstance relevant in the delimitation of the continental shelf beyond 200 nm (as was mentioned above, Bangladesh waived its 'most natural prolongation' in *Bangladesh v. India*). However, geology and geomorphology could still be a losing argument. After all, natural prolongation in the context of LOSC Article 76 is something a coastal state either have or does not have. Also, as a matter of cost-effectiveness, it is doubtful whether any court or tribunal ever will put the parties to the vast expense of gathering all the necessary technical data to prove which one has the 'most' natural prolongation for the purpose of delimitation.

Second, the physical configuration of the Bay of Bengal seabed in terms of geological and geomorphological characteristics. Having disregarded the relevance of natural prolongation, it was clear that the geological and geomorphological factors at issue appeared to apply equally to all coastal states in the Bay of Bengal. Thus if factors like the location of the foot of the slope or the depths of sediments were relevant to one state, they would be relevant to others as well.[97] Of course, in other cases the configuration

[96] The Court argued: 'Since the development of the law enables a State to claim that the continental shelf appertaining to it extends up to as far as 200 miles from its coast, whatever the geological characteristics of the corresponding sea-bed and subsoil, there is no reason to ascribe any role to geological or geophysical factors within that distance either in verifying the legal title of the States concerned or in proceeding to a delimitation as between their claims.' Ibid., [35].

[97] For an overview of the role that seabed characteristics may play in the delimitation of the continental shelf beyond 200 nm, see D. Colson, 'The Delimitation of the Outer Continental Shelf Between Neighboring States,' (2003) 97 *American Journal of International Law* 91, 102–107.

of the seabed may be very different, making geology and geomorphology more opportune considerations in the delimitation of shelf areas beyond 200 nm.

13.4.2 Grey Zones

Since the Bay of Bengal cases were the first two instances where the judiciary dealt with the concept of grey zones, what the ITLOS and the Tribunal had to say in that respect is important. The approach and conclusion were similar in both cases.

Deviating from the equidistance line beyond 200 nm creates grey areas with attendant practical difficulties for the neighbouring states with respect to the exercise of jurisdiction. However, the creation of grey zones did not prevent continuation of the delimitation beyond 200 nm, nor did it affect which method of delimitation to be employed. The argumentation that entitlement to a continental shelf within 200 nm should have primacy over continental shelf rights beyond 200 nm was rejected.

In light of the LOSC provisions, this is a highly welcome result. There is nothing in the LOSC to indicate that a state's rights to an EEZ should trump another state's continental shelf rights beyond 200 nm, nor does it fit well contextually either. States must, for instance, accept to carry out their rights to fish and navigate the high seas, although a coastal State exercises jurisdiction with respect to the seabed underneath. Despite the substantive integration of rights and uses of the continental shelf and the EEZ, the grey zone is legally possible. Important to the judiciary in this context seems to be that state practice indicates that reasonable agreements and practical arrangements for the exercise of coastal state's respective rights in such areas can be achieved.[98]

A remark should be made with respect to the way in which the ITLOS and the Tribunal chose to treat the issue of grey areas. The issue was not dealt with specifically when examining what was/what was not a 'relevant circumstance.' Yet, the anomaly of grey areas was taken up by Myanmar in the ITLOS decision as an argument for not deviating from the

[98] *Bangladesh v. India*, n. 4, [472]. Ibid., Award, [508]. One example to illustrate that coastal states may choose to avoid any such cooperative arrangements, however, is the 2010 Barents Sea Treaty, under which Norway and the Russian Federation instead favoured to transfer jurisdiction in the grey area resulting from the delimitation. See Ø. Jensen, 'The Barents Sea: Treaty between Norway and the Russian Federation Concerning Maritime Delimitation and Cooperation in the Barents Sea and the Arctic Ocean,' (2011) 26 *International Journal of Marine and Coastal Law* 151.

equidistance line beyond 200 nm.[99] One would perhaps expect that the ITLOS then dealt with the concept of grey areas in the pool of potential 'relevant circumstances.' Grey areas were, however, singled out from the exercise of delimitation: in both cases, the issue was in substance considered as a practical *result* of the delimitation beyond 200 nm, not a factor that possibly could influence the outcome of the delimitation itself. The rather lengthy and theoretical observations on grey areas by both the ITLOS and the tribunal make a fairly useful clarification of an important area of law. In terms of maritime delimitation, however, such remarks *obiter dicta* obviously do not form a necessary part of the rulings.

13.5 Conclusions

Although maritime boundary delimitation has long been dealt with by the international judiciary, it is only in recent years that it has ruled on disputes relating to the delimitation of the continental shelf beyond 200 nm. In the context of Article 76 of the LOSC, with its deadlines for submitting continental shelf submissions to the CLCS, it comes as no surprise that international litigation with respect to continental shelf delimitation beyond 200 nm is increasing. For international courts and tribunals set to deal with this issue for the first time, however, this entails being entrusted with a fundamental and challenging role. Particularly for the ITLOS in the *Bangladesh/Myanmar* case, this meant finding a way for dealing with a complex body of substantive law, one which hovers between generality on the one hand, and very technical issues on the other.

As only two cases have been rendered on delimitations beyond 200 nm, what the ITLOS said in *Bangladesh/Myanmar* and what the Arbitral Tribunal said in *Bangladesh v. India* is important. This also implies that there is every reason for critically examining the both tribunals' reasoning and conclusions. For instance, the dispute resolution bodies are not particularly convincing in explaining why the same delimitation methodology should be applied beyond and within 200 nm, especially since the former concerns the seabed exclusively and not the superjacent waters. However, it appears that this almost is a default mechanism: the delimitation line beyond 200 nm shall be implemented using the same methodology and follow the same direction as within 200 nm. That is not to say the

[99] As noted in *Bangladesh v. India*, India did not address the issue of grey zones, holding that no relevant circumstances called for an adjustment of the provisional equidistance line, which would have resulted in the absence of a grey area.

result is necessarily incorrect – but fuller reasoning might have made the conclusion more credible. In the view of this writer, a weak point is also the ITLOS' reasoning with respect to the substantive relationship between entitlement and delimitation, i.e., the significance of the term 'natural prolongation' in Article 76 of the LOSC. Neither has the case law thus far provided answers to all substantive issues relating to relevant circumstances for the delimitation of the continental shelf beyond 200 nm, such as the possible relevance of geology and geomorphology in the adjustment of the provisional equidistance line.

The fact that only two cases have been rendered so far makes it impossible to speak of any consolidated case law with respect to the delimitation of the continental shelf beyond 200 nm. The precedential value of the Bay of Bengal cases to other delimitation disputes beyond 200 nm might also be more limited than would otherwise be the case, given the identity with respect to the area of delimitation, the parties involved and nature of the proceedings. In that light, it is hardly surprising that *Bangladesh v. India* largely mirrors the ITLOS' judgment in *Bangladesh/Myanmar*.

There are several pending cases relating to delimitation of the continental shelf beyond 200 nm, from which further substantive answers are likely to emerge,[100] for instance with respect to grey areas.[101] It will, however, also be interesting to see whether the ICJ in any way feels bound by the reasoning in the Bay of Bengal cases. In that respect, a general observation should be made in relation to the ICJ's statement in *Libya/Malta* on consistency and predictability:[102] should consistency and predictability be realized by relying on the already established principles for delimitation

[100] These include, first, *Question of the Delimitation of the Continental Shelf between Nicaragua and Colombia beyond 200 Nautical Miles from the Nicaraguan Coast (Nicaragua v. Colombia)* (Judgment, Preliminary Objections), 17 March 2016, available at the website of the ICJ (www.icj-cij.org/docket/files/154/18956.pdf). The second case is *Maritime Delimitation in the Indian Ocean (Somalia v. Kenya)* (Judgment, Preliminary Objections), 2 February 2017, available at the website of the ICJ (www.icj-cij.org/docket/files/161/19330.pdf). The third pending case is the *Dispute concerning Delimitation of the Maritime Boundary between Ghana and Côte d'Ivoire in the Atlantic Ocean (Ghana/Côte d'Ivoire)* which also seems to be concerned with delimitation of the continental shelf beyond 200 nm. See *Request for the Prescription of Provisional Measures Submitted by the Republic of Côte d'Ivoire under Article 290, paragraph 1, of the United Nations Convention on the Law of the Sea, 27 February 2015*, [7] and Sketch-map 1. Available at the website of the ITLOS.

[101] In *Nicaragua v. Colombia*, Nicaragua argues that the Nicaraguan Rise allow extension of its continental shelf beyond 200 nm and into the EEZ projected by Colombia's islands or mainland. Thus the ICJ may also in this case be obliged to consider the status of a grey area.

[102] *Libya/Malta*, n. 30, [39].

within 200 nm, or should the judiciary seek to adopt a distinct methodology for the delimitation of the shelf beyond that distance?

This appears to be one of the most critical issues in the matter of delimitation of the continental shelf beyond 200 nm. By simply continuing in 'the same direction' as within 200 nm, the Bay of Bengal cases indicate that there is nothing peculiar about delimitation beyond that distance. Certainly, that approach seems appropriate on the basis of the applicable law, as there is in international law – both in terms of entitlement and delimitation – only one continental shelf. Future case law may, however, find the approach in the Bay of Bengal cases too narrow and rather focus on the fact that there are two distinct parts of the continental shelf that requires separate consideration. For instance, the equidistance/relevant circumstance approach should not always be the appropriate starting point for the delimitation of the continental shelf *beyond* 200 nm because a provisional equidistance point in some cases will be located beyond the area of overlapping entitlements, making it wholly inappropriate as a provisional delimitation line. And, after all, both the law of the LOSC and the practice of the international judiciary for drawing terrestrial boundaries, first and foremost calls for balancing all interests at hand and point to the need to attain an equitable delimitation result.

14

Conclusions

Taking Stock and Looking Ahead

ALEX G. OUDE ELFERINK, TORE HENRIKSEN, AND SIGNE VEIERUD BUSCH*

14.1 Introduction

This concluding chapter is intended to look at a number of common themes that emerge from the preceding chapters. Its purpose is not to repeat the findings of these individual chapters in full. The focus of this volume has been on the case law on the delimitation of the continental shelf and the exclusive economic zone. As is set out in Section 1.1, this choice is explained by the fact that the majority of the case law has been concerned with the delimitation of these maritime zones, while the territorial sea has been at issue in a much more limited number of cases. In addition, it was observed that the delimitation of the continental shelf and the exclusive economic zone has led to much more controversy and debate as regards the content of the applicable rules and their application to the individual case. At the same time, Chapter 1 submitted that an analysis of the case law on the delimitation of the territorial sea might enhance our understanding of the case law on the delimitation of the continental shelf and the exclusive economic zone. Chapter 2 draws attention to the fact that a major difference between Article 15 of the United Nations Convention on the Law of the Sea (LOSC) on the delimitation of the territorial sea and Articles 74 and 83 of the same on the delimitation of the exclusive economic zone and the continental shelf is that the former contains a clearly stated delimitation provision and the latter do not. As Chapter 2 indicates, this implies that 'aside from [Article 15's] interpretation and application, there is not much room for judicial "development," nor indeed any legal basis for its amendment by means of judicial practice.' However,

* The authors would like to thank Glen Jeffries for his research assistance in the preparation of this chapter.

Article 15, like Article 6 of the Convention on the Continental Shelf,[1] fails to include a mechanism for assessing the relationship between equidistance and special circumstances. This may make the task of the judiciary more similar in both cases than a simple comparison between Articles 15, 74, and 83 of the LOSC would suggest. As Chapter 2 also points out, a main distinction between these Articles concerns the area to which they apply, within the 12-nautical-mile limit of the territorial sea as compared to the 200-nautical-mile limit for the exclusive economic zone and in certain circumstances even beyond that for the continental shelf. This difference has two significant and closely related implications. First, within the territorial sea, factoring in specific circumstances in general will only have a limited impact on the course of the boundary line as compared to the exclusive economic zone and the continental shelf. Second, the limited dimensions of the territorial sea leave less room for shifting a provisional line. The limited scope for adjusting the provisional (equidistance) line also indicates that it will in most instances be in the range of what constitutes an equitable result.

The remainder of this chapter consists of the following sections. Section 14.2 looks at the general rules on delimitation contained in multilateral conventions and customary law and assesses how these rules have been provided further, specific content by the case law. The next two sections consider the consistency and predictability of the case law. Section 14.3 considers how the terms consistency and predictability should be understood and how they relate to each other, while Section 14.4 makes an assessment of the consistency and predictability of the case law. Section 14.5 looks at the normative nature of the process of maritime boundary delimitation. Is this process only characterized by the basic rules contained in the relevant provisions of the LOSC and the Convention on the Continental Shelf or is the three-stage approach as developed by the case law part and parcel of the law? Section 14.6 briefly considers how the case law on the delimitation of maritime boundaries may develop in the future, taking into account the analysis of the existing case law in this volume.

14.2 The General Rules and the Case Law: A Failure to Connect?

The general rules in relation to the delimitation of the continental shelf and the exclusive economic zone are contained in Article 6 of the 1958

[1] For a further discussion of Art. 6 on this point, see below, the text at n. 4.

Convention on the Continental Shelf,[2] Articles 74 and 83 of the LOSC and customary international law. As the analysis of Chapter 4 indicates, these general rules largely are empty shells. As regards Articles 74 and 83 of the LOSC, this conclusion hardly should come as a surprise. The Third United Nations Conference on the Law of the Sea (UNCLOS III) had tried to reach agreement on a substantive rule for the delimitation of the continental shelf and the exclusive economic zone for almost a decade, seeking to reconcile the proponents of equidistance and those of equitable principles.[3] In the end, the matter was settled by including neither of these concepts in the relevant provisions, but instead Articles 74 and 83 refer to delimitation in accordance with international law. In respect of Article 6 of the Convention on the Continental Shelf, the submission that it is an empty shell might seem to be more surprising. Article 6 contains a method of delimitation and specifies when that method should be applied and when it should be varied. However, as Chapter 4 observes:

> [t]he rather opaque formulation of [Article 6] left unclear how the rule was to be applied. Certainly, one could start by looking for agreement, but after that was equidistance the primary rule and 'special circumstances' the exception, or in the absence of agreement did one first test for 'special circumstances' and resort to equidistance as a last resort.[4]

As Chapter 4 further submits, the methodological question whether one should first apply the equidistance method and then check for the presence and significance of special circumstances 'was never resolved and remains at the heart of controversies over the applicable law in delimitation.' This

[2] *Convention on the Continental Shelf* (signed 29 April 1958; entered into force 10 June 1964), 499 UNTS 311.

[3] For the drafting history of Arts. 74 and 83 of the LOSC, see further e.g. S. N. Nandan and S. Rosenne (eds.), *United Nations Convention on the Law of the Sea 1982: A Commentary*, vol. 2 (Martinus Nijhoff Dordrecht 1993) 796–816 and 948–985.

[4] It may be noted that the Committee that advised the International Law Commission to include the equidistance method in a rule on the delimitation of the continental shelf observed that the equidistance line might not always lead to an equitable solution (see Doc. A/CN.4/61/Add.1, reproduced as an Annex to the Report of the Special Rapporteur (*Yearbook of the International Law Commission* 1953, vol. 2, 75–79, at 79). During the 1958 Geneva United Nations Conference on the Law of the Sea, the notion that the delimitation of the continental shelf had to be either equitable or fair was present in statements of both those states wishing to put greater emphasis on equidistance and those supporting the reference to special circumstances (see the statements of the Venezuelan representative (*United Nations Conference on the Law of the Sea; Official Records*, vol. 6, 92, [19]), the UK representative (ibid., 93, [1]), the Italian representative (ibid., [5]), the US representative (ibid., 95, [21]), and the Iranian representative (ibid., [96])). Although this indicates the existence of an overarching principle against which to assess equidistance and special circumstances, it does not resolve the question concerning the relationship of the two.

may be illustrated by the case law's current approach to the delimitation process. The three-stage approach to delimitation avowedly in principle starts with the determination of an equidistance line and subsequently looks at relevant circumstances that may require an adjustment of the equidistance line. However, as Chapters 4, 8, and 9 set out, the first stage of drawing an equidistance line is permeated by the second stage of considering relevant circumstances. As these chapters observe, the equidistance line in a number of recent cases has not been determined objectively on the basis of the relevant baselines of the parties that are in accordance with the baseline rules contained in the LOSC and customary international law. Instead, in determining the equidistance line, the case law has discarded valid baselines, infusing the first stage of the delimitation with subjective calls concerning the relevance of these baselines.

The observations concerning the indeterminacy of the law as contained in Articles 6, 74, and 83 also apply to customary international law as originally formulated by the International Court of Justice (ICJ) in *North Sea Continental Shelf* as 'delimitation is to be effected by agreement in accordance with equitable principles, and taking account of all the relevant circumstances.'[5] The Court itself in *North Sea Continental Shelf* was not required to apply the law as thus stated in the determination of boundary lines between the parties. As McRae submits in Chapter 4, in subsequent cases there 'has never been a straightforward implementation of what was articulated in *North Sea Continental Shelf*. Rather when "equitable principles" have been invoked it has often been in conjunction with other approaches and principles of delimitation.' The *North Sea Continental Shelf* customary rule subsequently was discarded. Following the entry into force of the LOSC, the ICJ on a number of cases has affirmed that customary international law is reflected in Articles 74 and 83 of the LOSC.[6]

The state of the law as contained in Articles 6 of the Convention on the Continental Shelf and Articles 74 and 83 of the LOSC, which reflect customary law, required its further operationalization.[7] As was observed in

[5] *North Sea Continental Shelf (Federal Republic of Germany/Denmark; Federal Republic of Germany/The Netherlands)* (Judgment) [1969] ICJ Rep. 54, [101(C)(1)].

[6] See *Maritime Dispute (Peru v. Chile)* (Judgment), [2014] ICJ Rep. 61, [179], where reference is also made to earlier cases.

[7] That requirement in any case applies to the case law. A mere reference to the law as contained in Arts. 6, 74, and 83 and customary law and the determination of a boundary line would not be in accordance with the requirement that a 'judgment shall state the reasons on which it is based' (Statute of the ICJ, Art. 56; LOSC, Annex VI, Art. 30).

Chapter 1, and this is a generally shared view, that operationalization has been achieved by the case law. Before further commenting on that point, the limited role of state practice in this respect merits some further attention. State practice in this field abounds, raising the question why it did not make its imprint on the law. A short answer may be provided by referring to the drafting history of Articles 74 and 83 of the LOSC. States had (and continue to have) opposing views on what the content of the law should be and, as was also pointed out above, those views were reconciled by a delimitation provision without substance. A look at state practice allows giving this explanation more substance. National legislation on the continental shelf and the exclusive economic zone in general will contain a provision on the delimitation of these zones. However, this legislation witnesses the same divide as the negotiations on Articles 74 and 83 of the LOSC.[8] Moreover, there currently are more than 200 bilateral agreements on the delimitation of maritime boundaries. That treaty practice differs in one important respect from national legislation. It includes treaties concluded between states from both delimitation groups at UNCLOS III and such treaties might perhaps reflect a common understanding of the applicable law. However, a review of some of this practice shows that this is not the case and that this is at least in part explained by the nature of maritime delimitation.[9] Bilateral boundary delimitation does not require the formulation of rules applicable to future conduct, but involves the establishment of a specific line. The latter exercise can be carried out without prior agreement on the applicable rules and may be, and in fact is, achieved through compromise offers, with each state reserving its position on the applicable law.[10]

The relationship between the applicable law as contained in Articles 6 of the Convention on the Continental Shelf and Articles 74 and 83 of the LOSC, which reflect customary law, and specific concepts figuring in the case law occupies a number of the preceding chapters to a lesser or larger extent. Two central themes seem to emerge from this volume. First, notwithstanding the apparent systematization the case law has achieved since *Black Sea*'s cogent formulation of the three-stage approach to

[8] A comprehensive overview of national legislation on this matter is accessible through the page *Maritime Space: Maritime Zones and Maritime Delimitation* (www.un.org/Depts/los/LEGISLATIONANDTREATIES/regionslist.htm) of the website of the Division of Oceans Affairs and Law of the Sea of the Secretariat of the United Nations.

[9] See further A. G. Oude Elferink, *The Law of Maritime Boundary Delimitation: A Case Study of the Russian Federation* (Martinus Nijhoff Dordrecht 1994) 365–373.

[10] Ibid.

delimitation, the case law has failed to provide a coherent explanation how the central concepts employed in the case law are exactly defined and how they are related. For instance, Chapter 4 concludes that 'the three-stage approach does not provide any guidance on the key question in maritime delimitation – what weight is to be given to particular factors that arguably affect the equity of the final result?' Chapter 8, while focusing on the first stage of the delimitation process, observes that the actions of the judiciary in relation to that stage, with its promise of objectivity, do 'not match the language of distinct, successive stages.'[11] Apart from the argument that the first stage not only has to be objective, but also has to be 'appropriate for the geography of the area in which the delimitation is to take place,'[12] a reasoned justification for the judiciary's approach, which fuses the different stages, is lacking. Similarly, as is apparent from the analysis of Delabie in Chapter 6, the case law has failed to come up with an explanation of how equity and equitable principles are related to the three-stage approach. As a matter of fact, as Chapter 6 indicates, equity and equitable principles, seem to have receded to the background in the recent case law.

A second common theme emerging from the volume is what might be called the 'rise and fall' of central concepts of the law on maritime delimitation. While equidistance seemingly has gained in importance, the opposite seems to hold true for relevant circumstances and equity and equitable principles. Relevant circumstances in a number of recent cases seemingly have had a limited impact and equity and equitable principles seem to have been given short shrift in recent judgments. On closer consideration, the current analysis suggests a more complex picture.[13] First, while equidistance seemingly has moved centre-stage, relevant circumstances continue to exercise an influence in the background. As was already observed, the discarding of basepoints at the first stage of the three-stage approach, has introduced relevant circumstances at that stage, although this is not explicitly acknowledged by the judiciary. At times, this implies that the provisional delimitation line differs radically from the strict, and thus objective, equidistance line. Second, the case law's silence in relation to equitable principles does not imply the absence of evaluative assessments in all the three stages of the delimitation process. This is readily apparent from a reading of the recent case law. In that light, it may be questioned

[11] For another example in this respect, see the text after n. 41 below.

[12] *Maritime Delimitation in the Black Sea (Romania v. Ukraine)* (Judgment) [2009] ICJ Rep. 61, 101, [116].

[13] See also the discussion in Section 1.4.2 below.

whether the abandonment of an assessment of the individual case on the basis of equitable principles has contributed to the transparency of the deliberative process.

14.3 Understanding Consistency and Predictability

The common question we asked our contributors to consider was to what extent the case law on the delimitation of the continental shelf and the exclusive economic zone has been consistent and predictable. In order to assess the outcomes of this exercise, it is first of all necessary to have a closer look at these two terms. It would seem that these two terms are two sides of the same coin. Consistency would of necessity seem to imply predictability. A consideration of the dictionary meaning of both terms allows a better understanding of their relationship. The *Oxford English Dictionary* defines the term consistency as 'the quality of achieving a level of performance which does not vary greatly in quality over time.'[14] Predictability is defined as 'the ability to be predicted' while the verb to predict is defined as to 'say or estimate that (a specified thing) will happen in the future or will be a consequence of something.'[15] These dictionary meanings indicate that consistency has to do with the way in which courts and tribunals execute the functions entrusted to them and predictability has to do with what can be said about the outcome of a future case, based on an assessment of how courts and tribunals have executed their functions in the past. Put differently, consistency is concerned with past performance, while predictability is concerned with making projections about the future on the basis of past performance. The former is concerned with an evaluation of performance across different cases, while the latter has to do with an assessment of the individual case. Moreover, while the former has to do with the identification of the applicable law and methodology, the latter is concerned with their application to the individual case. At the same time, both issues have an obvious relationship. Absence of consistency will make it difficult if not impossible to predict the outcome of future cases.

The Court's proviso in its judgment in *Libya/Malta* that there has to be *a degree of* predictability, while it applied no such conditionality in the case of consistency,[16] suggests that an assessment of the possible outcome of a future case, with its individual idiosyncrasies, is fraught with more difficulty than securing consistency in defining the applicable law

[14] A. Stevenson (ed.), *Oxford Dictionary of English*, 3rd ed. (available online). [15] Ibid.

[16] *Continental Shelf (Libyan Arab Jamahiriya/Malta)* (Judgment) [1985] ICJ Rep. 13, [45].

and methodology. The difference between these two aspects may be illustrated by an example from the case law. As discussed in Chapter 8 of this volume, the judiciary in the recent case law has taken the approach that the process of selecting the provisional delimitation line at the same time has to be objective and appropriate in light of the geography of the particular case, i.e., certain basepoints may be disregarded in drawing a provisional equidistance line. While this implies consistency, it does not necessarily imply that the implications of this approach may be readily predictable for future cases. On the basis of the Court's explanation in *Black Sea* as to why Serpents' Island should be disregarded as a basepoint, it would have been difficult to predict that the ITLOS in its judgment in *Bangladesh/Myanmar* would disregard the much larger and inhabited St. Martin's Island, which was also differently placed in relation to the mainland coasts.

14.4 The Consistency and Predictability of the Case Law

14.4.1 Introduction

In view of the distinction that can be made between the issues of consistency and predictability they will be addressed separately in respectively Sections 14.4.2 and 14.4.3. In this connection, particular attention will be paid to the three-stage approach to maritime delimitation, which is at the heart of the current maritime delimitation case law. Before embarking on this exercise, this introductory section will briefly consider some of the recent literature that submits that the recent case law displays consistency and predictability, in order to get a better idea on what basis such claims are made.

Churchill, in a commentary on the judgment of the ITLOS in *Bangladesh/Myanmar*, concludes that it 'is notable for maintaining what appears now to be the settled case law of international courts and tribunals regarding delimitation of single maritime boundaries' and that the Tribunal 'followed the now well-established case law.'[17] This conclusion primarily seems to be based on the fact that the Tribunal applied the three-stage approach. Churchill's review of the judgment among others indicates that he does not question the Tribunal's approach to the first

[17] R. R. Churchill, 'The Bangladesh/Myanmar Case: Continuity and Novelty in the Law of Maritime Boundary Delimitation,' (2012) 1 *Cambridge Journal of International and Comparative Law* 137, 138, and 151.

stage of the delimitation process, which included the selection of basepoints, instead of using valid basepoints of the parties to arrive at an objectively determined equidistance line.[18] Degan submits that the predictability of the case law was initiated with the 1993 judgment in *Jan Mayen* and that there has been 'a tendency in the judicial and arbitral practice to define some simple and general rules leading to predictable results in their application.'[19] His analysis of the four cases subsequent to *Jan Mayen* – *Eritrea/Yemen*, *Qatar/Bahrain*, *Cameroon v. Nigeria* and *Barbados v. Trinidad and Tobago* – is largely descriptive in nature and does not question the approach to the law in these cases.[20] Shi, who focusses on the case law of the ICJ, concludes that 'the jurisprudence of the Court has evolved. It now establishes a set of unified principal steps for maritime delimitation.'[21] Shi identifies six steps the Court will normally follow. These steps include the three stages of the three-stage approach.[22] Shi indicates that the Court may vary its approach under the three stages of the three-stage approach, but Shi does not question whether this has any implications for the conclusion that the Court has a 'set of unified principal steps for maritime delimitation.'[23] Tanaka in his discussion of the judgment in *Black Sea* observes that the Court's incorporation of the equidistance method, being an objective method, in the delimitation provisions of the LOSC 'will enhance predictability in the application of those provisions.'[24] Tanaka does discuss the leeway courts and tribunals have afforded themselves in selecting the basepoints of the provisional equidistance line.[25] He commends the judiciary for taking this approach as it avoids an inequitable outcome of the delimitation process.[26] While it may be true that the use of certain basepoints might lead to an inequitable result, the pertinent question rather would seem to be how the selection

[18] Ibid., 143. It may be noted that Churchill does question the fact that the Tribunal again considered St. Martin's Island, which was disregarded at the first stage, at the second stage of the process, but he does not consider that the relevance of the island should only have been considered at the second stage (ibid., 144).

[19] V. Degan, 'Consolidation of Legal Principles on Maritime Delimitation: Implications for the Dispute between Slovenia and Croatia in the North Adriatic,' (2007) 6 *Chinese Journal of International Law* 601, 609.

[20] See e.g. ibid., 614–619, which largely consists of quotations from the award in *Barbados v. Trinidad and Tobago*.

[21] J. Shi, 'Maritime Delimitation in the Jurisprudence of the International Court of Justice,' (2010) 9 *Chinese Journal of International Law* 271, 290.

[22] Ibid., 290–291. [23] Ibid.

[24] Y. Tanaka, 'Reflections on Maritime Delimitation in the Romania/Ukraine Case before the ICJ,' (2009) 56 *Netherlands International Law Review* 397, 426.

[25] Ibid., 420–422. [26] Ibid., 422.

of basepoints in determining the provisional equidistance line affects the use of the objective method of equidistance at the first stage of the delimitation process and why the (in)equitability of the objectively determined equidistance line is not rather considered at the second stage of the three-stage approach.

This brief review allows making a number of observations. First, as long as the three-stage approach is considered at face value, it conveys the image of consistency. However, to get a clear understanding of the consistency of the case law, it is necessary to probe the veil of the three-stage approach and to check what is actually going on in the execution of each of the stages of the three-stage approach. Second, three of the articles concerned, by Churchill, Shi and Tanaka, seem to raise questions about the consistency of the case law on specific points. However, this does not lead to questioning the conclusion that the law displays or is moving towards consistency. Again, this may be explained by the fact that the focus is more on the overall approach and outcomes of the delimitation process than its constitutive elements. In addition, as will also become apparent from the following discussion, to some extent consistency and predictability are in the eye of the beholder, or, to put in in modern-day idiom, it is a matter of framing.

14.4.2 Consistency

As was concluded in Section 14.3, consistency as understood in the present chapter has to do with the approach to the law across cases. The individual chapters of this volume do not all point in the same direction as far as consistency is concerned. In part, this is explained by the paucity of the case law on specific topics. For instance, the issue of provisional arrangements, which is discussed in Chapter 5, has only been considered in *Guyana v. Suriname*. However, the comparison of the case law on provisional arrangements and provisional measures does suggest some emerging patterns and commonalties. For instance, Chapter 5 observes that the recent provisional measures order of the ITLOS in *Ghana/Côte d'Ivoire*[27] may inform certain aspects of the interpretation and application of Articles 74(3) and 83(3) of the LOSC dealing with provisional arrangements. The chapter also posits that it is possible to draw a number of more general connections between provisional arrangements and provisional measures.

[27] *Dispute concerning Delimitation of the Maritime Boundary between Ghana and Côte d'Ivoire in the Atlantic Ocean (Ghana/Côte d'Ivoire)* [2015].

The delimitation of the continental shelf beyond 200 nautical miles, which is discussed in Chapter 13, is another matter that has a limited track record in the case law. This notwithstanding, it raises an interesting question concerning the consistency of the case law. In *Bangladesh/Myanmar*, the ITLOS had to consider whether the three-stage approach that was developed in the context of the delimitation of 200-nautical-mile zones was also applicable beyond that distance. The Tribunal found this to be the case, but in doing so reformulated the case law justifying this approach, which is concerned with the relationship between entitlement to maritime zones and delimitation methodology, beyond recognition.[28] Apparently, consistency at the level of methodology (i.e., using equidistance/relevant circumstances within and beyond 200 nautical miles) was considered to be more important than consistency at the level of principle (i.e., the relationship between entitlement and delimitation). A possible explanation may be the recent case law's focus on process and methodology and the more limited attention to matters of principle. That may make it more appealing to muddle the waters at the level of principle than to propose an altogether new methodology.

Other chapters of the current volume also do not indicate that the different basis of entitlement beyond 200 nautical miles has had an impact on the delimitation process. The approach to relevant coasts and relevant area, relevant circumstances and the disproportionality test thus far does not display any differences within and beyond 200 nautical miles.

The other chapter on the delimitation of the continental shelf beyond 200 nautical miles, Chapter 12, deals with procedural issues, in particular the relationship between the establishment of the outer limits of the continental shelf involving the coastal state and the Commission on the Limits of the Continental Shelf (CLCS) and the delimitation of the continental shelf beyond 200 nautical miles between neighbouring states. There is a larger body of case law on this matter, which is mostly of the last decade. The question that has faced the judiciary in a number of cases is whether a court or tribunal may proceed with delimitation in the absence of

[28] In *Libya/Malta*, the Court observed that there is a logical connection between the distance-based entitlement to the 200-nautical-mile zone and the distance-based equidistance method (*Libya/Malta*, n. 16, [61]). In *Bangladesh/Myanmar* the Tribunal submitted that there was such a connection between the combined equidistance/relevant circumstances method and 'the recognition that sovereignty over the land territory is the basis for the sovereign rights and jurisdiction of the coastal State with respect to both the exclusive economic zone and the continental shelf' (*Bangladesh/Myanmar*, Judgment of 14 March 2012, [455]).

certainty about the outer limits of the continental shelf.[29] The most recent case law of the International Tribunal of the Law Of the Sea (ITLOS) and the ICJ suggests that they have worked out a common approach, but this has only been accomplished after a tortuous journey that does not indicate consistency. This may in part be explained by the fact that the Court first addressed this matter in a *dictum* in *Nicaragua v. Honduras* without the benefit of pleadings of the parties, which had not raised this issue. Moreover, it seems that, generally speaking, the judiciary has shown hesitance in cases in which the states concerned had not yet made a full submission to the CLCS.

The remaining chapters all deal with topics that have been part and parcel of the case law since its inception with *North Sea Continental Shelf*, such as the relationship between entitlement to maritime zones and their delimitation, that between equidistance and relevant circumstances, and the concept of relevant coasts. All of these chapters thus have considered a period in which the applicable law changed both as regards the basis of entitlement and the delimitation rules. As was set out in Chapter 1, continental shelf entitlement according to the Court's interpretation of Article 1 of the Convention on the Continental Shelf was based on natural prolongation from the land, not distance. Subsequently, distance became the dominant criterion within 200 nautical miles even prior to the adoption of the LOSC in 1982 and, until recently, the case law was almost exclusively concerned with the delimitation of 200-nautical-mile zones. The delimitation provision as contained in Article 6 of the Convention of the Continental Shelf went through two permutations. First, the Court defined a different rule of customary law in *North Sea Continental Shelf*, while UNCLOS III resulted in the anodyne delimitation provisions of Articles 74(1) and 83(1) of the LOSC, which according to the Court now reflect customary law.

The changes in the applicable law are most directly relevant to Chapter 3 dealing with the relationship between entitlement and delimitation and Chapter 4 dealing with the applicable law and to a lesser extent Chapter 6

[29] It has been submitted in the literature that the establishment of outer limits is indeed a prerequisite to proceed with delimitation (see B. Kunoy, 'The Admissibility of a Plea to an International Adjudicative Forum to Delimit the Outer Continental Shelf prior to the Adoption of Final Recommendations by the Commission on the Limits of the Continental Shelf,' (2010) 25 *International Journal of Marine and Coastal Law* 23; B. M. Magnusson, 'Is There Really a Temporal Relationship between the Delineation and Delimitation of the Continental Shelf beyond 200 Nautical Miles?,' (2013) 28 *International Journal of Marine and Coastal Law* 465).

dealing with the of role of equity, equitable principles, and the equitable solution and Chapter 8 dealing with the provisional equidistance line.

Chapter 3 submits that the *acquis*of the case law as far as the relationship between entitlement and delimitation is concerned is captured by the principle of 'the land dominates the sea.' At the same time, Chapter 3 points out that the 'conceptual bridge between *entitlement* and *delimitation* has been a far more difficult issue to tackle.' This in particular is the case in relation to the recent case law on the delimitation of the continental shelf beyond 200 nautical miles. As Antunes and Becker-Weinberg observe on the *Bay of Bengal* cases, '"[n]atural prolongation" (*basis of entitlement*) has apparently been given no relevance, either in establishing the provisional line or for purposes of adjustment thereto.' The authors also conclude that the case law has struggled with conceptualizing the relationship between the entitlement of islands and their role in the delimitation process. The treatment of islands 'has not contributed to certainty and predictability [. . .] [and] much can be improved as a matter of legal argumentation and judicial discourse.'

As Chapter 4 points out, the case law, with *North Sea Continental Shelf* being the only exception, has equated the different sources of the applicable law. A clear case of consistency. For anyone even moderately familiar with the delimitation case law this will hardly come as a surprise. However, as is argued by McRae, this equation of the sources of the law is not without problems. The formulation contained in Articles 74 and 83 was intended to overcome the stalemate between the equidistance and equitable principles group. As McRae observes, the case law has 'articulated a process to give effect to the basic rule of Article 74/83 of the LOSC.' This could be said to be a 'considerable development in the applicable law relating to maritime boundary delimitation.' However, under this process 'equidistance has been elevated into an almost mandatory provision – a result that seems at odds with the objectives behind Article 74 and 83.'[30] Second, the ultimate goal of the law at present is achieving an equitable

[30] Initially, the case law took a different approach to the delimitation provision contained in Arts. 74 and 83. The Court in *Tunisia/Libya* concluded:

> Treaty practice, as well as the history of Article 83 of the draft convention on the Law of the Sea, [which is identical to article 83 of the LOSC], leads to the conclusion that equidistance may be applied if it leads to an equitable solution; if not, other methods should be employed (*Case concerning the Continental Shelf (Tunisia/Libyan Arab Jamahiriya)* [1982] ICJ Rep. 246, [109]).

solution, as is explicitly stated in Articles 74 and 83. However, according to McRae:

> The jurisprudence has responded to this in ways that are not entirely clear or consistent. Three formulations can be identified. First, by developing a three-stage process for delimitation; second by endorsing the 'equidistance-relevant circumstances' approach; and third by saying that resort to equitable principles may also be appropriate. In doing so, they have blurred any dividing line between delimitation law and delimitation method.

An important theme of Chapter 6 is the shift from equity and equitable principles to the focus on the need to achieve an equitable solution. This development is in line with the explicit reference to the need to achieve an equitable solution in Articles 74 and 83. As the Court observed in *Black Sea*, the second and third stages of the three-stage approach are intended to achieve an equitable solution.[31] As was also observed above, the rebalance of the law in the direction of the three-stage approach and the equitable solution has taken place simultaneously. At the same time, the absence of attention for equitable principles in the more recent case law perhaps is one of the major deficiencies of the current law. As is submitted by McRae, the case law has failed to provide an objective basis for assessing the presence and impact of relevant circumstances, making the three-stage approach a cover for the application of equidistance. Equitable principles as first formulated by the Court in *North Sea Continental Shelf*, which are of a more general nature than relevant circumstances, could have provided the starting point for making the process of assessing the presence and impact of relevant circumstances more objective and as a consequence more consistent.

The advent of the distance-based 200-nautical-mile zone provided an important impetus to the acceptance of equidistance as the starting point for the delimitation of that zone.[32] At present, the equidistance method seems to be at the heart of the delimitation process. However, as the current volume indicates, this may be a pyrrhic victory. First, as detailed in Chapter 8, the determination of the provisional equidistance line in

[31] *Black Sea*, n. 12, [120] and [122].

[32] As a matter of fact, in *North Sea Continental Shelf*, Denmark and the Netherlands had already argued that such a link between entitlement and the equidistance method existed (n. 5, [39] and [44]). However, the Court in its judgment rejected that the notion of adjacency, which was the basis for coastal state entitlement to the continental shelf, implied a title based on proximity. Instead, the Court submitted that this basis of entitlement was the geophysically-based notion of natural prolongation. Ibid., [40–46].

most recent cases has become a subjective process, due to the selection of basepoints the judiciary considers appropriate, instead of using the validly determined basepoints of the coastal states involved.[33] Second, as is argued in Chapter 9, some of the recent case law in the second stage of the delimitation process has abandoned the equidistance line altogether. In the Bay of Bengal cases, the ITLOS and an arbitral tribunal adopted an azimuth as the final boundary instead of the equidistance line. It would not be an exaggeration to say that this constitutes a return to *Tunisia/Libya*, which is considered to be the high point of equity and unpredictability. In *Tunisia/Libya*, the Court submitted that equidistance could be applied if it led to an equitable solution, 'if not, other methods should be employed.'[34] The Court adopted such other methods on the basis of the consideration of the relevant circumstances of the case. In view of its reference to equidistance, it is safe to assume that the Court considered and rejected that equidistance led to an equitable solution. This results in a perfect match with *Bangladesh/Myanmar*. In that case, the ITLOS considered equidistance and concluded that it did not lead to an equitable solution and instead adopted a different method of delimitation on the basis of the relevant circumstances of the case. That different method was in no way linked to the provisional equidistance line, which had been established at the first stage of the three-stage approach.

Strict equidistance has been applied in a number of cases in the process of determining the provisional equidistance line. Chapter 8 discusses *Qatar/Bahrain* in some detail. Other cases in which strict equidistance was applied in determining the provisional delimitation line of the exclusive economic zone and the continental shelf include *Guyana v. Suriname* and *Barbados v. Trinidad and Tobago*. While in the latter case there does not seem to be any reason to discount specific features in determining the equidistance line – basepoints are located on the island of Barbados and a number of small islands that are very close to the island of Tobago – in the former two cases, baseline issues could have well led to the selection of basepoints in order to depart from the strict equidistance line. Chapter 8 discusses this point for *Qatar/Bahrain*. In *Guyana v. Suriname* the parties differed about the validity of newly charted basepoints depicted on Dutch chart NL 2218 and Guyana submitted evidence that the baseline was at a different location.[35] The tribunal concluded on this point that it was:

[33] For possible explanations of this approach, see Section 14.6 below.

[34] *Tunisia/Libya*, n. 30, [109].

[35] *In the Matter of an Arbitration between Guyana and Suriname (Guyana v. Suriname)* [2007] 30 RIAA 1, [395].

> not convinced that the depiction of the low-water line on chart NL 2218, a chart recognised as official by Suriname, is inaccurate. As a result, the Tribunal accepts the basepoint on Vissers Bank, Suriname's basepoint S14.[36]

Recent case law disregarding specific basepoints has failed to explain what distinguishes it from those cases that did apply strict equidistance at the first stage.[37]

Chapter 8 also raises the question whether stricter adherence to equidistance at the first stage of drawing the provisional delimitation line, i.e., using all valid basepoints of the parties, instead of making a subjective selection of some of those basepoints while disregarding others, would have led to different results. Chapter 8 submits that in many cases it probably would not have mattered. As has been argued elsewhere, in some cases a stricter adherence to equidistance at the first stage likely would have led to a different outcome.[38] Stricter adherence to the equidistance line at the first stage of the delimitation process could in some instances also have led to a final boundary that would have been an adjusted equidistance line.[39] This would have avoided the approach of abandoning the equidistance line altogether at the second stage of the delimitation process. As argued above, this approach makes the first stage of the three-stage approach largely irrelevant and implies a return to *Tunisia/Libya*. In conclusion, the approach of the case law to the determination of the provisional equidistance line can only be called consistent in the sense that the judiciary has taken much latitude in selecting base points.

Chapter 7 on the relevant coasts and the relevant area concludes that the case law on these issues has been far from consistent. One problem that was identified is that the general criteria formulated in *Tunisia/Libya*, which have been accepted by a considerable number of cases, do not allow the identification of meaningful relevant coasts and a meaningful relevant area in all geographical situations. Second, these general criteria have not been applied consistently in the context of individual cases. The same applies if different cases are compared. For instance, in some cases seaward projection is understood as a projection that is (approximately) perpendicular to the general direction of the relevant coasts, but in other cases areas well beyond a perpendicular projection from the relevant coasts have been included in the relevant area.

[36] Ibid., [396]. [37] For possible explanations of this approach, see Section 14.6 below.

[38] See A. G. Oude Elferink, 'International Law and Negotiated and Adjudicated Maritime Boundaries: A Complex Relationship,' (2015) 58 *German Yearbook of International Law* 231, 252–255.

[39] Ibid.

Chapter 9 seemingly reaches a positive conclusion on the consistency of the case law as regards the issue of relevant circumstance. After quoting the judgment in *Libya/Malta*, which found that 'justice according to the rule of law [. . .] looks with particularity to the peculiar circumstances of an instant case, it also looks beyond it to principles of more general application,'[40] the chapter submits that 'the conclusion must be that it is met, since those more general principles concerning relevant circumstances can – and, it is hoped, here have been – identified and presented in a sufficiently coherent and consistent fashion.'[41] However, Chapter 9 also submits that:

> Even after the introduction of the three-stage approach, [relevant circumstances] appear to be as open-textured and as decisive – yet as nebulous – as ever, and continue to operate at all stages of the delimitation process as a means of influencing its outcome, however described or addressed.

As is also argued by Evans, this evinces the consistency of the case law on this point, albeit not in a way that contributes to the transparency and predictability of the process.

Chapter 10 on third states reveals perhaps one of the most fundamental challenges of the case law as far as consistency is concerned. On the one hand, Chapter 10 indicates that the case law has been careful to avoid prejudice to the positions of third states. This has been mostly achieved by not determining maritime boundaries between the parties to a case in an area in which a third state also has claims. On the other hand, the presence of third states and their potential boundaries with the parties to a case continues to be taken into account in determining what constitutes an equitable solution between the parties. Looking beyond the bilateral boundary relationship of the parties may be unavoidable in ensuring an equitable solution to both parties – as only that wider context identifies the extent of their maritime zones – but at the same time implies a pronouncement on the delimitation context involving the parties and the third state.

The focus of Chapter 11 is on the third-stage (dis)proportionality test. Tanaka concludes that the test has not been consistently applied in the recent case law. In most recent cases, the judiciary has presented specific figures for the length of the relevant coasts and the size of the relevant area and compared those figures. However, this has not been done in other

[40] *Libya/Malta*, n. 16, [45].

[41] For a more pessimistic assessment in this respect, see Chapter 4 of this volume. The relevant point is also discussed above in this section.

recent cases such as *Nicaragua v. Honduras* and *Maritime Dispute (Peru v. Chile)*. Tanaka in discussing the latter case submits that 'serious doubts could be expressed with regard to the objectiveness of the broad assessment of disproportionality in this case.' As the analysis in Chapter 7 suggests, this failure to resort to specific calculations may not so much be due to some inherent shortcoming of the third stage, but rather may be explained by the fact that these cases did not allow a meaningful definition of the relevant coasts and relevant area on the basis of the approach to these matters developed in the case law. Tanaka also observes that there is:

> excessive subjectivity with regard to the evaluation of (dis)proportionality [. . .]. On the basis of the jurisprudence in this field, it is difficult to identify an objective standard for determining disproportion between the ratio of the relevant coastal lengths and maritime areas belonging to each party.

A final point to be noted about the disproportionality test is that it has always been met. It is submitted that this can hardly be otherwise. Prior to the third stage, a court or tribunal will have established an appropriate provisional line and assessed all the relevant circumstances that may or may not lead to an adjustment of this line. In other words, these aspects of the process have been fully considered. Not meeting the disproportionality test would imply that a court or tribunal in applying the first two stages did not 'get it right' and has not properly applied the law to the circumstances of the case. Still, this does not mean that the disproportionality test is without purpose. First, it creates the impression of a check on the first two stages. Second, it cannot be excluded that the test is used during the internal deliberations of courts and tribunals to assess the equitability of different possible outcomes. If that were to be the case, it could well be said that this would be the most important function of the disproportionality test.

An overall assessment of the case law's consistency is a daunting task. First, how should clear outlier cases be judged?[42] Are these part of a broader pattern of inconsistency, or should they rather be viewed as anomalies, that may moreover be explained by the peculiarities of that individual case. Second, the development of the law likely has impacted on the approach of the case law to delimitation. Finally, how should consistency be judged? The clearest example in this respect is the first stage

[42] For an example of such an outlier, see the discussion in Chapter 8 of this volume of *Maritime Dispute (Peru v. Chile)*.

of the three-stage approach, that has been infused with subjectivity by the judiciary. Moreover, in taking this approach the judiciary has introduced the second-stage consideration of relevant circumstances, without saying this with so many words, into the first stage of the process. The case law could be said to be consistent in the sense that this is now the standard approach. However, it is not consistent if it measured against the purpose of the three-stage approach of infusing the delimitation process with objectivity. Another example is the three-stage approach itself. It has become the standard for dealing with delimitation cases. However, the adoption of that standard approach has not accomplished consistency in relation to the individual stages of that approach. As the preceding analysis points out, depending on the answers that are given to the above questions, different assessments of the case law's consistency are possible.

14.4.3 Predictability

Predictability is concerned with the ability to predict the outcome of future cases on the basis of the existing case law. Taking the formulation of the Court in *Libya/Malta* again as our starting point, it should be recalled that the Court considered that there only was a need for 'a *degree* of predictability.'[43] No such condition was attached to the requirement of consistency by the Court.[44] This difference is explained by the different purposes of the two concepts.[45] While consistency is concerned with the formulation of the law and the process that needs to be followed in effecting maritime boundary delimitation, predictability refers to the individual future case. That individual case may display characteristics that were not previously considered by the case law and such characteristics may require a different approach to the operationalization or application of the law.

The existence of predictability can be assessed both by looking at a specific past case and trying to determine whether the outcome could have been predicted on the basis of the then existing case law and by looking at cases that are currently pending before the judiciary. To start with the former, in Section 14.3 above it was already argued that the treatment of St. Martin's Island at the first stage in *Bangladesh/Myanmar* would seem to

[43] *Libya/Malta*, n. 16, [45] (emphasis provided). [44] Ibid.

[45] At the same time it has to be acknowledged that both concepts are closely related. Lesser consistency would result in greater unpredictability, and little predictability could be the result from inconsistency.

have been difficult to predict on the basis of the Court's assessment of Serpents' Island in *Black Sea*. Second, in *Bangladesh/Myanmar* the ITLOS had to consider the relationship between entitlement of the continental shelf beyond 200 nautical miles and delimitation methodology. The Tribunal's approach hardly could have been predicted on the basis of the findings of previous cases on the relationship between entitlement to and delimitation of maritime zones.[46] Another example is provided by *Barbados v. Trinidad and Tobago*. The arbitral tribunal considered that the significant disparity between the relevant coasts of the parties constituted a relevant circumstance, but only adjusted the provisional equidistance line to a limited extent to give effect to that circumstance. In particular the judgment in *Jan Mayen* would have led one to predict a different impact of this relevant circumstance on the provisional line.[47] However, it is submitted that these examples do not reflect a broad pattern of unpredictability. For instance, small islands have been routinely disregarded in determining a mainland-to-mainland boundary or have been enclaved in 12-nautical mile territorial sea and specific relevant circumstances introduced by the parties have been routinely dismissed.

Turning to the pending cases of *Ghana/Côte d'Ivoire* and *Somalia v. Kenya*, we will at this point attempt to make a forecast on the basis of the existing case law. First, there is no reason to assume that the Court and the Chamber of the ITLOS will not apply the three-stage approach. Second, the coastal geography of both cases is such that we expect that a strict equidistance line, or an equidistance line very similar to the strict equidistance line, will be adopted as the provisional delimitation line. Third, we do not expect a radical departure from the equidistance line after the second-stage consideration of the relevant circumstances of each case.[48] Hydrocarbon licensing is likely to be considered as a potential relevant circumstance in both cases, but it is not expected that this practice requires a shifting of the provisional line. Fourth, the fact that Kenya's boundary

[46] For a further discussion, see above and Chapter 13 of this volume.

[47] For a further discussion of the comparison between *Barbados v. Trinidad and Tobago* and *Jan Mayen*, see Oude Elferink, n. 38, at 256–259.

[48] One note of caution is, however, necessary. We currently do not have access to the exact location of the continental shelf beyond 200 nautical miles in either case. If the equidistance line would lead to an unequal division of that area, presuming further that the Court and the Chamber will conclude that it is possible to proceed with that delimitation, that circumstance might lead to a shift of the provisional equidistance line beyond 200 nautical miles.

with Tanzania and the equidistance line between the former and Somalia further seaward move closer is unlikely to lead to the conclusion that the latter line leads to a cut-off or otherwise requires an adjustment of the final delimitation line.

Finally, we expect that the Chamber and the Court will have no difficulty in determining the relevant coasts and the relevant area. In the case of Somalia and Kenya it seems likely that the Court will at least select all of the coasts of the parties within 200 nautical miles of their common land boundary and possibly also the coast of Kenya up to its land boundary with Tanzania and for Somalia the coast up to Mogadishu or possible even some distance further north. For this latter definition, it is to be expected that the relevant area would be bounded by the relevant coasts, a perpendicular to the northern terminus of the relevant coasts, the outer limits of the maritime zones of the parties and the maritime boundary between Kenya and Tanzania. Turning to *Ghana/Côte d'Ivoire*, for Ghana, different options to define the relevant coast could be entertained: the coast from its land boundary with Côte d'Ivoire up to Cape Three Point, after which the coast clearly changes direction; the coast up to 200 nautical miles from that land boundary; or the entire coast of Ghana.[49] In the case of Côte d'Ivoire it may be expected that the Chamber will either adopt the coast up to 200 nautical miles from the land boundary with Ghana or the entire coast of Côte d'Ivoire. The relevant area can be expected to be bounded by the relevant coasts and the outer limits of the maritime zones of the parties. Depending on the definition of the relevant coasts, the lateral limits of the relevant area will be either perpendiculars to the general direction of these coast, lines of longitude (meridians) or the (potential) maritime boundaries with neighbouring states. We are confident that the third-stage test will point out that an equidistance boundary does not lead to disproportionality in either case.

Our assessment of *Ghana/Côte d'Ivoire* and *Somalia v. Kenya* strongly suggests that the law and methodology as developed by the case law result in a degree of predictability. It would not even seem unreasonable to submit that these cases suggest a high degree of predictability. At the same time, a word of caution is needed. *Ghana/Côte d'Ivoire* and *Somalia v. Kenya* are two cases with an uncomplicated coastal geography. In that respect, confidently predicting the approach and outcome in *Maritime Delimitation in the Caribbean Sea and the Pacific Ocean (Costa Rica v.*

[49] These different definitions are unlikely to have an impact on the outcome of the case, as they do not seem to lead to significantly different outcomes of the disproportionality test.

Nicaragua) that is currently pending before the Court would seem to be a much more difficult task.[50]

14.5 The Normativity of the Current Delimitation Process[51]

The corpus of the law as contained in the Convention on the Continental Shelf and the LOSC is limited to the statement of general rules. These general rules required further operationalization to allow application to the individual case. This raises the question whether this operationalization involves the development of these general rules into more specific rules, or the exercise of wide discretionary powers, without necessarily specifying the general rules.

As a point of departure, the judgment in *Black Sea*, which provided a cogent formulation of the three-stage approach, may be considered. In the section discussing the applicable law, the Court refers to Articles 74 and 83 of the LOSC, but adds that 'the principles of maritime delimitation to be applied by the Court in this case are determined' by these articles.[52] The Court does not further elaborate on the nature of these principles.

The discussion of the three-stage approach in the judgment in *Black Sea* is contained in a section entitled 'Delimitation Methodology.'[53] The

[50] This assessment calls to mind the observation that:

> the oscillation between predictability and flexibility seems set to remain a feature of the jurisprudence, with relatively 'easy' cases (such as [*Black Sea*]) being used to flagship the merits of the fairly formal application of objective criteria whereas the more complex (such as [*Territorial and Maritime Dispute (Nicaragua v. Colombia)*]) will continue to pull in the direction of a more results-oriented approach.

(M. D. Evans, 'Maritime Boundary Delimitation,' in D. R. Rothwell, A. G. Oude Elferink, K. N. Scott, and T. Stephens (eds.), *The Oxford Handbook of the Law of the Sea* (Oxford University Press Oxford 2015) 254, 278).

The authors consider that further comment on *Maritime Delimitation in the Caribbean Sea and the Pacific Ocean (Costa Rica v. Nicaragua)* would not be proper in view of the fact that one of them is acting as counsel for Nicaragua in that case.

[51] For a more detailed, but dated, discussion of this matter, see e.g. P. Weil, *The Law of Maritime Delimitation: Reflections* (Grotius Cambridge 1989) 159–185 and 279–288; N. Marques Antunes, *Towards the Conceptualisation of Maritime Delimitation* (Martinus Nijhoff Leiden 2003) 226–238.

[52] *Black Sea*, n. 12, [41]. The Court's current view on the normative nature of the delimitation process differs from that expressed in the past. Equitable principles were considered to be part of the normative framework to be applied (see e.g. *Libya/Malta*, n. 16, [46]). The demise of the concept of equitable principles, which is linked to a change in the applicable law, as detailed in Chapter 6 of this volume, explains this difference in approach.

[53] *Black Sea*, n. 12, 101.

Court starts out by observing that '[w]hen called upon to delimit the continental shelf or exclusive economic zones, or to draw a single delimitation line, the Court proceeds in defined stages.'[54] This formulation does not suggest an *obligation* to proceed in these defined stages, and the Court subsequently observes that in this respect it is acting 'in keeping with its settled jurisprudence on maritime delimitation.' Again, the Court is not indicating that there is a requirement to do so – the doctrine of *stare decisis*is not applicable to the Court – but it does suggest that it may at least be expected that the Court will act in accordance with the three-stage approach.[55]

The award in *Bangladesh v. India* is a clear departure from the Court's view on the delimitation methodology involving the three-stage approach as expressed in *Black Sea* and other recent decision of the Court. As the tribunal observed:

> [t]he ensuing – and still developing – international case law constitutes, in the view of the Tribunal, an *acquis judiciaire*, a source of international law under article 38(1)(d) of the Statute of the International Court of Justice, and should be read into articles 74 and 83 of the [LOSC].[56]

To determine the implications of this position, it is first of all required to consider Article 38(1)(d) of the Statute, which provides that:

[54] Ibid., [115].

[55] In another recent case, the Court again distinguished between the applicable law as reflected in Arts. 74 and 83 of the LOSC and the delimitation methodology as reflected by the three-stage approach (see *Maritime Dispute (Peru v. Chile)*, n. 6, [179]–[180]). In referring to this methodology, the Court repeatedly qualified it by the word 'usual' (see e.g. ibid., [180] and [184]). A similar reference is contained in *Territorial and Maritime Dispute (Nicaragua v. Colombia)* (Judgment) [2012] ICJ Rep. 624, [198].

[56] *In the Matter of the Bay of Bengal Maritime Boundary (Bangladesh v. India)* PCA Case 2010-16, [339]. The idea of *acquis judiciaire* had previously be formulated by Judge Wolfrum in a declaration appended to the judgment in *Bangladesh/Myanmar (Delimitation of the Maritime Boundary in the Bay of Bengal (Bangladesh/Myanmar)* [2012] ITLOS Rep. 4, Declaration Judge Wolfrum, 137). In *Bangladesh v. India*, Wolfrum acted as president of the five-member tribunal. The term *acquis judiciaire* is reminiscent of the term *acquis communautaire*, which is used in European Union law. This acquis has been summarized as:

> the collective legal term for European Union law. It stands for the whole body of written and unwritten EU laws, the EU's political aims, and the obligations, rights, and remedies the Member States share and must adhere to with regard to the EU. It is thus not a source of law itself, but a heterogeneous and amorphous blend of politics and laws of different hierarchical order, setting the benchmark for the current state of European integration. (M. Hilf, 'Acquis communautaire,' in *Max Planck Encyclopedia of Public International Law*, online ed.; last updated July 2009, [1])

The *acquis communautaire* as thus defined would seem to be closer to the settled practice to which the ICJ refers then to the tribunal's definition of the *acquis judiciaire* as a source of law.

> subject to the provisions of Article 59 of the Statute], judicial decisions and the teachings of the most highly qualified publicists of the various nations, as subsidiary means for the determination of rules of law.

Article 38(1)(d) of the Statute does not refer to judicial decisions as sources of international law, as the award does, but 'as subsidiary means for the determination of rules of law.' Reading the case law on maritime boundary delimitation into Articles 74 and 83 of the LOSC is not using that case law as a subsidiary means for the determination of rules of law, but instead is replacing Articles 74 and 83 by other rules of law. Still, it can be argued that there is a normative basis for the three-stage approach. Following the methodology that is usually applied in the delimitation of maritime boundaries would be in accordance with the general principle of proper administration of justice, without that methodology in itself in its totality acquiring normative force.[57]

The analysis and conclusions of some of the chapters of this volume do suggest that normativity in the delimitation process extends beyond the basic rule as contained in Articles 74 and 83 of the LOSC as reflected in customary international law. For instance, Chapter 9 concludes that 'it may be going too far to claim that particular matters or issues *will be* relevant circumstances as a matter of customary international law,' but 'recourse to relevant circumstances within the delimitation process represents a principle of customary law,' while McRae in Chapter 4 observes that 'it may be suggested that the applicable law today consists of a requirement to utilize a particular methodology and to engage in a particular process of assessment within that methodology in order to delimit a boundary.' Other chapters confirm that, whatever way the normativity of the law is defined, the rules are impressionistic rather than objective and precise. This leads Tanaka to conclude that '[i]t seems questionable whether the disproportionality test developed through the jurisprudence is adequately objective and scientific as a norm of international law.' Coming up with such rigid rules would in any case not seem to be appropriate in this field of the law. As was written almost thirty years ago by Weil:

> none of the concepts making up the delimitation process has so far been the subject of any scientific, or even reasonably rigorous, definition; all depend, in various degrees, on the qualitative and therefore intuitive assessment of the judge: 'I know it when I see it.'[58]

[57] For the Court's view that the proper administration of justice is a general principle of law it is required to apply, see e.g. *Certain Phosphate Lands in Nauru (Nauru v. Australia)*, [2002] Judgment, ICJ Rep. 240, [69].

[58] P. Weil, n. 51, 287 (footnote omitted).

Even though the law has evolved much since that time and we conclude that the case law has perhaps displayed too little consistency on certain points, these words still hold true today. A good judgment will involve translating intuition into an elegant legal argument.

14.6 The Future of the Case Law

The maritime delimitation case law has a history of almost fifty years. In light of the number of currently pending delimitations and the slow pace at which they are being resolved, it seems likely that its future will span at least a couple of decades. What does this future hold in store? Central to this question would seem to be the fate of the three-stage approach.

As a number of chapters in this volume suggest, the transparency and objectiveness of the process of maritime delimitation could be reinforced by avoiding subjectivity at the first stage.[59] If it is possible to determine an equidistance line, which almost invariably will be the case, that line should be determined objectively on the basis of the relevant basepoints.[60] Only after this equidistance line has been determined, it should be assessed at the second stage of the process whether certain of these basepoints or the features on which they are located constitute relevant circumstances that would require a shift of the provisional equidistance line. This would allow (and require) a more detailed assessment of such basepoints than is now often the case at the first stage of the delimitation process. How likely is it that the judiciary might adopt this approach in the future?

The past case law perhaps would seem to be the best starting point for answering the question whether there will be a sharper distinction between the first two stages of the delimitation process in the future. As is set out in Chapter 8 and Section 14.4.2 above, that case law has already taken this approach in a number of instances, showing that it is almost always perfectly feasible. So, why not do so always? A possible answer to

59 The same point has been made by S. Fietta and R. Cleverly, *A Practitioner's Guide to Maritime Boundary Delimitation* (Oxford University Press Oxford 2015) 579 *et seq*. The importance of this point is forcefully made by Lathrop in Chapter 8 of this volume:

> When a sound procedural methodology has been developed and a court or tribunal claims to apply it, that application should be faithful to the process as described. Courts and tribunals that ignore or distort their own process undermine the legitimacy of their decisions unnecessarily.

60 As Chapter 8 explains, this does require a prior determination as to whether the basepoints concerned have been established in accordance with the relevant rules as contained in Parts II and VIII of the LOSC.

this question is provided by Chapters 4, 8, and 9 of this volume. First, as McRae points out, it avoids the need for a fuller explanation, as would be required at the second stage of the process. Second, as Lathrop observes 'by cloaking subjective considerations of equity and appropriateness in the language of objectivity [at the first stage], judges [may be] attempting to avoid the critique of arbitrariness and imprecision often leveled at the second stage consideration of relevant circumstances.' Finally, Evans suggests that judges may favor making judgment calls at the first stage, because it has been much less open to scrutiny than the second stage. The recent attention to this aspect of the case law might suggest that these considerations, to the extent they play a role, might perhaps have somewhat less traction in future cases.

Other chapters in this volume also have made suggestions concerning the approach of the case law to delimitation methodology. For instance, Chapter 7 suggested that a preferable approach to the concepts of relevant coasts and relevant area 'might have been to solely rely on more general precepts underlying maritime delimitation law. That approach would have provided the flexibility to deal with the particularities of the individual case and avoids relying on general criteria that cannot be applied (equally) to all individual cases' as is currently the case. Another example is provided by Chapter 11 in which it is suggested that the disproportionality test either 'should be limited to the situations where a provisional equidistance line would create the cut-off effect by a markedly concave or convex coastline' or otherwise, if the test continued to be applied to all situations, its objectiveness should be enhanced.

If the past of the case law is taken as the point of reference, we submit that it is unlikely that the future case law will be characterized by new approaches. It seems more likely that courts and tribunals will gloss over the difficulties they encounter in dealing with factual circumstances that are difficult to fit into the existing general concepts and approaches. In that connection, it seems likely that they will either seek to square their own solution with the existing general concepts and approaches or instead look for a different approach without being very explicit that this implies a departure from the existing standard. Both Chapters 7 and 11 are a case in point in this respect. This point may be further illustrated by the delimitation of the continental shelf beyond 200 nautical miles. As Chapter 13 indicates, in certain cases a provisional equidistance line may not provide an appropriate starting point because that line is located beyond the area of overlapping entitlements that need to be delimited. This lack of a direct relationship between the equidistance method of delimitation and the basis of continental shelf entitlement would seem to make equidistance an inappropriate starting point as a matter of principle. This notwithstanding, we would expect that a court or tribunal that would be faced with this situation would not opt to openly reject the approach of the ITLOS and the arbitral tribunal in the Bay of Bengal cases, but would rather refer to the judgment in *Black Sea* where the Court noted that a provisional delimitation line has to be determined 'using methods that are geometrically objective and also appropriate for the geography of the area in which the delimitation is to take place,'[61] i.e., it could apply a line different from equidistance without the need for an open departure from the Bay of Bengal cases.

In light of these thoughts on the future of the maritime delimitation case law and the preceding analysis, it should be clear that research into the consistency and predictability of the case law on maritime delimitation is likely to remain relevant in the years to come.

[61] *Black Sea*, n. 12, 101, [116].

BIBLIOGRAPHY

Adede, A. O., 'Toward the Formulation of the Rule of Delimitation of Sea Boundaries between States with Adjacent or Opposite Coasts,' (1979) 19 *Virginia Journal of International Law* 207.

Anderson, D., 'Bay of Bengal Maritime Boundary (Bangladesh *v.* India),' (2015) 105 *American Journal of International Law* 146.

'Maritime Delimitation in the Black Sea Case (Romania *v.* Ukraine),' (2009) 8 *Law and Practice of International Courts and Tribunals* 305.

'The Principle of Reasonableness in the Law of the Sea,' in H. P. Hestermeyer, D. Köning, N. Matz-Lück, V. Röben, A. Seibert-Fohr, P.-T. Stoll, and S. Vöneky (eds.), *Coexistence, Cooperation and Solidarity, Liber Amicorum Rüdiger Wolfrum* (Martinus Nijhoff Leiden 2012) 667.

'Recent Judicial Decisions Concerning Maritime Delimitation,' in L. del Castillo (ed.), *Law of the Sea, from Grotius to the International Tribunal for the Law of the Sea* (Brill/Nijhoff Leiden 2015) 500.

Antunes, N. M., *Towards the Conceptualisation of Maritime Delimitation* (Martinus Nijhoff Leiden 2003).

Árnadóttir, S., 'Termination of Maritime Boundaries due to a Fundamental Change of Circumstances,' (2016) 32 *Utrecht Journal of International and European Law* 83.

Attard, D. J., *The Exclusive Economic Zone in International Law* (Oxford University Press Oxford 1987).

Bankes, N., 'The Relationship between Declarations under the Optional Clause of the Statute of the International Court of Justice and Part XV of the Law of the Sea Convention' (K. G. Jebsen Centre for the Law of the Sea blog, available at http://site.uit.no/jclos/files/2017/02/The-relationship-between-declarations-under-the-optional-clause-of-the-Statute-of-the-International-Court-of-Justice-and-Part-XV-of-the-Law-of-the-Sea-Convention.pdf).

Bardonnet, D., 'Equité et frontières terrestres,' *in Mélanges offerts à Paul Reuter. Le droit international: unité et diversité* (Pedone Paris 1981).

Becker-Weinberg, V., *Joint Development of Hydrocarbon Deposits in the Law of the Sea* (Springer Hamburg 2014).

Bianchi, A., and Peters A. (eds.), *Transparency in International Law* (Cambridge University Press Cambridge 2013).

Bonafe, B., 'Interests of a Legal Nature Justifying Intervention before the ICJ,' (2012) 25 *Leiden Journal of International Law* 3, 739.

Bowett, D. W., *The Legal Regime of Islands in International Law* (Oceana Publications New York 1979).

Brower, C. H., 'Arbitration,' in *Max Planck Encyclopedia of Public International Law* (online ed.; last updated February 2007).

Brown, C., 'Article 59,' in A. Zimmerman et al. (eds.), *The Statute of the International Court of Justice: A Commentary* (Oxford University Press Oxford 2012) 1434.

Brown, E. D., *Legal Regime of Hydrospace* (Stevens and Sons London 1971).

Sea-bed Energy and Minerals: The International Legal Regime (Martinus Nijhoff Leiden 1992).

'The Tunisia-Libya Continental Shelf Case: A Missed Opportunity,' (July 1983) *Marine Policy* 142.

Buga, I., 'Territorial Sovereignty Issues in Maritime Disputes: A Jurisdictional Dilemma for Law of the Sea Tribunals,' (2012) 59 *International Journal of Marine and Coastal Law* 27.

Busch, S. V., *Establishing Continental Shelf Limits beyond 200 Nautical Miles by the Coastal State: A Right of Involvement for Other States*? (Brill Nijhoff Leiden 2016).

Cazala, J., 'Retour sur les méthodes de délimitation juridictionnelle d'espaces maritimes mises en œuvre dans quelques affaires récentes,' (2008) 54 *Annuaire français de droit international* 411.

Charney, J. I., 'Ocean Boundaries between Nations: A Theory for Progress,' (1984) 78 *American Journal of International Law* 582.

'Progress in International Maritime Delimitation Law,' (1994) 88 *American Journal of International Law* 227.

Churchill, R. R., 'The Bangladesh/Myanmar Case: Continuity and Novelty in the Law of Maritime Boundary Delimitation,' (2012) 1 *Cambridge Journal of International and Comparative Law* 137.

'Dispute Settlement in the Law of the Sea: Survey for 2014,' (2015) 13 *International Journal of Marine and Coastal Law* 585.

Churchill, R. R., and Lowe A. V., *The Law of the Sea*, 3rd ed. (Manchester University Press Manchester 1999).

Colson, D., 'The Delimitation of the Outer Continental Shelf between Neighboring States,' (2003) 97 *American Journal of International Law* 91.

Cooper, J., 'Delimitation of the Maritime Boundary in the Gulf of Maine Area,' (1986) 16 *Ocean Development and International Law* 59.

Corten, O., *L'utilisation du 'raisonnable' par le juge international: discours juridique, raison et contradictions* (Bruylant Bruxelles 1997).

Cottier, T., *Equitable Principles of Maritime Boundary Delimitation: The Quest for Distributive Justice in International Law* (Cambridge University Press Cambridge 2015).

Crawford, J. (ed.), *Brownlie's Principles of Public International Law*, 8th ed. (Oxford University Press Oxford 2012).

Currie, J., 'Maritime Boundary Delimitation in a Federal Domestic Setting: The Newfoundland and Labrador *v.* Nova Scotia Arbitration,' (2004) 17 *Leiden Journal of International Law* 155.

Daillier, P., Forteau, M., and Pellet, A., *Droit international public* (LGDJ Paris 2009).

Davenport, T., 'ASEAN Approaches to Maritime Boundary Disputes: Wider Implications for ASEAN,' (2013) 107 *Proceedings of the Annual Meeting of the American Society of International Law* 281.

Degan, V., 'Consolidation of Legal Principles on Maritime Delimitation: Implications for the Dispute between Slovenia and Croatia in the North Adriatic,' 6 (2007) *Chinese Journal of International Law* 601.

Delabie, L., 'Le fragile équilibre entre prévisibilité juridique et opportunité judiciaire en matière de délimitation maritime: l'arrêt de la Cour internationale de Justice du 19 novembre 2012 dans l'affaire du différend territorial et maritime (Nicaragua c. Colombie),' (2012) *Annuaire français de droit international* 223.

del Castillo, L. (ed.), *Law of the Sea, from Grotius to the International Tribunal for the Law of the Sea, Liber Amicorum Judge Hugo Caminos* (Brill/Nijhoff Leiden 2015) 58.

Eiriksson, G., 'The Bay of Bengal Case before the International Tribunal for the Law of the Sea,' in L. del Castillo (ed.), *Law of the Sea, from Grotius to the International Tribunal for the Law of the Sea, Liber Amicorum Judge Hugo Caminos* (Brill/Nijhoff Leiden 2015) 514.

Evans, M. D., 'Delimitation and the Common Maritime Boundary,' (1993) 64 *British Yearbook of International Law* 283.

'Maritime Boundary Delimitation,' in D. R. Rothwell, A. G. Oude Elferink, K. N. Scott, and T. Stephens (eds.), *The Oxford Handbook of the Law of the Sea* (Oxford University Press Oxford 2015) 255.

'Maritime Boundary Delimitation: Whatever Next?,' in J. Barrett and R. Barnes (eds.), *Law of the Sea; UNCLOS as a Living Treaty* (British Institute of International and Comparative Law London 2016) 41.

'Maritime Boundary Delimitation: Where Do We Go from Here?,' in D. Freestone, R. Barnes, and D. Ong (eds.), *The Law of the Sea: Progress and Prospects* (Oxford University Press Oxford 2006) 155.

'Maritime Delimitation and Expanding Categories of Relevant Circumstances,' (1990) 40 *International and Comparative Law Quarterly* 1.

Relevant Circumstances and Maritime Delimitation (Oxford University Press Oxford 1989).

Fietta, S., 'International Court of Justice Judgment on Sovereignty over Disputed Islands, and Delimitation of the Territorial Sea, Exclusive Economic Zone, and Continental Shelf Guyana/Suriname' (2008) 102 *American Journal of International Law* 119.

Fietta, S., and Cleverly, R., *A Practitioner's Guide to Maritime Boundary Delimitation* (Oxford University Press Oxford 2016).

Forlati, S., *The International Court of Justice, an Arbitral Tribunal or a Judicial Body* (Springer Switzerland 2014).

Franck, T. M., *Fairness in International Law and Institutions* (Clarendon Press Oxford 1995).

Friedmann, W., 'The North Sea Continental Shelf Cases – A Critique' (1970) 64 *American Journal of International Law* 229.

Gao, J., 'Comments on *Guyana v. Suriname*,' (2009) 8 *Chinese Journal of International Law* 191.

Giraudeau, G., 'La remarquable entrée en scène du TIDM dans le contentieux de la délimitation maritime: l'arrêt du 14 mars 2012 relatif au différend entre le Bangladesh et le Myanmar dans le Golfe du Bengale,' (2012) 17 *Annuaire du droit de la mer* 105.

Guillaume, G., Speech by His Excellency Judge Gilbert Guillaume, President of the International Court of Justice, to the Sixth Committee of the General Assembly of the United Nations, 31 October 2001.

Gutteridge, J. A. C., 'The 1958 Geneva Convention on the Continental Shelf,' (1959) 53 *British Yearbook of International Law* 102.

Higgins, R., *Problems and Process: International Law and How We Use It* (Clarendon Press Oxford 1994).

Ibler, V., 'Jus cogens and the Law of the Sea,' in M. G. Cohen (ed.), *Promoting Justice, Human Rights and Conflict Resolution through International Law: Liber Amicorum Lucius Caflisch* (Brill Leiden 2007).

Ida, R., 'The Role of Proportionality in Maritime Delimitation Revisited: The Origin and Meaning of the Principle from the Early Decisions of the Court,' in N. Ando et al. (eds.), *Liber Amicorum Judge Shigeru Oda* (Kluwer The Hague 2002) 1037.

Jagota, S. P., *Maritime Boundary* (Nijhoff Dordrecht 1985).

Jensen, Ø., 'The Barents Sea: Treaty between Norway and the Russian Federation Concerning Maritime Delimitation and Cooperation in the Barents Sea and the Arctic Ocean,' (2011) 26 *International Journal of Marine and Coastal Law* 151.

'Maritime Boundary Delimitation beyond 200 Nautical Miles: The International Judiciary and the Commission on the Limits of the Continental Shelf,' (2015) 84 *Nordic Journal of International Law* 580.

Jiménez de Aréchaga, E., 'The Conception of Equity in Maritime Delimitation,' in P. L. Zanardi et al. (eds.), *Le droit international à l'heure de sa codification. Etudes en l'honneur de Roberto Ago* (Milan 1987) t. II, 229.

Johnston, D. M., *The Theory and History of Ocean Boundary-Making* (McGill-Queen's University Press Kingston-Montreal 1988).

Jouannet, E., 'L'impossible protection des droits du tiers par la Cour internationale de Justice dans les affaires de délimitation maritime,' in *La mer et son droit, Mélanges offerts à L. Luchini et J. P Quéneudec* (Éditions A. Pedone Paris 2003) 315.

Klein, N., 'Provisional Measures and Provisional Arrangements in Maritime Boundary Disputes,' (2006) 21 *International Journal of Marine and Coastal Law* 423.

Kolb, R., *Case Law on Equitable Maritime Delimitation: Digest and Commentaries* [Jurisprudence sur les deélimitations maritimes selon l'équite: répertoire et commentaires] (Nijhoff Leiden 2003).

Kunoy, B., 'The Admissibility of a Plea to an International Adjudicative Forum to Delimit the Outer Continental Shelf Prior to the Adoption of Final Recommendations by the Commission on the Limits of the Continental Shelf,' (2010) 25 *The International Journal of Marine and Coastal Law* 237.

Kwiatkowska, B., 'Submissions to the UN CLCS in Cases of Disputed and Undisputed Maritime Boundary Delimitations or Other Unresolved Land or Maritime Disputes of Developing States,' Farewell Lecture of Prof. B Kwiatkowska, 9 December 2011, http://dspace.library.uu.nl/handle/1874/23543019.

Lagoni, R., 'Interim Measures Pending Maritime Delimitation Agreements,' (1984) 78 *American Journal of International Law* 345.

Lando, M., 'Judicial Uncertainties Concerning Territorial Sea Delimitation under Article 15 of the United Nations Convention on the Law of the Sea,' (2017) 66 *International and Comparative Law Quarterly* 589.

Lathrop, C. (ed.), *International Maritime Boundaries*, online ed. (Martinus Nijhoff Dordrecht 2015).

Legault, H., and Hankey, B., 'Method, Oppositeness and Adjacency, and Proportionality in Maritime Boundary Delimitation,' in J. I. Charney and L. M. Alexander (eds.), *International Maritime Boundaries*, vol. 1 (Martinus Nijhoff Dordrecht 1991) 203.

Lowe, V., *International Law: A Very Short Introduction* (Oxford University Press Oxford 2015).

Lucchini, L., 'La delimitation des frontiers maritimes dans la jurisprudence international: vue d'ensemble,' in R. Lagoni and D. Vignes (eds.), *Maritime Delimitation* (Martinus Nijhoff Leiden 2006) 1.

Lucchini, L., and Vœlckel, M., *Droit de la mer tome II, Delimitation* (Pedone Paris 1996).

Magnusson B. M., *The Continental Shelf beyond 200 Nautical Miles – Delineation, Delimitation and Dispute Settlement* (Brill/Nijhoff Leiden 2015).

'Judgment in the Dispute Concerning the Delimitation of the Maritime Boundary between Bangladesh and Myanmar in the Bay of Bengal,' (2012) 27 *International Journal of Marine and Coastal Law* 623.

McDougal, M. S., and Burke, T., *The Public Order of the Oceans* (Yale University Press New Haven 1987).

Merrills, J. G., *International Dispute Settlement*, 5th ed. (Cambridge University Press Cambridge 2011).

Miyoshi, M., 'Considerations on Equity in Maritime Boundary Cases before the International Court of Justice,' in N. Ando, E. McWhinney, R. Wolfrum, and B. Baker Röben (eds.), *Liber Amicorum Judge Shigeru Oda* (Brill/Nijhoff Leiden 2002).

Ndiaye, T. M., 'The Judge, Maritime Delimitation and the Grey Areas,' (2015) 55 *Indian Journal of International Law* 493.

Nelson, L. D. M., 'The Roles of Equity in the Delimitation of Maritime Boundaries,' (1990) 86 *American Journal of International Law* 837.

Newton, M., and May, L., *Proportionality in International Law* (Oxford University Press Oxford 2014).

Olorundami, F., 'The ICJ and Its Lip Service to the Non-Priority Status of the Equidistance Method of Delimitation,' (2015) 4(1) *Cambridge Journal of International and Comparative Law* 53.

'Objectivity versus Subjectivity in the Context of the ICJ's Three-Stage Methodology of Maritime Boundary Delimitation,' (2017) 32(1) *The International Journal of Marine and Coastal Law* 36.

Ong, D. M., 'Joint Development of Common Offshore Oil and Gas Deposits: "Mere" State Practice or Customary International Law?,' (1999) 93 *American Journal of International Law* 771.

Orrego Vicuña, F., 'Le pied du chancelier continue de s'allonger: les principes généraux et l'équité en droit international: à la recherche de limites à la flexibilité du droit,' in M. Kohen, R. Kolb, and D. Liva Tehindrazanarivelo (eds.), *Perspectives of International Law in the 21st Century: Liber Amicorum Professor Christian Dominicé in Honour of His 80th Birthday* (Martinus Nijhoff Leiden 2012) 81.

Oude Elferink, A. G., 'Article 76 of the LOSC on the Definition of the Continental Shelf: Questions Concerning Its Interpretation from a Legal Perspective,' (2006) 21 *International Journal of Marine and Coastal Law* 269.

The Delimitation of the Continental Shelf between Denmark, Germany and the Netherlands; Arguing Law, Practicing Politics? (Cambridge University Press Cambridge 2013).

'Does Undisputed Title to a Maritime Zone Always Exclude Its Delimitation? The Grey Area Issue,' (1998) 13 *International Journal of Marine and Coastal Law* 143.

'The Impact of the Law of the Sea Convention on the Delimitation of Maritime Boundaries,' in D. Vidas and W. Østreng (eds.), *Order for the Oceans at the Turn of the Century* (Kluwer Law International The Hague 1999) 462.

'International Law and Negotiated and Adjudicated Maritime Boundaries: A Complex Relationship,' (2015) 58 *German Yearbook of International Law* 231.

'ITLOS's Approach to the Delimitation of the Continental Shelf beyond 200 Nautical Miles in the Bangladesh/Myanmar Case: Theoretical and Practical Difficulties,' in R. Wolfrum, M. Seršić, and T. Šošić (eds.), *Contemporary Developments in International Law – Essays in Honour of Budislav Vukas* (Brill/Nijhoff Leiden 2015) 230.

The Law of Maritime Boundary Delimitation: A Case Study of the Russian Federation (Martinus Nijhoff Dordrecht 1994).

'Slovenia/Croatia arbitration Is – the territorial sea delimitation inconsistent with the case law on maritime delimitation?', *JCLOS Blog* of 16 August 2017, http://site.uit.no/jclos/2017/08/16/sloveniacroatia-arbitration-is-the-territorial-sea-delimitation-inconsistent-with-the-case-law-on-maritime-delimitation/.

Oxman, B. H., 'International Maritime Boundaries: Political, Strategic, and Historical Considerations,' (1994–1995) 26 *University of Miami Inter-American Law Review* 243.

Paik, J.-H., 'The Role of Proportionality in Maritime Delimitation: State of Jurisprudence,' in H. P. Hestermeyer et al. (eds.), *Coexistence, Cooperation and Solidarity, Liber Amicorum Rüdiger Wolfrum*, vol. 1 (Nijhoff Leiden 2012) 199.

Pellet, A., 'Land and Maritime Tripoints in International Jurisprudence,' in H. Hestermeyer et al. (eds.), *Coexistence, Cooperation and Solidarity: Liber Amicorum Rüdiger Wolfrum* (Martinus Nijhoff Leiden 2011) 245.

Prescott, V., and Schofield, C., *The Maritime Political Boundaries of the World*, 2nd ed. (Martinus Nijhoff Leiden 2005).

Punzhin, S. M., 'Printsipy Razgranicheniia Morskikh Prostranstv,' in R. A. Kolodkin and S. M. Punzhin (eds.), *International Law of the Sea: Essays in Memory of A.L. Kolodkin* (Statut Moscow 2014) 61.

Reichler, P., 'A Case of Equitable Maritime Delimitation: Nicaragua and Colombia in the Western Caribbean Sea,' (2013) 2(3) *Revista Tribuna Internacional Volumen* 129.

Reismann, M. W., 'Eritrea–Yemen Arbitration (Award, Phase II: Maritime Delimitation),' (2000) 94 *American Journal of International Law* 734.

Reuter, P., *Le développement de l'ordre juridique international, écrits de droit international* (Economica Paris 1995).

Rosenne, S., 'The Case-Law of ITLOS (1997-2001): An Overview,' in M. H. Nordquist and J. Norton Moore (eds.), *Current Marine Environmental Issues and the International Tribunal for the Law of the Sea* (Nijhoff The Hague 2001) 127.

Intervention in the International Court of Justice (Martinus Nijhoff Leiden 1993).

Rothwell, D., and Stephens, T., *The International Law of the Sea* (Hart Oxford 2009).

Ruiz-Fabri, H., 'Sur la délimitation des espaces maritimes entre le Canada et la France, sentence arbitrale du 10 juin 1992,' (1993) 97 *Revue générale de droit international public* 67.

Schachter, O., 'Linking Equity and Law in Maritime Delimitation,' in N. Ando, E. McWhinney, R. Wolfrum, and B. Baker Röben (eds.), *Liber Amicorum Judge Shigeru Oda* (Brill/Nijhoff Leiden 2002) 1163.

Schoolmeester, T., and Baker, E. (eds.), *Continental Shelf; The Last Maritime Zone; Status in Sept. 2010* (UNEP/GRID-Arendal Arendal 2011) 16.

Scobbie, I., 'Res Judicata, Precedent and the International Court: A Preliminary Sketch' (1999) 20 *Australian Year Book of International Law* 299.

'Tom Franck's Fairness,' (2002) 13 *European Journal of International Law* 909.

Scovazzi, T., 'Libya-Tunisia,' in J. I. Charney and L. M. Alexander (eds.), *International Maritime Boundaries*, vol. 2 (Martinus Nijhoff Dordrecht 1993) 1663.

Shah Alam, M., and Al Faruque, A., 'The Problem of Delimitation of Bangladesh's Maritime Boundaries with India and Myanmar: Prospects for a Solution,' (2010) 25 *International Journal of Marine and Coastal Law* 405.

Shi, J., 'Maritime Delimitation in the Jurisprudence of the International Court of Justice,' (2010) 9 *Chinese Journal of International Law* 271.

Smith, R. W. (ed.), *Maritime Boundaries of the World*, Limits in the Seas 108, 1st rev. (US Department of State Washington, DC 1990).

Sorel, J.-M., 'Le juge international face à l'équité dans le règlement de différends territoriaux,' in P. Weckel (ed.), *Le juge international et l'aménagement de l'espace: la spécificité du contentieux territorial* (Pedone Paris 1998) 161.

Talmon, S., 'The South China Sea Arbitration and the Finality of "Final" Awards,' (2017) 1 *Journal of International Dispute Settlement* 388.

Tanaka, Y., *Predictability and Flexibility in the Law of Maritime Delimitation* (Hart Oxford 2006).

'Reflections on Maritime Delimitation in the Cameroon/Nigeria Case,' (2004) 53 *International and Comparative Law Quarterly* 369.

'Reflections on Maritime Delimitation in the Romania/Ukraine Case before the ICJ,' (2009) 56 *Netherlands International Law Review* 397.

'Reflections on the Territorial and Maritime Dispute between Nicaragua and Colombia before the International Court of Justice,' (2013) 26 *Leiden Journal of International Law* 909.

'Unilateral Exploration and Exploitation of Natural Resources in Disputed Areas: A Note on the Ghana/Côte d'Ivoire Order of 25 April 2015 before the Special Chamber of ITLOS,' (2015) 46 *Ocean Development and International Law* 315.

Tanja, G. J., *The Legal Determination of International Maritime Boundaries* (Kluwer Law Deventer 1990).

Thirlway, H., *The International Court of Justice* (Oxford University Press Oxford 2016).

'The Law and Procedure of the International Court of Justice 1960–1989: Part Thirteen,' (2003) 74 *British Yearbook of International Law* 1, 52.

The Law and Procedure of the International Court of Justice: Fifty Years of Jurisprudence, vol. 1 (Oxford University Press Oxford 2013).

Vallat, F., 'The Continental Shelf,' (1946) 23 *British Yearbook of International Law* 333.

Van Logchem, Y., 'The Scope for Unilateralism in Disputed Maritime Areas,' in C. Schofield, S. Lee, and M.-S. Kwon (eds.), *The Limits of Maritime Jurisdiction* (Martinus Nijhoff Leiden 2014) 186.

Vidas, D., 'The UN Convention on the Law of the Sea, the European Union and the Rule of Law: What Is Going on in the Adriatic Sea?,' (2009) 24 *International Journal of Marine and Coastal Law* 1.

von Mühlendahl, P., 'Tiny Land Features in Recent Maritime Delimitation Case Law,' (2016) 31 *International Journal of Marine and Coastal Law* 1.

Wang, Z., 'Disputes over Fishery Resources and Maritime Boundary Delimitation of the Diaoyu Islands: An Analysis,' (2009) 1 *China Oceans Law Review* 310.

Watts, A., *The International Law Commission 1948–1998*, vol. 1 (Oxford University Press Oxford 1999).

Weil, P., 'Délimitation maritime et délimitation terrestre,' in Y. Dinștein and M. Tabory (eds.), *International Law at a Time of Perplexity: Essays in Honour of Shabtai Rosenne* (Martinus Nijhoff Leiden 1989) 1023.

The Law of Maritime Delimitation: Reflections (Grotius Cambridge 1989).

'Le droit international en quête de son identité: cours général de droit international public,' (1992) 2 *Collected Courses of the Hague Academy of International Law* 245.

'Towards Relative Normativity in International Law,' (1983) 77 *American Journal of International Law* 413.

INDEX

For EU product safety concerns, contact us at Calle de José Abascal, 56–1°, 28003 Madrid, Spain or eugpsr@cambridge.org.

www.ingramcontent.com/pod-product-compliance
Lightning Source LLC
LaVergne TN
LVHW052021200926
848481LV00005B/1552
* 9 7 8 1 1 0 8 4 4 0 9 4 3 *